C0-ALZ-535

CONCISE ENCYCLOPAEDIA OF ARABIC CIVILIZATION

STEPHAN AND NANDY RONART

CONCISE ENCYCLOPAEDIA OF ARABIC CIVILIZATION

THE ARAB WEST

FREDERICK A. PRAEGER, Publishers
New York • Washington

Also by Dr. S. Ronart:

ALBANIEN VON HEUTE, Vienna 1932
BULGARIEN VON HEUTE, Vienna 1933
GRIECHENLAND VON HEUTE, Vienna 1935
TÜRKEI VON HEUTE, Vienna 1936
The last mentioned work has been translated into
English: TURKEY TO-DAY, London 1937
French: LA TURQUIE D'AUJOURD'HUI, Paris 1937.

The preceding volume, CONCISE ENCYCLOPAEDIA OF ARABIC CIVILIZATION, *The Arab East*, was published by Frederick A. Praeger, Inc., Publishers in 1960

BOOKS THAT MATTER

Published in the United States of America in 1966
by Frederick A. Praeger, Inc., Publishers,
111 Fourth Avenue, New York, 3 N.Y.

Library of Congres Catalog Card Number: 66 - 13401

Printed in the Netherlands

PREFACE

We have little to add to the lines introducing the first part of this Concise Encyclopaedia. There we treated of the cultural, social, economic and political aspects of the eastern section of the Arab world, and tried to show the issues, events and ideas, the achievements of its thinkers and the actions of its leading figures, which shaped its development. Here we have endeavoured to shed a similar light on the principal driving forces behind the evolution of the countries in the Arab West or Maghrib - Morocco, Algeria, Tunisia and Libya. There has also been embodied, though without entering into details, the Arab era in the Iberian Peninsula, the time of al-Andalus, whence for several centuries rich currents of science, philosophy, literature and artistic inventiveness were flowing into North Africa and fructifying the intellectual and material life of its society.

This volume is a self-contained book. It is intended to serve without requiring consultation of its companion which preceded it. In order to avoid duplications, however, certain basic Islamic concepts and institutions which were dealt with there, have had here to be omitted, but short explanatory remarks have been added whenever it was thought this would make it easier to understand a particular situation. As in the first part, the text had been divided into individual entries arranged in alphabetical order, asterisks being placed after certain words referring to special articles and to invite connected reading.

We know that a great deal which still could have been said will be found missing. It was with great regret that often we had to force ourselves to abridgements and omissions so as not to exceed the limits of space imposed by the general frame. On the other hand, we are well aware that in some instances we cannot escape the criticism of having used too much room where less might have sufficed. In these cases, the particular attraction we personally felt for the subject is our sole excuse. We hope that notwithstanding these shortcomings - and others that will undoubtedly come to light — our efforts at presenting a work which aims at supplying information on a part of the world today very much in the limelight will prove useful.

STEPHAN AND NANDY RONART

NOTE ON TRANSLITERATION

The precise rendering of some particular Arabic sounds requires a system of diacritical marks placed under or above the vowel or consonant signs of the European alphabet. To the non-Arabist they hardly convey anything, therefore we have omitted them except for the dashes which indicate long vowels: ā as in far; ī as in feel; ū as in lose. We used the conventional signs ʿand ' representing respectively the Arabic consonants *ain* (a very strong guttural produced by compression of the throat and expulsion of the breath) and the *hamza* (a click produced by a quick compression of the upper part of the throat). The *th* has the value of the English th as in think; the *dh* has the value of the English the as in this; the *kh* is a guttural ch as in the Scottish loch; the *q* is a k-sound produced in the throat; and the *gh* indicates a hard sound between a snarling pronunciation of *gh* and r.

For familiar place names we used the current English spelling; for others, less widely known the transliterated form. The names of contemporary Arab and Berber personalities presented a particular problem. In literature and in the press they appear in most of the cases in a French transformation of the original. We have decided to use this commonly known form, adding occasionally the Arabic way of spelling in brackets.

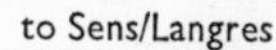

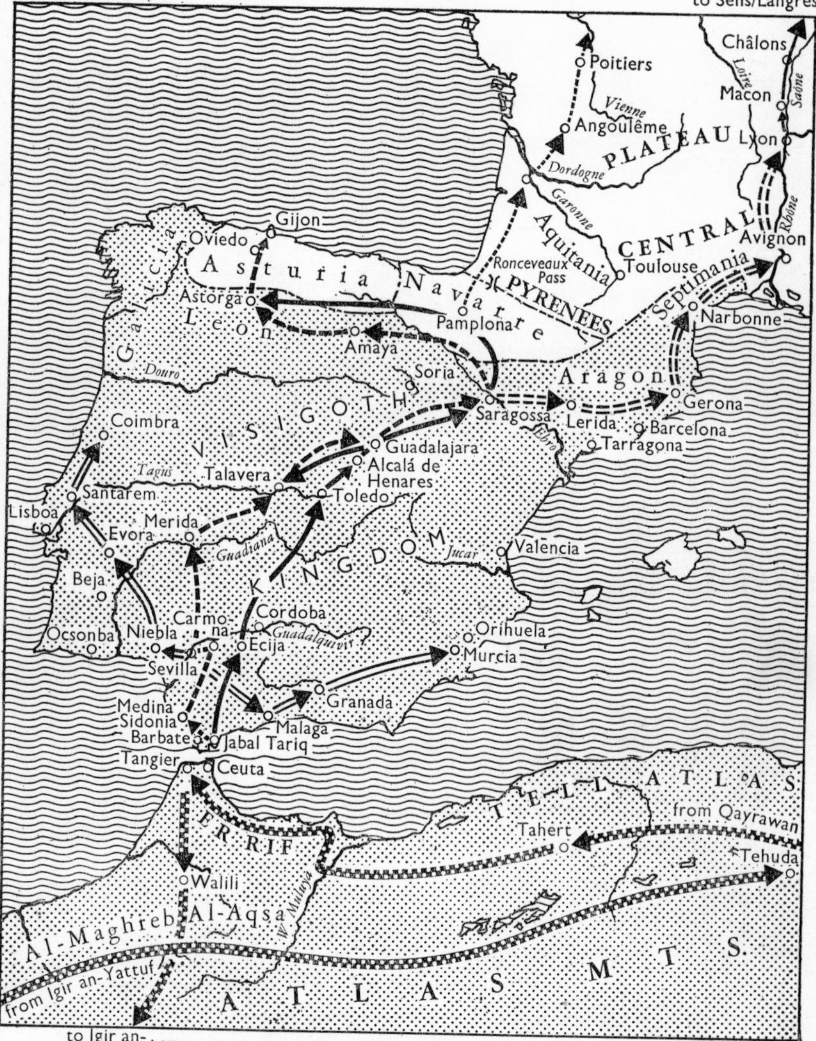

AFRICAN AND EUROPEAN CAMPAIGNS
THE MUSLIM EXPANSION IN THE WEST

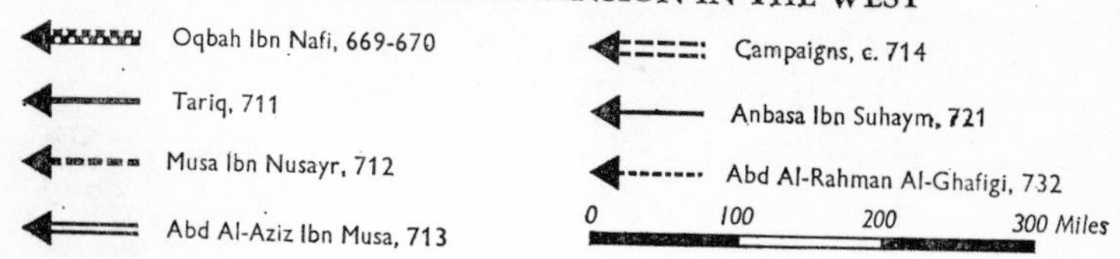

A

ʿABBĀDIDS, *Banū ʿAbbād*, a Hispano-Arab dynasty (1013-1091) of Seville, which, when at the summit of power, extended its domain over most of the south-western sector of the Iberian peninsula. Seville, thanks to its port on the Guadalquivir, navigable for sea-going vessels as far upstream as the city, maintained a profitable trade with the Moroccan commercial centers on the Atlantic coast, and was second only to Cordova, the wealthiest and most influential of the Andalusian towns. It was the seat of an old Arab nobility which proud of its pure Arabian blood, owned all the fertile land in the Guadalquivir valley. Supported by substantial political and economic prerogatives it had little esteem for the neighbouring Berber notables nor was it willing to submit to the orders of native Moslem (*muwalladūn**) or Christian (Mozarab*) government or court officers.

The scions of one of these families which claimed descent from the Lakhmid kings of al-Ḥīra, Abū al-Qāsim Muhammad Ibn-al-ʿAbbād, son of a reputed scholar of canon law and himself cadi of Seville, succeeded in taking the power into his hands, at first in the name of the caliph and finally in his own. His heir was his son Abū ʿAmr (1042-1069), better known by his surname al-Muʿtadid bi'llāh (The Seeker of Strength from God), the prototype of the strong-willed, merciless autocrat impelled by a limitless ambition that ignored any inhibitions as to the choice of means, yet gifted with a keen sense of political and military realities. Playing upon the anti-Berber feelings always more or less dormant among the upper-class Arab society he knew how to create the atmosphere for the aggrandizement of his realm at the expense of the minor city-dynasts, the so-called Party Kings*, many of them of Berber extraction or relying on Berber sympathies. He also knew how to gain the support of the masses and local leaders by exploiting the popular belief that the Umayyad Caliph Hishām II, who some years earlier had been deposed and most probably assassinated, was still alive in some hiding place and awaiting his restoration. Under the pretext of acting for the legitimate sovereign, al-Muʿtadid by force of arms and treachery - one day he invited a number of potential antagonists into his palace and had them suffocated in their baths - made himself master of most of the important towns in the region. He did not hesitate to have his eldest son Ismāʿīl executed because of his attempt at cutting out for himself an independent kingdom when commanding one of his father's conquering expeditions.

Al-Muʿtadid left to his son Muhammad (1069-1091), surnamed al-Muʿtamid bi'llāh (He who relies on God), a heritage which comprised the territories of the majority of the ephemeral city-princes whom the dissolving Umayyad caliphate had allowed to come to the surface. Al-Muʿtamid further enlarged it by adding Cordova (1078) which he made his capital as well as the land lying between the Guadalquivir and the Guadiana in the kingdom of Toledo, and Murcia with the area around

it. Although al-Muʿtamid controlled a territory and a military force, which made him unquestionably the strongest among the Andalusian rulers of his time he finally was compelled to recognize the overlordship of Alfonso VI, King of Castile and Leon. The diplomatic talents of his vizier, the poet Ibn ʿAmmār* and the payments of heavy tributes staved off for a while more serious dangers. Soon, however, Alfonso and his vassal Rodigro Diaz de Bivar, the 'Cid', resumed their incursions. Al-Muʿtamid, joined by the emirs of Badajoz and of Granada, called to his help the powerful leader of the politico-religious Almoravid* confederation, Yūsuf Ibn Tāshufīn*, then master of practically the whole of Morocco and part of Algeria. He came and at al-Zallāqa* near Badajoz (1086) defeated the Christian army, but thereupon went back to Africa. Two years later al-Muʿtamid again sollicited his help, and again Yūsuf Ibn Tāshufīn crossed the Straits but the rivalries among the Andalusian emirs soon caused him once more to return to Africa. In the course of a third Almoravid expedition, this time directed against the Party Kings, al-Muʿtamid's son al-Ma'mūn fell in battle at Cordova, Seville was captured (1091) and al-Muʿtamid taken first to Tangier, then to Meknès and finally to Aghmāt where he died (1095) in complete destitution. His beloved Iʿtimād (also known as al-Rumaikīya) whose sligthest whims it once was his pleasure to fulfil, remained faithfully at his side. Their tombs are still shown at Aghmāt.
Both al-Muʿtadid and al-Muʿtamid were cultured lovers of refinement and luxury, holding a splendid court and surrounding themselves with poets - Ibn Zaydūn* and Ibn ʿAmmār were among their closest entourage - men of letters and scholars. As much, however, as the Arab authors depict the father as a cruel and vindictive despot, they extol in words of highest praise the son's affability, delicate liberality and sensitive aestheticism, and assign him a place next to the most brilliant artisans of Hispano-Arab civilization. Muʿtamid himself was a poet, and the verses he found to sing his love for Iʿtimād and his deep-felt words of longing, in exile, for the lost beauty of al-Andalus continued to evoke for many years to come the admiration of all, including the severest critics of his capacities as a ruler.

ABBĀR Ibn al-, ABŪ ʿABD ALLĀH MUHAMMAD, Andalusian man of letters (1199-1260) born in Valencia where he moved in the scholarly circles of highest standing and fulfilled a distinguished function first in the service of the Almohad* governor of the town, then under its semi-independent, ephemeral ruler of the Mardanīsh* family. During the siege of Valencia by James I of Aragon, his sovereign sent him to the court of Tunis in order to sollicit the help of Emir Abū Zakariyyā' (1228-1249)* which he did in the form of a much admired poem composed for the occasion. It did not secure the requested substantial assistance but gained for its author the emir's favour, who after the fall of Valencia (1238) accorded him and his family liberal hospitality and appointed him chief of the chancellery. Replaced, however, after a while by a native notable he was thrown into prison because of his disrespectful attitude. There he wrote, and dedicated to the emir his *Iʿtāb al-Kuttāb* (Rehabilitation of the Scribes), a series of remarkably erudite and well-written stu-

dies dealing with the lives of court secretaries or chancellors fallen into disgrace and subsequently taken again into their high patron's favour. The book - it has been preserved - seems to have pleased and he was pardoned and after the death of Emir Abū Zakariyyā' distinguished with high honours by the emir's son and successor, Caliph al-Mustansir (1249-1277)*. Yet he was dismissed a second time, probably one of the victims of a court intrigue, accused of lese-majesty and cruelly executed. His body together with his writings was committed to the flames.
The best known among the works of Ibn al-Abbār's pen which have come down to us is his *Kitāb al-Takmilah li-Kitāb al-Silah* (appr. Supplement to the Book of Relation), a collection of biographies of Arab scholars of al-Andalus*, which completes the biographical dictionary by Ibn Baskuwāl* (1101-1183), itself the continuation of a similar work of the early XIth century by the biographer Ibn al-Faradī*. In addition to it Ibn al-Abbār wrote a second collection of biographies, entitled *Kitāb al-Hullah al-Siyarā'*. A rare connoisseur of the refinements of diction and phraseological intricacies, he was, while in charge of the official correspondence, one of the first to use in the Tunisian state documents that grandiloquent style and bombastic vocabulary which for several centuries were the pride of the bureaucracy of the Arab countries.

ʿABD ALLĀH IBN YĀSĪN, a Berber theologian of the Malikite school, professing extremely puritan convictions (†1059), descended from the Jazūla, one of the veil-wearing members *(Mulaththamūn*)* of the wide-spread Sanhāja* family of tribes nomadizing in the Mauretanian parts of the Sahara. Invited by the chieftain of the two allied, also veil-wearing Sanhāja sister tribes, the Judāla and Lamtūna, he went preaching among them in order to eradicate their pagan practices still alive under a varnish of Islam. Soon, however, the tribesmen grew weary of his unyielding missionary zeal so that upon the death of his host he withdrew to an island in the Senegal River, accompanied by two Lamtūna chieftains, the brothers Yahyā Ibn ʿUmar and Abū Bakr Ibn ʿUmar, and a few faithful followers. There they assumed the half monastic, half war-like way of life in a *ribāt**, devoted to the Holy War *(jihād)* for the defence of the spread of the faith. Within a short time this small community of *murābitūn** (people of the *ribāt)* was joined by new adepts. By their eloquence and the use of the sword they made a rapidly increasing number of proselytes among the neighbouring Sanhāja groups, ʿAbd Allāh Ibn Yāsīn assuming the spiritual and Yahyā Ibn ʿUmar the military leadership. Their first major expedition was directed against the town of Sijilmāsa (in the Tāfīlālt on the south-western slopes of the High Atlas), then ruled by a clan of the Maghrāwa* tribes, the Banū Khazrūn. They conquered the town and the near-by oases (1053 and 1054) and instituted a new public order based on ʿAbd Allāh Ibn Yāsīn's strict puritanism: no wine shops, no musical instruments, no taxes which were not prescribed in the Koran, and one fifth of the booty - comprising 50.000 camels, according to the historiographers - distributed among the men of religion and religious law. The following year the people of Sijilmāsa revolted and in the ensuing fights Yahyā Ibn ʿUmar met his death (1055 or 1057). His brother took his place, subdued the rebels and with renewed impetus continued the war of the conquest which within two years made the growing army of desert tribesmen, inspired by ʿAbd Allāh ibn-Yāsīn's word, masters of the Wādī Darʿā and the Wādī Sūs and the fertile region between the Atlantic coast and the Atlas mountains with the flourishing town of Aghmāt, center of southern Morocco and residence of the Maghrāwī ruler. Thence they pushed northwards into the area of the Tādlā in central Morocco, the territory of the Banū Ifrān*, and everywhere ʿAbd Allāh Ibn Yāsīn's doctrine became the law. He fell, sword in hand, in the course of the further advance northward in the Barghawāta* country (near Karīfla appr. 35 miles east of Casablanca) on the seashore where his alleged burial place is still to be seen. With his death the religious motif ceased to be the driving force, but the Murābitūn, or as they are called by the occidental historians, the Almoravids*, were well on their way to a history-making conquest.

ʿABD al-HAQQ, the last Moroccan sovereign of the Marīnid* dynasty (1421-1465), put on the throne after the assassination of his father Abū Saʿīd ʿUthmān (1398-1421), while he was one year of age, by the all-powerful clan of the Wattāsid*, who in the course of the five or six decades of the fictitious reigns of child-monarchs had usurped all the key-functions in the state and made themselves its actual masters. Favoured by a lucky star he had, unlike most of his last predecessors, survived several critical periods in the struggle for supremacy among his Wattāsid viziers and provincial governors, and thought the general emotion caused by the Portuguese advance along the Moroccan coasts propitious for ridding himself once for all of the degrading tutelage and refurbishing the ancestral glory. He started by having the entire Wattāsid clan assassinated except two brothers, Muhammad al-Halū and Muhammad al-Shaykh who succeeded in escaping, the founder to be of a new reigning dynasty. In order to consolidate his own authority he tried to dam, or at least to counterbalance, the all-pervading influence of the various kinds of marabouts and religious brotherhoods* by exalting the traditional prestige of the Sharīfian aristocracy, the - real or alleged - descendants of the Prophet, and in particular of the house of the Idrīsids*, one-time rulers of Morocco. Very timely in this connection was the discovery in Fez of the miraculously preserved body of Mūlāy Idrīs II*, the founder of the city and, as it were, its patron saint. To what extent ʿAbd al-Haqq might have been successful it is difficult to judge, since one great mistake which he committed was to frustrate all his efforts, to cost him his life and bring about the fall of the Marīnid dynasty. Pressed by the need to resplenish the depleted treasury he abolished the prebends and tax exemptions until then liberally accorded to the holy men and fraternities. Infuriated, they called down upon his head the curse of godlessness. While he was away fighting the Portuguese invaders in the region of Ceuta, Ibn ʿAbd Allāh Muhammad Ibn ʿImrān al-Jūtī, the head *(naqīb)* of the Idrīsids, stirred up a revolt, declared ʿAbd al-Haqq destitute of his rights and had himself proclaimed Imam, the worldly and spiritual leader by the will of God. ʿAbd al-Haqq returned to Fez and was savagely murdered in a mosque by the fanaticized mob. Through a peculiar turn of the popular mind his memory lived on for many years as that of a saint whose mystical, wonder-working blessing *(baraka)* was firmly believed in by the Zanāta* people, the tribe of the Banū Marīn.

ʿABD al-KARĪM, in occidental texts usually spelt Abdel Krim or Abdelkrim, with his full name Muhammad Ibn ʿAbd al-Karīm al-Katabī (1882-1963), a Berber warlord and founder of the short-lived „Republic of the Rif", (1922-1926). He was born in the village of Adjir near the Mediterranean coast west of Melilla on the slopes of the Rif, on the site of the one-time Nakūr of the Sālihid* princes. There his father held the office of a caid *(qā'id*)* in his tribe, the great and warlike Banū Uriaghel. Together with his brother Muhammad, his faithful companion in the turbulent events of his career, he was given a good education in Spanish and Arabic; became, so it seems, a member of the Darqāwā* brotherhood, served for a time as chief judge *(qādī al-qudā')* in the region of Melilla and edited a Melilla newspaper of strong anti-French colour. Involved in a conflict with the Spanish authorities at the end of the first World War, presumably because of his political attitude which evoked French protests, he was sentenced to prison, escaped and was recaptured, but fled again and succeeded in reaching the safety of the mountains, where the prestige of his learning and of his courage in his quarrels with the powerful foreigners immediately won him the esteem of the tribesmen. Joined by his brother, a mining engineer in Spain, and like him, thenceforth an implacable enemy of the Spanish and French and not less hostile to the Sultan who inactively submitted to their rule, he soon had all the Banū Uriaghel up in arms (1921).

In a series of fierce battles Abdel Krim completely routed the Spanish corps which was meant to suppress the revolt; drew all the Moroccans in its ranks onto his own side; captured an enormous booty of arms, amunition and war supply; came close to the gates of Melilla; and pressed the Spaniards back onto the narrow strip of land on the coast. All over the Rif from Melilla to Tetuan he was cheered by the tribal world as the victorious hero, the liberator and defender of Islam and recognized as leader. Without losing time, so as not to let the enthusiasm fade and become overshadowed by hereditary clannish rivalries, he consolidated his success with the same skill as he had shown in his warlike operations, and on the basis of the time-honoured tribal institutions built up a body politic, primitive yet perfectly adapted to the mentality of the tribesmen. He called it the Republic of the Rif *(Jumhurīya Rīfīya)* and had himself proclaimed President.

Throughout three years Spain attempted in vain to regain her lost position either by direct military action or by stirring up and exploiting the antagonism of local chieftains, but with little practical results. In 1924 Abdel Krim launched a new offensive, forced the Spanish to retreat into Tetuan with heavy losses, occupied Shashāwan (Xauen), then turned southward and crossed the border of the zone of the French Protectorate*. In April 1925 his horsemen were within twelve miles of Fez. In July a Franco-Spanish Conference in Madrid decided, not without having to overcome considerable dissensions, upon the measures to be taken in common to stop the Berber advance. A more or less disguised offer to recognize the autonomy of the Rif tribes remained ignored by

Abdel Krim. His struggle against European colonial rule had by then awakened a loud echo not only in the Arab East and in the Syrian and Lebanese groups in Brazil, Argentina and the United States but also in Germany and even in France, where a communist-sponsored „Committee against the War in Morocco" carried on an active propaganda in his favour and even seems to have lent him material support. Combined French-Spanish operations were at last started with some 250.000 men and every type of modern armament in the field. In September 1925 a Spanish corps landed at Alhucemas and penetrated deep into the Rif. Simultaneously French and Spanish troops pressed from Melilla southward, and a French army advanced step by step northward. Negotiations for peace were initiated but soon broken off again and Abdel Krim, crushed by the weight of what he called the „iron civilization of the Occident" and trusting in the promise that his personal freedom would be respected, surrendered to the French (May 27,1926). The promise was not kept and he was deported with his numerous family, close friends and servants to Reunion Island in the Indian Ocean. There he set up a Berber village with its seigneurial *qasaba** and during the 21 years of his exile lived the life of a Berber chief, sharply observing, however, the political development in the Arab world and fluctuations in the international configuration.

In the Rif Abdel Krim is still remembered as the great popular hero surrounded with the glory of his exploits and succumbing only to the overwhelming number and technical superiority of his enemies. From his native mountains the legend of his fame took its way into Moroccan nationalist writing, making him rather anachronistically the first standard-bearer in the struggle for Moroccan independence. Detached from the emotional background, however, his revolt might probably appear as just another episode in the long story of the inveterate reluctance of Berber mountain society to submit to any outside authority. Abdel Krim, it is true, turned his arms against the Protectorate Powers, but because it was they who controlled the machinery of the state and forced his people into its wheelwork. Later, in his exile, it is equally true, this Berber regionalism gave way to aims of a nationwide, even Pan-Arabic scope. However, his republican conviction and his hostility against the ʿAlawid* dynasty remained what they were in the days of the Republic of the Rif, whereas to Moroccan nationalism Sultan Muhammad Ibn Yūsuf* became the embodiment of all its patriotic ideals and dynastic loyalty was a matter beyond dispute.

Thus when at last the French government decided Abdel Krim's transfer to France, the intention to use this divergency as a means of weakening the nationalist camp was presumably not absent from its motives. Yet in April 1947 during a call at Port Said he left the ship, was granted asylum by the Egyptian government and took refuge in Cairo, then the most active center of Moroccan, Algerian and Tunisian nationalist propaganda. There the Liberation Committee of the Arab West, the so-called Maghrib Bureau*, chose him as its president, but disappointed by the discord in its midst and all sorts of intrigues he resigned five years later. Notwithstanding his - apparently not more than superficial - reconciliation with King Muhammad V, who even came to see him in his Cairo villa and allotted him a pension, he refused to return to Morocco or to any of the Maghrib countries as long as there was still one French soldier on its soil. He died, 81 years of age, on February 6,1963 and was temporarily buried with full honours in Cairo pending the solemn funeral in Morocco.

ʿABD al-MU'MIN, with his full name Ibn ʿAlī Ibn ʿAlwī Ibn Yaʿlā al-Kūmī, the first ruler (1133-1163) of the Almohad* empire which he built up from the politico-spiritual community founded in the Atlas mountains by his teacher, the religious reformer Ibn-Tūmart*. He was born in a village near Tlemcen (in the present-day Algerian department of Oran), the country of the Kūmya member tribe of the Berber Zanāta* confederation, which at his time apparently was already completely arabicized. While still a youth - the year of his birth is not known - he left his home to study in the Arab East at the famous seats of religious learning, but decided to discontinue his journey and join Ibn Tūmart when he heard him preaching in a suburb of Bougie. Pious legend has surrounded with miraculous glamour the circumstances of this meeting as well as his early childhood and even his mother's dreams before his birth. Thenceforth ʿAbd al-Mu'min remained his master's most faithful disciple who shared in all the vicissitudes of his wandering westwards, together with him rallied under the Almohad flag the Masmūda* tribes of the Atlas, calling them up to the Holy War against the Almoravid* régime; and was closest to him in the organization and governance of the Almohad state in the making. It was he whom the Mahdi Ibn Tūmart shortly before his death instituted as his successor (1130), but only three years later upon his return from a victorious expedition was the succession solemnly recognized by the community.
By a patiently proceeding policy which associated the forces inherent in tribal cohesiveness with the spiritual and revolutionary élan released by the Mahdi's powerful personality, he brought on to his side first all the still hesitant Masmūda clans, then an increasing number of the Zanāta, his own tribal family, and finally more and more of the Sanhāja*. By his growing religious, political and military prestige he forged these heterogeneous groups into a solid coalition under his firm authority. For a while it was his tactics to lead his warriors into the plains only to harass the enemy by surprise attacks, avoiding whenever possible all serious encounters and quickly retreating into the safety of his mountains. As soon as he felt certain of his numerical superiority he started to push forward (about 1140) into the Sūs and along the slopes of the High Atlas. While one column secured the possession of the central section of the Middle Atlas, a second column penetrated through the valley of the river Ziz into the oases of the Tāfīlālt on the eastern side of the Atlas. Undeterred by occasional even heavy setbacks he continued his offensive northwards over Taza, the first larger town which fell into his hands, into the Rif, conquered Nakūr and Tetuan, then turned eastward and captured Melilla. With the death in battle (1145) of his most dangerous antagonist, the Catalan Reverter (al-Ruburtayr), commander of an Almoravid élite troup of mercenaries, which he presumably took over into his own services, his final victory was no longer doubtful. Oran,

Oujda and Tlemcen were taken, Fez (1145) capitulated after a nine-month siege, Meknès and Salé fell soon afterwards, Ceuta and with it the Almoravid fleet surrendered. Marrakesh, the Almoravid residence, was taken by assault after desperate resistance (1147) and Isḥāq Ibn ʿAlī, the last Almoravid ruler, with all his notables and the majority of the population - as in most of the other conquered towns- were put to the sword. Rebellions which broke out, partly on religious, partly on political grounds, among some of the tribes in the plain on the Atlantic coast, and spread to the north as far as the Rif as well as over the Sūs into the Tāfīlālt, were suppressed not without difficulty and punished with the execution of all those, allegedly some 30.000, supposed to have been guilty of insufficient loyalty to the Almohad cause.
Having brought under his sway, in a struggle of nearly twenty years, the whole of Morocco and a large section of Algeria, ʿAbd al-Muʾmin was now ready for carrying the Holy War either into Spain or into eastern Algeria and Tunisia, where the Zīrid* and Ḥammādid* emirs at al-Mahdīya and Bougie defended their shrinking realms with little hope for survival against the twofold pressure of the Arab Bedouin tribes and the Normans of Sicily. He assembled his army in the area of Salé on the Atlantic coast (1151), then led it in a northerly direction, to all appearance prepared for crossing the Straits, but suddenly turned eastward and in a forced march over Tlemcen arrived at the gates of Algiers, which the Ḥammādid governor left without striking a blow while one of his sons conquered and destroyed the stronghold of al-Qalʿa. Following the occupation of Bougie and the surrender of Yaḥyā Ibn al-ʿAzīz, the last Ḥammādid emir, whom he sent into honourable exile to Marrakesh, he routed at Sétif (1153) in a heavy battle, an army of Bedouin warriors, mainly Banū Hilāl* and Sulaym*, formerly in Ḥammādid pay and unwilling to submit to the new and much stronger master.
Engaged in the urgent task of organizing his vast territories and settling certain unavoidable internal frictions, ʿAbd al-Muʾmin had to let several years pass before planning for the conquest of the remaining parts of the North African coastal areas. Finally, after careful preparation, he set out (1159) for Tunisia with an army, according to contemporary chroniclers, of some 200.000 men and a fleet of 70 ships, strong enough to face the Norman navy. In the same year Tunis, at that time under an independent Ṣanhāja dynasty, surrendered, and al-Mahdīya, the one-time residence of the Zīrid emirs, then in the hands of King Roger II of Sicily, capitulated after a seven-month siege. Greeted everywhere as the liberator from Norman rule, he occupied in quick succession Sousse, al-Qayrawān, Sfax, Gabès and Tripoli, as well as wide stretches of the interior (1160). As in Algeria, the unruly Arab Bedouins had to be reduced to obedience by the force of arms but thereupon were treated as equals, and while the arm-bearing were incorporated in the Almohad army, a great number of the families were moved into Morocco and assigned new pasture grounds there.
Less successful had until then been the Almohad Holy War in al-Andalus* among the confusing constellation of ever changing city-potentates (Party Kings*) or semi-independent Almoravid governors and their vague alliances and uncertain loyalties. The first to espouse the new

doctrine was the Almoravid admiral of Cadiz, followed by the emir of Jaen, whereas others had to be subdued one by one by ʿAbd al-Mu'min's generals. Repeated revolts, however, of the citizenry everywhere and especially the daring raids of the lord of Valencia and Murcia, Ibn Mardanīsh*, not only delayed further advance, but even brought about the loss of earlier conquests. Thereupon ʿAbd al-Mu'min, just back in his capital Marrakesh, left for al-Andalus, fortified Gibraltar as his operational basis and concentrated an army in the area of present-day Rabat, protected by a fortress he had erected (today the Qasba of the Ūdāya), but his plans of invasion were cut short by his death (1163). He was buried in Tinmāl beside the tomb of Ibn Tūmart.
In spite of his designation by the venerated Mahdi, ʿAbd al-Mu'min did not ascend to the leadership of the community without encountering serious resistance. This emanated in general from the Masmūda confederation because of his coming from an alien tribal group, and in particular from Ibn Tūmart's relatives, who felt frustrated in what they had considered their legitimate title to the supreme position. By his skill in dealing with people, ranging from subtle adaptability to calculated cruelty, and, thanks to the unflinching support he found at all times with Abū Hafs ʿUmar*, the influential mountain chieftain and first-hour protector of the Mahdi, he finally imposed his undisputed authority, efficiently emphasized by his own tribe, the Kūmya, who were made to migrate from their homeland into the area of Marrakesh, and constituted his personal guard, allegedly some 40.000 strong. As *Amīr al-Mu'minīn* (Commander of the Faitful), the secular and spiritual head of the State, he further elaborated for the requirements of an empire the system of public administration, devised by Ibn Tūmart and founded on a combination of tribal institutions, a kind of religious hierarchy and military structure, with governors of the provinces and larger towns selected from among his own or Abū Hafs ʿUmar's clan. Everywhere a network of missionaries spread and kept alive the tenets of the Almohad faith and the principles of the theocratic movement which rested upon it. The heritage which ʿAbd al-Mu'min left to his son and successor Abū Yaʿqūb Yūsuf* (1163-1184) was one of the most powerful, largest and most solidly constructed empires in the history of the Arab West.

ʿABD al-QĀDIR IBN MUHYĪ al-DĪN, in the Occident better known as Abdelkader, the great popular leader (1808-1883) in the armed resistance against the French expeditions undertaken for the conquest of Algeria in the years between 1830 and 1847. His family, which claimed descent from the Prophet Muhammad had moved, prior to his birth, from the Rif region into the area of Mascara (western Algeria), where his father was held in high repute for his pious way of life and profound knowledge in matters of religion. ʿAbd al-Qādir, educated in the same spirit, dedicated himself to the current theological studies and at the age of twenty had already twice undertaken the pilgrimage to the Holy Cities. After their occupation of Algiers (July 1830) and the principal coastal towns between Oran and Bône, the French tried to win over his father to their side, hoping to appease through his intervention the restless population of the hinterland, with the result that both father and son took the lead in a quickly spreading movement of a Holy War against the invaders.

ʿAbd al-Qādir, twentyfour years old assumed the time-honoured title *Amīr al-Mu'minīn* (Commander of the Faithful) and started a most tenacious guerilla warfare. Although his attacks on Mostaganem and Oran failed, mainly owing to the defection of some Kabyle* tribal groups, the French commanding general thought it advisable to negotiate for a truce and recognize him as emir (February 1834). A few months later, however, ʿAbd al-Qādir again took up arms, came dangerously near to Algiers, and inflicted serious losses upon the French in an encounter in the swamps - they have since been drained - south of Mostaganem. All over the Arab West his name was hailed as that of the great new hero of Islam. Although he had to evacuate Mostaganem, lost Mascara and suffered several other setbacks, he succeeded, by exploiting the difficult situation of the French troops in the area of Constantine, in bringing about (May 1837) the so-called agreement on the Tafna (a river north of Tlemcen), by which France restituted Mascara and turned over to him almost the entire province of Oran as well as large sections of the province of Algiers in the hope of securing his allegiance and thus the control over the country.

The calculation proved wrong. ʿAbd al-Qādir immediately set about organizing his territory but he recognized the sovereignty of Sultan Mūlāy ʿAbd al-Rahmān of Morocco and in return received much needed war supplies and financial aid. Establishing his capital at Tagdempt (near the coast, some 60 miles east of Algiers) he trained and regrouped his troops, extended his hegemony over most of Kabylia, installed his governors in the more important localities and finally penetrated southward as far as the fringe of the Sahara, using the force of arms when persuasion was ineffective. After new and protracted pourparlers with the French had proved resultless, he proclaimed again the Holy War, invaded the Mitīja (the plain extending south of Algiers) and prepared to attack Algiers. This time, however, his luck deserted him. He was driven out of Tagdempt and Mascara (May 1840), the ideological foci of the resistance, and within two years lost one after the other of his strategic key-positions in northern Algeria thus having to shift continually the large encampment *(zmāla*)* which thenceforth was his residence, headquarters and rallying point of his warriors after each of their roving expeditions. When it was conquered while stationed at Tanuine, south of Reibell (May 1843) he passed over into Morocco whence he carried the war across the border, everywhere aided by the people and actively encouraged by the sultan. Only by a two-fold military intervention, at sea by shelling Tangier and Mogador, on land by the defeat of a Morrocan army in the Isly valley near Oujda, could France put a stop to Moroccan assistance without, however, obtaining ʿAbd al-Qādir's extradition. Supported by the Berber frontier tribes and the religious brotherhoods*, especially the local Darqāwā* branches, he reappeared in Algeria and again roused up the fighting spirit of the people, Berber and Arab, against the French intrusion. It took a most strenuous winter campaign (1845/46) to push him back into Morocco, and strong pressure

upon the Moroccan government to have him declared a rebel and his pursuit obtained. Caught between two Moroccan army detachments in the valley of the Muluya river ʿAbd al-Qādir, trying to escape southward and seek refuge with some tribes in the Sahara, was encircled by French troops and surrendered (December 1847). It was the end of his epic struggle.
After three-year's internment in France he was released and, having pledged himself to refrain from all further interference in Algerian matters was granted for himself and his descendants a permanent allowance which only recently was discontinued by the French government. With his family and those of his followers who had accompanied him into exile he went first to Brussa, then to Constantinople and finally settled in Damascus, where the seigneurial home of Emir al-Jazā'irī - from *Barr al-Jazā'ir*, Algeria - during the tragic persecution of the Christians (1860) protected the refugees it could shield from the fanatical mob. The place is still inhabited by members of his family, quite a few of whom today are prominent in Syrian intellectual life. One of his grandsons, Emir Khālid, a French officer, was in the 1920's one of the first to claim equal rights in the military and civil services for the native Algerians, many of whom in the World War had fought in the ranks of the French army. Thereupon Emir Khālid was exiled. In the history of Algerian nationalism, at least in its popular versions, the figure of ʿAbd al-Qādir appears surrounded with the glory of the pioneer on the road to independence.

ʿABD-RABBIHI, IBN, a Hispano-Arab poet and man of letters (860-940). He was born in Cordova where he spent most of his life, except for a short stay at the court of the Banū Hajjāj, the ephemeral self-styled 'Kings' of Seville, and a sojourn in the Arab East in order to acquaint himself through personal contacts with the intellectual currents of the great Arab literary and scientific centres. He was the official court poet of four Umayyad emirs. His creation, which comprises panegyrics in honour of his patrons, satires, love poems and, in his later years, ascetic poetry, is said to have filled twenty volumes. The work which established Ibn-ʿAbd Rabbihi's reputation is the *Kitāb al-ʿIqd al-Farīd* (The Unique Necklace), an encyclopaedic compilation of the principal aspects of the world of Islam down to his days. It consists of 25 books in two sections, separated by book thirteen which is called *Al-Wasita* (the middle), while each of the twelve books of the first and the second section bear the name of a different gem. The material used by Ibn-ʿAbd Rabbihi, the manner in which he elaborated it, and the interest the *ʿIqd* met with the West as well as in the East illustrates the intense interchange of ideas between the two parts of the Arab world.

ʿABD al-RAHMĀN I IBN MUʿĀWIYA, called Benemaugius (756-788) by the Latin chroniclers of the Middle-Ages, the founder of the Umayyad dynasty of emirs, later caliphs, in al-Andalus*. Grandson of Caliph Hishām (724-743) and son of a Berber slave girl, he was born and brought up in Damascus, and almost miraculously survived, together with his infant son Sulaymān, two sisters and some cousins, the wholesale murder of his family (750) by the first ʿAbbāsid caliph al-Saffā. Sheltered by a group of Bedouins encamped near the Euphrates, he was, however, discovered by his enemies, but escaped by swimming across the river, and in constant danger of his life made his way into Palestine where he was joined by his freedman Badr*. Throughout four years they wandered across Egypt and all over North Africa among the Berber tribes until at last were in safety with the tribe of ʿAbd al-Rahmān's mother. There, ʿAbd al-Rahmān seems to have thought for the first time of rebuilding the Umayyad throne in the Spanish province of the ʿAbbāsid caliphate.

In June 754 Badr crossed the Straits into al-Andalus in order to explore the prospects of such an undertaking. About a year later he returned, after having set up the nucleus of a pro-Umayyad organization ready to take up arms for the pretender. In August 755 ʿAbd al-Rahmān, trusting in the prestige of his name, set foot on Iberian soil halfway between Malaga and Almeria, and established himself in the stronghold of one of his supporters in the region of Granada. Skilfully playing upon the hereditary antagonism dividing Arab tribal society into the two factions of Qays and Kalb - the people of the South and the people of the North - and the feuds among the Berber chiefs, he rallied enough followers to move forward. In March 756 he was enthusiastically acclaimed in Seville; in May he beat the troops of the ʿAbbāsid governor on the banks of the Guadalquivir, and was master of Cordova; and a few days afterwards he had himself proclaimed Emir of al-Andalus. Soon the solemn mention of the caliph's name was omitted from the Friday sermon, yet without ʿAbd al-Rahmān letting his own name be substituted for it. All he did was to call himself „the son of the caliphs" ʿ*(ibn al-khalāʾif)*.

It took ʿAbd al-Rahmān - *al-Dākhil* (the Immigrant) as he was frequently spoken of by his biographers - four more years to break the resistance of the ʿAbbāsid governor. Combining patient negotiations and persuasion with severity and even cruelty, he consolidated his authority in the face of the multitude of fickle and turbulent local leaders. He subdued revolts of malcontent Arab chieftains, some of which were fomented by ʿAbbāsid agents in Toledo, Seville and in the southern regions of present-day Portugal. Then he quenched a tenacious Berber uprising in the southwestern sector of the peninsula, stirred up by a fanatical 'prophet', probably in spiritual relation with the heretic Barghawāta* community in western Morocco. At the same time he had to ward off his Christian neighbour in the north, the King of Asturia, and an incursion (778) of the Franks led personally by Charlemagne, which after a fruitless siege of Saragossa ended with the retreat of the Frankish army through the pass of Roncevalles. The epic death in battle of Roland is immortalized by legend and the 'Chanson de Roland'.

The Umayyad restoration carried into Spain both from North Africa and the Arab East, especially from Syria, a wave of immigrants, among them ʿAbd al-Rahmān's cousins with their clientele, who were invested with military and administrative key-positions. Also his young son Sulaymān was brought over, whereas his sisters, treated with distinction by the caliph, preferred to remain in the home country. How strongly ʿAbd al-Rahmān himself felt attached to it he showed when building his palace near Cordova which he named *al-Rusāfa* after his grandfather's pleasure seat in an oasis between Palmyra and the Euphrates. There he planted a solitary date palm from Syria, inspiring him, at least so it is said, to elegiac verses of home-sickness. The village of Arizafa, now on this site, perpetuates the name of the emir's residence. From Syria, too, he introduced apricot, peach and pomegranate trees which until then were unknown in Spain.

Under ʿAbd al-Rahmān's reign Cordova began to assume the first features of the splendid capital into which it was soon to grow. He remodelled and extended the fortifications; built quarters for the government offices; and purchasing from the Mozarab* community the second half of the city's principal church - one half had been turned into a mosque at the time of the country's occupation - laid the foundation of the famous Great Mosque of Cordova. He strengthened the public administration and reorganized the army, which he based on a corps of mercenaries recruited from among Berber tribes, and on military slaves. At his deathbed he designated as his successor his second-born son Hishām, whose two brothers, the older Sulaymān and the younger ʿAbd Allāh, emigrated to Morocco after a short attempt to reverse in their favour their father's decision by the force of arms.

ʿABD al-RAHMĀN II, the fourth Umayyad emir of al-Andalus* (822-852). After his father, Emir al-Hakam I (792-822) had forged the political and religious unity by instituting the Malekite school of juridico-theological thought as the sole official doctrine, ʿAbd al-Rahmān II, ascending the throne at the age of thirty, could look forward to a reign of peace, prosperity and cultural evolution. Apart from the usual summer incursions *(saifa*)* into the neighbouring Christian states no warlike events disturbed the generally quiet atmosphere except minor feuds among Arab chieftains and Berber clans and uprisings in Toledo, Merida and Algeciras. Fighting also took place on the northern frontiers against the Basques (Vascones, *al-Bashkūnish)* around their stronghold Pampeluna (Banbaluna, from Pompeiopolis) - the region out of which in later years was to grow the Kingdom of Navarre - and against their ally, a rebellious governor of Tudela.

The only real alarm was caused by the first appearance (844) at the Andalusian coast of the brown sails of some hundred vessels of filibustering Normans *(al-Urdumāniyūn)*. They landed at Lisbon, were repelled, but proceeded southwards and entered the estuary of the Guadalquivir. Sowing death and destruction in the nearby villages they arrived at Seville that was abandoned by most of the panic-stricken inhabitants. The city was sacked and whosoever was still found in hiding was massacred. Soon, however, the Andalusian troops, rapidly assembled from every part of the country, defeated the invaders in the plain of Tablada south of Seville - today an airport - and exterminated everyone who could not regain a ship. A few isolated groups who escaped into the marshland of the lower Guadalquivir surrendered, embraced Islam, settled in the neighbourhood of Seville and in the course of a few generations became peaceful peasants. Thenceforth all along the Atlantic

coast a system of fortified outposts *(ribātāt,* sing *ribāt*)* was established and garrisoned with volunteers who performed there the pious duty of combining religious exercise with military service.
Of refined taste, well-read and interested in philosophy, medicine and astronomy - or rather astrology - ʿAbd al-Rahmān II assembled at Cordova a galaxy of scholars, men of letters, poets and musicians, among whom the theologian Yahyā Ibn Yahyā al-Laithī*, the savant ʿAbbas Ibn Firnās*, the poet al-Ghazal* and the musician-composer Ziryāb* were the most brilliant lights. Consigning into oblivion the enmity which so long had opposed Umayyads and ʿAbbāsids he sent his agents to the centres of learning in the Arab East to acquire the manuscripts of its great thinkers, and Arabic translations of Greek and Persian authors. Also in setting up or remodelling the pattern of the administration and finances of the state he was to a certain extent guided by what he was able to learn about the public institutions of the Baghdad caliphate. Concentrating in his person all military, executive and judicial power he devoted particular attention to the strengthening of the army - and after the Norman invasion also of the navy - by greatly increasing the body of mercenaries and military slaves. One of the wealthiest monarchs in the western Arab world, he purchased precious works of art, silken fabrics and jewelry for his court and household. He erected a new palace within the precincts of his residence; enlarged and embellished the Great Mosque at Cordova; and built smaller mosques in a number of towns. The diplomatic mission sent to Cordova by the Byzantine Emperor Theophilus in order to win ʿAbd al-Rahmān for an alliance against the Aghlabids* of Tunisia and the splendid reception which the bearer of his answer, al-Ghazal, was given in Constantinople reflect his prestige. He died at the age of sixty and was succeeded by his son Emir Muhammad I (852-912).

ʿABD al-RAHMĀN III, an outstanding ruler of the Spanish Umayyad dynasty (912-961). At the time he ascended the throne at the age of 23 in succession to his grandfather ʿAbd Allāh (888-912) the influential families in the provinces and larger towns recognized the central government at Cordova hardly more than by name. The Berber tribes of the highland devastated the fertile coastal regions. The newly converted peasant population *(muwalladūn*)* revolted, and so did the Christians incited by the zealotry of some of the priests and monks. Incessant feuds among the Arab landed lords and the sedition of the adventurer and popular hero ʿUmar Ibn Hafsūn shook the structure of the state to its very foundation. The danger was increased by the aggressive spiritual and political imperialism of the Fātimids, threatening to spread from the African coast across the straits into Spain; and by continuous attacks of the kings of Leon, Castile and Navarre, aiming at territorial expansion if not at complete conquest.
Step by step ʿAbd al-Rahmān subdued the disloyal grandees and Ibn Hafsūn's revolutionaries; pacified the religious excitement in Moslem as well as Christian quarters; and established his authority in all parts of the country. To counter the heterodox Fātimid propaganda he had himself proclaimed caliph (929), with the epithet *al-Nāsir li Dīn Allāh*

(Defender of the Religion of God), and *Amīr al-Mu'minīn* (Commander of the Believers). He fortified the Andalusian coasts; equipped a strong fleet; and by skilful political moves made first one and then another chieftain of the Berber Miknāsa*, Banū Ifrān* or Maghrāwa* recognize him as protector. Having thus gained a foothold in North Africa he occupied and fortified Ceuta (931), then Tangier and Melilla. In a series of succesful campaigns the Christian kings were pushed back, their frontier strongholds destroyed, and the war was carried into their own territories. Notwithstanding a heavy defeat in a battle near Salamanca in 939 inflicted on the Arab army by the allied troops of Leon and Navarre, attemps at further attacks from the North were checked by large-scale devastations of the frontier areas.
ʿAbd al-Rahmān's army with his body-guard of 4000 foreign military slaves *(saqāliba*)* blindly devoted to him was now the strongest and best-disciplined of his time. Hated as much as dreaded by the proud Arab nobility it prevented the very thought of disobedience from whatever side, and protected the peasant, artisan and tradesman from oppressors and brigands. Al-Andalus enjoyed a hitherto unknown prosperity, rooted in a well-diversified agricultural and industrial production, a flourishing horticulture - one of the date groves laid out at that time in the province of Valencia has survived to this day - and a lucrative over-sea commerce. Considerable reserves in the public treasury permitted the caliph to give rein to the display of splendour and the patronage of arts. Near Cordova he erected a palace called *al-Zahrā'* (The Bright One) after his favourite slave girl, on which 10.000 workmen are said to have worked for 20 years. It must have surpassed in magnificence any other royal residence, even discounting as a play of over-imaginative enthusiasm of the contemporary chroniclers some of the 4300 columns imported from Constantinople, and some of the 1500 doors and many multi-coloured marble halls decorated with rock crystal, ebony, ivory and ornaments of chased gold. Cordova's beautiful mosques, public baths and gardens, its schools and scholarly circles were rivalled only by those of Baghdad. Even in Fez the minaret of the Qarawīyīn Mosque was built upon his order and at his expense. Al-Andalus under ʿAbd al-Rahmān III was one of the leading powers of the world.

ʿABD al-RAHMĀN IBN HISHĀM, a Moroccan sultan (1822-1859) of the ʿAlawid* family, designated by his uncle, Sultan Mūlāy Sulaymān (1792-1822), as his successor and immediately recognized all over the country - a rather rare case in Moroccan dynastic history. His first care was directed towards the reconsolidation of the authority and the finances of the State, which had badly suffered in the last years of his predecessor. On the one hand, he encouraged the formation of alliances among the strong Arab and Berber tribes, counting on their loyalty to strengthen his comparatively small body-guard garrisoned in the principal towns; and, on the other, he tried to base public administration and tax collection, especially in the mountains and the remote regions south of the Atlas, as far as possible upon the co-operation of the powerful local chieftains to whom he entrusted high governmental positions. It was a somewhat labile apparatus of government requiring a well-balanced dosage of firmness and negotiating abilities, both of which he expertly applied, but above all support by the mass of the people. To secure this he completely reversed the attitude of disapproval, taken by his uncle, of the activities of the religious brotherhoods* by associating their influence with his policy, and drawing the heads of some of them into his closest surroundings.

Nevertheless Mūlāy ʿAbd al-Rahmān had to face some serious seditions of the restless Arab tribes, in particular of the Ūdāya, once the élite troop of the army *(jaish)* which he disbanded and resettled in separate small units; and of the Sharrarda, a Maʿqil* branch in the area of Marrakesh under the obedience of a warlike marabout* whom he transferred together with his people into the region of Meknès. Others, in the Tādlā, north of the Middle Atlas and around Rabat, were subdued and severely punished. Berber revolts broke out on the western slope of the Middle Atlas and in the oases to the south, while in the Tazarwalt, in the southeastern corner of the country, a grandson of the marabout-prince al-Samlālī*, set up a sort of miniature state which maintained itself until the establishment of the French Protectorate* in 1912.

For a while Mūlāy ʿAbd al-Rahmān continued the old practice of lending a more or less veiled patronage to the activities - disguised as Holy War - of the Moroccan pirate fleets of Rabat-Salé and Larrache in return for a part of the booty. He discontinued it only after the Austrian navy had shelled Larrache (1830) and destroyed the pirate ships in the port in reprisal for the capture of Austrian merchant vessels and their crew. Then he concluded an alliance (1856) with England whereby English trade was accorded a preferential position, and England in compensation - and also to forestall the implantation of another European power in front of Gibraltar - guaranteed the inviolability of Moroccan territory. In these years there took place the French occupation of Algiers (1830), an event that was to be conducive to far-reaching political and cultural consequences for the entire Arab West. As its immediate result Morocco became involved in a war with France, the issue of which could not but be unfortunate. It began when the sultan, perhaps more under the pressure of public opinion than on the ground of a well weighed policy, decided to lend his help to Abdelkader (ʿAbd al-Qādir Ibn Muhyī al-Dīn*), the hero in the struggle against the foreign invader. At last he declared the Holy War against France. The French riposte was the shelling of Tangier and Mogador, followed by an offensive advance in the region of Oujda, which led to the defeat of the Moroccans in the nearby valley of the Isly river (August 1844). One month later peace was concluded at Tangier, and in compliance with the conditions imposed by the victor, the sultan thenceforth not only had to cease assisting Abdelkader but also to outlaw him and participate in the operations against him, which however he did very reluctantly. Subsequently the Franco-Moroccan convention of Lalla Marnia (1845) in parts delimited the border between Algeria and Morocco from the small coastal town of Port-Say some 80 miles southwards to the pass of Teniet Sassi and left to France a free hand for further operations in Algeria.

Mūlāy ʿAbd al-Rahmān died while conducting a campaign against seditious Berber tribes, and was succeeded by his son Sīdī Muhammad

(1859-1873), who already for quite some time had held the highest administrative and military functions.

ʿABD al-WĀDIDS, Banū ʿAbd al-Wād, also known as Banū Zayyān, a Berber dynasty (1236-1550 with several interruptions) in Tlemcen with a territory covering approximately the present-day Algerian province of Oran and at the periods of its greatest expansion reaching as far as Algiers. The Banū ʿAbd al-Wād were a clan of the Banū Wasīn, a branch of the Zanāta* family of tribes, and related with, but in hereditary feud opposed to, the Morroccan dynasty of the Marīnids*, with whom in their earlier history they had lived side by side on the northern fringe of the Sahara until under the pressure of the advancing Arab Banū Hilāl* and Sulaym* both of them migrated northwards. The Banū ʿAbd al-Wād were assigned pasture grounds in the West-Algerian tablelands by the great Almohad conqueror ʿAbd al-Mu'min* (1133-1163), which they gradually extended over the region of Bougie, remaining, although with occasional frictions, loyal servants of the Almohad régime. In the years of its decline their chieftain Abū Yahyā Yaghmurāsan (also mentioned as Yaghamrāsan and Ghamarāsan) Ibn Zayyān was governor of the town of Tagrart, a foundation of the Almoravid* ruler Yūsuf Ibn Tāshufīn* (1061-1107) which with the neighbouring, much older town of Agadir was to grow into the city of Tlemcen. He shook off a no longer more than nominal suzerainty and thus became the first (1236-1282) of the long line of ʿAbd al-Wādid - or Zayyānid - princes.
Until his death Yaghmurāsan remained the patriarchal chieftain of his tribal community, which only slowly and incompletely turned to a sedentary mode of life. Deeply respected for his just and wise leadership and political insight he set up a rudimentary but solid governmental structure; had his chamberlain *(hājib)* and viziers selected from among close relatives; a staff of scribes, presumably Andalusians-he himself knew only his Zanāta dialect - and summoned distinguished doctors of the religious sciences to teach at the Great Mosque, while not omitting to keep at his court poets who had to sing his praise. He sent and received ambassadors, and concluded alliances with the Sultan of Granada and the King of Castile against his old-time enemies, the Banū Marīn. Berber tribesmen constituted the main body of his armed forces, but he also recruited a corps of Turkish and Christian mercenaries from the Almohad army in dissolution. He was not, however, strong enough to resist the expansive pressure of his neighbour in the East, the Hafsid* emir Abū Zakariyyā'* (1236-1275) of Tunisia. During five years he had to leave his capital to the victorious aggressor and to recognize his overlordship before being permitted to return. The marriage between his son and successor Abū Saʿīd ʿUthmān (1283-1303) with a Hafsid princess consolidated for some time the good-neighbourly relations.
The hostilities, however, between ʿAbd al-Wādids and Marīnids lasted intermittently almost for generations and several times took an extremely critical turn for the far weaker rulers of Tlemcen. Under Abū Saʿīd ʿUthmān the ʿAbd al-Wādid territory was repeatedly overrun, and its capital besieged during eight years by the Marīnid Abū Yaʿqūb Yūsuf* (1286-1307) who built up his camp some two miles from Tlemcen into a

regular town, al-Mansūra (The Victorious), and made it the centre of a splendid court life and a lively trade. Only his assassination saved Tlemcen at the last minute from surrender and the dynasty from a sudden end. After the withdrawal of the invaders al-Mansūra remained abandoned, even when they returned somewhat later for a second siege, soon again terminated, during the reign of Abū Zayyān's brother Abū Hammū Mūsā (1308-1318). Immediately upon his accession to the throne the new ruler, energetic, authoritative and regardless of difficulties, devoted all his efforts to the task of restoring the fortifications, repairing the damages of the war, reconsolidating the dynasty's prestige, badly shaken by the occupation, and reorganizing the affairs of the state. Rebellious tribes were subdued, and from all clans and families of any standing, even in the villages and towns, hostages with their wives and children were interned in the vast compound around his residence where they were well treated, built their own houses and did business with the townspeople. Simultaneously the apparatus of government, which had been adequate for a mainly nomadic or semi-nomadic community, was gradually adapted to an increasingly complex social and economic structure. The steady influx from al-Andalus* of people trained in clerical work supplied the personnel for the new administrative and financial offices, as well as the sultan's advisers for the organization of an appropriate government framework.

Abū Hammū Mūsā was assassinated under the eyes and perhaps with the connivance of his son Abū Tāshufīn ʿAbd al-Rahmān (1318-1337) who continued his father's modernizing policy. Luxury-loving, appreciative of cultural refinement as well as of the more trivial types of distraction he changed the traditional rustic simplicity of the royal household into a ceremonial court atmosphere, and embellished Tlemcen with a number of religious and profane buildings, some of them accounted by chroniclers among the outstanding monuments of the time. Attracted by a flourishing trade, wealthy Andalusian merchants sought a new home in the expanding ʿAbd al-Wādid capital, which developed into a key-point in the traffic with the interior of Africa and with Europe. Their seigneurial residences, tastefully laid-out pleasure gardens, and their mode of life in elegant Andalusian style, set the fashion for the native upper classes. At the same pace there evolved fruitful intellectual activities brought by the theologians and jurisprudents who came to Tlemcen from abroad. Hand in hand with these scientifically orientated religious studies radiating from each newly created *madrasa* (school mosque) there went on as in neighbouring Morocco and Tunisia a deep-going mystical movement which centred around numerous saintly men (marabouts*) held in veneration by rich and poor alike. It was on the whole a reasonably prosperous society without sharp economic contrasts, blending Berber, Andalusian and Bedouin elements in its leading groups - tribal chieftains, court dignitaries, men of learning and well-to-do merchants - as well as in the broad urban middle-class in which close contacts with the floating, semi-sedentary population of the surroundings kept alive the memory of its own not so distant nomadic past.

Over-confident in his miltary strength Abū Tāshufīn attempted a territorial aggrandizment at the expense of his Hafsid neighbours, a policy which was soon conducive to a Moroccan-Tunisian alliance and furnished the ambitious Marīnid Abū al-Hasan ʿAlī (1331-1351) with the welcome pretext for a large-scale offensive against the ʿAbd al-Wādid domain. Within a short time the whole country was overrun, but Tlemcen resisted three years before it was conquered in embittered street-fighting in which Abū Tāshufīn was taken prisoner and killed. The Marīnid interregnum was to last over two decades, interrupted only (1348-1352) in the troubled years of Abū al-Hasan's fall from power and the struggle for the throne by his son Abū ʿInān Fāris* (1351-1358). To al-Mansūra, promoted again to the rank of the ruler's permanent headquarters, it brought a splendid resurrection. The victor's first care was to provide it with an imposing defensive system of a fifteen foot high and two foot thick circumvallation with eighty massive built-in towers. Then he completed the Great Mosque which had been left unfinished since the death of the city's founder some thirty years earlier, set up a monumental gate and a minaret, about 50 foot high, with a spiral ramp inside instead of stairs, broad enough for two persons to ride on horseback to the top. Very little of the mosque has been preserved: a few column capitals and shafts of onyx, a fountain basin of green porphyry, parts of the minaret and the gate, but they evidence the perfection which hispano-moresque architecture and decorative arts had by then reached. Of the sultan's palace - Palace of the Victory, as it was called - hardly more than traces have remained. Still in use, however, there is in al-ʿUbbād, (today called El-Eubbad or popularly Sīdī Bū Madin, half a mile from Tlemcen) the mosque built by Abū al-Hasan ʿAlī adjacent to the mausoleum of Tlemcen's great patron-saint Abū Madyan*, and nearby a *madrasa*, a public bath for the use of the pilgrims, and other minor structures, all with elaborately finished decorative details.

The dynasty's restoration, due chiefly to the support of Arab tribes of the Maʿqil*group, was the achievement of one of its most popular figures, Abū Hammū II Mūsā (1359-1389). Born and brought up in al-Andalus he was conversant with the scholarly and literary currents of his time, occasionally also giving rein to his poetical propensities and to philosophico-political speculations. In friendly relations with the Hafsid princes at whose court in Tunis he had spent several years, he seized the opportunity of Abū ʿInān's* assassination at a time when the never very close Hafsid-Marīnid sympathy was once more cooling off, had himself entrusted with the command of a Hafsid army and reconquered the ancestral throne. His reign was far from peaceful. He had to repress several rebellions, to combat his own son who sided against him with the Marīnid enemy, and was even forced to a temporary abandonment (1370-1372) of his capital and the major part of his territory to a Moroccan army while taking refuge with some tribes in the desert. Yet, whenever peace was re-established he assembled at his court poets, men of letters and learning - the historian Yahyā Ibn-Khaldūn* was his personal friend and confidential secretary - for scholarly and literary debates or the recitation of poems, often himself participating in the discussions and keeping for these entertainments the doors of the palace open to everyone, down to the humblest of his people. Abū Hammū fell fighting against

another invading Marīnid force conducted by his rebellious son Abū Tāshufīn II ʿAbd al-Rahmān, who succeeded him to the throne (1389-1393), after having recognized Moroccan sovereignty.
Within its geographical limitations Tlemcen under the ʿAbd al-Wādids maintained its place in economic and cultural spheres undiminished for a century-and-a-half longer; politically it was thenceforth reduced to an entirely passive rôle. Concessions of ever larger portions of the state domain to the Maʿqil chieftains in return for military service; endless family feuds, conspiracies and rebellions; an unfortunate sequence of weak and incapable rulers - all combined to make Tlemcen a mere stake in the contest of other powers for supremacy in North Africa: Morocco, Tunisia, Spain and Turkey. The seven sultans who in the following two decades occupied the throne in quick succession were Moroccan vassals. Under their three successors, by turns installed, deposed and installed again by the Hafsid Abū Fāris ʿAbd al-ʿAzīz*, Tlemcen and whatever was left of its former territory became a Tunisian dependency (1424). It remained under Tunisian control until the end of the century, notwithstanding an occasional attempt at emancipation by one or other of the ʿAbd al-Wādid princes, which mostly ended with the rebel's withdrawal to a tribe in the desert and his replacement by a less ambitious family member.
Then the political and military configuration shifted. Neither did the Hafsids nor the Wattāsid* rulers of Morocco count any longer as factors in the competition for influence, and Spain could pursue practically unhindered a systematic policy of expansion along the Moroccan and Algerian coasts. By 1510 Spanish garrisons lay in Melilla, Oran, Bougie, Algiers and Tripoli; an organization of partisans in the hinterland was built up; raiding expeditions pushed into the interior; and Spanish tutelage was imposed upon Tlemcen. Already, however, the Turkish advance westwards was in motion, impelled by the two brothers ʿArūj and Khair al-Dīn Barbarossa, maritime adventurers just then at the beginning of a career which was to make them the founders of the threehundred-year Ottoman rule in Libya, Tunisia and Algeria. Around 1510 they had their vessels and stores of war supply in most of the small Algerian ports and their allies among the surrounding population. ʿArūj conquered (1516) the town of Algiers - but not the sea-fort, the so-called Peñon, erected by the Spanish - and made his entry into Tlemcen (1517). He was welcomed by the populace, while the ʿAbd al-Wādid Abū Hammū III Mūsā (1517-1527), who had just ascended the throne by overthrowing his nephew, was forced to flee in all haste. Supported by the Spanish protector he returned a year later and ʿArūj was killed, but the Turkish party in Tlemcen did not cease to gain influence. With its help a coup d'état carried the pro-Turkish Abū Zayyān III Ahmad to power (1540-1550), and when the Spanish governor of Oran through armed intervention tried to replace him by one of his brothers, a popular rising quickly ousted the Spanish protégé. His son al-Hasan Ibn ʿAbd Allāh renewed the experiment but again it miscarried. By then Spain's position in North Africa was at the beginning of its decline, while Morocco under the forcefully emerging Saʿdians* reappeared in the field, and a Moroccan army on its march eastwards against the Turks found the

gates of Tlemcen wide open. Al-Hasan sought refuge with his Spanish suzerain (1550) and disappeared from the stage. He was the last of the line. Soon afterwards the Moroccans had to withdraw, and Tlemcen was permanently incorporated in the Turkish regency of Algiers.

List of the ʿAbd al-Wādid rulers:

Abū Yahyā Yaghmurāsan Ibn Zayyān	1236-1282
Abū Saʿid ʿUthmān I Ibn Yaghmurāsan	1282-1303
Abū Zayyān I Muhammad Ibn ʿUthmān	1303-1308
Abū Hammū I Mūsa Ibn ʿUthmān	1308-1318
Abū Tāshufīn I ʿAbd al-Rahmān Ibn Mūsā	1318-1337
First Marīnid Occupation	1337-1348
Abū Saʿīd ʿUthmān II Ibn ʿAbd al-Rahmān and his brother Abū Thābit	1348-1352
Second Marīnid Occupation	1352-1359
Abū Hammū II Ibn Abī Yaʿqūb	1359-1389
Abū Tāshufīn IIʿAbd al-Rahman Ibn Mūsā	1389-1393
Abū Thābit II Yūsuf Ibn ʿAbd al-Rahmān	1393
Abū Hajjāj Yūsuf Ibn Mūsā	1393-1394
Abū Zayyān II Muhammad Ibn Mūsā	1394-1399
Abū Muhammad ʿAbd Allāh I Ibn Musā	1399-1401
Abū ʿAbd Allāh Muhammad I Ibn Mūsā	1401-1411
ʿAbd al-Rahmān Ibn Mūsā	1411
Abū Saʿīd Ibn Musā	1411
Abū Mālik ʿAbd al-Wāhid Ibn Mūsā	1411-1424
Abū ʿAbd Allāh Muhammad II Ibn ʿAbd al-Rahmān	1424-1427 and 1429-1430
Abū al-ʿAbbās Ahmad Ibn Mūsā	1430-1461
Abū ʿAbd Allāh Muhammad III al-Mutawakkil Ibn Muhammad	1461-1468
Abū Tāshufīn III Ibn Muhammad al-Mutawakkil	1468
Abū ʿAbd Allāh Muhammad IV al-Thābit Ibn Muhammad al-Mutawakkil	1468-1504
Abū ʿAbd Allāh Muhammad V al-Thābit Ibn Muhammad IV	1504-1517
Abū Hammū III Mūsā Ibn Muhammad III	1517-1527
Abū Muhammad ʿAbd Allāh II Ibn Muhammad III	1527-1540
Abū ʿAbd Allāh Muhammad VI Ibn ʿAbd Allāh	1540
Abū Zayyā n III	1540-1550
Al-Hasan Ibn ʿAbd Allāh	1550

ʿABDARĪ al-,MUHAMMAD, the author (XIII/XIVth cent.) of one of the best-known so-called travel books *(rihla*)* a literary genre much in favour at the time of the outgoing Middle-Ages. No biographical data have been transmitted except that he was born in Valencia, established himself in Morocco and lived for a while in the area of Mogador before setting out for the pilgrimage(1289). His work, the *Rihla al-Maghribīya*, is an account of this journey and of his prolonged stay in the larger towns on his way through Algeria, Tunisia, Tripolitania through Egypt to Arabia. Its value consists not so much in the geographical and topographical descriptions, which in many instances are mere repetitions of the observations recorded already by others, but in the fact that al-ʿAbdarī felt principally attracted by the life and activities of the intellectual groups. Hence he concentrates on the ways and methods of teaching at the various scholarly centres in the Arab West; on the savants he met and whose courses he often attended himself; and on the manuals used in the various branches of study such as grammar, Koran reading and interpreting, or poetry. In this respect al-ʿAbdarī's *Rihla* represents from the present-day point of view a source of information of considerable interest. His contemporaries may also have appreciated his rhetoric, high-sounding style as well as the moral aims he pursued, clearly revealed by the emphasis laid upon what he considered the marks of a spiritual and material decadence. Al-ʿAbdarī was currently read and valued as an authority by the geographers and historians in the Arab West as late as in the XVIIIth century.

ABDELKADER see ʿABD al-QADĪR IBN MUHYĪ al-DĪN

ABDELKRIM see ʿABD al-KARĪM

ʿABDŪN IBN, MUHAMMAD IBN AHMAD, al-TUJIBĪ, a *muhtasib* (municipal officer in charge of the market and public morals police) in Seville (XI/XIIth cent.). Besides the similarity of the name he has nothing in common with the poet Ibn ʿAbdūn* except being his contemporary and compatriot. No other biographical information has been transmitted, but a treatise from his pen has come down to us, suggesting the codification of the rules which in his opinion were to govern the discharge of the public offices in Seville. Its interest lies in the insight which it opens up into urban life in al-Andalus* under the Almoravid* régime (translated by E. Lévi-Provençal, Séville musulmane au début du XIIe siècle, Paris, 1947).

ʿABDŪN IBN, ABŪ MUHAMMAD, al-FIHRĪ, Hispano-Arab poet (†1134). Born in Evora (Portugal), at that time within the territory of the Aftasid* rulers (1022-1095), of Badajoz, he served as secretary to ʿUmar Ibn al Aftas al-Mutawakkil (1065-1095), the last of his line. When the dynasty was overthrown by the Almoravids*, Ibn ʿAbdūn whose reputation as a poet was already solidly established, still spent some time in al-Andalus* until ʿAlī Ibn Yūsuf* summoned him to the Almoravid court at Marrakesh. Towards the end of his life Ibn ʿAbdūn returned to his native Evora, where he died. His fame rests in particular on one ode, *al-Bashshāma*, dealing with the tragic end of the Aftasids. Subsequently it was twice commented upon from the point of view of its historical background, and reproduced by the historian ʿAbd al-Wahīd al-Marrākushī* (XIIth cent.) in his *Kitāb al-Muʿjib* (French version of the poem in the translation of Marrākushī's work by E. Fagnan, Histoire des Almohades, Alger 1893).

ʿABĪD al-BUKHĀRĪ, colloquially Buākhar, the Moroccan soldiery of negro slaves (*ʿabīd*, sing *ʿabd)* recruited by the ʿAlawid* Sultan Mūlāy Ismāʿīl*(1672-1727) from among the mass of Sudanese slaves dispersed everywhere in the towns and among the tribes. Some of them were descended from the prisoners made in the Sudanese campaign under the Saʿdian* Sultan Ahmad al-Mansūr* (1578-1602), others were subsequently imported. Mūlāy Ismāʿīl bought them or acquired them in other ways, had them registered as his personal property in strict observance of all legal requirements. They were bound to him by a solemn oath sworn on the venerated collection of the *hadīth* (Tradition of the Prophet), compiled in the IXth century by al-Bukhārī, whence their designation. Together with a number of negro women purchased at the same time, they were settled in a large encampment in the plain of the Gharb, halfways between Meknès and the coast. There they underwent a special military training such that they could be garrisoned, after a careful selection, either in the sultan's palaces or in the fortresses erected in the neighbourhood of the principal towns or along the important lines of communication and in tribal districts difficult to police. After a certain period of service, however, they were returned to their permanent camp in exchange for others. Every year their children were sent for some time to the sultan's residence, where the girls were employed in the royal household or placed in the harem, and the boys were trained in various kinds of minor handicraft as a sort of pre-military instruction. The total of this particular type of black population is variously reported by the contemporary chroniclers, but it seems that the system proved satisfactory and that under Sultan Ismāʿīl the Morrocan army thus comprised a thoroughly reliable, well-trained and well-equipped combative corps of about 50.000 men. Although of little military value, they stood high in the sultan's favour, received preferential pay, and the officers of higher rank acquired not only considerable wealth, but also political influence. In the years of a state authority almost completely dislocated after Mūlāy Ismāʿīl's death, this élite troop, too, rapidly deteriorated. Their discipline vanished, and making up for overdue pay by plundering and highway robbery, they deserted the outpost garrisons and flocked into Meknès, the capital, and the larger provincial towns, thus adding a new unruly element to the easily irritated city proletariate. Others spread over the countryside becoming in time agricultural labourers or peasants. Those who remained under arms were only a small minority but a ready tool in every court conspiracy or subversive movement. When under some of the later sultans the reins of government were again in firmer hands, especially under Sīdī Muhammad Ibn ʿAbd Allāh (1757-1790) and Mūlāy Sulaymān (1792-1822) the 'Buākher' corps numerically much reduced, was several times reorganized, subjected to stricter discipline and assigned quarters on the outskirts of Rabat, Meknès and Fez, where it could be kept under control, but without regaining its one-time military virtues. As time went on, its members, in return for their service, were alloted smaller or larger rural properties cultivated by their families and after their discharge, by themselves. Yet it was obviously impossible to train them in the spirit of military order and obedience, and even to prevent them from selling their arms, horses and equipment. Finally, towards the end of the last century the institution of the 'Buākher' was abolished, except for a picked body of men serving as the king's personal guard which is still a section of the Moroccan army.

ABŪ BAKR ABŪ YAHYĀ, a Hafsid* caliph (1318-1346) who in his early years was appointed governor of Constantine by his brother, Caliph Abū al-Baqā' (1309-1311), but soon declared himself independent. While his brother was deposed by a collateral, Ibn al-Lihyānī, who for the next few years held the throne of the caliphs in Tunis (1311-1317), Abū Bakr conquered Bougie after heavy fighting against the town's governor and was acclaimed sovereign in the western part of the Hafsid realm. As soon as he felt his own position sufficiently consolidated, the cordial relations between the two Hafsid princes quickly deteriorated. Open warfare broke out, and within three years Abū Bakr was master of central and northern Tunisia. Ibn al-Lihyānī left the country, and his son Abū Darba, caliph for nine months (1317-1318), was pushed back to the coast and enclosed in the fortified town of al-Mahdīya. Abū Bakr was recognized as caliph and the Hafsid territories were again in one hand, as they had been under his brother Abū al-Baqā'.

For more than a decade the new caliph still found himself confronted by most serious difficulties. It took twelve years to subdue three 'legitimist' rebellions: one was led by Ibn al-Lihyānī's son-in-law, who in alliance with a chieftain of the Sulaym* three times in succession forced his way into Tunis and was proclaimed anti-caliph by the populace; the second was carried on by Abū Darba from al-Mahdīya, likewise with the help of the Sulaym, and, after his withdrawal to the ʿAbd al-Wādid* court at Tlemcen, by his brother who also penetrated into Tunis and maintained his position there for about two weeks; and the third, was instigated by the ʿAbd al-Wādids in common with the Sulaym, and led to another temporary occupation of Tunis. During these combats and the ensuing weakness of the central government, the city notables of Biskra, Gabès, Tripoli and the smaller places in eastern and southern Tunisia, often engaged in internecine rivalry, cut out for themselves a position of autonomy which in many cases came very near to complete independence. The ʿAbd al-Wādids who had their hand in these and other subversive movements and gave a liberal asylum to all malcontents and conspirators, did not cease by repeated incursions into Tunisian territory to add fuel to the flame. At last Abū Bakr brought about an alliance (1331) with the Marīnids* of Fez, which was sealed by the marriage of his daughter Fātima with the heir to the Marīnid throne, Abū al-Hasan ʿAlī* - and when she had perished together with the other women of his household in the disastrous battle at Rio Salado (1340) he married another of Abū Bakr's daughters - and this led within a few years to the Marīnid conquest of Tlemcen (1337).

Thenceforth Abū Bakr, assisted by his strong-minded and ambitious chamberlain Ibn Tāfārāgin*, could turn all his energy towards the pacification of his country, and still find time for composing poetry. The refractory Arab clans were brought to submission, the island of Djerba, lost under Caliph Abū Hafs ʿUmar* (1284-1295), was reincorporated, and the various local power groups were made to renounce their autonomous aspirations, while close members of the family, each one seconded by an experienced chamberlain *(hājib)*, were entrusted as emirs with the administration of the provinces. Yet neither the Marīnid alliance and marriage relations nor the efforts at consolidating the governmental system proved to be of any avail; hardly one year after Abū Bakr's death most of his sons had either killed one another in the struggle over the heritage or perished otherwise, and his Marīnid son-in-law, Abū al-Hasan ʿAlī, had invaded the country and although his power was to last little longer than one more year he made himself master of the Hafsid territories.

ABŪ FĀRIS ʿABD al-ʿAZĪZ, popularly known as ʿAzzūz, a ruler (1394-1434) of the Tunisian dynasty of the Hafsids* and one of its most remarkable figures. As soon as he ascended the throne in succession to his father Abū al-ʿAbbās (1370-1394) he mastered the insubordinate governors - all his brothers or cousins - of Bône, Sfax, Bougie and Constantine; the rebellious Bedouin chiefs in the area south of Bougie; and the recalcitrant city notables of Tripoli, Gafsa, Tozeur and Biskra; and finally occupied Algiers which was to serve as the operational basis against the ʿAbd al-Wādids* of Tlemcen whom he forced to recognize his suzerainty.
Also in these early years of his reign he succeeded in averting consequences which might have taken a perilious turn, namely a foolhardy raid upon the Spanish village of Torreblanca near Valencia by Tunisian pirates who captured the inhabitants, desecrated the church and carried off its silver ciborium. Valencian and Majorcan galleys thereupon plundered and burnt down the town of Tédellis (Dellys, east of Algiers), at that time still in ʿAbd al-Wādid territory, and killed or carried off into slavery many of the people. A modern painting in the church of Tédelis commemorates the pious legend which tells of how the ciborium with the consecrated hosts was miraculously restored to the village. In the following year a combined fleet of Valencia and Majorca sailed out against Bône, but too weak for an assault withdrew a few days later. In both instances, the diplomatic skill of Abū Fāris kept the strong maritime forces of Aragon and Sicily out of these enterprises upon which the blessings of the Pope had bestowed the merits of a crusade.
As in the past, Tunisia's relations with the Christian Kingdoms and city-republics of the Western Mediterranean were governed by mutual economic interests expressed in a series of treaties and negotiations with Pisa, Venice, Sicily, Aragon, Genoa and lastly with Florence. From time to time, it is true, the peaceful climate was troubled by one side or the other, neither of them being any too scrupulous about policing the piratical instincts of its seafaring nationals or of their financial backers. More serious was an Aragonian invasion of the Kerkena islands in which several hundred inhabitants were killed in battle and two or three thousand men, women and children dragged into captivity (1424). The Tunisians retaliated by a raid on Malta, which in turn provoked an Aragonian landing on the island of Djerba and an encounter between Spanish and Tunisian troops under the personal command of King

Alfonso V and Caliph Abū Fāris. It ended with the enforced re-embarcation of the invaders and the reconciliation of the two sovereigns.
In the annals of the Hafsid dynasty, the reign of Abū Fāris is remembered as an era of inner order, stability and prosperity. Pious, cultured and a friend of scholars and men of letters; carefully balancing the various religious and social power groups in the state; furthering the interests of artisans and small merchants by a considerate fiscal policy, he gained and preserved the respect of the upper classes as well as lasting popularity among the people. By a reorganization of the public finances he restricted the functions of the finance minister *(sāhib al-ashghāl)*, put the supervision of the State's revenues and expenditures in the hands of a special court dignitary, the *munaffidh* (the treasurer of the royal household), and thus in practice kept the use of all State money under his personal control. In this way he was able to lay out a line of strong fortifications along the north-eastern coast; to provide the capital, Tunis, with urgently needed cisterns, reservoirs for drinkingwater and public fountains; to build hostels for travellers, night shelters for the poor and a hospital *(māristān)*; and to organize a regular library service in the Great Mosque of Tunis, to which he donated an important collection of manuscripts. Abū Fāris fell in a campaign against the emir of Tlemcen, who had tried to regain independence. He was succeeded by his grandson Abū ʿAbd Allāh Muhammad al-Muntasir (1434-1435).

ABŪ HAFS ʿUMAR, the fifth ruler (1284-1295) of the Hafsid* dynasty, a son of its founder Abū Zakariyyā'*. Helped by the Kuʿūb, a branch of the Sulaym* - a help rewarded by considerable financial privileges *(iqtā*)* - he reconquered for his family the throne which had been usurped by the 'impostor' Ibn Abī ʿUmāra* (1283-1284) and for a time re-established internal peace and order. Very much against his intentions he found himself drawn into the conflicts among the great Italian city-republics of Venice, Genoa and Pisa; although the skirmishes often took place in Tunisian waters, he managed to maintain with each of them the traditional and indeed very profitable trading relations. He was unable, however, to prevent the loss to the Aragonian admiral, or rather freebooter, Roger de Lauria, of the island of Djerba on the southern end of the Gulf of Gabès, of the Kerkenna islands at its northern end opposite the town of Sfax, and of several points on the coast; and the sale on the Sicilian slave markets of a few thousand male and female inhabitants. At the same time he had to face the attacks of two pretenders: one was easily repelled. It was launched by the sons of the last Almohad* ruler Abū Dabbūs with the support of the Aragonian navy. The other, of much more serious and far-reaching consequences was launched by his own nephew Abū Zakariyyā', the only one of Emir Abū Ishāq Ibrāhīm's (1279-1283) five sons who had survived their father in the tragic struggle against Ibn Abī ʿUmāra. By a well-planned coup-de-main, Abū Zakariyyā' occupied the towns of Bougie and Constantine and the areas as far as Algiers. Everywhere he was acclaimed as emir and established his headquarters at Bougie. Failing to seize the Hafsid capital, Tunis, he pushed southwards, forced the governor of Gabès to surrender, and had already penetrated deep into Tripolitania, when upon Abū Hafs ʿUmar's request for help, an army of the ʿAbd al-Wādids* advanced from Tlemcen and compelled him to a precipitate return to Bougie. Nevertheless his prestige continued to grow and a few years later, shortly before Abū Hafs ʿUmar's death, the town of Biskra with the entire region of the Zāb - the southern part of the present-day Algerian department of Constantine - and also Gabès again recognized his sovereignty. It was the first split of the Hafsid realm.

ABŪ HAFS ʿUMAR IBN YAHYĀ al-HINTĀTĪ, the chieftain (ca 1090-1176) of the Hintāta, or Īnta in the Berber language, a Masmūda* branch in the High Atlas. He was one of the first and closest disciples of the founder of the Almohad* doctrine, the Mahdi Ibn Tūmart*, and the ancestor of the Tunisian dynasty of the Hafsids (1228-1575). He protected and supported Ibn Tūmart and his small groups of followers when they were still persecuted everywhere as subversive, fanatical heretics, and with his men stood in the forefront of the religio-political revolution which ultimately overthrew the Almoravid* régime and carried the Almohads to victory. It was Ibn Tūmart who caused him to change his original Berber name Faskāt u M'zāl to that of one of the Prophet Muhammad's companions, perhaps wishing to exalt his own prophetic mission, and who assigned him a rank of first importance in the Council of Ten (*jamāʿa*), the highest governing body of the community. Under Ibn Tūmart's successor ʿAbd al-Mu'min* he remained the thoroughly loyal though never blindly submissive second-in-command, always at the head of his troops in battle, victorious in Africa and al-Andalus*, sternly subduing rebellious tribal chiefs, forcefully using the weight of his word in matters of internal administration and inflexible whenever he thought the Mahdi's spiritual heritage involved in the slightest degree. In the somewhat confused situation which arose concerning the succession to the throne after ʿAbd al-Mu'min's death (1163), he seems to have favoured at first another of the deceased ruler's sons, Muhammad. But having recognized, after long hesitation, Abū Yaʿqūb Yūsuf*, he served him as faithfully as he had served his father. Abū Hafs ʿUmar spent the last years of his long life in al-Andalus engaged in military operations, and died in Salé (near Rabat) as he was returning to Marrakesh. His sons held the highest offices in the Almohad empire. One of them, Abū Muhammad ʿAbd al-Wāhid, called al-Sāmit (the Taciturn), was appointed governor of Tunisia (1207), and his son Abū Zakariyyā' had himself proclaimed independent emir.

ABŪ al-HASAN ʿALĪ, a Marīnid* ruler of Morocco (1331-1351) and one of its most remarkable figures. His reign began with the suppression of a serious revolt and the execution of its leader, his brother Abū ʿAlī, and ended with his defeat in battle by his son Abū ʿInān*. The two decades in between were a period of internal peace, wealth and high artistic and scholastic performance - with one interruption by another rebellion stirred up by his son Abū ʿAbd al-Rahmān - but beyond the borders a period of nearly continuous warfare. In the West, it was the traditional Holy War in alliance with the Nasrid* sultans of Granada against the Christian Kingdoms in Spain. Notwithstanding the retaking by his son Abū Malik, of Gibraltar - which had been lost by his father Abū Sāʿid ʿUthmān - and the destruction of the Castilian navy by his fleet of some hundred vessels it was a failure. Abū Malik lost his life in a skirmish and Abū al-Hasan ʿAlī himself, heavily beaten by a combined Castilian and Portuguese army at the Rio Salado (1340), north of Tarifa, escaped the same fate only by a precipitate flight across the Straits. Soon afterwards Algeciras fell into Castilian hands in spite of tenacious resistance. Thereupon he abandoned for good every ambition to retrieve in al-Andalus* the Moroccan hegemony of Almohad* days.

Not so in the East. There, the first stage of his exploits was the campaign, in alliance with the Hafsids* of Tunisia, against his neighbours and traditional rivals, the ʿAbd al-Wādids*, an alliance strengthened for the time being by his marriage with a Hafsid princess. He fought his way as far as Algiers, and then, after bitter street fighting, entered Tlemcen. The congratulations and gifts of honour sent by the Mamluk Sultan of Egypt and the Emir of the Sudan marked the prestige acquired by the Marīnid State. To commemorate his triumph, he set up a splendid mosque, lavishly decorated with mosaic work, around the nearby tomb of the city's patron saint, the great mystic Abū Madyan* (1126-1197). Here were also erected a group of new lodgings and public baths for the pilgrims, all well-preserved down to this day. Piety was presumably his prime motive, but the consideration of winning the sympathy of his new subjects and of extolling the majesty of the new régime may not have been entirely absent. In Morocco, however, his religious policy followed somewhat different lines. There he obviously aimed at diverting popular piety from the growing trend of a mysticism often tinged with heterodox leanings, which took ever more distinct shape with the appearance of numerous saints and religious brotherhoods* all over the country. These efforts at emphasizing the concepts of strict orthodoxy appear in the systematic creation of official theological schools *(madrasas)* in every town of any importance, among them in Fez, the brilliantly decorated Masbahīa and Sabbaiyīn - both still in existence - which at the same time supplied his chancelleries with a staff of devoted clerks of all grades.

Abū al-Hasan's friendship with the house of the Hafsids, on both sides strongly tinged with caution especially after the death of his wife, lasted about a decade, until their dynastic conflicts over the succession provided him with a welcome pretext for armed intervention (1347). In a sweeping expedition, he took Bougie and Constantine, which surrendered without resistance, turned southwards and occupied Biskra, penetrated as far as Tripoli and at last victoriously entered Tunis, the Hafsid capital. The Almohad empire in Africa was resurrected, the great dream of his life had materialized, and sovereigns like the King of Castile and the Sultan of Mali thought it wise to convey their solemn congratulations and to court his goodwill.

It was to be an ephemeral glory. His garrisons, well-disciplined, held the towns securely. The citizenry, on the whole, either remained indifferent to the change of rule or even welcomed it, impressed by the magnificence of the court, the galaxy of scholars and craftsmen it attracted, and the wider commercial possibilities it promised. In the country the situation was different. There, strong Arab tribes, mainly groups of the Sulaym*, were the undisputed masters. The Hafsids, whom experience had made familiar with the ever changing alliances and feuds of the clans and who knew when and with whom it was possible to enter into appropriate arrangements, had learned how to keep the unruly Bedouins under control and how to use their warlike disposition. Abū al-Hasan ʿAlī lacked this experience. Hardly a year had elapsed when he was confronted with a powerful coalition of hostile tribes. The encounter, which took place between al-Qayrawān and Tunis, ended in a débâcle. His troops were dispersed, the towns, fearing the vengeance of the tribesmen, closed their doors, Tunisia had to be evacuated, and Tlemcen was recaptured by the ʿAbd al-Wādids (1348). With utmost difficulty Abū al-Hasan ʿAlī reached Tunis, where he maintained his position for a few months but was then forced to withdraw. He left by sea and landed in Algiers, saved from shipwreck by a hair's breadth while all the ships of his escort were lost. Destitute, he arrived in Morocco, where in the meantime his son Abū ʿInān Fāris, believing him dead had himself proclaimed his successor. He refused to hand over power to his father, and in the ensuing struggle Abū al-Hasan ʿAlī's followers were beaten (1351). Soon afterwards he died in the Atlas mountains and was buried with high honours in the family necropolis at Chellah, in the mausoleum he had built for himself and his wife, Abū ʿInān's mother, a Christian converted to Islam. Abū al-Hasan ʿAlī was doubtless a great general and possessed with political abilities, but these gifts were not matched by that of shaping the territories which his sword and his policy had assembled, into an organically structured whole. This deficiency was at the root of his tragic fate.

ABŪ al-HASAN ʿALĪ, called Bū Hassūn, the last of the Moroccan dynasty of the Wattāsids* (1472-1554) and one of its most remarkable figures. Gifted with as much will-power and tenacity as political versatility, he was the driving force of the régime during the reign of his weak and irresolute nephew, Abū al-ʿAbbās Ahmad (1524-1549, with a short interruption), particularly during the period of the latter's captivity in the hands of his Saʿdian* antagonists. Having brought to his side an influential group of religious brotherhoods* and, at the same time, the Ottoman Sultan Sulaymān the Magnificient, he repelled the Saʿdians who were advancing against the Wattāsid capital Fez, and through the intervention of the men of religion, obtained the liberation of Abū al-ʿAbbās Ahmad in exchange for the surrender of Meknès. Forced to flee after the conquest of Fez (1550) by the Saʿdians, he refused to accept the defeat of his family as final and crossed over to Spain where he tried to enlist the interest of the regent, prince Maximilian, son of the German Emperor Charles V, in his cause but failing to overcome the latter's hesitation, he travelled to Germany and started negotiating with the emperor personally. There he served for some time in the imperial army, then he returned to Spain with another of the emperor's sons, the future Philip II of Spain, without, however, having obtained the assistance he had hoped for. Thus he left for Portugal and, slightly more successful there, was given six vessels with which to attempt a landing in Morocco, but with his small fleet he was captured by Turkish pirates and taken to Algiers. Helped by his former friendly relations with the Sultan he gained the confidence of the beylerbey, persuaded him to undertake an expedition against Morocco and after a victorious advance with the Turkish army entered Fez, which had been abandoned by the Saʿdian ruler. He was enthusiastically received by the people, made the Turkish soldiers withdraw from the city, gathered together an army of mercenaries, and allied himself with Ahmad al-Aʿrāj, the brother of the Saʿdian sovereign Muhammad al-Shaykh al-Mahdī. In the fighting which ensued, he beat the Saʿdian troops, but the messenger he sent to bring the good tidings to his ally, fell into the enemy's hands and a message announcing defeat was substituted. Thereupon al-Aʿrāj, discouraged, called back his men, and this time Bū Hassūn lost the battle and his life (1554). The rest of his troops went over to the victor and his sons, while trying to escape by sea, were captured by pirates and put to death.

ABŪ ʿINĀN FĀRIS, a Moroccan ruler (1351-1358) of the Marīnid* dynasty, the first to bear the title *Amīr al-Mu'minīn* (Commander of the Faithful), but the last who actually exercized sovereign power. At the age of twenty-two, he had himself proclaimed successor to his father Abū al-Hasan ʿAlī* (1331-1351). The latter was believed to have been killed in flight after a disastrous campaign in Tunisia (1348), but at last returned safely from his perilious wanderings. In the armed clashes between his own and his father's partisans, Abū ʿInān Fāris came out victorious. During the negotiations which followed, his father suddenly died, but it took several more years before the internal unrest, kept active by one of his brothers, was brought to an end.
According to his biographers, the young prince was highly cultivated and distinguished by a sound literary and juridico-theological education. Like his father, he was a munificient builder - down to this day the splendid Madrasa Bū ʿInānīya in Fez testifies to the artistic genius of this period - and was intent on enhancing the prestige of his court by the reputation of men of science to whom he extended liberal patronage. The great ambition of his life, like that of his father's, was to remake the Almohad* African empire, but like his father, he failed. He conquered Tlemcen (1352), abandoned by the ruling ʿAbd al-Wādids*, obtained a foothold in Western Algeria, pushed further eastwards and even for a time made himself master of Tunisia. Unable, however, to keep discipline among his Arab auxiliary troops, he soon had to withdraw again into Morocco. Shortly afterwards, he fell victim to a conspiracy of his courtiers and was strangled by his vizier, who put his ten-year old son on the throne.
A few months later the boy-sultan, too, met with a sudden death in the course of another court intrigue, headed this time by his uncle and successor Abū Sālim (1359-1361). Somehow the scholar Ibn Khaldūn*, then at the beginning of his career, seems to have had a hand in this affair, for one of the new sultan's first acts was to free him from an imprisonment of nearly two years and appoint him chief of his chancellery (*kātib al-sirr wa al-inshā'*).

ABŪ QURRA, a politico-religious leader (VIIIth century) of the Berber Banū Īfran*, adherents of the heterodox Khārijite sect. Around 765 he was established near Tlemcen, at Agadir (today in ruins); as the 'Caliph' of his community, but while trying to expand his domain, he came into conflict with the government of the caliphate and was forced to retreat into Agadir. A few years later, he renewed his attempt in alliance with other Khārijite groups, besieged the Arab governor of the province in the town of Tobna (on the outskirts of the Aurès) but, allegedly bribed, gave up the struggle and withdrew. Shortly afterwards he participated in an assault on al-Qayrawān with another Khārijite ally, ʿAbd al-Rahmān Ibn Rustum*, formerly governor of the town, who had been expelled by the troops of the Caliph, but suffered a crushing defeat. Whereas Ibn Rustum withdrew westwards and built up in Tāhart (present-day Tiaret in the Algerian department of Oran) a sort of theocratic Khārijite state, Abū Qurra, with the fragments of his warlike sect, returned to Agadir, which still retained for some time its religious prestige as the centre of Khārijism, although without aspirations after worldly power. In 786, it was conquered by the great Maghrāwa* chieftain, Muhammad Ibn Khazar, and three years later, when Idrīs I*, successfully propagating among the tribes of northern Morocco his version of orthodox sunnism, entered the town, Agadir lost also its spiritual significance.

ABŪ YAʿQŪB YŪSUF, the second Almohad*ruler (1163-1184) *Amīr al-Mu'minīn* (Commander of the Faithful) - one of the many sons ofʿAbd al-Mu'min* (1133-1163). He was born in Tinmāl in the High Atlas, the fountainhead of the Almohad faith, and through his mother was related with one of the great Masmūda* families of tribes, which formed the core of Almohad power. He spent his early years at the court of Marrakesh, but while still a youth was sent to Spain, where he grew up in the refined environment of Andalusian life, and was invested with high government offices, albeit assisted by experienced advisers. He was governor of Seville when called to the throne. According to some authors this took place after the brief reign of his elder brother Muhammad, which was ended by a coup d'état, while according to others, ʿAbd al-Mu'min had disinherited Muhammad some years previous to his death. Three younger brothers, the governors of Fez, Bougie and Cordova, refused to recognize him, but two of them having suddenly died, the third one finally acquiesced.

Abū Yaʿqūb's reign meant for the empire on the whole, a period of order, safety and well-being. He had to subdue two tribal uprisings in the Rif south of Ceuta (1163, 1167); the revolt of a local chieftain in central Tunisia (1180), who tried to make himself independent in the region of Gafsa; and the incursion into Tunisia of a Turkish adventurer, Qarāqūsh, who penetrated from the Cyrenaica and Tripolitania with bands of military slaves. With the help of some tribes in the Nafūsa mountains (in the north-western corner of Tripolitania) he occupied Tripoli, where he established his seat. Yet this temporary unrest in the far confines of the vast realm was hardly felt in the interior and in no way disturbed peace and prosperity in town and country. Neither did it divert Abū

Yaʿqūb from what he considered his prime task: the pacification of the Andalusian province and the Holy War against the Christian kingdoms. Having defeated his most recalcitrant opponent in al-Andalus*, Ibn Mardenīsh*, the proud lord of Murcia and Valencia, whose family and adherents he gained for the Almohad creed and cause - he even married his former enemy's daughter - he tenaciously waged war along the continually fluctuating borders. Trying to play off one against the other the Kings of Portugal, Castile and Leon, at times pushing forward deep into their territories, then again remaining on the defensive, he gained here and there a town or even larger region, but no decisive success.

Abū Yaʿqūb Yūsuf still was able to uphold the former power and prestige of the empire as well as the authority of the dynasty. He entrusted with influential positions in the state - besides close relatives - mainly members of the family of Abū Hafs ʿUmar*, all of whom proved to be faithful servants of the régime. Although of deep religious feeling and at all times a convinced and generous patron of theological science, he was no longer given to the rigorous puritanism so strictly observed and enforced by the first adherents of the Almohad doctrine. With a remarkable broadness of mind, probably a fruit of his upbringing in the Andalusian atmosphere, he drew into his close circle scholars, philosophers or poets of whom none had much in common with the rigidity of the Almohad tenets. One may cite the great Aristotelians Ibn Tufayl* and Ibn Rushd* (Averoes) or the physician and poet Abū Bakr Muhammad Ibn Zuhr*. With these scholarly and literary inclinations, especially a predilection for the epic tales of the heroic Bedouin life, went a marked taste for contemporary Hispano-Arabic art and architecture, to which the extensive building activity promoted by him and his dignitaries opened wide doors on North-African soil. The new style and technique practiced by Andalusian craftsmen and artisans began to supersede that of the Syrians, and Egyptians, until then prevalent particularly in the eastern sections of the empire.

On an expedition planned against Lisbon, Abū Yaʿqūb Yūsuf was wounded in a battle before the walls of the city of Santarem (north-east of Lisbon) in which his troops suffered a heavy defeat. He died on the road to Evora. His son and successor, Abū Yūsuf Yaʿqūb*, took his body to Seville, his favourite residence, whence it was later taken to Tinmāl to be buried beside his father and the Mahdi Ibn Tūmart.

ABŪ YŪSUF YAʿQŪB al-MANSŪR, the third Almohad* ruler (1184-1199), proclaimed in Seville after the death of his father Abū Yaʿqūb Yūsuf* (1163-1184), under whom he had served as vizier. The opposition of some of his relatives, who alleged that his way of life in earlier years had been somewhat frivolous, was overcome thanks to the support of the influential clan of Abū Hafs ʿUmar*, most loyal servants of the dynasty, sharing the highest functions of state with members of the ruler's own family. Twice subsequently, however, he was faced by a rebellion instigated by two of his brothers and one of his uncles and subdued only by their execution.

Abū Yūsuf Yaʿqūb's outstanding military achievement, to which he also owed his title of honour, *al-Mansūr* (the one rendered victorious, i.e.

by God), was his brilliant victory (1195) at the great battle at Alarcos* (al-Arak, in the southern part of present-day New Castile, near Calatrava) which completely routed the army of King Alfonso VIII of Castile. For quite some time this victory held back the menacing tide of the Christian advance in al-Andalus*. Exploiting his advantage, he pushed deep into Spanish territory, as far as Madrid and Guadalajara. Along with the Almoravid* victory, won a century earlier by Yūsuf Ibn Tāshufīn* at al-Zallāqa* (1086), Alarcos has inspired a great many romantic stories dealing with the feats of the Almohad knights and their adventures. Less spectacular were his accomplishments in the eastern provinces of the empire, where the clan of the Banū Ghānīyah* had risen in open revolt against the central government. These emirs of the Balearic islands and leaders of what may be called the Almoravid legitimists had started by gaining a foothold on the Tunisian coast, then formed an alliance with a number of strong Bedouin tribes. At the same time they made common cause with Qarāqūsh, the same chief of bands of slave-soldiers who had revolted against Abū Ya‘qūb Yūsuf and kept all southern Tunisia and Tripolitania under their sway. Notwithstanding a severe defeat inflicted upon them by the Almohad army (1187) the Banū Ghāniyah withstood all attempts to reduce them to submission. Although in the writings of some of his biographers, Ya‘qūb al-Mansūr does not appear to have been a convinced believer in the Almohad creed as it had been preached by Ibn Tūmart*, and in particular not in its tenet of the exalted position of the Mahdi, he realized its fundamental significance as the raison d'état of his empire. Thus all missionary activities were systematically continued, yet he did not lose sight of the mystical trends taking an ever firmer hold upon the minds of the masses. These currents led to the emergence everywhere of pious men, devoted to a life of asceticism and solitary meditation, and of the popular veneration they enjoyed. Ya‘qūb al-Mansūr, Commander of the Faithful *(Amīr al-Mu'minīn)* omitted no occasion to manifest his esteem for these holy men, presumably finding his personal religious convictions in accordance with the requirements of his dynasty and state policy. In line with both this policy and his own soldierly inclinations was his consolidation of the so far loosely organized tribal army - as it was often unwilling to obey - through the incorporation of mercenary troops, most of whom were recruited after the victory over the Banū Ghāniyah from among their slave soldiery more accustomed to discipline. Probably also motivated more or less equally by the political consideration of emphasizing the power of the realm, and by the ambition of giving himself an imperishable monument, was the plan to create a grand new capital. It was to be built on the site of the assembly place of the troops in his grand-father's and father's days - he called it *Ribāt al-Fath* (present-day Rabat), the stronghold of victory, in memory of his victory at Alarcos. It was to have an impregnable circumvallation and the largest, most richly decorated gates ever seen in the Arab West, and in its midst a mosque with room enough to accomodate a whole army at prayer, with a fifty-feet high minaret adorned with glazed tiles and elaborate sculptures. Throughout his reign no efforts were spared in carrying on the work of construction, but after his death it was no longer continued and

gradually fell into ruins, but what has been preserved of it - the gates of Rabat, the minaret and some of the columns of the mosque, the so-called Mosque of Hassan - bears witness to the aesthetic inventiveness of the architects and the mastership of the craftsmen.
Taken seriously ill during one of his frequent tours of al-Andalus, Abū Yūsuf Yaʿqūb appointed as his successor his son Muhammad, who subsequently ascended the throne as Muhammad al-Nāsir(i.e. *lī Dīn Allāh*, the Defender of the Religion of God, 1199-1213). According to some historians, he seems to have retired completely from all public activities, giving himself up to prayer and pious works for the short time he still had to live. He was buried in Tinmāl next to the tombs of his father, of Ibn Tūmart and ʿAbd al-Mu'min*.

ABŪ YŪSUF YAʿQŪB, the second Marīnid* ruler (1258-1286), heir to Yahyā Ibn ʿAbd al-Haqq, the head of the warlike Zanāta* clan, of the Banū Marīn, who had wrested almost the whole of Morocco from the Almohads*. It took eleven more years of fighting and the suppression of several rebellious movements, until the conquest of Marrakesh and the death in battle of the last Almohad sovereign Abū Dabbūs gave him victory (1269). The next step was to consolidate what this victory had brought him, a task which this tribal chieftain, though without experience in statecraft, undertook with noteworthy skill.
He started by systematically incorporating into his army of tribal warriors - his own men and those of allied Berber and Arab chiefs - Turkish and Kurdish military slaves and Christian as well as Moslem mercenaries recruited in Spain, and knew how to secure the loyalty of this heterogenuous soldiery, to maintain it in discipline and keep up its fighting spirit. Simultaneously he strengthened such strategically important positions as the port of Badis halfway between Ceuta and Melilla (today an insignificant village); Salé with its shipyards and arsenal; and the ramparts of the city of Meknès. At the same time he proceeded to move the seat of the central government from Marrakesh, too profoundly impregnated with Almohad ideology, to Fez, but also laid out a new strongly-fortified section, called *Madīnat al-Baīdā'u* (the White City), nowadays *Fās al-Jadīd* (New Fez). Within its walls were built his palace and the barracks for his bodyguard; the offices of the chancellery; and the residences of the Zanāta and the Arab dignitaries with their staff of scribes, mainly Andalusians, who were entrusted with the high-ranking offices in the government apparatus. His son and successor Abū Yaʿqūb Yūsuf surrounded the new city with vast gardens planted, according to contemporary sources, with the most beautiful flowers, for which an ingenious system of irrigation, fed by an enormous hydraulic wheel - its foundations are still in existence - provided the necessary quantity of water. Close by was established somewhat later a quarter for the Jews *(malla)*. In the course of time quite a few members of this community found the way to distinction and influence at the Marīnid court, thanks to their financial ability as the bankers of the State.
Realizing how important it could be for him to ingratiate himself with the populace by manifestations of his piety, he followed the example of

his predecessor - perhaps to some extent inspired also by real conviction - and gave far-reaching support to the marabouts* and religious brotherhoods*, which were surrounded by the halo of sanctity. He gave it, however, in no less measure to the orthodox theologians. He founded the first theological academy in Morocco, the *Madrasa al-Saffariyīn* ('of the coppersmiths', so called after the quarter where it was located) in Fez, which he endowed with a rich collection of manuscripts; built several mosques among which is the Great Mosque in *Fās al-Jadīd*; and enlarged or munificiently embellished older ones. In the same light, but also as a matter of prestige, must be regarded the attempts at renewing the Almoravid* and Almohad policy of expansion in al-Andalus*. Yet none of the four expeditions undertaken under the flag of the Holy War was marked by particular success although he was able to gain a victory at Ecija (1275), to enter triumphantly Malaga (1277) and to occupy Carthagena, Cadiz, San Juan and Niebla. He died on Andalusian soil and his body was taken to Morocco and buried in Chellah on the outskirts of Rabat. Abū Yūsuf Yaʿqūb left to his son Yaʿqūb Yūsuf (1286-1307) the largest and most powerful realm in the contemporary Arab West.

AFTASIDS, Banū Aftas, also occasionally called Banū Maslama, an arabicised Hispano-Berber dynasty (1022-1095) springing from the group of Miknāsa* clans settled in the region north of Cordova. They ruled for a time over almost the entire western sector of the Iberian peninsula, which stretches from the valley of the Guadiana deep into present-day Portugal, including Lisbon, with their seat at Badajoz. The founder of the family, ʿAbd Allāh Ibn Muhammad Ibn Maslama, surnamed al-Aftas, had held a high-ranking position at the court of an usurper of the power in this territory, a freedman of the Umayyad Caliph al-Hakam II, and ascended the throne after the death of his sovereign. Both ʿAbd Allāh (1922-1045) and his son al-Muzaffar (1045-1065) were cultured patrons of men of learning and letters, but were lacking in political and military gifts. So was al-Muzaffar's son and successor ʿUmar al-Mutawakkil (1065-1095), who lost one part of his realm after the other to the ʿAbbādid* rulers of Seville and to the Kings of Castile and Leon who also imposed upon him the payment of a tribute. ʿUmar made several attempts to reconsolidate his weakening position, first by trying to bring Yūsuf Ibn Tāshufīn*, the great Berber chief of the Almoravid* theocracy in North Africa, on to his side, and then by turning to the Christian kingdoms for help. In 1095, his capital Badajoz was conquered by an Almoravid army, which was amiably received by his own subjects. He and two of his sons fell into the hands of the enemy and lost their lives. A third son and some of his followers found refuge with King Alfonso and were converted to Christianity.

AGADIR, plur. *igudar*, a Berber word denoting in Morocco a fortified granary for common use by a number of families with a separate storage room for each one of them. This served not only for the safe-keeping of the harvest but also as a stronghold in the frequent local feuds. The families constituting such *agadir* communities, which may go back to a considerable length of time, are connected either by blood ties through the father, or through neighbourhood relation in their village. With the disappearance of general insecurity, the considerations of safety have lost their former prime significance, and although the old, fortress-like *agadir* is still maintained in serviceable condition, it functions today simply as a sort of co-operative storehouse for grain. Its one-time rôle as a fortification is, however, remembered in the names of localities in the Sūs, the Atlas and the Rif in which the word *agadir* occurs accompanied by a second, topographical specification as in Agadir N Irir (the port-town on the Atlantic coast, severely damaged by the earthquake in March 1960), Agadir Izanaguene, Agadir Tesguent and others, apart from the ancien town of Agadir - today in ruins - which gave birth to present-day Tlemcen (Algeria). The institution of the community fortress-storehouse is found, though under various other names, also in Tunisia and Algeria in the areas inhabited by a Berber population.

ĀGDĀL, a Berber word - in French texts spelt Aguedal - which infiltrated into Arabic and denoted originally in the Arab West pasture grounds in private property of an individual owner and serving only his own herds. In Morocco around the XIIth century, this meaning underwent a change and from then on the term was used to designate the vast tract of crown-land, covering several square miles, bordering the residential quarters of the sultan and surrounded by fortified walls with monumental entrance gates. It contained spaces for the encampment of troops, especially cavalry, grounds for grazing and parks provided with water basins and canals for irrigation. Some of the Almohad*, Saʿdian* and ʿAlawid* sultans showed special inclination for the horticultural embellishment and architectural ornamentation of the *āgdāl*, turning it gradually into the combination of an imperial pleasure garden and a site for military parades and equestrian games. In the early years of the present century, these areas were either parcelled out, such as the *āgdāl* of Rabat, into high-class suburban residential quarters and sports-grounds; or converted into orchards and parks open to the public, as in Marrakesh; or used partly as agricultural research stations, as in Meknès.

AGHLABIDS, an Arab dynasty of emirs (800-909) who, except for a merely symbolic recognition of the sovereignty of the Baghdad caliphs, ruled in complete independence over a territory comprising present-day western Libya, Tunisia and the greater part of the Algerian department of Constantine, and for a certain period also Sicily. The name al-Aghlab appears for the first time as that of an army commander who was sent with his troops from Khurāsān (Persia) to this restless African province of the caliphate, but fell while fighting a rapidly spreading subversive movement. Practically lost to the rebels, the province was reconquered by his son Ibrāhīm, who thereupon (800) was appointed hereditary governor by Caliph Hārūn al-Rashīd.
Ibrāhīm Ibn al-Aghlab, possessed of remarkable military and statesmanlike qualities, and according to his biographers, also of theological erudition and poetic gifts, began his reign by moving the seat of his government out of the precincts of al-Qayrawān, the old provincial

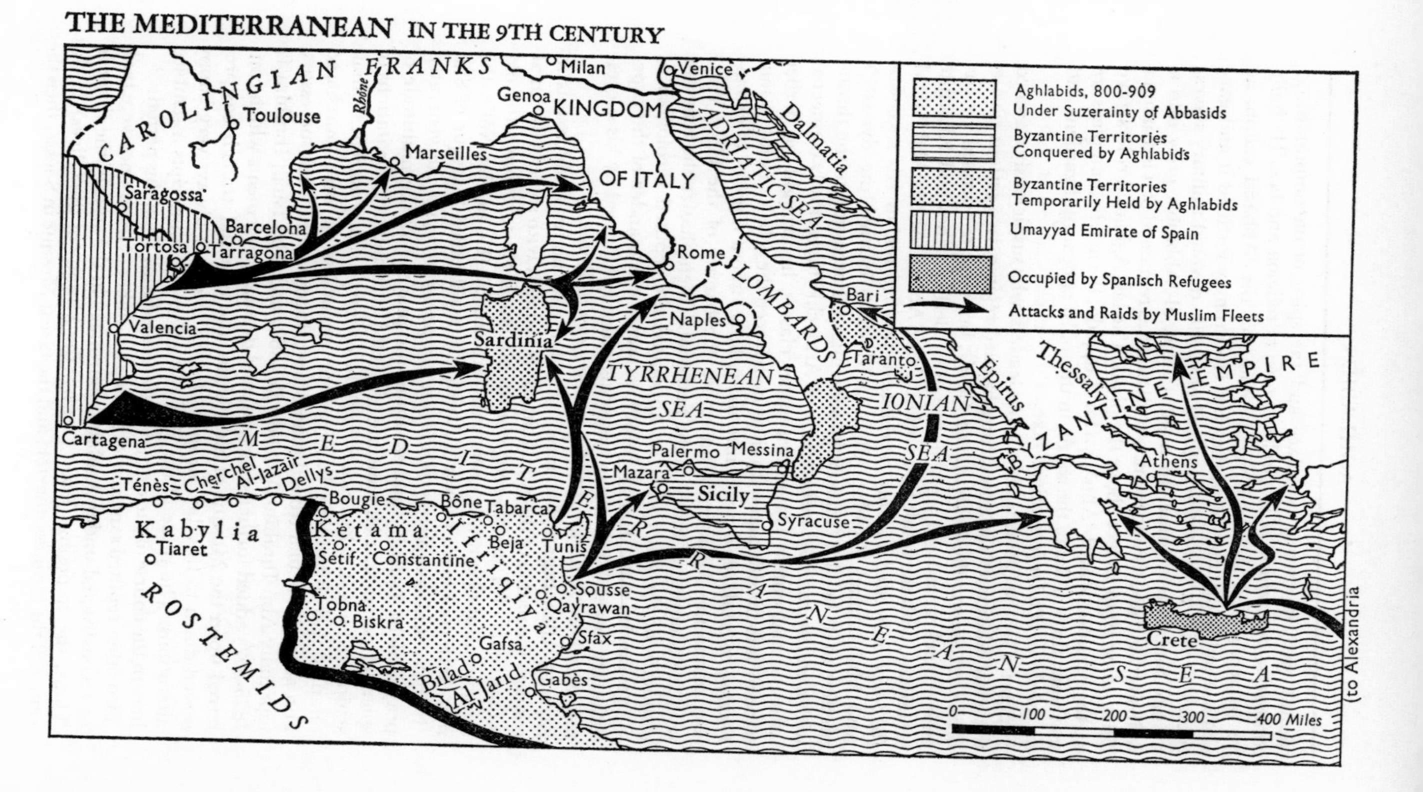
THE MEDITERRANEAN IN THE 9TH CENTURY
Aghlabids, 800-909
Under Suzerainty of Abbasids
Byzantine Territories
Conquered by Aghlabids
Byzantine Territories
Temporarily Held by Aghlabids
Umayyad Emirate of Spain
Occupied by Spanisch Refugees
Attacks and Raids by Muslim Fleets
CAROLINGIAN FRANKS
KINGDOM OF ITALY
LOMBARDS
BYZANTINE EMPIRE
ROSTEMIDS
Kabylia
Ketama
Ifriqiya
Bilad Al-Jarid
ADRIATIC SEA
TYRRHENEAN SEA
IONIAN SEA
MEDITERRANEAN SEA
Toulouse
Rhône
Marseilles
Genoa
Milan
Venice
Dalmatia
Saragossa
Barcelona
Tortosa
Tarragona
Valencia
Cartagena
Sardinia
Rome
Naples
Bari
Taranto
Epirus
Thessaly
Athens
Crete
Palermo
Messina
Mazara
Sicily
Syracuse
Ténès
Cherchel
Al-Jazair
Dellys
Bougie
Bône
Tabarca
Tiaret
Sétif
Constantine
Beja
Tunis
Sousse
Qayrawan
Tobna
Biskra
Gafsa
Sfax
Gabès
0 100 200 300 400 Miles
(to Alexandria

capital, with its unruly populace and the spirit of uncompromising, combative puritanism of its circles of men of religion and law. He built his palace, called al-ʿAbbāsīya in honour of the ʿAbbāsid caliph, at about a mile's distance from the city. He strongly fortified it and garrisoned it with a war-trained guard of wholly devoted military slaves, mainly Sudanese negroes. In a short time, al-ʿAbbāsīya grew into a well-sized and flourishing town, but all that has remained of it is a mound rising some 10 to 15 feet above the plain. The last Aghlabid rulers gave up their residence at al-ʿAbbāsīya for Raqqāda, the newly built pleasure seat some three miles to the south, in the midst of beautiful gardens and on the shore of a large artificial lake.

Supported by the Qayrawān religious leaders, who suspiciously watched the consolidation of the new strong-handed régime, two serious revolts broke out among the Arab militia *(jund)*, but were suppressed by the emir's black guard. So were uprisings of Berber tribes and Khārijite sectarians, with the result that Ibrāhīm's son Abū al-ʿAbbās ʿAbd Allāh I (812-817) inherited a firmly established, pacified realm. His successor Abū Muhammad Ziyādat Allāh I (817-838) carried the dynasty's prestige to its height. Confronted soon after his accession to the throne with a widely ramified insurrection of Arab chieftains closely connected with the malcontent Qayrawān upper classes, he brought the Berber tribesmen to his side and with their help forced the rebels to submission. Having re-established peace internally, he set about a policy of expansion across the Mediterranean under the banner of the Holy War, with the conquest of Sicily as the first goal. To emphasize the religious character of the enterprise, he appointed the reputed theologian of al-Qayrawān, Asad Ibn al-Furāt*, supreme commander of the expeditionary forces. This course was systematically followed by his successors who bore Arab arms as far as the gates of Rome.

Ziyādat Allāh began that munificent building activity which was to connect the names of the Aghlabid emirs lastingly with some of the finest monuments of Tunisian religious architecture. He tore down the old mosque at al-Qayrawān, originally erected by ʿUqba Ibn Nāfiʿ, the first Arab conqueror of North Africa - it is still called 'Mosque of Sīdī ʿUqba' - and completely rebuilt it. He preserved only the venerated prayer niche *(mihrāb)* and set up in the prayer-hall the multitude of splendid columns, rich paneling of glazed tiles and ornamentations of sculptured wood, taken either from the country's many ancient Roman temples and Byzantine basilicas, or regardless of cost, purchased abroad, in particular from the famous workshops of Iraq. His successors, especially Abū Ibrāhīm Ahmad (850-863) and Abū Ishāq Ibrāhīm II (875-902) added further structural and decorative elements which conferred upon the Mosque of Sidi ʿUqba the essential traits it has preserved down to this day, in spite of some later not always very happy alterations. The pride of the rich collection of manuscripts assembled here in the course of the centuries are those dating from this period.

Two other reputed sanctuaries among a number of lesser ones were built or reconstructed under Aghlabid patronage in the style of the time: in Tunis, the imposing *Jāmiʿ Zaytūna* (the Mosque of the Olives) in the centre of the business quarter; and the Great Mosque in Sousse, then the most important Tunisian seaport. Outside the field of these pious works fall such architectural and engineering constructions as the huge water-storage basins of al-Qayrawān and Raqqāda - both still in existence - and those of al-ʿAbbāsīya; a number of aqueducts and bridges; various water-works, modelled after those left by the Romans and Byzantines; and the complex sewerage system of al-Qayrawān. Neither the frequent feuds among the numerous members of the dynasty, nor the repeated revolts nor, finally, the undisguised opposition of the groups to whose puritanism the sumptuous court-life of the luxury-loving emirs could not but appear sinful and objectionable, prevented the country, in particular the towns, from enjoying great prosperity. Its source was agriculture, caravan traffic and a lively maritime trade, more often than not closely bordering on piracy. A belt of strongholds *(rābita*)* and signal towers, mostly also inherited from the Byzantine era, protected the coastline and the vulnerable sections of the inland frontiers.

The decline of the Aghlabid rule set in with Emir Abū Isḥāq Ibrāhīm II. He had to combat the attacks of the Tulūnid rulers of Egypt, who were eager for conquest; to suppress at the price of heavy losses of men, horses and material uprisings of local chieftains in several parts of the country; and to face the increasing general dissatisfaction caused by the devastations of war, heavy taxation and by his own despotic temper. At last he was forced to abdicate in favour of his son, went to Sicily and in the course of an expedition against Italy, died before Cosenza. The last of the Aghlabids, Abū Mudar Ziyādat Allāh III (903-909) who had his father and several other members of his family assassinated in order to clear for himself the way to the throne, lost it to the precursors of the Fātimid conquest of North Africa, Abū ʿAbd Allāh al-Shīʿī and his followers, from among the Berber Sanhāja*, the tribe of the Kutāma - the Kabyles* of today. In the name of the expected Mahdi - the God-guided Saviour - they conquered Raqqāda and al-Qayrawān and soon were masters of the whole Aghlabid realm. After a hairbreath escape Ziyādat Allāh III fled to Egypt, from there to Palestine, and died in Jerusalem.

1. Ibrāhīm Ibn al-Aghlab 800-812
2. Abū al- ʿAbbās ʿAbd Allāh I 812-817
3. Abū Muhammad Ziyādat Allāh I 817-838
4. Abū ʿIqāl 838-841
5. Abu al-ʿAbbās Muhammad 841-856
6. Abū Ibrāhīm Ahmad 856-863
7. Ziyādat Allāh II 863-864
8. Abū al-Gharānīq Muhammad 864-875
9. Abū Ishāq Ibrāhīm II 875-902
10. Abū al-ʿAbbās ʿAbd Allāh II 902-903
11. Abū Mudar Ziyādat Allāh III 903-909

AGRICULTURE. Of the roughly 300.000 square miles or 192 million acres which constitute the surface of Morocco, Algeria (without the Sahara regions) and Tunisia, about two-fifths are barren rocks and desert. The other three-fifths of productive soil are covered, according to estimates, by 20 million acres of forests including several areas of cork-oaks; 8 million acres of esparto grass, the raw material of high-class paper; 22 million acres of pastures, some of which might be turned into arable land; 10 million acres of olive and fruit trees, vegetable gardens, vineyards and date groves; and by some 55 million acres given to the cultivation of cereals, of which one half is actually ploughed and sown every year while the other half is lying fallow. In all three countries agriculture and stock breeding furnish, except in a year of drought, 35 to 40 per cent of their total national produce; as much of their total national revenue; and, in good and bad years alike, are the sole source of livelihood for 20 million out of their 25 million people. The real significance of these figures appears, however, only in the light of certain particularities of the socio-economic structure. One is what has been called a 'demographic explosion': the annual increase of the population at the rate of 2.5 to 3 per cent, which means that every year 600.000 to 700.000 people more will have to be fed, clothed and housed. Another one lies in the striking inequality of the distribution of the land. And a third one springs from the differences in the manner and way of its exploitation. In the period of French political supremacy a comparatively small number of French settlers ('colons') acquired the best soils, approximately 10 million acres, and in some cases built up enormous estates. In Algeria this process set in soon after the beginning of the occupation specially through confiscations and re-allotments of the state domains and the landed property of some hostile religious brotherhoods*, tribes and notables. At the outbreak of the revolution in 1954 there were 20.000 or so smaller or larger French landholders installed, many of them already for several generations. Some 300 among them owned very imporant property: about a dozen owned two-and-a-half thousand acres each; and three powerful concerns controlled a total of more than 200.000 acres, one of which, the 'Compagnie Algérienne', on a concession granted by Napoleon III at a rental of one Franc per hectare (2.47 acres). In Tunisia some 2400 French and Italian settlers had acquired one-and-a-quarter million acres either through advantageous purchases or on still more favourable terms in the form of concessions from state domains. In Morocco about 1.6 million acres were partitioned into some 900 estates, and one million acres into 3000 lesser farms. This foreign colonization used up-to-date techniques and mechanized equipment, was run on commercial management principles. It disposed of adequate capital or easy credits, specialized in high-quality crops for the European markets and yielded appreciable returns.

The native sector, for the most part fields of barley or wheat and pastures, producing almost exclusively for home consumption, is either split into a multitude of dwarf-holdings - mainly a consequence of the Islamic laws of inheritance which easily lead to extreme fragmentation; or is divided into collective clan or tribal land and mortmain of pious foundations *(habūs)*; or has come, particularly at the time of the

French régime, into the hands of influential sheikhs or caids. With rare exceptions archaic methods of cultivation, rooted in the lack of both the technical knowledge and means for modernization, and hence low yields, are the rule. In fact none of the three countries can dispense with import of cereals, canned or powdered milk and sugar, although, as their own and foreign experts agree, they normally could produce these basic foodstuffs in sufficient quantities and save expenditure of much needed foreign currency. A far more serious consequence of this stagnation is the depressing poverty of the rural masses: peasants on their own tiny piece of land from which they derive an income estimated for Morocco at one-twentieth, and for Algeria at not much higher than a thirtieth, of the average income of the European farmer; tenants working on a contract *(khāmisat)* of crop-sharing under which they receive one-fifth *(khāmis)* of the harvest - in Algeria raised by a decree of 1956 to one-half - whereas the landlords provides the seed, stock and sometimes the tools, and retains the other four-fifths; finally all the landless labourers, the few who are permanently employed on the modern estates, and the many who are hired for seasonal work, but the rest of the time are left without earning.

As the number of this peasantry grows - and the rate of its growth is one of the fastest in the world - its level of living is still more deeply depressed. There lies the source of the currents of migration which in the last few decades have populated the slums of the Moroccan, Algerian and Tunisian cities and their belts of 'bidonvilles' (petrol-can towns). They have shifted half a million Algerians into similar slums and shanty-towns in the surroundings of Paris and other industrial centres of France. It was calculated that the savings they send back to their families equal approximately one-third of the earnings of the entire agricultural labour force in Algeria.

The few incoherent and hesitant attempts made by the French administration to find a way out of this critical situation were each time quickly abandoned when it became manifest that to pursue them would affect powerful French interests, so that inevitably for Tunisian, Algerian and Moroccan nationalism of whatever shade 'economic liberation' became but another aspect of the struggle for political independence. It was equally obvious that land reform was found to hold a rank of priority as soon as independence was obtained. To have the State take over and parcel out the tribal and *habūs* land could be regarded as a purely internal question and its solution is well on its way. More complex were the matters, specially those of a financial order, involved in the re-purchase of the big estates of French 'colons', which could be dealt with only in inter-governmental negotiations including the grant of long-term loans. Most of the major obstacles were overcome once the bitterness of the revolutionary years had begun to subside. Simultaneously the new States embarked on a variety of plans to promote social and economic development, but it was soon realized that land reform, indispensible as it was, would by itself neither solve the problem of unemployment nor make the countries self-supporting in essential food products. What the planners advocated was the formation of adequately organized peasant co-operatives under expert management, capable of using scientific farming techniques on a large scale. They would take over the great modern estates, as well as the small plots of the many individual owners following their consolidation in holdings of a rational size. A system of agricultural schooling and training, coupled with the provision of credit facilities for the benefit of the peasantry at large, is to lead to more efficient use of the land and improvements in yield, to a profitable marketing of the crops and thus to higher family incomes. The creation of industries for the processing of the domestic natural resources, preferably away from the great cities, is to open up employment for the surplus of manpower in the country side, and to replace some of the imports of finished products. Within the framework of such Two-, Five-, and also Ten-Year Plans a number of projects have already materialized or reached an advanced experimental stage with the technical and financial assistance supplied by international agencies and various foreign governments. They all are based on a combination of economic liberalism and State control, the dosage of which differs according to the particular ideological and political pattern of each State.

In MOROCCO, a few of the measures inaugurated by the Protectorate have survived after certain re-adaptations, such as agricultural co-operatives and pilote farms; some credit-societies advancing money and distributing seed-corn and fertilizers, which in 1962 were combined in a 'Caisse Nationale de Crédit Agricole'; or a service for the 'Defence and Restoration of the Soils' (D.R.S.), for the prevention of soil erosion and the encouragement of afforestation, and the plantation of fruit trees and vines. A number of 'Secteurs de Modernisation du Paysannat' (S.M.P.) were transformed into so-called 'Centres de Travail' (C.T.) and in August 1957 entrusted with what has become known as the 'Opération Labour' (Operation Ploughing). They put to work 570 tractors purchased by the government controlled 'Centrales des Travaux Agricoles' (C.T.A.) in an area of 750.000 acres - the late King Muhammad V himself on the wheel of a tractor ploughed the first furrow - and sold to the peasants on easy terms seeds, fertilizers and minor implements, trying to induce them to a temporary assembling of their holdings into fields of rational dimensions. The following year the 'Operation Labour' was repeated on an area twice the size, and it was decided to extend it gradually over a surface of two-and-a-half million acres. Within the framework of the new Five-Year Plan an autonomous 'Office Nationale de la Modernisation Rurale' (O.N.M.R.) created in 1962 is to integrate the development of the entire rural economy in co-operation with the 'Office Nationale de l'Irrigation' (O.N.I.) and the National Institute of Agricultural Research as well as with the village and tribal communities and the various agricultural schools.

In ALGERIA it was for the first time the Free French government in exile (Comité de la Libération Nationale) that in 1943 turned serious attention to the situation of the peasantry. A specially appointed 'Commission des Réformes Musulmanes' worked out a country-wide long-term plan for the raising of the rural proletariat, and in pursuance of its recommendations an autonomous body of regional 'Secteurs d'Améliorations Rurales' (S.A.R.) was instituted. In co-operation with a governmental 'Service de Défence et de la Restauration du Sol' it was to distribute vacant land in adequately sized plots to the landless labourers and the owners or tenants of the uneconomic miniature holdings; provide credit and supply appropriate tools; and through a staff of monitors sharing the peasants' life teach the use of rational methods, promote collective cultivation and organise the sale of the harvest surplus. The number of the S.A.R. increased from 12 in 1946 to 103 in 1948, but owing to budgetary curtailments only to 175 in 1952 and to 200 in 1954. By then they tutored some 75.000 settler families, while the total of 600.000 initially assumed as being most urgently in need of their assistance had in the meantime grown to 800.000. Thenceforth the action of the S.A.R. was tuned down to the concept of a series of pilot projects and gradually faded out altogether. There followed two Four-Year 'Plans de Modernisation et d'Equipement' (1949-52 and 1953-56) to be financed by a 'Caisse d'Equipment pour le Développement de l'Algérie', but whatever their practical value might have been, in those years of revolutionary passion and the dislocation of the rural population they could hardly be expected to bring results.

A third comprehensive and development programme scheduled for a period of 15 or perhaps 25 years was formulated in 1959. Based like its predecessors on the assumption of an 'Algérie Française', this so-called Plan of Constantine - announced in a speech delivered by General de Gaulle in that city - was intended, in the words of its 'Orientation Générale' to repair century-long retardations and to accord the underdeveloped Algerian economy to the rhythm of the modern world. Preparatory steps were begun immediately under the direction of a 'Conseil Supérieur du Plan de Constantine', but left little room for optimistic expectations while the hostilities continued. The Franco-Algerian agreement concluded at Evian in March 1962 and establishing the independence of Algeria, contains circumstancial provisions for the financial and technical assistance France would extend for the implementation of the Plan to the Algerian government, which since then has announced its intention to devote more than one-third of the capital investments to the improvement of rural life.

In March 1963 the Algerian government confiscated the large domains held by Algerian nationals branded as 'enemies of the people' because of pro-French sympathies in the years of the Revolution. Simultaneously the biggest, and soon also the medium-sized estates of the French 'colons' and in October all French agricultural properties, were nationalized as a 'preventive means for the sake of public order'. The question of indemnification was left to subsequent negotiations between the Algerian and French governments. Each estate was turned over for collective management to a three-level workers' organization: at the bottom, the general assembly of all the workers of Algerian nationality, permanently occupied on the estate; then a workers' council elected by the assembly for a period of three years; and finally a management committee renewable at the rate of one-third of its members every year. In every municipality a 'stimulating council for self-management' helps to set up these managing bodies and assists them in their activities. It consists of the chairmen of the managing committees, representatives of the authorities, of the trade unions and of the Party (the National Liberation Front*). A government agency originally called the 'National Bureau for the Protection and Management of Vacant Properties', subsequently renamed, 'Bureau of the Socialized Sector', supervises the functioning of this organization and appoints for every estate a responsible body for maintaining all operations in conformity with the principles laid down in the Plan. An 'Office Nationale de Commercialisation' is in charge of the sale of the harvest. The profits are divided among the members of the general assembly after deduction of the taxes, remuneration for exemplary work and premiums accorded for good management. Periodically the functioning of the system and the problems arising from it are discussed at national peasants' congresses, the first of which convened at Algiers in October 1963 with the participation of some 2500 delegates.

In TUNISIA the Protectorate authorities began as early as 1884 the survey and registration of the state domains, the collective tribal land and the properties of the pious foundations. The primary purpose was to facilitate the allocation of land to foreign - mainly French - colonists and to provide a legal title for these acquisitions. By the end of the Protectorate about one-quarter of the cultivable surface was registered, but the only noteworthy effect with a bearing on the peasantry was the settlement between 1920 and 1938 on partitioned state domains, of 8700 landless families, of which 1500 acceded to full ownership. Foremost also in the interest of the foreign colonization was the construction, terminated in 1957 of the two great barrages in the area of Souk el-Arba on the Wādī al-Līl and the Wādī al-Mallègue. It was followed by various schemes for the development of the irrigated land and the promotion of the use of tractors, chemical fertilizers and up-to-date methods of cultivation. Compared therewith the increase in the productivity of the date plantations and orchards in the oases of the south through the boring of artesian wells, or through the installation of motor pumps in some sections of native agriculture in the coastal areas must appear as modest. In the first years of independence the Tunisian government took over the land of the pious foundations - about one-quarter of the country's cultivable surface - and of the religious brotherhoods. It was placed under the administration of an 'Office des Terres Domaniales' in charge of improvements and of the sale in adequately sized plots on easy terms, while the National Agricultural Bank (established 1959) provides the necessary credit at a low rate of interest. Simultaneously a two-fold reform programme was set in operation: on the one hand, the assemblage into economically exploitable holdings of the fragmented properties; and on the other, the division of the vast stretches of collective land of the tribes, and the apportionment to their individual families of its cultivable sections. Hand in hand with this there goes an educational, technical and social assistance project intended to guide the nomads in the transition to a settled mode of life.

In 1963 these measures were supplemented by new legislation with the purpose of increasing the productivity of the insufficiently utilized cultivable soils, which implied the redistribution of some 2400 square miles. It distinguishes between the irrigable but not yet irrigated areas mainly situated in the northern parts of the country, and the regions in the centre and the south. In the former it establishes a strictly determined size for all holdings, to be obtained through the reduction, by way of expropriation, of the over-sized properties and the grouping of the smaller plots into appropriate units. Once this operation is terminated the State is to undertake the improvement of the land and turn it over to the owners for collective cultivation. In the other regions the small holdings are to be assembled into domains of a rational size in accordance with the type of the soils which are to be cultivated by co-operative organizations following the plans worked out by the government.

The modalities of the re-purchase of the large French estates, but only in so far as they are given to cereal growing, were finally determined in an agreement with France in March 1963 after complicated negotiations which had dragged on for several years. According to its terms the transfer of the properties with their live-stock and mechanical equipment was to take place in two stages, one during 1963 comprising 360.000 acres, the other during 1964 comprising 120.000 acres, whereby the French Treasury would undertake the compensation of the owners on behalf of the Tunisian government, which for these payments was granted a long-term credit. The retrocession of the remaining portion of some 300.000 acres was left in abeyance.

In the first years of independence took place also the experiment of the so-called 'Chantiers de Développement', devised to absorb about half of the 300.000 or so unemployed or under-employed agricultural labourers through general improvement works such as road building, tree planting or the digging of wells and irrigation channels. They were paid partly in cash and partly in wheat and flour contributed by the United States as a non-repayable aid. This action, started with more enthusiasm than foresight as to its technical and economic implications, was discontinued in 1961 when it became evident that the effects were a long way out of line with the charges provided for in the budget. On an entirely different basis there were founded two recent, comprehensive development schemes promising highly beneficial results for the peasantry. One, in the Mejerda Valley, financed about half-and-half by the State and the American International Co-operation Administration and managed by the autonomous Mejerda Valley Authority, is concerned with the conversion into arable soils through a drainage and irrigation system covering some 35.000 acres of unproductive land and its distribution to landless families. The other, planned by the U.N.O. Food and Agricultural Organization (F.A.O.) which eventually may contribute to the expenses an amount of $ 900.000, is meant to improve some 100.000 acres of steppe and poor soils in the region east of the Tell and to raise the standard of living of the cattle-breeding nomads and small peasants. Both schemes fit into a Ten-Year Development Programme (1961-1970), set forth in the 'Perspective Décennale de Développement', which in the domain of agriculture is to promote the co-operative organization of the peasantry and the village artisans.

In all three countries the prime difficulty at present is the shortage of personnel possessing sufficient knowledge and experience to organize and keep functioning all the institutions, especially at the medium and lower levels, made necessary by the multiplicity of tasks. Thus an appraisal of the work so far accomplished and still ahead will have to include one essential factor - time.

AHMAD BĀBĀ, TINBUKTĪ al-, the name under which the jurist and biographer Abū al-ʿAbbās Ahmad al-Takrūrī al-Massūfī (1556-1627) is usually quoted. Born in Timbuctoo (Sudan) of a family whose members for generations had held juridical and religious posts, he was known far beyond his native country for his erudition, particularly in the field of canon law according to the Mālikite school of thought dominant in the Arab West. When the Saʿdian* ruler of Morocco, Ahmad al-Mansūr* (1578-1603) conquered the Sudan (1592), al-Tinbuktī was arrested because of his antagonistic attitude, and deported to Marrakesh, but after a while set free on condition that he would not leave the city. Upon al-Mansūr's death, he was permitted to return to Timbuctoo, where he spent the rest of his life. Al-Tinbuktī wrote a great number of juridical treatises on subjects of Mālikite canon law, but of basic significance for modern research, in particular for the detailed biographical and bibliographical information it contains is his *Nayl al-Ibtihāj bi-Tatrīz al-Dibāj*, a dictionary listing the Mālikite doctors of law and the most venerated saints of Morocco. This work, compiled during the author's stay in Marrakesh, supplemented and brought up to date a similar work of the XIVth century. Subsequently an abridged version was prepared by the author himself.

AHMAD al-MANSŪR, ABŪ al-ʿABBĀS, one of the most prominent sultans of Morocco (1578-1603), the sixth of the line of the Saʿdians*, proclaimed on the battle-field at the Wādī al-Makhāzin (the so-called Battle of the Three Kings*) by his victorious troops after the death of his brother, Sultan Abū Marwān al-Malik (1576-1578). Highly cultured, occasionally also trying his hand at poetry, and keeping his court at Marrakesh wide open to scholars and men of letters, to some of whom he was bound in real friendship, this 'savant of the caliphs and caliph of the savants', as his biographers called him, was at the same time an excellent statesman. He proved equally skilful in foreign relations; in using the Sharīfian* family prestige for controlling the critically increasing secular ambition of the religious brotherhoods* and marabouts*, and in exploiting all possible sources of state revenues, including the taxation of the proceeds from smuggling and piracy, while now and then himself embarking as a sleeping partner in a profitable trading transaction. He devoted particular care to the building up of an army which could command respect, composed of a standing corps of Turkish, Kabyle* and Morisco* (Spanish Moslems) mercenaries, well-trained in the use of fire-arms, and of unswerving loyalty, supplemented by a reserve of - not quite so reliable - Bedouin warriors. His work, too, was the construction of the still existing 'Bastiun' in Taza with its walls more than three feet thick, heavily-gunned and capable of withstanding the strongest then known cannon bombardment, as well as of the two heavy towers (*burj*, plur. *burūj*), also preserved, in the northern and southern sections of the circumvallation of Fez, and a number of

fortresses at strategically important places. It was probably due to his military preparedness not less than to his diplomacy that under his reign the country enjoyed an era of peace, apart from some minor tribal disturbances and revolts of insubordinate family members, all of which were suppressed without difficulty.
Al-Mansūr's only warlike undertaking on a large scale was an expedition into the western Sudan against the Negro kingdom of Sanghoy in the region of the great loop of the Niger, ruled by the royal dynasty of the Askīya and widely thought to possess fabulous wealth of gold. He established an operational basis in the oases of southern Algeria and then his troops, some 4000 men with 8000 camels and 1000 baggage horses, set out (1591) on a three-month march across the Sahara. Under great hardship, they reached the Niger at Gao; annihilated the Sudanese army which although much superior in numbers, had only arrows and spears to oppose to their guns, and became masters of Timbuctoo. Al-Mansūr rejected a request for peace, substantiated by the offer of a large tribute, and dispatched reinforcements and transport vessels, which could be taken to pieces and reassembled whereever needed, to carry on the offensive down the river. Thus the conquest of the Askīya kingdom was completed, Sultan Ishāq II, the last of the Askīya, fell in battle, and masses of prisoners, among whom the well-known scholar Ahmad Bābā al-Tinbuktī*, were taken back. There was also a rich booty of gold, although not as enormous as it appeared to the enthusiasm of the chroniclers, to which he owes his surname *al-Dhahabī* (the Golden). Yet the precious metal continued to flow in, although gradually diminishing, for some ten to fifteen more years, until the sovereignty over the Sudan had faded away, but in the meantime the high standard of its coinage made Morocco a very desirable partner in international trade.
It was just another aspect of al-Mansūr's policy of securing peaceful relations with the great Powers and internal stability that he gave impressive displays of grandeur and opulence: an elaborate court ceremonial; resplendent military parades; and the luxury of his palace in Marrakesh, the famous *Qasr al-Badīʿ*, for the construction of which, according to contemporary reports, architects and craftsmen were called from Florence, marble columns and sculptured ornaments ordered in Pisa, and works of art imported from everywhere in the Orient. At the same time, he was a most conscientious pater familias who, judging from his letters to his son Abū Fāris, kept a close eye on the affairs of his household, from protective measures against infection from the plague to care for his personal wardrobe and concern for the proper attendance to his favourite horse.
Ahmad al-Mansūr died at an advanced age, himself a victim of the plague, and was buried in the dynasty's necropolis at Marrakesh, in the sumptuous sanctuary which he himself had built. Its refined architectural elegance, the softness of the plaster-carved arabesques lining the walls, in perfect harmony with the subdued lustre of the glazed tile marquetry which a fortunate fate has preserved almost unimpaired, bear witness to the artistic achievements this era was able to attain.

ʿĀ'ISHA al-MANNŪBĪYA, also called Sayyida Lālla Mannūbīya or popularly simply *al-sayyida* (The Lady), the most highly reputed among the saintly women who from time to time made their appearance in the Arab West towards the end of the Middle Ages († appr. 1255). Born in the village of La Manouba (Mannūba, about 3 miles south-west of Tunis), she is said, already at the age of twelve, to have shown signs of her visionary gift and miraculous powers. She then left her home for Tunis. There she seems to have been accepted among the disciples of the mystic Abū al-Hasan al-Shādhilī and, grown up, mixed with the poorest classes, miserably dressed herself, and, while strictly maintaining her dignity, disregarded the social restrictions imposed upon women by the conventional moral code. Notwithstanding, or perhaps because of certain excentricities of her behaviour, she commanded the respect of the crowd to the extent that the authorities protected her against the hostilities of the theologians who wanted to have her arrested and expelled. She died at an advanced age, widely venerated for her saintliness, and was buried allegedly on the high ground south-west of Tunis, where her tomb became a much visited shrine, especially by women afflicted with sterility. She herself, it is said, indicated the most propicious days of the week for these visits. Popular poetry in praise of her virtue, her saintliness and the miracles she performed has kept her name alive down to this day.

AISSAOUA see ʿĪSĀWA

AIT, also *aith* or *īt*, a Berber term meaning the 'sons of', equivalent to the Arabic *banū* and *awlād*, and used only in combination with proper nouns as the indication of the name of a tribe, e.g. Ait Atta, etc.

ʿALAWIDS, ʿAlawī or ʿAlawīya, the reigning dynasty of Morocco which emerged out of the political confusion in which the country was left by the last Saʿdian* sultans (1554-1659). Tracing their descent to the Prophet's grandson al-Hasan, and hence of Sharīfian* nobility, they came into Morocco towards the end of the XIIIth century in the wake of the Maʿqil* invasion, and settled south of the High Atlas in the oases of the Tāfīlālt (whence also called Fīlālī, the people from the Tāfīlālt). In the first quarter of the XVIIth century, the chroniclers mention a chief of their clan, Mūlāy ʿAlī al-Sharīf, in connection with his feuds with the marabout-prince al-Samlālī*. For unknown reasons the family leadership was entrusted to his son Mūlāy Muhammad, while he himself was taken prisoner by al-Samlālī, but soon again released. Accompanied by his second son al-Rashīd, he withdrew to Sijilmāsa (about 1659) where another son, Mūlāy Ismāʿīl, was born to him. He died in Sijilmāsa at an advanced age, apparently without having taken further part in the events of his time. His tomb at Rissānī (some 13 miles south of Erfūd), called the *Zāwiya Mūlāy ʿAlī*, is still in existence. It fell to his three sons, Muhammad, al-Rashīd and Ismāʿīl successively to prepare, build up and consolidate the reign of the ʿAlawid dynasty.
Mūlāy Muhammad (1636-1663) was soon involved in an open conflict

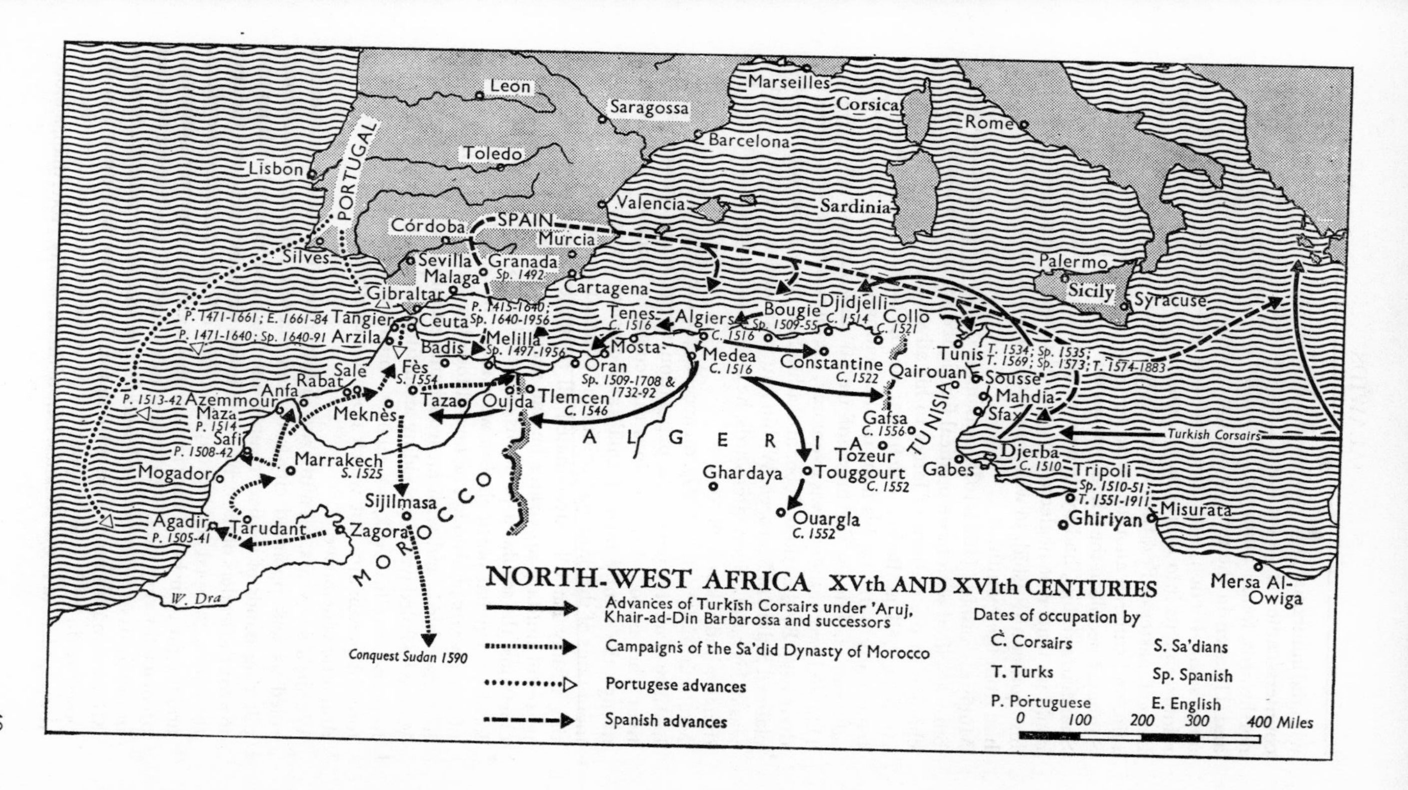

Leon
Saragossa
Marseilles
Corsica
Rome
Toledo
Barcelona
Lisbon
PORTUGAL
Valencia
Sardinia
Córdoba
SPAIN
Murcia
Silves
Sevilla
Granada
Sp. 1492
Malaga
Cartagena
Palermo
Sicily
Syracuse
Gibraltar
P. 1415-1640; Sp. 1640-1956
Ceuta
P. 1471-1661; E. 1661-84 Tangier
P. 1471-1640; Sp. 1640-91 Arzila
Badis
Melilla
Sp. 1497-1956
Tenes
C. 1516
Algiers
C. 1516
Bougie
Sp. 1509-55
Djidjelli
C. 1514
Collo
C. 1521
Mosta
Oran
Sp. 1509-1708 & 1732-92
Medea
C. 1516
Constantine
C. 1522
Tunis
T. 1534; Sp. 1535; T. 1569; Sp. 1573; T. 1574-1883
Qairouan
Sousse
Mahdia
Sfax
Sale
Rabat
Fès
S. 1554
Anfa
P. 1513-42 Azemmour
Maza
P. 1514
Safi
P. 1508-42
Meknès
Taza
Oujda
Tlemcen
C. 1546
Marrakech
S. 1525
Mogador
A L G E R I A
Gafsa
C. 1556
Tozeur
TUNISIA
Gabes
Djerba
C. 1510
Tripoli
Sp. 1510-51; T. 1551-1911
Turkish Corsairs
Ghardaya
Touggourt
C. 1552
Ouargla
C. 1552
Sijilmasa
Zagora
MOROCCO
Agadir
P. 1505-41
Tarudant
W. Dra
Ghiriyan
Misurata
Mersa Al-Owiga
Conquest Sudan 1590
NORTH-WEST AFRICA XVth AND XVIth CENTURIES
Advances of Turkish Corsairs under 'Aruj, Khair-ad-Din Barbarossa and successors
Campaigns of the Sa'did Dynasty of Morocco
Portugese advances
Spanish advances
Dates of occupation by
C. Corsairs
T. Turks
P. Portuguese
S. Sa'dians
Sp. Spanish
E. English
0 100 200 300 400 Miles

with the influential Dilā'yūn* sheikh Muhammad al-Hajj but in two encounters came off as the loser. Undeterred by this setback, he moved northwards, found allies in the kindred Maʿqil of the region of Oujda and Tlemcen in the territory of the Turkish Regency of Algeria, and after some friction with the Ottoman pasha, returned with large reinforcements into Morocco. Although he tried twice in vain to make himself master of Fez, then a sort of city-republic under an Arab chieftain, and suffered another defeat by the Dilā'yūn partisans among the Sanhāja* people in the Middle Atlas, the ʿAlawid clan, supported by its Sharīfian prestige, had by then developed into a factor of power which could no longer be neglected. Mūlāy Muhammad fell fighting against his brother al-Rashīd, to whom an irreconcilable enmity had opposed him from their youth.

Mūlāy al-Rashīd* (1664-1672) was imbued with the same warlike spirit, but was gifted with more political foresight and greater ability to turn changes in the pattern of forces to his advantage. His allies included Arab as well as Berber chieftains; he operated without haste, but tenaciously pursuing his aim, in eliminating one after another of his adversaries. Finally the most influential and obstinate of them, the Dilā'yūn brotherhood, was overcome, dissolved and its stronghold was destroyed. By the end of 1666, al-Rashīd had entered Fez and was proclaimed Sultan of Morocco. Within four years almost the entire country was in his hands. Soon afterwards, he lost his life in an accident, but the dynasty had taken firm root.

Mūlāy Ismāʿīl* (1672-1727), on acceding to the throne, had to face the hostility of a large part of the population, stirred up by his nearest relatives who exploited the feelings that could be invoked by the call to avenge the saintly men of Dilā', and carried the rebellion from the mountains of the Sanhāja far into the plains. In years of ceaseless fighting Mūlāy Ismāʿīl exterminated all resistance, mercilessly using the powerful military apparatus he had set up, until the pride of the tribal chieftains, the secular aspirations of the religious brotherhoods and the local or regional particularism were made to bend to his will. In the fifty-five years of his reign he bound together the territories his brother had assembled, and with an iron hand established order and safety. Where he failed was in providing an institutional structure solid enough to perpetuate his work, a weakness which had been covered up by his forceful personality but which upon his death became manifest with dramatic vehemence.

Within a few years, all authority disintegrated. Garrison commanders ruled as self-appointed city-lords and masters over the countryside; pilfering bands of soldiers roamed the land and ravaged villages and towns; the leaders of the urban mob levied taxes and laid down the law; the tribes, grouped and regrouped in fluid alliances, invaded the plains, and fought their hereditary feuds without any of them ever gaining supremacy for very long. Trade came to a standstill, the harvest perished in the fields or was destroyed, and famine spread threatingly. Eight of Mūlāy Ismāʿīl's many sons were in turn raised to the throne and deposed again by military captains, a powerful governor of a province, or the populace of Fez or Meknès. One of them, Mūlāy ʿAbd Allāh, a bloodthirsty tyrant, took four, according to some sources five times the place of a less fortunate brother. It was his sole merit to have complied at the beginning of his last reign (1745-1757) with the demand of the people of Marrakesh and appointed his young son Mūlāy Muhammad governor *(khalīfa)* of the city. His accession to the throne marked the first step out of this anarchy.

Sīdī Muhammad Ibn ʿAbd Allāh (1757-1790), pious and highly cultured, energetic and tenacious yet pliable when the expected result would not seem to warrant the costs, knew how to command respect and obedience. He reorganized the military apparatus, secured financial stability and revived economic activities by building up a system of trade agreements with a number of the European maritime countries and with the United States of America (1786). He imposed his authority upon the tribes, negotiating whenever possible, using force when inevitable, and displacing those who proved intractable. Of a similar elasticity was his policy towards the sheikhs of the great religious brotherhoods* and marabouts* who, willingly or not, had to bow to him as the country's supreme spiritual head. As his lasting monument stands the city of Mogador that he erected on the site of a former Portuguese seafort and developed into an important shipping centre for the caravan trade from Mauretania, the Senegal and the Niger regions, which still flourished in the first quarter of this century until it was gradually surpassed by Safi and Agadir.

His death heralded two troubled years with his elder son on the throne, the dissolute and incapable Mūlāy al-Yazīd (1790-1792). His assassination opened the way to the younger Mūlāy Sulaymān Ibn Sīdī Muhammad (1792-1822) against whom two of his brothers took up arms in the Rif and on the plains of the Atlantic coast. They had to be brought to submission in long-drawn fighting. Nevertheless, minor armed expeditions at more or less frequent intervals, particularly in the remoter parts of the country, remained indispensable in order to collect the taxes which were usually two or three years in arrears, or as a demonstration of power to restrain refractory tribal instincts. Continuing his father's efforts at promoting trade with the occidental countries, Sultan Sulaymān granted them substantial reductions of import duties, exemption from the taxes levied on their commercial establishments in Moroccan ports, and extended their privilege of consular jurisdiction. Special facilities were conceded to the United States of America in return for a donation by Congress of 20,000 Dollars, which George Washington (1795) announced to the Sultan in a personal letter. Subsequently, they were incorporated in the so-called Treaty of Meknès (1836) and retained a certain significance as an instrument of American policy well into the era of the French Protectorate.

Profoundly religious, like his father, but of a much sterner orthodoxy, Mūlāy Sulaymān felt strongly attracted by the radical Wahhābite puritanism just then carried by the Bedouin warriors of the Ibn Saʿūd clan at the point of the sword all over Central Arabia. The first half of his reign remained unaffected by any intolerance, particularly in the thorny question of the relation between the State and the brotherhoods. To some of them, such as the Darqāwā* and the Tijānīya*, he even showed far-reaching benevolence, motivated presumably by political opportunism. Then, however, his attitude suddenly changed. A delegation of theologians and legists headed by one of his sons, was commissioned to discuss with the Saʿūdi leaders the question of how to apply the principles of Wahhābism in the conduct of government affairs. Under the impression of their report, he had an ordinance proclaimed at the Friday sermon *(khutba)* in mosques of every town, condemning all forms of the marabout cult, all public manifestations of worship *(mūsem*)* at the tombs of saints, and the extravagancies of the brotherhood rituals. It was a serious underestimate of the forces of maraboutism and of the violence of its reaction: insurrections of the tribes, Berber and Arab, in which his son lost his life; a revolt of the people of Fez; insubordination in the army; a rebellion of his nephews - all these were the result of his mistake which practically undid his prior achievements and nearly cost him the throne.

His nephew Mūlāy ʿAbd al-Rahmān Ibn Hishām* (1822-1859) repaired the damage. He reconciled the brotherhoods and calmed the popular passions; secured the obedience of most of the great chieftains and replenished the state treasury. Less fortunate was his policy of siding with Abdelkader* against French penetration into Algeria, which ended with his defeat on the Isly river (1844). His son Sīdī Muhammad (1859-1873) similarly overrated Moroccan military strength and allowed a series of incidents at the frontiers of the Spanish territory of Ceuta to degenerate into a war with Spain. The result was a two-year occupation (1860-1862) of Tetuan, the enforced grant of an extensive fishing concession at Ifni* and the payment of a heavy indemnity. Only England's intercession saved Morocco from the loss of the entire coastal area on the Straits.

Thenceforth the sultans no longer entertained any illusions as to the value of their army as a factor in their foreign relations, but used it merely for large-scale police operations *(harka*)*, for the pacification of unruly tribes or the collection of taxes. It was essentially for this purpose that Sultan Mūlāy al-Hasan Ibn Muhammad (1873-1894) devoted much effort to its modernization. He engaged French, English and Italian instructors, purchased quick-firing rifles and light field artillery in Europe and with the help of an Italian technical mission built in Fez a large armament factory, the so-called Makina, today the site of several sorts of industry. Thus he consolidated the authority of the central government *(makhzan*)* in three-quarters of the Moroccan territory, while this area *(bilād al-makhzan*)* was no more than one-third when he ascended the throne. Equally efficient proved his tactics in the international field where he adroitly played on the rivalry for colonial expansion, so that at the Madrid Conference* (1880) France was thwarted in her designs of gaining an exclusive footing in Morocco. His success survived him just two decades, but in Morocco he is still commemorated as one of the prominent rulers. He died suddenly while conducting a *harka* in the Middle Atlas, but his chamberlain *(hajīb)* Bā Ahmad Ibn Mūsā, keeping his death secret, had the defunct monarch propped up on a litter and carried back to Rabat. There he had the youngest son, the thirteen year old ʿAbd al-ʿAzīz (1894-1908), proclaimed sultan.

For seven years Bā Ahmad, the son of a negro slave girl of the royal harem, ruled as the boy-sultan's tutor with dictatorial firmness but competently and as a faithful servant of the dynasty. Upon his death ʿAbd al-ʿAzīz took the reins of government into his own hands but with far less success. His disregard for time-honoured usages and the meticulous court ceremonial; his naive admiration of European style and the most futile objects of European make which filled the palace; and the motley crowd of Europeans whom he drew into his close surroundings could not fail to give offence to the conservative, religious as well as secular, upper-class society. Military discipline deteriorated; the *bilād al-makhzan* shrank and the public revenues critically diminished. His attempts, well-intended but inadequatly implemented, at modernizing the administrative and fiscal system violated deepseated privileges, hurt the bureaucracy and heightened the general dissatisfaction until it all culminated in the revolt of Bū Hmāra* which spread very dangerously. Pressed by inextricable financial difficulties and sensing the menace to his throne, ʿAbd al-ʿAzīz accepted the onerous terms of the loans offered by the French banks and appealed for French military assistance. Thenceforth France was firmly implanted in Morocco. Although the terms of the Act of the Algeciras Conference* (1906) prevented an actual occupation, they accorded France a privileged position and in essential domains of government submitted the sultan to international control. In the atmosphere of wide-spread irritation at the foreign interference, ʿAbd al-ʿAzīz, held responsible for it, lost also the support of those who until then had remained loyal to him, until his own brother ʿAbd al-Hāfiz declared the Holy War gainst him and the French, and was proclaimed Sultan by the people of Marrakesh (June 1908). After some vain attempts at resistance ʿAbd al-ʿAzīz gave up all further struggle and withdrew to Tangier under the protection of the foreign legations.
Mūlāy Abd al-Hāfiz (1909-1912), the „Sultan of the Holy War", began his reign with the so-called Hāfizīya Proclamation in which he announced the abrogation of the privileges conceded by his brother; the dismissal of all foreign advisers; and the expulsion of the French troops. Yet after a while he submitted to the inevitable, acknowledged the Act of Algerciras and was recognized in due form by the signatory Powers. He made serious efforts to restore the authority of the state and the prestige of the dynasty and to save as much as was still possible of the country's independence. He suppressed the uprisings, put Bū Hmāra to a cruel end and had another revolutionary leader, the highly esteemed head of the Kattānīya brotherhood, ʿAbd al-Kabīr al-Kattānī* bastinadoed to death. Most of these operations were conducted with an iron hand by his Grand Vizier, Maydānī al-Glāwī, of the Glāwa* family, the undisputed lord of all the country around Marrakesh and the principal artisan of his rise to power, but also of his fall. Exacerbated at the brutal and unscrupulous manner in which the all-powerful minister exploited his function, the tribes over almost all the northern regions rose, enclosed the sultan in Fez and began to sack the city. ʿAbd al-Hāfiz owed his life to French troops (1911), and a year later signed the treaty of Fez which instituted the French Protectorate*. Soon afterwards he abdicated and was replaced by his brother Mūlāy Yūsuf, upon whose death, after a

reign entirely under the shadow of the French Governor-General, his young son Muhammad ascended the throne. Sultan - later King - Muhammad V Ibn Yūsuf* (1927-1953 and 1955-1961), to his people the incarnation of the victorious struggle for national liberation, left to his son King Hassan II a heritage of ways, wide-open though certainly not unimpeded into a new era of cultural and economic development.

ᶜAlawid Rulers:

Mūlāy ᶜAlī al-Sharīf	1631-1636	
Mūlāy Muhammad Ibn al-Sharīf	1636-1663	
Mūlāy al-Rashīd	1664-1672	
Abū al-Nasr Mūlāy Ismāᶜīl	1672-1727	
Ahmad al-Dhahabī Ibn Ismāᶜīl	1727-1728	
Mūlāy ᶜAbd Allāh Ibn Ismāᶜil	1728-1757	(with several interruptions)
Sīdī Muhammad Ibn ᶜAbd Allāh	1757-1790	
Mūlāy Yazīd	1790-1792	
Mūlāy Sulaymān Ibn Sīdī Muhammad	1792-1822	
Mūlāy ᶜAbd al-Rahmān Ibn Hishām	1822-1859	
Sīdī Muhammad Ibn ᶜAbd al-Rahmān	1859-1873	
Mūlāy al-Hasan Ibn Muhammad	1873-1894	
ᶜAbd al-ᶜAzīz	1894-1908	
MūlāyᶜAbd al-Hāfiz	1909-1912	
Mūlāy Yūsuf	1913-1927	
Muhammad V Ibn Yūsuf	1927-1961	
Hasan II	1961-	

ALGECIRAS CONFERENCE, an international attempt at solving the 'Moroccan question', which at the time of the reign of Sultan ᶜAbd al-ᶜAzīz (1894-1908) had reached a critical stage as a result of the German resistance to a further expansion of the French colonial empire in North Africa. The Conference, convened at the sultan's request, but inspired by Germany, was held from January 16th to April 7th 1906 at Algeciras (on the southern coast of Spain, in front of Gibraltar) by the governments of 14 states: Austria-Hungary, Belgium, Denmark, France, Germany, Great Britain, Italy, Morocco, the Netherlands, Portugal, Russia, Spain, Sweden and the United States of America. The final Act of the Conference, drawn up in 7 chapters and 123 articles, established three basic principles: the sovereignty and independence of His Majesty the Sultan; the integrity of Moroccan territory; and economic freedom without restriction. The most important points embodied in the Act concerned reforms of the Moroccan police with the assistance of Belgian, French and Spanish instructors, under the supervision of a Swiss officer; the suppression of the smuggling of arms; the creation of a state bank of issue with the participation of the signatories; the institution of an international organization for the award of contracts for public works; the reorganization of the customs administration under the control of a special international body; the introduction of certain taxes; the establishment of uniform import duties, excluding all preferential rates; and the specific confirmation of the privileges already held by the foreign

Powers, which conferred the jurisdiction over their citizens in Moroccan territory upon their own consular courts.
The Act of Algeciras passed over in silence and thus left unaffected the previous (1902 and 1904) agreements by which Italy and Great Britain had conceded to France, in return for certain compensations, full freedom of action in Morocco. Yet it made the consent of all signatory powers necessary before France could realize her plans of establishing the Protectorate* over Morocco. A few years later (1912) they gave this consent. The Act of Algeciras, in fact, did not save Morocco from losing her independence, but it preserved the country as a territorial unit within its boundaries until it regained its full sovereignty in 1955.

ALGERIA, officially the Democratic and Popular Republic of Algeria, *Al-Jumhurīya al-Jazā'rīya al-Dimuqrātīya wa-l Shaʿbīya*, (about 850.000 sq. miles and 10.300.000 inhabitants in 1964) was designated by the Arab geographers and historians of the Middle Ages *al-Maghrib al-Awsat* (the Middle West, i.e. the central portion of the Maghrib* or Arab West). Only much later was the country given its present name, derived from the name of Algiers *(al-Jazā'ir*, the islands), the principal city, itself so called because of a row of little rocky islands a short distance off the shore, which had provided a natural anchorage until they were incorporated into the construction of the port.
Measured in square miles, Algeria surpasses by far her two neighbours, Tunisia in the East, and Morocco in the West. However, nearly nine-tenth of her surface, south of the broad chains of the Atlas of the Sahara, belong to the Saharan desert - bare, stony plains and highlands *(hamada)* alternating with depressions below sea level, enormous stretches of pebbles and of sand dunes *(erg)*, which may reach a length of 10 to 15 miles and a height of 800 feet or more; here and there interspersed with oases occasionally quite extensive fed by subterranean water courses and artificial irrigation; and in the south-east the black granite massif of the Hoggar *(Atakōr N Ahaggar)* rising to nearly 10,000 feet and falling off northwards and southwards to high tablelands *(tassili*, the Berber equivalent of the Arabic *hamada)* intersected by deep canyons and somewhat broader valleys with comparatively good pastures. According to the census of 1960, some 580.000 people live in the Algerian Sahara. Some are camel-breeding nomads - Arabs on the slopes of the Atlas, and veil-wearing Tuareg Berbers around the Hoggar who have their main camp near Tamanghassat. Others are settled in the oases in villages *(ksour)* or semi-rural towns, cultivating wheat, vegetables and also tobacco in between their date groves. This mode of living prevails in the M'Zab, the seat of the Mozabite* community (50.000 inh.) or around Wargla (with the surrounding area approximately 30.000 inh.), near the once prosperous Sadrata, today in ruins, which after the collapse of the Rustumid* emirate had grown into an important centre of the Ibadite sect; or further south in the region of Touat, where the work of centuries has created 1300 miles of underground irrigation channels (appr. 40.000 inh.), whose southernmost outpost, the group of ksours of Reggan, in the last years before Algeria became independent was chosen as

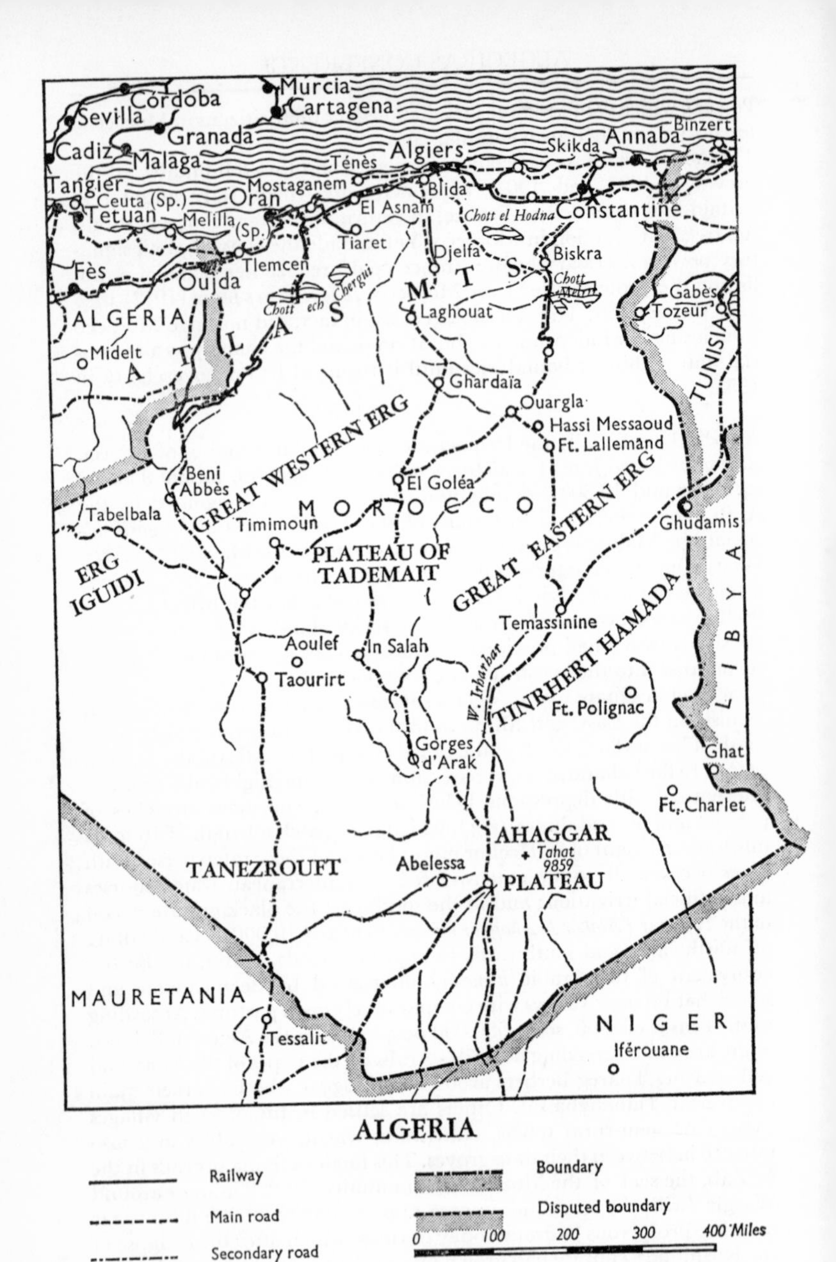
Murcia
Cartagena
Córdoba
Sevilla
Granada
Cadiz
Malaga
Tangier
Ceuta (Sp.)
Tetuan
Melilla (Sp.)
Oran
Mostaganem
Ténès
Algiers
Blida
El Asnam
Skikda
Annaba
Binzert
Constantine
Chott el Hodna
Tiaret
Tlemcen
Oujda
Fès
Djelfa
Biskra
Chott Melrir
Chott ech Chergui
Laghouat
Gabès
Tozeur
TUNISIA
ALGERIA
Midelt
ATLAS MTS
Ghardaïa
Ouargla
Hassi Messaoud
Ft. Lallemand
GREAT WESTERN ERG
Beni Abbès
El Goléa
Tabelbala
MOROCCO
Timimoun
PLATEAU OF TADEMAIT
GREAT EASTERN ERG
Ghudamis
ERG IGUIDI
Temassinine
TINRHERT HAMADA
Aoulef
In Salah
Taourirt
W. Irharhar
Ft. Polignac
LIBYA
Gorges d'Arak
Ghat
Ft. Charlet
AHAGGAR
Tahat 9859
PLATEAU
TANEZROUFT
Abelessa
MAURETANIA
Tessalit
NIGER
Iférouane
Railway
Main road
Secondary road
Boundary
Disputed boundary
0 100 200 300 400 Miles
ALGERIA

the 'Centre d'Essai d'Engins Spéciaux' or, in other words, a testing station for atomic bombs.

Hardly touched by the currents of history, the world of the 'Saharan sea', troubled only by the Bedouin raids against its islands of oases, remained unchanged for time immemorial until in the last century France began to build up a colonial empire in Africa. Then it rapidly assumed strategic importance. Military expeditions penetrated ever deeper into its vastness, garrisons were stationed in the oases; Bedouin warriors were recruited for a camel corps, the so-called 'Compagnies méharistes'; an administrative organization policed by the army was set up; research institutions were created such as the Observatory in Tamanghassat, the 'Laboratoire Saharien' in Beni Abbès or the 'Institut de Recherches Sahariennes' with its seat at Algiers. Five trans-saharan 'imperial tracks' from north to south and linked by west-east connections, totalling 16.000 miles, were laid down and served by regular motor-bus traffic and a chain of rest-houses, to which subsequently several air lines were added.

To strictly delimit Algerian, Tunisian and Moroccan territories in the uniform expanse of the desert was not a matter of particular concern as long as all three countries were under French control. In 1912, the so-called Varnier Line (named after the French official responsible for its demarcation), rather a roughly sketched belt, marked for purposes of the local administration, the Moroccan-Algerian frontier southwards from the pass of Teniet Sassi (east of the Moroccan town of Oujda), assigning Colomb-Béchar to Algeria and Figwig to Morocco. In 1928, Sultan Muhammad recognized the Varnier Line, but as affirmed on the Moroccan side, under the pressure of the French Protectorate* authorities. Subsequently, it was continued to the south-west by a similar but still vague 'Trinquet Line' through the parts of a broad border zone known as the 'Confins Algéro-Marocains', which finally was lengthened as far as the Spanish colony of the Rio de Oro. There it included - reaching into Algerian territory - the oasis settlement of Tindouf with the surrounding country, which in 1934 had been occupied by French troops stationed in Morocco, according to the French version in the name of France, but following the Moroccan interpretation in the name of the sultan. In an equally fluid manner the Algero-Tunisian and Algero-Libyan confines were traced out in the indistinguishable sameness of the desert. Then, however, came the discovery that there was rich mineral wealth never before suspected in, or comparatively near, those border regions drawn more or less haphazardly on maps far from precise. Thus what until then had been a question of minor significance became suddenly a major economic and political problem. Morocco found in her history the basis for a 'Greater Morocco', rejected the artificial frontiers and demanded the reincorporation of Mauretania and about one-third of the Algerian Sahara including the 'Confins' with the mining* districts of Colomb-Béchar, Tindouf and Zegdan. Tunisia laid claim to a stretch of the desert, corresponding in size to nearly one-fifth of her territory, which would open a passage into the oil* bearing region of Hassi Messaoud. Libya apparently waited for the occasion to call for the rectification of the frontiers in the oil-field area of Edjeléh, Zarzaitine and Tingentourine. These claims remained in abeyance so long as the outcome of the Algerian Revolution* was still undecided, although in 1961 they had been the subject of secret discussions with the Provisional Government* (G.P.R.A.) in Tunis. However, immediately after the war of liberation had been won, they were brought up, in particular by Morocco, with increasing insistence, but only to evoke the equally firm Algerian refusal to consider territorial concessions and the tension between the two countries sharpened. In October 1963 it came to armed clashes between the frontier police, military detachments and tribesmen, with killed and wounded on both sides.

About one half of the remaining tenth of Algeria's territory, the so-called High Plateau, extends between the ranges of the Atlas of the Sahara and the Atlas of the Tell; large, undulating, treeless steppes, which gradually decline from a height of 3800 feet in the West to the 1300 feet high Hodna mountains in the East. Tracts of bare earth alternate with expanses of brushwood, shrubs and low grass, the home of flocks of gazelles, mouflons and all sorts of birds - only the oistrich has been exterminated in hundreds of years of ruthless hunting - and the pasture grounds of the herds of goats, sheep, cattle, camels and horses, raised by the semi-nomadic Berber and Arab tribes. Esparto grass *(cellunaf* in the local parlance), the raw material of high quality paper, covers some ten million acres and adds a quarter of a million tons annually to Algeria's exports. This rather remunerative trade is controlled by a few French concerns, but the cutting, conditioning, packing and transport of the grass supplies a livelihood to quite a number of workers, and has also brought into existence some sizable settlements at the assembling stations such as Marhoum, south of Saida; Bouktoub still further south; Ain Oussara (formerly Paul-Cazelles) in the midst of the 'esparto sea'; or Hassa Bahbah south of Tiaret. Only one river, the Chélif, finds its way to the sea through the steppes, where heat, dryness and violent winds permit only on rare, privileged sites a modest agriculture yielding very irregular harvests. When rain falls, a thin sheet of flood water remains for a while on the soils without vegetation but short river beds continuously changing their course soon drain it off into wide-spread depressions. There it dissolves the salt contained in the earth and evaporates on the shallow shores leaving them covered with layer upon layer of pure salt and forming endless stretches of salt-marshes *(sebkha)*, while it fills the deeper parts *(shatt**, colloquially *shott)* with a quivering quagmire of earth, sand and sodium sulphate. The string of these basins begins with the Chott Gharbi (*gharbi*, the western *shatt*) near the Moroccan border at an altitude of about 3500 feet, spans the steppe from south-west to north-east, and with the Chott Melghir at ten feet below sea level joins the line of the Tunisian *shatts* which come to an end at the Gulf of Gabès. Its two Algerian centre-pieces are the Chott Chergui *(sharqi*, the eastern *shatt)*, approximately 100 miles long and 10 miles broad, and the Chott el Hodna with a surface of some 350 square miles. On the basis of studies of the hydrological conditions, it is assumed that subterranean drainage could recover for irrigation purposes a great deal of the water - for the Chott Chergui estimated at no less than one billion gallons - which at present is lost through evaporation.

Beyond the mountain seam of the steppes and reaching the sea with its coastline of some 600 miles, lies Algeria proper, forming a sort of distorted quadrangle at an average altitude of about 3000 feet. This is the so-called Tell, to the people of the steppe and the desert something like the Land of Promise, well watered, bearing rich crops and abounding in fresh, green pastures. In fact, the North African dialectical use of the Arabic word *tell* (regularly meaning a hill) for the dark, heavy and fertile soils may be a heritage from Roman times, supported by the assonance with the Latin *tellus* denoting the idea of the fruit bearing, life-giving earth. However, much of this wealth is more apparent than real. The yields of agriculture*, in particular as regards cereals, vary greatly from year to year according to whether the spring and automn rains come in time or are late. Besides, they fall in extremely violent showers washing off the top soil at a rate estimated to amount to over 4000 acres every year, and turning every river bed *(wādī,* colloquially *oued)*, waterless for the rest of the year, into a devastating torrent. The construction of barrages to control the flood waters was begun around 1920. Thirteen, capable of storing a total quantity of six million gallons, function at present. The largest three are one over the Oued Fodda near Orléansville (1,400.000 gallons); one over the Chélif west of Médéa (1,740.000 gallons); and one at Oghli Emda in the Kabylian mountains (900.000 gallons). They were planned to irrigate 450.000 acres, but in the meantime it was found impossible to protect the reservoirs from the danger of silting up, which would limit their life-time to fifty years. This meant that the land put under irrigation would have to produce so much better yields, and hence so much higher taxes, that the increase over this period would at least cover the cost of new barrages - improvements that reasonably could be expected only from the combination of high-quality soils, up-to-date mechanized techniques and rational management, or in other words, from large-scale agricultural enterprises. Thus the secondary network of feeder channels has been developed only on less than half of the irrigable surface, of which more than three-quarters were in French hands. The native peasants *(fellahīn)* on their tiny, dispersed holdings still draw water out of wells with buckets on a wheel driven by a camel or horse, or at the time of the flood build up primitive dams and dig equally primitive grooves to lead the water over their plots. From these they derive per acre about one-quarter of what the modern estates bring to the 'colons'.

As the string of chotts lies across the High Plateaux, so there lies embedded in the western section of the highland of the Tell a double ribbon of plains. One begins in the area of Oran, continues through the valley of the Chélif, and ends near Algiers in the wide tract of the Mitidja where it is closed up not far from the sea by the long hill range of the Sahil; the other runs from the Moroccan border north-west from Tlemcen as far as the oak and cedar forests of the mountain mass of the Ouarsenis (appr. 6400 feet). All this land is intensively cultivated: fields of wheat, barley, oats or maize alternating with vegetable gardens and orchards, and everywhere on the sunny slopes with nearly one million acres of vineyards which before the outbreak of the revolution produced over 11 million gallons of wine annually. There, too since the French occupation a number of larger and smaller towns have developed into seats of regional administration and centres of the agricultural export trade and of minor industrial activities. Many stand on, or near the site of a Punic, Roman or Byzantine settlement which was destroyed or fell into decay in the course of the turbulent events of the Arab conquest and of the wars between the great Berber tribes. They owe their resurrection to new prosperity to one of the Zīrid*, Almoravid*, Almohad* or ʿAbd al-Wādid* princes who wanted to be remembered as munificient builders and patrons of the arts and sciences. Later, a few came into Spanish hands, until all North Africa except Morocco was incorporated into the Ottoman Empire. To the Algerian towns except Algiers and to some extent Bône, the Turkish rule meant an era of economic stagnation and a shrinking number of inhabitants. Then, in the wake of the gradual consolidation of the French régime, more and more European settlers arrived until there were finally over a million, by far most of them in the towns. They built their own quarters, away from the old Moslem *madīna*, with broad, chess-board patterned avenues, with French street names, French shops, offices and schools, and evolved their own mode of life, while in the surroundings there grew up and expanded unchecked vast agglomerations of miserable huts and tin-can shacks populated by the crowds who were attracted from their poverty-stricken villages by the hope of earnings. This picture prevailed, apart from variations in size, throughout the period of the 'présence française', be it in the two largest cities and sea-ports, the capital Algiers (in 1960 estimated at 835.000 inhabitants, including the suburbs) and Oran (300.000), or the strongly fortified naval base of Mers al-Kebir, or in Tlemcen, (75.000), Blida (70.000), Mostaganem (60.000), Mascara (40.000), Médéa (26.000) or in one of the smaller places such as Cherchel (17.000), Miliana (16.000) or Ténès (11.000). These were the figures returned by the last census in 1954. Since then the dislocations brought about by the seven years of revolution and thereafter by the disappearance of nine-tenths, if not more of the French element, have altered most probably the number, but certainly the social, economic and cultural structure of this urban population. It is still too early for an appraisal of the degree and the effects of these modifications.

Further eastwards the landscape changes. Flanking the Gulf of Bougie in a wide semi-circle and cut by deep ravines rises to over 6000 feet the massif of the Kabyle* mountains. It is separated into the Greater and Lesser Kabylia by the deep depression of the Summam Valley*, in the seclusion of which the revolutionary leaders gathered in 1956 to take some of the most momentuous decisions in the history of their struggle. The Kabylia is the region of forests: cedars crowning the peaks, then giving way to pines; lower down, cork-oaks, ash-trees and carobs; then woods of fig- and olive-trees; and in between, on even the tiniest parcel of arable land, cereals and vegetables. It is one of the most densely populated and also one of the poorest parts of the Tell. From hill-top to hill-top and along the crests of the mountain ridges a chain of villages spans the narrow, entangled alleys of one-roomed and more often than not windowless houses divided by a matting into one compartment for the family and one for the animals. A dense network of roads, primarily conceived for the purpose of policing the headstrong clans, connects the villages with one another as well as with the sea and, at the mouth of the Summam valley and by the town of Sétif (55.000), with the great highway which begins at Oran, and skirts the Kabyle mountains until they fuse with the Atlas of the Tell.

There it reaches Constantine, the principal city (150.000) in eastern Algeria, in the middle of a high well-watered tableland with good agricultural soils in some parts, and in the less favoured ones with wide stretches of grazing grounds for the herds of the semi-nomadic tribes. Towards the sea, this highland gradually falls to a wide plain comparable, by its rich cornfields, vineyards and the variety of fruit-trees to the Mitidja, yet surpassing it by the expanse of the tobacco plantations held and cultivated in small plots by many hundreds of individual growers who associate, however, in co-operative organizations for the processing and marketing of the tobacco. The great commercial and shipping centre of this region and, in fact of the entire Algerian East, is Bône (115.000), the ancient Hippo Regius where St. Augustine, its bishop, was killed in 430 when it was conquered by the Vandals. Among the Algerian ports, Bône ranks third by the tonnage handled but first by the weight of freight, principally phosphate and iron-ores extracted in the mining districts in the area of Tebesa (26,000). Towards the South, the Constantine table-land ascends to the wildly romantic mountain mass of the Aurès, culminating in the Jabal Chélia and the Kef Mahmel (7400 feet), the highest summits in Algeria. It dominates the passage into the Sahara. Covered with forests of cedars, pines, oaks and on its northern foothills, of walnut- and fig-trees, it provides room for the date-palm in the canyon-like valleys which split its steep, southern walls of bare rock and allow free access to the hot winds of the desert. In these mountains, homeland of the rough Shawīya Berber, cousins of the Kabyles, the French occupational forces laid out a military camp to protect communication between the Tell and the Sahara, which developed into the town of Batna (22.000). The Roman emperors had done so before them as is witnessed by the imposing ruins of their two cities of Lambaesis (today the village of Lambèse) and of Thamugadi (nowadays Timgad), the 'Algerian Pompeii'. Their most advanced fortified outpost on the fringe of the desert has grown into the oasis town of Biskra (37.000) with the neighbouring village of Sidi Okba. There, surrounded by some 100.000 date-palms, lies buried the Arab conqueror ʿUqba Ibn Nāfiʿ in an ancient mosque from the minaret of which the eye embraces the endless sweeps of the Saharan sand-dunes.

A glance at a relief map will clearly show how a line traced from Algiers in a south-easterly direction would divide Algeria into two sharply contrasting halves: one, the wide stretch of open, easily accessible plains in the West; and the other, the seclusive, compact mountain mass of Kabylia, the Aurès and the Hodna. The dichotomy of the physical features revealed its history-making significance soon after the generals of the Umayyad caliphs (661-750) had brought war across North Africa and subdued the tenacious Berber resistance. This was inspired first by the Kāhina*, the half-historical, half-legendary 'prophetess'; then by the influential chieftain Kusaila*; and finally by the Khārijite

revolutionary Abū Qurra*. Their defeat paved the way for the religion - with all its doctrinal variations - and the language, the aesthetic concepts and intellectual aspirations of the Arabs, and lastingly brought the Berber people into the orbit of Arab civilization. Politically, however, the achievements of the conquerors survived only the life-span of a few generations.
Then there emerged a mosaic of independent emirates and tribal confederations within fluctuating boundaries, out of which grew the Almoravid* and Almohad* empires and which finally crystallized in Morocco and Tunisia. The existence of Algeria as a body politic which gradually evolved its own characteristics does not begin until the XVIth century with the administrative delimitation (1587) of the North African provinces by the Ottoman Government. In the intervening period, the country's two geographical halves each had a fate of their own, interwoven on the one side with Moroccan, and on the other with Tunisian history.

THE MUSLIM WEST IN THE MIDDLE AGES
TRADE ROUTES AND MAIN PRODUCTS

☆ Copper, Tin Lead, Iron
★ Gold, Silver
Rice
Dates, Olives, Fruits and Foodstuffs
Cotton
Wool
△ Hides
Land Trade Routes
Precious Woods
Horses
Fish
Shipbuilding
Textiles
Leatherwork
Leading Centres of Trade
Sea Trade Routes

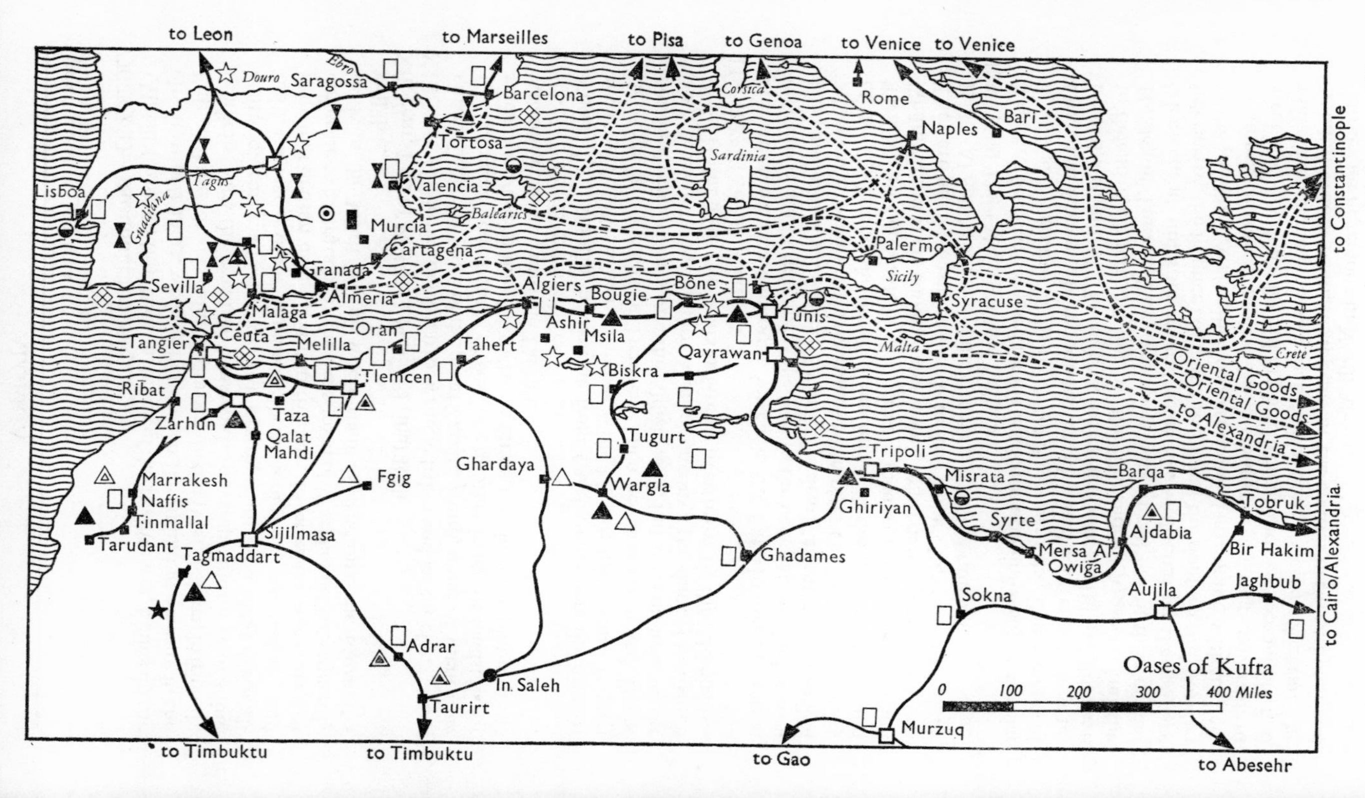
to Leon
to Marseilles
to Pisa
to Genoa
to Venice
to Venice
Douro
Ebro
Saragossa
Barcelona
Corsica
Rome
Bari
Naples
Tortosa
Sardinia
Lisboa
Tagus
Guadiana
Valencia
Balearics
Murcia
Cartagena
Granada
Sevilla
Almeria
Malaga
Algiers
Bougie
Bône
Tunis
Palermo
Sicily
Syracuse
to Constantinople
Ashir
Msila
Tangier
Ceuta
Oran
Melilla
Tahert
Qayrawan
Malta
Crete
Biskra
Tlemcen
Ribat
Taza
Zarhun
Qalat
Mahdi
Tugurt
Oriental Goods
Oriental Goods
to Alexandria
Tripoli
Marrakesh
Fgig
Ghardaya
Wargla
Misrata
Barqa
Naffis
Tinmallal
Tarudant
Sijilmasa
Tagmaddart
Ghiriyan
Syrte
Tobruk
Ajdabia
Ghadames
Mersa Al-Owiga
Bir Hakim
to Cairo/Alexandria
Aujila
Jaghbub
Sokna
Adrar
Oases of Kufra
In. Saleh
0
100
200
300
400 Miles
Taurirt
Murzuq
to Timbuktu
to Timbuktu
to Gao
to Abesehr

WESTERN ALGERIA

776-907 The Rustumid Emirate
ʿAbd al-Rahmān Ibn Rustum, imam of the Ibadite sect, builds up the city-state of Tāhart, wedged in between the Aghlabid emirate in the East, and the Idrīsid realm of Morocco in the West. Tāhart, in friendly relations with the Spanish Umayyads, develops into a flourishing centre of learning and trade. It is destroyed by Abū ʿAbd Allāh al-Shīʿī, the leader of the Kutāma tribesmen of the Lesser Kabylia and principal artisan of the Fātimid dynasty. Most of the survivors first emigrate to Sadrata near the oasis-town of Wargla and subsequently settle in the Wādī M'Zab where their descendants, the Mozabites still live.

Xth cent. End of Period of Berber Tribal Rule

XIth cent. Confederations of tribes, single tribes and larger clans under enterprising chieftains of the great Zanāta group, none of them able to organize a body politic, oppose one another in sterile feuds. Their raids extend deep into Morocco, as far as Fez, into the plains of the Atlantic coast and into the Tāfīlālt.

1082-1145 The Almoravid Era
Yūsuf Ibn Tāshufīn, advancing from Oujda, conquers the ancient town of Agadir, which together with his fortified camp Tagrart develops into the city of Tlemcen. Then he takes Oran and Ténès, continues victoriously into the Algiers area, but stops on nearing the Kabyle mountains. Western Algeria remains a province of the Almoravid realm until two years before its overthrow by the Almohads.

1145-1239 The Almohad Era
Notwithstanding a temporary set-back, ʿAbd al-Mu'min's conquest of Tlemcen and Oran opens the way to the occupation of all of western, and soon also of eastern Algeria. For nearly a century the whole of Algeria is incorporated in the Almohad empire. The Mitidja, the valley of the Chélif and the fertile plains and hillsides between Oran and Tlemcen are laid waste by the incessant incursions of the Berber Banū Ghāniya and their confederates from the predatory Bedouin tribes. They are finally mastered thanks to Abū Yahyā Yaghmurāsan of the Banū ʿAbd al-Wād, one of the strongest Zanāta branches.

1236-1550 The ʿAbd al-Wādid Sultans
Yaghmurāsan, as a reward for his services is appointed supreme chief of all Zanāta groups in the region of the present-day departments of Oran and Algiers. He repudiates the Almohad sovereignty, now no more than nominal. Throughout their reign, the ʿAbd al-Wādids have to defend their territory against the Marīnids of Morocco and the Hafsids of Tunisia. They are repeatedly forced out of their capital Tlemcen, at times for several years. Notwithstanding the military inferiority, the frequent dynastic feuds and the domineering position of the stubborn Arab tribal lords, they build up, mainly with the help of immigrants from al-Andalus, a comparatively solid government structure, develop a flourishing intellectual and commercial life, and make Tlemcen a focus of urban civilization in western Algeria. The ʿAbd al-Wādid realm disappears in the contest between Spain and Turkey for hegemony in North Africa.

EASTERN ALGERIA

800-909 The Aghlabid Emirate

Ibrāhīm Ibn al-Aghlab, governor under the ʿAbbāsid Caliph Hārūn al-Rashīd of a province covering what is today Tunisia and eastern Algeria, rules in almost complete independence. So do his descendants until they succomb to the onslaught of the Berber Kutāma tribes breaking forth from the Lesser Kabylia under the fervent Fātimid apostle Abū ʿAbd Allāh al-Shīʿī.

900-973 The Fātimid Era

While in the spiritual sphere the Fātimid doctrine prevails until 1045, the dynasty's secular sovereignty becomes merely nominal from 973 onwards. The Khārijite 'prophet' Abū Yazīd and his coalition of warlike Zanāta tribes pushing from the Aurès and the Hodna mountains into Tunisia, conquer al-Qayrawān, besiege the Fātimid residence at al-Mahdīya on the Tunisian coast and start negotiating an alliance with the Spanish Umayyads, the keen antagonists of the Fātimids in North Africa. The faithful Fātimid vassal Zīrī Ibn Manād, chieftain of a strong Sanhāja clan, subdues the revolt and is appointed governor over Tunisia and western Algeria north of the desert. He sets up the stronghold of Ashīr south-east of Algiers and establishes his residence there but falls in battle against other Zanāta allies of the Umayyads.

973-1017 The Zīrid Emirs

Zīrī's son Buluggīn succeeds his father as governor and is raised to vice-regal rank when the Fātimids move their seat to Cairo. Continuing hostilities against the Zanāta, he temporarily occupies Tlemcen, Fez and Sijilmāsa and advances as far as the Atlantic coast. The Zīrids transfer their seat from Ashīr into Tunisia and entrust Hammād Ibn Buluggīn, the head of a side-line with the governorship of the region of Ashīr.

1017-1152 The Hammādid Emirs

Hammād Ibn Buluggīn builds a new, strongly fortified residence, al-Qalʿat, in the Hodna mountains and declares himself independent. After some vain attempts to bring him to submission, his Zīrid cousins agree to the partition of their realm. The Hammādids, favoured by the decline of the Zīrid power under the onslaught of the Hilālian Bedouins, expand their domain over the Tunisian coast as far as Tripoli; penetrate into the oases of the Sahara; halt the Almoravid advance; and make Bougie their second capital. The increasing pressure of the Banū Hilāl forces them back to a narrow strip on the coast until the remainder of their troops are annihilated by the Almohad armies.

1152-1236 The Almohad Era

In a short campaign the Almohad armies under ʿAbd al-Mu'min occupy Algiers; inflict a decisive defeat upon the Hammādid troops at the gates of Bougie; conquer al-Qalʿat and in a three-day battle at Sétif break the resistance of the Arab tribes. Some thirty years later the Banū Ghāniya, lords of the Balearic isles, with a corps of Almoravid refugees, try to overthrow their Almohad enemies. They land

EASTERN ALGERIA, continued

at Bougie; take Algiers and Miliana; then, in alliance with a number of Arab chieftains, al-Qalʿat and Constantine. Beaten back, they withdraw into Tunisia but for nearly five decades they extend their devastating raids deep into Algeria.

1236-1575 The Hafsid Era

The Almohad governor of Tunisia, Abū Zakariyyā', a descendant of Abū Hafs ʿUmar, the pioneer of the Almohad movement, declares himself independent. His territory includes the present-day department of Constantine which thenceforth remains a Hafsid possession, either as a province administered by a Hafsid prince or divided into short-lived miniature emirates under dissident members of the dynasty. Bône, Collo and Bougie enjoy considerable prosperity owing to a lively over-seas trade and equally profitable piracy. The rise of autonomous city republics and tribal domains escaping government control heralds the disintegration of the Hafsid realm, which is consummated in the struggle for expansion in North Africa, in which Spain and the Ottoman Empire are opposed.

By contrast with the advance over-land of the horse- and camel-mounted armies of the Arabs, the Turkish occupation began by sea as a private undertaking of two daring Turkish corsairs of Albanian origin, the brothers ʿArūj and Khair al-Dīn Barbarossa. What they wanted was to secure for their operations bases on the Algerian and Tunisian coasts, most of which, however, Spain had wrested between 1505 and 1510 from the ʿAbd al-Wādids and Hafsids. With the help of the local population, the Barbarossas soon had stores of their war supplies in nearly everyone of the small Algerian fishing ports. In 1516 ʿArūj could make himself master of Algiers - although not yet of the Spanish island-fortress of the Peñon some 350 yards off the shore - and, penetrating into the hinterland, took the Mitidja, Miliana and Médéa. He fell in an encounter with the Spaniards at Tlemcen, but in the meantime the Ottoman Sultan Selim had seen in the two brothers' success prospects for Turkey of territorial expansion. He bestowed upon Khair al-Dīn the title of Pasha, sent janizary troops, equipment and money, and what had started as a privateering adventure became a protracted Turko-Spanish colonial war and ended with the victory of the Turks.

By the close of the century Algeria, except for Oran and Mers el Kebir which continued as a Spanish enclave until 1791, was in Turkish hands southwards as far as Biskra, Touggourt and Wargla, with its eastern and western frontiers approximately as they are today. At no time, however, was this far-away province or 'regency', as it was officially called, much more than in name a part of the Ottoman Empire. Nor did after a while the sultan's sovereignty go far beyond the confirmation in the office of regents of those who more often than not by the assassination of their predecessor had seized control of public affairs: until 1587 a *beylerbey (bey* of the beys)* whose jurisdiction extended over Algeria, Tunisia and Tripolitania; then, after the separation of these three areas, until 1659 a *wālī* (governor) bearing the title of pasha with a three-year term of office; thereafter, until 1671 the *aghas* (commanders) of the corps of the janizaries *(ojak)* every two months in rotation; and finally, until 1830, deys* elected for life by the *aghas*. Yet the authority of those regents, whatever their title, was more apparent than real. Corsairs and the janizary soldiery, who together had founded and consolidated the Turkish rule, remained the two pillars on which it rested; the former, by the resources derived from privateering - especially from the ransom of the captives of whom at times 30.000 were kept in Algiers - and by protecting the legitimate trade by sea from the equally ruthless European pirates; the latter by policing the unruly tribes, enforcing the payment of taxes, and fighting the wars with the Beys of Tunis and the Moroccan Sultans. Solidly organized in a 'Corporation of the Corsair Captains' and a 'Council *(dīwān)* of the Aghas', and bound to one another by their closely connected interests, they together held the levers of power in the State. Leadership ambitions and all sorts of rivalries often opposed one of these ruling classes to the other or split each one into enemy factions, but never let them lose sight of their mutual dependence when it came to defending their privileges.

For quite a time there seemed to be nothing which could shake the stability of this peculiar type of oligarchic republic controlled by a Turkish military caste from the central government at Algiers down to the smallest provincial township. The countryside was left to itself so long as the taxes were paid and the general order was not too seriously disturbed. Uprisings of the peasantry, when the fiscal burden was too heavy to bear, were suppressed with utmost cruelty, and the world of the tribes was kept in check by exploiting the jealousies of its petty chieftains and their trivial feuds to prevent concerted mass revolts. Most of the maritime European Powers found it to their advantage to buy the safety of their shipping by substantial payments in gold instead of continued armed interventions which had always proved fruitless. They thenceforth maintained a lively trade with the corsair captains who had become shrewd merchants and sold them wheat, raisins, dates, figs, tobacco and leather in exchange for the products of their industries. Until the end of the XVIIIth century, Algiers, the principal seat of this profitable commerce, as before of privateering, was according to the descriptions of contemporary travellers a thriving city with a wealthy Turkish bourgeoisie; a proletariat of some 100.000 Arabs, Berbers, Negroes, Jews; and a changing number of Christian slaves cared for as well as possible by religious orders. Then, however, the inability to understand, or reluctance to adopt, the modern economic, technical and political tendencies quickly undermined the structure of this medieval State and in a few decades sealed its collapse.

On the 25th of May 1830, a French expeditionary corps sailed from Toulon and on the 19th of June, at Ataoueli near Algiers defeated the troops of the Dey. He capitulated on the 5th of July, was permitted to leave the country, but had to abandon to the victors his Treasury with over 15.000 pounds of gold and 200.000 pounds of silver, while the French commander-in-chief reported to Paris that the 'whole kingdom of Algeria' would be occupied within two weeks without another French shot fired. He was mistaken. The Turkish rule was over, but the brotherhoods* and marabouts* called to the Holy War against the Christian invaders, and the tribesmen took up arms. In the area of Constantine and in the Aurès they rallied under Ahmad Bey, the former commander of the region, who resisted for eighteen years before he surrendered. In the Rif and the Mitidja, Abdelkader* who for a time had two-thirds of Algeria under his control and was only in 1847 forced to submission. In the Greater Kabylia, the rising, inspired by a woman, Lalla Fātima, had its centre at Icheriden, and several years of exhausting mountain warfare were necessary before it was crushed. However, it broke out again in 1871, spread southwards as far as Touggourt and Wargla and kept 80.000 soldiers at bay for nearly a whole year. All in all the 'total occupation' required almost four decades of hard fighting, with hundreds of villages burnt and harvests destroyed, olive-and palm trees cut down and oases laid waste, with many thousands of Algerians sentenced to death, and captured French soldiers mutilated and assassinated.

However, when deciding on the Algerian expedition the government of King Charles X had as little thought of territorial expansion as had the Ottoman Sultan three centuries earlier. Intended was merely a quick and spectacular success expected to bolster up the unpopular régime. The pretext advanced was the Dey's insulting attitude in claiming reimbursement of the money France owed since the days of the French revolution and the Napoleonic wars for the purchase of large quantities of Algerian wheat. The success of the expedition did not save Charles X from being dethroned, and for a while the ministers of his successor Louis-Philippe were at a loss as to what to do with the strip of African coast. Finally Parliament consented to the continuation of the venture. For several years it vacillated, primarily because of the financial implications, between a 'limited occupation' with the idea that it might open to France a new sphere of influence, and 'total conquest' and 'complete domination'. These doubts were reflected in the succession, between 1830 and 1848, of thirteen generals placed in charge of the supreme command in the theatre of operations officially designated as the French possessions in North Africa. In March 1848 the Provisional Government of the Second Republic brought the argument to an end by declaring Algeria an integral part of France to be defended like any other portion of French soil. Thus was born the myth of an 'Algérie Française' which was soon to assume in French public opinion the force of a patriotic axiom and died only with the end of the chaos and terror of the Algerian Revolution.

The 'Présence Française' began in 1832 with a small group of poor emigrants on the way to America who, victims of swindle, were put ashore near Algiers, cared for by the army and given a modest piece of ground. Ten years later, Trappist monks established a seat at Staouéli, bought some land and developed it into a prosperous farm of 2500 acres. Retired Foreign Légionaires and also some enterprising young French peasants mainly from the south and from Corsica - sons of families too numerous for their small holdings - followed their example once Abdelkader ('Abd al-Qādir Ibn Muhyī al-Dīn*) was forced out of the Mitidja and the confiscated properties of his supporters became available for distribution. In 1841 the number of settlers was estimated at 37.000. As pacification proceeded and the administrative apparatus gradually functioned in widening sections of the country, colonization was officially encouraged by the granting of land concessions and tax reductions, so that more and more people of every walk of life, not only Frenchmen but also Spaniards, Italians, Greek, Maltese or Cypriots, sought a new home across the Mediterranean. When it appeared, however, that among these *colons* - nicknamed 'pieds noirs', black feet, because of the many who arrived destitute and barefoot - the foreigners outnumbered the French immigrants, French citizenship was automatically accorded to all Europeans in Algeria as well as to the native Algerian Jews.

Thus the French-Algerian population steadily grew by continued immigration and natural increase: from 55.400 in 1841 to 152.300 in 1851; to 235.000 in 1872; to 633.850 in 1901; to 791.400 in 1921; and to somewhat over a million in 1960, the year of the last census. Simultaneously it lost its original, preponderantly agricultural character. There were still the 20.000 or so pioneer families given to farming, vegetable gardening, fruit- and wine-growing. The majority, however, flowed into the towns and monopolized the multiple functions of the country's increasingly complex economic and administrative machinery - public officials of all ranks, teachers, technicians, physicians, merchants of every type and grade, artisans, specialized workers or commercial employees. Far less than half, perhaps not even a quarter, were actually of French descent, but in a generation or two inter-marriage, the school, military service, the Church, business, and later the press, the cinema and radio effaced the differences of origin, made French the common language, although with certain dialectal peculiarities ('patahouet'), and impressed the French stamp on everyday life. However, the emotional, mental and also physical traits of the various ethnic components of this human mixture; the influence of climate and environment; and the specific political and cultural interests springing from their position in the midst of the native population nine times as numerous - all combined to generate a set of attitudes, loyalties and standards of behaviour, which distinctly marked off the average neo-Frenchman from his fellow-countryman in metropolitan France.

It must remain undecided whether or not it would have been possible to level the barriers of race, religion and mode of living which separated the two communities enrooted on Algerian soil, commonly but improperly referred to as European and Arab, and overcome the superiority complex of the one and the feeling of frustration of the other. The 130 years of French rule are rich in administrative, legislative or institutional reform schemes which show how in the minds of many within the policy-making circles in Paris the principle of unrestrained colonial exploitation originally commanding the whole system of governing slowly gave way to concepts of a 'constructive association'. Some were debated by Parliament, and a few became law but were either not at all applied or much watered down and retarded or after a while revoked, when endangering the interests in agriculture*, industry*or mining* of financial power groups in France and Algeria. Considered individually they appear devoid of any but episodic significance but as a whole they assume a very emphatic meaning in the fabric of disillusion, embitterment and hatred which makes up the background of the Algerian Revolution. Resented just as bitterly, if not more as time went on, was the kind of intellectual colonialism which determined the development of public education. By 1868, twenty years after Algeria had been solemnly declared an integral part of France 'one and indivisible', there were in the country apart from the primitive and antiquated Koranic schools, all in all 35 so-called Franco-Arabic primary schools for a Moslem population of nearly three million. Eighty years later these government schools attended by one group of pupils in the morning and by a second group in the afternoon, had just enough class-rooms and teachers for one-tenth of the Moslem children from 6 to 14 years, and by 1957 for one-eight. These are average figures; in the countryside they were as low as one twentieth and in many regions still lower. In the same year the 48 lycées and colleges, established in the meantime, had 32.000 pupils, of whom 6500 were Moslems, while among the 5500 students enrolled in the four faculties of the University of Algiers the Moslems numbered some 500. About a thousand students whose families could afford it, studied at universities in France and quite a number in Cairo. The language of instruction in the schools of all levels was French, with Arabic as optional taught in a few primary schools in the larger towns for two hours a week. Although in conformity with the Algerian Statute of 1947 which re-affirmed the equality of the Moslem population 'in all respects', Arabic was to be accorded in every school the position of a native tongue, this provision, like others of the same law, was never put into practice except in the three 'Lycées Franco-Musulmans' of Algiers, Tlemcen and Constantine with in all 450 pupils; there were furthermore in 1957 some 6500 Moslem boys in various technical schools. In the middle of the second quarter of this century a beginning was made, springing from reformist currents among certain groups of theologians, with the modernization of some of the old Koranic schools, particularly upon the initiative of the Association of the Algerian ʿUlamā'* which by 1955 maintained about 200 primary and intermediary Arabic schools, arranged courses for the training of teachers and supported the Pedagogic Institute Ben Bādīs in Constantine.

Whatever might have been the aims of this French educational policy, judged by its results it was most unfortunate both for France and the Algerian people. It implanted the use of French as a sort of lingua franca but left three-quarters of all Moslems illiterate in Arabic, and nine-tenths illiterate in French, unfit for any work of a somewhat higher type and without prospects of a change. From their midst came the 300.000 to 400.000 day-labourers and unskilled Algerian workmen in the industrial centres of France and Belgium whose savings supported their families at home, and the 60.000 or so military auxiliaries *(harkīs*, derived from *harka*)* of the French troops in Algeria for whom this mercenary service was the sole means of subsistence. But to the overwhelming majority the call to revolution meant the promise of a better future, and from among them the Army of Liberation* recruited its rank and file but also some of its most unconciliatory leaders.

Gradually, however, the youth grown up in the French school atmosphere emerged in the pattern of the native bourgeoisie. Its bottom layer constituted a white-collar, lower-middle class of high school graduates proud of knowing how to speak, read and write French and indoctrinated with French official propaganda. They supplied the departments of the central government with minor clerks; and the administrative, fiscal and police officers in the countryside and those attached to the tribes with interpreters, tax collectors and intermediaries, anxious to keep a comparatively well-paid job and to prove their zeal by carrying the catchwords of the régime to the uneducated masses. Then, step by step up the social and educational ladder, there came the members of the township and cantonal councils of the Financial Delegation - later transformed into the Algerian Assembly - and the 22 deputies whom it sent into the two Chambers of the French Parliament. They all were either nominated by the Prefects of the Departments or issued from admittedly 'pre-fabricated' elections which returned mainly 'Beni-Oui-Oui'. Still higher up stood the sons of the wealthy land-owning and merchant families, enjoying the particular favours of the authorities, distinguished by the Légion d'Honneur or other awards, holding seats in the Agricultural Committees and Chambers of Commerce, and given the benefit of all sorts of profitable transactions. Finally, there began to evolve towards the end of the First World War a thin intellectual upper stratum, the 'Evolués'* as they were called, cast in the French academic moulds. With rare exceptions they came home inspired with the aim to reconcile French cultural values with those rooted in Arabo-Islamic tradition, and convinced that they could find for their people within the social and political fabric of France the directives for modern progress. This conviction they defended by word of mouth and in their writings in the face of the growing movement for national autonomy, which soon became an ever more strongly voiced demand for complete independence. At last, however, most of all those belonging in whatever capacity to these various groups espoused sooner or later, openly or under cover, the nationalist cause, helped spread and tighten the revolutionary underground network, or whole-heartedly joined the Front of National Liberation*. The others sought refuge in France while there was still time or else fell victims to the vengeance released by the revolt.

Soon there arose voices in the midst of these and other groups, which more and more loudly insisted that this development, lest it deprive Algeria of all national individuality, must be primarily the responsibility of the Algerians themselves. Some of them, not rejecting French sovereignty, demanded a more or less far-reaching autonomy, others, more radical, full independence. These currents crystallized in a number of political parties reflecting most of the ideological, educational, and economic facets of Algeria's Moslem society. They ranged from the progressive yet rigorously Islamic Association of the Algerian Popular Union* (U.P.A., 1938) and its offsprings, the Friends of the Manifesto and of Liberty* (A.M.L., 1944) and the Democratic Union of the Algerian Manifesto* (U.D.M.A., 1946), all inspired by Farhat Abbas, to reach their left wing in Messali al-Hajj's labour-class North African Star* (1935) from which sprang the Algerian People's Party* (P.P.A.,

1937), the Movement for the Triumph of the Democratic Liberties* (M.T.L.D., 1946), and finally the Algerian National Movement* (M.N.A., 1955). In spite of all sorts of repressive measures, including imprisonment and deportation, and notwithstanding internal dissensions and conflicts among the leaders - temporarily bridged in the Common Front for the Defence of, and the Respect for Liberty* (1951) and the North African Unity and Action Front* (1952) - the movement expanded, its forms of expression grew sharper, and on November 1, 1954, the Front of National Liberation (F.L.N.) gave the signal for the outbreak of armed insurrection. It absorbed the political parties- except the closest followers of Messali al-Hajj - and gradually was joined by the majority of those who for some time had not dared, or had hesitated to espouse the national cause. There were, it is true, also others who, guided mainly by personal interests, stayed neutral or remained undisguisedly on the French side. The mass of the tribesmen, urban workers, small peasants and landless agricultural labourers, however, regardless of all hardship, carried on the merciless guerilla warfare throughout eighty-nine months. On March 18,1962, the Agreement of Evian terminated the Algerian Revolution, but for some time afterwards the French counter-revolutionary O.A.S. (Organisation de l'Armée Secrète) desperately tried to reverse the outcome by terror, the indiscriminate murder of Moslems, and blind devastation. The agreement was confirmed by a referendum of the French and Algerian people, and on July 3, 1962, Algeria was solemnly proclaimed independent. In the same year the first Algerian National Assembly designated Ahmad Ben Bella Prime Minister of the first Algerian Government, and in September 1963 he was elected President of the Republic by universal suffrage.
The great task ahead of the young state was to prepare the transition from the turbulence and lawlessness of the revolution to a new peacetime order in accordance with the ideals that had inspired the struggle. Everything had to be shaped, built up and installed anew. The French administrative, financial and economic apparatus was thenceforth obsolete. The French officials, from the department heads to the typists, had left for France; records had been destroyed or had disappeared. The mass departure of Europeans crippled industrial production, trade and communications, critically increased unenploymemt, reduced the tax revenues, deprived the schools of their teachers, and hospitals of their doctors and nurses. Peasants, workers and the indefinable many who in one way or the other had taken part in the fighting or at least borne their share of the suffering claimed the fruit of 'their' victory. They occupied the abandoned French flats and shops in the towns, and seized factories and farms. Passionate conflicts, ideological or merely personal, on the leadership level nourished deep-rooted regional and local antagonisms, heating the climate of anarchy to a point dangerously near civil war. The sole factor of stability was that well-disciplined sector of the Army of Liberation, to which the armistice had opened the way into Algeria from its training camps in the Tunisian and Moroccan border areas, and Ahmad Ben Bella knew how to win over their commander, Colonel Hūarī Būmedienne to his socio-economic programme. Silencing without

bloodshed nearly all opposition, he remodelled the Front of National Liberation and turned it into the constitutional instrument of the 'specific socialism' which holds now rule in the country's vital domain of agriculture and marks the development of its industry. Lack of experienced personnel and financial limitations, imposing more often than not proceedings by trial and error, do not always allow the results to come up to expectations, without shaking, however, the confidence in final success. Quite a number of young Algerian physicians, engineers or agriculturists, having studied abroad in the years of the revolution, began to come home. Within the scheme of technical assistance provided for by the Evian Agreement some 7000 French advisers of various grades have been engaged in the service of the Algerian government in the fields of public works, agriculture, public administration and industrial production, besides those, less numerous, supplied by other countries. Some 9000 French and Egyptian teachers and a great many enthusiastic young men and women from all over Algeria hastily trained by correspondence courses, made it possible to send one million children to school in the first year of independence. The Saharan oil* and natural gas furnishes industry with a practically unlimited flow of cheap energy, and, last but not least, the state treasury with an appreciable source of revenue. As far as relations with France are concerned, such as they were determined at Evian, there remain a number of points which in Algerian opinion are contrary to important national interests. However, as Ben Bella phrased it, 'the Agreement of Evian is not the Koran', and amiable though most tenacious bargaining by both parties seems to lead step by step to satisfactory results.

ALGERIAN NATIONAL MOVEMENT, generally known by its French designation as Mouvement National Algérien (M.N.A.), a political party founded in April 1955 by Messali al-Hajj (Masālī al-Haʿj) after the split in his Movement for the Triumph of Democratic Liberties* (M.T.L.D.), resulting in the secession of the so-called Centralists, the adherents of the more radical doctrine which the party's Central Committee stood for. While the majority of Messali's opponents joined the revolutionary National Liberation Front* (F.L.N.) in whose ranks many were subsequently to play prominent rôles, his prestige, particularly as the champion of the social and economic emancipation of the Algerian proletariat, was sufficiently strong to rally quite an important following both in Algeria and among the numerous communities of Algerian labourers in France and in Belgian and German mining districts. From his enforced residence in France at Angoulème he set up a solid party structure, published a monthly paper, 'La Voix du Peuple', and called into life a labour federation movement which crystallized in the Union Syndicale des Travailleurs Algériens (U.S.T.A.).
The political programme of the M.N.A. included as principal points the recognition of an Algerian nation; the free election of a Constituent Assembly by all Algerians; the release of Algerians interned by police decisions; and, as the ultimate goal, the establishment by mutual consent of Franco-Algerian relationships based on friendship and French assistance to the new Algerian State. Upon the whole, its position did not

differ very noticeably from that of the F.L.N. except for its more conciliatory attitude, so that Messali was often thought of as a possible mediator by some political circles in Paris.
Several attempts made by Messali to bring about an understanding with the leaders of the insurrection such that there should be a shared conduct of operations evoked, it seems, highly insulting answers. These were responsible in a large measure for the exacerbation of the conflict between the two groups, that marked the entire period of the Algerian war and has continued into the era of independence. The bands of M.N.A. supporters in Algeria, which under the command of Muhammad Bellunis waged their guerilla warfare against the French, were soon involved in an ever more implacable fight with the F.L.N. partisans, so that the losses suffered by both of them through French repressive actions were probably not heavier than those they inflicted upon each other in their internecine feuds in Kabylia, in the southern parts of the departments of Algiers and Constantine, in the Hodna mountains, around Biskra and down south in the border areas of the Sahara. Yet when Bellunis learned of the massacre by F.L.N. partisans of some 300 inhabitants of the village of Melouza near the town of Aumale (Sūr Ghazlān) who were suspected of having supported the M.N.A. forces, he went over to the French side in November 1957 with some 2000 of his men, continuing, however, to stand firmly for Algerian independence. He deserted a few months later and with a number of his troops was killed in combat.
Unable to benefit from the supply of funds and arms sent from Egypt, Syria, Irak and Saudi Arabia in aid of the revolution but channelled all to the F.L.N. through its agents abroad, the M.N.A. quickly lost significance as a military factor, but for some time retained its weight in Algerian public opinion. Still stronger remained its influence among the Algerian emigrants in Europe, but there too it gradually lost ground to the F.L.N.'s „Federation in France", not without frequent and violent clashes with the latter's adherents in the Algerian slums on the outskirts of the French industrial centres. After his release in December 1959 from Angoulème, Messali moved his headquarters to Chantilly and several times tried to win over the F.L.N. for plans of common 'pourparlers' with France, but his suggestions were either ignored or harshly rebuffed. In 1961, when officially entering into negotiations with France about a cease-fire and the recognition of Algerian independence, the F.L.N. made it a condition that Messali was in no way to be associated with the discussions.
Hoping to gain a place in the political life of the new Algerian republic he changed in 1962 the name of the M.N.A. to that of its predecessor in the first days of the nationalist struggle, the Algerian People's Party* (P.P.A.) but again found his way barred by the inflexible enmity of his old-time antagonists, now ministers in the Provisional Government of the Algerian Republic*.

ALGERIAN PEOPLE'S PARTY, generally known by its French designation as Parti Populaire Algérien (P.P.A.), founded in March 1937 by Messali al-Hajj, in Paris in succession to his North African

Star*, yet in contrast to it concentrating on the uncompromising struggle for an independent Algerian state, firmly Islamic in essence and guided by a working-class - though not communist - ideology. Set up on the basis of the membership it had inherited from its predecessor, together with its paper *al-Umma* (The Nation), the new party, supported by a solid structure of local cells, followed closely the congenial patterns of the Tunisian Destour* party and the Bloc of Moroccan Action* *(Kutla al-ʿAmal al-Maghribī)* with the addition of an autonomous section in France, particularly strong in Paris and Lyons. In June, Messali returned to Algiers, and, as was formerly always the result, by his oratorical verve rallied several thousand militant followers under the call of independence. On the 14th of July, the French national holiday, the green and white Algerian flag was publicly carried through the streets of Algiers. One month later Messali was sentenced to two-years' imprisonment for inciting to acts against the sovereignty of the State. But while in prison, he carried with an overwhelming majority a seat in the cantonal election. The result of the election was annulled, but the party continued its activities and published a second journal, 'Le Parlement Algérien', which remained in circulation until the outbreak of the Second World War. Messali, just released from prison, was interned and in March 1941 sentenced for sedition to 16 years' hard labour and a heavy fine. The party was dissolved and most of its prominent members were imprisoned or exiled. Pardoned in 1943, he was banished to Reibell, a village some 140 miles south of Algiers, and in the course of the suppression of the uprising in 1945 to Brazzaville in French Equatorial Africa. Yet the party lived on secretly, its vitality undiminished, and published a clandestine paper, 'L'Action Algérienne'; and at the first-of-May parade in 1945 had its members again display the green and white Algerian colours.
In 1946 Messali was released and assigned a residence under police supervision at Bouzaréa (at a distance of about 6 miles from Algiers). Enthusiastically acclaimed by his partisans as the Great Leader *(al-zaʿīm)*, he immediately began campaigning for the coming elections to the French National Assembly, launched a new journal, *Al-Saut al-Ahrār* (the Voice of the Free) which replaced 'L'Action Algérienne'; and constituted a new political party which under the somewhat clumsy but harmless-sounding name of 'Movement for the Triumph of the Democratic Liberties'* (M.T.L.D.), was intended as a cover for the still outlawed but still strongly organized People's Party. At the same time there was formed an underground framework of revolutionary combat groups, the so-called 'O.S.' (Organisation Secrète)*. The Algerian People's Party, screened behind the M.T.L.D., remained most active. It infiltrated youth organizations, students circles', scout groups, religious associations and even women's clubs. It operated also an efficient propaganda apparatus, closely following the instructions it received from the Central Committee of the M.T.L.D. Finally, in April 1953 it was absorbed by the M.T.L.D. In June 1962 Messali attempted to revive it and have it officially registered in preparation for the plebiscite held on the establishment of the Algerian Republic, but in this he was unsuccessful.

ALGERIAN POPULAR UNION, Union populaire algérienne (U.P.A.), a political organization stimulated by Farhat Abbas, one of the outstanding figures of the Algerian Revolution*, and set up in Algiers in 1938 by a group from among the progressive Moslem intelligentsia, the 'Evolués'*, as they liked to call themselves. Their purpose was to rally the broad masses around a programme aiming at close Franco-Algerian cultural and political co-operation with equal citizen rights for the members of both nations, yet with due recognition of the peculiarities of Algeria as to religion, language, traditions and customs. Farhat Abbas was born of a middle-class family in the department of Constantine, the son of an official in the Algerian civil service. Educated in French schools, he served in the French army in the First World War and after his return graduated in pharmacy at Algiers university, where he became president of the Algerian Moslem Students' Association. Then he married the daughter of a French settler, opened a dispensary in Sétif and was elected to the municipal council of the town, to the Financial Delegation and the Superior Council - one of the respectively 21 and 9 Moslems accorded a seat in these two consultative bodies of the administration. His attitude, forcefully asserted in a number of articles and studies (Le Jeune Algérien, Algiers 1931) and fully shared by his friends, was that of formal negation of the existence of an Algerian nation and, hence of the logic of an Algerian nationalism. It was coupled, however, with an equally strong opposition to the colonialist concepts widely prevailing in France and among the European settlers in Algeria, that implied the refusal to accept the Algerian Moslems as morally, politically and economically equal. Inevitably the U.P.A. encountered the antagonism not only of such nationalist protagonists as the Association of the Algerian ʿUlamā'* and Messali al-Ḥajj's North African Star*, but also of the more aggressive elements among the Evolués. Notwithstanding internal resistance and the disappointing rigidity of the French, Farhat Abbas and his friends of the U.P.A. did not lose hope. At the outbreak of the Second World War he enlisted, forty years old, in the French army. Upon his return to Sétif after the defeat of France in 1940, he reassumed the leadership of the U.P.A. and in April 1941 exposed his ideas in an explicit memorandum to Marshall Pétain, only to receive a polite but evasive answer. Equally discouraging was the reaction of the Free French military authorities to similar steps undertaken by the U.P.A. after the Vichy régime had come to an end in North Africa. A profound change of mind thus moved Farhat Abbas and those around him ever closer to the nationalist camp. In February 1943 they signed the 'Manifesto of the Algerian People'* which a year later gave birth to a new political organization, the Friends of the Manifesto and of Liberty* (A.M.L.).

ALGERIAN REVOLUTION. The conviction that their country's independence would never be achieved by peaceful means but only by some form of popular uprising began maturing in the minds of most Algerian nationalists since the sanguinary events of 1945. On the 8th of May in the town of Sétif on the southern slopes of Kabylia, at the celebration of the victory of the Allies a Moslem crowd shouting such slogans as

'Down with colonialism', 'We want equal rights' or 'Freedom for Algeria' clashed with the police and was dispersed. But in small bands the demonstrators penetrated into the French quarters, set shops and some buildings on fire, and killed a number of Europeans. The troubles spread into the mountains and the surrounding countryside with more burning, pilfering and killing, whereby nearly two hundred more French people lost their lives. Repression was carried out with utmost brutality by the French Foreign Legion; fighter planes bombed the settlements in the interior; the navy shelled the coastal villages, and civilian commandos shot indiscriminately every Moslem they laid hands on. The figures for the number of victims vary: somewhat over one thousand according to the official data; 6000 to 8000 according to French private sources; and some 20,000 according to foreign newspaper correspondents. Algerian nationalists maintain that at least 40,000 villagers were savagely killed. Yet whatever the figures were, those days of May 1945 have, in the words of the Algerian writer Katib Yassin, cemented Algerian nationalism.

In the following year the first terrorist groups recruited and trained by the 'Organisation Secrète'*, made their appearance. By 1950 most of them had fallen into the hands of the authorities, but the others continued to widen the network of underground cells until their Committee of Unity and Action* felt ready for a concerted rising. It broke out on the 1st of November 1954, the day set by the Committee, with attacks on French military outposts and isolated farms, the ambushing of motorbuses and the blowing up of railway lines in seventy different places all over Algeria. Simultaneously tracts distributed throughout the country announced the creation of the Front of National Liberation* (F.L.N.), the political organ of the Revolution, and of its military arm, the Army of National Liberation* (A.L.N.). The insurrection had its centre in the Aurès, whence it soon took root in the southern regions of the department of Constantine and in the Kabylia, thanks to the support of the local population. Notwithstanding considerable reinforcements the French troops, unfamiliar with guerilla tactics, were unable to check this growth. Yet at that time there was certainly nobody in France or Algeria who could have imagined that three years later the rebellion would officially be spoken of as the 'Algerian war'; that eight successive governments and seven successive commanders-in-chief would for the lenght of more than seven years try in vain to bring it under control and that it would end with the recognition of Algerian independence and sovereignty.

One year later, uniformed warriors of the A.L.N. marched in military formation through the streets of Philippeville, and rebel bands swarmed all over Eastern Algeria, murdering farmers, destroying the harvest, devastating orchards and vineyards. The French forces countered with mass executions and punitive expeditions, but the rebellion expanded into the hitherto quiet western parts of the country. At the same time the F.L.N. scored its first diplomatic success at the General Assembly of the United Nations, which by 28 votes to 27, with five abstentions, endorsed a motion of the Afro-Asian delegates stressing the right of the Algerian people to self-determination and recommending negotiations.

This was of merely moral significance, but as a symptom of world opinion may in a certain measure have furnished the incentive to the attempts made to find a platform for such negotiations, which were undertaken while the Assembly was still in session. On three occasions, in Cairo, in Belgrade and in Rome, French politicians, with the tacit consent of the government, had their first contacts with F.L.N. emissaries. They came to nothing, but the threads were taken up by King Muhammad V* and President Bourguiba, who resolved that Morocco and Tunisia would jointly propose their good offices, and the French Prime Minister promised that the four Algerian delegates partaking in the preliminary consultations - Ben Bella, Ait Ahmad, Muhammad Būdiaf and Muhammad Khidr - should have a safe passage between Rabat and Tunis. While in the air, however, their plane received orders from the French Intelligence authorities to land in Algiers. They were captured, handcuffed and taken to France (October 1956). Thenceforth there was hardly anybody in Algeria who believed any longer in the use of legal methods. Having witnessed how their Moroccan and Tunisian neighbours had succeeded in throwing off the French Protectorate only by resorting at last to force of arms, the mass of the people was now convinced that there was no alternative for Algeria. One after another the political parties joined the camp of the insurgents, and in their wake came more and more of those who until then had hesitated to depart from a cautious wait-and-see attitude.

A few months previously, preparations for providing the revolution with a solid structure had begun and in August 250 leaders assembled at the Summam Valley Congress*, set up the organization which was to plan and direct the political orientation and the strategy of the war: the National Council of the Algerian Revolution* and the Committee of Coordination and Execution* - the future Provisional Government of the Algerian Republic* - while an External Delegation* in Cairo was in charge of what may be called diplomatic and intelligence tasks. This apparatus functioned, although not without friction, upon the whole quite efficiently as long as hostilities lasted. Still in the same year terrorism, indiscriminate and uncompromising, was carried right into the heart of Algiers. A bomb exploding in a crowded café gave the signal for the start of this 'battle of Algiers' in which the rebels had on their side, in some form or other, practically the entire population of the city - workers, students, office clerks, merchants of the bazaar, dock - hands - while the police and gendarmery were replaced by paratroop batallions and units of the Foreign Legion with a network of richly paid informants and traitors. The battle was fought on both sides with utmost savagery: tenement buildings were blown up; women and children mutilated and killed; thousands arrested for questioning and dying under torture or summarily executed without proof of guilt or shot 'while trying to escape'. By the middle of 1957, the army had gained control of the situation and one of the most pathetic chapters in the story of the revolution was over.

The loss of many of their most daring protagonists was a severe blow to the rebels, but the scattered guerilla troops were reorganized, the levers of command readjusted and the fighting continued with undiminished tenacity in spite of the increasing difficulties and the hardship it entailed for the whole population. By the end of 1958, France had nearly 400.000 men in the field. Along the Tunisian border the electrified 'Morice Line' - so called after the officer who conceived it - and a similar barrier on the Moroccan border cut off, or at least greatly reduced, the inflow of arms and ammunition. Airborne expeditions penetrated into the roadless mountain regions and the desert highland. To stop the peasants from hiding the rebel bands and supplying them with food or information, they were herded together in thousands in large, more often than not extremely primitive 'relocation centres' while their fields lay waste, their olive groves remained unattended and the abandoned villages were destroyed. In 1961, according to French sources, 1,625.000 persons lived in 1,881 such camps - mainly old people, women and children, since the able-bodied men had in time disappeared. As a corollary of the 'relocation' ever wider spaces were declared 'forbidden zones' (zones de contrôle militaire renforcé) where air-force planes could - and did - shoot at sight at who ever they saw. The guerilla fighters however were still far from beaten, and when in October 1958 General de Gaulle, then Prime Minister invested with extraordinary powers, alluded to a 'peace of the brave' who would receive honourable treatment if they were to 'wave the white flag of truce', this offer was immediately rejected. So was four months later another approach couched in much the same terms and interpreted as merely another summons to surrender.

As time went on, the French government found it increasingly difficult to ignore the voices which in France called ever more loudly for an end to 'this stupid war without issue', accompanied by those, softer but not sparing in similar suggestions, of the foreign chancelleries. Yet there were others, more clamorous, decrying every move towards an understanding as the abandonment of a part of the national territory and equal to high treason: those of the European community in Algeria, echoed by powerful pressure groups in Parliament and in the press; and those, less and less undisguisedly menacing, of the army claiming to speak in the name of all French patriots.

In September 1959 General de Gaulle, by then President of the Republic, in a broadcast to the nation 'taking into account all the factors inherent in the Algerian as well as in the national and international situation', for the first time proclaimed the right of the Algerian people to self-determination, which they would be free to express by referendum 'after peace had been restored'. Yet there was still a long and tortuous way ahead. Two attempts at blocking it came dangerously near civil war: an uprising in Algiers of the right-wing, in fact, fascist 'Front National Français' in alliance with like-minded factions of the army in the 'Barricades Week' of January 1960; and in the 'Generals' Revolt' in April 1961, led by two former commanders-in-chief of the forces in Algeria with several high-ranking officers, and spreading widely throughout the upper levels of the civil administration. They collapsed, but not without having sown the seeds for a most tenacious counter-revolutionary movement, the extremist 'O.A.S.' (Organisation de l'Armée Secrète), provided with arms from pilfered military armouries. Under the flag of 'Algérie Française' it waged its own terrorist war, branched out into

France - de Gaulle himself miraculously escaped assassination - and continued with blasting public buildings, looting banks and inciting to street riots well after peace had been made. The Algerian Provisional Government, on the other hand, sternly refused to consider a cease-fire, or, in de Gaulle's words, 'to leave the knives in the cloak-room' unless previously assured of the impartial conducting of the referendum - contrary to the electoral consultations in the past; of 'territorial integrity' implying unrestricted sovereignty over the Sahara, and hence an adequate share in its oil and natural gas wealth; of the future status of the Europeans in Algeria - meaning an end of their privileged position; and finally of its recognition as the sole authorized spokesman of the Algerian people.
In the meantime de Gaulle's nation-wide radio and television addresses, press conferences and speeches to the people everywhere in the provincial towns brought step by step the majority of public opinion nearer to reconciling itself with the idea of Algerian independence, while talks between his agents and representatives of the Provisional Government went on in secret. The first official preliminary pourparlers took place in June 1960 at Melun near Paris. They fell short, but in the course of the following six months de Gaulle, cautiously hinting at further concessions, repeatedly proposed to re-open the discussions, until in February 1961 the French Prime-Minister and members of the Provisional Government discreetly met in Switzerland and arranged a full-dress peace conference. It convened on May 20 at Evian on the French shore of the Lake of Geneva, was broken off in June, resumed in July and dragged on, until on the 18th of March 1962 understanding was reached: the cease-fire was to come into force immediately; France, relinquishing all claims to the Sahara, would recognize Algeria as a sovereign and independent state; all French troops would be withdrawn from Algerian territory within three years, except from the naval base at Mers el-Kebir and from the nuclear testing station at Reggan in the Sahara, both leased to France for fifteen years; the European population would be free to choose between French or Algerian citizenship. A number of questions concerning the economic, financial, technical and cultural co-operation as well as the exploitation of the Saharan oil* and gas deposits were dealt with in broad outline but the details were left to later bi-lateral expert consultations. Already during the summer, the Algerian people were to be asked to approve the agreement by a referendum organized and controlled by a 'Provisional Executive' consisting in equal parts of French and Moslem members, that would, for the transitional period, also assume governmental powers and subsequently turn them over to the Government of the Algerian Republic.
The practically unanimous votes of the Algerians validated the Evian agreement in the referendum held on July 1, and two days later the proclamation of independence sealed the victory of the revolution. Its costs in lives, misery and suffering are beyond evaluation; to France it had caused real financial expenses, according to French estimates of approximately 50 billion New Francs or some 10 billion Dollars.

ʿALĪ IBN YŪSUF, the second Almoravid* ruler (1107-1143), the son of the founder of the dynasty, Yūsuf Ibn Tāshufīn* and his Christian wife, a former Spanish captive, was born and brought up in Ceuta. Unlike his father, the desert chieftain, ʿAlī lived throughout his formative years - he was twenty-three when called to the throne - in an urban environment and an atmosphere far more Andalusian than African. He was the friend of scholars and poets, a lover of art and fine buildings, and deeply religious. Yet it was not given to him to impose his authority upon the proud tribal chiefs who were his generals and provincial governors; and he was all too willing to bow in all matters to the opinion of the doctors of theology and law *(fuqahā)* who formed his permanent entourage. Nor was he possessed of sufficient energy to dam the interference in the affairs of the state exercized by the women of the powerful clans - perhaps a survival of a one-time matriarchal order in Berber society, difficult to eradicate, but a source of constant internal frictions. These weaknesses were balanced by a remarkable capacity, on the one hand, in selecting men of universal culture and organizational skill, most of them Andalusians, for his chancellery and the key positions in the central administration; on the other, in building up under the orders of a loyal servant of the dynasty, the Catalonian condottiere Reverter *(al-Ruburtayr)* a militia of mercenaries devoted heart and soul to his cause. Recruited among the Spanish Christians, they had their own priests and churches. In the African provinces their officers were in charge of the collection of taxes and of general police duties. In al-Andalus* the Berber warriors - the 'Veiled Ones' *(mulaththamūn*)* - represented a force which for some time was strong enough to repel the incursions of the Aragonian, Castilian and Catalan troops and keep the unruly Arab and Berber grandees in check. Notwithstanding the loss of Tudela (1114), of Saragossa (1117) and a defeat at Armisol near Lucena (1125) the Almoravid realm flourished, economically and also in the realm of letters and higher learning, almost until the end of ʿAlī's reign. Then the Almohad* movement, whose underground propaganda had been active for some years among the Masmūda* tribes in the Atlas region, came forcefully into the open. Four years after his death, the Almoravid régime collapsed.

ALJAMIADO LITERATURE, the literary products in *aljamía*, (the Spanish transliteration of the Arabic *al-ʿajamīya*, the parlance of the *ʿajam*, i.e. all Non-Arabs), a term which in the late Middle-Ages came into use in the Spanish Kingdoms to denote the literary products in the Romance dialects spoken by the native population of al-Andalus*, but written in Arabic characters. The authors were Christians (Mozarabs*), mainly from among those who had emigrated from a Moslem territory into a neighbouring region under Christian rule, as well as Moslems (Moriscos*), particularly in the Morisco communities which settled in the North African countries after their expulsion from Spain. Numerous Aljamiado manuscripts dealing with a variety of subjects have been preserved: religious poetry and prose, legends and pious stories and also private letters. These writings, while of no special literary value, present great linguistic interest and afford a good insight into the intellectual and emotional atmosphere prevailing among those groups who exercized considerable economic and occasionally also political influence in their new homeland.

ALMOHADS, Spanish form of *al-Muwahhidūn* (Unitarians), used in occidental literature to designate a Berber dynasty (1133-1269) which shattered the Almoravid* realm and for more than a century ruled over an empire comprising practically the entire Arab West - present-day Morocco, Algeria, Tunisia and Tripolitania - and al-Andalus*. By virtue of its military power and political prestige, its organization, economic development and general cultural level it held a foremost rank in the contemporary world. The State was built upon a spiritual doctrine taught by the religious reformer Ibn Tūmart* and was firmly implanted by him among his fellow tribesmen, the Berber Masmūda* of the High Atlas. It had its centre in the little mountain town of Tinmāl. His teaching emphasized the dogma of the Unity of the Godhead *(tawhīd)*, clothed in a socio-political code which, for the mass of the faithful, crystallized in the commandments of strict austerity in private and public life; absolute obedience to the infallible God-guided leader, the Mahdi; and the propagation of the creed, whenever necessary by ruthless use of the sword. Translated into the reality of the religious, social and political order prevailing in his day in the countries under Almoravid sovereignty, this meant open rebellion and the call to the Holy War.
Ibn-Tūmart's disciple and successor in the leadership of the community, ʿAbd al-Mu'min* (1133-1163), a Zanāta* tribesman, and his mountain warriors carried the master's word at the point of the sword, as had been his orders, all over the Atlas, the Rif and then on to the plains. They were as much inspired by their inveterate enmity with the tribes of the desert, the Sanhāja*, the pillars of the Almoravid régime. Yet, ʿAbd al-Mu'min, an eminent general as well as a far-seeing statesman and organizer, gradually turned most of them into adherents partly by the force of arms, partly by missionary propaganda, until finally first-hour believers and neophytes coalesced to form one single militant body animated by the same crusading spirit. By 1147, all Almoravid territory was in their hands, five years later Algeria, and some eight years later also Tunisia and the vital regions of Tripolitania. The Almoravid governors in al-Andalus and most of the semi-independent city potentates, the so-called Party Kings*, either voluntarily espoused the cause of the victors or were compelled to surrender. Thenceforth closer ties than ever before bound this over-sea province to the African regions of the realm, especially since ʿAbd al-Mu'min's son, Abū Yaʿqūb Yūsuf* (1163-1184) had chosen Seville as a residence, where he spent the greater part of his life, and still more so after the victory at Alarcos (1195) won by his son Abū Yūsuf Yaʿqūb al-Mansūr (1184-1199) over Alfonso VIII, King of Castile. Notwithstanding the defeat inflicted upon his son and successor, Muhammad al-Nāsir (1199-1213) by the allied Spanish Christian States in the battle of Las Navas de Tolosa* (1212) the Almohad rule in al-Andalus was to remain unshaken for some time to come.
It was the great achievement of these first generations of Almohad sovereigns to have realized that their sweeping conquests of enormous

THE MUSLIM WEST IN THE EARLY 13TH CENTURY (THE ALMOHADS)

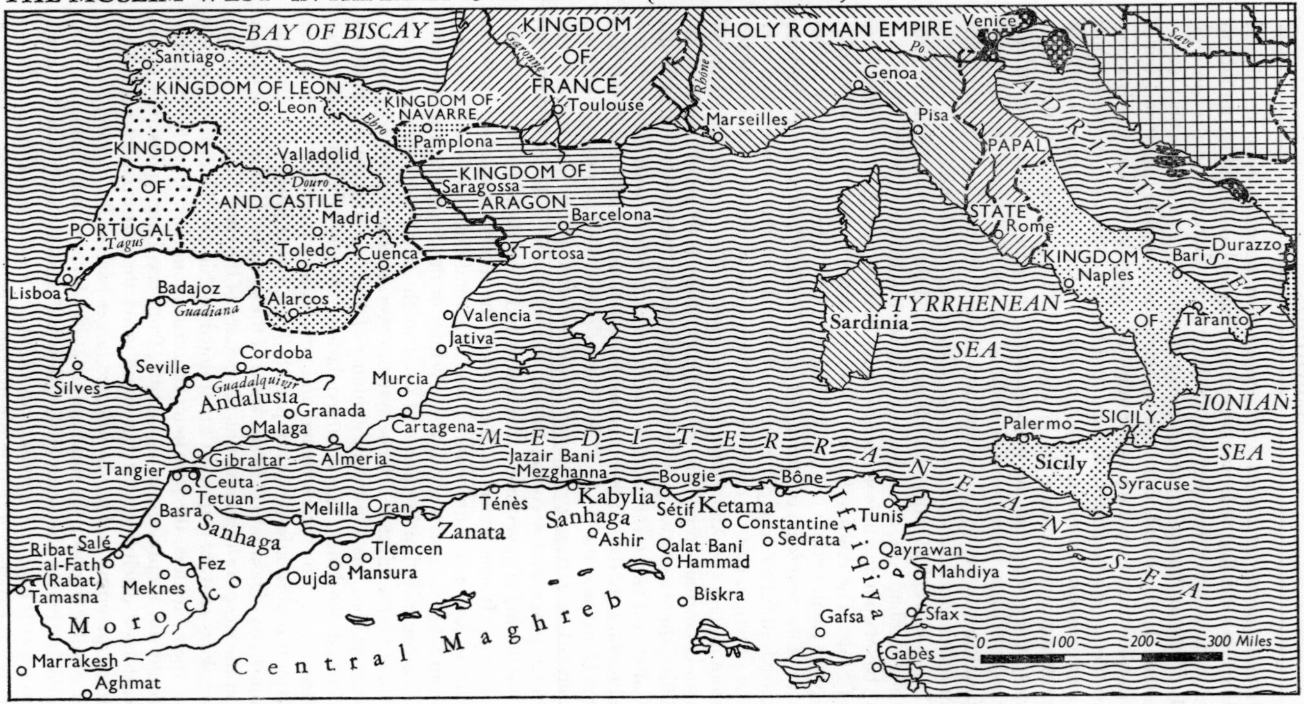

BAY OF BISCAY
KINGDOM OF FRANCE
Garonne
Rhône
HOLY ROMAN EMPIRE
Venice
Po
Save
Santiago
KINGDOM OF LEON
Leon
Ebro
KINGDOM OF NAVARRE
Toulouse
Marseilles
Genoa
Pisa
Pamplona
KINGDOM OF PORTUGAL
Valladolid
Douro
AND CASTILE
KINGDOM OF ARAGON
Saragossa
Madrid
Barcelona
Tagus
Toledo
Cuenca
Tortosa
PAPAL STATE
Rome
ADRIATIC SEA
KINGDOM OF Naples
Bari
Durazzo
Taranto
Lisboa
Badajoz
Guadiana
Alarcos
Valencia
Jativa
Cordoba
Seville
Silves
Guadalquivir
Andalusia
Murcia
Granada
Malaga
Cartagena
Almeria
Gibraltar
TYRRHENEAN SEA
Sardinia
IONIAN SEA
Palermo
SICILY
Sicily
Syracuse
MEDITERRANEAN SEA
Jazair Bani Mezghanna
Bougie
Bône
Tangier
Ceuta
Tetuan
Basra
Sanhaga
Melilla
Oran
Ténès
Kabylia
Sanhaga
Sétif
Ketama
Constantine
Tunis
Zanata
Ashir
Qalat Bani Hammad
Sedrata
Qayrawan
Mahdiya
Ifriqiya
Ribat al-Fath (Rabat)
Salé
Fez
Tlemcen
Mansura
Oujda
Meknes
Tamasna
Biskra
Morocco
Central Maghreb
Gafsa
Sfax
Gabès
Marrakesh
Aghmat
0 100 200 300 Miles

heterogeneous territories with peoples entrenched in their tribal and local loyalties had to be supported by solid and at the same time adaptable institutions lest they remain little more than ephemeral episodes. Ibn Tūmart had thought out the institutional framework which was to channel all spiritual, social and military resources into the service, first of his miniature theocracy at Tinmāl, then of the Empire and the dynasty: at the top, the infallible Mahdi, and hence repudiation of the caliph's overlordship; second in power, a council *(jamāʿa)* of ten chieftains of proven devotion, assisted by an assembly of forty delegates of the tribes; next, the body of faithful propagators of the religio-political tenets and their disciples; then the house of the Mahdi and his close entourage; and finally a military and governmental aristocracy constituted by the clans or tribes which had been the first followers of the Mahdi.
This hierarchical order was left unchanged throughout the duration of the Almohad rule. Soon, however, an administrative superstructure had to be set upon it, made necessary by the growing complexity of the affairs of State. The Andalusian courts supplied the model of the office of a Royal Chamberlain or Crown Minister *(hājib)*, held usually by a relative of the sovereign or a member of the Hafsid* family, for a long time most faithful servants of the throne. From al-Andalus too was taken over the system of court secretaries *(kuttāb)*, most of whom were appointed from among the Andalusian learned circles. To forestall the arising of non-conformist trends among the population little accustomed to stability, there were assigned to each army group, tribe and tribal faction a Caller to Prayer *(mu'adhdhin*, muezzin); an officer watching over the observance of the religious and moral tenets *(muhtasib)*; and Readers of the Coran and the Book of Ibn Tūmart *(ahl al-hizb)*. At the same time a network of garrisons stationed at well-selected points had to maintain inner peace and security, protect the caravan trade, guarantee the functioning of government machinery and the collection of the land-tax *(kharāj)*. It was levied on the basis of the newly established cadaster which, although rudimentary, was apparently quite efficient, judging from what is known about the revenues of the State and the dynasty. This organization in charge of what might be called police activities hinged on a military defence system covering most of the particularly vulnerable areas. Under the guidance of Andalusian architects and specialized workmen the circumvallations of every larger town were strengthened or reconstructed and new ones erected. Notwithstanding later transformations, the ramparts of Taza, Fez or Salé; the walls of the inner city (Qasaba*) of Marrakesh; or the so-called Kasba of the Ūdāya on the steep rocks dominating the estuary of the river Bū Ragrāg at the outskirts of Rabat, they all attest down to this day the circumspection of their builders, the first four Almohad monarchs. Unruly chieftains could not be prevented, to be sure, from revolting against this unaccustomed discipline, but for many years the disturbances were kept from spreading and hardly affected larger parts of the empire. Nor was it possible to check the steady infiltration of marauding Bedouin tribes, mainly clans of the Banū Hilāl*, Sulaym* and Maʿqil*, which pushed westwards from the Egyptian and Libyan deserts, pilfering and devastating the oases and fertile plains; but they were policed, turned to a

more peaceful pastoral life, and gradually quite a few of them settled in permanent villages.

While in the rural population the interpenetration of Arab and Berber elements slowly but steadily progressed, in urban society the generations of Arabs in every walk of life had been shaping, intentionally or not, an assimilation of Hispano-Arabic civilization rooted in the communion of age-old traditions, religion and a hereditary code of ethics. It appeared in the structure of the towns; the style and decoration of their buildings; their intellectual and emotional atmosphere. In this framework the Almohad dynasty traced the lines for an evolution which was to fit its double function as the guardian of a creed whose fundamental symbol was rigorous puritanism, and of the grandeur and prestige of a throne commanding a measure of power and wealth unique in the contemporary world. It confronted the architects and craftsmen who built their mosques, and majestic city gates with the task of finding the artistic expression for this dualism. The few monuments which have survived destruction or adulteration evidence their creative inventiveness in harmonizing structural austerity with the idea of stateliness conveyed by mass and dimension, and sobriety in ornamentation with the intricate refinement of the arabesques and the lustre of enamel. In Seville, the 'Giralda', the minaret of the Great Mosque which is now superseded by the cathedral; or in Marrakesh the 'Bāb Aguenaou', the richly decorated gate which gave access to the ruler's residence, and the mosque called *Kutubīya (al-kutubiyīn,* of the booksellers) with its minaret emphasizing the simplicity of the contours by the deep greenish-blue pattern of glazed tiles and the crown of three gold-plated balls which replaced, it is said, originals of pure gold; or in Rabat the Hassan Tower *(Manāra Hassan,* a name perhaps derived from the name of a tribe, the banū Hassan), facing the remains of the three hundred columns and hundred pillars which were to be built into a mosque planned - but left unfinished - to hold a whole army at prayer: all these occupy a foremost rank among the masterpieces of the Middle-Ages.

This golden age of the arts was parallelled by a comparable efflorescence in the field of thought, called forth by the same strong will to accord apparently disparate principles of governing. Whilst extreme orthodoxy was the strictly enforced law for the multitude, at the court philosophical speculation, regardless of inevitable contradictions with dogmatic teaching, enjoyed far-going freedom and even munificent encouragement. The extraordinary honours reserved for scholars devoted to the search for a fusion of religion with philosophy such as Ibn Tufayl*, Ibn Rushd* (Averroës), Ibn Sabʿīn* and many lesser lights, manifest the determination to counterbalance official doctrinal narrow-mindedness by the liberty accorded to those superior minds, provided their written or spoken word did not go beyond the circle of the enlightened. Inevitably, however, certain undercurrents of mysticism in their truth-finding endeavour joined in one way or another the mystical trends in the simple faith of the people and thus contributed, if only in a round-about manner, to the prodigious growth of saint-worship and religious brotherhoods*. This was thenceforth for many years to come to mark the spiritual and political life of the Arab West.

Simultaneously and notwithstanding the militant crusading spirit, a driving force both of Almohad thought and of the contemporary Christian world, a beginning was made to promote and regularize trade relations between the maritime emporia of the Italian coasts and the ports of the Almohad empire. The first steps in this direction were probably the treaties concluded with Genoa (1154) and Pisa (1157), fore-runners of the numerous future agreements following their pattern. They stipulated the mutual protection of sea traffic and laid down the terms for the use by Italian merchants of certain African ports; their right to establish warehouses, offices, lodgings, a public bath and a bakery and the amount of taxes they had to pay. Similar arrangements were concluded with Marseille, Venice and Sicily.

With the death of the fifth Almohad monarch, Muhammad al-Nāsir the first symptoms of decline became noticeable in the tenacious rebellion of the Banū Ghāniya* and their allies; the rivalries within the supreme councils of the 'Ten' and the 'Forty'; family feuds over the succession to the throne; the weakening of control over the provincial administration; and the slackening discipline of the army commanders. Gradually also the belief in the exalted mission of the Mahdi Ibn Tūmart dwindled until the mention of his name on state documents and the coinage was discontinued by Abū al-ʿUlā al-Ma'mūn (1227-1232), who was of Spanish blood on his mother's side, and by his upbringing and outlook fully estranged from, and even hostile to Almohad traditions. Although shortly before his death he re-established some of the institutions created by the Mahdi, the cohesion of the different tribal communities and their loyalty to dynasty and empire irretrievably gave way. ʿAbd al-Wāhid al-Rashīd (1232-1242) was still able to preserve a nominal suzerainty over the strong Zanāta clan of the ʿAbd al-Wādid* whose emir, Yaghmurāsan Ibn Zayyān, was in fact master of the strong town of Tlemcen and of large territories extending deep into Algeria. He could, however, no longer prevent the Ḥafsids*, throughout generations devoted servants of the dynasty and practically the hereditary governors of Tunisia, from declaring themselves independent (1236). Thenceforth the empire disintegrated rapidly. On its southern fringe another Zanāta branch, the Banū Marīn*, northwards pressing, allied themselves with Arab and dissident Berber chieftains, and established their hegemony in the plains of central Morocco. Taking foreign mercenary troops in their pay and exploiting the dynastic conflicts, they conquered one by one all larger towns and finally Marrakesh, the capital (1269). In the Andalusian towns local leaders shook off their suzerainty, but only to be expelled after a few years in power by the advancing armies of the Kings of Castile and of Aragon. In Granada alone the Nasrid* sultans maintained an unshakable independence as the sole Moslem power on Iberian soil. The last Almohad ruler, ʿUlā Idrīs al-Wāthiq, surnamed Abū Dabbūs (1266-1269) met his death in battle. It was the end of the empire and the beginning of the Marīnid era. A handful of fanatics desperately resisted for some time in the mountains of Tinmāl until they too were exterminated and the town destroyed. The mosque built by ʿAbd al-Mu'min, where he and his first three successors lay buried, was desecrated but its ruins are still standing. Two of Abū Dabbūs' sons, Abū

Mālik ʿAbd al-Wāhid and Abū Saʿīd ʿUthmān, found refuge with their families at the court of Alfonso III, King of Aragon, and entered his service, as some of their relatives, converted to Christianity, had already done. With the king's help, ʿAbd al-Wāhid - called 'Abdelhehit, filius Amir Alumenin' in the Aragonian documents - tried to reconquer the Almohad heritage, landed at Tripoli (1288) and with the support of Arab tribes obtained some success against the troops of the Hafsid sultan Abū Hafs ʿUmar (1284-1295). After his death, his brother continued the struggle but finally was forced to withdraw, apparently into the island of Jerba, then in Aragonian hands. He renewed his attempt a few years later, but again failed and for the rest of his life retreated into an oasis in Tripolitania.

The Almohad doctrine and institutions, although diluted as time went on, survived in Tunisia throughout almost the whole of the Hafsids' reign (1236-1575). They were descendants of Ibn Tūmart's and ʿAbd al-Mu'min's faithful second, Abū Hafs ʿUmar al-Hintātī*, and considered themselves the trustees of the Mahdi's spiritual heritage. His name continued to be mentioned in the Friday sermon, to appear on the coinage and in the inscriptions on public buildings. The fundamentals of his teaching were upheld for quite a long time in the theological schools under Hafsid patronage against the defenders of strict orthodoxy. The descendants of his first supporters at Tinmāl occupied key-positions in the administration of the State and high ranks in the army. These Almohad clans, each one under its own head *(mazwār*, in Berber *amzwar)*, constituted a communtiy of their own, were allotted special prebends in money and in kind *(iqtā'āt)*, and maintained the ancient hierarchical order under the traditional body of the 'Forty', called the 'great sheikhs', which were headed by the group of the 'Ten'. Their supreme chief, the *Shaikh al-Muwahhidīn*, appointed for life by the sultan from among the members of the Hafsid family and one of the most influential figures of the State, was also occasionally invested with the highest government functions such as the powerful chancellor Ibn Tāfarājīn* or Ibn al-Lihyānī who even acceded to the throne. About the middle of the XVth century this ascendancy of the Almohad clan began to vanish, but its prestige endured until the end of the Hafsid reign.

The Almohad Rulers:

The Mahdi Muhammad Ibn Tūmart	†1130
ʿAbd al-Mu'min	1133-1163
Abū Yaʿqūb Yūsuf	1163-1184
Abū Yūsuf Yaʿqūb al-Mansūr	1184-1199
Muhammad al-Nāsir	1199-1213
Abū Yaʿqūb Yūsuf al-Mustansir	1213-1224
Abū Muhammad al-Wāhid called al-Mahlūʿ (The Deposed)	1224
Abū ʿAbd Allāh Muhammad al-ʿĀdil	1224-1227
Abū al-ʿUlā Idrīs al-Ma'mūn	1227-1232
Abū Muhammad ʿAbd al-Wāhid al-Rashīd	1232-1242
Abū al-Hasan ʿAlī al-Saʿīd	1242-1248
Abū Hafs ʿUmar al-Murtadā	1248-1266
Abū al-ʿUlā Idrīs al-Wāthiq called Abū Dabbūs	1266-1269

ALMORAVIDS, transcribed form coined by the Christian chroniclers of the Middle-Ages from the Arabic term *al-Murābitūn**, and currently used in modern literature to designate a Berber dynasty (1061-1147) which reigned in Morocco, western Algeria and al-Andalus*. The Almoravids were carried to power by a spiritual movement whose driving force was a sort of crusading puritanism and which was spread among some of the veil-wearing *(mulaththamūn*)* Sanhāja* tribes in the Sahara by the theologian ʿAbd Allāh Ibn Yāsīn* and his community of warrior-monks *(murābitūn)*. A relative of one of the first companions, Yūsuf Ibn Tāshufīn* (1061-1107) became the founder of the dynasty which notwithstanding its short life holds a foremost place in the political and cultural history of the Arab West.

Structurally the Almoravid state rested only on a loose organization of provinces whose governors jealously guarded their autonomous position. Yet while the puritan élan which had inspired its creation gradually vanished, the centrifugal trends were counterbalanced, at least for some time, essentially by two factors also of a religious nature: on the one hand, the support given to the régime by the influential class of the doctors of religion and law *(fuquahā)* and their numerous clientage; on the other, the passionate, though vague mysticism which around the turn of the XIth century had taken hold of the broad mass of the people. In this climate the heterodox beliefs which in Morocco might still have survived and endangered the political coherence disappeared; and in al-Andalus the pressure of the Christian kingdoms was resisted with fresh vigour. The policy of the rulers followed the same lines. They embellished and enlarged the mosques in the cities and built everywhere new ones, thus emphasizing their own piety and widening the range of religious teaching. They multiplied the frontier outposts *(ribāt*)* garrisoned with ascetic soldier-monks; strengthened the fortifications of the towns; recruited a war-trained, faithful militia of mercenaries; and made every effort to give their peoples a feeling of security and confidence in the stability of the empire.

Currents of another order acted towards the shaping of a cultural entity. They flowed from al-Andalus, politically reduced to the status of a province, but in the domain of the arts, refinement of life and intellectual accomplishments the master of her conquerors. Men of letters, scholars and poets felt attracted by the rising splendor of Marrakesh, the new capital, sought the favour of the sovereign and served at the court or in the chancellery; merchants and artisans found a ready market for the amenities and luxuries which had made the reputation of the Andalusian cities as focus-points of elegance, taste and savoir vivre. Yūsuf Ibn Tāshufīn, at the beginning of his reign, was seen forming with his own hands the bricks of clay for the mosque in Marrakesh. Under his son ʿAlī, Andalusian architects and craftsmen designed the plans, elaborated the embellishment, taught the African builders Andalusian techniques, and adapted the architectural and decorative concepts of Egypt and Iraq, which had never ceased to exercise their influence upon the art of the Arab West since its emergence from the Byzantine heritage. Thus they prepared the evolution in North Africa of the characteristic West-Arabic 'moresque' style with its own, particular traits. Most of the

Almoravid monuments have fallen victim to destruction by time or enemy action. Some of them can be imagined only on the basis of the descriptions of chroniclers, such as ʿAlī's palace in Marrakesh, the *Dār al-Hajar* (Abode of Stone); others are in ruins, such as some castles in the Rif; but a few have remained, either in their original form, such as in Marrakesh some gates of the rampart, flanked by pairs of heavy towers; or in Tlemcen the Great Mosque, with its remarkable *mihrāb*, the best preserved of all; or incorporated into later buildings, such as portions of the Qarawīyīn Mosque in Fez and of the Great Mosque of Algiers.
Neither ʿAlī, however, nor still less his son Tāshufīn (1143-1145), nor his grand-son Ibrāhīm, who was deposed after a brief reign, nor the last of the line, Ishāq Ibn ʿAlī (†1147) were possessed of the qualities of leadership which had distinguished the ancestor of the dynasty. The theologians remained entrenched in the position of infallibility which as the principal pillars of the régime they had gradually been allowed to assume. They lost the incentive to engage in scholarly activity and inquiry into sources, even in more serious learning and were satisfied with repeating the texts of manuals sanctioned by unquestioned practice. Islam, limited to the narrowest, strictly literal and anthropomorphic conception of the word of the Koran, fell into rigidity, and this state of mind became the sole permissible principle in the spheres of thought as well as in public life. Deviating opinions were condemned as heresy, such as the writings of the famous, deeply religious scholar al-Ghazzālī (1058-1111) which were publicly burnt and forbidden to be read under penalty of death. Opposition, spiritual and soon also political, starting among the intelligentsia, began to spread among the people at large. In the Andalusian province it led to a new disintegration into a multitude of city-states under ephemeral Party-Kings*; and in the Atlas mountains south of Marrakesh to a revolt of the Masmūda* tribes, inspired by the preaching of a religious reformer, the Mahdi Ibn Tūmart*. It was tenaciously carried on by his disciple ʿAbd al-Mu'min*, who entered victoriously Marrakesh (1147) after the faithful commander of the Almoravid mercenary troops, the Catalonian Reverter (al-Ruburtayr) had fallen in battle. Ishāq Ibn ʿAlī and most of his followers were put to death; the time of the Almoravids had ended and the Almohad* era, in Africa and in Spain, began.

The Almoravid Rulers:

Yūsuf Ibn Tāshufīn	1061-1107
ʿAlī Ibn Yūsuf	1107-1143
Tāshufīn Ibn ʿAlī	1143-1145
Ibrāhīm Ibn Tāshufīn	1145
Ishāq Ibn ʿAlī	1145-1147

A.L.N. see ARMY OF NATIONAL LIBERATION

ʿAMAL al-, a term of Islamic jurisprudence, denoting, in particular in the countries of the Arab West, the practice of the courts in recognizing and applying local custom *(ʿurf*, literally 'that which is known') and usage *(ʿāda)* as a law-creating principle supplementary to the *sharīʿa*,

the formal, positive corpus juris established according to the official juridico-theological doctrine. Only interpretations of the text, carried out by a recognized scholarly authority *(mujtahid)* are admissible, while all practice not traceable to the Prophet or his companions is rejected as condemnable innovation *(bidʿa)*. Yet as time went on the change in conditions and needs, springing from the evolution and ramification of social relationships, confronted the judge *(qāḍī)* as well as the scholarly jurist *(faqīh)* more and more frequently with cases or situations either not foreseen by the *sharīʿa*, or in which by then its strict application was felt as leading to inequity.
Consequently, judicial decisions had to draw on the locally prevailing usages and customs as a second source of law and this dualism became accepted as one imposed by the public interest *(al-masālih al-ʿamma)* or the necessities *(al-darurāt)* of every-day life. Theoretically this practice was to remain in conformity, if not with the letter, at any rate with the spirit of the *sharīʿa* law. However, it inevitably modified, quite often essentially, what had been, and in the conservative, strictly orthodox conception still is regarded as an immovable system of sacrosanct law. An extensive juridical literature of which the Moroccan scholar ʿAbd al-Rahmān al-Fāsī* (1631-1685) is a characteristic representative, reflects the efforts to reach a compromise in this conflict and to integrate somehow the application of customary law into the *sharīʿa* framework. The rapid infiltration in recent years from the Occident of new attitudes and modes of conduct, of new concepts in the fields of science and techniques, and as a result in the philosophy of law, considerably accelerates this process of cautious adaptation of the traditional jurisprudence and judicature to the new conditions.

AMIS DU MANIFESTE ET DE LA LIBERTE see FRIENDS OF THE MANIFESTO AND OF LIBERTY

ʿĀMIRIDS, the descendants of the great statesman and general in al-Andalus*, Muhammad Ibn AbīʿĀmir al-Mansūr*, a dynasty of Party-Kings* reigning in Valencia from 1021 until 1085.

A.M.L. see FRIENDS OF THE MANIFESTO AND OF LIBERTY

ʿĀMMA, plur. *ʿawāmm*, a term used originally in al-Andalus* for the *muwalladūn** (the aboriginal Christian population, mainly serfs or freedmen converted to Islam, and their decendants), and later generally in the Arab West to designate the broad, inarticulate and uneducated mass of the people, the 'misera plebs', as opposed to the *khāssa*, the cultured, spiritually and ethically superior élite. This differentiation whose origin can be traced back to Plato and Aristotle was dealt with repeatedly in Arabic philosophy, particularly by al-Ghazzālī (1058-1111), Ibn Rushd* and later by Ibn Khaldūn.* In the mouth of the theologian, jurist, mystic and philosopher the notion of *ʿāmma* assumed a distinctly pejorative nuance implying, however, the moral and religious obligation of helping this populace find the means of expression for its dormant better faculties, correct its errors and restrain its brutal instincts and vicious passions. The awareness of this duty and of the spiritual, material and political problems involved, was a main driving force in the rise and expansion of the religious brotherhoods* and was a much discussed subject - and to some extent still is - in the literature of the Arab West.

AMMĀR IBN, ABŪ BAKR MUHAMMAD, a Hispano-Arab poet and statesman († 1086) of humble origin, born in a small country-town in the neighbourhood of Silves, on the southern coast of present-day Portugal, particularly reputed for the pure Arabic spoken in this area, allegedly of Yamanite parentage. Ibn ʿAmmār had his first schooling in Silves and then went for some time to Cordova to round off his education and familiarize himself with the concepts and technique of contemporary poetry. Gifted with natural intelligence, adaptability and real poetical talent, he spent the following years wandering about and making a living by singing the praise of everybody who was willing to pay for it. Thus he came to Seville and had the good fortune of winning the sympathy of the sovereign, the ʿAbbādid* al-Muʿtadid (1042-1068) who gave him a place in the circle of his court poets. Displeased, however, after a while, with the intimate friendship which soon began to tie his romantically inclined son, the 13 year old Muhammad, to the vagabond poet, he sent Ibn ʿAmmār into honourable exile to Saragossa. After Muhammad - himself a gifted poet - had ascended the throne as al-Muʿtamid billāh, he appointed his friend first governor of Silves and then minister of state.
In this position Ibn ʿAmmār had ample opportunity to prove his diplomatic skill by playing off one of the many diminutive city princes, the so-called Party Kings*, against the other and thus to contribute in no small measure to the aggrandizement and consolidation of the ʿAbbādid realm. On the other hand, his readiness to turn from the subtlest flattery to the most perfidious slander and his ruthless ambition brought upon him the enmity of most other high dignitaries and in particular of the poet Ibn-Zaydūn* whose removal from the court he finally obtained. At last, however, his boundless desire for power brought about his own downfall. Entrusted with an expedition against Murcia, he conquered the town, but assuming all the marks of sovereignty, having his name mentioned in the Friday prayer, and negotiating in his own name with foreign rulers, he openly showed himself to be in rebellion against his sovereign. Arab chroniclers give an account of the correspondence, all in verse, between al-Muʿtamid and Ibn ʿAmmār, wich grew increasingly heated until an offensive poem of Ibn ʿAmmār's sealed the break-up of their friendship. It was also the end of the poet's career. Expelled by the people of Murcia, he tried in vain to win new supporters among the various city lords, until one of them took hold of him and sold him - by auction, it is said - to Muʿtamid who had him first exposed to the derision of the mob, and then thrown into prison. Once more, thanks to his poetic persuasiveness he came near to being pardoned but again his loose tongue, for which enemies, especially the sons of Ibn Zaydūn, were only too willing to provide an appropriate echo, was his ruin. Ibn ʿAmmār found his death in prison, killed by al-Muʿtamid's own hands, but upon order of the prince was buried with all honours. A great number

of extracts from his poems are contained in the writings of several later historians.

ANDALUS al-, or *bilād al-Andalus* (the country of Andalus), a rather fluid geographical concept used by the Arab authors of the Middle-Ages for those parts of the Iberian Peninsula, which at any given time were under Muslim rule. During this era the territory comprised under this name varied considerably, and gradually shrank until it was reduced to the area of the city of Granada and its immediate surroundings. The term 'people of Andalus' *(ahl al-Andalus)*, on the other hand, denoted all Muslim inhabitants of whatever sector of Spain, whether under Muslim or Christian authority. The origin of the word, which as early as 716 appeared on a coin with Latin and Arabic inscriptions, has remained unexplained. The hypothesis, maintained for some time, of an etymological connection with the name of the Vandals, the groups of Teutonic tribes passing through Spain in the early fifth century before settling in Africa, has been abandoned. In its modern Spanish form of Andalucia it designates the roughly triangular region lying between the Mediterranean and the Sierra Morena, which includes the eight provinces of Almeria, Granada, Malaga, Jaén, Seville, Cadiz and Huelva.
At the period of the great Arab expansion in the VIIth century, the country was a Visigoth kingdom in which a small minority of German conquerors kept under sway a mass of landless serfs, and artisans of latinized Ibero-Celtic stock. Sectarian divergencies and feuds amongst the nobles repeatedly taxed this unbalanced political structure to breaking point. It was at a time of such a crisis that Arab troops under Mūsā Ibn Nusayr, on their victorious march over North Africa to the Atlantic coast, found themselves facing the narrow straits which separated them from the prospect of new success and booty. A reconnoitring raid of a few hundred men under Tarīf, one of Mūsā's subalterns (July 710), met with no resistance and was soon followed by a stronger expedition under Tāriq Ibn Ziyād whose memory survives in the name of Gibraltar *(Jabal al-Tāriq)*, the Mountain of Tāriq. With 5.000 men Tāriq beat the Visigoths near the town of Xeres, and headed for the capital Toledo which soon surrendered. In the meantime, Mūsā set out with the bulk of his troops, conquered the strongholds which his lieutenant had passed by, and joining forces with him, advanced as far as the foot of the Pyrenees. Within three years almost the whole of the peninsula was a province of the Arab empire, administered by an emir. The desire to extend their easy gains prompted the Arabs to repeated inroads across the Pyrenees. Notwithstanding a heavy defeat in the field at Tours and Poitiers in 732 *(Balāt al-Shuhadā'*, The Pavement of the Martyrs) the towns of Avignon, Arles and Lyons were plundered; Narbonne was seized and for forty years remained an Arab fortress. At last Arab Spain - or al-Andalus - found its borders on the mountain highlands of Galicia and the Asturias, and on the Spanish March set up by Charlemagne.
Less successful were the victors in building up a body politic sufficiently coherent to control the tensions in their own midst and among the various section of their subjects. By far the majority of those warriors who had crossed the straits and settled in the conquered country were

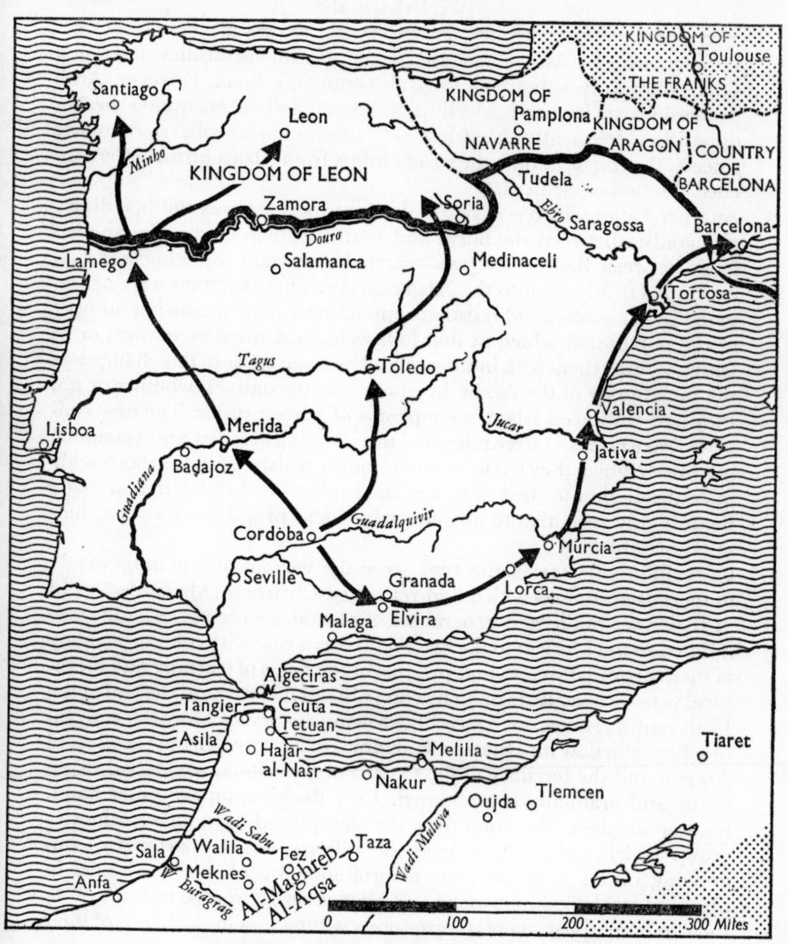

THE UMAYYAD CALIPHATE
SECOND HALF OF THE 10TH CENTURY

Berbers, who in Africa had joined the advancing armies and for a time voluntarily submitted to Arab command. Soon, however, Arab pretensions to lasting leadership could not fail to encounter Berber opposition frequently breaking out into open revolt, particularly since in the course of time the steady influx from Africa further strengthened the Berber element.

Another factor which weakened the Arab position was the hereditary antagonism between the north and south Arabian clans - the ancient feuds between Kalb and Qays - carried over from the homeland and continued until well into the XIth century. These frictions were aggravated by the underhand resistance spreading among a growing number of the population which at first had welcomed the new masters or at least accepted them with indifference. The main cause of this change was the racial pride of the Arabs, in whose eyes the natives, whether or not they had embraced Islam, were people of a lesser order. The new converts *(muwalladūn*)* were relegated to a standing of social and economic inferiority which they felt to be all the more offensive as it was thoroughly in contradiction to their notion of the brotherhood of Islam and made them highly receptive to all subversive ideas promising a rise in their inferior status.

Of a different, more static type were the various and comparatively numerous groupings which had remained Christian (Mozarabs*), but in their way of life and general set of attitudes were almost fully assimilated to the Moslem majority. Treated as a rule with tolerance, many of them acquired wealth and prestige in the fields of learning and literature, yet exercised little influence on political life. Around the end of the IXth century, however, a steadily growing current of Mozarab emigration began to flow into the new Kingdoms of Navarre, Leon, Castile and Aragon and the territory of the Counts of Barcelona, which had taken shape and gradually consolidated. Very decisive, on the other hand, became at about the same time the rôle played by another minority group which, originally a body of military slaves *(saqāliba*)*, was growing into a powerful caste of professional soldiers. Garrisoned in places of strategic importance and always ready to give free course to their fighting spirit, these troops were a willing tool in the hands of their captains.

Some thirty emirs following one another in rapid succession maintained in the name of the caliph a precarious authority until in 755 ʿAbd al-Rahmān Ibn Muʿāwiya*, one of the few surviving members of the Umayyad dynasty, landed on Spanish soil. Within a few months he was firmly established, set up his residence at Cordova and was acclaimed sovereign ruler. With ʿAbd al-Rahmān I begins the reign of the Umayyads, who held the throne of al-Andalus for nearly three centuries, first as emirs and after 929 as caliphs. Except for short intervals, however, under the firm hands of ʿAbd al-Rahmān I (756-788), ʿAbd al-Rahmān III* (912-961) and his grandson al-Hakam II (961-978) and during the dictatorship of Caliph Hishām's II all-powerful chamberlain al-Mansūr* (died 1002) the country was incessantly shaken by insurrections of the unruly Berber and Arab lords, seditions of the urban populace or peasant revolts. The suppression of such unrest, which usually remained local and upon the whole did not affect the general well-being or disturb intellectual and artistic activities, was considered as falling within the normal tasks of government. In some cases, it is true, the consequences were more serious, as in the so-called Revolt of the Suburb* at Cordova in 818, or the rebellion of ʿUmar Ibn Hafsūn who from the end of the IXth until the beginning of the Xth century was master of the entire southern regions.

Between the Umayyad caliphs and the neighbouring Christian princes in whose minds the thought of reconquering the Moslem lands for the Cross was at all times alive, hostilities continued, though restricted to never very serious encounters in the frontier areas during the summer months *(sā'ifa*)*. With the chieftains of the great confederations of tribes in North Africa, the court of Cordova maintained friendly but never more than loose relations uncoloured on either side by political ambitions. The situation changed when towards the tenth century the Fātimid religio-military advance over present-day Tunisia and Algeria and along the Moroccan coast suddenly upset the pattern of power and recalled to memory the Arabo-Berber conquest of Spain two hundred years earlier. Emir ʿAbd al-Rahmān's riposte was to proclaim himself caliph, a step which rallied the forces of orthodoxy against the Fātimid heresy and possible attemps at creating a 'third column' on Andalusian soil. Then he occupied and fortified Ceuta, Tangier and Melilla so as to forestall an attack by sea. Playing upon the inveterate tribal antagonism in the Berber world he inaugurated a policy of alliances which in a fluid constellation drew now one, then another group into the Umayyad orbit, until it changed over for a while to the Fātimid side and was replaced by a rival. Caliph Hakkam II and al-Mansūr continued this diplomatic game and occasionally supported it by direct armed intervention. Even Fez was temporarily occupied (986) and large regions in northern Morocco placed under the control of Umayyad governors, yet all these moves for securing hegemony in the territories across the sea were of a merely defensive character and ceased as soon as the Fātimid danger disappeared.

The death of al-Mansūr gave free rein to the manifold and mutually competing ambitions for power, which the weak and effeminate caliphs of the following three decades were no longer able to keep in check. They destroyed the structure of the state and brought about the downfall of the dynasty. Hishām III, the last of the Umayyad line, miserably ended his life in prison (1031) and after the short Hammūdid* interlude, a council of regents declared the abolition of the caliphate of Cordova. For some sixty years al-Andalus was split into innumerable emirates, 'kingdoms' and city-states.

It was an era of utter confusion and anarchy, inviting the Spanish monarchs to incursions which brought them unhindered deep into the heart of the country and forced most of those so-called Party-Kings* into their vassalage. Divided among themselves by dynastic rivalries and conflicting territorial ambitions they were satisfied with this sort of loose suzerainty which avoided more serious collisions and added substantial tributes, collected without effort, to their none too abundant revenues. To their vassals, on the other hand, it afforded the security of their throne and all the material and intellectual enjoyments which a refined court-life and the patronage of artists, men of letters and philosophers could procure. Although some of them, such as particularly the 'Abbādids* of Seville, succeeded in rounding off their area at the expense of weaker neighbours, this mosaic of Andalusian miniature states and their relations with the Spanish overlords remained, notwithstanding occasional frictions, upon the whole remarkably stable until in the last quarter of the XIth century the emergence of two new centres of power, one in Spain, the other in Morocco, upset the balance.

In Spain, Alfonso VI, King of Castile and Leon, by then commanded sufficient strength to turn the 'protectorate' into full sovereignty, occupied more and more Andalusian territory, triumphantly entered Toledo (1085) and prepared a large-scale campaign for further conquests. In Morocco, Yūsuf Ibn Tāshufīn*, the apostle of the renovation and expansion of Islam, forged the loose Berber confederations into the great Almoravid* realm, and in the eyes of the Andalusians, especially of the men of religion, appeared as the saviour from absorption by the advancing Christians. He followed their call for aid, took his army across the Straits and by his victory in the battle of Zallāqa* and the garrisons he left behind when returning to Morocco, thwarted King Alfonso's plans. Soon, however, quite a few of the Andalusian princes found the rough Berber warriors and the uncompromising Almoravid puritanism far heavier to bear than the former Christian dominance which had never interfered with their affairs as long as the tributes were paid. Increasingly the discontent crystallized in secret alliances with the Spaniards against the burdensome Africans, and it took Yūsuf Ibn Tāshufīn more than a decade of hard fighting to subdue all resistance. By the beginning of the XIIth century the Party-Kings had disappeared and al-Andalus was an Almoravid province.

Fifty years later Almoravid dominance collapsed under the blows of the Almohad* empire-builder 'Abd al-Mu'min*. Upon the first signs of his success al-Andalus broke into rebellion. The admiral of the Almoravid fleet in Andalusian waters went over to the victors, and most of the governors of the towns followed his example or were driven out by their own men or the populace. Old Party-King-dynasties reappeared, new ones came to the surface, and again particularistic tendencies were given free play. Some of the city-lords, such as Ibn Mardanīsh* of Murcia and Valencia, tenaciously defended their independence; others paid homage, voluntarily or under compulsion, to the Almohad sovereign; still others became vassals of one of the Christian kings; and many changed sides whenever the vicissitudes of war seemed to favour one party or the other. Ceaseless fluctuations of imperfect loyalties and frequent desertions, of internal discord and divergent interests were the dominant traits in the picture of Andalusian history throughout the XIIth century.

In the background, however, a profound change began to take place, called forth by the crusading enthusiasm which had taken hold of the Christian world and imparted a fresh incentive to the idea of the 'Reconquista'. English and German knights on the way to the Second Crusade stormed Lisbon and turned it over to Alfonso Henriquez, the first king of Portugal; the half-monastic and half-military orders of Calatrava, Alcantara, Evora and Santiago supplied the Kings of Castile with shock troops; an Aragonian and Catalan army conquered Tortosa and Lerida; and everywhere the pressure, although still incoherent and slow, steadily grew. For long years an almost uninterrupted, inconclusive war with few major encounters dragged on between smaller and larger Almohad and Spanish army groups, until Abū Yūsuf Yaʿqūb*, the third Almohad ruler, routed the Castilians under Alfonso VIII at the battle of Alarcos* (1195), penetrated into the region of Toledo and pushed his raids as far as Madrid. It was not a lasting success. With the blessing of Pope Innocent III, a coalition of Aragon, Castile and Navarre under Alfonso's direction won a decisive victory over Abū Yūsuf Yaʿqūb's son and successor Muhammad al-Nāsir in the great battle at Las Navas de Tolosa* (1212), which put an end to all attempts at securing the preponderance of the Almohad cause in al-Andalus, although it neither advanced the position of the Christians nor stopped the feuds among the turbulent petty states.

The decline of the Almohad power coincided with the appearance on the Spanish stage of two energetic and far-seeing monarchs, both endowed with remarkable generalship, James I of Aragon and Ferdinand III of Castile and Leon. Joining their efforts, but careful to limit in advance their fields of operation, they started a series of systematically planned campaigns which led them from victory to victory and from conquest to conquest. To Aragon fell the Balearic Isles (1229-1235) and the whole region of Valencia (1238), into Castile were incorporated Cordova (1236), Jaén, Seville (1249), Xeres, Cadiz and the area of the lower Guadalquivir and finally Murcia (1266). With the exception of the territory of Granada, which until 1492 remained in the possession of the Nasrid* dynasty, the Reconquista was completed. Abū Yūsuf Yaʿqūb*, the second Marīnid* sultan, endeavoured to recover at least some of the loss and to carry the Holy War into Spain. He occupied Malaga (1277) and a few smaller places in southern Spain, but they were soon again evacuated. The Christianization of the Moslem population (*Mudejares**, after the fall of Granada called *Moriscos**) was a much slower process. For a long time the Christian states pursued a policy of considerable tolerance towards their Muslim subjects, as the Muslim rulers had done towards the native Christians in al-Andalus. Soon after the fall of Granada, however, the idea gained ground that the propagation and defence of the Catholic faith within the borders of the State were the sacred duty of Church and King, and that this implied the suppression of all differing beliefs. Thus started under the pressure of the Inquisition a period of *Morisco* persecution, of enforced conversions, confiscation of property, emigration and revolts, which ended with the expulsion from Spain of the remaining Moslems (1609-1614), allegedly some 300.000, who found new homes in the countries of North Africa.

Al-Andalus evoled a characteristic culture of its own borne by the vehicle of the Arabic language, and created an intellectual and aesthetic atmosphere which, though decidedly Moslem and Arabic in essence, was readily accepted by all inhabitants in spite of ethnic and social differences, regional and personal antagonisms, and all the agitations which marked its history and even survived its existence as a geographic entity. It blended the elements drawn from Damascus, Baghdad or Cairo, and amalgamated the temperament and faculties of Ibero-Celtic, Visigoth and Berber communities. Yet it did not develop a sense of national unity, neither did it at any time show tendencies towards exclusiveness. The native Romance parlance vigorously survived throughout the centuries with its folklore and the popular literature which has come down to us in the so-called Aljamiado* manuscripts. Arising on the soil of a prosperous agriculture, artisanry and trade, and fertilized by the most manifold contacts with the Arab East, the Latin West and the North African tribal world, Andalusian civilization brought forth fruits of universal value. The designs, forms and ornamentations, invented and elaborated by Andalusian builders and sculptors, of which the Alcazar in Seville and the Alhambra in Granada have survived as world-famous monuments, embellished the towns in North Africa and left their traces in the development of occidental architectural style. The troubadours of southern France were inspired by the love-songs and ballads, the mode of lyric and metrical expression created and popularized by Andalusian poets such as Ibn ʿAbd Rabbihi*, Ibn Zaydūn* or Ibn Quzmān*. From the universities of Cordova and Granada or from such seats of higher learning as Seville, Toledo and Malaga came historians and biographers among whom stand out Ibn al-Qūtīya*, Ibn Hayyān*, al-Dabbī*, Ibn al-Faradī*, Ibn Bashkuwāl*, Ibn al-Abbār*; geographers and authors of travel-books such as al-Bakrī*, Ibn Jubayr*; astronomers and mathematicians such as al-Majrītī or al-Bitrūjī*; physicians and herbalists such as Ibn al-Baytār*, al-Zahrāwī* or the Ibn-Zuhr* family; or men of universal scholarship such as Ibn-Hazm* or Ibn al-Khatīb*. The most illustrious achievements were unquestionably attained by the Andalusian philosophers - Ibn Bājja*, Ibn Rushd*, Ibn Tufayl*, Ibn ʿArabī, to name some of the most celebrated ones - among whom an outstanding share falls to Jewish thinkers such as Salomon Ben Gabīrōl and Ibn Maymūn, the latter distinguished also as an astronomer and physician. They reconciled and harmonized Aristotelian and Platonic philosophy with a monotheistic faith, and within this framework evolved systems of their own. By way of Toledo, the great centre of systematic translating, much of this wealth in ideas and inspiration reached medieval Europe, and for many years to come influenced scientific thought and speculation of the Occident.

ʿARAFA IBN, ABŪ ʿABD ALLĀH MUHAMMAD, a Tunisian theologian and jurisprudent (1316-1401) considered in his time all over the Arab world in North Africa and al-Andalus* as one of the highest authorities in his field, whose memory Tunisian theological circles still hold in high esteem. Descended from the Berber Warghamma tribe in the south-eastern section of Tunisia, he studied in his home-country and then until the end of his life held the functions of an *imām* (leader in prayer) and *khatīb* (preacher in charge of the solemn Friday sermon, the *khutba)* at the Great Mosque in Tunis. It was, however, in his position as a *muftī* (juridical expert) where his erudition in scholastic theology as well as in the domains of religious law and jurisprudence gave a determinant weight to his opinion. It was his voice that decided the appointment

of the holders of all religious offices of any importance - as a rule his own disciples through whom his influence made itself felt in almost any sphere of life. Even the famous historian Ibn Khaldūn*, then in high favour at the court, thought it wiser to withdraw from Tunis than to risk a conflict with him on the ground of their divergent doctrinal views. Severe with himself as with others, keeping aloof from worldly pleasures and refusing to be drawn into the play of court ambitions and rivalries, he did not disdain, however, profitable commercial transactions. This might at least be judged from the fortune which according to his will was invested in pious foundations after his death.
The results of Ibn ʿArafa's studies and scientific thought have become known to us partly through the writings of his disciples and are partly found embodied in his two books: the *Mukhtasar al-Fiqh al-Kabīr*, an encyclopaedic work in several volumes which covers the entire system of law *(fiqh)* with its whole bearing on man's duties towards God and his social relationships; and the *Hudūd*, also called *Taʿārif*, a compilation of juridico-religious terms and institutions, still valued today.

ARMY OF NATIONAL LIBERATION, usually quoted by its initials A.L.N. (Armée de la Libération Nationale), denoting the militant forces in the Front of National Liberation* (F.L.N.), the organization behind the Algerian Revolution*. The French authorities first learned of its existence towards the end of 1954 when a 'standing order' fell into their hands, which enjoined upon all men between the ages of 18 and 40 the sacred duty to enlist, and asked those who would have been drafted to stay at home and await further orders. Its nucleus were the terrorist bands, probably not more than some 500 men, or rather what remained of them, trained and armed by the revolutionary Organisation Secrète* (O.S.) around 1946 and 1947, who after their discovery by the police in 1950 were either thrown into prison, went into hiding or escaped to Cairo. Within the next four years, however, the Revolutionary Committee for Unity and Action*, the forerunner of the F.L.N., reconstituted the underground apparatus, divided the Algerian territory into six operational wilayas, and appointed for each one a military commander. With the consolidation and expansion of the F.L.N., the systematic drilling of volunteers, especially in the mountain villages, and the increasing flow of deserters from the Muslim units in the French army, swelled the number of terrorist bands in the towns *(fidayūn)* and of guerilla-fighters in the countryside. Meanwhile arms and war supplies of Czecho-Slovakian, Belgian, East-and West German or Italian manufacture were smuggled in from Morocco and Tunisia. Wilaya commanders held three of the five seats in the supreme executive body of the revolution, the Committee of Coordination and Execution* (C.C.E.) created at a meeting of the Summam Valley Congress* (August 1958) and subsequently transformed into the Provisional Government of the Algerian Republic* (G.P.R.A.).
When, by the end of 1958, the French succeeded in practically stopping all further gun-running into Algeria, the F.L.N. set up recruiting centres and military camps in the Moroccan and Tunisian frontier areas,

where a well-equipped force estimated at some 15.000 to 25.000 men was given regular military training. At the same time a former sub-commander in the Oranian wilaya, Colonel Hūarī Būmedienne, was appointed Commander-in-Chief of the Army of Liberation with headquarters in the Tunisian border village of Ghardimaou on the right bank of the Majarda river. What the leaders of the revolution had in mind was not to conduct an offensive from outside, which obviously would have offered no prospect of success, but to wear the French out by incessant guerilla warfare in the interior and after the victory, to have a disciplined troop ready to re-establish order and security - and to enforce their own authority - in the war-torn, disorganized country. Their plans did actually, though incompletely, materialize.
Even before Algeria was officially proclaimed independent (July 3, 1962) the G.P.R.A. had split into two antagonistic factions: Colonel Būmedienne, siding with the one headed by Ben Bella, Būmenjel and Muhammad Khidr, later the so-called group of Tlemcen, began a vehement campaign over his broadcasting station at Ghardimaou against the other, the so-called group of Tizi-Ouzou in the Kabylia, led by Belkacem Krim and Muhammad Būdiaf. When the G.P.R.A. pronounced Būmedienne deposed and degraded for insubordination, he and his friends declared this measure illegal on the ground that the army was not subordinate to the government but responsible only to the revolutionary 'parliament', the National Council of the Algerian Revolution*. The majority of superior officers remained faithful to the Commander-in-Chief, others remained neutral, and still others turned against him. When the Tlemcen group set itself up as the 'Political Bureau of the F.L.N.' which assumed ever wider governmental prerogatives, the conflict in leadership rapidly sharpened and found its reflection on the level of the wilayas. The guerilla warriors refused to disband, set up 'wilaya councils', and, arms in hand, entered the contest for power: those in the Kabyle areas under the widely respected chieftain Mohand ou al-Ḥajj on the the side of the Tizi-Ouzou group and subsequently of its offspring, the Party of Socialist Revolution and the Front of the Socialist Forces; and the others for the most part in support of the Political Bureau.
All through the second half of 1962 and well into 1963, the skirmishes between the hostile camps continued, occasionally interrupted by attempts at negotiating a compromise but more frequently degenerating into serious encounters with quite a number of dead. Nearly 15.000 men wearing some kind of uniform or military attire swarmed about the country under the headmen of their clans or a leader of the moment, occupying one another's villages or the quarters of a town. Step by step, however, Colonel Būmedienne, Minister of Defence in the first cabinet of the Algerian Republic, presided over by Ahmad Ben Bella, incorporated some of them into his regular army (thenceforth renamed the People's National Army (A.N.P., Armée Nationale Populaire) while the others were gradually persuaded to return to civil life. By careful but rigorous sifting, the effective strength of this force was brought down to 30.000 men, and at the same time the division into wilayas, which had well answered the needs of the revolutionary struggle, was replaced by

an organization of military districts with a network of garrisons corresponding to the army's peace-time functions.

ʿARŪS IBN, ABŪ al-ʿABBĀS AHMAD, popularly known as Sīdī Ben ʿArūs, a Tunisian saint († 1463) born around the end of the XIVth century of a poor, probably Berber, family in the region of Bône. While still a youth, he left his native village for Tunis, where he acquired with the rudiments of theology a certain knowledge of different trends of mystical thought, earning a less than modest living in a variety of humble occupations. Then he began wandering all over Tunisia and thence by frequent and prolonged stages over Algeria into northern Morocco as far as Ceuta. Intent on deepening his experience in mysticism by staying for a while wherever possible with some religious brotherhood* or men revered for their piety and virtue, he at last returned to Tunis. With as his shelter for the night the corner of a dilapitated building, he spent the day in the court of the Great Mosque or strolling through the *sūq*. His queer utterances and still queerer attitudes, often very closely bordering on, if not transgressing, the limits of decency, did not take long to be held by the credulous masses for manifestations of supernatural inspiration. Gradually, the belief in his saintliness and miraculous power found its way into more critical circles, until Sultan Abū Fāris* (1394-1434) assigned to him free lodgings in a *funduq* (a commercial building combined with an inn) which his successor, Sultan al-Mustansir (1434-1435) converted into a regular *zāwiya** (the seat of a religious brotherhood) with ample quarters for the saint's already considerable number of adepts. It was to be his burial place, and, considerably enlarged towards the end of the XVth century and embellished in the XVIIth cent. is still in existence. Ibn ʿArūs moved from his room on the ground floor to a hut of mattings on the terrace - hence his surname *sāhib al-satah,* the lord of the terrace - where only a selected few were admitted while all those who sollicited his blessing had to call up to him from the street and place their pious gifts in a basket which he let down and drew up on a cord. Notwithstanding the mistrust in his wonder-working nature openly voiced by quite a number of the theological doctors, his prestige did not cease to grow even among the high-ranking officialdom and court society. Royal princes and the most prominent religious dignitaries headed the throng of mourners at his funeral.
The memory of Sīdī Ben ʿArūs, greatly embellished by legend, is down to this day vividly present in the minds of the people of Tunis, although the brotherhood which claims him as its founder, the ʿArūsīya - also known as Salāmīya after ʿAbd al-Salām al-Asmar who thoroughly re-organized it at the end of the XVIIIth century - has lost most of its former importance. The story of his life and of the miracles he performed *(manāqib*)*, recorded with a wealth of picturesque details by one of his disciples, ʿUmar Ibn ʿAlī al-Rāshidī, drastically illustrates the currents of popular thought in his time.

ʿASKAR IBN, ABŪ ʿABD ALLĀH MUHAMMAD, Moroccan biographer (1530-1578), a descendant on both his father's and mother's side of a branch of the Idrīsid* dynasty. Born in Shafshāwan (French Che-

chaouene, Span. Xauen, south-east of Tetuan), at that time a main centre of the Holy War against the Portuguese, he began his studies in his home town, and in a roving life which took him all over northern Morocco followed the courses of a great many religious doctors as well as the teaching of various saintly men and mystics, and twice held the offices of a cadi and mufti. Finally he took up residence in Fez but in the struggle for the throne between the Saʿdian* sultan Muhammad, the later al-Maslūkh (1574-1576), and his uncle ʿAbd al-Malik (1576-1578), he followed the former and with him fell in the battle of the Wādī al-Makhāzin (the so-called Battle of the Three Kings*, 1578).
Ibn ʿAskar left one single work, usually quoted under the abridged title *Dawhat al-Nāshir* (French translation by A. Graulle, 'La Daouhat en-nāchir de Ibn ʿAskar', Paris, 1913; and a condensed English version by T. H. Weir, 'The shaikhs of Morocco in the XVIIth Century', Edinburgh, 1904). His book was the first in the wide field of that particular type of biographical literature which deals with the lives of, and miracles performed by the saints. Although restricted to the adepts of the doctrine of al-Jazūlī* and without going very much into the events of historic significance nor evidencing any great precision as to dates, it conveys a vivid picture of the religious atmosphere of the time and of the movement of mysticism that was taking ever firmer root in the minds of the masses.

ASSOCIATION OF THE ALGERIAN ʿULAMĀʾ, constituted in Algeria by scholars of Moslem theology and law (*ʿulamāʾ*, sing. *ʿālim*) in May 1935 after an informal existence of several years for the pursuit of strictly religious and cultural aims, but gradually drawn into the sphere of politics, if only by the individual activities of a great many of its members. It developed into a principal factor in the awakening of an Algerian consciousness. Its leading spirit was the highly reputed Sheikh ʿAbd al-Hamīd Ibn Bādīs of the region of Constantine, a scion of the princely house of the Zīrids* (reigning in Tunisia, Algeria and al-Andalus* between the Xth and XIIth cent.), who came from the theological academy of the Zaytūna in Tunis and was a fervent protagonist for the then vigorously growing Islamic renaissance movement. Around 1930 he began to carry his ideas, rooted like those of the contemporary Salafīya* in the teaching of the great reformer Muhammad ʿAbduh, both by word of mouth and through his paper *al-Shihāb* (The Meteor) over practically all Algeria until most of the progressive religious circles were on his side. After his death (1940) his place at the head of the Association was taken by the equally energetic Sheikh Tālib al-Bashīr Brahimi (al-Ibrāhīmī). The Association strove for the purification of Islam from the medieval superstitions which had overgrown it, from the saint-worship and the misconceived mysticism of the brotherhoods* and their hold on the uncritical mind of the masses. Hand in hand therewith it advocated the adaptation to modern requirements of the antiquated educational system, accompanied by a corresponding revival of Arabic - the language of Islam, of the great Arabic civilization and of the speech of the Algerian people. It was but a further step along this line of thought to postulate the recognition of an Algerian nation as evidenced by its unity of religion, language, traditions and culture, which had evolved in its particular territory, like all other nations, in the course of historical events. The differences between Algeria and the Algerians on the one hand, and France and the French on the other, were of a nature, Sheikh Ibn Bādīs insisted, which excluded all assimilation, leaving open, however, the way to a mode of coexistence possibly in the form of the relationship between a British Dominion like Canada and Great Britain. The Association propagated these tenets in the sermons at the mosques; in the more than 200 schools for children and adults which it founded; in the courses it established in the larger towns for the formation of teachers, in the pedagogical Institute Ben Bādīs in Constantine; and in the lectures it arranged for the working classes in Algiers, all under the slogan: 'Islam is my religion; Arabic my language; Algeria my country.'

The Association met with a twofold opposition, Moslem as well as French. The former too ran in two disparate currents: one sprang from among the intellectual élite in the occidental - which meant French - mould, the 'évolués'*, maintaining, as did at that time in his writings also the young Farhat Abbas, one of the foremost figures in the Algerian Revolution*, that there never had existed an Algerian nation, that the cultural and economic future of Algeria, for a century a part of French territory, was indissolubly tied to France, and that nothing in the precepts of Islam prevented an Algerian Moslem from being and feeling French; in the second current converged the hostile feelings of the ultra-conservative elements who felt their prestige dangerously menaced: the brotherhoods and marabouts, and the holders of religious or religio-juridical offices - the imams, muftis and cadis, all of undisguised pro-French leanings. The French authorities, alarmed at the growing resonance the Association found, reacted by submitting its members to close supervision and forbidding them to preach in the public mosques (the much criticized 'circulaire Michel', called after the official responsible for its issue). In 1938 Ben Bādīs was put under arrest, yet the Association's influence continued undiminished and its strictly Islamo-Arabic conception of Algerian nationalism remained unshaken, notwithstanding an occasional collaboration with nationalist parties of a variety of political shades. So too for some time did its belief in negotiations as the means of achieving its goals, and its refusal to use violence. Early in 1956, however, it espoused most of the programme of the militant Front of National Liberation* (F.L.N.), was represented in the External Delegation of the Algerian Revolution in Cairo by its Secretary-General Tawfīq al-Madanī who after the achievement of independence held a seat in the Provisional Government of the Algerian Republic* (G.P.R.A.).

AVENZOAR see ZUHR IBN

AVERRÖES see RUSHD IBN,

ʿAWWĀM IBN al-, ABŪ ZAKARIYYĀʾ YAHYĀ, a Hispano-Arab author of Seville (XIIth century). He left few biographical traces, but his *Kitāb al-Falāha*, an extensive work on agriculture and cattle breeding, sheds an interesting light on the economic conditions in the Spain of that epoch. It has been translated into Spanish (J. A. Banqueri, 1802), and French (Clément-Mullet 1864).

ʿAYYĀSHĪ al-, ʿABD ALLĀH IBN MUHAMMAD, a Moroccan author (1628-1679) born of a family of the Berber Ait ʿAyyāsh tribe living in the region of the High Atlas which extends from the Jabal ʿAyyāshī southwards along the valley of the river Zīz into the fertile area of the Tāfīlālt. There his father was at the head of a *zāwiya** (a branch seat) of the Nāsirīya* confraternity of which he himself was a most devoted member. Al-ʿAyyāshī studied religious science in Fez, especially the mystical aspects, and then travelled about in the Arab countries of the East with long stays in Mecca and Medina, Jerusalem and Cairo, either teaching or attending the lectures of the prominent scholars of the day. He wrote a number of works on religious and philological subjects, but his reputation rests on his *Māʿal Mawāʿid* (appr. Voyage or Exploration), a travel book *(rihla*)* containing detailed information on the men of letters, theologians and on the intellectual activities in general of the places he visited. (French translation by A. Bergbrugger, 'Voyages dans le sud de l'Algérie et des Etats barbaresques . . .', Paris, 1846; and extracts by Motylinski, 'Itinéraires entre Tripoli et l'Egypte', Alger, 1900). Al-ʿAyyāshī's travel book which has been used as source of reference by numerous later authors, enjoyed wide popularity and is read and often quoted down to this day, perhaps also because it is one of the rare works of its kind which conveys information on the ways of thinking and attitudes of the mass of the common people *(ʿāmma*)*, to which as a rule the intellectual groups attached no interest whatsoever.

ʿAYYĀSHĪ al-, MUHAMMAD IBN AHMAD, one of the saintly men (marabouts*) in Morocco (†1641) who in the troubled times of the dissolving Saʿdian* reign used their spiritual influence upon the masses to create for themselves practically independent principalties, ephemeral, but sources of permanent unrest while they lasted. No data as to al-ʿAyyāshī's early years are known except that he came from the Arab tribe of the Banū Malik in the Gharb in north-western Morocco, was highly reputed for his ascetic life and theological knowledge, and seems to have been associated with a brotherhood* of Jazūlīya* affiliation. Preaching the Holy War against the Portuguese, he gathered a number of warriors, gained some success in the region of Azemmour and was appointed governor of the town by Sultan Abū al-Maʿālī Mūlāy Zaydān (1603-1628). Fallen into disgrace, he had to flee, and turned to Morisco* refugees in Rabat-Salé, who under the hegemony of the warlike Hornacheros*, readily responded when he appealed to their hatred of the Christian intruders. With fresh impetus he pushed into the plains bordering the Atlantic coast (1614/15) and as he advanced increasing the number of his troops and the spread of his prestige, he was soon master of the entire region of the Gharb. Yet, while venerated as a holy man and commanding undisputed respect as a warlord, he lacked the capacity of political leadership and could not impose his authority upon the people when fighting was over. Thus he took up arms again with the same success as before, penetrated northwards as far as Larache and even into the area of Tangier (1640) and southwards to Mazagan. Then, however, his friendship with the Moriscos began to cool off and, probably through his clumsiness in negotiating, turned into open enmity. He attacked and occupied Rabat and Salé with the result that his former allies asked the strong Dilā'yūn* fraternity for help. In the encounter which ensued, al-ʿAyyāshī was defeated and killed.

B

BADR, a freedman and servant of ʿAbd al-Rahmān Ibn Muʿāwiya*, the first Umayyad ruler of al-Andalus* (756-788), and his faithful companion on his flight from his enemy, the first ʿAbbāsid caliph Abū al-ʿAbbās ʿAbd Allāh al-Saffāh* (750-754). Having succeeded in gathering together some gold and jewelry from his master's family treasure, Badr joined ʿAbd al-Rahmān in Palestine and shared with him the vicissitudes of his adventurous five years' peregrinations in North Africa. Finally, crossing the Straits of Gibraltar, he set out on a reconnoitering trip into southern Spain and enlisted for a while in the army. There he won for ʿAbd al-Rahmān's cause the first adherents among the still quite numerous Umayyad partisans. With the money they contributed he purchased a small craft, and accompanied by a dozen of his newly gained friends, took ʿAbd al-Rahmān into the country over which thenceforth the Umayyads were to reign for nearly three centuries. In the turbulant events which filled Emir ʿAbd al-Rahmān's reign, Badr repeatedly proved his military talent and apparently also his ability in acquiring wealth for himself. Subsequently, however, he became guilty of some insurrectional scheming, was sent into exile and lost his fortune but was afterwards pardoned. According to some authors it seems that he became again implicated in a conspiracy, and this time had to pay for his too far-reaching ambitions with his life.

BAIDHAQ al-, ABŪ BAKR IBN ʿALĪ al-SANHĀJĪ, Berber chronicler (XIIth century) of the Almohad* period, one of the first adherents of this doctrine and devoted follower of its founder, the Mahdi Ibn Tūmart* († 1130) and of his disciple and successor ʿAbd al-Mu'min* (1133-1163). Only vague information has so far become available on his origin, his youth and the circumstances of his first contacts with Ibn Tūmart, dating back probably to the Mahdi's arrival in Tunisia after his stay in Egypt. From that time onwards he shared the master's and his few acolytes' long peregrinations, leading, as he reports, their only beast of burden, and deeply impressed by the miraculous signs of the Mahdi's divine mission which he was convinced to recognize in the manifold occurences of the journey and described with many picturesque details. Later, at the Almohad court, he continued to register even seemingly insignificant events, yet apparently always keeping in the background without aspiring after any official position. Only al-Baidhaq's name and some passages of his writings, quoted by other authors, were known until in the 'twenties of this century, 36 pages of a manuscript in the Escurial Library (Madrid), were identified as a portion of his chronicle, although the beginning, the title and the author's name were missing (published by E. Lévi-Provençal in 'Documents inédits d'histoire almohade,' Paris, 1928). These 'Mémoires' constitute a valuable source of information on the first years of the Almohad movement and its final triumph, although they do not always coincide with the descriptions given by others.

BĀJJA IBN, ABŪ BAKR MUHAMMAD IBN YAHYĀ, called Avempace in the medieval Latin of the scholastics, a Hispano-Arab philosopher, mathematician, astronomer, physician who was also known for his predilection for music and poetry (†1138). He was the son of a goldsmith - hence frequently mentioned as *Ibn al-Sāʾigh* - in Saragossa but when the town was conquered by Alfonso I of Aragon (1118),he left for Seville, then moved to Granada and finally settled in Fez where he held high positions in the Almoravid* chancellery. There he died, still in his young years, poisoned, it was said, at the instigation of some physicians, jealous of this successful newcomer. Yet in the short span of his life he acquired an outstanding rank in the history of Arabic philosophy and exercized a remarkably fertilizing, long-lasting effect upon the philosophical speculation in the Christian world of the Middle Ages, reflected particularly in some aspects of the teachings of St. Thomas Aquinas and Albertus Magnus. Besides commentaries on several of Aristotle's treatises, he wrote various studies, allegedly some twentyfive, on mathematical, astronomical, medical and philosophical subjects, all lost except for one. This is embodied in a farewell letter to a friend on the eve of his departure for a voyage, which is reproduced as the *Epistola Expeditionis* in a Latin version of Ibn Rushd's* writings. Also his great work, the *Tadbīr al-Mutawahhid* (The Régime of the Solitary) was known only through an analysis and quotations contained in a Hebrew commentary of the end of the XIVth century on Ibn Tufayl's* *Hayy Ibn Yaqzān* until the recent discovery and publication of the major part of the original. (Spanish translation, Avempace, El régimen del solitario by M. Asin Palacios, Madrid-Granada, 1946).

Ibn Bājja continued with certain modifications along lines traced by his predecessors in the Arab East. He starts from the thesis that the perfect State in which every member has attained to the highest degree of perfection accesible to human beings, and thus has ceased to be what mystical theology termed a stranger *(gharīb)* in his society, can be brought about only if everyone adopts the way of life, or régime, which it is the task of the 'solitary' to develop and implant. To explain this régime Ibn Bājja builds up a profound system which, reduced to its simplest expression, can be defined as resting on the distinction between two categories of 'spiritual forms': the one, inherent in the material bodies; and the other, the 'separate substance' without relation to matter, as it were, the idea of all ideas, the essence of all essence, including the very essence of man. The study of the speculative sciences in an ascetic and solitary life will lead human intellect to the re-union *(ittisal)* with the Agent Intellect *(ʿaql faʿʾāl)* - the nearest in the hierarchy of the spiritual above man and his world - of which it is an emanation. In this re-union the Agent Intellect operates on man's latent, potential faculties, arouses them to activity and develops his 'acquired intellect' *(ʿaql mustafād)* which perceives and assimilates the 'separate substances'. It is the aim of the 'solitary' to produce this stage which opens the way to supreme beatitude. This solitary, purely intellectual search for the ultimate goal of human existence was, however, in Ibn Bājja's teaching in no way connected with religious life. Assigning to the Koran and Revelation merely the function of a moral support for the masses, and neither desirous nor capable of philosophical reasoning, he could not fail to be stamped as an atheist by the theologians.

BAKRĪ al-, ABŪ ʿUBAYD ʿABD ALLĀH IBN ʿABD al- ʿAZĪZ, Hispano-Arab scholar (†1094), especially in the field of geography but reputed also as a theologian, philologist, botanist and poet. His family, the Bakrids*, ruled for a short time over the town of Huelva and then withdrew to Cordova, or, according to other sources, to Seville, while Abū ʿUbayd was still a boy. He studied with the best-known teachers of his time, spent some years in Almeria and at several others of the many small courts in al-Andalus*, and finally settled in Cordova. Only little is known about his writings on religion, linguistics and botany, except that a book on various plants, whose entries were arranged in alphabetical order, served later authors as a source of reference.
Al-Bakrī's scholarly merit rests on his *Kitāb al-Masālik wa al-Mamālik* (Book of the Roads and Kingdoms) - a title used also by other geographers - to which we owe a great deal of our knowledge of the political, social, economic and cultural life in Arab Spain and North Africa down to about the middle of the XIth century. He himself apparently had never travelled abroad but most conscientiously gathered together earlier as well as contemporary studies and data from the official archives at Cordova, supplementing them by the oral accounts from people personally familiar with the situation across the Mediterranean. Critically comparing, sifting and elaborating his vast source material, he arrived at remarkably precise descriptions embodying a considerable amount of political and social history and ethnography. Only fragments of this voluminous work have come down to us, some of which were translated into French (Descriptions de l'Afrique Septentrional by de Slane, Algiers 1911/13 and re-edited 1960). In the 1930's additional portions were brought to light. They were incorporated in the manuscript of a Hispano-Arab historian who had omitted to mention that they were quotations. They were, however, identified and also translated (Lévi-Provençal, La Péninsule Ibérique au Moyen Age, Leyden 1938). Of lesser importance is al-Bakrī's second geographical work, the *Muʿjam mā Istaʿjam* (edited under the German title 'Das geographische Wörterbuch', Göttingen, 1876), which deals shortly with Arabia in general, describes the pasture grounds of the important tribes and enumerates the places occuring in ancient Arabian poetry.

BAKRIDS, one of the many dynasties of the so-called Party Kings* in al-Andalus*, founded by Abū Zayd Muhammad al-Bakrī who at the time of the dwindling Umayyad power was governor of Huelva. This was at that period a small but flourishing town deriving its wealth from the trade of its port and the metal works on the nearby island of Saltès, where the copper from the neighbouring Rio Tinto deposits of pyrites was extracted. Upon the downfall of the Umayyad caliphate he made himself independent (1012), but his son ʿAbd al-ʿAzīz - the father of the well-known geographer Abū ʿUbayd al-Bakrī* - lost the town (1051) to the ʿAbbādids* of Seville, to whom he soon afterwards also sold the island with his ships and war materials and took residence in Cordova or, as some authors report, in Seville.

BARBARY, probably derived from the Greek and Latin word *barbaria*, i.e. a country inhabited by outlandish people *(barbaroi*, a word presumably imitative of unintelligible speech) and designating a region beyond the hellenic and Roman civilization, later outside the pale of Christianity. In the outgoing Middle Ages, to the world of the Occident 'Barbary' meant the countries of North Africa, and in this sense the term remained in use until well into the XIXth century. European travellers, consular reports and diplomatic documents speak of the 'Barbary coasts', the various 'Barbary Powers', the 'corsairs of Barbary' or of the Sultan of Morocco as the 'King of Barbary', and the English 'Barbary Company' (founded 1585) had the exclusive concession for 'the royal trade' with the Atlantic ports of Morocco. The meaning of the term, however, varied. It may comprise the entire region of the North African coast approximately from Tripoli to the Straits of Gibraltar and even further on along the Atlantic shore as far as the most southern point of Morocco; but it also may be applied either to Morocco alone or only to the Ottoman territories of Algeria and Tunisia. In Arabic writings the word Barbary does not occur, but with similar vagueness were used *Ifrīqīya** (Little Africa) for the region embracing approximately Tripolitania, Tunisia and eastern Algeria, and al-Maghrib* for the areas extending westwards over the greater part of Algeria and Morocco.

BARGHAWĀTA, one of the strong historic Berber confederations of tribes in Morocco, a member of the Masmūda* group, which lived dispersed in numerous villages and small townships in the plains between the Atlantic coast and the slopes of the Middle Atlas. In the second half of the VIIIth century they built up a sort of theocratic state which was to last about four hundred years. Its origin goes back to a revolt (740-742) started conjointly by the Barghawāta, Miknāsa* and Matghāra under the leadership of a warlike Khārijite fanatic, the Berber Maisara al-Matghārī,* a former water-carrier in al-Qayrawān. The rebels conquered Tangier, and in the so-called Battle of the Nobles* *(ghazwat al-ashrāf)* inflicted a heavy defeat upon the caliph's troops, hastily sent over from Spain. The rising was finally suppressed, but the son of one of Maisara's close companions, Sālih Ibn Tarīf (appr. 749-795) came forth as a new prophet. Only vague information has been transmitted on his doctrine which apparently presented a peculiar mixture of orthodox Sunni and heretic Khārijite teaching, strongly tinged with astrology and pagan beliefs. According to Arabic annals it was formulated in a Holy Book in the Berber language - a distortion of the Koran - but no text has come down to us.
Sālih was succeeded by his son Yasaʿ (795-842) who seems to have still hesitated to break openly with orthodox Islam, but his grandson Yunūs (842-885) and Yunūs' nephew, Abū Ghufayl (885-913) firmly implanted Sālih's doctrine in the Barghawāta territory, spread it in the surrounding

areas, and made it the basis of a religio-political organization solid enough to secure for their people a comparatively high degree of prosperity and military efficiency. By the tenacious defence of its realm against all predatory incursions the confederation steadily consolidated its power and increased its prestige far beyond its immediate surroundings. Even Caliph Hakam II of al-Andalus* (961-976) did not hesitate to receive an ambassador of the Barghawāta prince Abū Mansūr ʿIsā, regardless of the scandal which, as recorded by Arab historians, the appearance of the hated heretics provoked at the rigorously orthodox court of Cordova.
Towards the end of the Xth century the relations between the Barghawāta and Umayyad Spain deteriorated: twice within a decade Spanish expeditionary corps were sent against them but both were forced to withdraw, notwithstanding simultaneous incursions into the Barghawāta territory by Fātimid* armies. Soon afterwards, Umayyad allies the Banū Īfran* of the Zanāta* group, steadily permeating into the neighbouring regions, maintained throughout the first half of the XIth century a guerilla warfare of agression against the Barghawāta domain. Although dangerously weakened, the sect was still possessed of enough vitality to survive the assaults of the Almoravids*, whose spiritual leader, ʿAbd Allāh Ibn Yāsīn*, fell in one of these battles (1059). Ninety years later, after a desparate resistance it succumbed under the blows of the conquering Almohads* (1149) and disappeared as a religious group as well as body politic.

BASHKUWĀL IBN, ABŪ al-QĀSIM, a Hispano-Arab biographer (1101-1183) well versed also in the science of *hadīth** (Tradition of the Prophet) and in Andalusian history. He spent the greater part of his life in his home town Cordova and in Seville. Of his numerous works - allegedly some 50 - only two have come down to us, one of which in particular enjoyed great popularity. It is a collection of the life-histories of imams of al-Andalus* *(al-Kitāb al-Sila fī Ta'rīkh A'immat al-Andalus)*, which supplements an earlier work of the same kind by Ibn al-Faradī* (962-1012) and was continued some fifty years later by Ibn al-Abbār* (1199-1260).

BATTLE OF ALARCOS, *al-Arak* in Arabic, in the present-day Spanish province of New Castile, in which the Almohads* under Abū Yūsuf Yaʿqūb* routed (July 10,1195) the army of King Alfonso VIII of Castile, a victory much extolled by contemporary chroniclers and greatly adorned by legend. It could not prevent the final reconquest of al-Andalus* by Spain, but certainly contributed to retard it.

BATTLE of LAS NAVAS DE TOLOSA, called *al-Hisn al-ʿUqāb* (the Eagle's Castle) in Arabic chronicles (the present-day village Miranda del Rey on the southern slopes of the Sierra Morena some 70 miles east of Cordova) in which the Almohad* sovereign, Muhammad al-Nāsir (1199-1213) was severely beaten by the combined forces of the Kings of Aragon, Navarra and Castile, and a contingent of Templars and French knights (July 16, 1212). The coalition was brought about by the ceaseless efforts of the Bishop of Toledo, Rodriguez Jimenez de Rada, who saw it as a sacred duty of entire Christendom to avenge the defeat suffered by King Alfonso VIII of Castile at Alarcos* in 1195 by Muhammad al-Nāsir's predecessor, Abū Yūsuf Yaʿqūb al-Mansūr*, and obtained from Pope Innocent III the proclamation of a Crusade against the Almohads. Although this victory of the Spanish kings did not seriously affect the Almohad position, it certainly acted as a strong incentive in preparing for the Reconquista.

BATTLE OF THE NOBLES, *Ghazwat al-Ashrāf*, the name given by Arab historians to an encounter in the valley of the Sebū river (northern Morocco) in 740 between the troops of the Umayyad Caliph Hishām (724-743) and a coalition of the Berber tribal groups of the Barghawāta*, Matghāra and Miknāsa*, all adherents of the Khārijite heterodoxy and in revolt against Arab domination. The rebels, who under their fanatic 'Caliph' Maisara* of the Matghāra tribe had conquered Tangier, repelled under his successor several government contingents and inflicted a heavy defeat on the Arab troops in the 'Battle of the Nobles'. Although the rebellion was subdued in two heavy battles near al-Qayrawān, the unrest among the Berber population continued.

BATTLE OF THE RIO SALADO, called after a small river on the most southern point of the Iberian Peninsula (November 1340). In the long-drawn out war between King Alfonso XI of Castile and the Marīnid Sultan Abū al-Hasan ʿAlī* of Morocco, a combined Moroccan-Tunisian fleet destroyed the Castilian naval forces in an encounter in the Straits. Thereupon the sultan laid siege to the town of Tarifa, but a hastily assembled army of Castilian and Portuguese troops penetrated by surprise into the town, together with the garrison inflicted a heavy defeat on the Moroccans and captured a considerable booty. The sultan, crossing the Straits at night, escaped with great difficulty and thenceforth gave up further plans of expansion into al-Andalus*.

BATTLE OF THE THREE KINGS, or of the Wādī al-Makhāzin, fought on August 4,1578 near Qasr al-Kabīr in north-western Morocco some 20 miles from the Atlantic coast, by the Saʿdian* Sultan Abū Marwān ʿAbd al-Malik and his brother, the future Sultan Abū al-ʿAbbās Ahmad al-Mansūr, against an invading Portuguese army under the young and adventurous King Sebastian, obsessed by the idea of a conquest of Morocco, and the dethroned Sultan Abū ʿAbd Allāh Muhammad who hoped to regain his throne with Portuguese help. The Moroccans had 20 cannon in the field as compared with 36 of their enemies,' but were superior in number, particularly by their mountain tribes eager to throw the Christian invaders back into the sea. The battle ended with the disastrous defeat of the Portuguese and the death of both Don Sebastian and his Moroccan ally, drowned in the near-by river *Wādī al-Makhāzin*, while Sultan ʿAbd al-Malik, who had been carried seriously ill to the front in a litter, died in the course of the fighting. He was the first Saʿdian sovereign buried in the dynasty's splendid necropolis at Marrakesh. The King's body was taken to Portugal. The corpse of Abū

ʿAbd Allāh Muhammad, cursed as a traitor to the faith, was skinned - hence his surname *al-Maslukh*, the skinned one - and the skin, stuffed with straw, was carried through the streets of the Moroccan towns. King Sebastian's scheme was without doubt chimerical, and the glorification by the Moroccan historiographers of the victory somewhat out of proportion. Yet the fact remains that never before in its history, and rarely later, was Morocco as a result of this military success so highly respected, or did the European courts show a similar interest in maintaining friendly terms with the Sultan - quite aside from the appreciable revenues which the Treasury derived from the ransom for the great number of Portuguese prisoners. For Portugal, however, the Battle of the Three Kings meant far more than a miscarried military adventure: the death in his youth of King Sebastian, still without heir to the throne, brought for 60 years the Kingdom, with all its rich possessions in Africa, Brazil and East Indies, under the Crown of Spain.

BATTLE OF al ZALLĀQA, today Sagrajas in the Spanish province of Estremadura, won (Oct. 23, 1086) by the Almoravid* ruler Yūsuf Ibn Tāshufīn* called to help by some of the so-called Party Kings*, over King Alfonso VI of Castile and Leon, who one year before had occupied Toledo and thus regained for the Christians the first important city in al-Andalus*. The success of al-Zallāqa, due to the superior Almoravid tactics and the use of war-trained camels, was hailed as a compensation for the humilating loss of Toledo and appears much adorned by legend in the annals of the Arab West.

BATTŪTA IBN, MUHAMMAD IBN ʿABD ALLĀH, an Arab globe-trotter and author (1304-1377) of a well-known travel book *(rihla*)*, born in Tangier, whence at the age of twenty he set out on the first of his many long travels. He undertook four times the pilgrimage to the Holy Cities and on these occasions visited Tunisia, Libya, Egypt, Iraq, Persia, Anatolia and the Crimea. One of his journeys, undertaken in the company of a Byzantine princess, led him to Constantinople, whence he proceeded into southern Russia allegedly as far as the Volga, and then into India across Bukhara and Afghanistan. Having held for some time the office of a cadi in Delhi, he left for Ceylon, journeyed to Bengal, the East Indies and further on to China as far as Canton, and returned to Arabia via Sumatra. His last trip took him deep into Africa, to Timbuctoo and across the Sahara. After some 26 years of travelling he settled in his home country Morocco, and had the account of his observations brought into literary form by a secretary of the chancellery of the Marīnid* court in Fez, especially attached to him for this purpose. This work, the *Tuhfat al-Nuzzār fī Gharā'ib al-Amsār wa-ʿAjā'ib al-Asfār*, approximately rendered by 'Gift of the Man who sees rare Sights and does wonderful Travelling', constitutes in many respects, particularly concerning the topographical descriptions and certain economic aspects, a very valuable source of information that supplements the work of his slightly older Italian contemporary Marco Polo (French translation by C. Defrémery and B. R. Sanguinetti, Paris, 1853/58.; English translation by H. A. R. Gibb first of selected sections under the title 'Ibn Battūta, Travels in

Asia and Africa, 1325-1354', London 1929, then followed by the translation of the complete work, Cambridge 1962; Italian translation of selected parts under the title of 'I Viaggi di Ibn Battuta' by F. Gabrieli, Florence 1961).

BAYTĀR IBN al-, ʿABDULLĀH IBN AHMAD, a Hispano-Arab botanist born in Malaga (†1248). In order to study the known plants in their native habitat, and in search for unknown ones, he travelled all over al-Andalus* and North Africa. When he reached Cairo, his reputation was established and resulted in his appointment as 'Chief Herbalist' at the court of the Ayyūbid Sultan al-Mālik al-Kāmil (1218-1238). Subsidised by his patron, he continued his exploration in Syria and Anatolia, and finally settled in Damascus where he stayed until his death. Ibn al-Baytār left two main works. One, the *Jāmiʿ fī al-Adwiya al-Mufrada* (Collection of simple Drugs, generally known under its Latin title 'Simplicia') is an alphabethical compilation of some 1400 'simple remedies' - as opposed to 'compound remedies' - extracted from animal, mineral and vegetable substances, following old Greek, Arabic and his own prescriptions. The second, *al- Mughni fi al-Adwiya al-Mufrada*, a Materia Medica (pharmacological treatise) contains a classification of drugs arranged according to the diseases against which they were applied. The Latin version of the 'Simplicia' remained in use at the European medical schools until the middle of the XVIIIth century (French translation under the title of 'Traité des simples remèdes par Ibn al Beïthar' by L. Leclerc, Paris 1877).

BERBERS, the great NorthAfrican stock known already to the Phoenicians at the end of the second millenium. The name (Arabic *barābir* or *barābira*, sing. *barbarī)* presumably stems from the Greek word *barbaroi*, latinized *barbari*, which denoted people neither Greek nor Roman, and hence of outlandisch manners. The Berbers themselves generally use the individual tribal names, and only seldom the collective designation *Imazighen*, sing. *Amazigh*, i.e. free men. Their origin, as well as their ethnical and language relationship with any other Mediterranean or African race, present or extinct, is still a matter of conjecture. There exist no monuments of art or in writing which might supply a clue in the search for their early history. The first known Berber authors belong to the Roman and Byzantine cultural spheres, and wrote in Latin and Greek. Thenceforth the literary language of the intellectual groups was Arabic. The scarce prose literature in Berber language is of comparatively recent date: some short religious works in Arabic script and inspired by Arabic texts; a few secular books of didactic character are results of the encouragement by European scholars. Richer is the flow of folklore, mainly transmitted by the women, and of popular poetry, some of which has been collected by occidental ethnologists, such as the songs accompanying the village dances or the wailings for the dead. There still wander about some professional poets singing of love and the feats of war or of the high mind of a generous patron, but their creations leave no lasting impression on the memory of their audience.
According to Arab historians, the Berber people were divided long

before the Arab conquest into two groups of families of tribes, the Butr and Barāni. At an early date some of the Butr moved from the steppes and the highlands between the Nile and southern Tunisia into the Jabal Nafūsa in Tripolitania and into Algeria, where they settled in the regions of Tiaret and Tlemcen, while others continued into Morocco, spread in the country of the Mulūya and Sabū rivers and on the fringe of the Sahara.

Some of the Barāni wandered from the Aurès mountains (in the present-day department of Constantine) and the Kabylia*, into the area of Oran and further on into central Morocco and parts of the Rif. It remains doubtful how far, if at all, the different families of tribes were conscious of their being a part of either one of the two groups unless they might have felt the inveterate enmities opposing some of them to others as the heritage of a dark past. Within each one of them, however, the feeling of belonging together formed a solid moral tie notwithstanding their later separation and dispersal.

Recorded Berber history begins in the VIIIth century with the gradual incorporation of North Africa into the caliphate, but for a long time legend and picturesque details filled the gaps in the chroniclers' knowledge of the actual events and situations. Yet even in this vague framework three great tribal families and their significance for the coming military, political and social evolution are clearly discernible: the Masmūda*, the most numerous of them, scattered in many prosperous villages and small towns; the Sanhāja*, about one third of the total population, nomads in the Sahara, peasants in the valleys and on the mountain slopes, and sheep breeders in the hill-lands; and the Zanāta*, the most ramified of the three, famous horsemen, pushing steadily from the fringe of the desert westwards through the plains to the Atlantic coast.

Their attitude towards the Arab advance was twofold. Berber warriors fought on the side of the Arabs on their march through North Africa against the Byzantine forces. Tarīf and his 400 men, the first to cross the Straits into Spain, were Berbers; so were Tāriq Ibn Ziyād and his troop of 12.000 who took the Visigoth capital Toledo; the main body of the army which conquered most of the Iberian Peninsula and pushed deep into France consisted of Berber contingents; and in a continuous current Berber families and clans of practically every tribe followed the army and settled in al-Andalus*, the new province of the Arab caliphate. At the same time, in other parts, the Arabs soon were confronted with an obstinate resistance roused by misadministration, high taxation, and, in general, their haughty behaviour. The initial stages are reflected in the half-legendary stories about the revolts of the Kāhina* and of Kusaila*, cases still of minor import. More dangerous was the insurrection of a large tribal confederation under Maisara al-Matghārī*, which in the last days of the Umayyad caliphs led to the defection of the whole Berber country. For a few years the ʿAbbāsid Caliph al-Mansūr forced some of it back into obedience, but the separation from the Arab East was definitively sealed, when the Idrīsids* (788-974) and Aghlabids* (800-909) established the first more or less firmly structured independent Berber states.

Inseparably connected with, and often even overshadowing, the political character of this opposition, is its religious aspect in the form of mass-adherence to the Khārijite doctrine. This heresy, revolutionary from the point of view of orthodox sunnism on which the caliphate rested, was nearing its decline in the eastern provinces of the Arab Empire when missionaries of both its main sub-sects, the Ibādīya and the Sufrīya, found a fruitful field among all malcontents in the West. The rapidly growing number of their Berber proselytes came from among early converts to Islam but still more from pagan tribes and the Christian townspeople. The first to bind together Khārijite communities in a rudimentary body politic was Abū al-Khattāb who ruled as Imam (758-761) over a territory covering Tripolitania, Tunisia and the eastern half of Algeria. It needed a forceful military expedition to break his power, but similar heterodox Berber theocracies were built up in the VIIIth century by the Rustumids* in Tāhart (Tiaret); the Banū Midrar in Sijilmāsa extending eastwards into the Jabal Nafūsa in Tripolitania; by Abū Qurra* in Agadir (near present-day Tlemcen), by the Barghawāta* confederation on the Atlantic coast; and a number of half-secular, half-spiritual city republics. The revolt at the end of the Xth century of the fanatic Abū Yazīd*, directed against the nascent Fātimid régime, was the last flare-up of militant Khārijism. Upon the whole, however, its driving power abated with the disappearance of the political incentive. At the time of the Sanhāja Almoravid* dynasty, rigorous sunnism had for ever replaced Khārijism in Morocco and Algeria, except for some clusters which continued here and there. In Tunisia Ibādite islets maintained themselves longer in cohabitation with the sunnite majority, especially among the Berber Jarāba in Jerba (the island on the Gulf of Gabès) notwithstanding the efforts of some Hafsid* sultans who tried to lead them to orthodoxy by arranging dogmatic discussions between their religious chiefs *(ʿazziben)* and theologians of high repute. Khārijite Berber groups have survived in Tripolitania in the Jabal Nafūsa; in Tunisia on the island of Jerba and in the oases of the Jarīd; and in southern Algeria in the Wādī M'Zab, where they constitute the Mozabite* community. All together they number at the utmost some 125.000 believers.

Longer than to the temporal authority of the Arab caliphate and to its official version of Islam, the Berbers remained refractory to the penetration of its language. Points of a limited radiation of Arabic appeared first in Tunisia, where al-Qayrawān was the seat of the caliph's provincial administrator; then in Morocco, where Idrīs II* (804-828) transformed his father's half-rural residence of Madīnat Fās into a town modelled on Arabic patterns, and populated it with Arabs or arabized Berbers from al-Qayrawān. After the 'Revolt of the Suburb'* in Cordova, refugees from al-Andalus, settled also in and around Meknès and Ceuta and in a few villages on the coast, while in the flourishing market-town of Sijilmāsa there grew up a colony of Arab traders. Borne by the social and commercial relations of the immigrants with the Andalusian home-country, Arabic took its way slowly but continuously throughout the IXth and Xth centuries into most of the towns of northern Morocco. It acquired a place of prominence as the exclusive vehicle of learning in al-Qayrawān and Fez, which developed into the two outstanding centres of Islamic studies in North Africa. These infiltrations were purposefully stimulated into a vigorous inflow of Arabic literary and scientific thought, art and mode of living in the Almoravid (1061-1147) and Almohad* (1132-1269) era, which saw Arab Spain and, for a time, the entire Berber country, bound together in one single Berber empire whose rulers and high dignitaries surrounded themselves with men of letters, poets, jurists and philosophers from al-Andalus, and had their palaces and mosques built and decorated by Andalusian architects and craftsmen.

The process of arabization, which until then had been confined to a social and intellectual élite, was carried into wide strata of the population under the impulse of two historic events, unrelated to one another, but of complementary effects. One was the Bedouin invasion which at the end of the XIth century began to sweep wave after wave, the Banū Hilāl*, Sulaym* and Maʿqil* and affiliated Arab tribes from Egypt over the Libyan desert and the Cyrenaica into Tripolitania, the plains of Tunisia and the Algerian highland. They moved further on into Morocco, some of them driven by newcomers, others under the pressure of the Almohad government which hoped thus to neutralize certain unruly Berber elements. Pushing in between the Berber tribes and villages everywhere except in the mountains, at first plundering and devastating, but as time went on finding the ways to peaceful arrangements, most of them turned from their nomadic to a semi-sedentary and often gradually to a wholly sedentary mode of life. They traded with townspeople, their warriors served in the army, their chieftains held government offices, and married their daughters to the Berber Marīnid*, Hafsid* and 'Abd al-Wādid* sultans and royal princes. Thus, through an ever denser network of major or minor cells, Arabic steadily pervaded the Berber texture.

It was not only the language enjoying the prestige of both the Koran and the power of the irresistible invader which the Berber peasant and shepherd began to use. Needing in the various difficulties of everyday-life the support of the influential Arab clan or tribe in his region, he found the way of securing it by seeking acceptance into their community. To become one of them he took on an Arabic name, on the force of which his children or grand-children easily discovered, and soon also firmly believed in an Arab lineage which oral tradition with all its genealogical details corroborated for later generations. Yet this assimilation did not remain one-sided. Under the influence of the intimate contacts in every phase of their spiritual, economic and political life, Berber and Arab groups transmitted to each other enough of the complex tissue of their habits, their concepts of ethics and law, their attitudes and behaviour, to bring forth a type of civilization marked by its own proper characteristics.

The conquest, step by step, of al-Andalus by the Christian Powers - the 'Reconquista' - was the second historic event in the wake of which Arabic speech, mode of living and ways of thinking took their way into Berber society. Around the XIVth century more and more Moslems - Arabs of pure blood, arabized Berber and Mozarabs* (descendants of the native Visigothic and Celtic population) - began to seek new homes in the Berber sultanates of the Marīnids in Morocco, the ʿAbd al-Wādids in Tlemcen and the Hafsids in Tunisia. During the following two-hundred years this movement gradually gained momentum as ever larger territories changed from Moslem to Spanish sovereignty, especially after the fall of the last Arab state in the Iberian peninsula, the emirate of Granada (1492), and subsequently to the repression of the Morisco revolts in the XVIth century. The expulsion between 1609 and 1614 of all remaining Moslems who refused conversion, turned the steady current of voluntary emigration into a torrent of some 300.000 refugees. These were mainly townspeople of a variety of occupations, skills and professions - craftsmen and artisans, merchants, men of religion, clerks, scholars with their circles of disciples. They settled in and around the towns on or near the coast in Morocco, Algeria and Tunisia, built their houses and quarters in Andalusian style, exercised their trade, served in the government's offices, acquired land in the surroundings, and for quite a time continued to live a life of their own. Yet as the years went by, the interpenetration of Berber and Arab elements took place in the urban atmosphere as it had done in the rural environment, but with a distinct predominance of the Arabic forms of thought, artistic expression and scholarly learning, favoured by the concentration of commercial, political and scholarly activities.

This century-long process made Arabic the mother-tongue of today for roughly two thirds of the people in the North African countries, with dialects still reflecting its principal stages: the period of the first Arab conquerors; the invasion of the Banū Hilāl and their sister tribes; and the influx of the Moriscos. The Berber language *(tamasight)* is still spoken by altogether some seven to eight million people: some 40 to 45 percent of the population of Morocco - in the Rif, in the Atlas and in the Sūs, in the oases of the Figwig and the Tāfīlālt, in the valley of the Dadès; by about one third of the Algerians - in the Kabylia, in the Aurès, in the mountain region south of Blida and on the high plateaux of the Algero-Moroccan border and by the small community of the Mozabites*; by about one eight of the people of Libya - in the mountaneous country of Biskra, in the Jabal Nafūsa and in some of the oases; and by about one per cent of the Tunisians - in a few villages on the island of Jerba and the near-by coastal areas and where the Jabal Nafūsa reaches from Libya into Tunisia; and thereto will have to be added the Touareg in the Algerian Sahara and Mauretania.

The age-old social and economic order with its judicial and administrative arrangements has lived on, although with minor local variations, everywhere within this wide-spread Berber society. Its cell is the 'joint family' - the closely knit natural collectivity of several generations related by blood ties from the paternal side under the patriarchal authority of the oldest male member. Its living quarters are a structural whole built around a common courtyard with a single entrance and one common well, which is held in undivided ownership. So are virtually the arable land, orchards and herds of animals, of which the individual small families of the group are assigned portions for inalienable use. They are transmissible by inheritance, but in the male line only. While the exclusion of women, based on the concept of a group economy of

which females do not partake, conflicts with the Koranic as well as the state legislation in force, practice has developed various kinds of compromise. Among the nomads, the 'joint family' houses are replaced by clusters of tents set up at an appropriate distance from one another. Those of the joint families which trace their descent to a - frequently imaginary - common ancestor constitute a sort of administrative and political unit, the *ighs* (called *kharrūba* in Kabylia). Their organ is the assembly of the family heads *(jamāʿa)* under the guidance of an elected *amghar* (sometimes called *muqaddam*). It deliberates, often very circumstantially, and by common consent decides, on subjects of community interest such as the maintainance of the collective granary *(agadir)*, or questions connected with the pasture grounds, water rights or relations with the government authorities. To some extent it is also concerned with judicial issues. In accordance with customary law *(izref, ittifāqāt)* which is essentially based on the principle that private justice lies in the hands of the family, it functions in criminal as well as in civil matters much rather as a council of arbitration than as a court. Transmitted only by word of mouth, customary law varies greatly from region to region, but owing to the efforts of some European ethnologists a few codifications were recently compiled and appeared also in print. For political reasons the régime of the French Protectorate* in Morocco accorded in 1930 official recognition to this Berber popular law and its dispensation by tribal courts, but nation-wide opposition soon again enforced the revocation of this so-called Berber Edict* as far as penal jurisdiction was concerned. Since the achievement of independence, the legal process has passed into the competency of a regular judicial apparatus.
The units on the next higher levels, often also believing in a common, rather legendary ancestry, are the village, or among the nomads and semi-nomads the *dūwār* (in French texts spelt 'douar'*), which consist, depending upon their size, of two or more *ighs*; and, made up of several villages, the tribe *(taqbilt)*. Both, village and tribe, have each its own *amghar* or *muqaddam* and its own *jamʿa* constituted by the delegates of the lower-grade assemblies. Yet, besides these more formal and limited gatherings, all the village people meet, discuss their affairs and thus build up public opinion at the tribe's weekly market *(sūq)* held as a rule at a centrally situated locality on a wide, open square with a row of booths and store-rooms along its sides. In former times a number of tribes, members of the same great tribal family, occasionally combined under a common elected chief in a confederation for the pursuit of special, political and warlike enterprises directed against other tribal associations or the established government. If such a chieftain commanded sufficient power, he often succeeded in establishing a more or less independent territorial sovereignty whose duration, in some cases throughout several generations, depended upon the cohesion of the confederation. Such tribal confederations were at the origin of two of the Berber ruling families in Morocco, the Marīnids and the Wattāsids, and of the ʿAbd al-Wādids in Tlemcen. In a skilful combination with elements of a religious character they served two other Berber dynasties, the Almoravids and the Almohads, to forge the largest empires of their time. Quite another type of association, also temporary, which binds

together different villages or even parts of them is the so-called *suff*; or a number of tribes or tribal groups, often widely dispersed, is the so-called *leff** concluded for a variety of purposes, but seldom solidly enough to resist internal rivalries which in the long run do not fail to arise. While the tribal confederation has by now lost all significance except for the nomads as a means of regulating the use of the pasture grounds, the *leff* is still an institution very much alive and may have been of considerable importance in the organization and the conduct of the Algerian Revolution*.

BERBER EDICT, *al-Ẓahīr* al-Barbarī*, a much discussed decree innovating the system of jurisdiction in Morocco, promulgated by the young Sultan Muhammed V* on March 16, 1930 upon the proposition of the French Resident-General - a proposition which according to the terms of the Protectorate* was not to be disregarded. It instituted for the Berber communities the administration of justice according to their tribal customary law by their local assembly *(jamāʿa)*, as opposed to Koranic law *(sharīʿa)*, in all matters of personal status, inheritance and civil or commercial litigation, and establishing the competency of French jurisdiction in criminal cases. Allegedly intended to protect and preserve Berber customs and traditions it was in fact an instrument of Protectorate policy, designed to counterbalance the refractory attitude of Arab urban society by exploiting the hereditary individualistic inclinations of the Berber tribal world, and did not escape the severe criticism of political and also academic groups in France. In Morocco, it evoked immediate and sharp reaction by the men of religion as an act which excluded Moslems from the Law of God such as it was laid down in the Koran, but also deep indignation among large sections of the bourgeois classes of various cultural, educational and ideological shades. They considered it a decidedly retrograde measure which institutionalized practices of a time-worn civilization; a condemnable step along the lines of the colonial 'divide and rule' maxim; or a phase in a planful process of 'de-islamisation' and conversion to Christianity, especially since it coincided with the increased missionary activities of French Catholic orders, and with the efforts of some French officials to introduce converts as secretaries into the *jamʿa*.
Violent attacks were launched on two planes: in the press, especially in the two Moroccan periodicals in French language, political papers in Arabic being prohibited at that time- '*Al-Maghrib*', published in Paris, and 'L'Action du Peuple', in Morocco; and in the mosques, mainly in Fez, Rabat and Salé. There followed turbulent street manifestations which were rigorously suppressed by the police. A delegation of '*ulamā*', notables, men of letters, artisans and farmers submitted to the sultan a memorandum demanding the abrogation of the edict; the re-establishment of the unified judicial system; the stopping of the missionary activities; and the institution of Arabic as the official language and the general language of education. The campaign found a loud echo almost everywhere in Moslem lands, where it was voiced in protests transmitted to the great international organizations, and by committees for the defence of the Moroccan Moslems, which were set up in a number of European,

African and Asian cities. In 1934 another *zahīr* partly re-established the competency of the *sharīʿa* and vested again the pashas and caids* of the Berber districts with penal jurisdiction in minor offences, while the High Sharīfian Court in Rabat was to administer justice in more serious cases and to hear appeals against the sentences of those officials. Otherwise the Berber Edict remained in force until it was repealed by the Moroccan government after the achievement of independence in the course of the re-organization and modernization of the judicial system inherited from the Protectorate. Its historic significance, however, was that it released in widely different strata of the population currents of a resistance against the French régime, out of which emerged the first Moroccan political party, the *Kutla al-ʿAmal al-Maghribī** and with it Moroccan nationalism.

BEY, a title which came into use in Algeria and Tunisia under the Turkish régime towards the middle or end of the XVIth century for certain high government officers invested with military and administrative powers in a particular territory *(beylik)* and especially responsible for the collection of taxes. The majority made their way up from the ranks of the slave soldiery recruited from among Christian prisoners who had been captured by pirates, embraced Islam, were given a military training and assumed Turkish names.
In Algeria, a bey was at the head of each of the three territories of Constantine, Titteri (or Médéa) and Oran, into which the administration of the Regency was divided. They were subordinate to the chief-bey *(beylerbey* or *beglerbegi)* who resided in the separate district of Algiers as the representative of the Ottoman government. Between 1587 and 1671 the beylerbeys were replaced first by governors with the title of pasha appointed for three years, then by aghas. From 1671 onwards the holder of the highest executive office bore the title of dey*.
In Tunisia, the number of beys was greater, and the *beylik* comprised mainly the tribal areas. Some beys ascended to high functions at the court of the Dey* - the title of the Tunisian rulers from 1590 to 1640 - and in the central administration, so that at the beginning of the XVIIth century one of them, Murād, formerly Moratto from Corsica, was able to acquire considerable power as the Dey's chief lieutenant, and after the latter's death took the reins of government openly into his hands. He became the founder of the reigning line of the Murādid Beys*. Thenceforth the title of Bey was the prerogative of the Tunisian sovereign while the term '*beylik*' remained synonymous with 'state' or 'regency' until the end of the French Protectorate* (March 20, 1956). The last Bey of Tunisia, Sīdī Lamine *(al-Amīn)* Bey was deposed in July 1957 when the Tunisian Constituent Assembly abolished the monarchy and proclaimed the Republic.

BILĀD al-MAKHZAN, Morrocan term (coll. *bled el-maghzen)* denoting the territory *(bilād* pl. of *balad*, tract of land, district) controlled by government authority *(makhzan,**)*, as opposed to *bilād al-sība*, the territory of dissidence. The extent of the areas where an orderly administration functioned, where the regular collection of taxes could be secured and public law enforced, varied in the course of history according to the amount of power which the central government commanded and which, on the other hand, depended essentially upon the personality of the - theoretically - absolute monarch. In general, these areas comprised all the plains including the region from Fez eastwards to Taza; the hillsides of the Rif; the Tāfīlālt; the accesible sections of the Atlas; and, although only intermittently, most of the oases on the fringe of the desert. It was primarily the ruler's skill in winning and maintaining the allegiance of the religious and political power groups in the towns and among the tribes; and in bringing his prestige as the spiritual head of the community into play in the domain of the secular government, that determined the expanse of territory within which, and the degree to which, the State was able to impose obedience and discipline.

Where, however, the insufficiency, or more often than not, the lack of communication made it practically impossible for the central authority to assert itself, as well as for the people to conceive a solidarity reaching beyond the seclusion of their mountain valleys or the vastness of the desert, there, in the *bilād al-sība,* continued the closely circumscribed local loyalties to clan and tribe, rooted in age-old customs and usages, and leaving no room for the recognition of any outside worldly power whatsoever. Yet just as little as the *bilād al-makhzan* could be considered a solid and durably structured entity, so was the *bilād al-sība* by no means to be regarded as being in a state of constant revolt against the institutional government. The attitude of the multifarious larger or smaller units into which this society was split, was much rather one of indifference, so long as from the other side of the extremely fluid borderlines no attempt was made at interfering with their affairs and forcing them into a system of authoritative administration. Yet also in the *bilād al-sība* the sultan's spiritual authority was never questioned.

This duality is currently explained by the inveterate weakness of the central government, its failure to open up the mountain districts by adequate roads, and its general inability to police the refractory tribal society. Recently, however, a different interpretation has been advanced from the Moroccan side, which sees in it an illustration of what may be called a consent theory. According to this conception, the sovereign power rests with the people who may or may not consent to its partial or entire delegation. In the *bilād al-makhzan* this consent was given without restriction, whereas in the *bilād al-sība* it was refused with regard to the secular power, and the recognition of this refusal implied ipso facto the recognition of the status of 'dissidence'. With the termination of the régime of the French Protectorate* and the beginning of the new era of Morocco's full independence, the *bilād al-makhzan* completely absorbed, according to this conception, the *bilād al-sība.*

BILĀD al-SĪBĀ' see BILĀD al-MAKHZAN.

BITRŪJĪ al-, NŪR al-DĪN ABŪ ISHĀQ, a Hispano-Arab astronomer (†appr. 1204) called Alpetragius by the medieval authors of the Occident. His best-known book, the *Kitāb al-Hay'a* on the movements of the planets, based on Aristotelian teaching, was considered at its time a complete innovation. A Latin translation by Michael Scot in Toledo, 1217 was followed by a Hebrew version, which in the XVIth century served as the basis for a second translation into Latin.

BLOC OF MOROCCAN ACTION, *Kutla al-ʿAmal al-Maghribī* (in French texts referred to as 'Comité d'Action Marocaine'), the earliest political party in Morocco, established in December 1934 after four years of informal existence as a loose group in whose midst the different, often contradictory currents then moving educated youth were represented: Islamic traditionalism and various trends of religious modernism; pan-Arabism of different shades; and socio-political ideologies ranging from conservatism to a moderate socialism. Their common platform was the resistance against the encroachment of the French Protectorate* authorities upon Moroccan national life, and the claims, still rather inarticulate, for more democratic freedom within the framework of the Protectorate, and in particular for educational reforms and political equality between Moroccans and Frenchmen on Moroccan soil. The leading spirits were young men most of whom subsequently were to play prominent rôles in Moroccan public life, such as Muhammad al-Wazzānī, ʿAllāl al-Fāsī, Muhammad al-Makkī al-Nāzirī, Muhammad al-Fāsī, Ahmad Balafrej (Bla Freej), ʿUmar ʿAbd al-Jalīl and Muhammad Lyazidi (al-Yazīdī).
They were actively encouraged by a circle of French left-wing politicians and journalists voicing their sympathies in a periodical under the title *al-Maghrib* (first issue Paris May 1933) edited by a grandson of Karl Marx with French and Moroccan contributors. Its distribution in Morocco was prohibited a year afterwards, but it was replaced (1936) by a news bulletin, *al-Mukhbir al-Maghribī* (The Moroccan Informer), intended for a more popular type of readers without finding, however, the hoped for resonance. In the meantime al-Wazzānī had started a periodical of his own, *al-ʿAmal al-Shaʿb* with the French subtitle 'L'Action du Peuple' (first issue Fez, August 1933), also in French, since political papers in Arabic were permitted only from 1937 onwards. It, too, was suspended by the Protectorate authorities after one year of existence and re-appeared only in April 1937 as 'Hebdomadaire de l'Action Nationale Marocaine', again under al-Wazzānī's direction.
Gradually also a propaganda apparatus was set in motion, built upon the mass distribution of popular pamphlets, patriotic slogans and songs which were taught to youth, and public lectures held mainly by ʿAllāl al-Fāsī at the Qarawīyīn* Mosque at Fez and later also in Tangier, Tetuan and Paris, where Muhammad al-Fāsī and Ahmad Balafrej were the driving forces of the North African Moslem Students' Association. Towards the end of 1934 ten members of the group, who became known as the 'Comité d'Action Marocaine', set about the formulation of a regular party program, the so-called 'Demands of the Moroccan people' *(Matālib al-Shaʿb al-Maghribī)* and presented a 'Plan of Reforms' to the Sultan, the Resident General and the French Prime Minister (published in Arabic, Cairo Sept. 1934, and in French, Paris, November 1934). It enumerated in 15 sections a series of political, administrative, economic and social measures, designed to lead to a greater degree of autonomy

but respecting the institution of the Protectorate. It remained unanswered, and in October 1936 the party submitted a second list of reforms, the so-called 'Urgent Reforms'. No practical results, however, were achieved, except, perhaps, that three new publications could make their appearance in 1937: two weeklies in Rabat, '*al-Atlas*', the first periodical permitted in Arabic, and 'L'Action Populaire'; and a monthly in Paris, 'La Voix du Maroc', catering mainly for readers among the Moroccan workers in France.

When the party's voice became increasingly louder and its resonance grew stronger, the authorities of the Protectorate, under pretext of certain formal irregularities declared it illegal and closed its offices (March 1937). But by then its organization was solid enough to remain unimpaired, and also its press continued to appear. But fissures in the leading set, noticeable already for quite some time, were now coming to light with acuteness. Arising mainly from differences of temper and divergencies of opinion - divergencies not as to fundamental aims but as to methods and means to be used - they caused al-Wazzānī to organize a new party, the 'People's Movement' *(al-Haraka al-Qawmīya)*, whose principal centre was in Casablanca, while ʿAllāl al-Fāsī with Muhammad Lyazidi, Ahmad Balafrej and ʿUmar ʿAbd al-Jalīl rallied most of the former members of the *Kutla* in the 'National Party for the Realization of the Demands' *(al-Hizb al-Watanī li Tahqiqi al-Matālib)*. In the wake of wide-spread disturbances in the French zone (October 1937), both parties were dissolved and their publications suspended, while ʿAllāl al-Fāsī and al-Wazzānī were exiled, the former to Gabon, the latter into the Sahara, where they had to remain until 1946. Alhmad Balafrej escaped into the international zone of Tangier and returned to Rabat early 1943. A few months later he founded the *Istiqlāl** which was to grow into Morocco's most influential political party.

BUĀKHAR see ʿABĪD al-BUKHĀRĪ

BŪ HMĀRA, colloquially for Abū Himāra, meaning the man on the she-ass, the commonly used nickname of Jilālī Ibn Idrīs al-Zarhūnī, a Moroccan revolutionary leader (1865-1909), who during seven years kept in uproar the entire north-eastern section of the country. He was born in the Zarhūn mountains north of Meknès among a tribal population very much given to primitive mystical beliefs. He accomplished some studies in engineering, held for a time an office in the public administration, but, implicated in an intrigue, was sentenced to two years' imprisonment. After his release, he travelled about for a while in Algeria and Tunisia, then went to stay with the Ghiyāta tribe in the area of Taza. Cleverly playing upon the credulity of his hosts all sorts of tricks, he was soon regarded with awe as one gifted with miracle-working faculties, and next as the elder brother of the reigning Sultan ʿAbd al-ʿAzīz (1894-1909), Mūlāy Muhammad who had been disinherited by his father because of his disorderly conduct and lived in Meknès in strict seclusion. His influence spread, and in the atmosphere of general dissatisfaction at the tax reforms introduced by ʿAbd al-ʿAzīz, he had himself proclaimed sultan by all the tribes in the region (1902) an event not without precedence in Moroccan history. At the head of the Ghiyāta warriors he occupied Taza, while others seized the fortress at Sefrou and raided Meknès. Within a few months he had all eastern Morocco on his side, was master of Oujda, the principal town of the area, twice beat the government's troops and prepared to march against the capital Fez. Although he was repelled, wounded in the fighting and temporarily had to evacuate Taza, he reorganized his forces, made contacts with other seditious movements that had their seats in Tangier and in Oran, and the struggle dragged on with occasional negotiations for a compromise. Again defeated, he found refuge in Melilla, discussed with the Spanish authorities the grant of a concession for the exploitation of the near-by iron-and lead-ore deposits - today San Juan de las Minas of the Compagnie des Mines du Rif with a yearly production of about one million tons - but called back by his followers, who meanwhile had gathered new strength, he re-occupied Taza and again stood menacingly near Fez (June 1908). A few months later, however, he was decisively beaten in several combined French and Moroccan actions, was taken prisoner, sent to Fez in a cage and executed. His house in Taza is still standing and shown as an attraction to tourists.

C

CARPETS. Among the various branches of handicraft*, all of them once highly prosperous and flourishing but in the course of the last hundred years gliding deeper into obviously irreversible decadence under the pressure of machine-made products, carpet weaving and knotting have continued in widely spread, undiminished activities, One type, which has its seat in the towns, was introduced around the end of the XVIIth century by the Turks from Anatolia into Tunisia and Algeria whence it found its way into Morocco. It still keeps going quite a number of hand-looms in and around Constantine, Tunis and Rabat, whose products once ranged among the valuable gifts of honour offered by the Sultans of Morocco to kings and ministers, and today holds in all three countries a minor yet not negligeable rank on the list of their exports. Of an entirely different kind are the so-called Berber rugs, at home since time immemorial in the mountain villages and in the Bedouin camps, made from the wool of their sheep. They serve as separating curtains in the tent, take the place of a bed, and on festive occasions are hung on the walls. The taste and traditions of each region or tribe have created patterns of seemingly endless combinations of larger and smaller stripes and rhomb-shaped facets, curiously resembling those of Roman and Byzantine mosaics, and equally varied assortments of vivid reds, blues, yellows, greens and black, or all white with a loose borderline or a small center design. The natural dyes extracted from roots, bark, flowers and fruits are more and more giving way to imported chemical colourings, but the inherited technique has remained unchanged, and the age-old interpretations or beliefs attached by the people to the meaning of the patterns are still alive. A third group is that of the so-called *hanbels*, a thinner and lighter yet very strong fabric without knots, not of such elaborate workmanship as the carpets, but just as diversified and used for the same purposes.

CAÏD see QĀ'ID

C.C.E. see COMMITTEE OF COORDINATION AND EXECUTION

C.N.R.A. see NATIONAL COUNCIL OF THE ALGERIAN REVOLUTION

COMITE D'ACTION MAROCAINE see BLOC OF MOROCCAN ACTION

COMITE DE COORDINATION ET D'EXECUTION see COMMITTEE OF COORDINATION AND EXECUTION

COMITE REVOLUTIONNAIRE POUR L'UNITE ET L'ACTION see REVOLUTIONARY COMMITTEE FOR UNITY AND ACTION

COMMITTEE OF COORDINATION AND EXECUTION, commonly referred to as C.C.E., the initials of its designation in French (Comité de coordination et d'exécution), an organization of the Algerian Revolution*, created by the Summan Valley Congress* in August 1956. Appointed by, and responsible to, the National Council of the Algerian Revolution (C.N.R.A.)* established on the same occasion, the C.C.E. consisted, at the time of its constitution, of five members: the commanders of the Oranian, North-Constantine and Kabyle wilayas, Larbi (al-ʿArabī) Muhammadī, soon afterwards captured and killed after torture; Yūsuf Zighūt, and Belkacem Krim (Karīm Bilqāsim); the Algerian trade-union leader Ayssat Idir, then in prison and soon to die of the wounds inflicted, it is said, in the course of his interrogation; and the impetuously radical Kabyle partisan chief Ramdān Abbān. The C.C.E. was invested with military and political competencies, being put in charge of the supreme command in the field, as well as of the control over the External Delegation*. It established its seat in the heart of the city of Algiers which for the following twelve months was to be the stage of the most reckless terrorism and a no less violent repression by the French paratroop regiments. When in summer 1957 it had become obvious that the revolutionaries had lost the 'battle of Algiers' and that the struggle would go on still for a long time, the C.N.R.A., at a meeting in Cairo, reorganized the C.C.E. which in the meantime had moved to Tunis. By its departmental structure and bureaucratic machinery but especially by the prestige enjoyed by the men of whom this new C.C.E. consisted, it resembled already very closely the apparatus of a government in exile which, in fact, it was shortly to become. It comprised five of the 'historical chiefs' of the revolution: Ahmad Ben Bella (Ibn Ballā), Husain Ait Ahmad, Muhammad Būdiaf, Muhammad Khidr and Rabah Bitat - all at that time in French prisons; three members of the External Delegation: ʿAbd al-Hamīd Mahrī, its representative in Damascus; Farhat Abbas (Farhāt ʿĀbbas), the head of the Democratic Union of the Algerian Manifesto* (U.D.M.A.), and Muhammad Lamīn (al-ʿAmīn) Dabbaghin, one of the first and most prominent Kabyle members of the one-time Algerian People's Party* (P.P.A.); then three military commanders: ʿAbd al-Hāfiz Būssuf who was among the first to join the Revolutionary Committee of Unity and Action* (C.R.U.A.); Mahmūd Sharīf a former officer in the French army; and Lakhdar (al-Akhdar) Ben Tubbal, the commander of the North-Constantine wilaya; furthermore three members of the original Committee: Belkacem Krim and ʿUmar Amrān, both of whom had played first-rank parts in the Kabylia section of the Organisation Secrète* (O.S.); and Ramdān Abbān, who soon lost his life, allegedly seriously wounded in battle.
In September 1958 the C.C.E. was transformed into the Provisional Government of the Algerian Republic* (G.P.R.A.).

COMMON FRONT FOR THE DEFENCE OF, AND RESPECT FOR LIBERTY, Front Algérien pour la défence et le respect de la liberté, a loose association formed in August 1951 by three Algerian nationalist groups: the Movement for the Triumph of Democratic Liberties* (M.T.L.D.), the Democratic Union of the Algerian Manifesto* (U.D.M.A.), the Association of the Algerian ʿUlamā'*. They were joined by the Algerian Communist Party (P.C.A.), and by three Frenchmen in sympathy with Algerian nationalism. The general purpose of the Front was to give greater resonance to the claim of independence, and in particular to demand the release of the numerous political prisoners, the assurance of orderly elections, and the freedom of opinion of the press and of association. The significance of this somewhat disparate alliance lies not in its achievement, which was practically nil, but in the fact that it was the first step towards combined action for a common ideal, which a few years later led to the establishment of the revolutionary National Liberation Front* (F.L.N.).

CONSEIL NATIONAL DE LA REVOLUTION ALGERIENNE see NATIONAL COUNCIL OF THE ALGERIAN REVOLUTION

C.R.U.A. see REVOLUTIONARY COMMITTEE FOR UNITY AND ACTION

CRETE. In 827 a number of Andalusian refugees from Cordova, estimated at some 15.000 people, who in the troubled times of the Revolt of the Suburb* (814 or 818) had gained possession of Alexandria and established there a sort of republic, were forced out of the city and set sail for Crete. They succeeded in occupying the island which then was a part of the Byzantine empire. Thenceforth an Andalusian dynasty of emirs, founded by Abū Hafs ʿUmar al-Ballūtī, ruled in Crete for more than a century and a half. They maintained a flourishing trade with the Iberian and North African ports in goods derived to a great part from captured merchant vessels and raided towns of the Aegean Isles. In 840 the Byzantine Emperor Theophilus sent an embassy to Cordova, demanding the restitution of the island, but Emir ʿAbd al-Rahmān II* (822-852), through the envoy he sent to Constantinople, the poet al-Ghazal*, disclaimed any sovereign power over the Arabs in Crete. Several attempts undertaken by later emperors to dislodge them thoroughly failed. It was only in 961 that Nicephorus Phocas, great general and subsequently emperor himself (963-969), finally subdued their last ruler, Emir ʿAbd al-ʿAzīz Ibn Shuʿaib. The name of their principal stronghold and of the town which had grown up around it, Chandax (from ar. *kandaq*, moat), later transformed by the Venetians into Candia - today officially Heraklion - perpetuates the remembrance of these Andalusians' presence in Crete.

D

DABBĪ al-, ABŪ JAʿFAR AHMAD, a Hispano-Arab biographer and historian († 1203). He began his studies in his home town Lorca, and in their further pursuit travelled a great deal in North Africa with prolonged stays in Ceuta, Marrakesh, Bougie and finally Alexandria. After his return to al-Andalus* he spent the rest of his life in Murcia. He is particularly known by a compilation of biographies of Andalusian scholars, the *Bughyat al-Multamis fī Taʾrīkh Rijāl Ahl al-Andalus* (The Aim of the Investigator into the History of the famous Men of al-Andalus), which is preceded by a summary of the history of the Arabs in Spain.

DAHIR see ZAHĪR

DARQĀWĀ, a religious brotherhood* *(tarīqa)* named after its founder Abū Hāmid Mūlāy al-ʿArbī (popularly known as Mūlāy Larbi) Ibn Ahmad al-Darqāwī (1737-1823). His family, which claimed descent from the Idrīsid* dynasty and hence Sharīfian nobility, had its home in the southern part of the Rif among the Berber Banū Zarwāl in the village of Bū Barīh. He studied in Fez under ʿAlī al-ʿImrānī, the head of the Shādhilīya fraternity, who upon his death (1779) at the age of allegedly 105 years was given by the people a place of distinction among their many saints. Al-Darqāwī continued his master's teaching but after a while slightly modified it, added a number of liturgical rules including the ritual dance, and founded a mystical order of his own at his native Bū Barīh. His son tranferred it (1863) to the near-by Amajjūt.
By his piety, ascetic way of living and wisdom highly reputed among the Berber mountain tribes but equally among the urban middle class, and gifted with a remarkable organizing talent, al-Darqāwī attracted an ever growing number of followers. Devoted disciples spread his word all over northern and eastern Morocco and the neighbouring region of the Ottoman Regency of Algeria. In a short time there sprang up a number of Darqāwā branches, and the order grew into a factor of considerable political significance. Soon there arose frictions between an Algerian branch near Tlemcen and the Turkish governor *(beylerbey)*, which rapidly degenerated into open revolt. Thereupon al-Darqāwī incited the people in the area around Tlemcen to swear allegiance to Sulaymān, Sultan of Morocco (1792-1822), who first had encouraged his step but subsequently disavowed it under Turkish pressure. When the tension which now ensued between al-Darqāwī and the Sultan began to assume increasingly critical aspects, Sulaymān had a Friday sermon *(khutba)* read in every mosque, which stigmatized all religious brotherhoods* and their rites as a sinful innovation *(bidʿa)*. The result was a general rising of the Darqāwā and its partisans from among the tribes of the Middle Atlas. The rebels dispersed (1818) the army which was sent against them, besieged Meknès, took the Sultan prisoner and forced

him to conclude an armistice. Two years later, in alliance with the great Wazzānīya brotherhood and some malcontent notables they resumed hostilities, but had to make peace when al-Darqāwī fell into the hands of the governement and was kept as a hostage in honourable captivity. Sulaymān's successor, Sultan ʿAbd al-Rahmān (1822-1859) liberated him, but he died shortly afterwards and was buried in Bū Barīh.

Under his son Muhammad al-Tayyib, invested by his father's will with the leadership but not unanimously recognized, the Darqāwā continued to flourish. Under his grandson ʿAbd al-Rahmān (†1927) it further expanded, partly at the expense of older fraternities, into a variety of branches, each of which became the nucleus of new ramifications. Most of these assumed the names of their founders such as in Fez, the Dabbāghīya and the Fāsīya, founded by ʿAbd al-Wāhid al-Dabbāgh and Muhammad al-Fāsī in the Middle and High Atlas; the Badawīya, founded by Ahmad al-Badawī; or in Tetuan, the Harrāqīya, founded by the scholar and mystical poet Muhammad al-Harrāq. A number of Darqāwā offshoots spread into Tunisia, Tripolitania and Turkey. Others took root in Algeria, especially in Tlemcen, Sidi Bel Abbès, Saida and Mascara, the youngest, the Alīwaīya in Mostaganem. It was founded in 1913 by one Ahmad Ibn Mustafā Ibn Alīwa (†1934), a former shoemaker who had turned to theological studies, rejuvenated the time-honoured doctrine and modernized the ritual. Subsequently he went to France, preached among the Algerian workers, set up a number of daughter houses and also published a newspaper, *Lisān al-Dīn* (the Tongue of the Faith), printed on his own press.

In the spiritual sphere the various Darqāwā branches, upon the whole, continued the rules and traditions of the mother house with no or very little deviation. Administratively, economically and in their attitude towards the authorities of the country they followed their own, extremely flexible lines which were traced by local or regional, mainly tribal interests. In the internal unrest in Morocco, or in the conflicts with the Turks and later with the French forces in Algeria, some of them lent their support to one camp and others to its opponent, always ready for a change of sides. This conduct was also the rule in the agitated atmosphere of the Protectorate* in Morocco, particularly in the Spanish zone during the Spanish Civil War (1936-1939). During World War II American, British and Free French agents competed with one another in winning the friendship of the influential brotherhood. Upon the end of the war, the not all too reliable pro-American, pro-British or pro-French sympathies of the different Darqāwā groups quickly abated, and in the struggle for the abolition of the Protectorate they stood up, on the whole, for the national cause. Yet the approach attempted by various nationalistic parties for common action was met with the traditional mental reservation. Since the restoration of independence (1955), the Darqāwā, which among all brotherhoods in Morocco counts the largest number of sympathizers, has abstained from all but strictly local, political activities.

DEMOCRATIC CONSTITUTIONAL PARTY, *Hibz al-Dustūr al-Dimuqrātī*, often quoted as P.D.C. (the initials of its French designation Parti Démocratique Constitutionel), the name assumed in 1958 by the

Democratic Party of Independence* in Morocco.

DEMOCRATIC PARTY OF INDEPENDENCE, *Hizb al-Shūrā wa'l Istiqlāl*, often quoted as 'P.D.I.' (the initials of its French designation 'Parti Démocratique de l'Indépendance') founded in 1946 in the zone of the French Protectorate* in Morocco by Muhammad Hassān al-Wazzānī upon his return from exile. He had been a prominent member of the earliest nationalist party in Morocco, the Bloc of Moroccan Action*, and editor of one of the first nationalist papers, the 'Action du Peuple', as well as of its successor, the 'Action Nationale Marocaine'. After the dissolution of the Bloc (1937) he created the short-lived 'People's Movement' *(al-Haraka al-Qawmīya)*, which disappeared when he was sent into exile (October 1937) by the authorities of the Protectorate. The Democratic Party of Independence, which recruited its adherents, at least in the first years of its existence, almost exclusively from among the intellectual groups of French education, demanded the abolition of the Protectorate and the independence of Morocco under the reign of the 'Alawid* dynasty in the form of a constitutional, democratic monarchy. A treaty with France was to define the new economic, political and cultural relations between both countries. It claimed to stand for modern and progressive evolution contrary, so it asserted, to the tradition-bound and religiously tinged tendencies dear to the leading figures of its numerically far superior rival, the *Istiqlāl**.
The contrast of their characters which as far back as the years of the 'Bloc' had opposed to one another the two pioneers of Moroccan nationalism, al-Wazzānī and ʿAllāl al-Fāsī, the future leader of the *Istiqlāl*, was not appeased by their long separation. Thenceforth it was given expression on the personal as well as the party level in acrimonious press feuds between the *Istiqlāl's* paper *Al-ʿAlam* (The Flag) and the publication of the Democratic Party of Independence, the *Ra'y al-Amm* (Public Opinion) and its weekly in French 'Démocratie'. Yet both of them joined the parties in the Spanish zone, the Party of National Reforms* and the *Haraka al-Wahda**, in the common National Moroccan Front, which presented the Moroccan case in the lobbies of the United Nations, where al-Wazzānī with two of his party colleagues, Ahmad Ibn Sūda and Muhammad Sharqawī, acted on behalf of the Democratic Party of Independence (December 1952), while 'Abd al-Qādir Benjellūn in Casablanca assumed the party leadership. Subsequently Sharqawī returned to the French zone. Al-Wazzānī and Ahmad Ibn Sūda took up residence in Ceuta and with the assistance of the Spanish authorities organized the party also in the international zone of Tangier. Subsequently al-Wazzānī moved to Tangier and remained there until 1958. In the first Cabinet (7th December 1955) after the achievement of independence, the Party shared the ministerial posts with the *Istiqlāl* and some non-party independents, but soon the old rift, which had been patched up for a while, split open again. Ten months later, its ministers resigned in protest against its rival's alleged - and to some extent probably real - totalitarian aspirations and the Party went into opposition. Presumably to emphasize its own different ideology it changed its name into Democratic Constitutional Party* after having proceeded in 1958 with

the strengthening of its organization. It was represented again in government by Muhammad Sharqawī in the Cabinet set up by King Muhammad V* (26th May 1960) under the vice-presidency of his son Crown Prince Mūlāy Hassan. Al-Wazzānī who had been assigned a seat in the Constitutional Council instituted in November 1960, replaced him in the Coalition government of June 1961, presided over by King Hassan II himself.

DEMOCRATIC UNION OF THE ALGERIAN MANIFESTO, Union Démocratique du Manifeste Algérien (U.D.M.A.), an Algerian political party founded in 1946 by Farhat Abbas (Farhāt ʿĀbbas). He had worked out its programme during the one year he spent in prison after his arrest following the riots of May 1945 and the suppression of the association of the Friends of the Manifesto* (A.M.L.), and announced it in an 'Appeal to the French and Moslem Youth of Algeria.' He advocated close Franco-Moslem cooperation 'without assimilation or separation', but uniting all French and Algerian democratic forces in order to build up an Algerian Republic with its president, government, parliament and flag, freely associated with France on a federal basis. The realization of these aspirations, he insisted, would require patient efforts and the help of French advice, but also the disappearance, on the French side, of the 'colonial complex', and, on the part of the Moslems, of the 'medieval theocratic concepts'. By these postulates, diffused through his journal 'La République Algérienne', a dividing line was drawn between the policy of his new party and the currents of an intransigent nationalism, in which there moved, with sharp leftist leanings, Messali al-Hajj's (Masālī al-Hajj) Movement for the Triumph of Democratic Liberties* (M.T.L.D.) as well as the Association of the Algerian ʿUlamā'*. General de Gaulle, on the other hand, in his declaration in the course of the heated debates in the French National Assembly on a new Algerian Statute, made it clear that France would not cease to regard Algeria as an integral part of French territory or to limit her own sovereign powers. In fact, the Algerian Statute, enacted in September 1947, left French sovereignty and control as firmly anchored as before.
To this nationalist-reformist platform most of the Moslem urban middle-class groups rallied as well as large sections of the rural population. In view of the technique of admittedly 'managed' elections, used by the Administration, the party was well represented in the Algerian elected bodies, maintaining through its office in Cairo close relations with the Tunisian and Moroccan nationalists. Farhat Abbas held a seat first in the French Second Constituent Assembly, then in the French Parliament and in the Algerian Assembly created by the Statute. Notwithstanding their disappointment at the unyielding French attitude and in particular of the Algerian governors who, with rare exceptions, saw in a policy of the strong hand the only answer to the increasingly critical Algerian question, Farhat Abbas and his friends did not give up hope of a negotiated solution. They pleaded for moderation in the Common Front for the Defence of Liberty* in August 1951 and in the North African Unity and Action Front* in January 1952. Still shortly before the outbreak of the revolution in 1954 Farhat Abbas publicly declared his unshaken

belief in the possibility of cooperation with France for the formation of an Algerian State built upon the fraternal community of its inhabitants, whether Moslems or of European origin. Even afterwards he kept up for a while this position, although with much diminished confidence. By the end of 1955 the U.D.M.A. delegates ceased to attent the sessions of the Algerian Assembly, and in April 1956 Farhat Abbas, speaking at Cairo in the name of the party, submitted fully to the decisions of the revolutionary National Liberation Front* (F.L.N.).

DESTOUR, in occidental texts the usual spelling of *al-dustūr*, the currently used abridgement for the Tunisian *al-Hizb al-Hurr al-Dustrūrī* (Liberal Constitutional Party), established in February 1920 by members of the former Young-Tunisia Party*, who came again into the open after clandestine activity during the years of the First World War. The party's somewhat chequered story begins just after the armistice, when a delegation of Tunisian notables, headed by Sheikh ʿAbd al-ʿAzīz al-Tha ʿālibī and Ahmad al-Saqqa, a Tunisian lawyer practising in Paris, submitted to the Paris Peace Conference, to the French government and to President Woodrow Wilson their claim for the application to Tunisia of his famous Fourteen Points declaring the right of all peoples to self-government. They were left without answer. Then, al-Thaʿālibī and al-Saqqa published (June 1919) an anonymous pamphlet, 'La Tunisie Martyre', in which they maintained, with the support of eminent French jurists, that the treaties of Bardo (1881) and of La Marsa (1883), while establishing the French Protectorate*, had not abrogated the Tunisian constitution *(dustūr)* of 1857 and 1861; that its violation had reduced Tunisia to the status of a French colony; and that its legislative, judicial and administrative institutions had to come into force again. The publication remained practically unnoticed in France, but in Tunisia, although officially suppressed, found enthusiastic resonance.
In this atmosphere the Destour was born. Its first step was the promulgation of a manifesto demanding the abolition, by way of negotiation, of the Protectorate; a constitutional system of government under the dynasty of the Husaynid Beys*, with a parliament and municipal councils elected by Tunisians only; a national Tunisian army; and the retransfer into Tunisian ownership of the land that had been turned over to French settlers. There was, however, among the conservative elements, in particular the influential theologians of the Zaytūna Academy and the traditionalist bourgeoisie around them, considerable hesitation to join the movement which, they feared, might invite all sorts of extremist tendencies. Under their pressure a revised programme implicitly admitting of the continuation of the Protectorate, reformulated the party's aims: a national assembly elected by universal suffrage but with only advisory capacity, composed of Tunisian as well as French delegates; the separation of the legislative, judicial and executive powers; equal accessibility to public offices with equal salaries for Tunisians and Frenchmen; compulsory primary education; and the participation of Tunisians in the acquisition of state domains for colonization. Sheikh Thaʿālibī who continued in Paris his propaganda in the former more radical spirit, was deported to Tunis and kept nine months in prison.

Then, elected chairman of the party, he started its organization in the provinces, but in the wake of a dissension with Bey Muhammad al-Habīb, left Tunis and spent the following fourteen years in the Arab East and in India before returning from a more or less voluntary exile. His functions in the party were taken over by an Executive Committee directed by Ahmad al-Sāfī and Salāh Farhāt.

Reforms were indeed enacted but their intent - and in some measure also their effect - was to neutralize the currents of emancipation. Consolidating the prerogatives of the social and economic upper classes and granting French citizenship to selected groups of Tunisians, they introduced strong shades of pro-French sympathies into the political picture. The Destour, tuning down ever more its combativeness, receded farther and farther into a colourless background, and the broad public soon lost interest in the issues which had been raised in the days of post-war optimism. Not until the early 'thirties did the general indifference give way to a climate of highly strained sensibility, although more of a religious than nationalist nature, generated by some rather inconsiderate measures of the Protectorate authorities: appointments of French judges to Tunisian courts of law; the convention of an Eucharist Congress coinciding with the fiftieth anniversary of the French occupation and combined with a pageant of French youth in crusaders' costumes; or the attempt at enforcing the burial in Muslim cemeteries of Tunisians who had chosen French naturalization which implied the acceptance of French instead of Islamic law and jurisdiction, and hence in the eyes of many was equivalent to heresy. It was then that the Destour came again into the forefront, directing street manifestations, stimulating anti-French feeling and organizing strikes and boycotts of French products. The unrest found an echo in the labour troubles which were the source of the first purely national organization of Tunisian trade unionism*, the Conféderation Générale des Travailleurs Tunisiens (C.G.T.T.). The Protectorate authorities countered with mass arrests, imprisonments or banishments and the promotion of a western-oriented 'Reformist Party'. Finally the Destour was declared unlawful (May 1933) but after a while tacitly tolerated.

By then, the Party controlled, directly or indirectly, over twenty dailies or periodicals, had established more then eighty regional branches and a number of youth leagues, scout clubs and women's associations. Yet the wide range of spiritual, social and political values seeking expression, and the different tactics advocated for their pursuit, could no longer be contained under one single roof. The divergencies crystallized in an oppositional section of young intellectuals, to whose dynamic enthusiasm the majority and its aversion against energetic, mass-sustained action in all but religious questions, appeared too static and uninspiring. In March 1934 the split was consummated with the foundation of the Neo-Destour*, forcefully animated by its secretary-general Habīb Bourguiba, the future president of the Tunisian Republic, which soon drew into its ranks ever more like-minded members of the old party. Sheikh Thaʿālibī, returning in 1937, tried to bring about a reconciliation, but his sympathies went so openly to the 'Old Turbans', that he became himself involved in the conflict and after a while withdrew from public life (†1944).

More attempts were made but remained equally unsuccessful: one in 1945 when both parties with a number of non-political associations constituted a 'Committee of the Sixty' which formulated in the 'Manifesto of the Tunisian People' their demands for the fulfilment of the national aspirations; another one, in 1946, at a clandestine 'Congress of Independence' held by some 300 representatives of the same organizations, at which Salāh Farhāt for the Old Destour and Salāh Ibn Yūsuf in the absence of Habīb Bourguiba for the Neo-Destour set up a 'Common Front' for combining their efforts; a third one, in 1951, when the Old Destour tried to win over its rival to the idea of a National Front which by close collaboration with the Moroccan and Algerian parties as well as with the Arab League would, it was thought, command greater force in the struggle for independence. With the exception of these short intervals the feud went on in the most violent tones through the press and by mass meetings, but the Old Destour was the loser and after the abolition of the Protectorate gradually vanished from the political stage. In 1957 the last members joined the Neo-Destour.

DEY, a Turkish title (from the Turkish dāī, originally a maternal uncle), in Algeria and Tunisia borne in the first years of the Ottoman régime by the commanders of the Janizary brigade. In Algeria, from 1670 until the French occupation in 1830, a Dey, elected by the highranking officers and assisted by an officers' council *(dīwān)* was at the head of the Regency, but in most cases actual power was in the hands of the military. He resided in Algiers, at first in a vast and beautiful palace - restored after its destruction by fire in 1844 it became the residence of the archbishop, but still called *Dār es-Sultān* - and later in the Kasba*. The development in Tunisia was similar between 1590 and 1640, but then the place of the *deys* was taken by the Murādid Beys*, while *dey* thencefort was an honorary title which the *bey* conferred on court dignitaries and subsequently on high judicial officers.

DHŪ al-NŪN, the arabized name of the Banū Zannūn, a Hispano-Berber dynasty of Party Kings* in Toledo (1033-1085) and Valencia (1085-1092), descended from a clan of the Hawwāra tribe, which had come into Spain in the years of the Arab conquest or soon afterwards, and settled in the mountain region north-east of Toledo. They acquired considerable influence around the towns of Santaver, Huete, and Uclès, and through their unruly disposition frequently came into conflict with the central government, especially during the reign of Emir Muhammad I (852-886) and Emir ʿAbd Allāh (888-912). Mūsā Ibn Zannūn took possession of Toledo (888), the ancient Visigothic capital, which for a long time had proved refractory to the emir's authority. A few years later he lost it again to another powerful family, the Banū Qāsī. His eldest son Yahyā, after some years at the head of a band of brigands, entered the emir's army and died in battle. His second son al-Fath, lord of Uclès, took part in an uprising but was killed by his own men. His third son Mutarrif ascended to a commanding position in the emir's troops and ended his life as governor of the town of Guadalajara.
During the following two hundred years, the Banū Dhī al-Nūn continued

to rank among the great families, but held no particular place in Andalusian annals. In the second half of the XIth century, one of their members, the military commander of Santaver, was called upon by the people of Toledo to oust their ruler, and to occupy the throne of the city and its dependencies, which extended as far as the domain of the ʿAmīrid* kings of Valencia and that of the Banū Hūd, kings of Saragossa. He sent his son Ismāʿīl al-Zāfar, who died after a brief reign. Ismāʿil's son and successor Yahyā al-Ma'mūn (1038-1074) soon became involved in feuds with the Banū Hūd, to whom he lost the old family possession of Guadalajara. He concluded an alliance with Ferdinand I, King of Castile and Leon, which kept off his aggressive neighbours but made him tributary to his protector.

Notwithstanding the limitation of his sovereignty, al-Ma'mūn's reign was one of Toledo's most brilliant periods. He firmly organized public administration and finances, consolidated the discipline and preparedness of the army, and greatly enlarged his territory at the expense of the weaker city-states. The most valuable of these conquests was the city of Valencia (1065). His court became the meeting place of poets, scholars and distinguished theologians, who made Toledo an intellectual center reputed far beyond its borders and even in Christian Spain. His palace with its collection of works of art in the midst of luxuriant gardens, was the stage of festivities the like of which, according to contemporary chroniclers, had never before been seen in al-Andalus* and whose splendour became proverbial *(iʿdhār dhunnūnī*, the Dhū al-Nūn feasts). In the struggle among King Ferdinand's sons over the heritage, one of them, the later King Alfonso VI, was taken prisoner by his brother and sent into exile to Toledo. He was received with royal honours and spent his time hunting in al-Ma'mūn's forests or fighting in his battles, so that soon both princes were united in close friendship and remained friends even after Alfonso, upon his brother's death, was called home and ascended the throne.

Al-Ma'mūn died of poison in Cordova six months after his conquest of that city and was succeeded by his grandson Yahyā al-Qādir (1074/75-1092). Under the new ruler, the Dhū al-Nūn splendour rapidly tarnished. Court intrigues brought about the disgrace of faithful counsellors, serious disturbances in the country and the defection of the governor of Valencia who declared his independence. King Alfonso, asked for help, honoured his friendship with al-Ma'mūn and lent his support, but only in return for the payment of heavy tributes which exhausted the treasury, increased the burden of taxation and heightened still more the internal tension. One night, fearing for his life, al-Qādir secretly left Toledo, which was occupied by his neighbour, the Aftasid* King of Badajoz (1080). Alfonso, quickly expelling the usurper, re-installed al-Qādir but kept the city completely under the control of his troops until al-Qādir turned it fully over to him (1085) in exchange for the promise of assistance in the reconquest of Valencia. Thenceforth Toledo remained in Christian hands, but the promise was kept, and after a short campaign al-Qādir entered Valencia. He reigned, in name rather than in fact, owing to the protection extended to him first by Alfonso, then by Alfonso's powerful vassal, the Cid, but at costs which imposed upon his subjects unbearable taxes. At last al-Qādir lost his life in a revolt of the exasperated people. Valencia, for some time a sort of republic, was forced by the Cid to surrender. He had the leaders of the rebels executed and made the city his residence. After his death it was evacuated by his widow (1102) and occupied by the Almoravid* army.

DILĀ'YŪN al-, a Moroccan family springing from a clan of the Berber Sanhāja* of the Middle Atlas in the upper valley of the Umm al-Rabīᶜ, which during the five decades between the first and the third quarter of the XVIIth century acquired a dominant position in the great politico-religious brotherhood* movement; almost conquered the throne of the tottering Saᶜdian* dynasty (1554-1659); and finally succumbed to their more fortunate rivals, the first ᶜAlawid* sultans.
Their ancestor, Abū Bakr Ibn Muhammad (†1612), a disciple of well-known theologians and an adept of the great mystic al-Jazūlī*, founded a religious order with its seat *(zāwiya*)* at Dilā' on the left bank of the Umm al-Rabīᶜ - the site has not been localized with certainty - and by his piety, wisdom and hospitality attracted a rapidly growing number of adherents among the Ait Idrāsin, a Sanhāja group of mountain tribes. His son and successor Muhammad Ibn Abī Bakr (†1637) further increased the prestige of the Dilā' fraternity and extended its spiritual, and soon also secular influence southwards far into the Mulūya valley and thence further into the High Atlas. Under the guidance of the third sheikh, Muhammad al-Hājj (†1671), highly reputed as a saint and scholar, Dilā' became a favoured meeting place for the theological, juridical and grammatical discussions among men of religion and law, visited by pilgrims in every walk of life. At the same time it grew into a political factor more and more to be reckoned with. The master's word, carried by his brothers, sons and cousins, settled the feuds of rival chieftains, united antagonizing clans, built up intertribal leagues and confederations. The brotherhood now had at its call in the world of the tribes a mass of warlike members and sympathizers, all of them ready to follow the venerated leader, so that also north of the Atlas the towns in the Tādlā plain, and even Meknès and Fez bowed to the authority of Muhammad al-Hājj. It is not certain when he formed definite plans to forge for himself a throne out of the crumbling Saᶜdian realm, but around 1637 his men penetrated into the area of Salé and then along the coast as far as Casablanca. The following year he routed a Saᶜdian army under Sultan Muhammad al-Shaykh Ibn Zaidān al-Asghar (1636-1654), conquered the region of the Gharb with Arzila, al-Qasr al-Kabīr and Tangier, occupied Fez (1641) and everywhere installed his relatives and devoted followers as governors or military commanders.
Conflicts became inevitable between the Dilā'ī state in the making and the similar, half-monastic, half-worldly minor nuclei of power, then appearing almost everywhere in Morocco, on the one hand, and the forcefully ascending ᶜAlawid* clan on the other. The former were easily mastered. The encounter with the latter seemed at first also to turn to the Dilā'yūn's advantage. The ᶜAlawid chief, Muhammad Ibn al-Sharīf (1635-1663) was beaten, had to retreat into the Tāfīlālt oases south of the High Atlas, and to conclude a truce (1646). Three years later,

he resumed the struggle and incited, or at least supported, a revolt of the people of Fez against the Dilā'ī governor, but again suffered defeat. Equal failures were his subsequent attempts to take hold of the city. Dilā', so it seemed, had its ascendency unshakably established over the whole of central Morocco, the major section of the North and an important part of the South, while its light as a focus of learning shone brighter than ever before.

Within a few years, this vitality was spent. The first to shake off the overlordship of the Atlas warriors were the townspeople of Tangier. Next came those of al-Qasr al-Kabīr and the peasantry of the Gharb. Then Fez repudiated the Dilā'ī predominance. Soon afterwards the new 'Alawid sultan Mūlāy al-Rashīd Ibn al-Sharīf (1664-1672), himself not long ago one of the guests at Dilā', subdued some of Muhammad al-Hājj's allies in a three day battle near Meknès and forced the bulk of his troops back into their mountains. Thenceforth region after region, tribe after tribe began joining the victor, until Dilā' was conquered and levelled with the ground (1688). The members of the fraternity were dispersed and Muhammad al-Hājj, accompanied by his family, was sent into honourable exile to Tlemcen, where he died at a high age while his descendants soon afterwards were allowed to settle in Fez. There they were welcomed by the lettered élite in the same cordial spirit for which Dilā' had been renowned, and within a short time their name acquired a lasting place in the town's scholarly annals. One of Muhammad al-Hājj's grandsons, however, Ahmad Ibn ʿAbd Allāh, trying to revive the ancestral fame in the sphere of secular power, stirred up some tribal groups in the Mulūya valley, but after an ephemeral success was defeated and mysteriously vanished. A cousin of his, Muhammad, captured by a Christian pirate ship while on the pilgrimage to the Holy Cities, and taken to Italy, was converted to Christianity and entered the Jesuit order as Father Balthazar Loyola Mendez.

An exhaustive treatise on the Dilā'yūn family was compiled by the Moroccan biographer Muhammad Ibn ʿAbd Allāh al-Hawwāt (1742-1816). Beginning with Abū Bakr Muhammad, he deals with all those of its members who down to his days distinguished themselves in the learned society of Fez, reproducing portions of their writings and their correspondence with their colleagues. About the same time there appeared a similar, but less comprehensive, versified biography *(urjūz*)* of the family by another scholar of Fez. A third one in existence has been ascribed, although not with certainty, to the ʿAlawid Sultan Mūlāy Sulaymān (1792-1823).

DOUAR, the French transliteration of *dūwār* - called *dawār* in the Arab East - denoting a Bedouin encampment, by age-old practice set up in the form of a circle. By extension the term came to be used in Algeria for a territorial unit in the French administrative organization (comp. *dā'ira*, plur. *dawā'ira* circle, a district).

E

ETOILE NORDAFRICAINE see NORTH AFRICAN STAR

EVOLUES, a French term currently used in literature dealing with the development of Algerian nationalism and denoting certain progressive groups of the intellectual Moslem youth of the period approximately between the two World Wars. By the force of tradition and the ties of the patriarchal family they were emotionally rooted in the Islamo-Arabic social pattern and fully conscious of its cultural values. Yet brought up in the French educational atmosphere from elementary to academic levels - to such an extent that in many cases they were hardly, if at all, able to read or write Arabic - they reflected in their midst a wide range of contemporary socio-political ideologies and philosophies. Feeling themselves to belong by their mode of living to the world of modern civilization, and firmly believing in the need for, and also the possibility of, progressively adapting the mass of the people to the standards of that world, they deeply resented the French colonial policy which reduced the Arabs to a second-rate citizenship. They called, still rather confusedly for reforms consistent with the ideals of the French Republic: Liberté, Fraternité and Egalité. Those who held some of the few seats accorded to Moslems in the city councils and in the Financial Delegation and the Superior Council - the two consultive bodies of the Administration - were in a position to voice these claims in a political formulation. From among them Dr. Benjelloul (Ben Jalūl) constituted the 'Fédération des Elus' (elected representatives) and Farhat Abbas (FarhātʿᾹbbas) the Algerian Popular Union*. However passionately their demands may have occasionally been put forth, it was always within the framework of French sovereignty in the spirit of absolute loyalty to France that these programmes were conceived, contrary to the ideas of Algerian independence, which was the driving force of such movements as the North African Star* or the Association of the Algerian ʿUlamā'*. Yet in the years to come disillusion drove the majority of Evolués into the ranks of more extreme nationalism and eventually many into the camp of the revolution.

EXTERNAL DELEGATION OF THE FRONT OF NATIONAL LIBERATION, originally a small group of partisans of the terrorist Organisation Secrète* (O.S.), headed by Muhammad Khidr, Ḣusain Ait Ahmad and Ahmad Ben Bella (Ibn Ballā), who between 1950 and 1952 had escaped persecution, taken refuge in Cairo and there under the patronage of the Egyptian Government and the Arab League maintained a very active propaganda for the aims of the Algerian national movement. They were among the initiators of the Revolutionary Committee for Unity and Action* (C.R.U.A.) which prepared, and in 1954 decided the open outbreak of the insurrection. Thenceforth their more or less individual efforts were fitted into corporate forms, and branch offices were established in several Arab countries, especially after they were joined by an increasing number of politically prominent leaders, such as Muhammad Būdiaf; by Farhat Abbas, the head of the Democratic Union of the Algerian Manifesto* (U.D.M.A.), and his brother-in-law and close associate Ahmad Francis; by ʿAbd al-Rahmān Kiwān, one of the foremost 'Centralists' of the Movement for the Triumph of the Democratic Liberties* (M.T.L.D.); and Tawfīq al-Madanī, the secretary-general of the Association of the ʿUlamā'*. In February 1956 the External Delegation, as the group by then was currently called, constituted itself a military commission, responsible for the securing of material assistance to the fighting forces, such as money, arms, uniforms or medical supplies, and a political commission, in charge of creating an international atmosphere favourable to the aims of the revolution by the distribution of propagandistic literature, press conferences, travelling missions and similar means. In the reorganization of the revolutionary structure, undertaken by the Summam Valley Congress* in August 1956, the External Delegation was subordinated to the Committee of Coordination and Execution* (C.C.E.), the supreme commanding body of the operations in the field. Yet in October, Ben Bella, Ait Ahmad, Muhammad Būdiaf and Muhammad Khidr fell into the hands of the French, while flying from a meeting with King Muhammad V* in Rabat to Tunis, where they were expected to participate in a conference with the King and President Habīb Bourguiba. In April 1957 the External Delegation transferred its headquarters from Cairo to Tunis.

F

FAHRASA, a kind of catalogues which between the XIIth and the beginning of the XIXth cent. it was customary for everybody striving after scientific fame to leave. The author describes in full detail the phases of his scholarly career, beginning at his early youth, enumerating the teachers whose courses he attended; the books he studied, annotated and expounded; the works he wrote on the ground of his personal research; and the names of the students whom he taught and advised in the pursuit of their own learned activities. As a rule the *fahrasa* remains silent on anything concerning his person, family or events of his life; all this was left for his biographers. The rich *fahrasa* literature, regardless of whether the authors count among the major or lesser lights in their fields, gives a valuable insight into the development of Arabic scientific, religious and literary life and into the various social, emotional and political currents which moved it in the course of time.

FAQĪH MUSHĀWAR, the title used in Arab Spain for the members of the council of jurists who were appointed by the ruler to assist the judge *(qādī)* in the interpretation of the law, but frequently acted also as legal advisers to private persons. From the beginning of the tenth century onwards the *faqīh mushāwar* as a rule gave his opinion *(fatwā)* in writing, whereby all circumstances of the case without omission of even the most insignificant incidents were described in minute detail. Several collections of such *fatwās* have been preserved and give a good insight not only into the evolution of juridical practice but also into the manifold situations of every-day life and its major and minor problems.

FARADĪ IBN al-, ABŪ al-WALĪD ʿABD ALLĀH, one of the earliest Hispano-Arab biographers (962-1012). He was born in Cordova where he began to study history, canon law and the science of the *hadīth* (Tradition of the Prophet), and continued in al-Qayrawān, Cairo, Mecca and Medina. After his return to his home country, he taught for some time in Cordova and subsequently was appointed cadi of Valencia. He lost his life in one of the upheavals which marked the troubled years of the last Umayyad caliphs, while his rich library was pilfered or destroyed. Only his *Ta'rīkh ʿUlamā' al-Anadalus* (History of the Scholars of Arab Spain) has been preserved.

FĀSĪ al-, a highly reputed Moroccan family of scholars (the name is to be distinguished from *ahl-Fās*, meaning the inhabitants of Fez), a branch of the old Andalusian clan of the Banū al-Jadd, which towards the end of the XVth cent. in the course of internal disturbances had to emigrate from their home town Malaga and took residence first in Fez and then, because of the outbreak there of the pest, in al-Qasr al-Kabīr (on the road from Tangier to Rabat), where they were given their present

name by the people of the town.
Abū al-Mahāsin Yūsuf Ibn Muhammad (1530-1604), a grandson of the first Fāsī, went to Fez for his studies, settled there and founded a *zāwiya** (branch seat) of the Jazūlīya* fraternity, still in existence and known as the *zāwiya al-Fāsiyyīn*, of whose doctrine already his father was an adept. He is buried in Fez in the cemetery of the Bāb al-Futūh among the numerous mausolea of famous doctors of the Qarawīyīn* academy. Particularly renowned among his sons was Muhammad al-ʿArabī (1580-1642), jurist, poet and biographer of saintly men, especially of his own father and the circles in which he moved. He wrote also on the mystical movement exercising an ever increasing influence on all public life. Having travelled a great deal all over Morocco, he died in Tetuan, whence two years after his death his body was taken to Fez and buried in his father's tomb. His nephew and disciple ʿAbd al-Qādir al-Fāsī (1599-1680), head of the family *zāwiya*, where his tomb is still a much visited shrine, ranked among the widely recognized authorities on theology and law, but left no writings except for a short compilation of juridical interpretations. His son Abū Zayd ʿAbd al-Rahmān (1631-1685), on the contrary, was a highly prolific writer - he is said to have written some 170 books, presumably rather booklets for the greater part - on the most varied subjects in the fields of theology, jurisprudence and public administration, medicine and astronomy, besides historical and biographical studies. Among his writings, a number of which in accordance with an old practice are composed in verse as an aid to memory, have to be mentioned the *Kitāb al-Uqnūm fī Mabādī al-ʿUlūm* (appr. The Short Manual of the Principles of Science), an encyclopaedic treatise in nearly 15.000 verses of the *urjūza** type, of all that may be called the knowledge of his time; and the *ʿAmal al-Fāsī*, a sort of versified guide for the application of the customary law (*ʿamal**) by the cadi.
The lines which ʿAbd al-Rahmān's work had traced were followed by his son Muhammad (1648-1722), one of the highly distinguished savants in Fez at his days; as well as by his cousin Muhammad al-Mahdī (1625-1698) whom his pious and ascetic way of life secured a place of honour in the annals of the Jazūlīya fraternity of whose branch in Fez he was, like all the members of the family, a faithful adept. The lives of its founders and the activities of his disciples were the main themes of his writings besides subjects of theology and mystical speculation. The story of the scholarly accomplishments of the Fāsī family continues throughout the XVIIIth and XIXth centuries. It has been dealt with extensively in Moroccan biographical literature, and also invited modern research to reconstitute a picture of the cultural development in this part of the Arab West. Today, personalities such as ʿAllāl al-Fāsī, one of the protagonists in the struggle for independence and leader of the *Istiqlāl** party, or Muhammad al-Fāsī, the rector of the Moroccan university, occupy a foremost place in Moroccan scientific and public life.

F.D.I.C. see FRONT OF DEFENCE OF THE CONSTITUTIONAL INSTITUTIONS

FELLAGHA, a colloquial term denoting bandits, and by the French population in Algeria during the revolution used for the organized groups of nationalistic fighters. The nationalists themselves regarded it as title of honour.

FIRNĀS IBN, ʿABBĀS, an Andalusian scholar of Berber origin (†887), endowed with a poetical gift, who was the official court poet under three Umayyad emirs in succession: al-Hakam I (796-822), ʿAbd al-Rahmān II (822-852) and Muhammad I (852-886). He was possessed also of a remarkable talent in fields related to mathematics, astronomy and physics, judging from the information transmitted in a recently discovered part of Ibn-Hayyān's* *Muqtabis*. There it is reported that ʿAbbās Ibn Firnās acquainted the scholarly circles of his country with the system of Arabic numerals *(sindhind)*, the knowledge of which he had acquired on a voyage to Iraq; that he built for his royal patrons a mechanical clock *(manqāna)* and a so-called armillary sphere *(dhāt al-halaq*, i.e. a combination of metal rings representing the sky and the movements of the astral bodies); and that he constructed an apparatus for flying, which seems to have consisted of a kind of human-sized, feather-covered envelope with moveable wings. In experimenting with it, he jumped into a precipice, maintained himself - so Ibn-Hayyān says - some seconds in the air, and miraculously fell down safely onto the ground in the depths.

FISHTĀLĪ al-, ʿABD al-ʿAZĪZ IBN MUHAMMAD, a Moroccan historiographer and poet (1549-1621?) born in Marrakesh. He served in the chancellery of the Saʿdian* ruler al-Mansūr (1578-1603) of whose correspondence he was in charge. No biographical data are known nor have any of his works been preserved except for the title of one, the *Manāhil al-safā ʿfī akhbār al-Mulūk al-Shurafā'* (appr. The true Sources of the History of the Sharīfian Sovereigns), usually quoted simply as *Manāhil*, which allegedly consisted of 8 volumes. A great deal of its contents, however, is found in the form of quotations in the writings of later authors. It is a panegyric in praise of the Saʿdian dynasty, in particular of al-Mansūr, but its interest consists in the detailed description of the court life and the organisation of the public offices and the army. It records as minutely the various, major or minor events of his days such as the construction of the ruler's sumptuous palace *al-Badiʿ* - today in ruins - in Marrakesh, every one of whose marble blocks was imported from Italy and paid its weight in Moroccan sugar. All this gives a very vivid picture of the time, the leading groups and their ideas. In this framework al-Fishtālī, following a practice rather current in his days, inserted also a number of his poems.

F.L.N. see FRONT OF NATIONAL LIBERATION

FRIENDS OF THE MANIFESTO AND OF LIBERTY, currently quoted as A.M.L. (the initials of its French designation Amis du Manifeste et de la Liberté), a loose association of Algerian nationalists, organized by Farhat Abbas (Farhāt ʿĀbbas) in March 1944 after the refusal of the French authorities to grant the reforms called for in the Manifesto of the Algerian People*. The 'Friends' included nationalist groups of various ideologies, from the Association of the Algerian 'Ulamā'* to Messali al-Hajj (Masālī al-Hajj), the head of the radically leftist Algerian People's Party*. Their aim was to familiarize the population with the idea of an Algerian nation and to awaken the general aspiration after an autonomous Algerian republic federated with France. Within this framework there were demands for the abolition of all unjustifiably acquired economic, social and political privileges, whether by Frenchmen or Moslems, and for action against the colonial régime. A well-orchestrated propaganda through the association's weekly 'Egalité' brought the number of supporters within a few months allegedly up to about half a million, weakening, however, the influence of Farhat Abbas and his moderate group. The preponderance of the intransigent elements became manifest at the first congress of the association, one year after its constitution. There, an overwhelming majority declared itself against any sort of French guidance and for full freedom of the future Algerian State to choose whatever foreign relation it should see fit. The outbreak in the following month of sanguinary riots in Sétif and their still more sanguinary repression put an end to all further activities of the A.M.L. which was dissolved by government order. A great many of their sympathizers were sentenced to long prison terms, Farhat Abbas and Sheikh al-Ibrāhīmī, the head of the Association of the Algerian 'Ulamā', were arrested, and Messali al-Hajj was deported to Brazzaville in Equatorial Africa. Farhat Abbas and his friends, released a year later, created a solidly structured political party, the Democratic Union of the Algerian Manifesto* (U.D.M.A.).

FRONT ALGERIEN POUR LA DEFENCE ET LE RESPECT DE LA LIBERTE see COMMON FRONT FOR THE DEFENCE OF, AND RESPECT FOR LIBERTY

FRONT FOR THE DEFENCE OF THE CONSTITUTIONAL INSTITUTIONS, frequently referred to as F.D.I.C., the initials of its French designation 'Front pour la Défence des Institutions Constitutionelles', a political party in Morocco, created in March 1963 by Rashīd Ridā Guedīra, for many years connected in close friendship with King Hassan II and repeatedly entrusted with several ministerial posts. The creation of the party, shortly preceding the parliamentary elections of May 1963, was intended to counterbalance the growing influence of the opposition voiced particularly by the *Istiqlāl**, the National Union of Popular Forces* and the Trade Unions*, against what was considered the too authoritarian trend of government, inaugurated by the King. Contrary to expectations, the new party obtained only 69 of the 144 seats in the National Assembly, but a few weeks afterwards an overwhelming majority in the elections of the municipal councillors.

FRONT DE LIBERATION NATIONALE see FRONT OF NATIONAL LIBERATION

FRONT OF NATIONAL LIBERATION, usually denoted by the initials F.L.N. (Front de Libération Nationale), the name chosen by the so-called nine historical chiefs of the Algerian revolution - the Revolutionary Committee for Unity and Action* (C.R.U.A.) - at a clandestine meeting on October 10, 1954 for 'the national organization of the Algerian people in the struggle for independence'. On November 1st a widely distributed tract defined the goal of the F.L.N. as the 'restoration of the Algerian State, sovereign, democratic and social, within the framework of Islam, which would secure all fundamental freedoms, without distinction of race or religion'. The Army of Liberation* (A.L.N.), the tract announced, would carry on the struggle until this goal was attained, but 'in order to limit bloodshed' it proposed as a platform for discussion with the French authorities: 1) the recognition of Algerian sovereignty, one and indivisible; 2) the abolition of all measures of exception including the actions taken against the Algerian fighters for freedom, and the liberation of all political prisoners; and 3) the abrogation of all legal texts qualifying Algeria as French soil. In return the offer was made that: 1) French cultural and economic interests would be respected, as well as persons and families; 2) French citizens desiring to remain in Algeria would be free to opt for their original nationality and then be considered as foreigners; or for Algerian nationality with all its rights and duties; and 3) that the future ties between Algeria and France would be determined by an agreement between the two Powers on the basis of equality and mutual respect. Neither by the French authorities nor by Algerian public opinion was at that time the Committee's claim to speak in the name of the Algerian people taken seriously. Yet throughout the seven years of the Revolution, the F.L.N. did not deviate from this earliest outline of its policy, and at the end of the struggle had it embodied unaltered in the Franco-Algerian Agreement of Evian in March 1962. Within a year or so practically all nationalist groups sided with the F.L.N., namely: the Organisation Secrète*; the so-called Centralists, a dissident section of the former Movement for the Triumph of the Democratic Liberties*; the Democratic Union of the Algerian Manifesto* under Farhat Abbas; the Association of the Algerian ʿUlamā'*; the Union des Travailleurs Algériens; the Union des Commerçants Algériens; and the Union Générale des Etudiants Musulmans Algériens. Only the Algerian National Movement* of Messali al-Ḥajj and the Algerian Communist Party were not admitted. Thus the F.L.N. became in fact a coalition of the forces of Algerian nationalism. It branched out all over the country; had its agents in villages and among the tribes; and constituted a 'Federation in France' among the Algerian workers. It established the rudiments of a local administration with tax collectors, judges and political commissars; and issued several clandestine periodicals, among which in particular '*Al-Mujāhid*' (The Freedom Fighter), a monthly in French and Arabic; 'L'Ouvrier Algérien'; and 'Résistance Algérienne'. Created by the so-called Summam Valley Conference*, there functioned the nuclei of a parliament and of a government - the National Council of the Algerian Revolution* (C.N.R.A.) and the Committee of Coordination and Execution* (C.C.E.) - while an External Delegation* at first in Cairo, and later in Tunis, was in charge of international relations, finances and the purchase of arms and ammunition.

By the end of 1956 the F.L.N. had grown into a national mass movement. It had rallied the landless labourers of the plains and the sons of the middle-class merchants or prosperous land-owning families; the peasants of the Kabyle mountains and the graduates from the universities of Algiers, Paris or Cairo; the urban workers and the tribesmen of the Aurès. From among these it recruited its Army of Liberation: guerilla fighters in the countryside; terrorist bands in the towns; and a regular military force behind the Tunisian and Moroccan borders. From their midst came the men who at the headquarters of the army, in the meetings of the C.N.R.A. or as ministers of the Provisional Government of the Algerian Republic* (G.P.R.A.), directed the strategic, political and diplomatic conduct of the revolution. Rigorously enforced discipline founded on the principle of collective leadership silenced the differences of temperament, age or education, of cultural tradition or social and economic ideologies, and with rare exceptions kept all of them united in one solid 'Front'.

Simultaneously the F.L.N. secured its international standing. It maintained 'Algerian Bureaux' in Damascus, Beirut and Amman, and with the two ruling parties of Morocco and Tunisia, the Istiqlāl* and the Neo-Destour*, held the 'Conference for the Unification of the Maghrib' at Tangier in April 1958. It attented the conferences of independent African states at Accra (1958) and at Monrovia (1959), the former merely as observer, the latter already as an equal participant and displaying the green and white flag with red star and crescent of the Algerian Republic, for in the meantime the C.C.E. had been transformed into the Provisional Government of the Algerian Republic and was accorded official recognition by quite a number of countries. In December it participated in the Pan-African People's Congress which elected one of its leaders into its 'Standing Committee', and in January 1961 it was among the signatories of the 'Charter of Casablanca'. It had accredited ambassadors in the Arab states; unofficial agents in New Delhi, Djakarta and Tokio; delegates attached to the Arab embassies in most European capitals; and a well-staffed mission at the United Nations' headquarters at New York.

In January 1960, at a C.N.R.A. meeting in Tripoli the F.L.N. rules and regulations, still marked by its underground rebel past, were modified so as to correspond to its de facto position as the representative of a belligerant nation. In June after a great deal of tergiversation, the French government was ready to open serious pourparlers, conducted on the Algerian side by Ahmad Būmenjel and Ben Yahyā. It took a further year for these to mature into official peace negotiations in which the F.L.N. delegation was headed by Belkacem Krim, a Kabyle peasant's son and once a French army corporal, one of the 'nine historical chiefs' and three times sentenced to death in absentia by French court-martials. The result was the Agreement of Evian and the conclusion of the armistice, followed by the solemn recognition of Algeria's independence and sovereignty on the 3rd of July, 1962.

The F.L.N., as Yūsuf Ben Kedda, Premier of the G.P.R.A., proudly announced, had attained the aims for which it had fought but the end of the fighting meant also the end of its war-time solidarity. Complex and highly controversial questions demanded immediate answers and released the doctrinal and personal divergencies until then kept under cover. There were the 'bourgeois' and 'socialist', the 'moderate' and the 'radical' concepts of the State that was to be built up: of its type and régime, its economic and social order, its position in the Arab community and in the political configuration of the world. There was the disagreement about the competencies and prerogatives of the Front's vital organs in determining the future of the nation: the Provisional Government, the C.N.R.A. and the Army. There were those who returned from captivity, emerged from clandestinity or re-entered from beyond the frontiers to claim their share in the direction of the country: the five of the 'historical chiefs' - Ahmad Ben Bella, Husayn Ait Ahmad, Muhammad Būdiaf, Muhammad Khidr and Farah Bitat; the regional chiefs of the six military districts (wilayas) with their officers; and the supreme commander of the army, Colonel Hūarī Būmedienne and his staff at the head of their batallions. And on the lower levels there was the changing pattern of alliances and feuds among the headmen of clans and villages, strongly bound by ethnic and regional loyalties, particularly within the Kabyle population, who under the impulse of the moment joined and abandoned now one and then the other of the great rival camps. By the time of the cease-fire it was obvious that the fissures had gone too deep for a compromise.

At the end of June, a few days before the proclamation of independence, the Provisional Government, in the absence of Ben Bella, took the first openly hostile step by deposing and degrading Colonel Būmedienne because of alleged insubordination. Ben Bella and a number of sympathizers, foremost among them Muhammad Khidr, Bitat, Būmenjel and Colonel Būmedienne with some wilaya commanders, countered by declaring the Government's decision illegal. Assembling in Tlemcen, they constituted a 'Political Bureau of the F.L.N.' of six members with Khidr as secretary-general, that was to 'take the country's destiny into its hands' (July 1962). Then their men occupied the area of Tlemcen and soon afterwards most of the region of Constantine and the Aurès. Thereupon Belkacem Krim, Būdiaf and the old Kabyle warlord Mohand Ou al-Hajj with his followers formed the 'group of Tizi Ouzou', mobilized the Kabyle tribesmen in the mountains and the adjoining rural region of Algiers and prepared to take up arms against the 'Benbellist group of Tlemcen'. Both groups had their partisans in the C.N.R.A., while the Provisional Government, or rather what remained of it found itself reduced to the rôle of an impotent spectator. In the first few weeks of independence the dislocation of the Front had brought Algeria to the brink of civil war. It was averted only by a last-minute, half-hearted accord, but the contest for power continued.

The following three or four months were rich in dramatic episodes, vehement clashes–it even came to street fighting in Algiers, Oran and Constantine–and short-lived reconciliations, but then there was no longer any doubt that the victor would be Ahmad Ben Bella, one of the Front's youngest protagonists. A peasant's son of Marnia near Tlemcen, with strict but enlightened religious views, 'Ahimed', as the people familiarly called him, knew how to find their ear when he explained his notion of an Arab socialism rooted in the teaching of the Koran, animated by modern ideas, and supported by institutions of governance resting upon the will of the people. They were satisfied that the Front, reconsolidated and rejuvenated, was to be the artisan, under the guidance of the Political Bureau, of this construction of the State, and to protect it, with the help of the likewise re-organized army, against all possible neo-colonialist or counter-revolutionary ambitions. Behind him stood firmly Colonel Būmedienne's army and most of the peasantry, of the urban masses and the former guerilla fighters. Irreconcilable remained the group of Tizi Ouzou, entrenched in its Kabyle bastion, while some sections of the Federation in France, of the Union des Travailleurs Algériens and of the students' organizations showed a certain reluctance to follow him along a line which they suspected of leading to the monopolisation of power in one man's hands. These oppositional yet far from unanimous tendencies found expression under the roof of two new political parties, neither of them of particular numerical importance: the Party of the Socialist Revolution (P.R.S.) directed by Muhammad Būdiaf; and the Front of the Socialist Forces (F.F.S.) headed by Mohand Ou al-Hajj–he and his close adherents subsequently fell off again–and Husayn Ait Ahmad.

In the meanwhile the Political Bureau through a quickly expanding network of local 'committees of support' and by a very active propaganda was able to reforge the Front in most parts of the country and to restore its prestige of the days of the revolution. Thus it made itself the predominant factor in the nation's political life and assumed an ever wider range of governmental functions. At the same time Ben Bella, cautiously and not without occasionally very serious frictions, moving one by one his actual or virtual rivals out of the field, made it the platform for his ascent to the highest offices in the State, careful to have the people approve all major steps by referendum. The Political Bureau established the lists of the candidates for the election to the National Assembly held in September 1962, which under the chairmanship of Farhat Abbas designated the new government with Ben Bella as Premier (17.V.1963). Still in the same year the Political Bureau acquired the key positions in the Union Générale des Travailleurs Algériens, had the F.L.N. Federation in France dissolved, and the two parties of the opposition declared illegal. In April 1963 Muhammad Khidr had given up his position as secretary-general of the Political Bureau, which was taken over by Ben Bella. In June Būdiaf was arrested, and in August Farhat Abbas resigned the chairmanship of the National Assembly and was excluded from the Front because of his allegedly 'bourgeois and reactionary opinion'. In September the Algerian Constitution, elaborated by the Political Bureau and approved by the Assembly, was ratified by referendum. It declared the F.L.N. the sole political party in the country, exclusively authorized to designate the candidates for the National Assembly and the Presidency of the Republic. The following week Ben Bella was elected President of the Algerian Republic for a period of five years, combining with this office those of Premier of the cabinet of ministers, of High-Commander of the Army, and of President of the Front of National Liberation.

FRONT POUR LA DEFENCE DES INSTITUTIONS CONSTITUTIONELLES see FRONT FOR THE DEFENCE OF THE CONSTITUTIONAL INSTITUTIONS

FURĀT, IBN al-, ASAD, a scholar of theology and canon law (759-828), who in his early childhood came with his father from his home in the Arab East to Tunisia. He studied first in Medina with Mālik Ibn Anas, then in al-Kūfa with a disciple of Abū Hanīfa, the founders of two of the four basic schools of juridico-theological thought. Thus he manifested already at this formative stage of his career the inclination for eclecticism which marked the work of his later years, the *Asadīya*. Upon his return to Tunisia, having acquired an outstanding rank in his field, he was appointed cadi of al-Qayrawān by the Aghlabid* ruler Ziyādat Allāh I (817-838) but had to share his functions with a second jurist. His headstrong, impetuous disposition, which quickly drew his scholarly discussions with the other religious doctors at the Qayrawān Great Mosque into an atmosphere of heated altercation and quarrel, proved, however, fully in place when Emir Ziyādat Allāh entrusted him with the command of the expedition against Sicily. He landed successfully and, always at the head of his troops, advanced towards Syracuse but died suddenly, it is not certain whether of wounds or of the plague.

G

GHĀNIYA BANŪ, a family of the Lamtūna* tribe, headed at the time of the Almoravid* rule in Morocco and al-Andalus* by two brothers, Yahyā and Muhammad. In the days of its decline, Yahyā, who had been governor first at Valencia then at Cordova, died, whereas Muhammad gained power in Majorca, proclaimed himself Emir of the Balearic Islands and, refusing to reconcile himself with the new spiritual order instituted by the Almohads*, rendered homage to the ʿAbbāsid caliphs at Baghdad. His son and successor ʿAbd Allāh was dethroned, after a short reign, by his second son Ishāq, who took care to avoid an armed conflict with the Almohads, but received with open arms all their opponents seeking his protection. He was thus able to build up an army and navy of considerable fighting power, and not only to maintain himself against attacks of his Christian neighbours on the Iberian mainland, but at last (1183) also to break openly with the Almohad court.
Ishāq's son ʿAlī (1184-1188) succeeded his elder brother Muhammad, then carried the hostilities into Africa and landed at Bougie (1184). Helped by local Almoravid sympathizers, he easily captured the town and secured the alliance of the Arab chieftains in the environs, mainly branches of the Banū Hilāl,* but was driven back from the plains by the Almohad troops and for a while withdrew to the southern desert regions. From there he extended his raids into the areas of Tunis and Constantine and in the interior as far as Sijilmāsa, pillaging and devastating villages and towns, but retreating into the desert whenever he met serious resistance. When the number of his adherents from among the marauding tribes of the region began to grow, he entrusted his headquarters at Bougie to his brother Yahyā and first turned westwards, took Algiers and Miliana, then eastwards, conquered southern Tunisia and penetrated into Tripolitania, where he joined hands with a Turkish adventurer, Qarāqūsh, the chief of a band of Turkoman and Kurdish slave-soldiers and allied Bedouin tribes. Qarāqūsh established himself at Gabès on the Tunisian coast while ʿAlī had his seat further inland between Gafsa and the depression of the Jarīd. Both of them, recognizing the overlordship of the ʿAbbāsid caliph, were confirmed as the legitimate rulers in their territories delimited by common consent for the pursuit of their predatory expeditions.
The fourth Almohad sovereign, Abū Yūsuf Yaʿqūb al-Mansūr* (1184-1199), energetically attempted to pacify these far-away sections of the empire. In a combined operation by land and sea he succeeded in bringing most of Tunisia under control. ʿAlī and Qarāqūsh were beaten in open battle; the fortifications of Gafsa razed; a number of the turbulent Arab tribesmen transferred into central Morocco; and some of the Kurdish soldiery induced to take service in the Almohad army. Yet peace and order were of short duration. The Balearic Islands, occupied by the Almohad fleet, were reconquered by one of ʿAlī's

brothers, and as soon as the troops were withdrawn from Tunisia, plundering and destruction went on as before. ʿAlī Ibn-Ghāniya's successor, his brother Yahyā (1188-1236), after repeated conflicts with Qarāqūsh, feeling strong enough to dispense with his help, drove his former confederate first out of Gabès (1195) and then into the desert. An accomplished master of guerilla warfare, Yahyā with his allied tribal chieftains held all southern and central Tunisia as well as wide stretches of the coast under his sway, ruling in the manner of an independent prince without disguising his ambition of further expansion.
After some hesitation between a conciliatory policy and a war necessitating a fleet and an army organized for desert fighting, the fifth Almohad ruler, Muhammad al-Nāsir (1199-1213), decided for the latter when Tunis itself had fallen into Yahyā Ibn-Ghāniya's hands. In the course of two years the towns of the coast were taken; Yahyā and his Bedouin auxiliaries severely beaten; Tripolitania and Tunisia occupied and solidly garrisoned (1204-1206). Yet Yahyā, who was still able to rally a number of warlike chiefs and to constitute a widely-ramified Berber tribal confederation, reassumed his razzias, sowing everywhere ruin and destruction, until a decisive defeat forced him to take refuge in the desert. About the same time the Balearic Islands were incorporated into the Almohad empire. Yahyā's fighting spirit, however, remained unshaken. Taking advantage of the unsettled situation under al-Nāsir's weaker successors he repeatedly broke forth from the safety of his retreat, came dangerously near to another conquest of Tunis, harassed the entire region between Constantine and Bougie and for a while even held Tlemcen in his possession, until he fell in battle near Miliana (1236).

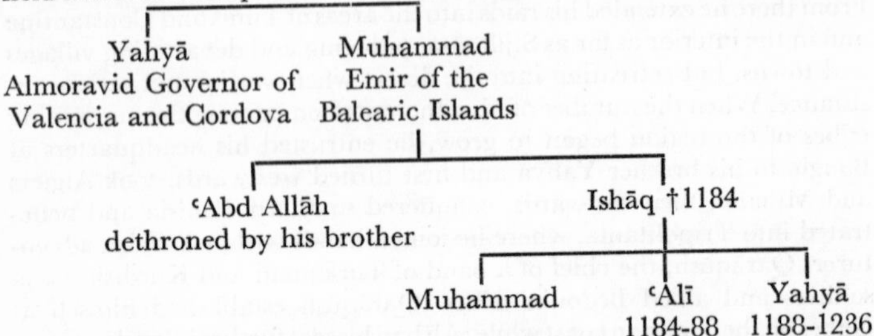

GHASSĀNĪ al-, MUHAMMAD al-WAZĪR, a Moroccan statesman, highly cultured man of letters and bibliophile, descended from an old Andalusian family (†1707). He served in several high court offices under the ʿAlawid* sultan Mūlāy Ismāʿīl* (1672-1727) who honoured him with his particular favour. He was entrusted with several diplomatic missions, amongst which one to Spain with the double task of ransoming Moroccan sailors of captured pirate vessels and of trying to trace and bring back ancient manuscripts that might have been left in former Andalusian mosques. After a leisurely voyage with prolonged stops at every place which aroused his curiosity, al-Ghassānī was splendidly received in Madrid by King Charles II (1665-1700). Upon his return he wrote a description of his travels, the *Rihla al-Wazīr fī Iftikāk al-Asīr*, partly translated into French ('Voyage en Espagne d'un ambassadeur marocain (1690-1961)', by H. Sauvaire, Paris 1884), which gives an interesting picture of contemporary Spanish court life and the impression it produced upon a member of the Moroccan élite.

GHAWTH, approximately 'one who accords help in time of distress', a term of Islamic mysticism, which according to some authors is more or less synonymous with *qutb** (i.e. one who has attained the supreme degree of saintliness), but according to others it designates one who holds a rank second to that of a *qutb* in the hierarchy of the saints.

GHAZĀL al-, a nickname meaning 'the gazelle' - because of his grace and slender stature while in the bloom of his youth - under which the Hispano-Arab poet Yahyā Ibn Hakam (†860) has become known in medieval Arabic literature, especially in the sphere of satirical poetry. A brilliant speaker in prose and verse, unscrupulously shedding his sarcasm on everybody and everything, and always ready, if attacked himself, with a quick and caustic repartee which made his opponent the laughing stock of the audience, he was one of the outstanding figures at the court of Emir al-Hakam I (796-822) and Emir ʿAbd al-Rahmān II (822-852). The latter sent him at the head of diplomatic missions to the Norman court and to the Byzantine emperor, and on both occasions his wit and conversational talent seem to have contributed a great deal to the success of rather delicate tasks. One of his most bitter enemies at Cordova and the permanent target of his satirical effusion was Yahyā Ibn Yahyā al-Laithī*, reputed scholar of theology and canon law (*faqih)*, who remained notwithstanding his influence powerless against the popular poet.

GHĀZĪ IBN, ABŪ ʿABD ALLĀH MUHAMMAD IBN AHMAD, a highly reputed Moroccan jurist (1454-1513), born in Meknès. There he began his studies, continued them in Fez, and returned subsequently to his native town. In Meknès he held the office of a *khatīb* (the official preacher of the Friday sermon, the *khutba)*, and later moved to Fez where he was invested with the functions of a *khatīb* and *imām* (the leader in prayer of the community) at the Qarawīyīn* mosque. While taking part in an expedition against the Portuguese, undertaken by the Wattāsid* Sultan Abū ʿAbd Allāh Muhammad al-Burtuqālī (1505-1524), he fell ill and soon afterwards died and was buried in Fez, the sultan in person attending his funeral. The mausoleum which some hundred years later was erected over his tomb is still in existence. Ibn Ghāzī wrote about a great many juridical, theological and literary subjects, but only about half of his writings have come down to us, while the others are known only by their titles. Of special interest from the modern point of view, is his *Rawd al-Hatūn* (abridged title) which was partly translated into French (O. Houdas, Monographie de Méquinès-Ibn Ghāzī, Er Rawd alhatoun, Journal asiatique, Paris 1885). It gives in three sections a history of Meknès, a detailed topographical description of the town and biographical information on some of its outstanding families and scholars together with a number of poetical quotations.

GHAZZĀL al-, ABŪ al-ʿABBĀS AHMAD IBN al-MAHDĪ, a Moroccan man of letters and dignitary (†1777), at the court of the ʿAlawid* sultan Muhammad Ibn ʿAbd Allāh, descended from an old Andalusian family of Malaga. He conducted successfully two diplomatic missions, one to Spain and the other one to Algiers, in charge of negotiating the exchange of prisoners-of-war. He left a very detailed description of the first of these voyages *(rihla*)* the *Natījat al-Ijtihād fi'l Muhādana w'al-Jihād* (appr. Conclusions of the exhaustive Studies on Peace and the Holy War), which constitutes an interesting source of information on the life and society of contemporary Spain.

GLĀWA, originally one of the minor branches of the great Masmūda* family of Berber tribes, which subsequently extended its influence over a region stretching south-eastward from Marrakesh in a broad belt across the chains of the High Atlas into the Dadès and Darʿa valleys. Except for an incidental mention as *Igelwān* among the first followers of Ibn Tūmart*, the founder of the Almohad* doctrine, they do not appear in the story of tribal events until the middle of the last century. At that time there emerges in their midst a sequence of outstanding figures who impose their authority upon the many clans and fractions composing the much divided tribal society of the area - the later Glāwa territory - so that finally their name completely superseded that of the Masmūda parent stock. It was still a regionally circumscribed preponderance, but was the platform upon which the Glāwa chieftains ascended to key positions in the state. The first to follow this path, at the time when Sultan Muhammad Ibn ʿAbd al-Rahmān (1859-1873) after his unlucky war with Spain was confronted with rebellions everywhere in the country, was one Muhammad al-Ibibat who from his stronghold at Telwat controlled the difficult passes on the important road from Marrakesh towards the Sahara. Carefully weighing the chances of the rebels and of the sovereign, he decided to join with all his warriors the forces of the government and in recognition of his services had his de facto predominance officially confirmed.
His successor in the leadership, al-Maydanī al-Glāwī, followed the same policy of calculated loyalty, and Sultan Mūlāy al-Hasan's (1873-1894) token of gratitude was one of the new Krupp canons. More by the cunning exploitation of the prestige which this 'artillery' gave him in the eyes of the tribesmen than by its actual military value, he established his overlordship in the ever widening Glāwa country and set up on all strategic points a kasba *(qasaba*)* for a caid *(qā'id**, the local government officer in charge of the dispensation of justice, the collection of taxes and the enlistment of troops) of his own choosing. Instituting his son ʿAbd al-Malik as his lieutenant in Denmat on the northern slopes of the Atlas, he ruled his vast community of tribes from his seat in Marrakesh, subtly blending traditional paternalism with autocratic firmness. With his support Mūlāy ʿAbd al-Hāfiz, the brother of Sultan ʿAbd al-ʿAzīz (1894-1908) and his bitter enemy, manipulated the threads of the insurrection which ended with the sultan's deposition, and a year later, with Mūlāy ʿAbd al-Hāfiz' accession to the throne. During his short reign (1909-1912), Maydanī al-Glāwī was his vizier,

an office which he made the source of more power and wealth in terms of money, land and water-rights. At first cautiously watching the violent but incoherent outbreaks of resistance against the establishment of the French Protectorate* (1912), but quickly realizing that in the long run the outcome could not be doubtful, he resolutely sided with the new régime, facilitated the occupation of Marrakesh by the French, and kept the Glāwa country quiet while everywhere else the mountain tribes stood in uproar. Upon his death (1918) his brother Tihāmī, eliminating all other heirs, took his succession and was appointed Pasha of Marrakesh, a position usually held by a member of the reigning dynasty, which elevated him to the highest ranks of state dignitaries. Al-Hajj Tihāmī al-Glāwī, entirely disregarding the theoretical sovereignty of Sultan Mūlāy Yūsuf (1913-1927), devoted himself with heart and soul to the French cause. The French Residents General, on the other hand, pursuing as the leitmotiv of government what was called the 'policy of the Grand Caids', let al-Glāwī Pasha, legitimately or not, bring more land into his possession and more tribes under his obedience, until from his sumptuous, strongly guarded palace at Marrakesh the 'uncrowned sultan of the South' controlled nearly one eighth of Morocco. He had an audience far beyond his domain proper, as the spokesman of the conservative elements, the big families in the countryside and a number of religious brotherhoods*, who, far from disapproving his methods and archaic ways of wielding his authority, saw in him the protector of the benefits which they reaped from their support of the French régime. With his close ally, Muhammad ʿAbd al-Haiy al-Kattānī, the head of the influential Kattānīya* fraternity and deadly enemy of the ʿAlawid dynasty, he was the exponent of all reaction against the various and still inarticulate but increasingly aggressive movements for the abolition of the French rule and the emancipation from the political, social and economic supremacy of its Morrocan defenders. During the second World War, around 1943 when it seemed as if the claim for independence was gaining favourable resonance in American policy-making circles, he cautiously tried to insert himself into the complex of the nationalist currents. At the end of the war however, he resumed still more tenaciously the persecution of the nationalist militants within his jurisdiction. At the same time, his attitude of contemptuous indifference towards the young Sultan Muhammad V* (1927-1961) turned gradually into undisguised hatred as public opinion, at least in the towns, manifested an ever firmer confidence in the sovereign as the embodiment of all patriotic aspirations. Resolved to bring about his downfall, al-Glāwī linked his partisans together in an 'Opposition and Reform Movement of the Pashas and Caids' - reforms involving an essential curtailment of the sultan's rights - which was to act as the instrument of the policy of force adopted by the Protectorate authorities. In February 1951, he marched his tribesmen against Fez and Rabat, and while they camped menacingly in front of the capital, the Resident-General forced the sultan to condemn solemnly the nationalist claims and to dismiss from his surroundings all those known for nationalist sympathies. The move, however, miscarried and, far from undermining the sovereign's position,

it increased his popularity, and gave further incentive to the patriotic sentiments.
Then Tihāmī al-Glāwī, backed by high Protectorate officials and influential French interests, set out upon a new attack which he intended to be decisive. In May 1953 his 'Movement' submitted to the French government a petition signed by an impressive number of pashas and caids, requesting the sultan's deposition, and in August, having sacrificed two black bulls at the sanctuary of Mūlāy Idrīs and taken an oath to have Muhammad V ousted, he and his caids and notables rallied the tribes for another march against the Palace. This time he was successful: the Resident-General declared the sultan deposed, had him deported and his uncle Muhammad Ibn ʿArafa put on the throne. The Pasha of Marrakesh triumphed. He was received as a guest of honour at the Académie Française in Paris and at the coronation of Queen Elizabeth in London. But his victory was short-lived. Instead of being forgotten, the 'martyr sultan' in exile, contrary to his enemies' expectations, became the symbol of the nation's struggle for independence. After two years of riots, strikes, terrorism and insurrection, al-Glāwī realized that his restoration was inevitable. Once more he sought a way into the nationalist camp and 'for the sake of unity and calm' announced his allegiance to the exiled monarch. In November 1955, Muhammad V was again recognized as the rightful Sultan of Morocco, and Tihāmī al-Glāwī prostrated himself at his feet and asked his forgiveness. Three months later, 83 years of age, he died, and all that has remained of the Glāwa splendour are the decaying kasbas where once Tihāmī's caids resided - landmarks in the southern valleys of the Atlas.

G.P.R.A. see PROVISIONAL GOVERNMENT OF THE ALGERIAN REPUBLIC

GOUVERNEMENT PROVISOIRE DE LA REPUBLIQUE ALGERIENNE see PROVISIONAL GOVERNMENT OF THE ALGERIAN REPUBLIC

H

HAFSIDS, Banū Hafs, a dynasty in Tunisia, eastern Algeria and Tripolitania (1236-1574), named after its ancestor Abū Hafs ʿUmar* (1090-1176), a chieftain of the Berber Hintāta tribe in the High Atlas, and one of the first adepts of the Almohad* doctrine. The long Hafsid line was started by his grandson Abū Zakariyyā'* (1228-1249), Almohad governor of Tunis, who a few years after his appointment declared his independence. He left to his son Abū ʿAbd Allāh Muhammad al-Mustansir* (1249-1277) a realm which included Tunisia, the present-day Algerian department of Constantine, and Tripolitania. It had a strong army, a comparatively smoothly running administrative machinery and maintained a profitable trade with the great Italian city republics.

Al-Mustansir, a far-seeing statesman, abstained from all conquering enterprises, enhanced the family prestige by securing his recognition as Caliph and *Amīr al-Mu'minīn* (Commander of the Faithful), a title, it is true, devoid by then of practical significance, but thenceforth borne by all Hafsid sultans but one. He strengthened the structure of the State, widened the sphere of its political and economic influence, and with only slight sacrifice steered clear of an invasion of the crusaders (1270). With his death began a century-long melodramatic sequence of dynastic rivalries, conspiracies and assassinations, leading to repeated partitions of the Hafsid possessions. His son and successor, Caliph Abū Zakariyyā' Yahyā al-Wāthiq (1277-1279) left the affairs of the State uncontrolled to his chancellor Ibn al-Habbabar, whose ambition, covetousness and ruthless persecution of real or potential rivals were the source of the most unscrupulous court intrigues. They were in no slight measure instrumental to al-Wāthiq being overthrown and put to death together with his three sons by his uncle Abū Ishāq Ibrāhīm, who after a previous miscarried revolt against his own brother al-Mustansir, had lived in exile at the Nasrid* court in Granada. He confiscated al-Habbabar's enormous fortune and had him put to the torture until he succumbed.

Abū Ishāq Ibrāhīm (1279-1283), presumably wishing to appear as the sole rightful heir to his father, Amīr Abū Zakariyyā', bore only the title of emir, as the latter had done, and not, like his two immediate predecessors, that of caliph. He subdued a sedition of his governor of Constantine and repelled the troops of the King of Aragon who in support of the rebel had landed at Collo (halfways between Bône and Bougie), but lost throne and life to the 'impostor' Ibn Abī ʿUmārā* (1283-1284). Another of the sons of Abū Zakariyyā', Abū Hafs ʿUmar* (1284-1295), made an end to the short-lived usurpation, but was unable to prevent the Aragonian admiral Roger de Lauria from seizing the island of Djerba and the Kerkenna islands. Under his reign occurred the first split in the dynasty, when his nephew Abū Zakariyyā' Ibn Abī

Ishāq tore off the entire territory of the present day Algerian department of Constantine, declared himself independent with the title of emir, and established his residence at Bougie (†1301). Caliph Abū Hafs ʿUmar was succeeded in the Tunisian sector by a fifteen-year old grand-nephew, usually mentioned by the Ḥafsid historiographers as Abū ʿAsīda, i.e. 'father of the wheat pap', from the liberal distribution of this kind of food to the poor by his tutor, a saintly man upon whose advice the caliph had passed over his own son and appointed him his heir. Abū ʿAsīda (1295-1309) tried in vain to regain the dissident emirate of Bougie. Upon his death it was the emir of Bougie, one of the sons of Abū Zakariyyā', Abū al-Baqā, who after a brief campaign entered Tunis, was acclaimed caliph and restored the unity of the Ḥafsid realm. His accomplishment was of short duration. In the West, his brother Abū Yahyā Abū Bakr*, the governor of Constantine, repudiated his allegiance and conquered Bougie. In the East a distant relative, Abū Zakariyyā' Ibn al-Lihyānī, the supreme Almohad Sheikh *(Shaykh al-Muwahiddīn)* and former head of the chancellery, rallied some Arab tribes and took hold of Tunis. Without attempting a counter-action, Abū al-Baqā abdicated, took refuge in Constantine with his brother, who received him, but only to have him assassinated. Thus for the second time, the Ḥafsid domain was parcelled off into a larger, eastern half with the capital Tunis, which extended somewhat beyond Tripoli, and a smaller, western section reaching approximately as far as Bône, with Bougie as capital.

Ibn al-Lihyānī (1311-1317) was a man of high culture, bound in close ties of friendship to the writer and chronicler al-Tijānī*, his chief chancellor. Open-minded in matters of religion, he allowed considerable freedom to the Christian missionaries, in particular to the Franciscan Friar Raymond Lulle (†1314), the famous controversionalist and intellectual parent of the first European college for the study of Arabic. The idea, however, entertained by King James II of Aragon in his three-year correspondence with Pope John XXII, that the 'King of Tunis' was ready for conversion to Christianity, was without doubt only wishful thinking. Ibn al-Lihyānī was, it seems, possessed of a high sense of justice, which even let him condemn to death by the cadi his own son accused of murder–he commuted the sentence into imprisonment–but he was no general. Scared by the first attack of his neighbour in the West, Abū Yahyā Abū Bakr, he sold everything of value in his palace in Tunis, including what had remained of the library collected by the first Ḥafsid ruler. Then he withdrew to Tripoli where he built for himself a new residence, al-Thārimat (1317), obviously hoping for a turn for the better. His son Abū ʿAbd Allāh Muhammad, called Abū Darba, (the one with the wound in the face), released from prison and proclaimed caliph by the people of Tunis (1317), resisted for a while but finally was defeated and died in exile in Tlemcen. Ibn al-Lihyānī left Tripoli for Egypt and spent the rest of his life at the Mameluke court in Cairo. The Ḥafsid territories were again united in the hands of Caliph Abū Yahyā Abū Bakr (1318-1346).

During the first half of his long reign, the new caliph had to contend against all sorts of adversities: family members disputing his title to the throne; turbulent Arab chieftains; particularistic ambitions of regional leaders; and the ʿAbd al-Wādids* of Tlemcen trying to fish in troubled waters. The struggle was hard but he won, seconded by his chamberlain *(hājib)* Ibn Tāfarājīn. With his death the fruits of the victory were lost. Twice in succession, if only for a short time, the Marīnid* sultans of Fez forced the Hafsids out of the country: first, Abū al-Hasan ʿAlī* between 1347 and 1349; then his son Abū ʿInān Fāris* in 1357. Neither of them could maintain himself against the hostile population. In the interval three caliphs of no more than episodic significance followed one another in Tunis, where the machinery of the State was actually run by Ibn Tāfarājīn, while various Hafsid princes ruled as independent emirs over the area of Constantine, Bougie and Bône.

This third split lasted until Abū Yahyā Abū Bakr's grandson, Caliph Abū al-ʿAbbās Ahmad (1370-1394), who had ruled as emir in Constantine, achieved the reunion first of the miniature emirates and then of the entire Hafsid territory, which for the following hundred years or so remained undivided in the hands of capable and energetic rulers. Abū al-ʿAbbās imposed discipline upon the Bedouins and the proud city lords; restored internal peace, at least to an extent which had been unknown for a long time past; and strengthened the authority of the government by installing his sons and his brother at the head of the administration in the provinces–a policy which previously had not always been conducive to the desired results. All this did not detract from his interest in the intellectual currents of his time, as was manifested by the patronage he extended to the universally famous historian Ibn Khaldūn*. Yet his ommission to curb the piracy operating with increasing audacity from the Tunisian ports began to disturb ever more seriously the country's relations with the great Italian trading centers, until Genoa, Venice, Pisa and Sicily assembled a fleet and occupied the island of Jerba (1388). The invaders were forced to withdraw, but two years later Genoa and France fitted out a second expedition, had it blessed by both the Pope of Rome and his rival of Avignon, landed near al-Mahdīya and laid siege to the town. Harrassed by the Tunisian troops and suffering from the heat and the shortage of supplies, they re-embarked after three months of resultless guerilla fighting. In the peace treaties concluded with the two Powers, the caliph secured appreciable advantages for the country's trade, but the pirates continued unchecked as before.

The political and social equilibrium established by Abū al-ʿAbbās was further consolidated by his son Abū Fāris ʿAbd al-ʿAzīz* (1394-1434), and successfully maintained by his great-grandson Abū ʿAmr ʿUthmān (1435-1488). He succeeded to the throne at the age of sixteen after the premature death of his elder brother al-Muntasir, whose name lives on in the oldest still subsisting *madrasa* in Tunis, the Muntasirīya. Each of them had first to reduce some all too ambitious relatives, some turbulent tribes or an overbearing clan in the larger towns, but such opposition was defeated without serious difficulties. The age-old caravan traffic with central Africa, Egypt and Arabia found increased incentive. It was paralleled by a thriving over-sea trade with the great Italian emporia, Sicily and Aragon, regulated by a series of diplomatic agreements and

upheld by minutely specified privileges which were granted to their commercial settlements in the principal Tunisian ports.
Armed interventions by one or the other of these Mediterranean Powers, called forth by an unscrupulous piracy affected, upon the whole, the Tunisian economy but little, and the less so when after the fall of Constantinople (1453) the Turkish advance forced them to shift to the North African ports of most their Levantine trade. Thenceforth the convoys of the so-called 'Barbary Galleys' left at regular intervals Venice and Syracuse for Tunis, continued either westwards to Bougie or eastwards to Tripoli and Alexandria; others connected Genoa with Tunis, Bône, Collo and Bougie, touching on their return journey the principal points on the Moroccan and Spanish coasts. It all was reflected in the higher profits of the upper business classes, and, although to a minor extent, in the greater well-being of the broad masses, but in particular in the increase of the state revenues from import and export taxes. The set-back caused by three devastating outbreaks of the plague (1443, 1453, 1468)–the most frightful calamity of the Arab West, periodically appearing since the end of the XIVth century and not completely rooted out until the middle of the nineteenth century–was of comparatively short duration. As little as their predecessors did these Hafsid sovereigns or their dignitaries think of displaying any of the marks of that splendour illustrated before their eyes at the contemporary Renaissance courts of the Sforza in Milan, the Malatesta in Rimini or the d'Este in Ferrara and Modena, whom Tunis supplied with high-priced Berber horses, lions, precious fabrics, carpets or ostrich feathers. Such luxury would in fact hardly have fitted into the traditional rôle they felt to be theirs as the custodians of Almohad puritanism, the patrons of theological scholars, of saintly men (marabouts*) and religious brotherhoods*.
Fissures in the structure of the state, which had appeared already in the few years of Abū ʿAmr ʿUthmān's three immediate, highly cultured successors, assumed critical proportions during the reign of Abū ʿAbd Allāh Muhammad (1494-1526) and became disastrous under his son Mūlāy al-Ḥasan (1526-1542). By the turn of the century, most of the larger urban centers such as Bougie, Constatine, Bône, Gabès or Tripoli with their surroundings were autonomous areas governed by families of notables. The great Arab chieftains, mainly of the Sulaym* group of tribes, held a position very close to independence in the rural districts which in the course of time had been assigned to them in full ownership or usufruct *(iqtā'*)*. Favoured by the decline of the central authority, new and sharply conflicting Spanish and Turkish aspirations began to take shape and were to produce deep-going effects in this section of the Mediterranean system of power. Owing to a superior armament as much as to skilfully playing upon the divergences of local interests, Spain gained possession of Mers al-Kabīr (1505), Oran (1509) and Algiers (1510) where on an island within cannon-shot range a heavy bastion, the so-called Peñon, was erected. In the same year the Spanish fleet, continuing eastwards along the Tunisian shores, occupied and fortified Bougie and Tripoli, and proceeded to attack the island of Jerba. There the advance came to an unexpected halt (1511), for by then Jerba had become a Turkish stronghold.

Turkish infiltration had started with the bold freebootery of the brothers ʿArūj and Khair al-Dīn Barbarossa. To them, around 1505 Sultan Abū ʿAbd Allāh Muhammad conceded, in return for a share in the ransom but also as a means of parrying in time the peril of a Spanish invasion, a base at La Goulette (at the entrance of the innermost part of the Gulf of Tunis) and later a second one on Jerba, appointing ʿArūj commander *(qā'id*)* of the island. ʿArūj repelled the assault on Jerba, but his attempts at reconquering Bougie failed. He dislodged the Spanish garrison from the town of Algiers–not, however, from the strong fort of the Peñon–and after his death in battle (1518) against the Spanish forces near Oran was replaced by the younger Khair al-Dīn. Although it is uncertain when the plan of establishing an Ottoman province in the Arab West came for the first time under serious consideration in Constantinople, the Barbarossa brothers could apparently from the beginning of their operations count on the assistance of the Porte. When Khair al-Dīn succeeded his brother, he had under his command a contingent of Turkish soldiers, received, so it seems, soon afterwards a substantial reinforcement of men and artillery, and was officially appointed commander-in-chief *(beglerbegi)* by the Ottoman government. In the contemporary, often contradictory reports dealing with the imbroglio of the Hispano-Turkish struggle whose stage thenceforth was Tunisian soil, only the main events stand out clearly discernible. Following the seizure of Collo, Bône, Constantine and the Peñon of Algiers (1529), Khair al-Dīn occupied Tunis, Bizerta, some of the ports on the eastern coast and even al-Qayrawān, which he turned over to the Shābbīya brotherhood. Mūlāy al-Hasan, expecting to obtain Spanish intervention, in the meanwhile withdrew into the desert (1534). Indeed, the year after, Emperor Charles V of Spain, embarked a strong force in Sicily, wrested Tunis and La Goulette from the Turks and reinstalled al-Hasan who submitted to Spanish vassalage. He was forced, however, to abandon La Goulette to Spain, and lost Sfax, Monastir and Sousse to Charles' faithful friend and ally, the great Genoese seaman Andrea Doria (1540). While attempting to reconquer al-Qayrawān he was taken prisoner, dethroned by his son Ahmad and blinded.

Under Sultan Ahmad (1542-1569), called Hamīda, courageous, enterprising but a ruthless despot, whatever had remained of the Hafsid realm continued to shrink in the protracted warfare between Spain and the Ottoman Empire or rather its governors in the Algerian Regency and their generals. Khair al-Dīn's devoted companion-in-arms, Darghūt, captured the Spanish stronghold of Tripoli (1551), then Gafsa (1556) and al-Qayrawān (1557) and won a decisive victory over a Spanish fleet near Jerba (1560). Taking advantage of a discord that had arisen between the Sultan and the Spanish commander of La Goulette, the Beglerbegi of Algiers, ʿEulj or ʿAlī Pasha, occupied Tunis, and Sultan Ahmad took refuge in the steppes of the Jarīd. After the almost complete destruction of the Turkish navy at Lepanto, however, the victor, Don Juan of Austria, recovered possession of Tunis (1573) and installed as ruler, under the tutelage of one of his officers, Sultan Ahmad's brother, Mūlāy Muhammad. He was the last of the long Hafsid line: a year later an Ottoman army reconquered Tunis and the fortress of La Goulette and made an end to his shadow reign. Ottoman sovereignty over the Arab West from Oran eastwards was definitively established for three centuries to come.

Hafsid Rulers of Tunisia:

Abū Zakariyyā' Yahyā I	1228-1249
Abū ʿAbd Allāh Muhammad I al-Mustansir	1249-1277
Abū Zakariyyā' Yahyā II al-Wāthiq	1277-1279
Abū Ishāq Ibrāhīm I	1279-1283
Abū Hafs ʿUmar I	1284-1295
Abū ʿAbd Allāh Muhammad II Abū Asīda	1295-1309
Abū Yahyā Abū Bakr al-Shahīd	1309
Abū al-Baqā Khālid I	1309-1311
Abū Yahyā Zakariyyā' I Ibn al-Lihyānī	1311-1317
Abū Darba	1317-1318
Abū Yahyā Abū Bakr	1318-1346
Abū Hafs ʿUmar II	1346-1347
First Marīnid Occupation	1347-1349
Abū al-ʿAbbās Ahmad al-Fadl	1350
Abū Ishāq Ibrāhīm II	1350-1369
Second Marīnid Occupation	1357
Abū al-Baqā Khālid II	1369-1370
Abū al-ʿAbbās Ahmad	1370-1394
Abū Fāris ʿAbd al-ʿAzīz	1394-1434
Abū ʿAbd Allāh Muhammad IV al-Muntasir	1344-1435
Abū ʿAmr ʿUthmān	1435-1488
Abū Zakariyyā' Yahyā III	1488-1489
ʿAbd al-Mu'min	1489
Abū Yahyā Zakariyyā' II	1489-1494
Abū ʿAbd Allāh Muhammad V	1494-1526
Mūlāy al-Hasan	1526-1542
Sultan Ahmad, called Hamīda	1542-1569
Mūlāy Muhammad	1573-1574

HAMMĀDIDS, Banū Hammād, a Berber dynasty in present-day Algeria (1014-1152), which had branched off from the Zīrids* of al-Qayrawān. Its founder Hammād Ibn Buluggīn was put in charge by his nephew, the Zīrid ruler al-Mansūr, of the fortified town of Ashīr (south-east of Algiers) and the western sections of the Zīrid realm. These he successfully defended against incursions of Zanāta* tribes, the hereditary enemies of his own tribal group, the Sanhāja*, as well as against a revolt of some of his own relatives. Presumably with a view of gaining full independence he built (1007) in the Hodna Mountains in the southern part of the present-day department of Constantine west of modern Sétif, a strong castle, *al-Qalʿat* (The Fortress), around which there soon developed a lively provincial town. It maintained a prosperous caravan trade with Egypt, Iraq, Arabia and western Africa, and was widely reputed for its beautiful Great Mosque and splendid palaces of the princely family, the *Qasr al-Manār* and the *Dār al-Bahr*. Today there stand only ruins, but their exploration, aided by the descriptions

of Arab historiographers, has given a fairly good picture of their architectural and decorative characteristics.
As soon as Hammād Ibn-Buluggīn felt solidly established he repudiated (1014) the suzerainty of his Zīrid cousins and of their common overlords, the Fātimid caliphs, and recognized the spiritual supremacy of the sunnite caliphate of Baghdad. After prolonged but fruitless attempts to subdue the rebellion, the Zīrid ruler al-Muᶜizz (1016-1062) had to consent to a partition, and to confirm it, following an equally unsuccessful siege of *al-Qalᶜat,* in an agreement with Hammād's son and successor al-Qā'id (1028-1055). Resuming the former friendly relations with the Fātimids, al-Qā'id made it possible for his line to exploit the tragic fate of its Zīrid rivals, who nearly succumbed under the onslaught of the Banū Hilāl* and the Sulaym* Bedouins.
Al-Qā'id's successor, BuluggīnIbn Muhammad (1056-1062), extended his heritage deep into Morocco and even temporarily occupied Fez. He was assassinated by his cousin al-Nāsir (1062-1088) who penetrated eastwards into the former Zīrid domain and established his influence on the coast from Sfax over Sūsa to Tripoli, and advanced southwards far into the Sahara. Then he built up the poor fishing village which has become the town of Bougie into a fortified port and made it his second capital, called after him al-Nāsirīya. Soon splendid government buildings, palaces surrounded by gardens and, allegedly with the help of Italian craftsmen, a Great Mosque after the pattern of the Qayrawān Mosque were to arise. It remains uncertain how much of these urbanistic achievements, known only by descriptions of later date, goes back to al-Nāsir, and how much to his son and successor al-Mansūr (1088-1104). All this illustrated the wealth of the Hammādid realm and formed an appropriate background for the flourishing trade, the scholarly activities and the luxurious, perhaps sometimes licentious life of which Bougie for the following fifty or sixty years was the centre.
At the time of al-Nāsir, the Hammādid power and prosperity attained their zenith. Under his son al-Mansūr, the Banū Hilāl began to draw their raids dangerously near *al-Qalᶜat,* and although al-Mansūr tried to buy the safety of the trade roads at ever increasing costs to his treasury, the town was soon left aside by the overland commerce and lost most of its inhabitants to Bougie. With some of the Arab clans in his pay, al-Mansūr still succeeded in halting the advance of the Almoravid* confederates, but after the short reign of his son Bādīs, his second successor al-ᶜAzīz (1105-1122) was no longer able to control the pressure of the Bedouin tribesmen irresistibly spreading over the inland plains, and had to shift the political and economic center of gravity of the shrinking Hammādid realm to the Algerian coast. His son Yahyā (1122-1152) was the last of the line. Having with difficulty mastered revolting Berber clans and Arab invaders, he was not strong enough to prevent a Norman fleet from occupying Jijelli (1143). A few years later, the Almohad troops took Algiers, beat his army at the gates of Bougie and completely dispersed it. Yahyā surrendered (1152) but was treated with honours and died in comfortable exile in Salé (Morocco).

1. Hammād Ibn Buluggīn	1014-1028
2. al-Qā'id Ibn Buluggīn	1028-1055
3. Muhsin Ibn al-Qā'id	1055
4. Buluggīn Ibn Muhammad	1056-1062
5. al-Nāsir Ibn ʿAlannās	1062-1088
6. al-Mansūr Ibn al-Nāsir	1088-1104
7. Bādīs Ibn al-Mansūr	1104
8. al-ʿAzīz Ibn al-Mansūr	1105-1122
9. Yahyā Ibn al-ʿAzīz	1122-1152

HAMMŪDIDS, an Arab dynasty in al-Andalus* and North Africa, one of the many branches of the Idrīsid* family, whose founders, the brothers al-Qāsim and ʿAlī Ibn Hammūd, at the time of the last Umayyad caliphs had left their homeland in the Rif mountains for al-Andalus. Caliph Sulaymān appointed al-Qāsim governor of Algeciras, Tangier and Arzila; and ʿAlī governor of Ceuta. Taking advantage of the troubled situation in the caliphate, ʿAlī declared himself independent, and with the connivance of the commander of the Berber troops stationed in the region of Granada, Zāwī of the house of the Zīrids*, made himself master of Malaga. Then he marched against Cordova, occupied it, and with his own hands killed Caliph Sulaymān. Thereupon, he had himself proclaimed caliph (1016-1018) and assumed the honorary surname *al-Nāsir*. It was the first time that the throne of the Spanish caliphate was not occupied by a scion of the Umayyad family. His brother al-Qāsim was installed as governor in Seville, while his elder son Yahyā took al-Qāsim's place in the family possessions in Africa, and the younger Idrīs in Malaga. Yet after a two-year reign al-Nāsir was assassinated by his servants in his palace.
In the week following al-Nāsir's death, al-Qāsim arrived in Cordova and was proclaimed caliph with the honorary title *al-Ma'mūn* (1018-1021). The first days of his high office were somewhat disturbed by the election of an Umayyad anti-caliph, who, however, after a brief career lost his life while attacking Zāwī Ibn Zīrī and his Berbers at Granada. Although al-Qāsim seems to have understood how to balance the various antagonistic currents at the court and in the town, a conspiracy instigated by his nephew Yahyā Ibn ʿAlī forced him to flee and to return to Seville. It was now Yahyā's turn to accede to the caliphal throne, but his influence hardly reached beyond the walls of the capital. Some eighteen months later, trusting no longer in the loyalty of the garrison, he withdrew to the greater safety of Malaga, and al-Qāsim went back to Cordova (early 1023). After remaining there half a year, he was driven out by a popular uprising, fell into the hands of his irreconcilable nephew Yahyā, was thrown into prison and assassinated. The following years again saw two Umayyad caliphs, both finding a premature death. Then Yahyā was called back to Cordova (1025). He came, after some hesitation, but having turned over to one of his lieutenants the office of caliph, by then devoid of all practical significance, he returned to his residence in Malaga. Under his descendants the Hammūdid heritage was lost to the Zīrid* rulers of Granada (1057) and to the ʿAbbādids* of Seville (1058).

HANDICRAFT. All over the Arab West generations of craftsmen, aided by the patronage of luxury-loving sultans, high dignitaries and the rich bourgeoisie, displayed during centuries in the embellishment of mosques, madrasas (theological schools) and seigneurial residences an artistic creativeness which inspired contemporary authors to enthusiastic descriptions and is today illustrated by quite a number of highly valued pieces in the collections of Arab and occidental museums. This source of inventiveness, taste and skill, which had its origin in al-Andalus*, began to flow more and more abundantly in the era of the Almohad* empire, during which the currents of art and thought found the ways wide open between the cultural centres of Arab Spain and North Africa. When subsequently the Moslem domain in the Iberian peninsula was pressed back into constantly narrowing limits, an ever greater number of Andalusian Moslems went to seek new homes across the Mediterranean until after the fall of Granada (1492) the Morisco* emigration, at first more or less voluntary, and then in the early XVII th century enforced, grew into a stream which according to estimates carried some 300.000 people into Morocco and Tunisia.
In these close contacts, and in the permanent interchange of skills and creative ideas, which went on for several hundred years between Seville, Cordova or Granada and Fez, Marrakesh, Rabat-Salé or Tunis, evolved a characteristic Moroccan-Tunisian blend of aesthetic concepts, enriched by Syrian, Egyptian and later on Turkish designs and techniques, and by Berber patterns and colour schemes. These were embodied in a large range of materials, treatments and objects: sumptuous mosaic work of rare woods and ivory; heavy bronze doors and chandeliers covered all over with a labyrinth of intertwained lines; wall adornments of glazed tiles *(zellīj)* shining in a play of lustre from soft white to light green, turquoise and deep violet; sculptured or polychrome gypsum and wood; richly tooled leather; some special types of carpets* and blankets *(hanbels)*; fine tissues of silk and wool; and embroideries of silver and silk threads in almost inexhaustible diversity. Within these trades, each one firmly organized in its own corporation or guild, there grew up in the course of time around one or the other family of masters and their apprentices some regional particularities, forms and methods, faithfully cultivated and developed, but upon the whole remaining confined to details. Gradually, however, the imaginative force and refined workmanship waned, and from about the middle of the XVIIIth century onward rapidly degenerated, with rare exceptions, into a monotonous and mediocre repetition of traditional models. Step by step the great majority of these craftsmen merged in the more modest artisanry which supplies the unpretentious needs of the broad masses in the towns and villages.
The penetration into all domains of every-day life, constantly gaining ground, of occidental habits and tastes, and in its wake the preference of the broad public for the occidental type of machine-made products and mass-confection - the import of second-hand clothes from America into Algeria alone amounted between the two World Wars to more than 9000 tons every year - pressed a great many of those humble weavers, tailors, tanners, sandal-makers, smiths or carpenters out of the lower

middle class and dangerously near to the borderline of poverty. Without savings and often in debt, continuing in their tiny workshops of the *sūq* their age-old methods, they have to support by their earnings, directly or indirectly, about one million people in Morocco, at least as many in Algeria and about 600.000 in Tunisia. In the development programmes which are in operation in all three countries various measures are being planned and partly implemented, in order to meet or at least keep within manageable dimensions the social and economic consequences of this apparently irreversible decline of the traditional handicraft production. They are designed to promote the training in efficient techniques, the introduction of mechanical equipment and the adjustment to the changed demands; to transform the ancient guilds into co-operatives for the extension of credit, the purchase of raw material and the sale of the products; and to facilitate the transfer into the modern factory sector of the largest possible number of those to whom handicraft can no longer offer any livelihood.

HARAKA al-SHAʿBĪYA see POPULAR MOVEMENT

HARAKA al-WAHDA al-MAGHRIBĪYA see MOVEMENT OF MOROCCAN UNITY

HARKA, colloquially for *haraka* (plur. *harakāt*), movement, in a wider sense military operation, a term which came into use in Morocco towards the end of the XVIIIth century to denote the military expeditions into the border areas between the *bilād al-makhzan** (territory controlled by government authority) and the *bilād al-sība* (territory of dissidence), undertaken mainly for the purpose of enforcing the payment of taxes, often several years in arrear, and to reconsolidate the prestige of the central government, at least theoretically and for a time. These campaigns, extending as a rule over several months, were conducted by specially assembled, regular armies under the personal command of the sultan accompanied by his court, his harem and the high government officers with their clerks, so that the current affairs of the state might be carried on without interruption. The *harka* moved very slowly, lived on the country and was rarely involved in real fighting, but by the sole weight of its presence made the people find it to their advantage to pay the taxes or rather bargain for a compromise, usually through intermediaries of religious prestige. A punitive raid into one or the other particularly refractory village or tribal area, resulting in devastated fields, burnt-down houses and the loss of the herds, helped all too reluctant negotiations forward. Yet since at heart both parties were equally desirous to arrive at a practical solution and animated by a similar conciliatory spirit, the *harka*, after all, was just a rather drastic and expensive instrument of governing. It worked in the easily accessible regions, but was of no avail in dealing with the warlike tribes in the rough Atlas mountains without roads, bridges or the space for laying out sufficiently large, fortified camps.

In the years of the Algerian Revolution* the word *harkī* came into general use as the designation of the Algerian Moslems who had enlisted in the French army and fought in the ranks of the French forces. Despised and branded as traitors by the revolutionaries, they were left upon the conclusion of the armistice practically defenceless against retaliation and persecution, notwithstanding the clauses granting them a theoretical safety. The French government had to ship nearly all of them, with their families, altogether ten to fifteen thousand persons, to France, to provide for them shelter, food, health-and medical services and the possibility of earning a livelihood.

HAYYĀN ABŪ, MUHAMMAD IBN YŪSUF, a Hispano-Arab philologist and theologian of Berber origin (1256-1344), born in Granada, whose studies took him practically all over the Arab world. Finally he settled in Cairo, where he taught the Tradition of the Prophet *(hadīth)* until his death. In the course of his long life he wrote numerous works - allegedly 65 - of which only 15 have come down to us. He dealt with historical, biographical and juridical subjects, but in particular devoted himself to grammar and linguistics, including Persian and - it is said - Ethiopian. Even when judged by modern scientific concepts, Abū Ḥayyān has to be accorded a high-ranking place in the field of grammatical research and comparative study. Among those of his works which have been preserved, especially outstanding are *al-Idrāk fī-Lisān al-Atrāk* (The Understanding of the Language of the Turks), the first Turkish grammar, and the *Manhaj al-Sālik* (The Road of the Seeker), a commentary including rectifications of the well-known *Alfīya* by Ibn Mālik, the grammar in 1000 verses.

HAYYĀN IBN, ABŪ MARWĀN al-QURTUBĪ, an outstanding Hispano-Arab historian (987-1086) of Cordova, of whom only scanty biographical data have been transmitted. He was a prolific author. He is said to have written some fifty works from among which a history of al-Andalus*, *al-Matīn* (The Truthful One), is reported to have consisted of about 60 volumes. The only book of which at least larger portions have been preserved, the *Kitāb al-Muqtabis fī Ta'rīkh Rijāl al-Andalus* (freely translated: Concise Compilation of the Biographies of famous Men of al-Andalus), usually quoted as *Al-Muqtabis,* constitutes a valuable source of information on the Umayyad period of Spain, and shows Ibn Ḥayyān's gift of keen observation and of colourful and occasionally extremely sharp writing. Of particular interest are some sections discovered in the library of the Qarawīyīn Mosque at Fez a few years ago (partly translated into Spanish by Garcia Gomez, Madrid). They contain extensive quotations from Ahmad and ʿĪsā al-Rāzī's* History of al-Andalus and from the works of two of their disciples, which otherwise would have remained unknown.

HAZM IBN, ABŪ MUHAMMAD ʿALĪ, a highly reputed Andalusian theologian, philosopher, chronicler and man of letters (994-1064). He was born in a village in the neighbourhood of Niebla of an originally Christian family, probably of Visigothic origin. His grandfather had embraced Islam, whereupon his father, who served in high offices at Cordova, had a genealogy made up intended to prove an ancient Irano-

Islamic descent. While still a youth, he felt attracted by a career of politics which suffered, however, many vicissitudes, leading him into prison in Almeria, from there to the position of a vizier in Valencia, then back into prison in Granada, and again to high honours in Cordova, but seven weeks later back into prison - all this was a result of the sudden changes in the constellation of the local groups in power, which marked the numerous city-states arising at the end of the Umayyad caliphate. Finally he withdrew from the intrigues and agitations of the courts, first to the quiet town of Jativa - famous for the art of its makers of fine writing paper, and in his later years to the family estate in his native village.

Ibn Hazm was a devout Moslem adhering to the rigid school of theological thought of the Zāhirites, allowing only strictly literal interpretation of the Koran and the Tradition of the Prophet *(hadīth)*. He stood up for his conviction with all the sharpness of a brilliant polemic, regardless of the standing or influence of his opponents, yet always fair enough to admit their argumentation when convinced of its correctness. Thus it is understandable that in spite of his prominent scholarly and literary qualities only a very close circle of friends remained at his side in the atmosphere of general animosity which his attacks aroused. He even had to witness the public burning of his books in the streets of Seville, but seems to have taken it with the disdainful equanimity of a mind certain of its unassailable superiority. Scholarly controversies on the merits and demerits of his doctrine continued for quite a time after his death. Yet besides those writings of an interest encompassed strictly by doctrinal theology, he left others which reveal him as a keen observer of the political events and their artisans, as well as a colourful portrayer of the Andalusian society of his days and of its everyday life.

It is said that Ibn Hazm wrote some 400 books, a figure which doubtless should not be taken too literally. Among those of a theological character which have come down to us ranges first the Book of Religions and Sects, *(Kitāb al-Fisal fī al-Milal wa al-Nihal)* which develops his doctrine and attempts a critical analysis of the Jewish and Christian religions (partly translated into Spanish by Miguel Asín Palacios, Madrid, 1936/39). He moves into quite different fields with a kind of psychological treatise with frequently interspersed passages in verse, on love and the lover's attitude, usually quoted by the abridged title *Tawq al-Hamāma*, 'The Dove's Neckring' (translated into English by A.R. Nykl, Paris 1932; into French by L. Bercher, Algiers, 1949; into German by M. Weisweiler, Leyden 1941; into Spanish by Garcia Gómez, Madrid 1952). Of his other works, in none of which he omits to illustrate the main subjects by his remarks on the various facets of Andalusian life, may be mentioned: the *Kitāb al-Akhlāq wa al-Siyar*, 'Book on Ethics and Conduct' (French translation by N. Tomiche, Beirut 1961) and the *Risāla fī Mudāwāt al-Nafs*, 'Epistle on the Treatment of the Soul', both translated into Spanish by M. Asín Palacios, Madrid 1936; the *Marātib al-ʿUlūm*, 'Classification of Sciences'; the *Risāla fī Fadl al-Andalus*, 'Epistle on the Excellence of al-Andalus'; and the *Kitāb Jamharat Ansāb al-ʿArab*, a treatise on the genealogy of the Arabs and Berbers in the Maghrib and Spain.

HILĀL BANŪ, a large, much ramified tribe which in the course of the suppression of the Qarmatian revolt in the ʿAbbāsid caliphate had been forced to move into Egypt. After a highly troublesome stay there of a century or so, they were urged by Caliph al-Mustansir (1035-1094) to start out together with their equally unruly sister-tribe, the Sulaym*, for the conquest of the realm of his disloyal vassals, the Zīrid* emirs, a territory covering present-day Tunisia and the eastern parts of Algeria. Thus began (about 1052) the great Arab tribal migration into North Africa, led by the Banū Hilāl and Sulaym and later continued by the Maʿqil* and others, generally referred to by the name of the strongest of them as the Hilālian invasion. They rushed over the Cyrenaica into the plains of Tripolitania, Tunisia and Algeria, devastating the fields, plundering and dislodging the native population. While the Sulaym for some time still remained in Tripolitania, the first Hilālian group, the Banū Riyāh, pushed straight into the Zīrid countries, where they were soon joined by the main body of the tribal masses. The Zīrid Emir al-Muʿizz, who in vain had tried to come to an understanding with their chieftain Mūnis was defeated in a heavy encounter near Gabès (1053) and in all haste evacuated his capital al-Mansūrīya. Within a short time, the Arabs were masters of most of the minor towns, where they installed tributary rulers of their own choosing, then forced their way into al-Qayrawān, which for many years did not recover from the destruction. In an attempt to save as much as he could, al-Muʿizz gave three of his daughters in marriage to three Riyāh chiefs and under their protection set up his residence in the strongly fortified al-Mahdīya (on the eastern Tunisian coast north of Sfax).

The Banū Hilāl, firmly implanted in Tunisia and in most of the present-day Algerian department of Constantine, continued their advance into Central Algeria. There, the Hammādid* emirs, having learned from the events in the neighbouring country, showed greater skill in negotiating than their Zīrid cousins. They made the invaders their allies, enlisted them for their army, and allocated them subsidies which soon took up half the yield of their country's harvest. But still they were unable to check the irresistibly swelling Bedouin flood, and considered it safer to transfer their residence from al-Qalʿat in the interior, to the coast where they built and fortified the port and town of Bougie. Moving in autumn southwards for the rainy season, and in spring up north again, the various Hilālian branches - Banū Riyāh, Sawāwida, Athbaj, Durayd, ʿIyād with all their sub-groups - gradually found each its particular pasture grounds. Their chieftains sold wheat, sheep and honey, partly the tribute levied on the villagers, or the produce of raids, to the townspeople in their area, who also had to keep in store for them the food needed by men and animals in the non-grazing period. They also discovered ways to advantageous arrangements whereby for an adequate compensation they abstained from robbing the carawans and kept the roads safe from the predatory instincts of other tribesmen. In spite of the rarely ceasing disturbances, there began in the countryside between Berbers and Arabs a slow but steady process of mutual adaptation which over several generations brought about a more or less peaceful mode of coexistence within the framework of the common religion and the same way of life

founded in the nature of the country. Yet it took a long time for recovery from the damage which every sphere of rural and urban economy had suffered.
The collapse of the Zīrid and Hammādid emirates under the blows of the Almohad* empire builder ʿAbd al-Mu'min* thoroughly modified this social and economic pattern. Suspecting that they might be deprived of their privileged position, the Hilālian tribes, allied in one strong coalition, refused to submit to the new ruler but were disastrously beaten in a four-day battle at Sétif (1152), and somewhat later again at al-Qayrawān. ʿAbd al-Mu'min followed up his victory by starting to shift more and more Hilālian groups into Morocco and to spread them over the thinly populated plains so as to keep them under closer control. The effects of this policy, continued by several of his successors, on the migratory mechanism of the tribes, was considerable. Whereas until then it had been moved only by their own volition or by the force of natural events such as drought or scarcity of grazing land, there was henceforth also an outside authority to command it, at least at times of strong governments. Such times, it is true, were none too frequent in Moroccan history. In the intervals, the Banū Hilāl as well as the Maʿqil appearing after them in Morocco, made themselves masters of ever wider regions in the plains and in the belts of the oases; imposed tributes on villages and towns; fought in the service of the sultan or took up arms for a rebel, changing sides without hesitation. However, also in Morocco the same economic, social and spiritual factors acting alike upon Arab and Berber communities, sedentary or nomad, were gradually conducive to forms of an association not differing from those in Algeria and Tunisia. In all three countries there still live here and there Hilālian clans as peaceful villagers.

HIZB al-DUSTŪR al-DĪMŪQRĀTĪ see DEMOCRATIC CONSTITUTIONAL PARTY

HIZB al-HURR al-DUSTŪRĪ see DESTOUR

HIZB al-ISLAH al-WATANĪ see PARTY OF NATIONAL REFORMS

HIZB al-ISTIQLĀL see ISTIQLĀL al-

HIZB al-SHŪRĀ wa'l ISTIQLĀL see DEMOCRATIC PARTY OF INDEPENDENCE

HORNACHEROS, or Hornachuelos, a turbulent, warlike community of Moriscos* (designation of the Spanish Moslems after the fall of Granada 1492) of the small town of Hornacho some 30 miles south-east of Mérida, who for years succeeded in deriving a prosperous livelihood from a combination of trade and high-way robbery. At last, in order to see them depart as smoothly as possible, the governor of the province authorized them to leave the country fully armed and with all their belongings (1608). They emigrated to Morocco and settled in Rabat, then very thinly inhabited, on the site of the present-day quarter of the

Ūdāya, which they strongly fortified. Soon they were joined by a few thousand other Moriscos expelled from Spain, who established themselves somewhat to the south, and erected that portion of the city's circumvallation which still bears the name of the 'Wall of the Andalusians'. Other Morisco newcomers settled on the opposite bank of the Bū Ragrāg River around Salé, the prosperous sea-port. Voluntarily submitting to the authority of the Hornacheros and practically maintaining no contacts with the native population, these Morisco colonies lived a life of their own according to their traditional Andalusian pattern, continued to speak their Spanish vernacular, and set up their own administration in a sort of semi-autonomous twin-city, subsequently called *Slā al-qadīm* (old Salé) and *Slā al-jadīd* (new Salé i.e. Rabat). Both names remained in use until late into the XVIIIth century.
Impelled, probably in equal measure, by the hate against their former Spanish overlords who had driven them out of their homes, and by the prospect of booty, the Moriscos of Salé-Rabat under Hornachero leadership began the Holy War against Spain and fought it in the form of a daring and profitable piracy. The Hornacheros provided the vessels, organized the expeditions, controlled the commercial and financial phases, and even concluded an agreement with the Saʿdian* Sultan Mūlāy Zaidān (1603-1629), to whom one-tenth of the proceeds was turned over. Emphasizing the religious tinge of their freebooting enterprises, which after a while were no longer confined to Spanish ships, they secured the political friendschip of some of the influential marabouts*, especially the widely popular Muhammad al-ʿAyyāshī*, who from the dislocating Saʿdian realm carved out nearly independent small kingdoms for themselves. In the confusion marking this period of Moroccan history, the Bū Ragrāg twin cities constituted a regular republic, governed by a Council in which the Hornacheros as well as the other Moriscos had their seats. It lasted for about fifteen years (1627-1641), although torn by incessant inner rivalries, with the people now of one, then of the other side of the river uppermost, each conspiring against the other and against the Hornacheros with the Saʿdian sultan, with al-ʿAyyāshī and with the Christian Powers. At last both of the two cities were occupied by al-ʿAyyāshī who, however, left unchanged their status as a self governing body politic. So too upon his death in battle (1641) did the Dilā'yūn* brotherhood, which incorporated the city republic into its territory; and likewise some 25 years later the ʿAlawid* Sultan Mūlāy al-Rashīd (1664-1672) after his victory over the Dilā'yūn. Thus the Morisco community of Rabat-Salé lived under Hornachero leadership, culturally, socially and economically a foreign body in the State, until the French King Louis XV, in order to curb piracy, had the cities several times bombarded, destroyed their fleet, and thus deprived them of the source of their wealth. Finally Sultan Mūlāy Ismāʿīl* (1672-1727) stationed a strong garrison in the Kasba of the Ūdāya. Sultan Muhammad Ibn ʿAbdallāh put an end to what had been left of Hornachero independence (1757).

HUSAYNID BEYS, the last Tunisian dynasty (1705-1957), whose reign ended with the proclamation of the Republic. It derived its name from Husayn Ibn ʿAlī, a Turkish *agha* of the spahees (cavalry commander), who in the three-year struggle for power after the assassination of the last Murādid* Bey had emerged as the victor. Following his recognition by the Porte a solemn assembly of high Turkish officers declared the succession hereditary in his family by seniority in the male line - a system conducive in most cases to open the way to the throne only to princes of an advanced age.

Throughout the first hundred years of their reign the Husaynids had to face revolts of pretenders; insurrections in the army; tribal disturbances; and aggressions by their neighbours, the Deys* of Algiers, who once even occupied and pillaged the capital Tunis (1756). The responsible positions in government and in the army were held by Ottoman subjects, mainly former Christians from Anatolia, Albania or Greece, captured while young by pirates, converted to Islam and bought on the slave market by the Bey who had them educated and trained for his service. With their offspring from Arab wives they developed into an oligarchical caste and through further intermarriage became in a few generations increasingly arabized. As their number grew, more and more of them infiltrated into the land-owning and merchant groups and thus became linked to the ruling circles. A wide cultural and economic rift separated these upper- and middle-classes, imbued with the orthodox teaching of the religious doctors of the great Zaytūna Mosque, from the poverty-stricken peasantry and urban proletariat. This mass readily followed the guidance of the marabouts*, of their descendants and adepts - some 40.000 by the middle of the last century- and of the sheikhs of the religious brotherhoods* with their 300.000 adherents.

Very few Beys of the long Husaynid line had capacities for real leadership. Ahmad Bey (1839-1855) abolished slavery and the restrictions to which the Jews were subjected; authorized schools run by Christian missionaries; and tried to modernize the army and navy. His successor, Muhammad Bey (1855-1859), built roads and bridges, laid the first telegraph lines and restored the ruined Roman aquaduct from the Zaghwān mountains to Tunis. He went also a step farther in the policy of liberal reforms and promulgated a 'Fundamental Pact' which granted equal civic rights to all Tunisians. He abrogated tax exemptions and private monopolies, and created a Supreme Council of 60 members, invested with legislative, supervising and judicial prerogatives which considerably limited the Bey's sovereign power. It was the first venture of this kind in an Arab country, and its application encountered serious obstacles. It was renewed in 1861 by the following Bey Muhammad as-Sadoq (al-Sādiq) in the form of a constitution *(dustūr)* by which he recognized 'side by side with his own sovereignty, the sovereignty of the Tunisian people'. Although this charter practically never came into force and was suspended soon afterwards in the course of a peasant revolution, it was not forgotten. Some sixty years later it supplied the protagonists of the Tunisian nationalist movement with an argument for their claims, and the two great Tunisian political parties, the Destour* and the Neo-Destour*, with a name of strong popular appeal.

None of these innovations went far enough to revive the prosperity which Tunisia had enjoyed in the XVIIth and during the greater part of the XVIIIth century, largely due to the skill and diligence of the immigrants from al-Andalus* (Moriscos*), and which unscrupulous dissipation and misgovernment had gradually allowed to deteriorate. For some time, loans advanced by French banks kept the state finances afloat until the interest charges, imposed at exorbitant rates, could no longer be paid. Under pressure of the creditors an 'International Finance Commission' was instituted (1869), headed by a Frenchman and, in order to save appearances, by the Tunisian general Khair al-Dīn, which controlled the operations of the State Treasury until the establishment of the Protectorate*. Aware of the political danger inherent in this financial dependence, particularly since the French aims at colonial expansion beyond the Algerian borders had become ever more evident, Khair al-Dīn sought in the dormant Ottoman suzerainty the means to forestall attempts of this kind. He brought about the issue of a *firman* (decree) by the Sultan, which reaffirmed the Bey's obligation to obtain the Sultan's authorization before declaring war, concluding peace or ceding a part of his territory, and in general before entering into negotiations with a foreign Power except on matters of internal bearing. Soon afterwards he was appointed Grand Vizier and endeavoured to reorganize the anachronistic public administration, to suppress corruption and to build up a staff of efficient civil servants, for which purpose he founded a school of higher learning, based on up-to-date pedagogic principles, the Sādiqi College, named after Bey Muhammad al-Sādiq. It is still in existence and counts among its alumni the President of the Republic, Habīb Bourguiba, and a great many of the men who have played a foremost rôle in Tunisia's recent history.

After six years in power (1872-1877) Khair al-Dīn was forced to resign, sold his large estate at Enfida (*Dār al-Bey*, on the Gulf of Hammamat), a gift of honour by the Bey, to a French concern, moved to Constantinople and for a while held the office of Grand Vizier under Sultan ʿAbdül Hamīd II. With his disappearance from the Tunisian stage the crisis approached rapidly. In 1881 Bey Muhammad al-Sādiq signed the Treaty of Kassar Said (The Bardo) and in 1883 the Convention of La Marsa which created the French Protectorate, although the Ottoman Government maintained the claim to Turkish suzerainty until Turkey's defeat in the First World War and the Treaty of Sèvres (1920). The Husaynid Beys had ceased to count any longer as a factor in Tunisian history, which for the following seven decades was shaped by the people's resistance against the enforced French rule. Two of them however sided openly with the nationalist parties against the Protectorate authorities: Naceur Bey (al-Nāsir) who in 1921 was on the point of abdicating in protest against the dictatorial policy of the Resident-General; and his son, Sīdī Muhammad al-Moncef (al-Munsif), spoken of by the people as the 'Bey of the Destour', sponsor of the Destourian youth organizations and ready to become the 'first President of an independent Tunisian Republic', but dethroned and exiled (1943) by the French government. On July 25, 1957 the Tunisian Constituent Assembly abolished the monarchy, deposed the 76 year-old Bey Lamine (al-Amīn †1962) and a few days later declared all possessions held by the hundred or so Husaynid family members the property of the State.

I

IBN ABĪ ZARʿ ABŪ al-HASAN al-FĀSĪ, a Moroccan historian of the XIVth century, author of much though often doubtful information on Moroccan history for the period which begins with the events leading to the establishment of the Idrīsid* dynasty and ends in the year 1324. The work, generally quoted by the abridged title *Rawd al-Qirtās* (appr. Garden of literary works, a bibliography) contains a great number of details regarding the reign of the first Marīnid* sultans. It was translated into German (Dombay, Geschichte der mauretanischen Könige, Agram 1794-97); Latin (Tornberg, Annales regum Mauritaniae, Upsala 1843-46); Portuguese (1824); and French (Beaumier, *Roudh el-Kartās*, histoire des souverains du Maghreb, Paris 1860). Nothing is known about the person and life of Ibn Abī Zarʿ.

ʿIDHĀRĪ IBN, ABŪ ʿABD ALLĀH MUHAMMAD al-MARRĀKUSHĪ, an Arab historian (XIIIth century) whose work *Al-Bayān al-Mughrib fī Akhbār Mulūk al-Andalus wa'l Maghrib* (appr. The History of the Sovereigns of al-Andalus and the Maghrib) usually quoted simply *al-Bayān* (translated into French by E. Fagnan, Histoire de l'Afrique et de l'Espagne, Alger 1901-4; a later translation by A. Huici, Tetuan 1953) constitutes an important source of information on the history and the cultural development of Arab Spain and North Africa down to the end of the XIIIth century. Incorporated are extensive passages from the writings of another chronicler, ʿArīb Ibn Saʿd, of which no other records have been preserved. The *Bayān* deals with the organization and the institutions of the Umayyad government in al-Andalus and greatly contributes to the understanding of Hispano-Arabic public life. No biographical data of either al-ʿIdhārī or ʿArīb Ibn Saʿd are extant. It may be noted that in the light of more recent research the French translation of *al-Bayān*, in particular of the sections of Ibn Saʿd's chronicle, appears to require certain rectifications concerning the meaning of a number of administrative terms and the functions to which they refer.

IDRĪS I, with his full name Idrīs Ibn ʿAbd Allāh, the founder of the first dynasty (788-974) in Morocco, descended from al-Hasan, son of ʿAlī, the Prophet's cousin and husband of his daughter Fātima. Idrīs, implicated in a revolt (785/786) in Medina against the ʿAbbāsid caliph, was forced to flee and, acompanied by his faithful servant, the freedman Rashīd, remained for some time hidden in Egypt. From there both of them wandered across North Africa, went to Tangier, and then, turning southwards, finally came into the territory of the Berber confederation of the Awrāba, mainly peasants and living in villages widely spread around the town of Walīlā, in the fertile Zarhūn mountains, perhaps identical with, but certainly near to, the ancient Volubilis of Roman

times. Well received by one of the major Awrāba chieftains, Idrīs started to preach Muhammad's message in a version close to moderate Shī'ism, among the Awrāba and the neighbouring tribes, most of them adherents of beliefs vaguely related to Christianity, Judaism or some kind of paganism. His word spread and took root. In a short time he made a great number of converts and was recognized as *Imām* - the spiritual and secular head of a half-religious, half-political coalition of Berber tribes in northern Morocco and in the Rif mountains.
By peaceful propaganda as well as by force of arms Idrīs extended his domain eastwards into the country of the Maghrāwa* tribes, conquered Agadir (789) - the later Tlemcen - and built a mosque there, appointed one of his relatives governor of the town, and concluded an alliance with the Maghrāwa chieftain, Muhammad Ibn Khazar, who also recognized his imamate. Thereupon he returned to Walīlā, but wishing to establish a residence of his own he laid out in the same year a simple fortified settlement with quarters for his retinue of Berber chieftains and their men, grouped according to their tribal affiliations. It contained besides a mosque and provision for a rudimentary public administration, also an installation for the minting of coins. Called Madīnat Fās - so far no valid explanation for the name has been found - it was the origin of the city of Fez. The rapid consolidation of the Idrīsid influence in this sector of the caliphate inevitably aroused the suspicion of the Baghdad government: in 791 Idrīs Ibn 'Abd Allāh died of poison a few months before the birth of his son, the future Idrīs II*, under circumstances which in the eyes of some of his biographers do not exclude Caliph Hārūn al-Rashīd's (786-809) participation. He was buried in Walīlā, today the town of Mūlāy Idrīs, a much venerated place of pilgrimage.

IDRĪS II, the second ruler (804-828) of the Idrīsid dynasty in Morocco. He was born after the death of his father Idrīs I* († 791), so that a regency had to be instituted which was first entrusted to his father's devoted companion, Rashīd, and then, after Rashīd's assassination - instigated, according to some authors, like that of Idrīs I by the caliph's court at Baghdad - to two tutors in succession. At the age of thirteen, Idrīs II was proclaimed *Imām* at the mosque in the town of Walīlā, founded by his father. The young ruler, contrary to his predecessor, based his government more on Arab than on Berber support, attracting from al-Andalus* and from the Aghlabid* emirate influential Arab chieftains with their warriors, from whose midst he chose his vizier, his scribes and cadis. With the aid of his Arab advisers he began the construction of a new town adjoining Madīnat Fās, the still primitive Berber settlement conceived and laid out by Idrīs I as the nucleus of his future capital. The new town was designed after Arab urban patterns, with the ruler's palace, the central mosque, the merchants' and artisans' quarters and surrounded by solid walls. It was named *al-'Alīya* (The High One) and drew within its precincts a rapidly growing population mainly from al-Qayrawān, the Aghlabid capital. Madīnat Fās was left to its Berber inhabitants, but only just for one more decade, until the arrival of a wave of refugees from Cordova subsequently to the so-called Revolt of the Suburb* (814 or 818), to whom Idrīs II assigned this still mainly

rural settlement. They did not take long to transform it into a town of the type of those in their home-country. Around it the Berbers rebuilt their dwellings in a belt of suburbs where also an apparently quite numerous Jewish community given to commercial activities was soon flourishing. Thus grew up the twin-cities Madīnat al-Qayrawāyīn, the town of the Qayarawānians, and Madīnat al-Andalusiyīn, the town of the Andalusians. Much later the name of Fās appeared again, but as the place-name for the entire urban agglomeration.
Idrīs II continued and consolidated the spiritual and political conquest initiated by his father. Contemporary sources do not shed much light on the organization he built up, but the heritage which he left to his sons has been described as the first commonwealth set up in accordance with the spirit of Islam on the territory of present-day Morocco. He is said to have died, like his father, in Walīlā. His burial place, since the XVth century believed to be in the Mosque of Mūlāy Idrīs in Fez, was enlarged and embellished in the XVIIIth century and completely rebuilt in the XIXth century. It is still one of Morocco's most holy shrines.

IDRĪSĪ al-,ABŪ ʿABD ALLĀH, an Arab geographer (1100-1156 or 1166), an offspring of the Idrīsid* dynasty of Morocco (788-974). He was born in Ceuta, studied in Cordova and travelled extensively until Roger II, Norman King of Sicily (1130-1154), summoned him to his court at Palermo. There he made his permanent residence, munificently assisted by the king in the preparation of the work of his life - a monumental geography of the world. Special investigators were sent out into different countries in order to collect, following his instructions, the information which was to complete, or to verify the data transmitted by previous geographers. The result was the so-called Rogerian Book *(Kitāb Rujār* or *Al-Kitāb al-Rujārī)* whose somewhat lengthy original title is usually quoted in the abridged form as *Nuzhat alMushtāq fī Ikhtirāq al-Āfāq* (freely translated as The Recreation of One longing for Travel) or simply as the *Nuzhat.* It gives a comprehensive description, illustrated by a variety of details, of the inhabited parts of the earth as far as they were known, including Scandinavia, Italy, France and Germany, besides sections of the African coast, Egypt, Syria and the region of the Niger. An outstanding feature which in particular has made Idrīsī's work famous, is the set of 70 maps which constitutes a complete and continuous picture of al-Idrīsī's world. Judged by the level of knowledge and the concepts of critical research of his time, Idrīsī's Rogerian Book must be ranked among the most prominent achievements in the history of geographical science.
Several manuscripts of the *Nuzhat* (in Paris, Oxford, Leningrad, Istanbul, Cairo) have come down to us. A rather defective summary with its maps was one of the first books printed in Arabic (Rome, 1592) and was used for an equally inaccurate Latin translation under the title of Geographia Nubiensis (Rome 1619) by two Maronite clerics, Gabriel Sionita and Joannes Hesronita (Jibrā'īl al-Sahyūnī and Yūhanna al-Hasrūnī). There exists a French translation of the complete text (A. Jaubert, Paris, 1836-40), and a critical edition of parts of it (Description de l'Afrique et de l'Espagne, R. Dozy and M. J. de Goeje, Leyden, 1866). Idrīsī

wrote a second book, this one for Roger's successor, King William I (1154-1166), entitled *Rawd al-Uns wa Nuzhat al-Nafs* (The Garden of Humanity and the Entertainment of the Soul), which is known only by abstracts contained in the writings of a later author. He is also reputed for two pieces of high craftsmanship in wrought silver which he constructed for King Roger: a celestial sphere and a picture of the world in the form of a disc.

IDRĪSIDS, the first independent dynasty (788-974) in the history of Morocco, called after its founder Idrīs I Ibn ʿAbd Allāh*. Systematically awakening and gradually strengthening the consciousness of a community of religious, military and to some extent also economic interests, Idrīs I and his son Idrīs II* (804-828) succeeded in linking together the autochthonous Berber tribesmen and the Arab clans immigrated from al-Andalus* and Tripolitania into one single body politic. While this Idrīsid state still lacked the coherence of an administrative structure, it was strong enough to supplant the sovereignty of the Baghdad caliphate. Its capital, *Madīnat Fās* - present-day- Fez - which the first two Idrīsids built at the crossing-point of its great historic roads, gained increasingly in importance, commercially, culturally and strategically, and under their successors saw the foundation (859) of a sanctuary, the Mosque of Fātima, which was to become the nucleus of the famous Mosque and Academy of al-Qayrawīyīn*, probably the largest of all mosques in Africa.

It was the fatal mistake of Muhammad Ibn Idrīs (828-836), the eldest son of Idrīs II, not to have understood the creative idea of his predecessors and to have distributed the heritage among eight of his brothers, although keeping for himself the city of Fez and retaining a sort of moral supremacy over the other portions. After a comparatively peaceful reign, disturbed only by occasional family quarrels, he was succeeded by his son ʿAlī (836-848), who was ousted by Yahyā, his own brother. Yahyā was followed by his son Yahyā II, expelled after a short while by the people of Fez, who took offence - as it seems not without reason - at his conduct toward their womenfolk. Thereupon his cousin and father-in-law ʿAlī Ibn ʿUmar, head of the Rif branch of the family, was called to the throne but lost it in the course of an uprising. Another Idrīsid prince, Yahyā III (880-905), re-established peace and order, but had to give way to a relative, Yahyā IV (905-923), who temporarily united in his hand most of the different minor family possessions.

Thenceforth the Idrīsids became intextricably involved in the contest for supremacy which opposed the Umayyad rulers of al-Andalus to the expanding religio-political Fātimid movement. The two great protagonists, careful to avoid a direct impact, had their battles fought by their Berber vassals, mainly the confederations of the Maghrāwa* and Miknāsa* tribes, who often changed sides without apparent motives. Fez and the other Idrīsid principalities were the major stake of these encounters, which alternately played them into the hands of one or the other of the tribal chieftains or an Idrīsid prince acting as an Umayyad or Fātimid governor. A great-grandson of Idrīs II, the warlike al-Hasan al-Hajjām, recovered the sovereignty over Fez and the surrounding region but, betrayed by one of the local leaders, lost his throne and life (926), while his brothers and their sons retreated northwards into the territory of the Berber Ghumāra tribes. There, around the towns of al-Basra - the ruins of its fortifications are still in existence - and Arzila, one of their branches, the Banū Muhammad set up the mountain stronghold *Hajar al-Nasr* (the Eagle's Nest, near present-day al-Qasr al-Kabīr) and maintained themselves for some fifty more years, manoeuvering between the Umayyad and Fātimid camps. Simultaneously a second group, the Banū ʿUmar, established their supremacy in the area extending along the coast as far as Tangier and Ceuta. During this time, the Idrīsids solemnly declared their submission to the Umayyad Caliph ʿAbd al-Rahmān III* (912-961), who received them with honours at his court, while bringing others forcefully to the recognition of his suzerainty.

Once more an Idrīsid prince, al-Hasan Ibn Gannūn, regained independence and mastery over the plain of the Gharb and the entire region extending to the North and the towns of Tangier and Tetuan. It required two years of military effort to break his resistance. The surrender of *Hajar al-Nasr* (974) meant the end of the Idrīsids as a reigning dynasty. Al-Hasan Ibn Gannūn with his family was taken to Cordova and accorded princely rank by Caliph al-Hakam II (961-976), while the Berber warriors who accompanied him were enlisted in the caliph's army. Finding his presence however too cumbersome, the caliph after some time had him and his relatives transferred to the African coast, whence they moved into Egypt and were given honorary asylum by the Fātimid caliph. A few years later, al-Hasan reappeared in the Rif, assembled troops and prepared for the restoration of his throne. Defeated by an Andalusian expeditionary corps and taken prisoner, he was assassinated on the way to Cordova (985). Most of the offshoots of the widely branched-out Idrīsid family with their followers then moved from Africa to al-Andalus and took service in the Umayyad army. From their midst sprang the short-lived dynasty of the Hammūdids* (1016-1058) who for a few years occupied the throne of the caliphs at Cordova.

The part which the Idrīsids held in the history of the Arab West was a three-fold one: spiritual, cultural and political. In a society still partly pagan and in a still greater measure adhering to the Khārijite heresy, they came forward, invested with the prestige of *sharīfs* - descendants in direct line of the Prophet - damming up the advancing schism, and preparing the ground on which everywhere orthodox Sunnism was to grow up as the dominant creed. Their residences, which not seldom developed from primitive tribal settlements into sizable towns inhabited in the midst of the Berber country by a great many Arabs from the East or from al-Andalus, became as many centers of religious and secular learning, with Arabic as the vehicle of spoken and written thought. The realm founded by the first and second Idrīsid did not withstand, it is true, the rivalries among their heirs and the particularistic inclination of the tribal population, but in the portions into which it was dismembered, the concepts, although still vague, of a public administration and of an organized State continued to germinate.

IFNI, a Berber word meaning 'rocky desert' and the name of an enclave (appr. 650 square miles) in the south-western part of the Moroccan territory on the Atlantic coast, which constitutes a province of Spanish West Africa (Africa Occidental Española). It is a poor country covered almost entirely by the last spurs of the Anti-Atlas rising from a narrow, flat strip of land along the sea to some 4000 feet. The meagre soil allows only a less than modest cultivation of wheat or barley and the raising of sheep, goats, donkeys and camels, to which the not very substantial proceeds of a coastal fishery have to be added. Yet all this is insufficient to provide a living for the 35.000 to 40.000 inhabitants, mainly sedentary Berber groups of the Ait Bā ʿAmrān tribe, so that regularly about one third, in a bad season up to one half of the men must seek work in Morocco. The only town is Sīdī Ifni (appr. 4000 inhabitants), some thirty years ago a few houses around the tomb of a local saint, at present the seat of the Spanish administration, of a hospital and a secondary school, and equipped with an airport, a cinema and a race course.
The first chapter in the history of this minimum-sized, far from remunerative Spanish possession goes back to the middle of the XVth century when the governor of the Canary Islands set up at a no longer identifiable site somewhere in this region a fortified fishery and trading station - primarily for slave-dealing - which became known as Santa Cruz de Mar Pequeña. The enterprise does not seem to have flourished much, partly because of its unhealthy conditions, partly because of unceasing attacks by the neighbouring tribes. In 1524 these captured and destroyed the fortifications, whereupon the place was abandoned. The second chapter opens with Sultan Mūlāy Muhammad Ibn ʿAbd al-Rahmān's* defeat by Spain in 1860 and the subsequent treaty of Tetuan, which stipulated that Morocco was to grant to the victor a perpetual concession for the reinstallation of the fishery in an area around Santa Cruz de Mar Pequeña. No mention, however, was made, whether purposely or not must remain undecided, of the transfer of territorial sovereignty. There remained the problem of locating this one-time settlement of which no traces were left, and since the Morroccan government was in no hurry to arrive at a solution, the discussions dragged on. A mixed Spanish-Moroccan commission in 1878 failed to reach a result; so did a second one in 1885, and the negotiations continued until the Franco-Spanish Convention of 1912, after the institution of the Protectorate*, officially declared the area of Ifni as identical with the ancient Spanish possession. The outbreak of the first World War, and after its end the difficulties encountered by France in pacifying southern Morocco, delayed the actual occupation by Spain until 1934. Then, however, arose the question of determining the boundaries which had been traced on the map: in the North, along a *wādī* which was unknown on the spot; in the South, a river bed visible in the stony surroundings only during the short rainy season; and in the East, a theoretical line drawn across ravines and rocks. The French and Spanish authorities eventually arrived at an agreement, and no particular incident occurred while the era of the Protectorate lasted, notwithstanding the active nationalist propaganda of the Istiqlāl* partisans strongly supported by the local branches of the Nāsirīya* brotherhood.

The end of the Protectorate in 1956 introduced the third chapter in the history of Ifni with the Moroccan claim for its retrocession on the ground that the recognition of Moroccan independence had implicitly abrogated the Convention concluded in 1912 between the Protectorate Powers. While the Spanish and Moroccan governments were considering a solution by international arbitration, the people of Ifni gave increasingly vehement expression to their wish for incorporation into Morocco. In June 1957 the Spanish authorities deported most of the Istiqlālists, whereupon the Ait Bāʿ Amrān, helped by tribal warriors from outside, attacked the Spanish frontier posts, which were captured and had to be evacuated. The troubles, directed by an Istiqlāl militant, Bū Hammū, continued throughout the winter 1957/8 and then gradually calmed down, but the Ifni question is still a matter of discussion between Morocco and Spain, although no particular obstacle to their friendly relations.

ĪFRAN BANŪ, one of the branches of the great Zanāta* family of tribes which from their pasture grounds in the southern sections of present-day Tunisia had at an unknown period migrated westwards and at the time of the Arab conquest lived on the fringe of the Algerian highlands in the areas of Tiaret and Tlemcen. Converted to Islam, they became zealous adherents of the Ibādite version of the Khārijite heterodoxy, and about the middle of the VIIIth century under their 'caliph' Abū Qurra* set up a sort of ephemeral, loosely knit Ibādite theocracy with Agadir (near Tlemcen, no longer in existence) as the centre. Although gradually turning to the orthodox sunnite creed, they followed in the second quarter of the tenth century the call of another Khārijite 'prophet' from their midst, the fanatical Abū Yazīd*, against the Fātimid caliphs, which ended with their defeat and migration into the plains around Mascara in the present-day Algerian department of Oran (about 950). There they were soon involved in sharp feuds with the kindred Maghrāwa*, lost a great many of their best warriors and their chieftain Muhammad Ibn Sālih, but recovered under Muhammad's son Yaʿla, who established his fortified headquarters at Īfgān (today the village of ʿAin Fekān some 15 miles south-west of Mascara).

In the struggle for supremacy in the Arab West between the Umayyads of al-Andalus* and the Fātimid caliphs, Ya ʿla sided with the former - although with occasional interruptions when his preference went to the latter - and was entrusted by the Umayyad ʿAbd al-Rahmān III* with the governorship of a region extending over his own area deep into Morocco, including the city of Fez. A few years later, however, the Banū Īfran were severely beaten (958) by a Fātimid army, Yaʿla fell fighting and Īfgān disappeared for ever. Thereupon a number of their clans sought new homes in al-Andalus while the mass of the tribesmen withdrew into the desert under Yaʿla's son Yuddū. Yet hardly a decade had passed when he led them back into their former domain, again took up arms for the Umayyad cause, was again beaten (972) by the faithful Fātimid paladin Buluggīn of the house of the Zīrids*, and once more the Banū Īfran were forced to migrate westward. They rallied in the plains of central Morocco, but there again came into conflict with their old enemies the Maghrāwa. Twice Yuddū succeeded in gaining hold of

the city of Fez, then governed in the name of the Umayyads by the Maghrāwa Emir Zīrī Ibn ʿAṭīya. At last, however, the Maghrāwa were victorious, Yuddū was killed in battle (994), the Banū Īfran were dispersed, and once more a number of them found their way into al-Andalus, where at the time of the declining Umayyad caliphate a few Īfranid families gained for a generation or two independence in a town or a small territory around a fortress (Party Kings*).
One of Yuddū's relatives, Hammāma, reassembled his people, led them still further westwards into the regions bordering the Atlantic coast around the lower Bū Ragrāg, expelled the Barghawāta from Chella, and on the opposite bank of the river built up a new settlement which was to become the town of Salé, and made it his residence. His brother Abū al-Kamāl Tamīm, who succeeded him, tore away under the battle-cry of the Holy War, large areas from the heretic Barghawāta* in the Tādlā plain on the north-western slopes of the Middle Atlas, and even displaced for a while the Maghrāwa emirs from Fez. After his death (1055), the miniature Īfranid kingdom of Salé and the Tādlā maintained itself for a few more years until it fell victim to the Almoravid* assault under Yūsuf Ibn Tāshufīn* notwithstanding tenacious resistance. Thenceforth the Banū Īfran lost their coherence as a tribe. Some groups finally settled in the region of Tlemcen and gradually were absorbed by the surrounding population.

ĪFRANĪ al-, ABŪ ʿABD ALLĀH MUHAMMAD, called *al-Saghīr* (The Little One), a Moroccan historian and biographer (1670-1751). Only scanty data on his life have been transmitted, except that he was born in Marrakesh where he began his studies in order to continue them at the Qarawīyīn* in Fez. Subsequently he held an office, probably as a scribe, in the chancellery of the ʿAlawid* sultan Mūlāy Ismāʿīl* (1672-1727). At an advanced age he had to struggle hard against poverty so that he was even forced to give up his library to his creditors. It was only after his death that he was accorded general recognition as one of the great historians of his time, whose writings speak of his wide general culture. A number of his works have been lost, but one among those which have been preserved, has remained a basic source of information on the period of the Saʿdian* dynasty (1554-1659), usually quoted by its abridged title the *Nuzhat al-Hadī* (French translation 'Histoire de la dynastie saadienne au Maroc, 1511-1670' by O. Houdas, Paris 1888/9). Its value from the present-day point of view is primarily based on its reliability due to the care the author took to place, contrary to so many others in his field, historical truth above the effort to please some high patrons by eulogistic descriptions of events or persons somehow connected with them.

IFRĪQĪYA, Little Africa, a term used by the Arab authors until approximately the Ottoman conquest for the areas extending over present-day Libya, Tunisia and the eastern sections of Algeria, while the western part of North Africa was called *al-Maghrib**.

IJĀZA, the written certificate delivered by a scholar to his students upon their request at the end of a course and attesting their attendance at his lectures. This practice originated in the IXth century in Baghdad and subsequently came into general use in the Arab West. No examination was required for its delivery yet it was considered as the valid expression of the master's conviction that its holder had acquired the necessary degree of knowledge to lecture in his name on all or some of the subjects he was professing himself. It was then up to his disciples to build up for themselves their scholarly reputation and to attract their own circle of students. Quite a number of such certificates going back several centuries have been preserved and open up an interesting insight into the development of scholarly life and the general trends of thought.

INDUSTRY, in the sense of production by machine techniques as opposed to handicraft*, made its first, stepwise appearance in the Arab West towards the end of the last century in Algeria, and only much later in Tunisia and Morocco. The reluctance of domestic capital towards investments other than in trade or land, coupled with the lack of a native managerial or technical personnel, left its development, location and type or quality of production entirely to French initiative and decision. In many cases there had to be taken into account, on the one hand, the absence of protective tariffs, or, on the other, powerful financial and economic pressure groups in France, trying to prevent, or at least, retard the implantation of competitors in a market they were accustomed to consider the domain of their own export trade. It moreover soon became clear that an abundantly available cheap but entirely unskilled labour could not compensate for the deficiency of qualified workmen in somewhat more complicated processes of production. Consequently the growth of this industry was slow; the factories, with few exceptions, were small; and their equipment old-fashioned. Its field comprised mainly repair work or the manufacture of simple tools and, as a kind of side-line of the French agricultural sector, the pressing of oil, flour-milling and the preparation of a limited range of other foodstuffs. Thus as soon as these countries had achieved political independence, their next goal was to free themselves from their economic dependency. Hence the particular attention given to the preparation of economic development programmes differing according to the prevailing socio-economic trends, but invariably directed towards the initiation of a process of accelerated industrialization. Aware of the limitations of their financial and technical resources they welcomed outside assistance and cooperation, taking, however, every possible precaution to keep the operations of foreign capital under control and to forestall all possible 'neo-colonialist' aspirations.

MOROCCO presents a more favourable picture thanks to the more abundant natural sources of energy: a hydro-electric power equipment with a capacity - by far not fully utilized - of nearly one and a half million Kilowatt; coal deposits; and since recently, oil. In fact there has grown up in the last three or four decades of the era of the Protectorate a small and medium-sized, rather diversified industry which contributes about one-sixth to the national produce and one-third to the national income. It is located mainly in or around Casablanca, rests almost entirely on

French capital investments, is operated by a French technical and commercial staff, and employs an unskilled or semi-skilled native labour force of about 70.000 stable and 30.000 temporary workers. To a limited extent only it processes domestic raw material as the lead foundry of the mines of Zellija (near Oujda); the petroleum refinery at Sīdī Qāsim (formerly Jean Petit) which treats about 180.000 tons per year; the superphosphate and hyperphosphate works near Casablanca; the cement factories, flower mills and tanneries; factories of fruit and vegetable preserves or, at the fishery port of Safi, for the canning of sardines - about one-and a half million cases per year - and other undertakings of lesser significance. Upon the whole, however, the raw and half-finished materials are entirely or at least for the greater part imported, as for the three great sugar refineries with an output of 270.000 tons per year; the refineries of vegetable oils, which produce some 50.000 tons annually, but utilize hardly 6000 tons of locally harvested olives and oleaginous grains; the various branches of the textile industry which cover one-third of the local requirements; the shoe factories turning out some three million pairs per year; different types of metal works, the manufacture of household articles and of uncomplicated kinds of machines.

With the achievement of independence a new industrial policy was inaugurated. Its aims were three-fold and closely interconnected: to reduce economically unsound imports and thus the expenditures in foreign currencies; to replace the exports of domestic raw material by the export of the finished products of domestic manufacture; and to secure steady work for the greatest possible number of the potential urban and rural labour force. The ground was laid by the introduction in 1957 of a protective tariff and the conclusion of a series of agreements with France, providing for technical and financial assistance which, however, matured only in July 1962 owing to a two-year break in Franco-Moroccan relations. In the meantime a formula was elaborated combining wide latitude for free enterprise with state control concerning the selection of the industries to be created, and their policy and management by financial participation in their investment capital. This formula was given expression by the organization in 1958 of the 'Bureau d'Etudes et de Participations Industrielles' (B.E.P.I.), an autonomous, semi-public body whose activities comprise general, economic, financial and technical research on a nation-wide level and publication of the findings; studies of individual projects; and participation of a financial as well as technical and managerial order in certain newly established concerns. A simultaneously promulgated 'Code d'Investissements' specified the categories of industrial production considered beneficial for the country's economic growth, and the fiscal advantages accorded to encourage the establishment of such enterprises.

As another instrument of industrial promotion, in particular through the grant in close contact with the B.E.P.I. of long-term credits, was founded in 1959 the 'Banque Nationale pour le Développement Industriel' with a capital of which two-thirds derive from Moroccan sources, private and public, while one-third was subscribed by French, American, Belgian, German and Italian banks. In this way already came, or in foreseeable time will come, into operation: two assembly plants for light motor cars, trucks and tractors, gradually to be complemented by the fabrication of parts in as wide a range as possible; a second petroleum refinery with a capacity of a million-and-a-quarter tons; a spinning-mill for 1700 tons of yarn; a sugar factory connected with new sugar-beet plantations in the Gharb; a cork-processing plant in Tetuan, conceived as a pilot project for the large-scale exploitation of the cork-oak forests in the Mamura area; and a factory of pharmaceutical products. especially antibiotica and medicines against tropical diseases. Under study are great steel-and-iron works as well as additional docks in the ports of Tangier and Alhucemas. In December 1961, after a two-year tug of-war entangling internal political antagonisms and sharp international business competition, King Hasan II laid at Safi the corner-stone of the most important of all these undertakings - a wide industrial zone for the treatment of some 900.000 tons yearly of phosphates, comprising an electric power station and the extension of the port, the railway network and the waterway system. The constructions which require an investment of 15 million Dollars will give work to 10.000 labourers during five years. The co-ordination of the industrial projects, public and private, with those initiated in the domain of agriculture and with the training of the necessary numbers of technicians, administrators and skilled workers is to be secured within the framework of a comprehensive Five-Year-Plan (1960-1964).

It would be premature to form an opinion on the method, the rhythm or the compass of this process of industrialization. Still more so would be any attempt at a forecast of its bearing on the social structure in each of the three countries. A great deal will depend on the extent to which new opportunities of earning are opened up and how much the standard of living will be raised for the mass of the people.

In ALGERIA, statistics indicate for 1900 a little over 10.000 enterprises occupying about 40.000 workers; 25 years later they numbered 20.500, all in French ownership, and the total of their workers 110.000. There appeared no noteworthy change until the outbreak of the Second World War. When the hostilities cut the channels of imports, some additional factories were put up on the spur of the moment, but most of them did not survive the return of peace. Agriculture* remained the sole source of subsistance for the overwhelming majority of the people, yet owing to the particularities of its structure and the increase of the population the average quantity of corn per day and inhabitant, which between 1911 and 1936 according to a survey of 1938 had shrunk from 2.6 lb to 1.8 lb, amounted by then to not quite 1.3 lb, and pauperization assumed ever more alarming proportions.

While the war was still on, a 'Commission des Réformes Musulmanes' recommended the creation of industries capable of absorbing the greatest possible number of Moslem workers, whereupon in 1946 a plan providing the grant of tax reductions and credit facilities for the foundation or extension of industrial enterprises was inaugurated. Within four years it resulted in a little over 80 new factories, mostly branches of important French concerns, with some 8000 workers. Hardly much more impressive were the achievements of two subsequent Four-Year Plans (1949/52 and 1953/56), except in the field of building materials, especially cement, owing to military requirements in those years of the Algerian Revolution*. Some of the new establishments, such as in Oran a large and well-equipped earthenware factory, or in Tlemcen a textile mill with a labour force of 1200, had to close down after a short, difficult life, either because of the sharp competition of French exporters or because of the extremely low purchasing power of the domestic market. There followed another plan, solemnly announced by General de Gaulle in October 1958 and thenceforth known as the Plan of Constantine. It conceived a framework of coordinated, all around educational, social and economic development during a period of from 15 to 25 years, and within it, as a means to overcome the critically progressing unemployment, a systematic process of intensive industrialization, decentralized as far as possible, so as to prevent the excessive growth of the old urban centres. The financial aspect comprised grants of subsidies, loans and tax exemptions, managed by a specially created public institution, the 'Caisse d'Equipement pour le Développement de l'Algérie' under a mixed Franco-Algerian board of directors. The task of acquiring and parcelling out the land for the new industrial constructions with a view to their appropriately balanced regional location was given to two other public bodies, the 'Caisse Algérienne d'Aménagement du Territoire' and the 'Bureau Public d'Industrialisation', which subsequently became the Algerian Ministry of Industrialization. Considerable investments of public funds - to a much lesser extent from private sources - have in fact, and notwithstanding the troubled situation, increased the industrial activities. By the end of 1962 there were completed or near completion: a great steel work near Bône with a productive capacity of 400.000 metric tons, combined with a zone of metallurgic industries to which the necessary 70 million cubic metres of water will be supplied by a new barrage irrigating at the same time some 50.000 acres of arable land; large chemical works at the gulf of Mostaganem-Azew with extensive port installations; textile mills at Tizi-Ouzou (in Greater Kabylia); an important industrial zone in the Rouiba-Reghaia area (about 20 miles south-east of Algiers); a rubber factory at Sati; a petroleum refinery at Algiers and some 150 minor concerns occupying a permanent labour force of about 20.000 workers. In the Agreement of Evian (March 1962) which determined the relations between France and the thenceforth independent Republic of Algeria, provision was made for the continuation of the Plan of Constantine by the Algerian Ministry of Industrialization in cooperation with the 'Caisse d'Aménagement'. In March 1963 the Algerian Constituent Assembly passed an 'investment code' defining the facilities accorded on the basis of the Plan to industrial enterprises which contribute to the economic development of the country by reason of their location, the kind of their activity, the amount of the invested capital and the number of workers.

With this policy, designed to attract desirable private investments from foreign sources, there appeared ever more distinctly the tendency of basing the process of industrialization on a system of state-partnership financed in each case by a special long-term foreign loan coupled with the purchase of the necessary equipment in exchange for Algerian agricultural products. Along these lines negotiations were initiated with

Italian, German, Spanish, Japanese and American groups, with Jugoslavia and with several countries of the Soviet bloc. Simultaneously was built up a socialized sector under the management of workers' committees through nationalization of a number of light-industry and commercial enterprises such as flour-mills, brick and cement works, factories of chemical and food products, and also hotels, cinemas or motor-bus companies, but all of them owned only by Algerian citizens. A 'Commission de Planification' with various branches on the national and district levels functions as the guiding and controlling organism of the government.

The industrial outfit which TUNISIA upon accession to independence inherited from the régime of the Protectorate* is described in an economic analysis by the authors of the 'Perspectives Décennales de Développement' (Secretariat du Plan et aux Finances, Tunis 1961) as geographically and structurally inarticulate and unbalanced. Geographically, because of its concentration up to more than four-fifths in the North - except the treatment near the mines of certain minerals - which consumes 90 per cent of the total electric power and is serviced by 97 per cent of the railway lines. Structurally, because up to three-fifths it comprises foodstuffs, beverages and tobacco, while the remainder is split into a wide and incoherent range of lines such as textiles, leather goods and shoes, furniture, metal goods and simple electrical appliances, chemical products and fertilizers, all of which also figure conspicuously on the list of imports, although normally domestic manufacture could cover the requirements. In the southern regions, industrial production is absent with the exception of some 60 mechanized oil presses, as compared with nearly 500 in the North, and some date-processing and fruit or vegetable preserving plants in the great oases.

These industrial activities began and gradually evolved between the two World Wars through the initiative and the investments emanating exclusively from industrial or banking concerns in France, following the trends of their business policy, whether or not they happened to coincide with the particular interests of Tunisia. The two development plans (1947-1952 and 1953-1956) left this dependency of the Tunisian economy upon outside decisions unmodified. They were financed to seven-eighths by the French Treasury and to one-eighth from the Tunisian budget, and primarily concerned with the repair of the war damages, road and railway construction, and measures of public health, but contained no programme for rational industrialization. They were elaborated in Paris, and the French government agencies responsible for their implementation did not interfere with the choice of the type and site of the enterprises which French industrialists intended to implant. Neither was Tunisian capital, on the other hand, familiar with investments in this field, which moreover was entirely under foreign administrative and financial control.

In 1956, immediately after the recognition of independence, the leader of Tunisian trade unionism* Ahmad Ben Sālāh outlined in a 'Rapport Economique' the objectives of a long-term, planned economic, social and financial development. Its economic aspects may be summed up as the disengagement from French colonial conceptions and the building

up of a system based on the coexistence, directed and co-ordinated by a state planning authority, of a co-operative organization in agriculture and handicraft; of state control in banking, mining and public transport; and of free enterprise in industry with far-going facilities extended to private capital investments within the scope of the general development programme.
Five years passed before Ahmad Ben Sālāh's ideas, formulated with slight alterations in the 'Perspectives Décennales', materialized in a Ten-Year Development Plan (1962-1971), with himself responsible at cabinet level for the implementation. The delay was caused primarily by the multiple frictions with France in the wake of the Algerian revolution, which culminated in the crisis over the evacuation of the French naval base at Bizerta. The French government interrupted the payments to the Tunisian treasury, which had been agreed upon, and the withdrawals of French private funds attained in one year one-sixth of the national income, losses which American aid compensated only to a minor extent. Still, a Directory of the Plan was instituted and undertook some preparatory studies. Two institutions for the financing of industrial projects were founded, the 'Société Tunisienne de Banque' and the 'Société Nationale d'Investissement'. To secure cooperation in all planning tasks between government departments and private interest groups a 'Conseil National du Plan' was created which under the chairmanship of the President of the Republic comprises most of the members of the cabinet, the managers of the banks and representatives of the industrial, agricultural and labour organizations. In 1961 the Directorate of the Plan was raised to the rank of a Secretariat of the State, which started the first triennial phase (1962-1964) of the Plan. After long-drawn-out negotiations, Franco-Tunisian relations returned to normal. At the same time the quotas of certain French imports were considerably reduced so as to provide protection for Tunisian industry in the making. For a number of large-scale projects the Tunisian government obtained loans in the United States, Poland, the Soviet Union and West Germany; concluded partnership agreements with big Italian, Swedish and French concerns; set up the 'Office Nationale de Textiles' for the promotion and diversification of the textile industry and the supervision of all textile imports; and acquired the majority in a vast holding company controlling a wide variety of industrial firms. Within the first two years of the Plan about one-half of the financial investments required by the programme of industrialization could be derived from foreign sources. There came more or less near to completion or were in an advanced stage of preparation: a petroleum refinery with a capacity of over a million tons near Bizerta; a plant for the treatment of phosphates and the production of chemical fertilizers in Sfax; a cellulose factory at Kessarine; a sugar refinery at Béja;an assembly plant for different types of machinery near Sousse; steel and iron works; chemical factories and textile mills. In March 1963 the continuation of these and other schemes was announced as scheduled for a second phase from 1965 to 1969.

IQTĀ, plur. *iqtā'tāt*, literally assignment or apportionment, an administrative term denoting the cession by the sovereign of the proceeds of a portion of the State domain or of the amount of the taxes paid by the inhabitants of a certain, determined region as a reward for services rendered, or expected to be rendered to the community. By an increasingly extensive interpretation this sort of gratuity developed in the Arab West into a firmly established institution, particularly in Tunisia under the Hafsid* sultans (1236-1575) who found it a convenient instrument of governing. Under this title were comprised the allocations accorded to the Almohad* sheikhs of various grades; the donation of a piece of land to saintly men held in veneration by the mass of the people; and finally the concession of levying for their own account the taxes in one or several towns or in a whole rural district, granted to Bedouin tribes either as a means of pacifying a turbulent chieftain or in order to secure his alliance against an outside enemy or a dangerous rebel. In many cases such a privilege, originally conceived as limited by the grantor's or the grantee's lifetime, lost this temporary nature and by its constantly practised renewal finally resulted in a hereditary tenure in spite of the objections voiced by jurists.

ʿĪSĀWA, in French texts usually spelt Aïssaoua, a religious brotherhood* founded in Morocco at the end of the XVth century by Abū ʿAbd Allāh Muhammad Ibn ʿĪsā (1465-1523 or 1526). Aside from the certainly fictitious genealogical tree established by some hagiographers crediting him with sharīfian nobility, no unquestioned data as to his descent have been transmitted. Little, too, is known about his life except that he started his religious studies in Fez and later was introduced to the teaching of the great mystic al-Jazūlī* († between 1465 and 1470) by some of the latter's disciples in Marrakesh and Fez. After a stay in the Arab East where he was initiated into the doctrines of other fraternities he returned to Morocco, and in Meknès laid down the rules of a new brotherhood, strictly in conformance, it seems, with the principles of orthodox sunnism. His high reputation of saintliness attracted an ever widening circle of adepts, one of whom, Abū al-Hajjāj Ibn Abī Mahdī ʿĪsā, established still during his lifetime a branch seat *(zāwiya*)* in the area of the oases of the Figwig (in the south-eastern corner of Morocco on the Algerian border) whence his teaching spread eastwards and westwards along the border of the desert. He died in Meknès, where some two hundred years after his death Sultan Muhammad Ibn ʿAbd Allāh, in recognition of the brotherhood's never failing loyalty to the dynasty, erected over the saint's tomb a splendid mausoleum still visited every year by several thousands of devotees.
According to a version which presumably mingles fact with fiction the ʿAlawid* Sultan Mūlāy Ismāʿīl* (1672-1727), when recruiting his negro soldiery, the so-called *ʿAbīd al-Bukhārī**, fresh converts to Islam but still strongly imbued with age-old fetishistic beliefs, made them adhere in a body to the ʿĪsāwa brotherhood, confident of turning them thus into good Moslems. Just the contrary happened. The mass injection of foreign cultural elements into the ʿĪsāwa spiritual spheres perverted the teaching of the founder and lastingly infected the ceremonial of the brotherhood with the rites and practices of a primitive culture, repugnant to all higher concepts. Notwithstanding the enmity of the other brother-

hoods condemning it as heretical, the ʿĪsāwa spread mainly among the uneducated classes in Morocco around Rabat, Meknès, Marrakesh and Fez; in Tunisia; and in Algeria in the regions of Bône, Constantine, Médéa, and Oran. By now it has lost its former importance, particularly since the recent prohibition of its religious meetings by the Moroccan and Tunisian governments.

ISTIQLĀL al-, Independence Party, with its full name *Hizb al-Istiqlāl*, the strongest and most solidly constructed political party in Morocco. It was founded in Rabat in December 1943 by a group from among the principal animators of the first Moroccan nationalist movement, the Bloc of Moroccan Action*, such as ʿUmar ʿAbd al-Jalīl, Muhammad Lyazidi (al-Yazīdī), Ahmad Mikawār, or Muhammad Zaghrawī, and some younger patriots such as Mahdī Ben Barka, ʿAbd al-Kabīr al-Fāsī or Hassan Ben Shikrūn, joined two or three years later by ʿAbd al-Karīm Benjallūn (Ibn Jallūn), ʿAbd al-Rahīm Būabid (Ibn Abi ʿUbayd) or Muhammad Laghzawī. All of them acceded to key positions after the achievement of independence. The guiding and organizing spirit was Ahmad Balafrej (Blā Freej), a graduate from the Paris Sorbonne, much travelled in England, Switzerland and Germany, who had just returned from an enforced several-year expatriation. Around this nucleus crystallized a following, not numerous at the beginning, but very energetic, which represented a fairly accurate cross-section of the intellectual urban middle-class with a certain religio-traditionalist bias.
The party program was submitted to the Sultan, the Free French Resident-General and the representatives of the Allied Powers whose armies at that stage of the war were in control of North Africa. It was formulated as a Manifesto which emphasized the right of the people to self-determination. On this ground it demanded the abrogation of the French and Spanish Protectorates*, the unification of the national territory, its recognition as an independent, constitutional monarchy under the crown of the ʿAlawid* dynasty, with Islam as the state religion and Arabic as the official language. The party explicitly declared, it would refrain from all acts of violence and pursue its objectives by the sole use of legitimate means.
Surprised by the resonance the program found within religious circles, at the court and within the population at large, the French authorities reacted by arresting Balafrej, Lyazidi and the most conspicuous members. The popular manifestations provoked by these measures in all larger towns quickly degenerated into serious riots (January and February 1944), in the course of which a number of people were killed and a great many sentenced to several years of prison. After the restoration of order and the liberation of most of the arrested leaders, a series of reforms was proposed by the French Protectorate authorities for deliberation by a joint Franco-Moroccan commission. Apparently with the Sultan's tacit consent, the proposal was rejected by the Party, which refused all cooperation as long as the principle of independence was not recognized. Favoured by a period of abated tensions, the *Istiqlāl* under Lyazidi's leadership rapidly expanded, and by the end of the 'forties seems to have reached a number of some 100.000 adherents and sympathizers

recruited among associations of college and high-school graduates, sport clubs and scout troops, many of which it had created. 'Free schools' established in many of the larger urban settlements became social and political rallying points for a membership spreading more and more among the broad working classes. In the countryside, the mountain villages and among the tribes, visiting traders from the towns explained the Party's aims as best they could, although with far less conspicuous results. Simultaneously it consolidated its political machinery which rested on a system of local units or 'cells' (*jamāʿa*, literally assembly) grouped into 'sub-sections' and 'sections', and combining administrative, propagandistic and educational activities. The supreme direction was assigned to a 'Higher Council' *(majlis al-ʿalī)*, but decisions of some importance were taken by a Political Committee and a small Executive Committee, practically controlled by Ahmad Balafrej, Muhammad Lyazidi and ʿAllāl al-Fāsī, who in 1946 was enthusiastically received by the people when returning from Equatorial Africa after a nine-year exile.

By his deep religiosity and theological learning, his ardent patriotism and brilliant eloquence, he had acquired still in his young years, as a teacher of the Academy of the Qarawīyīn* Mosque at Fez, a rare reputation far beyond this scholarly atmosphere. A firm believer in the doctrine of the *Salafīya**, he carried its spirit into the nationalistic ideologies as they were voiced in the early 'thirties by the Bloc of Moroccan Action. Back home, surrounded with the halo of a national hero, he was given by the *Istiqlāl* the title 'Leader of the Party' and entrusted with propagandistic activities in a world-spanning field. He set up a branch in the international city of Tangier (1947); represented the Party in the Maghrib Bureau* in Cairo; and in the 'Moroccan National Front', a temporary association of several nationalist parties constituted in Tangier; on behalf of the party he toured the Scandinavian countries, Switzerland, Belgium and Latin America (1952); and at the end of the year together with Ahmad Balafrej and Muhammad Laghzawī headed the - unofficial - Moroccan delegation sent to the session of the United Nations Assembly in New York, which gained valuable sympathies among international public opinion, although the practical accomplishments remained limited to a rather colourless resolution.

Two Moroccan Offices of Information supplemented the apparatus of public relations: one in Paris under the direction of Ahmad al-ʿAlawī, and very active among the North-African workers and students in France, the second in New York, with a branch in Washington, which issued two publications, the 'Moroccan News Bulletin' and 'Free Morocco'. Notwithstanding continuous frictions with the censor, the party press at home flourished: *Al-ʿAlam*, (The Flag), a daily in Arabic which maintained correspondents in Tangier, Damascus, Cairo, Paris, London and New York; two weeklies, *Ra'y al-Shaʿb* (The Opinion of the People) in French, subsequently replaced by *Al-Istiqlāl*, directed during a number of years by ʿAbd al-Rahīm Būabid; and *Al-Taqqadum* (Progress); another daily, *al-Maghrib*; a literary review, *Risālat al-Maghrib* (the Message of Morocco); the magazine *Sawt al-Shabāb al-Maghribī* (The Voice of the Moroccan Youths); and finally the weekly *Sahara al-Maghrib*. A cinematographic company, the 'Studio Maghrib', added to the persuasive power of the printed word. Within a decade the *Istiqlāl* had taken root everywhere in the country, although its force sprang from the towns, and most of the court dignitaries, in particular in the close surrounding of the Sultan and the Crown Prince Mūlāy Hassan, later King Hassan II, had joined it.

This ascending line was dramatically broken up by a riot which in December 1952 under circumstances never fully elucidated started in the slums of Casablanca, spread into the city center and was suppressed with utmost severity, resulting in an undetermined but doubtless heavy loss of lives. The *Istiqlāl*, suspected to have plotted the uprising in concert with communist agitators, was dissolved, its publications were suspended, and mass arrests left the Party without guidance and the country without the stabilizing weight of the most influential factor in its political life. A few of the higher leaders were able to find refuge abroad and to continue the struggle. When on August 20, 1953 Sultan Muhammad Ibn Yūsuf was deposed and deported, the general agitation rapidly reached the danger point. Terror bands sprang up, at first of three or four, with single firearms and primitive bombs, then joining in the 'Black Star', the 'Black Crescent' or the 'Black Hand', which closely collaborated with a 'Liberation Army' and the revolting Berber tribes in the Rif and the Atlas. Many party members and also some chiefs of units were in their ranks, but hardly any responsible party leaders. At the end of 1954 one of them, Muhammad al-Basrī - the *faqīh* (colloquially *fqih)* as he was commonly called - rallied a following from among the more radical elements in his 'Secret Organization' *(Munaddama Sirrīya)*. In the meanwhile the *Istiqlāl* branches and offices abroad created and nourished international goodwill for the Moroccan case and prepared the climate for subsequent negotiations; collected money, arms, amunition and supplies for the militants of the Liberation Army. The abrogation of the Protectorate régime, the Sultan's triumphant entry into Rabat (November 16, 1955) and the return of the nationalistic leaders from prison, exile or hiding, sealed the victory of the 'Armed Resistance'.

From the confusion of the battle the *Istiqlāl* emerged full of enthusiasm, yet far from unanimous as to the lines of policy to be followed in the great work of constructing the new State. For the first time in its existence it could hold in complete freedom a National Congress (December 1955), but too hastily prepared it was mainly a manifestation of the Party's significance in the life of the nation. It reflected unmistakably the ideological differences and divergent views over the politico-economic problems which separated the more moderate Old Guard or intellectual bourgeoisie from the left-wing groups, especially trade-union members and Liberation Army militants of various shades, as well as the specifically urban interests, from the aspirations of the rural masses, still inarticulate but beginning to find their spokesmen. The second National Congress in the following year formulated the programme, an obvious compromise between these conflicting trends and the Party's statute which was built upon a combination of elections, appointments and inspectorships bound by rules of a strict discipline. Nevertheless the Party successfully set about occupying in the government machinery the position it considered its due, and within two years was solidly implanted in public administration down to the most modest functions in the provinces; in the police under the firm direction of Muhammad Laghzawī; in school and in public or semi-public institutions in charge of laying down the country's economic policy; and, although to a lesser degree, in the army. It controlled the Consultative Assembly - the forerunner of a Parliament - and held the most important ministerial posts until the end of 1958. This predominance, judged by many as differing little from authoritarian or even totalitarian party rule, acquired and maintained with uncompromising sternness, could not fail to provoke an opposition that became increasingly aggressive. It was nourished, on the one hand, by the Democratic Party of Independence*, headed by ʿAllāl al-Fāsī's all-time antagonist al-Wazzānī, and on the other, by the forcefully expanding Popular Movement*. More critical still was the growth of dissidence in the Party's own midst, against which repeated purges and the rigorous sifting of membership candidates proved of no avail. Orchestrated at the upper level, it resounded forcefully among the younger middle-class intelligentsia and the industrial workers, resenting what they called the reactionary, feudalistic attitude of the party heads. By the end of 1958 the *Istiqlāl* government in power had to give way to an allegedly non-party cabinet, four of whose ministers, however, more or less openly showed their sympathies with the factionists. In January 1959 the scission was consummated by the expulsion of the dissenters who constituted the National Union of Popular Forces*.

Conscious of its diminished influence upon the mass of the population, the *Istiqlāl* at its Third Congress in 1960, called by the leading speakers a gathering of 'auto-criticism', resolved on essential reforms of its organisation and programme which the Fourth Congress in 1961 further elaborated. In the meantime, contrary to the National Union of Popular Forces which persisted in its rôle as opposition party, it participated together with the other parties in the coalition cabinet formed (May 1960) and presided over by King Muhammad V himself with his son, Crown-Prince Hassan, as vice-president. After his father's death (February 21, 1961) King Hassan II continued to combine the royal prerogatives with the presidency of the government, leaving the ministries of foreign affairs, national economy, finances and Islamic affairs as before to the *Istiqlāl*, still a factor of considerable weight in the political pattern. In its midst, however, resistance gained more and more ground against - as the King himself termed it - the system of 'personalized powers', and was formulated by its Fifth Congress at Tangier in July 1962 in a resolution expressing the 'conviction that the only régime suitable for Morocco was a constitutional monarchy'. By the end of the year King Hassan proclaimed the Constitution, but in the opinion of many it gave too much room to control by the Crown and too little to parliamentary party play. Although it was approved by referendum (December 1962) the *Istiqlāl* ministers resigned a month later and the Party passed into the ranks of the opposition, while with the King's blessing the director of the Royal Cabinet, Rashīd Ridā Guedīra, Minister of the Interior and Agriculture, set up a new party, the 'Front for the Defence of the Constitutional Institutions*. In the elections (May 1963) for the National Assembly it obtained 69 of the 144 seats, whereas 42 were carried off by the *Istiqlāl* and 28 by the National Union of Popular Forces. Since then in each of the two camps which together are to occupy the benches of the opposition, certain, though hesitating trends towards a reconciliation have begun to appear, but both oppostion parties boycotted the elections of municipal councillors held in the same month.

J

JAHWARIDS, a Hispano-Arab dynasty reigning in Cordova (1031-1068). The Ibn Jahwar were of Syrian origin, had settled in Spain in the early years of the Arab era and belonged to the small and exclusive set of the patrician families of Cordova, whose members, as a matter of traditional privilege, used to serve as high government officers and court dignitaries throughout the Umayyad régime. In the troubled atmosphere of the depostion of the last Umayyad caliph, Hishām III (1027-1031), it was mainly thanks to the general esteem enjoyed by Abū al-Ḥazm Ibn Jahwar that Cordova was spared serious disorder, and that under his leadership a council of notables continued the management of the affairs of the city in the form of an aristocratic republic. He was succeeded in his function by his son Abū al-Walīd al-Rashīd, who, however, soon afterwards was forced to give way to the ʿAbbādids* of Seville. Their court was the scene of the poet Ibn-Zaydūn's* amorous entanglements, which inspired some of the best lyric, and especially epistolary creations of his pen.

JAZŪLĪ al-, ABŪ ʿABD ALLĀH MUḤAMMAD IBN SULAYMĀN, or Gazūlī, (from his tribe, the Gazūla of the Sanhāja* group in the western portion of the Anti-Atlas), a highly reputed religious doctor († between 1465 and 1470) and founder of a school of mystical thought which gave rise to a great number of widely branched-out religious brotherhoods*. He began his studies in Fez at the Madrasa al-Saffarīn (of the coppersmiths, because of its location in the section of this trade), continued in Azemmour and Tīt (south-east of Mazagan, today in ruins) in the *ribāt** of the Amghar, originally a clan of warrior-monks immigrated from the Arab East. There he went deeply into the teaching of the mystic al-Shādhilī (1175-1250) which at that time began to attract an increasing number of adepts in the western Arab world. The pilgrimage which he then undertook, led him to a stay of many years in Mecca. Having spent some time in Fez, he withdrew again to Tīt, devoting himself to solitary meditation. Thence he moved to Safi where his fame as a scholar and holy man, which in the meantime had spread wide over the country, made him the centre of a varied multitude of reverent disciples. Probably at this stage of his life he was attributed with descent from the house of the Prophet and thus ranked among the families of sharīfian prestige, which may explain the pride or even haughtiness reflected in so many of his sayings transmitted by his biographers. It may also have been the reason why he came into conflict with the governor of the region, had to leave Safi, went into hiding into the village of Afūghāl (some 15 miles from Mogador) and there died of poison. His death nearly caused a revolution. One of his disciples, heading a crowd of fanatic followers, carried the master's body from place to place, sowing devastation wherever in his opinion the people were lacking in veneration for the saint's memory, until he was killed (1486) by al-Jazūlī's widow or sister whom he had forced to marry him. Al-Jazūlī was then buried first in Taghazūt (some 10 miles north of Agadir), later taken away by the people of Afūghāl and buried in their village, until about the middle of the XVIth century his body, miraculously preserved, it is said, was finally placed to rest in Marrakesh in the quarter called after him Sidi Ben Sliman (pop. for Sayyid Ibn-Sulaymān), in a mausoleum built by the Saʿdian* prince al-Aʿraj, and down to this day a much-visited shrine.

Al-Jazūlī's doctrine, roughly summarized, is based on the strict observance of the religious precepts, enhanced by the recitation *(hizb)* of particular prayers the frequent repetition of the ninety-nine 'excellent names' *(al-asmā' al-husnā)* of God, leading to the mystical nearness to the Divinity, and the profound veneration of the Prophet. Only few of his numerous writings have been preserved. The most popular among them, the'*Dalā' il al-Khairāt* (abridged title, approximately 'The Guide to Good Works'), is a collection of prayers for the Prophet, with the glorifying enumeration of his attributes, of which some elaborate, beautifully illuminated manuscript copies as well as several modern printed editions are in existence. Al-Jazūlī himself did not organize his adepts - allegedly some twelve thousand at his lifetime - into a specific community, but several ofhis prominent disciples, or their own disciples after them, taking their inspiration from the master's word, set up Jazūlīya fraternities all over the Arab West ,known by their founders' names and more or less differing in their ritual and structure. Quite a few of them are still flourishing although they are no more to be reckoned with as a factor in public life - such as the *ʿIsāwa** (Morocco, Algeria, Tunisia), the *Yūsufīya* (Algeria), the *Sharqāwāya* (Morocco), the *Shaykhīya* (Morocco and Algeria), the *Nāsirīya** (Morocco), the *Taibīya* (Morocco and Algeria) etc.

JUBAYR IBN, ABŪ al-HUSAYN MUHAMMAD, the author (1145-1217) of one of the best-known travel books *(rihla*)*. Born in Valencia, he studied law and theology in Játiva, and worked as a government clerk in Granada. He undertook the pilgrimage to the Holy Cities, then a second journey to the countries of the Arab East, extending his trips over a considerable length of time and making frequent stops at various places in North Africa, Arabia, Iraq, Syria and Sicily. His account of these travels is a valuable source of information on the customs and conditions of life in those parts of the world, especially in Sicily. He died in Alexandria while on a third voyage.

K

KABYLES, the collective designation (derived from the Arabic vocable *qabīla*, plur. *qabā'il*, tribes) used in occidental languages for the Berber groups, each one, in fact, bearing its individual name, but all stemming from ancient Sanhāja* stock. They inhabit the north-Algerian mountain region extending approximately from Algiers, or rather the Mitīja plain, eastward to the Wādī al-Kabīr. It is divided by the Summam River into a western sector, the so-called Greater Kabylia or Kabylia of the Jabal Jurjura, with the principal town of Tizi-Ouzou (ca. 30.000 inh.), and an eastern sector, the so-called Lesser Kabylia or Kabylia of the Jabal Babor. By extension, the name of the largest group in the Jurjura, the Zwāwa (in French texts spelt Zouaoua, whence Zouaves, a special unit in the French army), is often applied to the entire Kabyle population.
Known for its extremely difficult access - opened up as late as the XIXth century by the French administration, principally for strategic reasons, and now well provided with communications - and for the warlike spirit of its people, the Kabylia was long left aside by the Arab armies on their conquering advance into North Africa. Finally, with great efforts, superficially occupied and no more than loosely incorporated into the caliphate, it remained refractory to all outside authority under the Umayyad governors of Egypt as well as later under the Aghlabid* emirs. It took a long time for Arabic to find its way into the Kabyle mountains, and then only into their eastern part, the Lesser Kabylia, while Berber is still the dominant language in the Greater Kabylia. Islam, too, infiltrated but slowly and in somewhat vague forms, and is down to this day peculiarly impregnated with practices deeply rooted in an ancient social system and ethical code.
In this atmosphere the first missionary of the nascent Fātimid doctrine, Abū ʿAbd Allāh al-Shīʿī, started to preach the spiritual and political revolution against the established Sunnite order. From the midst of the Kutāma tribe in the small town of Ikjan in the Lesser Kabylia (no longer in existence, near the village of Chevreuil, founded by the French settlers north of St. Arnaud) his word spread rapidly all over the Kabyle mountains. Within not quite two decades the last Aghlabid Emir Ziyādat Allāh III was overthrown and al-Shīʿī with his Kabyle warriors entered Raqqāda, the Aghlabid capital (909). It was the beginning of the Fātimid rule in the Arab West, whose solid pillars were the Kutāma at the head of most of the other Kabyle tribesmen. They continued to hold this privileged position, owing certainly more to their military value than to their religious or political convictions, well into the XIth century under the Fātimid vassals, the Zīrid* emirs, and then under the house of the Ḥammādids*, long after the Fātimid centre of gravity had shifted into Egypt. For the following four hundred years or so the Kabyle people seem to have remained withdrawn in the seclusion of

their mountains, untouched by the stormy history of their surrounding world. Except for an occasional mention by one or the other Arab chronicler of the name of some tribe, more detailed information on the situation in the Kabyle country begins to come forth only in Spanish sources of the XVIth century.
At that time the population appears grouped into three 'states': the sultanate of Kūko (a village of the Ait Yahyā, east of the present day town of Michelet) in the Jurjura, extending down to the coast with the small port of Azzefūn (today Port-Gueydon); the sultanate of Labès (Banū ʿAbbās) in the Lesser Kabylia, originally founded and ruled by a family of marabouts*, with Qalʿat Banū ʿAbbās, the seat of the strong clan of the Banū Muqrānī; the principalty of the Banū ʿAbd al-Jabbār on the coastal area east of Bougie; and the loosely coherent but numerous and most combative Zwāwa confederation. They all were inevitably drawn into the struggle between Spain and the Ottoman Empire for supremacy in this section of the Mediterranean, which filled three quarters of the XVIth century and ended with the disappearance of the Ḥafsid* realm (1575) and the establishment of the Turkish Regency in Algeria. Sought by both sides as allies, but divided among themselves, and changing camps as it fitted into the changes in their own midst from friendship to feud, they finally all had to bow to the new Turkish overlord. In the ups and downs of these fights the sultanates of Labès and Kūko disappeared, presumably absorbed by the Zwāwa who readily enlisted in the army of the Turkish beglerbeg as readily as in the mercenary corps of his none too friendly neighbour, Sultan Aḥmad al-Manṣūr* of Morocco. All through the XVIIth century, the general unrest hardly ever ceased. Scarcely was one rebellious chieftain forced back to submission when another uprising flamed up somewhere else. At last the Kabyles acquiesced in the Turkish régime, which by a system of strongly fortified outposts (*burūj*, sing. *burj*) - they have remained a landmark of the country - and mobile military camps (*zmāla**), sustained a policy of pacification by the well-weighted dispensation of privileges, financial advantages and the patronage of religious brotherhoods*. For the rest it avoided all interference with the internal affairs of the tribes, provided a minimum of taxes could be collected.
Little, if at all, aware of the foreign control, each village (*thaddert*), grouping in a sort of federal community a number of *kharrūba's* - solidly coherent, clan-like units consisting of the families issued from the same ancestor - continued to live its own, closely circumscribed life as a self-governed social, economic and, as it were, psychological entity moulding its political attitudes, its administration and its concepts of right and wrong in the assembly (*thajemat*, Arabic *jamāʿa*) in conformity with age-old traditions. Its cultivable land is considered the community's property, of which each family holds in undivided use a share, as a rule fragmented in widely dispersed, exiguous lots, in proportion with the number of its members, or, more exactly, of the number of ploughs it possesses. It has a poor, stony soil which limits the remunerative yields to olives and figs, making a great many of the peasantry dependent upon the savings of their members working abroad, where they constitute the majority of the Algerian labour in France, Belgium and Germany.

Now and then some villages might combine to a tribe, loosely bound together by the legend of a common descent, and some tribes or tribal groups to a confederation *(leff*)*. Both, tribe and confederation, are easily dislocated by internal rivalries, but easily set up again after peace has been re-established. In between this rather vague and unstable superstructure there inserts itself the particular type of alliances between villages or parts of villages, the *suff*, quickly contracted and as quickly dissolved, and renewed in a different configuration. The alertness imposed by this social order and the permanent petty warfare springing up on quite trivial occasions but seldom causing much bloodshed or loss of property, has prevented the Kabyle community from social and mental stagnation notwithstanding its self-contained, static mode of living.
The occupation by France of Algiers (1830) and the principal points on the coast, soon followed by the withdrawal of the Turks from Algeria, opened a new chapter in Kabyle history. With a few exceptions, the Kabyles refused to become party to the long-drawn combat between the French and Emir ʿAbd al-Qādir*, suspecting either of them, not without reason, of designs running counter to that particularism which they felt to be the essence of their social and moral concepts. To defend it, after the emir's defeat, against the centralizing policy of the French colonial administration, they took up arms and fought for it to the utmost limit. The focus of the most tenacious resistance was in the Jurjura mountains, the homeland of the Banū Yanni, Ait Fraūsan and Ait Irtatan, which only the heavy guns of Fort National (south of the town of Tizi Ouzou), built at considerable cost on a dominating position over 3000 foot high, could finally overcome. Yet again, in 1871 upon the defeat of France by Germany, a new insurrection incited by the Muqrānī clan, rapidly spread from the Summam valley, and under the call to the Holy War, raised by the eighty year old Sheikh Muhammad Amziān Ibn al-Haddād, stirred up the whole Kabyle country to violent passion. It was suppressed after months of fierce fighting, but thenceforth the refractory spirit remained curbed for a long time by a series of draconic measures such as the imposition of heavy contributions, the confiscation of large tracts of landed property which was apportioned to French settlers, or the abolition of the autonomy of the villages which were placed under French military control.
Very gradually proceeding efforts at pacification paved the way for the second or third generation to a cautious acquiescence. Step by step the village self-government was, if only partly, re-established. Parcel by parcel some of the confiscated land was repurchased. New rural and small-town schools opened for quite a few the access to higher education. Thus there emerged in the last decades a body of teachers whose association published throughout nearly twenty years, until the beginning of serious nationalist unrest, its modest review, 'La Voix des Humbles', open to the most varied philosophic currents. Soon also the colleges and faculties in Algiers and in France formed a Kabyle intellectual élite at home as much in its native mountains as in the world of French letters and the professions: the writer and literary critic Jean Amrouche (†1962) or the poet Mūlūd Feraoun (assassinated 1962);

the lawyers ʿAbd al-Rahmān Farès, Ahmad Būmenjel and Hāshim Sharīf or the physicians Dr. Shawqī Mustafaī and Dr. Muhammad Lamīn (al-Amīn) Dabbaghīn, all of whom sooner or later joined the ranks of the Algerian Revolution*. Kabyles, too, were some of the fiercest revolutionary leaders, such men as Ait Hamūda Amirouche, ʿUmar Amran, Ramdān Abbān, Belkacem Krim (Karīm Bilqāsim) or Husayn Ait Ahmad. It was in the Kabyle mountains at the Summam Valley Congress* in 1956, that the foundation was laid upon which was set up the military and political structure of the revolution and, after the fighting, the organization of the Algerian Republic.

KĀHINA al-, the surname (fem. of *al-kāhin*, the seer) of the legendary Berber prophetess Daniya or Dinya (VIIth cent.) of the - perhaps - judaized tribe of Jawāra, a Zanāta* branch in the Aurès (northern Algeria). She is said to have assumed the leadership in the Berber resistance against the Arabs who under Hassān Ibn al-Nuʿmān al-Ghassānī, the Umayyad governor of al-Qayrawān, had driven the Byzantines out of Carthage (698) and the other smaller coastal towns, and penetrated further inland. The Kāhina, so the story goes, inspiring her people in some mysterious way, laid all the land waste before the advancing Arabs, inflicted upon them a heavy defeat and pushed them back beyond the borders of Ifrīqīya*. Magnanimously she set all the prisoners free, adopted one of them, Khālid Ibn Yazīd al-Qaysī, and was recognized as queen throughout the entire region. A few years later, however, the Arabs came back with fresh troops and the Berbers were decisively beaten near the old Roman port-town of Tabarqa, half ways between Bône and Bizerta. The Kāhina, pursued into the mountains and betrayed by Khālid Ibn Yazīd, was killed near a well still today called *Bīr al-Kāhina* (the well of Kāhina). Her sons following her advice joined the victorious Arabs.

KASBA see QASABA

KATTĀNĪ al-, in occidental texts often spelt al-Kittani, a sharīfian* family of Fez, tracing its descent to the Idrīsid* dynasty, which around the end of the last century acquired a prominent place in Moroccan scholarly and spiritual life. Among the first to establish this reputation was al-Ma'mūn Ibn ʿUmar (†1891) who wrote among other treatises a study on the earliest Muslim inhabitants of Fez and the biography of one of his relatives venerated as a saint, Mūlāy al-Tayyib Ibn Muhammad (†1837). It was further built up by Jaʿfar Ibn Idrīs (1825-1905), credited with over a hundred writings mainly of a biographical character; but especially by his son and pupil Abū ʿAbd Allāh Muhammad. He wrote a comprehensive bibliographic dictionary of the saints and famous savants buried in Fez, usually quoted under its abridged title *al-Salwat al-Anfūs*, which is valued as an essential work of reference. Its introduction offers a justification of the cult of saints, accompanied by a set of instructions as to the ritual to be followed on visits to their shrines. The main part consists of the stories of the lives of saintly men, of the members of the sharīfian families and of all those whose names stand out in the religious sciences, jurisprudence and, although with some omissions, historiography. The links of Muhammad al-Kattānī's chain of biographies are the burial places of the persons he studies. He begins at the sanctuary of the city's founder, Idrīs II*, and by an intricate itinerary from tomb to tomb, minutely recording all funeral inscriptions, he assembles a wealth of biographical and bibliographical information, concluding with a detailed list of his sources of information. His work throws much light on the intellectual currents in the last two to three centuries in the Arab West, and was made the subject of particular research (R. Basset, Recherches bibliographiques sur les sources de la *Salouat el-anfūs*, Alger 1905).

Around 1850 another member of the family, Muhammad Ibn ʿAbd al-Wāhid, guided by the teaching of the Darqāwa* fraternity, conceived the spiritual basis for a new religious brotherhood* *(tarīqa)*. Firmly organized some 40 years later by his grandson Muhammad ʿAbd al-Kabīr, the Kattānīya fraternity attracted a numerous membership in Fez, Rabat, Meknès and Marrakesh among the intellectual groups of conservative leanings, but also among the rural population of the environs. Shortly after the accession to the throne of Sultan ʿAbd al-ʿAzīz (1894-1909) the all-powerful vizier Bā Ahmad Ibn Mūsā, suspecting Muhammad al-Kabīr of subversive machinations, apparently not quite without ground, had him put into prison, while the Kattānīya was declared unlawful. Liberated after the vizier's death (1900) and again at the head of the order which had emerged from the suppression with still greater prestige, he took a leading part in the uprising which overthrew Sultan ʿAbd al-ʿAzīz, whom popular opinion held guilty of irreligiosity and of connivance with what today would be called European imperialism.

His successor, ʿAbd al-Hāfiz (1909-1912), unable to withstand the foreign pressure which was soon to result in the establishment of the Protectorate*, had to face the same dangerously spreading unrest, and again ʿAbd al-Kabīr al Kattānī with his brotherhood, planning perhaps as his final aim the usurpation of the throne, stood in the forefront of the rebels. He fell into the sultan's hands and was bastinadoed to death. The brotherhood was dissolved but continued underground until his brother ʿAbd al-Haiy, completely reorganized it (1920), whereupon it was authorized to resume its activities.

Muhammad ʿAbd al-Haiy al-Kattānī (1886-1962), known by his wide erudition - his library with the collection of rare, unpublished manuscripts was of much help to European orientalists - had studied and lectured in Damascus, Cairo, Jerusalem and Medina before his final return to Fez where he taught at the Qarawīyīn* University. In the mid-'twenties he was compelled to resign because of his anti-dynastic and pro-French attitude which evoked the passionate protests of the students, most of them fervent protagonists of the awakening Moroccan nationalism. In fact ʿAbd al Haiy al-Kattānī's hatred of the perpetrators of his brother's dishonourable execution identified the dynasty with all those who made the sultan's person, as it were, the sacro-sanct symbol of the resistance against the French Protectorate. Thus, in the further pursuit of this train of thought, he openly manifested his sympathy for the French régime and its policy, and together with the Pasha of Marrakesh, Tihāmī al-Glāwī, became one of the most active artisans of the deposition (1953) of Sultan Muhammad V*. He had to leave Morocco upon the sultan's restoration and the termination of the Protectorate (1955), notwithstanding his somewhat belated declaration of loyalty, and settled in the south of France where he died in September 1962. His library was confiscated and declared national property, while the Kattānīya brotherhood lost all practical significance.

KHALDŪN IBN, ʿABD al-RAHMĀN, one of the most brilliant philosophers, historians and social thinkers (1332-1406) produced by the world of the Arab West, whose theories, in many respects wholly foreign at his time, have preserved permanent interest and intrinsic value for ways of thought comprised very much later under the concepts of philosophy of history and sociology. Imbued with Islamic scholarship and conversant with Platonic and Aristotelian ideas; a sharp and critical observer gifted with the faculty of independent, synthetical reasoning; an experienced diplomatist familiar with the multifarious currents at the Arab intellectual and political centres as well as with tribal and small-town ideologies; free from national prejudices, broad-visioned yet fully realizing the material and situational limits, but strong-willed, unruly and extremely ambitious - thus appears the portrait of Ibn Khaldūn, which the numerous authors dealing with his work have drawn from the elements he himself provided in his autobiography.
Ibn Khaldūn was descended from a family of Andalusian patricians of Yamanite origin, settled since the first years of the Arab conquest first in Carmona, later in Seville, and at the time of the Almohad* régime on friendly terms with the town's governors of the house of the Hafsids*. One of them emigrated into Tunisia and entered the services of the first independent emir, Abū Zakariyyā' Yahyā *(1228-1249). Some hundred years later Ibn Khaldūn was born in Tunis and spent his early youth in the easiness of an upper-class, intellectual atmosphere hardly troubled by the Marīnid* occupation of the Hafsid countries (1347-1349), with prominent men of letters and religious scholars as his teachers, when at the age of seventeen he lost both his parents in an outbreak of the pest. Still studying and, not yet twenty, a scribe of the great chancellor Ibn Tāfarājin*- this master of versatility must have left a deep impression on the youth's susceptible mind - he abandoned his post upon a defeat of the Tunisian army and went over to the victor, the emir of Constantine. Yet, fascinated by the rising star of the young sultan of Morocco, the Marīnid Abū ʿInān Fāris*, and seeking a way into his entourage, he went to Biskra for a stay with the clan of notables of pro-Marīnid leanings, the Banū Muznī, and secured an appointment as secretary at the court at Fez. Soon enwrapped in a game of intrigues together with the Hafsid prince Abū ʿAbd Allāh, then in honourable captivity in Fez, he was put into prison and freed only a year and a half later by Abū ʿInān's successor who made him chief of the chancellery, without, however, assigning him more than a merely nominal rôle. Although disappointed in his expectation, he remained three years in the Moroccan capital, where he formed a close friendship with the

Andalusian statesman, poet and writer Ibn al-Khatīb*, and gained the favour of his sovereign, Muhammad V of Granada (1354-1359 and 1361-1391), a guest at the Marīnid court during the enforced interruption of his reign. Both of them welcomed him heartily when he appeared in Granada one year after Muhammad had reconquered his throne. There Ibn Khaldūn stayed three years, holding a foremost rank in the splendid court society, but unable to accede to one, equal to his ambition, on the higher government level. Thus he moved to Bougie, where in the troubled period of the split in the Hafsid dynasty Emir Abū ʿAbd Allāh, his acquaintance from Fez, had come to power. Ibn-Khaldūn served as his chamberlain *(hājib)* and taught law at the mosque of the Palace, where he also held the office of a preacher *(khatīb)*, but a year later was among the first to pay homage (1366) to a more fortunate rival, Emir Abū al-ʿAbbās Ahmad of Constantine, the future caliph of the re-unified Hafsid realm. Obviously, however, his loyalty to the new sovereign was subjected to too difficult tests, for he soon left the court of Bougie. During the following nine years or so he appears involved in an imbroglio of anti-Hafsid politics, which took him to the chieftains of the Arab Dawawīda on the highlands in eastern Algeria; to the Banū Muznī in Biskra; then for a while to the ʿAbd al Wādid* residence in Tlemcen; again to Biskra; and finally to Muhammad V in Granada, whence he was expelled when trying to save his friend Ibn al-Khatīb who had fallen into disgrace, from Muhammad's vindictive persecution (1375). After these peregrinations he felt the need for a complete seclusion to reflect on his manifold experiences, clarify his thoughts on the problems he had encountered, plan and draft the work which had occupied his mind throughout his restless activities and which was to make his fame. With his family he withdrew into a lonely Arab village in northern Algeria, Qasr Ibn Salāma (now called Tawghzūt, near present-day Fronda), and lived there for nearly four years, assembling, mainly from memory, his material, and began writing until stopped by illness and also by the necessity of consulting more informants, books and documents. Hoping to find in the intellectual atmosphere of Tunis what he required, he solicited, and obtained, from Caliph Abū al-ʿAbbas Ahmad (1370-1394) not only forgiveness for his past none too friendly attitude, but also generous interest in his efforts. Dividing his time between his work and a quickly widening audience of students, he settled, as he thought for good, in his home town. He was mistaken. May be because of an all too pronounced self-assertion in his commerce with other scholars; may be because his views, very advanced for his time, appeared offensive and unorthodox, in particular to the influential theologian and jurist Ibn ʿArafa*; or simply because of the jealousy of colleagues resenting what they considered a newcomer's intrusion into the sovereign's favours. After four years of fruitful research Ibn Khaldūn in the midst of his work - he presented a copy of the finished portion to Caliph Abū al-ʿAbbās Ahmad - he saw himself obliged to leave Tunis and, pretexting a pilgrimage to the Holy Cities, embarked for Alexandria. A month later he arrived in Cairo (1382). There he spent the last twenty-five years of his life.

As almost everywhere before, he was received with honours by the

Mamlūk Sultan al-Zāhir Barqūq (1382-1389 and 1390-1398) and continued his career as a scholar, teacher of the Law, Chief Judge *(qādī al-qudāt)* of the Malekite school of thought and courtier, but afflicted by the loss of all his family, which perished in a shipwreck on the way from Tunis to join him. After a pilgrimage to Mecca and some time spent in Arabia, he resumed his activities in Cairo, there as elsewhere previously the target of much criticism and enmity yet always supported by the sultan's confidence, which was once only temporarily shaken by his somewhat ambiguous conduct during a short interregnum. He enjoyed an equally privileged position under Barqūq's son, Sultan al-Nāsir al-Dīn Faraj (1398-1406), who made it possible for him to extend his research into Palestine and Syria as a member of his suite in a military expedition. A second time in Syria in a similar but far more critical situation he had the - entirely unlooked for - occasion of staying a month in the camp of the Mongol war-lord Tīmūr Lang (Tamerlan) at the doors of Damascus, with whom he negotiated the surrender of the town, and in two memorable meetings discussed with remarkable diplomatic skill the prevailing conditions in Egypt and the western Arab world. Although he could not prevent the plunder and destruction of Damascus, he obtained a safe-conduct of return for himself and his Egyptian friends. While Ibn Khaldūn found in Egypt all the material ease and freedom of mind, the scientific contacts and facilities for study and investigation he required for the pursuance of his scholarly activities, he never felt really at home there, and sentimentally and intellectually remained thoroughly attached to the West. It was there that he had conceived and shaped his ideas, drawing upon his erudition and his abundant experience with the variety of its social, ethnic and economic structures, and formulated most of his system. In Egypt he revised and re-wrote some sections, prepared the final version and completed the historical parts. He died in Cairo at the age of seventy-four, continuing to the last in his professional activities.

The complete title of Ibn Khaldūn's monumental work, generally quoted as *Kitāb al-ʿIbar*, is inserted in the text itself and runs as follows: *Kitāb al-ʿIbar wa-Dīwān al-Mubtada' wa-l-Khabar fī Ayyām al-ʿArab wa-l-ʿAjam wa-l-Barbar wa-man Āsarahum min Dhawī al-Sultān al-Akbar* (The Book of Instructive Examples and Register of the Origins and Events - literally subject and predicate - of the Days of the Arabs, Persians and Berbers and of their Contemporaries who were the Holders of Power). A Preface and the famous Introduction *(Muqaddima)* precede the historical study proper, which deals first with the Arab East and then with the peoples, states and dynasties of North Africa until 1394 (seven volumes including the autobiography in the edition of the Būlāq Press, Cairo 1867). Very early, although presumably not in conformity with the author's intention, the term *muqaddima* was understood to cover also Book One of the main body, and in the beginning of the XIXth century, translated as 'Prolegomena', became current also in occidental literature.

While the chronological enumeration of battles, revolutions and rulers, chosen by Ibn Khaldūn for his history of the East, has no particular claim to originality nor even always to accurate dating, his records of the events in the Moslem world of the West constitute in many cases a unique source of information. In this section he partly replaces the annalistic recording by a more synoptic presentation of the inner concatenation of the events, although here too the social and economic elements are almost completely left aside. Ibn Khaldūn's treatment, in the main purely descriptive, of historical themes has sometimes been judged as inconsistent with the theses advanced and systematized in the *Muqaddima*. It should not be overlooked, however, that he differentiates in history, the simple narration intended to meet the taste of the many, from its inner, philosophic essence, the study of which he considers a science by itself, calling for the attention of the learned élite. It is this 'science of culture' *(ʿilm al-ʿumrān)*, as he termed it, which he developed in the *Muqaddima*. Its scope is human culture - or, we may say, society - and it has to use methods of its own beyond the comprehension of the untrained mind: the critical examination of events in their relationship to a particular epoch, people and type of social order; the search into their causes and the circumstances of their origin; the discernment between what is inherent in man's nature and what is accidental; and the analysis of the continual changes, manifest or latent, in the structure and aspects of social life. Applying such scrutiny, in whose omission he sees the source of fundamental errors *(maghālit)* which he illustrates by a series of examples, he arrives at an explanation, entirely new for his time, of the socio-cultural processes and their psychological, economic, religious and political driving forces.

One of his focal points is the concept of *ʿasabīya* (social solidarity, esprit de corps, Gemeinsinn) as the primary impulse in the gradually progressing stages of human society, from the nomadic groups of camel breeders satisfying their simple needs in the way of life of a Bedouin–meaning primitive–culture *(ʿumrān badawī)*, to the life of cities generating a richly diversified civilization *(hadāra)* characterized by refinement and luxury, the practice of arts and sciences, and the specialization of economic activities, and calling into existence kingdoms and empires. In *ʿasabīya*, too, lies the origin of political control which prevents men from attacking one another. This control goes from tribal chieftainship to the government of the State, and is exercized either, as in the Caliphate, in its pure form, in accordance with the order of the Law of divine emanation *(siyāsa sharʿīya)*, or with an order evolved by human reason *(siyāsa ʿaqlīya)* which, if it is just, pursues the common good, *(masālih ʿāmma)* and, if unjust, the self-interest of a despotic ruler. Yet, in the course of these processes not only does *ʿasabīya* change in intensity but also of necessity remains open to interferences by climatic conditions, conflicts of desires, contacts with neighbouring cultures and other interrelated influences, thus leaving ample room for variation. Hence no type of social organization and its particular culture can ever be static, so Ibn Khaldūn deduces from his analysis of their component elements and from the data he derives from Muslim history. On this recognition he constructs a system of social dynamics determining a continuous cyclical change of growth, decline and disintegration as the essence of all human history. While viewed from the present day level of historical and sociological knowledge the range of the field attainable for his ob-

servation may not always appear adequate for his generalizing conclusions, in a great many respects he comes strikingly close to modern conceptions of the phenomena he deals with.
For a long time the *Kitāb al-ʿIbar* found among the Arabs themselves but surprisingly little resonance, and there still does not exist a satisfactory Arabic edition of the complete text, since the one of the Būlāq Press cannot any longer be considered satisfactory. The first occidental editions in Arabic of some important parts date from the middle of the XIXth century, and so do the first translations into French - by W. Mac. Guckin De Slane: the autobiography (Paris 1844); the 'Histoire des Berbères' (Alger, 1852-1856); and 'Les Prolégomènes (Paris, 1862-1868), which since then have been used by an ever increasing number of European and American social scientists. More recently also a broader public became acquainted with some sections of the *Muqaddima* through English, French and German commented versions, while scholarly studies from different points of view on the personality of Ibn Khaldūn or concentrating on special subjects treated in the *Muqaddima*, have appeared in practically every occidental language as well as in Turkish and Arabic. De Slane's 'Prolégomènes', at the time of their appearance extremely valuable but in the course of a century inevitably becoming antiquated, are now replaced by an up-to-date English version (The Muqaddimah - An Introduction to History by Ibn Khaldūn, translated by F. Rosenthal, with an extensive bibliography prepared by W. J. Fischel, New York, 1958) based on the critical examination of important manuscripts and other pertinent source material. Lately, too, was published a comparatively minor study by Ibn Khaldūn, developing his ideas on mysticism and some of its principal concepts under the title *Shifā' al-Sā'il li-Tandhīb al-Masā'il* (Appeasement of One who attempts the Clarification of the Problems). It was hitherto generally unknown, notwithstanding the existence of several manuscripts in private libraries and a photographic copy of one of the oldest of them in the Egyptian National Library. On the ground of different manuscripts two scholars, neither of them knowing of the other's work, undertook almost simultaneously these editions (Muhammad Ibn Tāwīt al-Tanjī, Istanbul, 1958 and Father Ignace-Abdo Khalifé, Beyrouth, 1959), which however, complement each other on quite a number of points.

KHALDŪN IBN, ABŪ ZAKARIYYĀ' YAHYĀ, younger brother of the famous philosopher and historian ʿAbd al-Rahmān Ibn Khaldūn*, the author of a history of Tlemcen under the ʿAbd al-Wād* (1333-1378). He studied presumably, like his brother, in his native town Tunis and spent some time together with him at the Marīnid* court at Fez, then in the suite of the Hafsid* emir of Bougie. He was taken prisoner when the town was conquered by the latter's rival, Emir ʿAbd Allāh of Constantine, later sultan of Tunisia. After his successful escape, he joined his brother who stayed with his friends, the Banū Muznī, the most influential family in Biskra, whence he journeyed to Tlemcen and was appointed to a high office in the chancellery by the ʿAbd al-Wādid ruler, Abū Hammū II. At the appearance of an invading Marīnid army he abandoned his position and entered Marīnid services. After a while he returned to

Tlemcen, still enjoying Abū Hammū's favours who made him his confidential secretary. A few years later he was assassinated, apparently the victim of the jealousy of other courtiers.
The work of his life, *Bughyāt al-Ruwwād fī Dhikr al-Mulūk min Banū ʿAbd al-Wād* (French translation 'Histoire des Beni ʿAbd al-Wād, rois de Tlemcen' by A. Bel, Alger, 1904/13), distinguished by its erudite and elegant style, is a most valuable source of information not only on the political history of Tlemcen but also on the scholarly and literary court society of which he himself was one of the prominent members.

KHĀSSA see ʿĀMMA

KHATĪB IBN al-, LISĀN al-DĪN, a Hispano -Arab writer, historian and statesman (1313-1374). He was born presumably in Loja near Granada, of a Syrian family of Yamanite origin, the Banū al-Khatīb, settled in al-Andalus* since the Arab conquest. Reputed, while still a youth, for wit, knowledge and accomplished manners, he succeeded his father who held a distinguished position at the Nasrid* court of Granada, and was soon appointed minister of State with the title *Dhū al-Wizāratayn*, Master of the two Vizirates, i.e. that of the pen and that of the sword. In this function he served under two Nasrid sultans, Abū-al-Hajjāj Yūsuf I (1333-1354) and Muhammad V (1354-58 and 1365-1390). When in the course of a family feud his sovereign was forced to abdicate and to seek refuge at the Marīnid* court in Morocco, Ibn al-Khatīb after a short imprisonment followed him, and returned with him to Granada after he had reconquered his throne. There Ibn al-Khatīb reassumed his high charge and his scholarly studies. Some ten years later, however, court intrigues brought about his disgrace and made it appear safer to him to leave the country. Thus he went back to Morocco, where he was received with great honours and entrusted with high offices by several of the short-lived Marīnid princes or their all-powerful Wattāsid*viziers. Meanwhile his enemies in Granada accused him of heresy and demanded his extradition, which was refused by two successive Marīnid princes. The third one, more submissive to the influential Sultan of Granada, brought him to trial and threw him into prison. There he was strangled to death by a fanatical mob incited by his personal enemies. The story of his life was written by the great scholar Ibn Khaldūn*.
Ibn al-Khatīb was famed as a refined poet and elegant stylist of vast erudition. His writings, allegedly some 60 works, of which only some twenty have been preserved, cover a wide field which includes mysticism, philosophy and medicine, as well as geographical descriptions and biographical studies of the rulers and prominent scholars of Granada. Of considerable interest is a treatise 'On the Plague', about the great epidemic which ravaged the world in his time. He was one of the few who understood, or at least suspected, its contagious nature, and in the face of the aggressive bigotry of certain theological circles fearlessly maintained that its spread was not to be fought by prayers but by avoiding occasions of personal contact. The most important work from his pen is *al-Ihātah fī-Ta'rīkh Gharnāta*, a detailed history of Granada, which furnishes valuable insight into the complex political currents of this period.

KHATTĀB ABŪ al-, ʿABD al-AʿLĀ al-MAʿĀFIRĪ, of Yamanite origin, the first *imām* in Tripolitania and Tunisia of the Ibādites, one of the more moderate branches of the heterodox Khārijite sect (middle of the VIIIth century). Sent out as a missionary from the Ibādite center at Basra to preach the doctrine in North Africa, where it had already a number of widely dispersed adherents, he successfully constituted a well-organized and growing community of his proselytes in the region around Tripoli and was elected imam. In a surprisingly short time he gained the Berber tribes all over Tripolitania for his creed and carried it into Tunisia. He made himself master of al-Qayrawān (758), where he installed as his governor one of his distinguished lieutenants, ʿAbd al-Rahmān Ibn Rustum, who was to become the founder of theRustumid* dynasty of Tāhart (Algeria). Abū al-Khattāb expanded his religio-political rule over a territory covering all Tripolitania, Tunisia and the eastern part of Algeria, and during two years repelled the troops of the ʿAbbāsid governor of Egypt, but his resistance was finally broken in a heavy battle near Tripoli (761), in which he and a great number of his followers, allegedly some 14.000, were killed. ʿAbd al-Rahmān Ibn Rustum was forced to flee and to leave al-Qayrawān in the hands of the caliph's army.

KUSAILA IBN LEMZEN, one of the earliest known Berber chieftains, the head of the tribe of the Awrāba in the area west of Tlemcen (end of the VIIth century), around whose exploits a fabric of more or less fanciful stories has been woven. It seems that Kusaila and his people who under Byzantine rule had become Christians, made their submission to the advancing Arab armies, but after a while revolted, were defeated and embraced Islam. When ʿUqba Ibn Nāfiʿ, the Arab general, undertook his victorious march across Morocco, Kusaila and his men, so it is told, were in the midst of his army, apparently under close supervision, perhaps as auxiliaries, perhaps as hostages. On ʿUqba's return eastwards, Kusaila succeeded in regaining his freedom of action, brought about a coalition of Berber tribes and Byzantine troops of which quite a few were still in the country, and - thenceforth the tales move on historic ground - attacked the Arabs. In a heavy battle near Biskra (683), ʿUqba and most of his army fell fighting, whereupon Kusaila and his Awrāba victoriously entered al-Qayrawān. He seems to have extended his rule over most of present-day Tunisia and a great part of what is today the Algerian department of Constantine. Finally he was defeated and killed (690) at the gates of al-Qayrawān by an army sent by the Umayyad Caliph ʿAbd al-Malik (685-705), but the Berber resistance against the Arab overlordship continued.

KUTLA al-ʿAMAL al-MAGHRIBĪ see BLOC OF MOROCCAN ACTION

L

LAMTŪNA, one of the large nomadic branches of the great Sanhāja* family of Berber tribes, belonging to the so-called *mulaththamūn** (veil-wearing) groups, with pasture grounds in present-day Mauretania and parts of southern Algeria. At the beginning of the IXth century they were united with neighbouring Sanhāja members in a strong confederation which under its leader Tilutan († 826) imposed its suzerainty upon the various negro kingdoms in the Sudan. In the first quarter of the Xth century internal conflicts broke up the confederation temporarily until the Lamtūna chieftain Tarsīna (about 1040) reconstituted it with two sister-tribes, the Gudāla and Massūfa, whereby the leadership was to alternate between Gudāla and Lamtūna. Tarsīna's successor, Yahyā Ibn Ibrāhim, a Gudāla chieftain married to a Lamtūna woman, invited the religious scholar ʿAbd Allāh Ibn Yāsīn* to preach the true precepts of Islam among his people, whose religious beliefs were still very much tinged with pagan concepts. ʿAbd Allāh Ibn Yāsīn followed the call, but after Yahyā Ibn Ibrāhīm's death had to give up his missionary activities among the recalcitrant tribesmen, and with two other Lamtūna headmen, the brothers Yahyā Ibn-ʿUmar and Abū Bakr Ibn ʿUmar, and a few devoted followers founded a *ribāt** (fortified monastery) on an island in the Senegal river. It became the nucleus of the politico-spiritual Almoravid* *(murabitūn*)* movement which the nephew of the two brothers, Yūsuf Ibn-Tāshufīn*, carried from the midst of the desert all over Morocco and al-Andalus*, making it the foundation of the powerful Almoravid empire (1061-1147). The Lamtūna remained one of its most solid pillars until it finally gave way under the religio-military impact of the Almohad* *(muwahhidūn)* doctrine. Under the reign of the Almohad ʿAbd al-Mu'min* (1133-1163), the Lamtūna fell out with the Massūfa and suffered a heavy defeat, whereupon some of them joined the Almohads. Thenceforth the Lamtūna tribe is no longer mentioned in Arabic annals.

LEFF, plur.*lfuf*, a Berber term of Arabic origin (comp. *laffa*, to roll up, to envelop), denoting in Morocco an ancient and very fluid type of tribal leagues or coalitions, current among Berbers but also among some Arab groups which played an important rôle in the relations within the world of the tribes, and hence in the history in the North African countries. According to circumstances, these ties binding for longer or shorter duration, may stress different political, military juridical or spiritual aspects, and greatly vary as to their numerical and territorial significance. The *leff* does not necessarily include all groupings within a tribe, or all parts of its area, nor does it prevent personal or clannish antagonisms, but repeatedly was an efficient instrument in the hands of revolutionary leaders who built up major or minor local sovereignties or even founded a reigning dynasty. In the last years detailed sociological research has been devoted to the social mechanism of the *leff*, which seems to have still preserved a certain importance, although no longer as a power-creating factor, yet as an element in modern political party life.

LIBYA, *Mamlakatu Lībiyā al-Muttahida* (The United Kingdom of Libya) covering approximately 680.000 squ.miles with a population estimated at 1,200.000, borders Egypt and the Sudan in the East; Tunisia and southern Algeria in the West; the young republics of Niger and Chad in the South; and the Mediterranean along a 1200 mile coastline in the North. There, around the Gulf of Sirte (Sidra), the desolate, storm-swept Sirtica Desert skirts the sea and separates in a breadth of more than 400 miles the two territories of Tripolitania (110.000 squ.miles, 820.000 inhabitants) and Cyrenaica (350.000 squ.miles, 320.000 inh.). Stretching southwards, it melts into the boundless expanse of the Libyan Desert with its scattered string of oases in the Fezzan (220.000 squ.miles, 60.000 inh.) - among them Sebha, where an entirely new town has arisen, the seat of the provincial government with a parliamentary building, a royal rest-house, modern villas for the high officials, a hospital, an agricultural school, a printing press and a handicraft training centre - and the Cyrenaican oases of Marada, Jālū and the two main seats of the Sanūsīya* Brotherhood, Kufra and Jaghabūb. Only east and west from the ends of the Gulf, a coastal strip, nowhere more than fifty miles wide, is favoured by fertile soils and a soft Mediterranean climate, although the periods of abundant winter rains frequently alternate with others of severe drought. Then, especially when also the parching winds from the South blow the sand and the dust from the desert over the fields and plantations, the antiquated irrigation system, fed in almost complete absence of perennial water courses from primitive wells, is unable to prevent the loss of most of the crops, sometimes for two years in succession.
In the 1930's, in the wake of the gradual pacification of the country, Italy began to turn over in various forms some of the best parts of the land to Italian settlers. Many left again during and after the Second World War, but quite a few stayed on and still operate a number of big, commercial estates equipped with up-to-date machinery, and several hundred smaller, well-managed family farms. They produce in good years with very remunerative results barley and wheat, olives, groundnuts, almonds, citrus fruit, bananas, a variety of vegetables, potatoes and many kinds of fruit. However, in four-fifth of the region the picture is dominated by the mass of poor, native peasants on dwarf-holdings which are owned as a rule by an absentee landlord. They still lift water from the well in buckets or bags *(dalūs)* of goatskin, till with the age-old wooden nail-plough and use the animal-drawn sledges for threshing. Imprisoned in a share-cropping system coming very close to usury, they remain indebted for life-time to the landlord and the local merchant. Along the coast runs the country's principal road, as already in Roman times, some 1150 miles in length from the Egyptian to the Tunisian border. It is a heritage of the Italian régime, constructed between the two World Wars as the main artery of a highway system of over 6200 miles, partly macadamized, partly rough roads and branching out in

desert tracks. It links villages and oases with one another and with the urban or semi-urban settlements on the sea. Its densest sections cover the areas of Tripoli and Benghazi, the two largest cities (about 150.000 and 50.000 inh.), provincial capitals and commercial centres, seats of university colleges, broadcasting stations and even of gambling casinos-patronized by foreign residents and tourists - which yield appreciable revenues to the municipal treasuries. More than three-quarters of Libya's almost entirely sea-borne trade passes through the port of Tripoli which is accessible to ocean-going ships of all sizes. Most of the remainder is handled by the Benghazi harbour, originally developed as an Italian naval base but now unable to admit even slightly larger vessels because of some war-time destruction and damage suffered through the impact of the storms and the action of the sea. In Tripoli in particular, the development in the last few years of numerous, small-scale factory industries and intensified commercial activities has stimulated the growth of a well-to-do bourgeois upper- and middle-class but also the afflux of country people in search of work resulting, on the one hand, in a building boom, in the central districts, of modern apartment houses, offices and shops, and, on the other, in the mushrooming of shanty-town agglomerations on the outskirts. Apart fròm the two minor ports of Derna and Tobruk, both lacking - and probably not needing - facilities for handling larger volumes of cargo, there are some fifteen or twenty anchorages serving coastal transport and occasionally sheltering the tunny and sponge fishing boats, mainly Italian, Greek or Maltese, licensed to fish in Libyan territorial waters.

Both the eastern and western sections of the coastal belt rise up to a moderately high hilly massif. In Tripolitania, the Jabal Nafūsa (appr. 1000 feet above sea-level) rests its steep northern escarpment on the sea, spans in a flat arc the Jefara plain, and with its southern slopes merges into the desert. In the upper parts of the Nafūsa, rain is plentiful and allows of permanent agriculture and extensive olive groves around the few villages. The spontaneously growing esparto grass, once covering wide expansions extending as far as the coast, has become increasingly scarcer because of irrational methods of picking. Although the entire process of its commercialization comprising the collection, grading, baling and shipping is entrusted to a government-controlled agency, the sale, exclusively to England for the manufacture of high-quality paper, diminished between 1954 and 1963 from 17 per cent to 3 per cent of the total domestic export value. The Jebara plain, very hot and interspersed with sand and moving dunes, especially in the 300 sq.miles of the so-called Sand Sea, still offers some land, mainly in common tribal ownership, suitable for grazing the sheep-and goat-herds of the nomads. The recent studies of the ground resources and of the possibilities of storing the flood water rushing down the hills may result in turning parts of the sandy area into irrigated farmland.

Parallel to the Cyrenaican coastline stretches the Jabal al-Akhdar (The Green Mountain) whose summits attain some 2500 feet above sea-level. Like the Jabal Nafūsa it falls off steeply to the sea and slopes gently down to the South while its western ridges span the flat basin of the Barce plain with a lake in the centre, filled, it is true, only for a while by the

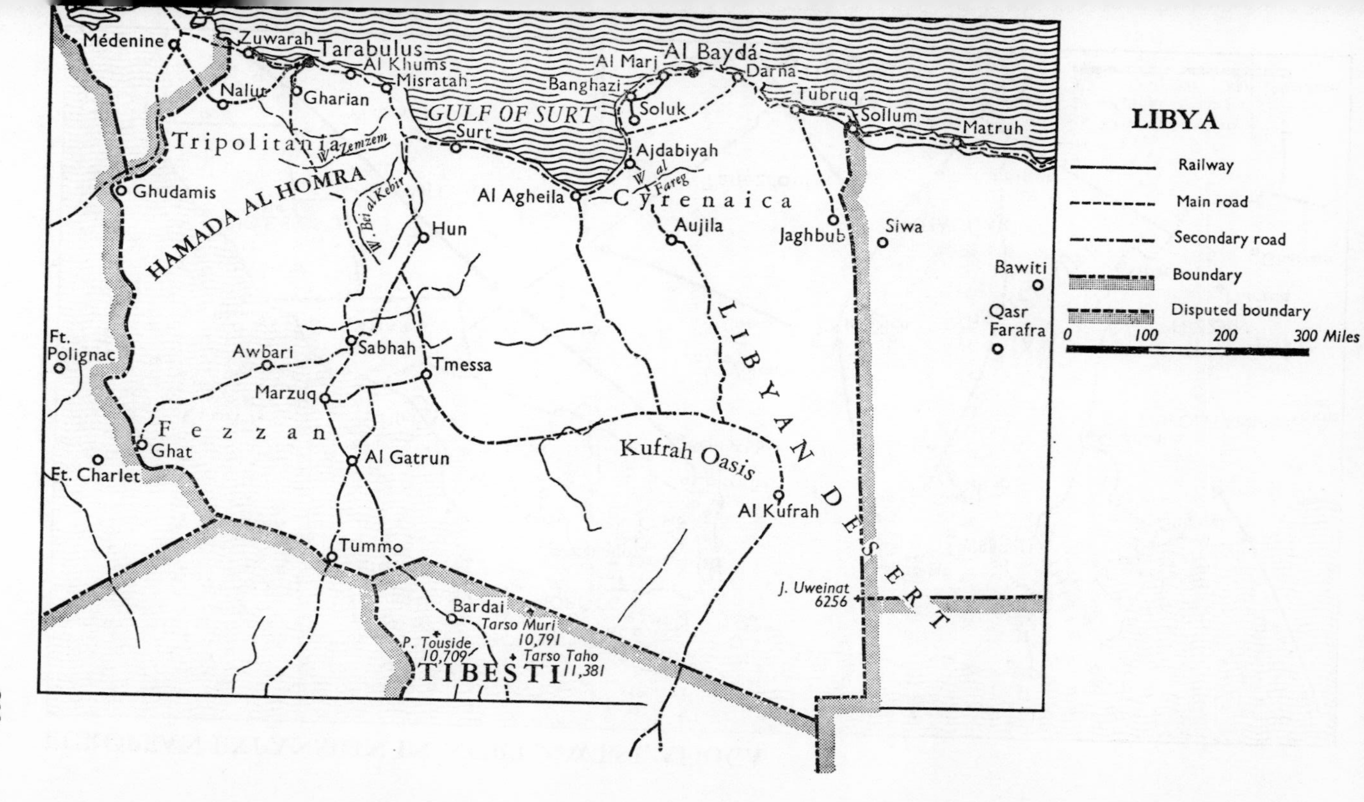
LIBYA
Railway
Main road
Secondary road
Boundary
Disputed boundary
0 100 200 300 Miles
GULF OF SURT
Tripolitania
Cyrenaica
Fezzan
HAMADA AL HOMRA
LIBYAN DESERT
Kufrah Oasis
TIBESTI
Médenine
Zuwarah
Tarabulus
Al Khums
Misratah
Nalut
Gharian
Ghudamis
Surt
Banghazi
Al Marj
Al Baydá
Darna
Tubruq
Sollum
Matruh
Soluk
Ajdabiyah
W. al Fareg
Al Agheila
Aujila
Jaghbub
Siwa
Bawiti
Qasr Farafra
W. Zemzem
W. Bei al Kebir
Hun
Sabhah
Tmessa
Awbari
Marzuq
Al Gatrun
Ghat
Ft. Polignac
Ft. Charlet
Tummo
Al Kufrah
J. Uweinat 6256
Bardai
Tarso Muri 10,791
P. Touside 10,709
Tarso Taho 11,381

EUROPEAN EXPANSION IN NORTH-WEST AFRICA

F.c. = French conquests
S.c. = Spanish conquests
0 100 200 300 400 Miles

winter rainfall and soon again drying up under the summer sun. The Jabal al-Akhdar owes its name to the 1500 or so square miles of shrub-oak and bushes which cover its upper regions and are cut, or often even uprooted, for firewood and the burning of charcoal with the inevitably ensuing erosion by the fierce desert winds and the torrential rains. Its lower parts and the plain contain some of Libya's best agricultural soils, while in the southern areas and on the fringe of the desert the nomadic or semi-nomadic tribes raise their herds of sheep and goats. In many cases the animals belong to a city merchant, are grazed by the herdsmen on tribal land, and driven on hoof across the border for sale at the nearest market in Egypt where they are fattened and slaughtered. This trade, the principal source of money-income for the Bedouins, is prominently reflected in the list of national exports, in which livestock holds the second place. According to foreign expert missions it might be rendered far more remunerative by combinations on the Libyan side of fattening stations, slaughter houses, refrigerating and cold-storage plants together with the provision for emergency supply of fodder so as to prevent the loss of animals in years of drought, which not seldom amounts to more than half of the herds.

All in all, less than one-tenth of Libya's total area can be regarded as economically useful. This has to provide a livelihood for approximately four-fifths of the population: some 7000 sq.miles by permanent farming; some 50.000 sq.miles of grazing-grounds by animal husbandry and in some parts by certain methods of shifting cultivation; and 4000 sq.miles though only to a limited extent, by forestry. The rest is desert except the oases in southern Cyrenaica and in the Fezzan. Barley constitutes over two-thirds, and wheat most of the other cereal crops, but notwithstanding the existence since 1958 of some government-owned modern silos, the majority of the peasants still adhere to the old traditional ways of storing the harvest in primitive containers kept in the house or in caves, which inevitably lead to considerable damage of the grain. Second in importance range olives. The well-tended groves of the large farms on the Tripolitanian coast with their modern equipment produce a superior quality oil, which finds open markets in Europe. Home-consumption so far has been satisfied with the oil of relatively high acidity content that comes from the numerous small-holdings in the Jabal Nafūsa, where the age-old types of presses made of a stone wheel, timber and ropes, and driven by a donkey or also by hand, are still very much in use. Groundnuts, almost completely unknown in Libya before the second World War and locally only gradually becoming popular, are now extensively grown in Tripolitania and have acquired first rank among the country's exports. Between 1943 and 1963 sales, mainly to Italy, Germany, Great-Britain and the Netherlands have been rising from roughly 200 tons to 10.000 annually. By improved grading of the nuts and especially by processing certain qualities into peanut butter and oil, far more substantial benefits will doubtlessly be derived once the projects of the required installations have materialized. Inversely, a domestic staple food, but which so far has been unable to enter successfully the occidental markets, is the Libyan date. The number of palm trees is estimated at between twelve and fourteen million, by far most of them in the Fezzan and

Cyrenaican oases, but the figures assumed for the harvest vary between 30.000 and 70.000 tons a year. A small quantity of the crop is used for distilling alcohol; the manufacture of date syrup intended to replace imported sugar, at least to a certain extent, is under study.
The sensational discoveries starting in 1955 of the rich deposits in the Libyan desert of oil* and natural gas, introduced a new, never before suspected element in this socio-economic pattern. In 1957 the expenditure by the prospecting concerns to Libyan contractors for locally purchased materials, on wages and inland transport, amounted to about four million pounds Sterling; a year later to twice as much; and in 1960 to some 19 million. It is true that the number of workers employed directly or indirectly by the oil companies is bound to decline to a small portion, probably not exceeding five or six percent, of the country's total labour force, once the exploratory and development stages are passed and the construction of the pipelines is completed. It is also true that with the exception of a small minority so far the mass of the peasants, agricultural labourers and shepherds has benefited very little, if anything at all, from the oil wealth. Yet in 1963, when the royalties began to flow into the Treasury, the government launched a new five-year development programme - after one of 1950 and a second one in 1956, both of which have remained more or less on paper - involving investments of 150 million pounds to be covered chiefly from 75 per cent of the oil revenues. It is based upon a survey organized in 1959 by the International Bank for Reconstruction and Development, and comprises the extension of irrigation; the gradual mechanization of farming and improvements in livestock; the promotion of light industries; more schools of various types and grades; the clearance of the 'shanty towns' on the outskirts of Tripoli and Benghazi; and, in general, measures apt to raise the economic and cultural level of the tribal population and the peasantry. A Ministry of Planning and Works is in charge of coordinating all activities within the framework of the programme.
The sudden rise of this lucky star was unforeseeable when at the end of the Second World War the United Nations Organization decided upon what was then called one of the boldest experiments: the creation, by joining together Tripolitania, Cyrenaica and the Fezzan, of the United Kingdom of Libya as an independent State. The experiment turned out a success although, in the words of a UNESCO report of 1952, few countries in the world were then less advanced economically; had a higher proportion of illiteracy - 90 per cent of the adult population; a lower per capita income - about 35 Dollars per year; had been longer under foreign domination; and were less prepared for self-government. There was, moreover, the immense no-man's land of the desert and, separated by hundreds of miles, in Tripolitania and Cyrenaica the closely circumscribed areas of fertile soils and grazing land, with, in the Fezzan, few groups of oases. Thus each of the three territories constitutes a distinct geographical unit with little incentive to mutual contact. Certainly, as early as the middle of the seventh century the advance along the coastal regions of the Arab armies had begun to draw Berber tribes and the townspeople - an ethnical mixture with a strong Roman element - into the Islamic orbit, a process which four hundred years later the invasion

of the Banū Hilāl* and Sulaym* carried into the interior. Yet also within this community of religion and language the differences of the environment kept the three units apart, as they had done while Phoenicians, Greeks, Romans, Vandals and Byzantine emperors were in turn masters of one or the other portion of the country.

As from time immemorial before, the desert remained the roaming ground of the nomads where Berber tribes thenceforth shared with the Arabs the control over the oases and the caravan routes. The settled regions, fitted as individual districts into the organization of North Africa under governors of the Umayyad and ʿAbbāsid caliphs, came under the rule of the Aghlabid* emirs (800) who about a hundred years later had to give way to the early Fātimid caliphs then still residing in Tunisia. The appointment by Caliph al-Muʿizz (953-975) of his vassal, the Berber warlord Buluggīn of the Zīrid* clan, as hereditary governor in North Africa made no change in this situation. When his descendants were driven back to a small strip on the Tunisian coast by the Banū Hilāl and Sulaym sweeping over Cyrenaica and Tripolitania, fields and orchards were laid waste, villages and towns fell into ruin and the country was reduced to misery and anarchy for many years to come. Thus by the middle of the twelfth century the Norman King Roger II of Sicily could without resistance occupy Tripoli as a foothold, and so hoped for the conquest of an African empire. It was only the new constellation of power far away in Morocco, which brought this first attempt at European colonial expansion on the African shore of the Mediterranean to an early end. As soon as the people of Tripoli learned of the triumphal march across Algeria and Tunisia of the Almohad* armies they massacred the Sicilian garrison and opened the gates of the city to the victors. Thenceforth for three hundred and fifty years it was the course of events first in the Almohad empire and then in Tunisia under the Hafsids*, which shaped the history of Tripolitania, while the Fātimid caliphs and after them the Ayyūbid and Mameluke sultans maintained Cyrenaica in the sphere of Egyptian influence.

A new era for the country that was to become present-day Libya began with the contest for hegemony in the Mediterranean basin, which opposed in the XVIth century Spain and the forcefully expanding Ottoman Power, and ended with the victory of the Turks. In 1510 the Spaniards were still able to seize Tripoli which Emperor Charles V turned over together with Malta to the order of the Knights of St. John after its expulsion from Rhodes by Turkey. In 1517 Egypt, and with it Cyrenaica, was conquered by Sultan Selīm I, and in 1551 Tripoli and its hinterland in the name of Sulaymān the Magnificent by his admiral Darghūt Pasha. During some 150 years the Porte exercized in the Libyan 'Regency' as in Algeria and Tunisia a more nominal than actual rule through governors, mainly Greek or Italian renegates, who resided in Tripoli and appointed a Bey with the seat in Benghazi as their - likewise almost autonomous - representative in Cyrenaica. In the early eighteenth century one of them, Ahmad Karamanli (1711-1745), shook off Ottoman suzerainty and secured for his descendants the hereditary succession in Tripolitania, Cyrenaica and the Fezzan. Privateering and the ransom for the captives or payments of 'protection money' constituted, also as in Algeria and Tunisia, a richly flowing source of income for the Turkish and Arab upper-caste until the beginning of the nineteenth century, notwithstanding repeated punitive expeditions by the British and French fleets, which once even brought Tripoli near to destruction. It also involved Yūsuf Karamanli, the last of the dynasty, in a four-year war (1801-1805) with the United States of America, in the course of which the newly formed American navy lost one of its best frigates, with captain and crew, in the waters of Tripoli but, on the other hand, succeeded in capturing Derna. Finally, however, Yūsuf, old and helpless, was forced to abdicate, while in the ensuing struggle between his son ʿAlī and other pretenders a Turkish fleet sailed into the port of Tripoli and deported the whole Karamanli family to Constantinople except Yūsuf and his harem and one of his sons, the governor of Benghazi, who escaped to Malta.

Although restive tribes, mutineering garrisons and local insurrections recurrently troubled the following period of direct administration by the not particularly efficient provincial bureaucracy of the Constantinople government, it was marked upon the whole by general progress, at least in the coastal areas. Export trade to Europe of livestock, wool, skins and hides, esparto grass, citrus fruit and dates developed; mulberry trees were planted and a fairly prosperous silk handloom industry came into being; a School for Arts and Crafts and a School for Industry along with some intermediary and secondary schools were established; a water-supply system for Tripoli was constructed; the first, though still rather primitive census was taken and a land registration prepared. In these years arose the Sanūsīya* brotherhood, founded by Ahmad al-Sanūsī, the ancestor of the present reigning family, and vigorously spread in Cyrenaica and the Fezzan. Notwithstanding the obstacles put in its way by the Turkish authorities, the order consolidated its spiritual prestige, foremost within the tribal society which readily recognized also its political guidance with unquestionable benefit for the economic well-being of the people of the oases and of the nomad herdsmen. This situation continued until towards the end of the century when the increasingly active Italian policy of 'peaceful penetration' began to foreshadow a new turn in Libyan history, particularly since the conclusion in December 1902 of an Italo-French agreement determining the 'special interests' which France claimed to have in Morocco and Italy in Libya. Playing upon the rivalries among the Great Powers, Turkey managed for a while to keep these interests within the limits of commercial privileges, but in September 1911 Italy, under a futile pretext, declared war, landed an expeditionary corps at the strategic points of the coast defended by altogether 5000 men in Tripolitania and 2000 in Cyrenaica. The Treaty of Ouchy (October 1912) terminated the war and the era of Turkish sovereignty, leaving certain hardly more than symbolic rights to the Sultan-Caliph as the supreme religious head of the Moslem community. Yet popular resistance against the invaders continued in Tripolitania well into the 1920's, and was carried on by the Sanūsī warriors in Cyrenaica and the Fezzan until the end of 1932. Then only were the three territories formally constituted as the Italian colony of Libya. Thinking of the conquered country primarily as an outlet for her rural over-population, Italy's first attention was directed to the creation of the structure for large-scale agricultural settlement schemes: harbour installations, roads, public utilities and housing, followed by land reclamations, experimental farms, the provision of modern farming equipment, cattle and seeds. In 1938 the first larger groups of emigrants took possession of their new holdings on Libyan soil. By 1940 about 4000 families were settled in Tripolitania and some 2000 in Cyrenaica. In 1942 the Italians in Libya numbered over a hundred thousand, about one-third of them in towns. All good farming land was turned over to the newcomers, and domestic handicraft was left unprotected against the importation of cheap Italian mass-production. After thirty years of Italian rule there were in Tripolitania for the Libyans altogether 88 elementary and 2 secondary schools with 15.000 pupils and 330 teachers, the majority unprepared for their task, as compared with the 72 elementary and 7 secondary Italian schools with 6300 pupils and 360 competent teachers. In Cyrenaica the situation was worse; in the Fezzan school education was practically non-existent. As a result, positions only on the lowest levels in the civil administration, the public services or in a banking and commercial enterprise were accessible to Libyans except the few who had been able to pursue higher studies abroad. Italy's defeat in the Second World War meant the end of the colonial venture and the loss of the considerable investments of capital and work it had entailed: in 1942 the whole Italian colony in Cyrenaica had to be evacuated, while in Tripolitania it had shrunk to some 35.000.

The intricate story of Libya's accession to independence opens with the expulsion around the end of 1942 of the last Italian troops and the German Afrika Korps from Cyrenaica and Tripolitania by the British. Incorporated in their ranks was the 'Libyan Arab Force' recruited by Sayyid Idrīs, the head of the Sanūsīya. At the same time the Free French advanced into the Fezzan. There followed seven years during which Tripolitania and Cyrenaica were under British, and the Fezzan under French military administration, but in these years crystallized Sayyid Idrīs al-Sanūsī's secular leadership in the fermentation of a nationalist movement - a Nationalist Party, a United National Front, a Free National Bloc, an Egyptian-Tripolitanian Union Party, a Labour Party, a Liberal Party and others - centering around a Cyrenaican and Tripolitanian 'National Congress'. On the international stage there were the discussions among the 'Big Four' - France, Great Britain, the Soviet Union and the United States - on the future of the former Italian colonies, which dragged on with less and less prospect of an agreement as the symptoms of the incipient 'cold war' increased. Equally unfruitful proved such expedients as the investigation by a Four-Power commission of the wishes of the Libyan people and of the social and economic situation of the country, or the consultations with nineteen other 'interested governments'. In view of the failure to arrive at a solution, the Libyan question was referred to the United Nations Organization, with the result that after long and arduous debates the General Assembly on November 21, 1949 passed a resolution which stipulated that within the following two years Libya was to be established as an independent and sovereign State; that representatives of the inhabitants meeting in a

National Assembly were to determine a constitution and the form of government; and that a United Nations Commissioner, aided and advised by an international Council of ten members, should assist them in formulating the constitution and setting up the government.
Thenceforth events proceeded at an accelerated rhythm, although not without heated controversies among the various Libyan interest-groups. In January 1950 the Commissioner arrived in Tripoli. In April the Council of Ten convened for the first time, and in July appointed a Preparatory Committee of the Libyan National Assembly, composed of seven members from each territory, known as the Committee of the Twenty-One. In October, this committee decided that the National Assembly should consist of sixty members who were to be selected, twenty from each territory, by Sayyid Idrīs, the mufti of Tripoli and the chief notable of the Fezzan. In November the Assembly inaugurated its session and in December it set to work. It decided on the fundamentals of the new State: a constitutional monarchy structured as a Federation with three provincial governments and legislative councils, and one Federal Parliament and Federal Government. It offered the throne to Sayyid Idrīs, referred to as the King-designate until the proclamation of independence. Thereupon it nominated a 'Committee on the Constitution', which in turn set up a six-member working group, two from each province, and established a provisional government. The Committee held twenty-five, and the working group ninety-six meetings until in consultation with the Commissioner and the King-designate a draft constitution was presented to the Assembly which adopted and promulgated it in October 1951. An electoral law was voted in November; governmental powers were gradually transferred from the British and French administrations to Libyan authorities; and on December 24, 1951 King Idrīs proclaimed Libya an independent and sovereign state at Benghazi.
From its very first steps into life there was no doubt that this rather weak child of the United Nations family would need a great deal of expert care to secure its survival, and it has had it indeed in almost every aspect of its development. With the help of United Nations consultants was opened a School of Public Administration, was set going the government apparatus and began functioning a Central Statistics Office. A mission of the Food and Agricultural Organization (FAO) included agronomists, horticulturists, livestock experts, a date specialist and an adviser on cooperatives. The World Health Organization (WHO) concentrated on measures to improve the general hygienic situation, especially on tuberculosis control, and established schools for nurses, medical assistants and sanitarians, and together with the United Nations Children's Fund (UNICEF) provided hospital equipment and medical supplies. UNESCO laid stress on adult and fundamental education, both rural and urban, and on the training of teachers and of technical and clerical personnel. The International Labour Organization (ILO) helped prepare and implement a social insurance law and modernize handicraft among the nomads. Partly in connection with these United Nations assistance projects, which make no provision for the funds to carry them out, was the aid, both advisory and financial, extended by Great Britain and the United States, covering among various minor

schemes the reconstruction of the Tripoli harbour; the extension of the road-network; water works and power stations; the supply of drinking water; the creation of a telecommunications system; construction of hospital and school buildings, popular housing and of office buildings in the new summer capital of al-Baīdā' in the Jabal al-Akhdar on the Cyrenaican coast-road; the foundation of the Libyan university; and, last but not least, the balancing of the state budget, where ordinary revenues met just half of the expenditures. However, the British and American money which has thus become available to Libyan economy can hardly be regarded as help in the strict sense of the word, but much rather as the financial compensation for the grant of far-going facilities for military purposes, such as the use of public lands and buidings, airfields and highways (Treaty of Friendship and Alliance with Great Britain of July 1953, to remain in force until 1973); and the lease of the important Wheelus Air Base on the outskirts of Tripoli (Agreement with the United States of America, September 1954, to remain in force until 1970).

While the ways were paved towards at least a temporary solution of the vital problems, the infant years of the Kingdom were by no means free from internal troubles. There were the conflicts between the federal and provincial authorities; between towns and tribes; between the entourage of the Palace, the Government and Parliament. There were movements gaining in strength which tended towards the transformation of the hereditary monarchy into a republic - with Sayyid Idrīs as the President for life and after him an elected president with a ten year tenure of office- and of changing the federal into a unitary system of government. There - were scandals about bribery and corruption in the awards of government contracts for public works; and there were rivalries and conspiracies within the royal house, which culminated in the assassination by one of the King's cousins of one of his most devoted councillors. There was even an attempt on his life. All this led King Idrīs, whatever his concepts of a parliamentary régime originally might have been, to take more and more of the power in the State into his hands; to dissolve all political parties; to banish most of his relatives to the desert; and, being without a son, to appoint as heir apparent his nephew al-Hasan al-Ridā. Finally, in December 1962, he had Parliament approve a Royal Decree which by an amendment of the Constitution assigned to the Federal Government nearly all matters of some significance, hitherto falling within the competency of the provincial executive. It was a great step towards closer administrative and political cohesion, particularly important in the perspective of the comprehensive economic and cultural development plans, whose realization the new oil revenues now make possible without foreign financial contribution. In fact, a year later Libya requested Great Britain and the United States to enter into negotiations on the abrogation of the treaties of 1953 and 1954, on the evacuation of their military bases and the withdrawal of their troops since, in the words of the Chairman of the Libyan Chamber, Libya henceforth would be in the position to dispense with all foreign subsidies.

M

MĀ' al-ʿAINAIN al-SHINGĪTĪ, Water of both Eyes, the surname - its meaning has not been elucidated - under which the religio-political leader Muhammad Mustafā Ibn Muhammad al-Fādil al-Shingītī of Mauretania (al-Shingīt) had become known († 1910). His father was an influential chieftain in the area of the town al-Shingīt, reputed for his piety and as the head of a religious brotherhood*, the *Fādilīya*, which he had founded. After his death (1869) Mā' al-ʿAinain who from his early youth had devoted himself to theological sciences, in particular to the teachings of the great mystics of the past, continued for a time in the seclusion of the *Fādilīya* an ascetic life given entirely to religious studies. Finally, he framed the rules of a brotherhood of his own, closely leaning to Sanūssī* and Wahhābite concepts, and established its seat at Smara in the Sāqīyat (Seguiet) al-Hamrā', the northern section of Spanish West Africa. Faithful disciples carried his fame as a scholar endowed with miracle-working gifts into the tribal world of Mauretania, the Sudan and Senegal and northwards into Morocco, spread his word and gathered a fast-growing number of adepts, while one of his sons set up a branch seat *(zāwiya*)* of the brotherhood in Fez. In Mauretania and the western Sahara his spiritual influence soon assumed the weight of a secular authority which policed the unruly tribes, secured the safety of the caravan roads, and promoted order and well-being. Mā' al-ʿAinain's voice found resonance in the immediate surroundings of Sultan Mūlāy al-Hasan (1873-1894), at whose court at Fez he was a frequent and honoured guest. These friendly relations in which propaganda for his brotherhood held an equal place with political activities and commercial interests, continued under Sultan ʿAbd al- ʿAzīz (1894-1908). He munificently patronized the establishment of a second Moroccan *zāwiya* in Marrakesh whence the master's teaching further radiated by word of mouth and his numerous lithographed pamphlets and treatises.

When in 1905 French columns penetrated into southern Mauretania and occupied the region of Tāgant with its main town Tijika, Mā' al-ʿAinain requested the sultan to declare the Holy War *(jihād)* against the invaders. This he refused to do, but following, it is believed, the suggestion of German advisers, claimed, although in careful terms, Morroccan sovereignty over Mauretania, and sent at first money and arms, then troops under the command of one of his relatives, which were, however, unable to stop the French advance. Mā' al-ʿAinain, forced to withdraw into southern Morocco, set up his headquarters at Tiznit, preached the Holy War and organized tenacious guerilla action sustained by most tribal groups in the coastal plains of the Wādī Nūn and the Sūs. He died at Tiznit but his son Ahmad al-Hība continued the warfare with equal obstinacy. After the conclusion by Sultan Mūlāy ʿAbd al-Hāfiz (1909-1912) of the Treaty of Fez which established (March 30, 1912) the French Protectorate*, Ahmad al-Hība declared the sultan deposed, proclaimed himself *Mahdī* and *Imām*, pushed northwards and occupied Marrakesh where he was acclaimed as sultan, but only to be driven out by the French a month or so later. Like his father, he retreated into the Sūs and kept up fighting until his death. His brother succeeded him as 'sultan' and under the flag of the Holy War relentlessly carried on resistance until the main body of his warriors was exterminated (1934) in the mountains of the Tazarwalt, the south-easternmost corner of the Anti-Atlas. The 'Sultan of the Jihād' and a number of his followers were given asylum by the Spanish authorities in the Rio de Oro, the southern section of Spanish West Africa. Until his death (1942) he remained implacably hostile to France, but during the era of the French Protectorate in Morocco and of the colonial régime in Mauretania there was no room on the political stage for the Mā' al-ʿAinain family and brotherhood. They began again to play their part, both openly and under cover, but as loyal subjects of the sultan, as soon as Morocco was independent, and voiced the old claim to some kind of a union with Mauretania - since 1960 the sovereign Islamic Republic of Mauretania.

MADRID CONFERENCE, convened in July 1880 upon the initiative of the Moroccan Sultan Mūlāy al-Hasan (1873-1894) and attended by delegates of Morocco and 13 occidental states: Austria-Hungary, Belgium, Denmark, France, Germany, Great Britain, Italy, the Netherlands, Norway, Portugal, Spain, Sweden and the United States of America. From the point of view of Moroccan policy the conference was intended as a forum where there were to be brought face to face the mutually conflicting colonial interests and aspirations of the European Powers and thus a compromise arrived at that would counterbalance the preponderant position France had acquired in Morocco. They all had, in fact, step by step secured various privileges and advantages, differing in extent and degree, especially regarding preferential import duties, tax reductions for their trading establishments and jurisdiction of their consular courts over their nationals, in some cases also over Moroccan subjects. The European governments, on the other hand, were primarily motivated by the wish to eliminate causes of mutual frictions and preserve the delicate balance of power from dangerous shocks. Seen from this angle, the international convention concluded as the result of the conference is to be considered a success of the Sultan, in so far as it established the principle of equality for all occidental signatories in their relations with Morocco, averted the danger of too far penetrativeFrench infiltration, and secured the status quo in Morocco for still some time to come.

MADYAN ABŪ, SHUʿAYB IBN al-HUSAYN al-ANDALUSĪ, popularly called Sīdī Bū Madin, an Arab mystic (1126-1197) still highly venerated as a holy man among the broad masses of the population in eastern Morocco, Algeria and Tunisia. He was born in a small town near Seville, of humble origin, and already in his early years felt inspired by deep religious emotion. Soon he left his home for Fez where he had his first introduction into the spheres of mystical thought, at that time in Morocco still of a somewhat simplistic nature, yet imbued with fervent piety.

Subsequently he undertook the pilgrimage to the Holy Cities, stayed some time in the Arab East at the centres of theological scholarship and became initiated into the speculative refinements of the great masters of Islamic mysticism. Then he returned to the West and settled in Bougie (Algeria). Within a short time he became widely known for his deep religiosity, his disregard for wordly goods and his ways of opening the hearts and minds of the common people as well as of the educated to the desire of attaining to a communion with God. In his mouth the doctrines of the scholarly mystical thinkers, accessible only to an intellectual élite, assumed the words of an easily understandable system of ethics founded upon the belief in a world of the supernatural and in the power of intercession with God which He bestows upon the saints (*awliyā'*, sing. *walī*, *murābit*, marabout*). While following an invitation by the Almohad* ruler Abū Yūsuf Yaʿqūb* (1184-1199) to the court at Marrakesh, Abū Madyan died on the way at Tlemcen and was buried in the nearby village of al-ʿUbbād, apparently already at his time the seat of a certain mystic-ascetic movement. His tomb around which the Marīnid* Abū al-Hasan ʿAli* (1331-1351) upon his conquest of Tlemcen erected a beautiful mosque, a madrasa (institution for theological studies) and other buildings for the use of the numerous pilgrims, has remained a much visited shrine down to this day. Abū Madyan left no writings, but generations of disciples have continued to keep alive his teaching which imparted to the powerful current of mysticism in the Arab West its particular shades.

MAGHRĀWA, one of the large historic Berber confederations of tribes, a member of the great Zanāta* group, which at the time of the first westward push of the Arabs around 650 had their pasture grounds in an area within the confines of present-day Algeria. They were among the first of the North African peoples who embraced Islam, recognized the spiritual supremacy of the caliph, and fought in the ranks of the Arab army led by ʿUqba Ibn Nāfiʿ into the Atlas regions and on to Tangier (682/683). In the long-lasting unrest stirred up by the Khārijite heresy they gained a sort of hegemony in the Zanāta family of tribes, but it is not known for certain whether or not they themselves adhered to this creed, although it seems rather probable. On no account did doctrinal considerations influence their political attitude. From the end of the eighth throughout the ninth century they repeatedly fought on the side of the Idrīsids*. In the early tenth century they were allied to the rigorously orthodox Umayyad emirs of al-Andalus*, and in their service the Maghrāwa chieftain Muhammad Ibn Khazar inflicted a heavy defeat upon the Umayyad rivals in Africa, the shīʿite Fātimids (924). His messengers of friendship were much honoured guests at the court of Cordova, but thirty years later the Maghrāwa were among the vassals of the Fātimid caliph al-Muʿizz (953-975). Muhammad Ibn Khazar's grandson, Muhammad Ibn al-Khair, remembering the former Spanish alliance and the subsidies flowing from it, changed colours again and took up arms for the Umayyad caliph al-Ḥakam II (961-976) against some of the strongest of the Fātimid auxiliaries, the Sanhāja* tribesmen under the leadership of the Zīrid* family. It was a move for which the Maghrāwa paid with a heavy loss in battle, and Muhammad Ibn al-

Khair with his life (971). The following year, the Sanhāja chieftain Bulug-gīn Ibn-Zīrī inflicted a second crushing defeat upon them, penetrated deep into their territory and exterminating, it is said, thousands of them, pushed most of the Maghrāwa people into central Morocco. Yet he was still far from having broken their warlike élan or shaken their loyalty to the Umayyad rulers, who offered to quite a number of clans new homes in the region north of Cordova, where in course of time their notables gained an important place in public life.

Some fifteen years later, the all-powerful regent of al-Andalus, al-Mansūr Ibn Abī Āmir* († 1002), appointed a Maghrāwa emir of the Khazar family, Zīrī Ibn ʿAtīya as governor of the western parts of Morocco with residence in Fez, received him splendidly in Cordova, and bestowed upon him the title of vizier. Zīrī returned the courtesy by sending to the Cordova court 200 thoroughbred Berber horses, some beautiful camels, an enormous panther and other rare animals. Having expanded his territory over all northern Morocco and the region of Oran in a tenacious warfare with the neighbouring Banū Īfran*, and transferred his seat from Fez to the newly founded, more easily defensible city of Oujda, he threw off Umayyad allegiance. Defeated three times in succession by al-Mansūr's son, he withdrew into the Sahara (998), but was pardoned the following year and reinstated in office and honours. His son al-Muʿizz (1001-1026) succeeded him as viceroy of the Maghrib with the exception of the town and surrounding area of Sijilmāsa, held in the name of the Umayyad caliphs by a second branch of the Khazar dynasty, and again made Fez his capital. Unhindered by the rapidly waning authority of the Cordovan government, he ruled practically in full independence until his death. So after him did his cousin Hammāma (1026-1039), great patron of scholars, and Hammāma's son Dūnās (1039-1060) whose sons, Futūh and ʿAjīsa, engaged in a struggle for the throne, which divided the people of Fez into two enemy camps and ended only with ʿAjīsa's death. The names of the two rival brothers have lived on in the names of two gates in the walls of Fez – the *Bāb Futūh* and the *Bāb Gīsa*. The end of the Maghrāwa rule, however, was rapidly nearing. Futūh, fleeing from the assault of the Almoravids* into the comparative safety of northern Morocco, was replaced at the head of the confederation by a relative, Muʿansar (1063), who four years later fell fighting on the walls of Fez. His son Tamīm resisted for a while. Then the city was conquered (1069) by Yūsuf Ibn Tāshufīn, the great Almoravid leader, and the last Maghrāwa emir of Fez, together with a great number of his warriors was killed.

Another line of Maghrāwa emirs of the house of Khazar was founded around 976 by Khazrūn Ibn Falfūl. Encouraged and probably helped by the Cordova government, he conquered the flourishing town of Sijilmāsa with the oases in the surrounding area south of the Middle Atlas from the Banū Midrār, a Miknāsa clan, and recognized what might be called an Ummayyad protectorate over his territory. For a while his son and successor, Emir Wanūdīn, continued to submit to Umayyad sovereignty, but then made himself independent and expanded his realm at the expense of his neighbours and Umayyad allies, the Maghrāwa of Fez, into the country of the Mulūya river. His son Masʿūd,

beaten by the advancing Almoravids, lost Sijilmāsa and his life (1053/4). Ten years later the last resistance of this Maghrāwa dynasty was irretrievably broken.
Thenceforth the Maghrāwa played only secondary rôles in the history-making events in Morocco. Today they live peacefully, mingled among other tribal groups in the area south of Taza and the Tāfīlālt.

MAGHRIB al-, the time and place of the sunset, and the designation of the ritual evening prayer *(salāt al-maghrib)*; in a geographical sense, the western part of the Arab world *(bilād al-maghrib*, the countries of the West, i.e. between Egypt and the Atlantic coast). Originally *al-Maghrib* denoted the regions comprising Morocco and the central and western sections of present-day Algeria, whereas for the areas extending eastwards as far as the border of Egypt, the term *Ifrīqīya** (Little Africa) was generally used throughout the Middle Ages.

MAGHRIB BUREAU, the commonly used designation of the Liberation Committee of the Arab West *(Lajna Tahrīr al-Maghrib al-ʿArabī)*, constituted in Cairo in January 1948. Presided over by the aged revolutionary Abdelkrim (Muhammad Ibn ʿAbd al-Karīm*), then living in exile in Cairo, it was actually directed for a few months by the head of the Tunisian Neo-Destour*, Habīb Bourguiba (Habīb Abū Ruqayba), the later president of the Tunisian Republic; and then by ʿAllāl al-Fāsī, the leader of the Moroccan *Istiqlāl**. Its members were the delegates of a number of the Algerian, Moroccan and Tunisian nationalist parties. Its main task was to create world-wide sympathies for the aspirations of the Arab peoples in North Africa under the French colonial régime, and to cultivate relations with the countries of the Arab East. To this effect it maintained branch offices in several occidental countries and in particular at the seat of the United Nations. After some time, internal divergencies of opinion and frictions with Abdelkrim, followed by his rather curt withdrawal in 1952 from his post of honour seriously impeded its activities and encouraged the creation of a competitive organization, the North African Unity and Action Front*. Following the attainment of independence by Morocco and Tunisia, and the establishment by the Algerian Front of National Liberation* (F.L.N.) of its propaganda apparatus, the Maghrib Bureau quickly lost ground and in 1956 ceased functioning.

MAHALLĪ ABŪ, ABŪ al-ʿABBĀS AHMAD, one of the influential and warlike Moroccan marabouts* (ca. 1555-1613), born in Sijilmāsa of a family of jurists, according to an almost certainly fabricated genealogy descended from the Prophet's uncle ʿAbbās Ibn ʿAbd al-Muttalib, but more probably of Berber origin. After having accomplished his theological studies in Fez, where he belonged to the circle of disciples around the well-known Sudanese scholar Ahmad Bābā al-Tumbuktī*, he undertook the pilgrimage to the Holy Cities. Upon his return to Sijilmāsa, he claimed to have received the sacred mission of re-establishing the unaltered teaching of Islam and demanded obedience as the Mahdi, the God-guided leader. Expelled by the authorities, he went into Algeria, and in the Saūra valley (some 60 miles south of Colomb Béchar), at that time most fertile and well populated, gathered a rapidly increasing number of adherents, secured the support of the Turkish pasha and declared the Holy War against the Saʿdian* Sultan Mūlāy Zaidān (1603-1628). Moving westwards, Abū Mahallī soon was master of the Tāfīlālt where all the tribes followed his call, conquered Sijilmāsa (1611), pushed into the Darʿa valley and across the High Atlas into Marrakesh, the residence of the sultan, who fled to Safi and even thought of taking refuge in Spain. While planning an invasion of North Morocco, Abū Mahallī was attacked by two other marabouts, Abū Zakariyyā' Yahyā Ibn ʿAbd Allāh and Abū al-Hasan ʿAlī al-Samlālī*, and was killed fighting at the gates of Marrakesh.

MAISARA al-MATGHĀRĪ, the leader of an insurrection against Arab domination of several Berber tribes (738-740) particularly exasperated by the hard rule of the Arab governor of Tangier. Maisara, a Mathgāra tribesman who formerly had made a poor living as a water-carrier in al-Qayrawān - whence his surname *al-Haqīr*, the One of Low Standing - brought about under the flag of the heterodox Khārijite doctrine a coalition of the Matghāra, Miknāsa* and Barghawāta* confederation. They took up arms, soon made themselves masters of Tangier and repelled the troops sent over from Spain to reestablish order. Maisara assumed the title of Caliph and with it such overbearing pride that he was deposed and assassinated by his own people. Under his successor Khālid Ibn Hamīd, a Zanāta* chieftain, the confederates conquered the plains of the Sūs on the Atlantic coast and completely routed an army of the caliph at the banks of the Sabū river in the so-called *Ghazwat al-Ashrāf*, the Battle of the Nobles* (740). A second army, allegedly some 70.000 strong, was beaten the following year, and the revolt spread. It was finally subdued in two battles at the gates of al-Qayrawān (742).

MAKHZAN, a term (derived from the verb *khazana*, to close in or to lock up) denoting in Morocco the central government. It came first into use under the Aghlabid* emirs of Tunisia (800-909) as the designation of the iron case in which the tax money was kept. Subsequently the word entered into the administrative terminology of the various states that arose in the Arab West, but in the wider sense of the locality where all the receipts from taxes, custom duties and other legal exactions, in many instances paid in kind, were stored and kept in safety (comp. its infiltration into European languages in the forms of magazine, magasin, Magazin etc.), while the office in charge of the administration of these revenues was known as the *bait al-māl* (lit. the house of property.).
In Morocco, at the time of the Saʿdian* sultans (1554-1659) this development of the meaning continued, and *makhzan* began to signify the State Treasury, probably without clear distinction between the sultan's and the state finances, and finally the entire apparatus of the supreme government which thus took over for itself the name of the source whence the means for its functioning were flowing. The territory, however, where the *makhzan* was strong enough to make itself respected, the so-called *bilād* (colloquially *bled) al-makhzan**, practically never comprised the

whole country; it was mainly confined to the plains, with very fluid delimitations, whereas the tribes in the mountain areas, the so-called *bilād al-sība* (the area of dissidence) refused to submit to any supervision by the central administrative authority. There, government was equivalent to the ability of exploiting the rivalries among the tribal chieftains, of using the influence of the religious brotherhoods* and of appropriately dispensing honours, privileges or advantages of a more tangible nature. The régime of the Protectorate* instituted by the Treaty of Fez (1912) added further, deep-going restrictions of a structural order by transferring to its own agencies the control over the army, police, communications and most economic and financial services. The *makhzan* by then had in fact lost all governing competencies, but the name remained and with it certain purely formal requirements such as the sultan's signature for the validation of more important decrees, which, however, in the normal course of affairs he could not afford to withhold.
The military occupation by the Protectorate Powers of the entire territory, achieved with great cost of lives, material and money, and the gradual implantation in all its parts of their own system of administration, effaced without doubt much, although by constraint and mainly outwardly, of the age-old contrast between *bilād al-makhzan* and the *bilād al-sība*. It needed the atmosphere of the nation-wide enthusiasm after the successful struggle for independence to start the process of their psychological integration. While here and there some resistance springing from the inveterate particularistic disposition still had to be broken, the unification can today be considered as completed and the social or economic conflicts, which certainly are not lacking, as having been channelled into the arena of political party strife.

MANĀQIB, sing. *manqaba*, an Islamic term denoting the ensemble of the conduct of life, the attitudes and acts regarded as miraculous of persons who in the course of time were surrounded by popular opinion with the halo of saintliness. Towards the end of the Middle Ages a vast *manāqib* literature, in many cases anonymous, began to flourish, particularly in the countries of the Arab West, consisting of the biographies of such saintly men. The great mass of this literature, intended for the broad, uncritical public, is marked by extreme naiveté of content, the simplistic representation and the colloquialism of vocabulary and grammar. This manner of approach to the mind of the people illustrates well some aspects of the general social and mental situation of the time. There exists also a biographical production of a higher level which attempts to situate the story of the saint's life, the description of his piety and his supernatural powers within the framework of his environment and epoch. It thus occasionally reflects a picture of appreciable historic interest, especially when a number of such individual biographies are assembled according to a geographical or chronological system. From the literary point of view, also this type of *manāqib* accounts, frequently written by one of the saint's descendants or an author commissioned by him is, with rare exception, only of a very limited value.

MANIFESTO OF THE ALGERIAN PEOPLE, a declaration prepared by Farhat Abbas (Farhāt ʿĀbbas) and signed by 55 prominent notables of various political shades, which in March 1943 was handed over to the Free French Governor-General in Algiers and the diplomatic agents of the Allied Forces in North Africa. It is a document at its time often termed the 'Algerian Charter', which marks a decisive phase in the developement of Algerian nationalism. It begins with a kind of circumstantial survey, exact in many points although less so in others, of the situation of social, economic and political inferiority to which French colonization had methodically reduced the Algerian Arabs. Decidedly discarding whatever policy of piecemeal reforms or promises of a change in a more or less distant future, the Manifesto demanded the abolition of the colonial system, to be carried into effect by immediate and irrevocable measures embodied in an Algerian Constitution which would grant: freedom and absolute equality of all inhabitants of Algeria without distinction of race and religion; a radical land-reform for the benefit of the agricultural proletariat at the expense of the large landlordism; recognition of Arabic as an official language equal to French; freedom of the press and association; free and compulsory education for the children of both sexes; religious freedom for all denominations and the separation of Church and State; the effective participation in government functions of Algerian Moslems; and the liberation of all political prisoners.

The story of the Manifesto must be viewed against the background, on the one hand, of the Atlantic Charter and the proclamation by the Allies of the right to self-determination of all peoples; and, on the other, of the need of the Free French to win the support of the native population for large-scale enlistment in their army. It started in December 1942 with a 'Message from the Algerian Moslems to the Authorities', in which Farhat Abbas and his political friends, mainly from among the Algerian People's Union*, requested the convocation of a conference of notables for the elaboration of an Algerian statute that should replace the colonial régime by a sort of Algerian Home-Rule. The Message was left without answer. Thereupon Farhat Abbas drafted the Manifesto, apparently in consultation with some liberally-minded superior French officials in sympathy with his ideas. Then he submitted it with a list of signatures to the Governor-General. It was turned over without delay to an ad hoc appointed Study Commission for Moslem Social and Economic Affairs which was to propose a programme of reforms suitable for implementation in war-time.

In May 1943, Farhat Abbas and a number of his Moslem colleagues in the consultative Financial Delegation submitted an 'Addendum to the Manifesto', intended to interpret some of the general and abstract terms of the first document. Yet by ommitting all reference to Algeria's relations to France and speaking of a 'sovereign Algerian nation' and an 'Algerian State', it went considerably beyond the original targets and was rejected, together with the Manifesto, by the Governor-General. Instead, a series of minor reforms was enacted, but was declared unacceptable by the partisans of the Manifesto. The disappointment evoked by this French attitude resulted in a menacingly spreading commotion and, in its wake, in a three-month internment of Farhat Abbas. Anxious to prevent an aggravation of the situation at this critical phase of the war, General de Gaulle and his French Committee of National Liberation decided upon a more liberal policy which de Gaulle himself announced at a great popular meeting in Constantine in December 1943. In accordance with the principles he had outlined, a second reform project was elaborated by another special commission of ten Frenchmen and four Moslems from among the conciliatory groups. This was judged thoroughly inadequate by Farhat Abbas and particularly by the two radical nationalist leaders, Sheikh al-Ibrāhīmī of the Association of the Algerian ʿUlamā'* and Messali al-Hajj (Masālī al-Hajj) of the Algerian People's Party*. The same fate was suffered by the Ordinance of March 7th, 1944, to a great extent based on the commission's report, by which the reforms, very much watered down, were given force of law. One week later, Farhat Abbas with a number of nationalists of various trends constituted a common front for concerted political action, the Friends of the Manifesto and of Liberty* (A.M.L.).

MANJŪR al-, ABŪ al-ABBĀ AHMAD IBN ʿALĪ, a Moroccan scholar (1520-1587), highly reputed for his universal erudition. He spent most of his life in his native Fez except for his annual visits to the court at Marrakesh of the Saʿdian* Sultan Ahmad al-Mansūr* (1578-1603), whom he prided himself to count among his numerous disciples. Al-Manjūr wrote a number of commentaries on theological and juridical works of various authors. One of his writings presenting a particular interest is his *fahrasa** (description of the author's studies) which conveys a good insight into the scholarly movement of his time.

MANSŪR al-, MUHAMMAD IBN ABĪ ʿĀMIR, called Almanzor by the medieval chroniclers in the Occident, statesman and general (†1002) in al-Andalus* whose family, of Yamanite descent, had settled in Spain at the time of the Arab conquest. He studied law in Cordova, and like his father started his career as a clerk in court service. Gifted with extraordinary social talent he soon gained the favour of the beautiful Sultana al-Subh (Aurora) who held the reins of the government in the name of her son, the boy caliph Hishām II, and rapidly climbed the steps of the hierarchical ladder. By a well-calculated generosity he made himself popular with the masses and won valuable friendships at the court and in the army, and while still rather young was appointed vizier. A number of successful campaigns against the Christian kingdoms on the northern frontiers finally advanced him to the position of *hājib* (the caliph's chamberlain), the highest office in the state.
Within a few years Ibn Abī ʿĀmir was in fact ruler of al-Andalus. Disbanding the caliph's guard of military slaves *(saqāliba*)* and replacing it by a newly formed body of Moroccan mercenaries; then substituting for the traditional tribal structure of the army a hierarchy of appointed commanders chosen from his entourage, he made the troops a strong and flexible instrument in his hands. His next step was to move the central government out of Cordova's atmosphere of intrigues and machinations into a new, strongly fortified town, *al-Madīna al-Zahīra* (The Beautiful

City) with his own splendid residence in its midst. The regular summer incursions *(sā'ifa*)* into the neighbouring Christian kingdoms, as a rule raids of no very great significance, became under his command victorious campaigns leading to feats of arms such as the conquest, although only temporarily, of Zamora and Barcelona, the destruction of the well-defended holy place of Santiago di Campostela (called *Shant Yāʿqūb* by the Arab chroniclers) - the saint's tomb was left undisturbed - and the occupation of the territory of León and the imposition upon the king of the payment of tribute to the caliph. In northern Morocco he continued the Umayyad policy of alliances with the Berber chieftains but emphasizing it by several armed expeditions. These resulted in the capture of Fez (986) and a number of smaller, but strategically important towns; in the installation of Umayyad governors in the districts of some of the unreliable chieftains and in the entlistment of numerous Berber warriors, who were incorporated into his army.
At the height of his triumph he assumed the epithet *al-Mansūr bi Allāh* (The Victorious by the Grace of God) to which he later added the title *al-Malik al-Karīm* (The Noble King). He had his name mentioned in the Friday prayer, and coins minted with his name as well as state documents issued with his instead of the caliph's seal. On official occassions he appeared in royal attire, but his political ability restrained him from proclaiming himself caliph. He died on his way home from his fifty-second campaign and in his tomb was put, according to his biographers, some of the dust of the many battle-fields, the scenes of his victories, which he himself had taken off from his armour and collected to be buried with him.
Ibn Abī ʿĀmir's son ʿAbd al-Malik al-Muzaffar inherited his father's high office and continued his policy and the wars against the Spanish kingdoms, but was poisoned (1008) by his younger brother ʿAbd al-Rahmān, surnamed Shanjūl (Sanjuelo, Little Sanjo) after his maternal grandfather Sanjo, King of Navarre. Heir to his father's pride and ambition but not to his statesmanship, he openly aspired after the caliphate and forced the weak caliph Hishām II to appoint him heir apparent. Yet the people of Cordova, stirred up by the Umayyad family, revolted and compelled Hishām II to abdicate (1009) in favour of one of his relatives. The new caliph occupied and destroyed *al-Madīna al-Zahīra*, arrested Sanjuelo and sentenced him to death. His son ʿAbd al-ʿAzīz escaped to Valencia, gained possession of the town and the surrounding area, and was recognized by the people as king (1021-1061). His descendants, known in Andalusian annals as the ʿĀmirids, held the throne for two more decades until they lost it (1085) to the Dhū al-Nūn*, another of the many dynasties of the so-called Party-Kings*. An ʿĀmirid client, Muhājid, founded an equally short-lived miniature kingdom in Denia (the chief town in the province of Alicante) and on the Balearic islands.

MAʿQIL, a nomadic Arabian tribe immigrated into Egypt, which followed the great tribal group of the Banū Hilāl* and Sulaym* into North Africa, and by the end of the XIIth century had its pasture grounds on the fringe of the Tunisian and Algerian deserts. Pressed by new-comers, some of them gradually moved northwards and came into the region of

Algiers, then further to the West into the southern parts of the present-day Algerian province of Oran and into the domain of the ʿAbd al-Wādid* sultans of Tlemcen. The majority continued along the southern slopes of the High Atlas into the belt of the oases of the Tāfīlālt, whence some groups went through the broad valley of the Darʿa as far as the plains of the Atlantic in the utmost South of Morocco and further northwards into the wide spaces of the Sūs, everywhere raiding villages, damaging fields and plantations, and escaping most of the time all control by the government authorities. In their wake came other Arab clans or tribal sections, which were accepted into their community and thus, increased in number and strength, the Maʿqil waves began to displace more and more of the native Berbers, who withdrew into the safety of the mountains. Under the first Marīnids* (1244-1465) they were several times driven back, but after a while advanced again, reached the surroundings of Rabat and Fez and roamed the Gharb. At the time of the Wattāsids* (1472-1554) they penetrated into the river valleys of the Middle Atlas - the Wādī Mulūya, the Wādī Umm al-Rabīʿ and the Wādī Sabū - but there the Berber mountain tribes stopped and repelled them.

The rulers of Tlemcen tried, not always successfully, to use their warlike temper and at the same time to check their predatory instinct within the framework of the army. In Morocco, the Saʿdians* (1554-1659) succeeded in transferring the main body of the Maʿqil from western and south-western Morocco into the plains around their capital Marrakesh, and recruited a number of their warriors for military service in a special auxiliary corps, *(jaish)*. In compensation, their chieftains were accorded certain tax privileges and later also pieces of state land in property or usufruct *(iqtāʿ*)*. The ʿAlawid* Sultan Mūlāy Ismāʿīl* (1672-1727), himself on his mother's side related to an influential Maʿqil clan, shifted most of those of their branches which were scattered south of the Atlas into the vast tracts bordering the Atlantic, others from the area of Marrakesh into the environments of his new capital Meknès. He enregimented all of them in the considerably reinforced *jaish*, which thenceforth remained constituted almost exclusively of Maʿqil tribes and was known by the name of the most outstanding among them as the *jaish* Ūdāya. Still, in the frequent periods of disturbances shaking Morocco in the following two centuries, the Maʿqil, like the entire tribal society, whether Arab or Berber, proved extremely hard to police, so that several times some particularly unruly clans were expelled from the *jaish* and resettled in smaller or larger groups in various parts of the country. Today the many Maʿqil branches, under different names, are fully integrated with the mass of the population, most of them hardly conscious of their agitated history.

MAQQARĪ al-, ABŪ al-ʿABBĀS AHMAD IBN MUHAMMAD, a man of letters (ca. 1591-1632) and an outstanding authority on the history of the Arabs in Spain. He was born in Tlemcen (Algeria) of a family of theological scholars which originally came from the small town of Maqqara (appr. 15 miles south east of Msīla, in the present-day Algerian department of Constantine). He began his studies in Marrakesh, continued in Fez and was appointed imam and mufti at the Qarawīyīn* mosque. Having spent some years in Fez he undertook the pilgrimage to the Holy Cities and subsequently taught in Cairo, Jerusalem and Damascus. Finally he returned to Cairo where he died. In Damascus he wrote the work of his life, usually quoted under its abridged title *Nafhu al-Tīb* (one portion dealing with the political history of al-Andalus has been translated into English by Pascal de Gayangos, 'History of the Muhammedan dynasties in Spain, London 1840). It is a biography of the famous vizier at the court of Granada, Ibn al-Khatīb* (1313-1374), equally outstanding as a man of letters and poet. Its most valuable part as a source of information on the political evolution, the literary activities and social conditions of al-Andalus* is the introduction. In eight chapters it gives a geographical description, narrates the events of the Arab conquest, continues with the history of the ruling families and biographies of Arab scholars in al-Andalus as well as of visiting scholars from the Arab East, and ends with the reconquest of al-Andalus by the Christians and the expulsion of the Arabs. Thanks to the many quotations contained therein a number of works lost in the meantime have partly survived.

MARABOUT, the corrupted form of the Arabic word *murābit* (comp. *ribāt**; in the Arab West colloquially *mrabet*, in Berber language *agurran*), denoting approximately the equivalent to the Christian concept of a saint. Nourished by the currents of mysticism which around the XIth century began to take their way from the Arab East, mainly across al-Andalus*, into North Africa, popular piety sought - and found - in saint veneration the medium of personalizing the abstractions of scholastic theology, which were far above its understanding and incapable of satisfying its emotional needs. Here and there, at first sporadically then more frequently, men and women withdrew from worldly life, devoted themselves to prayer, fasting and asceticism, and in the eyes of the people appeared as the friends *(awliyā'* sing. *walī)* of God, the intermediaries between Him and men, upon whom He had bestowed the blessing *(baraka)* of working miracles *(karāmāt*, sing. *karāmā)* for the benefit of the believers. This blessing they transmitted to their adepts whom they guided along the path to the nearness to God, and who shared in their sanctity. Upon the Master's death the disciples became new teachers of God-seeking devotees, all linked together, from generation to generation, as it were by a mystical chain.
For quite some time these expressions of a naive and unorthodox fervour were regarded with mistrust, as could hardly be expected otherwise, by the scholarly and religious élite and by the governing circles, and occasionally also branded as heresy. Not until the end of the XIIIth century did this attitude gradually change, when out of the motley crowd of marabouts, many of them, it is true, illiterate, grossly superstitious or inclined to all sorts of charlatanic practices, there emerged some profoundly pious thinkers, well-trained in theological reasoning, such as Abū Madyan* (1126-1197) or Ibn Mashīsh* († ca. 1228), who reconciled the formalistic requirements of the Law with the mystical experience of the soul in its longing for union with God. They and their circle of

disciples opened to the marabout ideologies the way to official recognition and even to high-ranking patronage, so that the following two hundred years witnessed the prolific spread of persons of every walk of life who felt, and followed, the call to saintliness. Towards the end of the XVth century there was throughout the Arab West hardly a town, tribe or larger village without their saints, called upon by the people as helpers in times of distress, as arbitrators in every-day conflicts and as mediators in difficulties with the authorities. Depending on the convincing force of the cycle of legends spun around them, the fame of their miraculous powers might remain confined to the more or less close neighbourhood of their abode, or extend over a large region and a whole country; it might soon sink into oblivion or continue as the hereditary privilege of one single marabout family, or also give rise to a widely branched-out religious brotherhood*. The saint's tomb might be an artless, whitewashed cublicle *(qubba*)* on the wayside; or it might be built up into a splendid mausoleum at the seat of a brotherhood claiming him as its spiritual patron, such as in Marrakesh the burial place of al-Jazūlī* († ca. 1465), the venerated teacher, it is said, of some 12.000 disciples; or in Tunis of his contemporary Ibn ʿArūs* († 1463) whose obsequies were attended by the whole population of the town, headed by the highest religious and court dignitaries.

By then 'maraboutism' had ceased to be a merely religious phenomenon. Adaptable to every local or regional particularity, it permeated all strata of the population, rural as well as urban. By its moral hold upon the mind of the masses it developed, without organization or formal authority, into a social factor possessed of potential forces sufficient to turn into a political, and eventually military power that was capable of endangering the very structure of the state. The sultans, aware of the danger, but anxious not to hurt public opinion, reacted in a twofold way. On the one hand, they intensified the diffusion of strict orthodoxy through the channels of new, richly endowed theological schools *(madrasas)* at various levels of learning; and on the other, took care to display their own veneration for the great popular saints and to use the marabout cult as an instrument for the consolidation of loyalty to sovereign and dynasty. For a while this policy seemed to work. It became immediately inefficient as soon as the ruler failed in his sacred duty as the defender of Moslem soil *(dār al-Islām)* against the Portuguese or Spanish invasions. In Algeria and Tunisia, the marabouts stood on the side of the Turks, who drove back the Christian aggressors and overthrew the crumbling ʿAbd al-Wādid* and Hafsid* thrones. In Morocco, at the time of the disintegrating apparatus of government under the Wattāsids*, and again somewhat later under the last Saʿdians*, it was maraboutism which came forth as the protagonist in the battle against the unbelievers. It raised the call to the Holy War; mobilized tribal chieftains, village headmen and leaders of the populace in the towns; collected funds for the ransoming of prisoners; and was the relentlessly impelling force of a most tenacious guerilla warfare. Quite a few of the holy men took up arms themselves, rallied the warriors of the area, and at their head added to the reputation of saintliness the glory of military feats.

While one or the other of a more enterprising mind even succeeded in building up a kind of rudimentary body politic, most of them were soon again forgotten, to be replaced by newcomers of equally ephemeral fame. Yet in the first half of the XVIIth century there emerged also figures of a truly commanding caliber, such men as Abū Mahallī*, al-ʿAyyashī* or al-Samlālī*, daring warlords, inspired without doubt by the sincere ardour of a fighter for the faith but as much, if not more, by the ambition for personal power, who knew how to crystallize all the nuclei of militant saintliness. For a generation or two it seemed as if thenceforth Morocco was to remain divided up into the half-religious, half-secular dominions which those marabout princes had forged in the atmosphere of the country-wide anarchy; but their ruin was the rivalry opposing one against the other and against the influential brotherhoods. Their last traces disappeared when the strong hand of the first ʿAlawid* sultans reforged the unity of the state.

The rather abrupt end of what may be called the heroic phase of maraboutism in no way affected its vitality. At least a hundred years earlier it had already discoverd a source of additional prestige, flowing ever more rewardingly as time went on, in the ideology of sharīfism, the genealogical relationship with the Prophet Muhammad. From the XVIth century onward there was hardly a saint of some repute, whether Arab or Berber, who - or his family for him even many years after his death - would not claim, and as a rule be readily accorded by public opinion, the supreme distinction of descendancy from the Prophet. Inventive experts in the science of genealogy *(nasab)* elaborated the intricacies of a lineage which associated him in the halo surrounding the religious aristocracy of *sharīfs** with the members of the reigning dynasties, the Saʿdians and the ʿAlawids, and with the luminaries of scholarship and letters. Biographers, either family members or professionals commissioned by them, related the story of his life with its mystic and magic experiences, his visions and voices, the methods and modes of his asceticism. The libraries in Morocco, Algeria and Tunisia contain a great deal of this rich hagiographic literature in the form of individual biographies or chronological and geographical compilations, continuing well into the present century. The omission, regrettable perhaps from folkloristic and sociological points of view, of the popular legendary ornamentation and in particular the restriction to urban saints of theological schooling, reflects a distinction by social and educational criteria which gradually separated the world of maraboutism into two classes of a superior and an inferior standing.

Until about the turn of the century this discrimination was practically of no more effect than other differentiating elements in the cultural fabric. By then the thought, born in the Arab East, of awakening Islamic life and civilization from their long stagnation took shape and gained momentum in such movements as the Salafīya* and later in the Association of Algerian ʿUlamā'*. They rose against the cult of the saints, which they denounced as the source of superstition and semi-pagan practices, clouding the purity of true faith, obstructing intellectual advancement and deadening the hope for material progress. They stood soon in a common front with the nationalist champions of political emancipation, but

thereby essentially modified their crusade for spiritual emancipation. They had to keep away from the village marabouts, upon whose attitude hinged the success of nationalist propaganda in the rural communities where the emissaries of a political party were not seldom, occasionally without objecting, taken for missionaries of a new religious brotherhood. Thus maraboutism continued to thrive among the peasantry in the plains and among the tribes in the mountains, but at last cautiously and with hesitation joined the ranks of the militant patriots.
In the towns, the struggle for enlightenment and for the national ideals went hand in hand, but there more than the beliefs and attitudes of a naive population had to be faced. Urban maraboutism had a two-fold organised support: on the one hand, the compact religious officialdom sensing the menace to its influence - imams, cadis and muftis, teachers at the madrasas and koranic schools, administrators of pious foundations; and, on the other, the French authorities realizing the significance of those tradition-bound elements for controlling the revolutionary dynamism. The final victory of the national revolution everywhere in the Arab West meant also the end of this alliance. Saint veneration, with many of the customs of a primitive piety, still lives on, but the political philosophy and the cultural values prevailing in the young independent states leave to maraboutism today only a very modest rôle.

MARDANĪSH IBN, ABŪ ʿABDULLĀH MUHAMMAD IBN AHMAD, one of the so-called Party Kings* in al-Andalus* (1124-1172), born of a Visigothic family–his name obviously is a corrupted form of Martinez, i.e. the son of Martin–converted to Islam. In the political and military unrest which accompanied the decline of the Almoravid* rule, he made himself master of Murcia and Valencia (1145-1147). Together with his father-in-law Ibn Hamushkū (called Rey Lope or Lobo by contemporary Christian chroniclers), the most influential of the local lords in the area of Jaén, he occupied Carmona and defeated the Almohad* army set against him. The situation changed when Abū Yaʿqūb Yūsuf* ascended the Almohad throne (1163-1184) and vigorously took up the campaign in al-Andalus. Two of his brothers at the head of a strong force beat Ibn Mardanīsh and his mercenary troops, mainly Spanish Christians, near Murcia (1165) but the city itself was not taken. Also in the course of a second expedition conducted by Abū Yaʿqūb personally Murcia resisted all assaults but at last most of the garrison deserted and Ibn Mardanīsh died (1172). His sons and his brother, the governor of Valencia, following the advice he gave them on his deathbed, surrendered and entered Almohad service. Three years later the nuptials of his daughter with Abū Yaʿqūb Yūsuf were celebrated in Seville.

MARĪNIDS, Banū Marīn, a Berber dynasty in Morocco (1244-1465), founded by a clan of one of the nomadic Zanāta* branches which had its pasture grounds on the fringe of the Sahara between the oases of the Tāfīlālt and the Figwig, but towards the end of the XIth century began moving into the central plains. Rough warriors and refractory to all rules of discipline excepting those of their own tribal code, they refused to be fitted into the politico-religious order of the Almohad* state and

THE MAGHRIB STATES XIIIth AND XIVth CENTURIES

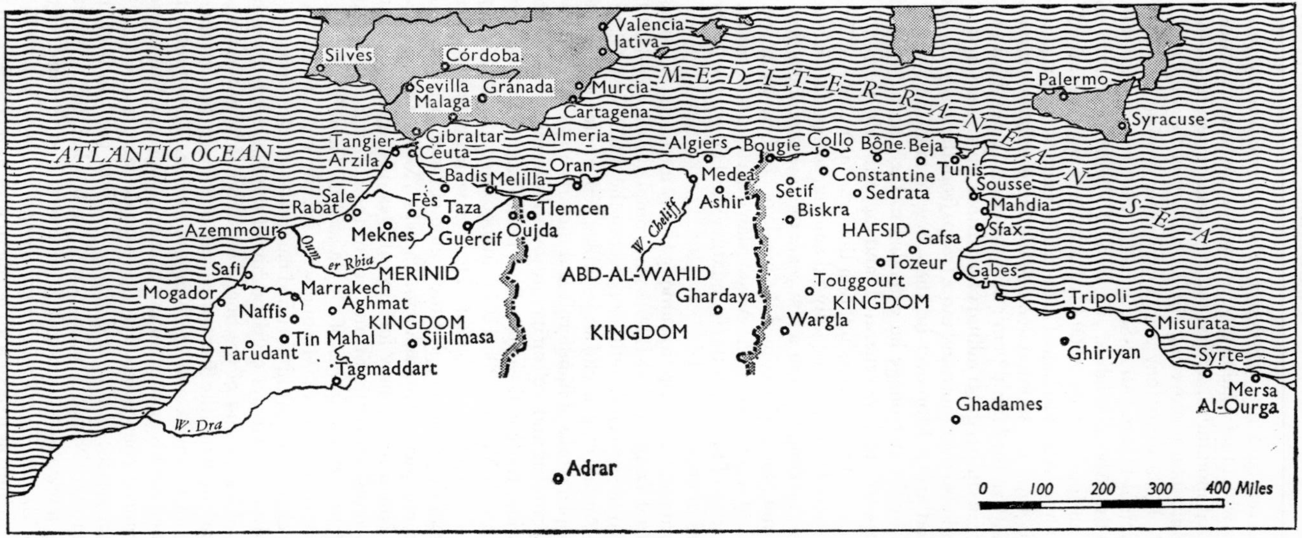

were driven back into the desert (1145). Some seventy years later, in alliance with other Zanāta groups, they pressed again northwards as far as the Rif mountains, at first pilfering and devastating wherever they came, but soon discovering the advantage of the imposition of taxes instead. For a while they were forced into obedience by the Almohad ruler Abū al-Hasan ʿAlī al-Saʿīd(1242-1248) and took part in his wars against the ʿAbd al-Wādids*, the lords of Tlemcen, their hereditary and most tenacious enemies. After his death, an energetic Marīnid chieftain, Abū Yahyā ʻAbd al-Haqq (1244-1258) resumed the struggle for power but this time far more systematically. Recognizing temporarily the suzerainty of the Hafsid* emir of Tunisia Abū Zakariyyā', he grouped his warriors into regular military formations; recruited foreign mercenaries; and won over more and more troops from the gradually disbanding Almohad army. Moreover he knew how to gain the sympathy of the masses by the patronage he extended to their holy men and women (marabouts*) highly venerated and accordingly influential in the atmosphere of mystical inclination that was taking an ever firmer hold on the popular mind. Steadily advancing, although with occasional setbacks, he conquered in a few years the towns of Taza, Fez, Meknès, Rabat and Salé and occupied the whole of northern Morocco. He died in Fez and was buried in the Andalusian quarter *(Madīnat al-Andalus)*. At the time of his death the foundation was laid for the Marīnid State that was to grow up.

The heritage, hotly disputed among family members, fell to his brother Abū Yūsuf Yaʿqūb (1258-1286)* who completed the conquest and made Morocco the strongest military power in the Arab West. Close contacts with al-Andalus*, peaceful and warlike, kept up steady currents of ideas and people, works of handicraft and the arts into Fez, the new capital, rapidly growing and well on its way towards the rank of a foremost centre of learning, trade and wealth. Abū Yūsuf Yaʿqūb's son and successor, Abū Yaʿqūb Yūsuf (1286-1307), inaugurated the Marīnid policy of eastward expansion. By-passing Tlemcen which withstood a more than eight-year siege, he occupied the region of Oran, penetrated deep into Algeria, conquered Mostaganem, Cherchel, Miliana and Médéa (1302). In the North he strongly fortified al-Qasr al-Saghīr, the point of the shortest crossing over the Straits; and on the eastern frontier strengthened the defences of the towns of Oujda and of Taza. There, in Taza he embellished the Great Mosque with its fine cupola and the famous bronze chandelier. At his fortified camp al-Mansūra opposite Tlemcen he received the envoys of friendship of the Hafsids of Tunisia, of the Sultan of Egypt and of the Sharīf of Mecca. He was less succesful in his relations with the two principal powers in Spain, the Nasrid* Sultans of Granada and the Kings of Castile. They broke the peace he needed for his venture in the East and which he had hoped to buy by territorial concessions. His fleet was defeated by Genoese ships in Castilian service (1291) and Tarifa fell into the hands of the allied Castilian and Nasrid armies. Nasrid troops landed in Africa, seized Ceuta - a few years later again turned over by the people of the town to their Marīnid lords - and his governor of Malaga, joining the enemy, stirred up into insurrection all northern Morocco (1306-7). In the same

year Abū Yaʿqūb Yūsuf was assassinated in al-Mansūra by his harem slaves and was buried in Chella.
His death concluded the first period of the Marīnid reign and introduced a quarter of a century of dynastic strife, mutinies of the mercenary troops and rebellions of the Arab tribes. Yet the disturbances affected neither the country's intellectual and artistic creativeness nor its economic prosperity resting upon an urban society that felt little concern about those conflicts unrelated to its own interests. Two strong-handed sovereigns, Abū al-Hasan ʿAlī (1331-1351)* and his son Abū ʿInān Fāris (1351-1358)*, made an end to the troubled interlude. They gained the support of the city people by the lavish construction of splendid mosques and monumental fountains. Their creation, in all larger towns, of theological schools *(madrasas)* dispensing rigorously orthodox instruction along the official lines of thought counterbalanced, at least for some time, the hold upon the mind of the masses of the growing number of saints and brotherhoods* not seldom tinged with heterodox beliefs and often of doubtful dynastic loyalty. Urged on by their ambition to resuscitate the grandeur of the Almohad African empire, they overran the ʿAbd al-Wādid and Hafsid countries – all of present-day Algeria and Tunisia – and for a short while Marīnid glory had attained its summit. With Ābū ʿInān's assassination it faded away, rapidly and irretrievably
Thenceforth viziers and provincial governors, most of them of the Wattāsid* clans which for generations had given to the dynasty its most trusted servants, controlled the country nominally for Marīnid sovereigns – often children of six or eight years, or even of one year as in the case of ʿAbd al-Haqq* (1421-1465) – whom they enthroned and dethroned as it happened to fit into the changing pattern of their own rivalries. The Marīnid state, never very solidly structured, came dangerously near to disintegration. In the mountains, the Berber tribes were undisputed masters and neither paid taxes nor supplied troops. In the plains, the great Arab chiefs of the Banū Hilāl* and Maʿqil* imposed their authority upon the whole countryside, making villagers and townspeople purchase at the price of heavy contributions a doubtful safety from pilfering raids. The towns lived their own independent life, engaged in endless feuds with one another; and venturesome commanders of Kurdish, Andalusian or Christian mercenaries waged their own wars.
In this climate of general anarchy, Fez still maintained its position as the center of gravity culturally, economically, and of whatever little of central authority was left. It was at the Marīnid court at Fez, whosoever might have been the Wattāsid vizier in power, that Morocco's external relations converged. Thence was directed the herditary war against the Banū ʿAbd al-Wād, in the course of which Tlemcen, lost after Abū ʿInān's death, was recaptured by Moroccan troops (1359), lost again, and again reconquered (1370) with most of the ʿAbd al- Wādid territory until its rulers were reduced to Morrocan vassals (1389). There, too, worked such scholars as Ibn al-Khatīb* and Ibn Khaldūn* and were invested with official functions. It was by exploiting the imbroglio of intrigues at the court of Fez that Muhammad V of Granada (1354-1358 and 1365-1390) replaced for nearly two decades the régime of the Wat-

tāsid regents by a veritable Nasrid tutelage.
The perpetual internal discord dangerously undermining the country's military force inevitably called forth offensive enterprises on the part of the Iberian Kingdoms, where the idea of maritime expansion was gaining ever more ground. The first victim was Tetuan, which had grown up in the shadow of a strong fortress erected by the first Marīnids, and was soon chosen as rallying point by a well-organized and thriving piracy operating along the African and Spanish coasts. A Spanish expeditionary corps razed the town to the ground and took the inhabitants into slavery to Spain (1399). Only a century later it was reawakened to life by Moslems expelled from Spain after the fall of Granada (1492). A far more serious loss was Ceuta, the prosperous centre of a flourishing trade with Marseille, Genoa and Pisa, conquered (1415) by a Portuguese fleet of 200 ships manned allegedly by 50.000 soldiers. Encouraged by this first success, the Portuguese thenceforth methodically concentrated their efforts at gaining a solid foothold in northern Morocco. Carefully but steadily expanding along the Straits, they attacked Tangier (1437), but having been repelled, took (1458) al- Qasral-Saghīr (The little Castle, Alcazarseguer, halfway between Ceuta and Tangier) and pressed forward on the Atlantic coast, nearer to their own ports. It was the first step in the series of their history-making oceanic adventures which led them to the circumnavigation of Africa by Vasco da Gama and the building up of their colonial empire.
With ʿAbd al-Haqq, ambitious, energetic and tenacious yet lacking in statecraft, the Marīnid line came to its end. He freed himself from the Wattāsid ascendancy by the wholesale murder of the family (1458) but was unable to prevent two of its members from getting safely away. One of them, Muhammad al-Shaykh*, ascended the throne as the first Wattāsid sovereign after ʿAbd al-Haqq had lost his life (1465) while trying to subdue a rebellion of the people of Fez. In the political evolution of the Arab West the Marīnid régime, notwithstanding its long duration, left no particularly noteworthy traces. In the history of the arts and handicraft it has acquired a lasting place by the munificent patronage it afforded to architects, sculptors and mosaic designers whose combined creative genius brought forth symphonies of lines, forms and colours which belong to the outstanding aesthetic achievements of all times. For the people of Morocco the name of the Marīnids lives on in the beautiful garden which has grown out of the necropolis of Chella on the outskirts of Rabat, built for themselves by the rulers of the dynasty's first hundred years, and in the row of mausolea, today in ruins, on a hill facing the old city of Fez, where those of the second hundred years were buried.
In the years of the dynasty's decadence a Marīnid branch established in the north-eastern regions of Morocco an independent emirate with its residence in the mountain fortress of Dabdū (some 30 miles south of Taūrirt). It maintained itself well into the first quarter of the XVIth century partly with the help of the Moslem and Jewish refugees from Spain, to whom it offered asylum after the fall of Granada (1492). The Wattāsid Sultan Muhammad al-Shaykh (1472-1505) having several times vainly attempted to subdue them, finally gave two of his daughters

in marriage to two sons of the emir of Dabdū and thus prepared the peaceful incorporation of the emirate into Moroccan territory.

List of Marīnid Rulers:

Abū Yahyā ʿAbd al-Haqq	1244-1258
Abū Yūsuf Yaʿqūb	1258-1286
Abū Yaʿqūb Yūsuf	1286-1307
Abū Thābit	1307-1308
Abū Rābiʿa	1308-1310
Abū Sāʿidʿ Uthmān	1310-1331
Abū al-Hasan ʿAlī	1331-1351
Abū ʿInān Fāris	1351-1358

Supremacy of viziers under 17 sultans 1358-1374
Tutelage of Muhammad V of Granada during the reign of 4 sultans 1374-1390
New supremacy of viziers under 3 sultans 1393-1421
ʿAbd al-Haqq 1421-1465 (Wattāsid regency 1421-1458)

MARRĀKUSHĪ al-, ʿABD al-WAHĪD, an Arab historian born in Marrakesh (1185). No data about his family and early youth have been transmitted. He studied in Fez, then went to Seville and afterwards to Cordova where he was given an official position at the court of the Almohad* governor. Extensive travelling which took him to Tunisia and Egypt, to Mecca and Baghdad widened the circle of his relations and enabled him to gain a close personal insight into the political situation of these years and the intellectual and literary currents. Finally he seems to have settled in Egypt. The fruits of his experience are embodied in the work of his life, *Al-Muʿjib fī Talkhīs Akhbār al-Maghrib* (appr. Compendium of the History of the Arab West) usually quoted simply as *al-Muʿjib*. It is one of our main sources of information on the history of the Arab West down to his time, especially of the Almohad régime, besides supplying interesting data on the literary activities in al-Andalus* during the period of the so-called Party Kings* (French translation by E. Fagnan, Histoire des Almohades, Alger 1893).

MASHĪSH IBN, ʿABD al-SALĀM al-HASANĪ, one of the most popular Moroccan saints († ca. 1228). He was born in the mountain region of the Jabal al-ʿAlam south-east of Tetuan, obviously of Berber origin but later attributed a genealogy going back to the Prophet's family, and thus elevated to sharīfian* rank. Only vague biographical data have been transmitted except that while still a youth he spent some time at the places of theological learning in the Arab East, and after his return joined the circle around the great mystical thinker Abū Madyān* at Bougie. Subsequently he withdrew into his native mountains for a life of meditation among a group of selected disciples, and seems to have enjoyed the prestige of a holy man throughout a fairly extensive area. He died assassinated by a 'false prophet', a partisan of the Marīnids* in their struggle against the weakening Almohad* rule, who apparently saw in the saint's influence upon the people a danger for his own politico-religious purposes. Around Ibn Mashīsh's name, whose tomb on the top of a mountain remained a place of local reverence, a circle of legends and tales about the miracles he had performed was woven in the course of time. Some two hundred years after his death his veneration began to spread all over northern Morocco, and from the XVIth century onwards he was revered in the Arab West as a *qutb** (a focus of mystical worship). His descendants ranked for many years among the highly respected sharīfian families in Morocco.

MASMŪDA, the most numerous of the great historic Berber families of tribes. The first more than fragmentary information as to their geographic distribution does not go back further than the XIth century, but it is generally assumed that already four centuries earlier, at the beginning of the Arab penetration into North Africa, their many branches and sub-groups occupied the major parts of Morocco: the Ghumāra all over the Rif as far as the Straits and southward into the plain irrigated by the Bū Ragrāg and Sabū rivers; their neighbours, the Barghawāta*, as far as the Umm al-Rabīʿ which separated them from the Dukkāla; then further south down to the Wādī Tansift, the Ragrāga; and gradually gaining the hill-lands, the H'āh'a and a number of minor groupings. None of these Masmūda communities in the fertile plains on the Atlantic coast, apparently a well-to-do, peaceful peasantry under the patriarchal guidance of elected headmen, seems to have opposed serious resistance to the advancing Arab army of ʿUqba Ibn Nāfiʿ (about 683) or later to Mūsa Ibn Nusayr (about 710) who incorporated the whole of North Africa into the empire of the caliphs of Damascus. It was he who on the slopes of the High Atlas built the town of Aghmāt – no longer in existence – which was chosen as a place of residence by some of the Masmūda chieftains until its conquest by Idrīs II (around 812). As time went on, the more or less compact Masmūda block disintegrated under the onslaught of the Arab Banū Hilāl* and Maʿqil*; under the pressure of other Berber tribes; and in the nearly incessant population shifts in the wake of dynastic struggles. Only the H'āh'a (Ihahane) still live in the region between Mogador and Agadir, and the name of the Ragrāga is in existence in the Dukkāla country and in the Sūs. It is borne, only by one family, once–and to some extent even today–held in the reputation of sanctity because of the many marabouts* who in a sort of hereditary succession came from its midst. Of a few other tribes remembrance has survived only in some geographic names such as the Peñon of Velez de la Gomara, the cape on the Rif east of Tetuan; or the Dukkāla country, the hinterland of Mazagan, inhabited for some five hundred years, if not longer, by an Arab population entirely unrelated to their Masmūda predecessors.
In the mountains the picture was different. In the High and Middle Atlas, the Mamsūda society, structured in small tribes and tribal sections, most of them under their own particular names, but combining in loosely knit, ever changing associations *(leff**, plur. *lfuf)*, continued undisturbed, except for internal feuds in its widely dispersed villages and hamlets. Once only were the Masmūda people of the mountains and those of the plains closely united in their common faith, in the religio-political doctrine preached by the Mahdi Ibn Tūmart* (middle of the

XIIth century) among the Hargha and Hintāta in the western region of the High Atlas. Their union–initial defections had been severely punished–forged the Almohad* empire, the mightiest concentration of power in the history of the Arab West, and the frame of some of its most splendid cultural attainments. When it began to lose coherence, another family of Masmūda blood, the Hafsids*, descendants of Ibn Tūmart's devoted follower Abū Hafs ʿUmar* of the Hintāta, built up their throne in Tunisia, which they held until well into the XVIth century. With the dislocation of the Almohad state the deeply ingrained particularistic spirit came again to the surface, and with it the old pattern of self-governing tribes, clans and village communities, each one jealously defending its independence. By adroitly exploiting a favourable situation, an energetic chieftain, a venerated marabout* or the head of a religious brotherhood* might occasionally constitute within somewhat wider confines a kind of miniature tribal republic, but in its attitude to the central government the Masmūda mountain remained the *bilād al-sība* (the territory of dissidence) refusing to recognize any authority that had not been freely accepted. Time has effaced also in the mountains, as it has done in the plains, the ancient tribal names except a very few, such as that of the Glāwa* (Igelwān) in the valleys of the Darʿa and the Dadès, while the mass of the Berber population in the High and Middle Atlas is known today as Shulūh (in French texts Chleuh), the true descendants of the ancient Masmūda.

MAWSIM see MŪSEM

MIKNĀSA, one of the large historic confederations of Berber tribes, belonging to the great Zanāta* family, which apparently in pre-Islamic times, it is unknown when, migrated from the regions of present-day Tripolitania and Tunisia into Algeria with Tiaret (in the department of Oran) as a centre. Many of its members then moved into eastern and central Morocco, gradually expanding in the Mulūya valley and further on into the Rif mountain lands as well as towards the plains bordering the Atlantic coasts. Some of their clans were among the troops which in the VIIth century under Tāriq Ibn Ziyād set out for the conquest of Spain, and others followed later at irregular intervals. These groups settled in the so-called *Fahs al-Bullūt* (Highland of the Acorn Fields, today Los Petroches) north of Cordova, from whose midst in the middle of the XIth century came the dynasty of the Aftasids*, rulers of nearly the whole western sector of al-Andalus*; and in the region of Saragossa, where the place-name of Mequinenza still recalls its one-time inhabitants. In Morocco, the Miknāsa laid out in a fertile countryside an agglomeration of settlements which were to develop into the city of Meknès; established in the great gap between the northern end of the Middle Atlas and the mountain system of the Rif, the town of Taza, important strategically as well as commercially throughout the Middle-Ages; and founded in the oases of the Tāfīlālt on the border of the Sahara, the town of Sijilmāsa whose ruins known as Madīnat al-Hamrā' (the Red City) still tell of its former significance.
Two outstanding Miknāsa chieftains, Masāla Ibn Habūs and his cousin

Mūsā Ibn Abī'l ʿĀfīya, played a noteworthy rôle in the contest for supremacy in North Africa, which throughout the Xth century opposed Spanish Umayyads and Fātimids. Masāla Ibn Habūs who had espoused the Fātimid creed and cause, subdued Tiaret (912), the former Rustumid* imamate, and was entrusted with the governorship of the town and the surrounding area. Next he conquered the Sālihid* principality of Nakūr (917), an Umayyad ally, which, however, was soon afterwards lost again by one of his lieutenants and became an Umayyad vassal state. Then he took the Idrīsid* capital Fez (922/23) and the mountain region eastwards as far as Tlemcen, over which Mūsā Ibn Abī'l ʿĀfīya was appointed governor with exception of the urban area of Fez entrusted to an Idrīsid prince. Finally he occupied Sijilmāsa. At the height of his success he was attacked by the Maghrāwa* chieftain Muhammad Ibn Khazar, at that time in friendly relations with the Umayyad court, and fell in battle. Tiaret became the heritage of his brother Yasal Ibn Habūs who was followed by his son Hamīd. Both father and son faithfully preserved the allegiance to their Fātimid overlords.

Mūsā Ibn Abī'l-ʿĀfīya was the acknowledged leader in Taza and in the region stretching between Fez and Tlemcen. For reasons which have remained obscure he suddenly went over into the Umayyad camp (931). Thereupon a Fātimid army, commanded by his nephew Hamīd Ibn Yasal, was sent against him, defeated him near Taza and forced him to withdraw into the mountains, and the territory he had held as a Fātimid fief was given to members of the Idrīsid family. After his death (939) his sons remained loyal to their Umayyad protectors.

A third Miknāsa group constituted a kind of city-state in Sijilmāsa and the oases of the Tāfīlālt under the house of the Banū Midrār (771-977) whose founder, allegedly a blacksmith from Cordova, had emigrated from al-Andalus and adhered to a sect of the heterodox Khārijite doctrine. Throughout the IXth century the people of Sijilmāsa maintained friendly relations with the Umayyad court at Cordova. Emir Muhammad I (852-886) seems to have greatly appreciated the 'intelligence service' – as it would today be termed – and the information it supplied on the political currents in the Arab East, which the Midrārid prince Abū Malik al-Mustansir had organized for the Cordovan chancellery. In Sijilmāsa, too, the Mahdi ʿUbayd Allāh, the apostle of the Fātimid creed, was temporarily put into prison when stopping there on his peregrination through North Africa (908/9), which led to the first encounter of the Midrārids with, and their defeat by, Fātimid troops. One of the later rulers, Muhammad Ibn al-Fath (943-959) turned from Khārijism to Sunnism and assumed the title *Amīr al-Mu'minīn* (Commander of the Faithful). He did not enjoy it very long; Sijilmāsa was captured by a Fātimid army and he lost his life. Shortly afterwards the Midrārid ruler al-Muʿtazz, the last of his line, tried his luck on Fātimid sides, but was beaten by an Umayyad vassal, the Maghrāwa chieftain Khazrūn Ibn Falful. He fell fighting (977) and his head was sent as a trophy to Cordova. Until the middle of the following century Sijilmāsa remained in the hands of the Maghrāwa.

Among all the tribes in central and northern Morocco the various

Miknāsa groups opposed the most tenacious resistance to the advancing Almoravid* armies impelled by the indomitable energy of their great leader Yūsuf Ibn Tāshufīn* (1061-1107). It was one of Mūsā Ibn Abī l'ʿĀfya's descendants, Emir Qāsim al-Miknāsī, who in a last desperate effort rallied his men against the enemy everywhere irresistibly gaining ground. Victorious in the first encounter, he lost the second decisive battle and also his life. The Miknāsa's élan was for ever broken, but down to this day a tribal group in the area of Taza still bears their name, while others in their neighbourhood, rightly or wrongly, claim to be their descendants.

MINING. While in Morocco, Algeria and Tunisia alike the yields of the soil are still far from nearing the full potential measure, the exploitation of the subsoil wealth has gone on for quite a time with incomparably higher efficiency and considerably more remunerative results.
In MOROCCO, mining supplies nearly 40 per cent of the value of the total exports and occupies 40.000 miners. Three-quarters, or eight million metric tons, in 1961 are constituted by the phosphates of the deposits at Khouribga (east of Casablanca) and Yūsufīya (formerly Louis Gentil, east of Safi), and make Morocco the world's second-greatest producer of phosphates. Shipping these, means to the port of Casablanca two-thirds, to the port of Safi more than four-fifths of all their tonnage handled, and to the Moroccan railways nearly half of their receipts. Extraction and merchandising are the monopoly of the 'Office Chérifien des Phosphates' (established in 1921), a stock-holding company whose shares are all in the hands of the government. In the world production of cobalt Morocco holds third place (mines at Bū Azar south of Warzazat in the Anti Atlas); of manganese, the fifth (mines at Imini north-west of Warzazat in the High Atlas, and at Bū Arfa north-west of Figwig on the High Plateau); and of lead, the seventh (mines in the area of Midelt in the upper Mulūya valley and at Khenifra). This quite respectable list comprises also iron (in the region of Mellila); coal (at Jerada south of Oujda near the Algerian border) in deposits estimated at about a hundred million tons; tin (at Bū Bekr and Touissit in the eastern parts of the country); copper; antimony; silver; wolfram; barytes; graphite; and salt. All these are private mining concerns, but in some thirty of the larger ones the State holds parts which may amount to half of their capital. The State exercizes, however, a general control over the entire mining industry through its 'Bureau de Recherches et de Participations Minières', a semi-public, technical and commercial institution (established 1928) which investigates, or assists and cooperates in the investigation of, mineral ressources and administers the share held by the State in private mining concerns.
ALGERIA, although not as rich in exploitable minerals, has valuable iron-ore deposits, estimated to amount up to a hundred million tons, near the Tunisian border north of Tebesa in the Jabal Ouenza, with the centre at Clairefontaine and in the Bū Khadra mountain near Morsott. Less abundant are those near Milliana in the Zaccar mountains and of Beni Saf on the coast south-west of Oran which are connected with the port by a tunnel. On the fringe of the Sahara, close

NORTH-WEST ARFICA

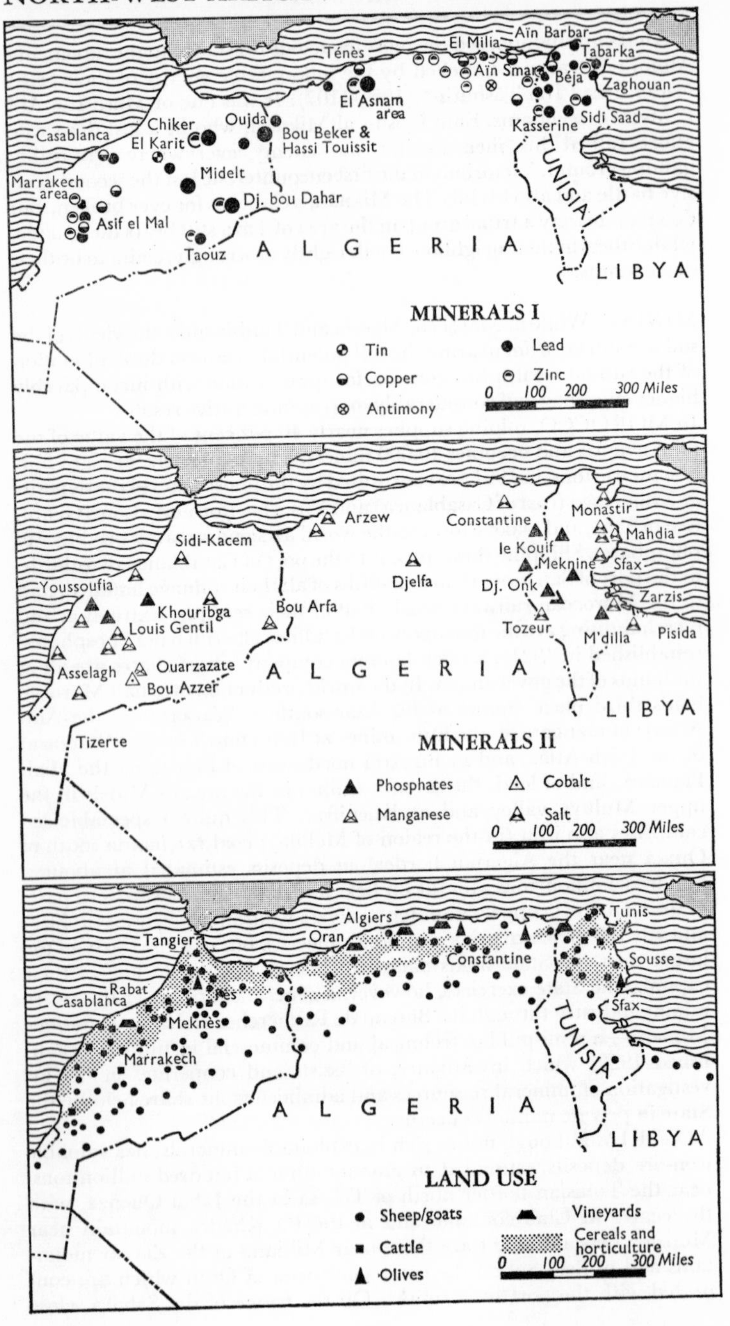

to the Moroccan border are the coal mines of Kenadza near Colomb-Béchar, employing some 3000 miners and connected by a 475-mile long railway line with Oran. There are furthermore important deposits of sulphate and soda at Zegdan in the so-called 'Confins Algéro-Marocains'; the large phosphate deposits of the Jabal Onk and the Jabal Kouif in the area of Tebesa, and minor ones at different places, occupying altogether a labour force of about 2000. Of lesser significance are the tin- and lead-ores in the Jabal Oudsta near Sakiet Sīdī Yūsuf close to the Tunisian border, and in the Jabal Maslūla near Clair-fontaine; tin, uranium and wolfram in the Hoggar mountain around Tamanghassat; and small quantities of barytes and mercury. Great hopes were raised by the discovery at Gara Jibilet east of Tindouf in the westernmost part of the Algerian Sahara – an area under dispute between Algeria and Morocco – of high-quality iron-ores in deposits estimated at some 4000 millions tons. They are expected to yield an annual output of five million tons, but depending on the construction of a railway line for the transport. All those mines are being exploited by French concerns. The Agreement of Evian (March 1962), which established Algeria's independence, created an autonomous Franco-Algerian 'technical organism' for the supervision of the rational exploitation of the country's mineral wealth.

Although in absolute figures the output of TUNISIA's mining industry stays behind that of Morocco and Algeria, it plays a considerable rôle in the country's economy: it supplies one-third of the total exports; over three-quarters of the transportation of the railways; nearly all the traffic of the port of Sfax; and two-thirds of the goods shipped abroad through the port of Tunis. The Tunisian output of phosphates occupies the fourth place in the world's total. Their deposits cover an area of some 200 sq. miles extending westwards from Gafsa to the Algerian frontier with Metlawi (formerly Philippe Thomas) as the centre, and occupy some 4000 workers. In 1959 the government controlled 'Société Nationale d'Investissements' acquired half the shares from the former sole owner, the 'Compagnie des Phosphates Sfax-Gafsa', which also built the 180-mile railway line from the mines across the steppe to Sfax. Other deposits lie in the middle of the Highland at Kalaat-es-Senaam and Kalaat-Jerda in the area of the town Le Kef. Abundant, too, is the output of iron-ore in quite a number of regions in the northern and central parts of the country, especially around Jeriss and at Nebeur in the Jabal Hadida (area of Le Kef). Various minor deposits of lead and zinc are worked to an extent which varies with the fluctuations of the demand on the world markets.

As a regulating factor of the principal source of income from the mineral resources in all three countries, a North African Phosphate Office was established in Paris in 1933, and re-organized after the Second World War in 1946 by agreement between the Office Chérifien in Morocco and the Algerian and Tunisian mining companies. It centralizes the sales, determines the prices in accordance with a scale of standardized qualities, balances the different costs of production and assigns to every one of the countries a proportional share in the exports.

Approximate Mining Output (metric tons) in 1963

	Morocco	Algeria	Tunisia
Phosphates	8.000.000	7000.000	2.250.000
Iron-Ore	1.260.000	3.300.000	1.000.000
Lead-Ore	135.000	15.000	38.000
Tin-Ore	105.000	55.000	7.000
Salt	35.000	100.000	100.000
Coal	465.000	300.000	
Iron-Pyrites	15.000	25.000	
Manganese	475.000		small quantities
Barytes	37.000	small quantities	
Copper-Ore	4.800		small quantities
Cobalt	12.000		
Antimony	575		

M.N.A. see ALGERIAN NATIONAL MOVEMENT

MORISCOS, 'Little Moors', a Spanish word (a diminutive of *Moro*, derived from the Latin *Maurus)* which after the capture of Granada (1492), the last Arab state on the Iberian peninsula, replaced the hitherto current term Mudejars* as the designation of the Moslems in Spain. The conditions of the surrender stipulated full freedom for the Moslem minority as to the practice of their religion, comprising the preservation of the mosques and the public call to prayer from the top of the minaret; the jurisdiction of the cadi in conformity with Islamic law; and the free disposal of their pious foundations *(waqf, habūs)*. Yet the initially loyal observation of these terms soon gave way to all sorts of vexations, at first in the former state of Granada, then also in the other Spanish provinces where until then the Mudejars had enjoyed far-going tolerance. Hardly a decade had elapsed when the high Catholic clergy, ever more forcefully insisted upon the eradication of heresy until pressure was brought to bear upon the Moriscos in order to obtain their conversion. This policy led, it is true, to mass-baptism, but most of the converts secretly continued to adhere to Islam, or after some time, more or less openly reverted to it, in either case drawing upon themselves the duress of the Inquisition. Arabic books were confiscated and either incorporated into Spanish libraries or else, if of a theological character, turned over to the mob to make bonfires of. The first Morisco reaction was a seditious outbreak in the city of Granada (1499), which the archbishop and the Grand-Cadi by their joint intervention were still able to calm down, but an upheaval, a year later, in the neighbouring areas was mastered only with considerably greater difficulties. The measures taken in the wake of the repression included the transfer of the pious foundations to the mortmain of the Church; the order to dress in Christian fashion; and finally the destruction of mosques. For the first time, too, was issued a royal decree enjoining upon the Moslems either to recant or to leave the country (1501). Subsequently several times renewed, it resulted every time in the same pseudo-conversions, but without turning the Moriscos into Spaniards. They trafficked with England and plotted with Turkey, both Spain's tenacious antagonists; they preached the Holy War in

Morocco, then Spain's ally; and inevitably in Spanish eyes seemed what today would be called a 'fifth column'. After long preparation, they rose again (1569) and the revolt spread from Granada all over the surrounding mountain regions. Yet the help hoped for from the Sultan of Morocco, the Saʿdian* Mūlāy ʿAbd Allāh al-Ghālib (1557-1574), did not eventuate. The Turks undertook two unsuccessful landings on the Andalusian coast, but after their defeat at Lepanto (1571) by the Spanish and Venetian fleets, gave up further interference. Left to themselves, the Morisco rebels were subdued, expelled from the area of Granada, and resettled in small groups among the Christian population in various provinces. Still, resembling in this respect the Spanish Jews, they remained a foreign body in the State whose historic mission the ruling classes, clerical and lay, as well as the people at large, conceived as the preservation and propagation of the unadulterated Catholic faith and the extermination of all heretic beliefs. Thus, when Spain suffered a succession of military reverses, and in particular the loss of its proud Armada in the great sea-battle in the Channel against England (1588), the nation saw in these calamities God's punishment for the sinful toleration in its midst of the mass of His enemies. Exposed to unrestrained popular hostility, Moslem emigration from Spain into the countries of the Maghrib, which for many years had been going on in waves following the gradual expansion of the Christian states in the Iberian Peninsula, strongly increased. Between 1609 and 1614, by several successive royal orders, all still remaining Moslems, estimated at about 300.000, were expelled and joined in the Maghrib countries those who had already preceded them there.

Victims of an enemy of the Ottoman Empire, they were helpfully received in Algeria and Tunisia, both under Turkish obedience. They established themselves on or near the coast, either setting up a new quarter in one of the towns or founding a new urban settlement. In either case they preserved a community organization under authorities from their midst, and firmly clung to their inherited mode of life, their institutions and idiomatic parlance. It took four or five generations for their amalgamation with the surrounding native population. In Morocco the situation was different. The greater part of the Mediterranean coastal regions were in Spanish hands or under Spanish control, except for a few smaller places populated by Andalusian Moslems who had left prior to the general expulsion. There their main streams converged and brought strong Morisco concentrations into existence, which before long became not only the seats of an organized, highly remunerative piracy but also, similar to the Hornachero* city-republic of Rabat-Salé, factors of considerable significance in the country's political pattern, negotiating on equal terms with European Powers, and maintaining themselves well towards the end of the XVIIth century.

MOROCCO, *al-Mamlakat al-Maghribīya* (The Kingdom of Morocco), in occidental texts often designated as the Sharīfian Empire in reference to the reigning dynasty's standing as *Sharīfs** (descendants of the Prophet Muhammad), covers approximately 170.000 square miles in the western corner of North Africa and in 1960 had a population of

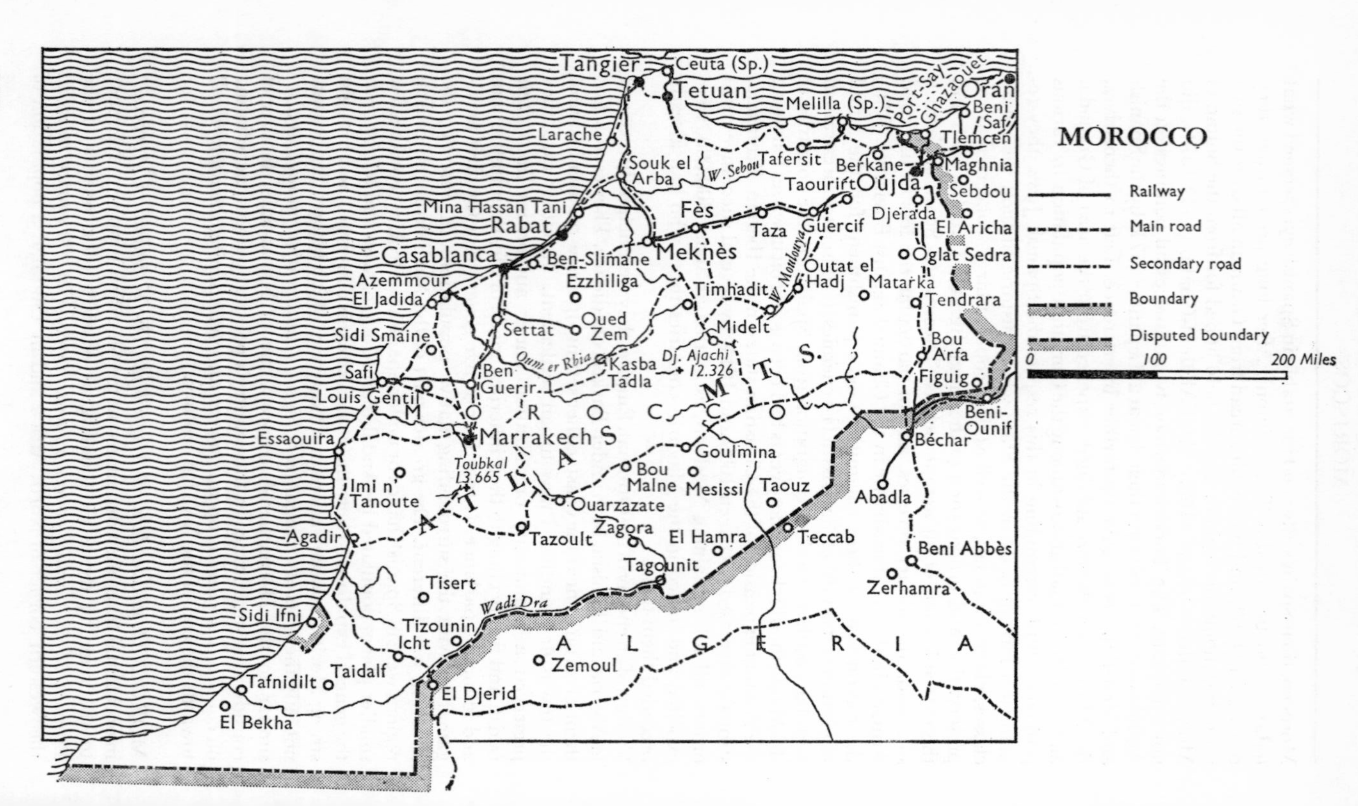
MOROCCO
Railway
Main road
Secondary road
Boundary
Disputed boundary
0
100
200 Miles
Tangier
Ceuta (Sp.)
Tetuan
Melilla (Sp.)
Port-Say
Ghazaouet
Oran
Beni Saf
Tlemcen
Maghnia
Sebdou
El Aricha
Oglat Sedra
Larache
Souk el Arba
W. Sebou
Tafersit
Berkane
Taourirt
Oujda
Djerada
Mina Hassan Tani
Rabat
Fès
Taza
Guercif
Casablanca
Ben-Slimane
Meknès
W. Moulouya
Outat el Hadj
Matarka
Tendrara
Azemmour
El Jadida
Ezzhiliga
Timhadit
Midelt
Settat
Oued Zem
Sidi Smaine
Oum er Rbia
Kasba Tadla
Dj. Ajachi 12.326
Bou Arfa
Figuig
Beni-Ounif
Safi
Ben Guerir
Louis Gentil
MOROCCO
ATLAS MTS.
Marrakech
Essaouira
Toubkal 13.665
Goulmina
Bou Malne
Mesissi
Taouz
Béchar
Abadla
Imi n' Tanoute
Ouarzazate
Agadir
Tazoult
Zagora
El Hamra
Teccab
Beni Abbès
Zerhamra
Tagounit
Tisert
Wadi Dra
Sidi Ifni
Tizounin
Icht
ALGERIA
Zemoul
Taidalf
Tafnidilt
El Djerid
El Bekha

approximately 11.600.000. From the promontory of Tangier, only 9 miles distant from Tarifa on the Iberian peninsula across the Straits of Gibraltar, its coast extends over 600 miles along the Atlantic shore, leaving out, however, the Spanish enclave of Ifni*; then stretches about half this length along the Mediterranean, with the exclusion, on that side, of the Spanish Presidios–the towns of Ceuta and Melilla and some small islands. The frontiers towards Algeria are determined with precision not more than 80 miles from the sea southwards at the small town of Port Say as far as the pass of Teniet Sassi by a line fixed in the peace treaty with France–the so-called convention of Lalla Maghnia–after the Moroccan defeat on the Isly river (1845). For the following 110 miles the line is replaced by a vague zone which runs from north to south through the desolate, almost waterless High Plateaux, called the Dahra on the Moroccan side. Then, determined by a Franco-Moroccan agreement of 1901, it encloses in a sort of loop the oasis of Figwig with its 200.000 date trees. Afterwards it turns sharply first west, then south and becoming again less definite in the so-called 'Confins Algéro-Marocains', continues for some 130 miles a little beyond the Tāfīlālt and the oases irrigated by the arms of the river Zīz and its affluents, the ancestral home of the ʿAlawids*. There amid the forests of half a million date palms, lie the ruins of *Madīnat al-Hamrā'* (The Red City), once the rich and powerful town of Sijilmāsa whose palaces and pleasure gardens inspired in the XIth and XIIth centuries the enthusiastic descriptions of the geographers al-Bakrī* and al-Idrīsī*. Thereabouts the border zone of the 'Confins' takes a turn to the south-west but soon vanishes for a stretch of 450 to 500 miles in the pre-Saharan desert where it has never been clearly defined. It reappears on the lower course of the river Darʿa, or rather its wide, sandy bed along a ten-mile wide valley, which carries water only after a rare heavy rainfall. Some 150 miles upstream from its estuary, the meridian 9°40′ west separates Morocco from the Algerian desert as far as the intersection with latitude 27°40′. This parallel delimits the Saqīyat al-Hamrā', the northern section of Spanish West Africa, from the Moroccan province of Tarfaya, the former southern zone of the Spanish Protectorate, which was retroceded in April 1958.

It is hardly surprising that public opinion should resent the continuation of the control by Spain over portions of the national territory after victory had crowned the struggle for the abolition of the Protectorate*, and that the political parties were unanimous in claiming the 'liberation' of the enclave of Ifni and of the 'Presidios'. Yet, while official policy after a miscarried insurrection in Ifni took care not to press the issue too far, the matter is certainly not forgotten and will presumably be brought up again sooner or later in some form or another. In the meantime the peculiar situation of the land frontiers has left open a field for questions which involve interests of considerably greater import. As early as April 1956 'Allāl al-Fāsī, the highly respected leader of the Istiqlāl* party, started campaigning for a Greater Morocco. In a widely publicized map he included in this 'national, historic, geographic and social entity' the whole Saharan region divided among the Spanish colony of Rio de Oro, Mauretania, the French Sudan and the western section of the Algerian Sahara. His weekly *Sahra al-Maghrib* (the Moroccan Sahara) forcefully voiced the arguments for their reunion with Morocco, while new party cells carried the propaganda among their population. For a while this action went on merely under the cloak of the party but soon was given official sanction. In November 1957 a special section of the Ministry of the Interior – subsequently detached and at present a separate Ministry – was put in charge of the affairs of the Sahara. Shortly afterwards, in February 1958, the late King Muhammad V* proclaimed at Mahāmīd south of Zagora on the fringe of the Sahara, in a much noted address to a tribal assembly called together from far-away desert regions, that efforts would not cease for the return to Morocco of the Sahara in accordance with the historic rights and the will of its people. This he solemnly repeated a few months later at a Congress of the Moroccan Sahara. His son and successor, King Hassan II, continued to sustain these, in his own words, inalienable rights, also after the accession to independence of the new Islamic Republic of Mauretania in November 1960. So does everybody of prominence in political life over the radio, in public declarations and in interviews in the western press. To whatever extent the Greater-Morocco question may belong to domains of an emotional order, the recent discovery of the rich iron- and copper-ore deposits in Mauretania, and above all of the enormous oil and natural gas reserves in the Algerian Sahara supply motives dictated by financial realism, particularly in view of the requirements of the country's economic and social development. Seen in this light, the frontier problem loses most of its purely territorial aspects and appears rather as a matter of agreements among the interested countries as to the exploitation and distribution of the mineral wealth there.

Contrary to what a first glance at the map might suggest, the limitless outlook over two seas has seldom in their long history awakened maritime inclinations in the Moroccan people. The merchants left the quite considerable over-sea trade in European hands, or had it carried by ships under the flag of Spain, Portugal, France and the Italian city republics. Very few sultans found it necessary to increase the fighting force of the army by an adequate navy. Recently, however, this indifference has given place to economic considerations mainly from the point of view of saving expenditures in foreign currencies, and if the plans for economic development materialize, the present rather insignificant mercantile fleet–in 1960 a total of 35.000 register tons besides the 16.000 register tons of 2.700 fishing boats–may enter on a period of reasonable growth. The formation of the coasts is indeed not of the kind to encourage seafaring ambitions, if the freebooting enterprises are excepted which between the XIth and XVIth centuries flourished all along the North African shores, in competition with the not much less active European pirates. On the Mediterranean side, the Rif mountains fall off steeply and wherever they are cut into and flattened to a beach, inland communication is extremely difficult. East of Melilla the lower course of the river Mulūya opens up a large gap, but this leads into inhospitable steppe land. Neither can the Atlantic coast be expected to generate mariner spirit. Throughout its extent it consists of a low barren platform changing now and then into stretches of gravel with swamps behind and rows of sandbanks before and occasionally receding into a broad roadstead or bay offers no protection against the violent gales and heavy billows. The great rivers streaming down from the Middle and High Atlas across the plains have, it is true, worked out wide estuaries which penetrate far into the coast: the Sabū river at Kunaitra (Port Lyautey); the Umm al-Rabīʿ at Azemmour; the Tansift between Safi and Assawīra (Mogador); the Sūs at Agadir; and the Darʿa, in the South. Yet they are either quite shallow and silted up if not most of the time almost waterless; or else impracticable because of the whirlpools thrown up by the oceanic counter-currents which gush in. In the last three or four decades modern engineering has provided what nature failed to supply, by creating the great port at Casablanca–over 4.000 miles of quays and approximately nine-and-a-half million tons of goods handled in 1961–as well as several minor ports at Kunaitra (appr. 700.000 tons handled), Safi (appr. 2½ million tons handled) or Agadir and others of local significance. A further incentive to sea traffic is hoped for from the development project of the port of Tangier announced in January 1962, which includes the installation of extensive dockyards, of several industrial plants and of a sector with free trade facilities.

It is thus understandable that the nearness to the sea should have exercised comparatively little influence on the social and economic structure or on the customs and attitudes of the people. These were primarily shaped by the interplay between continental factors: rough mountain masses accessible only through narrow, deeply cut-in river valleys or over steep, difficult passes; large arable plains and hilly pasture-grounds; stony table-lands, steppes and the pre-Saharan desert. Like an enormous belt the Atlas spans the country to the south-west and north-east and connects with the Rif which seams the Mediterranean, as it were, in the form of an arc resting its two ends at Melilla and at Tangier. Between the Atlas and the sea there expands the system of the Atlantic plains: the Gharb, Shawīya, Dukkāla, Abda and Chiadma–rich soils, blessed with abundant rainfalls and the water collected by innumerable streamlets in the mountains. These coastal plains are Morocco's granary: their crops of cereals, vegetable, fruit, grape, olives and tobacco; and their herds of cattle, sheep, goats, donkeys, horses and camels constitute the preponderant part of the country's agricultural produce. The vast expansions of pasture grounds and, where irrigated, of corn-land and orchards, prolong this system inland: one, the Tādlā, in between the north-western ends of the Middle Atlas and the area of the phosphate deposits of Khuribga; the other, its continuation to the south, the Hawūz and the Dīr with their nearly three million olive trees reaching as far as the spurs of the High Atlas. Further south, between Assawīra and Agadir, and bordered by the slopes of the High Atlas, lies first the hilly Hāhā country; and then, filling the angle formed by the High and Anti Atlas, the wide basin of the Sūs. Once it nourished a well-to-do peasantry, but later for centuries remained in decay until its redevelopment was started some twenty years ago. From the southern extension of the Sūs, the so-called Moroccan Sahil, a loose, sinuous string of oases leads eastward, inserted like green beads in the edgy greyness of the rocks between the bed of the lower Darʿa and the ridge of the Bānī mountains. Continuing further upstream it broadens beyond the area of Warzazat into a ribbon on both banks of the rivers Dadès, Todgha, Farkla and Gharis, closely encased by the bare, vertical limestone cliffs, and studded with clusters of peasant houses and, on the dominating points, with the reddish-brown kasbas *(qasaba*)*, the imposing–though not very solid–one-time strongholds of local lords. Finally the line of oases joins the Tāfīlālt and the valleys of the upper Zīz and its network of affluents.

A variety of age-old methods of artificial irrigation corrects or supplements the natural water supply over an area of about half a million acres. Some, such as the simple cisterns collecting the rainwater, are extremely primitive; or the precarious barrages *(sedd)* made of sticks and faggots and re-made at every seasonal swelling of the river, which tap its water and distribute it in accordance with time-honoured, inalterable rules over the fields of the neighbouring owners. Others are more complicated, such as the earth-built channels *(seguias)* which catch the river water, meander over the slopes of the valley and feed the numerous ditches on three or four terraced rows of fields somewhat down-stream. Still others bear witness to considerable ingenuity, such as the skilful combination of wells sunk sometimes as deep as 100 or 150 feet, with subterranean ducts *(ghettara, khottara* or *foggara)* leading the subsoil water for several miles to points lower than the bottom of the well. In the Hawūs there are nearly a thousand of these combinations in existence, and around Marrakesh some 450, said to date back to the time of the foundation of the city (1062) by the Almoravid* ruler Yūsuf Ibn Tāshufīn*, water the only palm groves prospering north of the Atlas. During 1961/1962 in the course of a government action to provide work for the unemployed, the so-called 'Promotion Nationale', some 1000 miles of *seguias* and *khottaras* were newly dug or repaired.

From the time of the French Protectorate* dates a modern network of primary and secondary irrigation canals fed by some of the great rivers. Parts of it are combined with large electric power plants, the most important of which is an artificial lake of nine-and-a-half million gallons, in the great barrage at Bīnal Widān (Ouidane) in the Middle Atlas. A 'National Irrigation Office', created in 1961 and invested with the right of expropriation and the re-allocation of holdings, is in charge of all studies concerning the country's water resources as well as of the technical management. For the time being not more than one-third of the 450.000 acres for which this system was conceived, benefits by it. The reason lies partly in the difficulty of getting the peasants to change from the traditional dry-farming to irrigated farming methods, which, however, it is hoped, appropriate guidance will gradually overcome. More serious is the fragmentation of the land into numerous small plots held by different owners, which often prevents the tracing of the necessary lateral channels. Their consolidation into economically exploitable, compact farm units involves a long and complicated process which in turn depends upon the progress in drawing-up a land register, decided upon in 1962. The irrigated or irrigable area amounts to but a minor portion of the more or less regularly cultivated 19 million acres, of which two-thirds to one-half are sown every year while the rest lies fallow. Improvements might render partially cultivable another 19 millions.

As throughout the Arab West, agriculture* and stockbreeding are main pillars in the country's economic and social edifice. They contribute over one-third - cereals, oranges, tomatoes, fresh and canned vegetables, eggs, olive oil, wine, wool, hides and leather - to the total value of its exports, principally derived, however, from the large properties of the foreign landowners. They have moulded the life of three-quarters of its people and occupy about two-thirds of its economically active male population, small peasants and landless farm-hands, but at best only during 150 days in the year, leaving them idle the rest of the time and yielding to their families only a quarter of the income per head earned by the workers in mining* and industry*. The full significance of this situation and the problems involved appear if viewed against their demographic background. In 1936, the returns of the census showed a native population of 6.3 million; in 1952, of 8.6. million; and in 1960, of 11.6 million. Estimates established on the basis of these figures, and considering the improvement of the sanitary conditions and hence the probable decline of the mortality rate, forecast a rise to 15 million by 1970 and to 19 million by 1977 if the present birth rate is maintained. Differently expressed this means the need to provide every year additional food, shelter and clothing for some 300.000 people; it means the continuous expansion of medical care, welfare facilities and public services; and, assuming an average family size of five members, it means creating 80.000 new earning opportunities every year not without forgetting the present under employment.

Still other shadows are brought into this picture by the current of migration to the towns, stimulated by the hope of escaping the poverty of the villages. During the last three decades some of these towns have seen the number of their inhabitants multiplied three-and fourfold by the steadily continuing population shifts from the border areas of the steppes, from the Rif and the Atlas mountains and to some extent also from the plains on the Atlantic coasts.

Number of inhabitants

	1936	1952	1960
Casablanca	257.000	682.000	965.000
Rabat	83.000	156.000	227.000
Kunaitra	18.000	56.000	87.000
Oujda (mining town)	35.000	81.000	128.000
Khuribga (mining town)	8.000	20.000	41.000

All in, all the native population of the towns, that is, a locality covering an area of over 10.000 inhabitants, grew between 1937 and 1952 from about 890.000 to 1,540.000 and until 1960 to 3,330.000. If forecasts prove right it will have grown by 1970 to 4.7 million and by 1977 to 6 million. A great many of the poorest people crowded together in the old quarters, and when these were filled up there arose on the empty space in the outskirts the vast tin-shak cities ('bidonvilles') around Casablanca (200.000 slum dwellers), Rabat (35.000), Kunaitra (40.000), Meknès (35.000), Fez (20.000), Marrakesh (30.000) and quite a few more, populated altogether by roughly half a million, though some 45.000

'economic' lodgings for 225.000 persons were built between 1944 and 1961. The expenditure on slum-clearance and low-cost housing in 1961 represented seven per cent of the public investments but only the synchronisation of the rural and urban improvement projects which have been elaborated, combined with the rationalization of agricultural production and the systematic industrialisation, can be expected to balance the demographic pressure.
Throughout most of Morocco's known history and probably long before, waves of tribes have swept from the mountains and the desert into the fertile plains. At times they were pushed back and after a while broke forth again; at times they stayed on, permeating the peasantry but preserving, often down to this day, their local speech and much of their particular customs. For the last three or four generations the population, with rare exceptions, has been settled. It lives in some 30.000 villages, some of them high up and isolated in the mountains; in numerous, small half-rural towns; and in some twenty larger cities, six considerably exceeding the hundred thousand mark and one coming near to one million. Among them there are the historic four 'imperial cities', the one-time residencies of the Moroccan dynasties: Fez (215.000), Marrakesh (145.000), Meknès (177.000) and the present capital Rabat (227.000). Still enclosed in their imposing medieval circumvallation, they present a maze of narrow streets and blind alleys faced by the blank fronts to time-worn houses, while at a distance of up to a mile or two the French town-planners set up the new quarters with the public buildings, modern shops and hotels.
Fez dates back to a camp laid out in 789 by Idrīs I*, and was built up and fortified by his son Idrīs II*, the city's patron saint, whose tomb in the heart of the *sūqs* is one of Morocco's most venerated shrines. Situated at the intersection of the ancient caravan roads from the Atlantic into northern Algeria and from the Sahara to the Mediterranean, Fez was for many centuries one of the richest and most splendid commercial, industrial and political centres in North Africa and the seat of a flourishing literary, philosophic and spiritual life which had its focus in the theological academy of the Qarawīyīn* Mosque. Marrakesh, in the midst of a wide belt of palm-and orange-groves, was founded in 1062 by the first Almoravid ruler Yūsuf Ibn Tāshufīn, enlarged by his successor ʿAli Ibn Yūsuf*, and adorned by the great Almohad* conqueror ʿAbd al-Mu'min* with the Kutubīya mosque, one of the masterpieces of the Andalusian architects and craftsmen whom he entrusted with the embellishment of his capital. More than 500 years passed before it was again elevated to the rank of a royal residence by the Saʿdian* sultan Ahmad al-Mansūr*, who wanted it to remain for all future with the dynasty and created there a sumptuous necropolis for his family. Meknès, perpetuating the name of the great Miknāsa* confederation, was long before the presence of the Arabs in Morocco one of the many primitive tribal settlements but, unlike others, survived and grew slowly and steadily until around the beginning of the XVIIIth century it reached its golden age during the fifty-year reign of the ʿAlawid sultan Mūlāy Ismāʿīl*. Rabat, a defensive outpost *(ribāt*)* of warrior-monks, judging from the so-called Hassan tower, the columns

in the ruins of the Hassan mosque and what still stands in the Kasba of the Ūdāya, might have become the most imposing monument of Almohad glory, had not death put an end to the ambitions of the builder, the third Almohad Abū Yūsuf Yaʿqūb al-Mansūr*. In the early XIIth century a group of emigrants from al-Andalus, the warlike Hornacheros*, made of Rabat together with Salé on the other bank of the Bū Ragrāg river a sort of independent pirate republic. Much later the ʿAlawid sultans remodelled the fortifications, erected their palace with the chancellery and the barracks for their negro guard. Still later, at the beginning of the forty-year era of the Protectorate it was chosen as the seat of the French Governor-General, and since then has remained the country's capital. Large-scale expansion added on the hills a district for the services of the French administration, now occupied by the Moroccan ministries; a modern down-town business section; and a garden-city with sportsgrounds. A special place in the urban pattern of the country is held by Casablanca. Its origin goes back to an age-old fishing village on the hill of Anfa, today the wealthy garden-suburb where in the second World War Roosevelt, Churchill and de Gaulle discussed the plan of the landing in Italy, and Sultan Muhammad V in a confidential meeting with President Roosevelt the prospect of Morocco's independence. In the late Middle-Ages it was one of the half-independent repairs of the North African corsairs, until between the end of the XVIth and the middle of the XVIIIth century it was in turn destroyed and occupied, evacuated and retaken and finally abandoned by the Portuguese when they were no longer able to defend it against the tribes of the surrounding area. The ʿAlawid Sultan Muhammad Ibn ʿAbd Allāh* (1757-1790) enlarged it and named it *Dār al-Baidā*, made known in the Occident by Spanish traders as Casablanca. From 1862 onwards French steamers maintained a regular connection with Marseille, and in 1906, when the town had grown to some 20.000 inhabitants, a French concern was granted the concession of constructing and operating a port accessible to small craft. Since then it has developed into one of the largest ports in Africa and handles some 10 million tons yearly, while blocks of eighteen-story buildings have sprung up in the commercial sections of the city which today is Morocco's economic capital.

Whether the reigning dynasties had their origin in a Berber tribe or traced their descent back to Muhammad, the men of letters, scholars of theology, craftsmen and merchants from al-Andalus found always the ways to the 'imperial cities' wide open. They made them in the midst of the Berber country focal points of Arabo-Islamic culture whence the currents of religious, intellectual and economic life flowed across the barriers of the language dychotomy and the contrasts of customs and traditions. Today, the schools of different types and grades provide training for the majority of the civil servants, political leaders and members of the liberal professions. At no time, however, has there been any thought of imposing by constraint or any kind of inducement the acceptance of Arabic upon the Berber population. Its arabization has been a natural, slow and far from country-wide process which has still left a Berber speaking minority of some 40 to 45 per cent.

Until very recently the central government exercised actual power only in certain sections of the country, the so-called *bilād al-makhzan** (the land under government control), while dealing as well as possible with the others, the *bilād al-sība* (the land of dissidence). There the sovereign tried to assert his authority by an occasional, half-warlike expedition *(harka*)* for the collection of taxes in arrear or the suppression of a revolt, more often, however, by negotiations with the powerful chieftains and influential religious fraternities. Yet notwithstanding the multifarious and contradictory tribal, regional or spiritual loyalties, making, as it were, every town, valley and plain an island by itself, there emerged comparatively early a certain feeling of somehow belonging together. It was of course far from the notion in its modern sense of a national unit, national territory and national will. Much of it was rooted in the concept of the brotherhood of Islam, much also in the need for self-defence, but behind the chronic anarchy and the unstability of the dynasties which colour Moroccan history, trends towards national unification became discernable at an early date.

683 First Arab conquering expedition under ʿUqba Ibn Nāfiʿ who seems to have penetrated westwards as far as Ceuta and then southwards through the plains on the Atlantic coast into the Sūs.

703-711 Second expedition under Mūsā Ibn Nusayr who follows apparently the same itinerary, but continues in the Dar ʿa valley and the Tāfīlālt without encountering serious resistance. Morocco is incorporated into the Umayyad caliphate, as part of the territory of the governor of Ifrīqīya, who resides in al-Qayrawān. Infiltration of Islam, mainly in the version of the heterodox Khārijite doctrine.

738-742 Berber revolts led by Maisara al-Matgharī under the flag of Khārijism and the defeat of the caliph's army in the 'Battle of the Nobles'. Foundation of the heretic Barghawāta confederation.

788-974 Idrīsid Dynasty
First attempt at setting up a body politic. Idrīs I lays out the fortified camp of Madīnat Fās, which is chosen by Idrīs II as his seat of residence and begins to assume the physiognomy of present-day Fez. Foundation of the Mosque of Fātima (875), the later Qarawīyīn Mosque. Sunnism gains preponderance and Arabic starts to radiate from the Idrīsid court.

Contest for hegemony between Spanish Umayyads and Fātimids. The conflicts of the two Powers are fought out by their Berber allies from among the Zanāta, Maghrāwa, Miknāsa and Banū Īfran families of tribes. Repeatedly changing sides in a fluctuating framework of confederations, they cover Morocco with a pattern of loosely-knit tribal kingdoms continuously involved in mutual feuds. Fātimid vassals of a Sanhāja group in present-day Algeria, the Zīrid emirs of Ashīr reach the coasts of the Atlantic (about 980).

1061-1147 Almoravid Dynasty
Unification of Morocco by Yūsuf Ibn Tāshufīn (1061-1107). Foundation of Marrakesh, the new capital (1062); conquest of northern Morocco and the adjoining Algerian territory (1062-1082); four expeditions into al-Andalus, (1086-1102); defeat of Alphonso VI, King

of Castile, in the battle of al-Zallāqa (1086); deposition of the Party-Kings of Granada, Malaga, Cordova, Ronda, Carmona, the ʿAbbādid emirs of Seville (1091) and the conquest of Valencia (1102), the stronghold of the 'Cid'. Yūsuf Ibn Tāshufīn and his son ʿAli* (1107-1143)rule over the whole of Morocco, western Algeria and the major part of al-Andalus. With ʿAli's death the decline of the Almoravid empire sets in.

1133-1269 Almohad Dynasty.

Ibn Tūmart formulates his doctrine, gains the adherence of most of the Masmūda tribes in the High Atlas and at Tinmāl elaborates the religious, political and military organization upon which the Almohad state was to rest. His disciple and successor, ʿAbd al-Mu'min (1133-1163), builds up an empire comprising Morocco, Algeria, Tunisia, almost the whole of Tripolitania and the western portion of al-Andalus, with Marrakesh as the capital. His reign introduces an era of efflorescense in the fields of science, philosophy and the arts under the impulse of close contacts with Andalusian civilization, accompanied by the spread of Arabic in the towns as the language of learning, and in the rural areas as a consequence of the increasing infiltration of Arab tribes. The victory of Yaʿqūb al-Mansūr (1184-1199) over King Alphonso VIII of Castile in the battle of Alarcos (1195) stems for some time the counter-offensive of the Christian Kings in Spain, notwithstanding Muhammad al-Nāsir's (1199-1213) defeat at Las Navas de Tolosa (1212). In the period of the waning Almohad power, which sets in with his death, the Andalusian possessions are gradually lost, while in Tunisia the Hafs ids, and in Tlemcen the ʿAbd al-Wādids arise as independent dynasties. The clan of the Marīnids, at the head of strong Zanāta groups, pushes from the southern regions into central and northern Morocco and conquers Marrakesh (1269). The Almohad line comes to an end with the death in battle of Abū Dabbūs.

1244-1465. Marīnid Dynasty

Abū Yūsuf Yaʿqūb (1258-1286) makes Fez his new capital, which, much enlarged and embellished, develops into a wealthy trading center and widely reputed seat of theological studies. The Marīnid sultans consolidate their throne by manoeuvering between the growing religious brotherhood and marabout movement on the one hand, and the influence of the orthodox theologians on the other. Attempts at regaining the possessions in al-Andalus are abandoned subsequently to defeat in battle at the Rio Salado (1340) for a policy of expansion in North Africa. Started by Abū Yaʿqūb Yūsuf (1286-1307) the eastward advance results under Abū al-Hasan ʿAlī (1331-1351) and Abū ʿInān Fāris (1351-1358) in the occupation of the ʿAbd al-Wādid domain of Tlemcen and the greater part of Hafsid Tunisia. Soon afterwards, the Marīnid reign declines under a succession of child sovereigns which favours the rule of all-powerful viziers, most of them of the Wattāsid family, yet unable to check the rivalries among court dignitaries and the feuds of tribal warlords. The weakness of the central government invites intervention in internal affairs by the Nasrid sultans of Granada; the implantation of the Spaniards and Portuguese along the coasts; and the rise all over the country of virtually independent principalities. The last Marīnid ʿAbd al-Haqq is assassinated in a revolt in Fez. Undisturbed by the political anarchy, urban scholarly and artistic life, fructified as before by Andalusian cultural currents, continues to flourish.

1472-1554 Wattāsid Dynasty

After a several-year struggle Muhammad al-Shaykh (1472-1505) conquers Fez from an Idrīsid scion proclaimed Imam by the population of the city, but neither he nor his successors are able to reforge the unity of the state. Even within the narrow limits of the territory where they are recognized as sultans they have to defend their authority against unsubmissive tribes and the secular aspirations of the marabouts or the heads of brotherhoods. Notwithstanding their desperate efforts to enlist help in Portugal, Spain and Germany, the third generation loses the throne to the Sharīfian family of the Saʿdians, who rally a rapidly growing number of followers from their seats in the Dar ʿa valley and irresistibly press northwards.

1554-1659 Saʿdian Dynasty

The Saʿdian Muhammad al-Shaykh al-Mahdī repels the Portuguese and is proclaimed sultan in Marrakesh, thenceforth the splendid Saʿdian capital. He conquers Fez (1554); concludes an alliance with Spain to counter the aggressive policy of the Turkish beylerbeg of Algeria; takes an energetic stand against the religious brotherhoods and marabouts; and strengthens the military and fiscal organisation. Mūlāy Ahmad al-Mansūr (1578-1603) beats the Portuguese in the battle of 'The Three Kings', and undertakes several successful expeditions into the Sudan. Under his reign Morocco enjoys considerable prosperity and great international prestige. Upon his death family feuds lead to the split into one Saʿdian Branch at Marrakesh (until 1659) and one at Fez (until 1626), neither being strong enough to cope with the 'marabout emirates' such as those of al-ʿAyyashī or al-Samlālī; with the Hornacheros city republic of Rabat-Salé and the powerful Dilā'yūn brotherhood, which for a time dominated nearly all northern Morocco.

1666- ʿAlawid Dynasty

Out of the anarchy emerges in the Tāfīlālt the dynasty reigning today, the Sharīfian house of the ʿAlawids, with Mūlāy al-Rashīd proclaimed Sultan in Fez (1666). His brother, Mūlāy Ismāʿīl (1672-1727) builds up a strong military system and makes his residence at Meknès the most formidable fortress in North Africa. Torn by thirty years of inner turmoil, the state comes near disintegration until his grandson Sīdī Muhammad Ibn ʿAbd Allāh (1757-1790) re-establishes order, restores the public finances and economic activities, and by the foundation of Mogador promotes a lively over-sea trade. Prosperity continues under Mūlāy Sulaymān (1792-1822) but his leaning toward Wahhābite puritanism causes serious insurrections among the tribes and the army. They are appeased by Mūlāy ʿAbd al-Rahmān (1822-1859), but his siding with Abdelkader against the French advance in Algeria results in the defeat on the Isly river (1844), while his treaty with England (1856) secures England's guarantee of the inviolability of Moroccan territory. Sīdī Muhammad (1859-1873) is forced, after a lost war, to grant a fishing concession at Ifni to Spain, on the ground of which this area is placed, and has remained until today, under Spanish sovereignty. By bringing about (1880) the Madrid Conference, Mūlāy al-Hasan (1873-1894) neutralizes for some time French commercial and financial infiltration. In the face of dangerous insurrections and diminishing public revenues, and increasingly dependent on French military and financial help Mūlāy ʿAbd al-ʿAzīz (1894-1908) cannot avoid the ever more frequent intervention of French troops. The Act of the Algeciras Conference (1906) confirms the country's territorial integrity and the sultan's sovereignty, yet paves the way to the establishment (1912) of the French and Spanish Protectorates under ʿAbd al-Hāfiz (1909-1912), and under Mūlāy Yūsuf (1913-1927) to the international agreement upon the Statute of Tangier (1924).

It took France and Spain twenty years of sustained efforts to master the tenacious guerilla warfare carried on against foreign rule by the tribes in the North under Abdelkrim* and in the South under Ahmad al-Hibā, the son of the widely reputed religious leader Mā' al-ʿAinain*. As pacification proceeded, French and Spanish administrative, judicial and financial systems were superimposed upon the traditional order, leaving Moroccans no room for any meaningful rôle. Roads were constructed, primarily with regard to military requirements, and in the French zone, new economic activities controlled by French capital developed in the fields of mining, industry and banking. In the major towns schools were established by the French and Spanish authorities with French and Spanish as the languages of instruction. When this penetration of foreign interests began to be felt, it evoked increasing discontent which found expression, no longer, however, in tribal revolts, but among urban intellectual youth and springing from a new, though yet vague and inarticulate nationalist spirit. In the country-wide excitement aroused by the so-called Berber Edict* (1930) which stressed and, as it were, institutionalized the social, cultural and language differences between the Berber and Arab communities crystallized the first Moroccan political parties: in the French zone the Bloc of Moroccan Action* (1934), and in the Spanish zone the Party of National Reform* (1936) and the Movement of Moroccan Unity (1937). This awakening nationalism accepted the principle of the Protectorate, but in the sense of a technical guidance towards development and progress without 'colonialist' implications. Its demands centered around the reunion of the national territory; the participation at an equal standing of Moroccans in the management of public affairs; a modern, national school system; and social and economic reforms which would raise the level of living of the masses. It was still confined within narrow circles of an educated élite and affected by ideological divergencies with internal dissensions in their wake; but it gained in strength, albeit along different lines in each of the zones. When the French authorities found it too clamorous they declared it illegal, imprisoned some of its leaders and exiled its two most prominent figures, ʿAllāl al-Fāsī and Muhammad al-Wazzānī (1937). In the first years of the World War, its voices remained subdued, but were no longer to be silenced. Soon they were raised again and then did not call for reforms, but for the abrogation of the Protectorate.

From that time on the struggle for independence and the efforts, after it was won, at constructing the new state, together with the dramatic events in the reign of Sīdī Muhammad Ibn Yūsuf are inseparably interwoven chapters of one single story. The issue of independence was raised on an international level in the Sultan's conversation in June 1943 with President Roosevelt and thenceforth remained the postulate of Moroccan nationalism. In the same year there came forth as its standard-bearer, the *Istiqlāl** party, followed in 1946 by the Democratic Party of Independence*. At first their adherents came only from among the enlightened bourgeois classes and even there often met with cautious hesitation. The peasantry and the tribes, however, either showed indifference or feared to antagonize the sheikhs of the religious brotherhoods and great chieftains, all more or less beneficiaries of favours on the part of the Protectorate authorities. It was Sultan Muhammad's widely re-echoed speech at Tangier in 1947, and regardless of French protests, his hardly disguised patronage of the *Istiqlāl* leaders which conferred efficiency on their proselytizing and organizing activities. Within a short time the nationalist movement spread through a country-spanning network into the villages of the plains, began to reach out into the mountain tribes and had a propaganda apparatus abroad, while the Sultan made himself its spokesman in Paris in his discussions with the French Cabinet and the President of the Republic. Dilatory proposals for reforms were the reply, and when these were rejected, suppression of the nationalist press, mass arrests and the imposition of exile. When popular unrest grew and at last culminated in violent riots, Sīdī Muhammad Ibn Yūsuf, the 'Sultan of the Istiqlāl', was deposed and deported to Madagascar (August 1953).

There followed two years of utter confusion, with Sīdī Muhammad Ibn ʿArafa, the shadow-sultan by the grace of the French Governor-General on the throne; with terrorist organizations and French counter-terrorists all over the country; with an 'Army of Liberation'; with martial law, death sentences and imprisonments incapable of dealing with the uproar. By the end of 1953 Ibn ʿArafa abdicated. Negotiations with Sultan Muhammad were opened in Madagascar, continued in France, and were brought to a conclusion by the 'Declaration of La Celle-St. Cloud' (November 6, 1955) which terminated the régime of the Protectorate. On the 16th of November Sīdī Muhammad Ibn Yūsuf was enthusiastically welcomed in Rabat, and three weeks later he appointed his first government in which the *Istiqlāl* held seven, and the Democratic Party of Independence four, out of fifteen seats. In a series of documents signed in Paris on March 2, 1956 France and Morocco, speaking as equal partners, acknowledged their new relationship of 'interdependence' and determined the changes by which unrestricted authority was restored to the Sultan. On April 7, he and General Franco signed a similar agreement by which Spain recognized Moroccan independence and unity, and on May 26, the Moroccan national anthem was heard for the first time over the Moroccan radio in the place of the Marseillaise. In November 1956 a formal Act drawn up by an eight-nation conference abrogated the Tangier Statute* and thus initiated the administrative and economic assimilation of the International Zone. Also the intricate question of the withdrawal of the French and Spanish troops was at last satisfactorily settled as was finally too the evacuation by 1963 of the American air and naval bases conceded in 1950 by the Protectorate authorities.

Then, however, it was the great and many-sided problem of the 'decolonization' which confronted independent Morocco in nearly every phase of national life. It required a two-fold yet simultaneous approach: to meet, if only temporarily, the pressing needs of the moment; and to prepare systematically and step by step durable solutions for the future. Of the 25.000 or so foreign officials who in 1955 served in various functions, one third had left by the end of 1957. The total in 1955 of 400.000 French inhabitants, among whom many skilled workers and experienced technical or commercial employees, had by the end of 1960 shrunk to 150.000. This meant filling immediately the most urgent vacancies as well as was possible and providing for the training of new Moroccan civil servants, judges, technicians, teachers, doctors and administrators. It meant 'moroccanizing' public administration and justice, and converting the multiple cells of the old tribal order into parts of the governmental machinery. It meant recruiting from among the 21.000 Moroccans in the French and Spanish armies and the 5000 warriors in the Army of Liberation the soldiers for the Royal Moroccan Forces. And it meant broadening, decentralizing and arabizing the educational system from primary to secondary and college levels and creating agricultural, technical and commercial schools.

Cultural and judiciary conventions concluded with France and the advisors supplied within the United Nations Technical Assistance Programme helped to secure specialized instructors. Thus were established a School for Public Administration and a 'Bureau of Popular Education' (B.E.P.). Then was set up a National Institute of Judicial Studies in charge of the unification of the system of law until then different in the three zones. Finally were built up faculties of Law, Science, Literature and–aided by grants from the United States and the United Nations Special Fund–a faculty of Engineering. At the same time the Moroccan Institute of Arabization elaborated modern school books in Arabic. Plans for the raising of agricultural productivity and the promotion of industrial production were elaborated and experimented with, but while indispensable foreign investments and loans were invited, care had to be taken to prevent the financial obligations from being turned into political ties. The nationalization of most of the railway lines and electrical power plants, all controlled by French capital, was prepared and after lengthy negotiations completed in 1963.

Among the different social and economic groups, united in a common front while the battle for independence was still to be fought, it was not long before dissensions as to the policy, methods and rhythm of the work of reforms began to arise and to assume ever sharper forms. In 1959 two new political parties appeared on the stage: the Popular Movement*, vigorously standing up for the peasant interest; and the National Union of Popular Forces*, closely connected with Moroccan trade unionism*, of leftist and increasingly radical orientation. Muhammad V allowed the various currents of opinion ample freedom of expression in the press, in the cabinet of ministers and in the Council he had charged with deliberation on a Constitution which he solemnly promised to promulgate by 1962. Yet he was at all times the absolute monarch taking undisputedly the final decision. This coexistence of autocracy at the top and democracy at the base, rooted in the profound esteem he enjoyed among the whole population, continued throughout his reign. When, however, after his death (February 16, 1962) his son, King Hassan II, began to put openly heavier weight on the authoritarian side of the balance, he was immediately confronted by an opposition that quickly strengthened and gained ground in both the conservative and progressist sections of public opinion. Dispensing with the Constitutional Council, he personally conceived and drew up a Constitution and after intense propaganda over the radio and television had it approved by referendum on December 7, 1962. It instituted a two-chamber parliament, leaving the king free, however, to reassume all powers. In contradistinction to the Algerian constitution and the actual situation in Tunisia, the one-party system is expressly declared inadmissible. In March 1963 was created by one of King Hassan's closest collaborators and personal friends, the government-sponsored 'Front pour la Défence des Institutions Constitutionelles'*. Notwithstanding the fullest official support this party obtained in the elections for the Lower Chamber in May 1963 only 69 of the 144 seats, and the opposition - *Istiqlāl* and National Union of Popular Forces - 70. In July, two weeks before the elections of the 11.000 municipal councillors – the electoral body of two-thirds of the Upper Chamber–the police discovered a conspiracy of high treason, and arrested the leaders of the opposition, which thereupon boycotted the elections and the government candidates won an easy victory.

MOUVEMENT BOURGEOIS DE TUNISIE, or, as it was also called, the Group of the Forty, a loose association set up in Tunis in 1883 by some young, middle-class intellectuals of various religio-cultural shades ranging from enlightened conservatism with pan-Islamic leanings to a more or less advanced liberalism. They advocated the assimilation of western modes of rational and scientific thought, and were united in the deep resentment of their country's occupation by France. The animator of the group was a Tunisian lawyer, ʿAlī Bāsh Hambah, a member of a renowned Turkish family, who after his schooldays in Tunis first at the academy of the Zaytūna Mosque and then at the Collège Sādiqī had made his academic studies in Paris, but soon after his return actively engaged in politcs. Close to him stood Bashīr Sfar (Safar), later professor at the Zaytūna and director of the administration of the pious foundations *(habūs)*. The 'Forty' also issued their own paper, *al-Hādhira*, directed by ʿAlī Abū Shūsha, and emphasizing Tunisia's need for cultural rejuvination within the great Islamic community. Yet after a while they split into two circles: the 'Khaldūnīya', named after the great Tunisian scholar Ibn Khaldūn*, rallying those of conservative and strictly Islamic-Arabic conviction (1896) under Bashīr Sfar; and the 'Alumni of the Sādiqī College (Les Anciens du

Collège Sādiqī) of westernizing and laïcistic tendencies, led by ʿAlī Bāsh Hambah. Notwithstanding their different philosophy of life both movements were inspired by the same desire for national emancipation, primarily in the social, economic and cultural domains. Both saw the way to it in the raising of the general level of education through extension and modernization of the school system, the spread of an Arabic press, and improved training of the Arab artisans suffering greatly under the competition of the native Jewish workers. Their political action was a campaign against the French project of granting French citizenship to the Tunisian Jews, which had to be withdrawn under the pressure of public opinion. Upon the whole, however, their efforts, too widely scattered and inco-ordinate, produced no tangible results so that in 1907 the two leaders decided the fusion of their groups. This was the origin of the first Tunisian political organization on a nationalist basis, the Young Tunisia Party*.

MOUVEMENT NATIONAL ALGERIEN see ALGERIAN NATIONAL MOVEMENT

MOUVEMENT POUR LE TRIOMPHE DE LA LIBERTE ET LA DEMOCRATIE see MOVEMENT FOR THE TRIUMPH OF LIBERTY AND DEMOCRACY

MOVEMENT FOR THE TRIUMPH OF LIBERTY AND DEMOCRACY, an Algerian political party, generally quoted as M.T.L.D., the initials of its designation in French (Mouvement pour le Triomphe de la Liberté et la Démocratie), founded in October 1946 by Messali al-Hajj (Masālī al-Hajj) after his return from exile in Brazzaville in order to mask the Algerian People's Party* (P.P.A.) which had been declared unlawful by the French authorities. From its seat at Bouzaréa, a locality near Algiers, which the police had assigned as residence to Messali al-Hajj, it branched out into the remotest parts of the country as well as among the Algerian labourers in France and in Belgium, everywhere widely diffusing its journals *Al-Maghrib al-ʿArabī* (The Arab West), later replaced by 'L'Algérie Libre', and *Saut al-Jazā'ir* (Voice of Algeria). Its programme, briefly summarized, called for Algerian sovereignty and a Constituent Assembly elected by universal suffrage without distinction of race and religion. The underground system of the P.P.A.'s cells was left intact and even strengthened, but a new and complex party hierarchy was erected with, at the top, a forty-men Central Committee, under the supreme authority of a small Executive Committee (Comité Directeur) which, at least in the first years, Messali had firmly in his hands. A National Council assembling in monthly meetings the leaders of the higher ranks in the party structure, transmitted the instructions of the directorate down to the lowest levels and assured the coordination of all party activities in Algeria and France, while an office in Cairo was in charge of external relations. Behind this apparatus the ideology of the illegal P.P.A. lived on as strongly as before. In fact, at the M.T.L.D.'s first National Congress in March 1947 it was resolved to continue the development in the authorized forms, but at the same time, well veiled, that of the People's Party and its special section, the Secret Organization (O.S.*). In the years to come the M.T.L.D. created also some affiliated, half-political, half-welfare organizations such as the Committee for the Assistance of the Victims of Repression or the Algerian Society of the Press and of Publications.

In the municipal elections of October 1947, the M.T.L.D. gained one-third of the seats in the city councils all over the country and in April 1948 nine seats in the Algerian Assembly which had been instituted by the Algerian Organic Statute of September 1946. These results were obtained although in many polling stations the ballot boxes admittedly were pre-arranged by the Administration in favour of more docile candidates, and although shortly before election day 32 of the party's 59 candidates were arrested for plotting against the security of the State. Although less successful in subsequent elections to various other public bodies, because of still more efficient precautionary measures taken by the Administration, its numerical and moral force did not cease to grow, and with it the prestige of Messali. After a pilgrimage to the Holy Cities and a stay in Pakistan, where he participated as vice-president of the World Moslem Congress of 1951, he arranged in Chantilly (France) a meeting of the Moroccan, Algerian and Tunisian nationalist party heads resulting in the establishment of the North African Unity and Action Front*. Then he started out for a propaganda and inspection tour intended to cover all Algeria. The four weeks of enthusiasm and patriotic fervor in every town and village where he appeared, the unlimited faith in his word, manifested by the masses hailing him everywhere as the great national leader, the *za'īm*, were the triumph of his career. It came to a sudden end by his arrest in May 1952 and his removal to France, where he was assigned residence under police supervision, first in Niort then successively in various other provincial towns.

For quite a time his popularity with the rank and file continued unshaken, especially among the Algerian proletariat in France, highly receptive to the well-calculated dosage of nationalistic, religious and socialistic militant catchwords. Among the party officers, however, in particular the young intelligentsia, a certain antagonism began to crystallize. On the one hand, they resented his increasingly marked authoritarian or, as it was termed, dictatorial attitude and what they criticised as 'personality cult', strongly encouraged by himself and his close surrounding; and, on the other, there were many who felt that the time for mere oratorical attacks or street demonstrations was over and that the moment had come for the arms to speak. The first source of these divergencies may have been no more than theoretical differences of opinion, but they were sharpened by temperamental contrasts and did not take long to degenerate into an open crisis.

A Party Congress arranged by Messali in July 1954 from his seclusion in Niort appointed him president for life, dissolved the Central Committee and designated one composed of reliable adherents. Another Congress convened by the old Central Committee expelled him and his friends from the party and declared itself the sole governing authority. Quarrels between the 'Centralists' and the 'Messalists' about the use of the party funds and party premises, and an embittered press feud between Messali's 'L'Algérie Libre' and the Centralists' new organ 'La Nation Algérienne' carried the conflict into the street and led to riots with a number of wounded and dead. All efforts at bringing about a compromise failed. Towards the end of 1954 it became obvious that the schism was not to be bridged. In November, upon the outbreak of the Algerian Revolution*, the offices of the party and its affiliated organizations were closed down, the publications of both factions prohibited and some of their most conspicuous members arrested. The majority of the Centralists joined the Front of the National Liberation* (F.L.N.). After a while Messali and his friends set up another party, the Algerian National Movement* (M.N.A.), but under the new name the old enmity lived on even more vehemently.

MOVEMENT OF MOROCCAN UNITY, *Haraka al-Wahda al-Maghribīya*, a political party in the zone of the Spanish Protectorate* in Morocco, founded in February 1937 by Muhammad al-Makkī al-Nāsirī in Tetuan, where he took residence after his expulsion from the French zone because of his activities in the Bloc of Moroccan Action* *(Kutla al-ʿAmal al-Maghribī)*. He started by issuing a bi-weekly in Arabic *(al-Wahda al-Maghribīya)* with a supplement in Spanish *(Unidad Marraqui)*, edited by ʿAbd al-Salām Tamsamanī, a native of the Rif and former companion in arms of the revolutionary leader ʿAbd al-Karīm* (Abdelkrim). The *Unidad Marraqui* published the Spanish translation of the 'Plan of Reforms' which the *Kutla* had established in 1934, but soon afterwards al-Nāsirī formulated a 'Plan' of his own. It emphasized the friendly attitude of General Franco's young régime towards the Moroccan nationalists as opposed to their persecution by the French authorities, and expressed the Movement's confidence in the achievement of its aims with the help of the Spanish people. With Spanish subsidies al-Nāsirī created branches in the principal towns of the Spanish zone and increased the number of adherents, mainly at the expense of his rival ʿAbd al-Khāliq Torres (al-Tarrīs), the leader of the Party of National Reform* *(Hizb al-Islah al-Watanī)*; then he acquired a printing plant, organized boy scout groups after fascist patterns, and founded an institute of higher education, the *Mawlay al-Mahdī*, followed later by a professional school, both of them under his direction.
In the uncertainty of the quickly changing events of which the Arab countries in North Africa were the stage during the Second World War, the Movements' sympathy inclined towards the German side, although it was careful not to commit itself while the final outcome of the war was not foreseeable. Upon the end of the war the re-establishment of the Tangier Statute* (1945) offered new opportunities for propaganda, and al-Nāsirī took the branch of Tangier in his own hands while turning the general leadership as well as the direction of the Institute *Mawlay al-Mahdī* over to Tamsamanī, whose popularity in the Rif region greatly furthered the spread of the Movement among the mountain tribes. There, however, soon a split took place and a new 'Rifian Party' came into being. Following the temporary closing of the Movement's offices by the authorities in the wake of nationalist riots in

Tetuan (1948), al-Nāsirī concentrated his activities on close collaboration with the political leaders in the French zone. Having started in Tangier a new daily, *al-Shaᶜb* (The People), which had some first-rank French contributors, and taken a leading part in the secret Trade Union movement in the Spanish zone, he set out on extensive journeys. In close co-operation with the Arab League he carried Moroccan propaganda to the United States, Pakistan, the Philippine Islands and Indonesia. In the tense period of Sultan Muhammad's V* exile, *al-Shaᶜb* was suspended and most of the members of the Movement joined the *Istiqlāl** Party.

MOZABITES, Banū M'Zāb, a Berber community of the heterodox Ibādite sect, the survival of the once flourishing Rustumid* imamate of Tāhart or rather of the city republic of Sadrāta (near Wargla in the Algerian Sahara) which succeeded it. Driven out also of Sadrāta about the middle of the XIth century, the faithful adherents of the creed, anxious to escape further persecutions, withdrew into the arid and inhospitable limestone highland of the Shabka (some 400 miles south of Algiers). There, in the Wādī M'Zāb–whence the name under which they are currently referred to–in centuries of hard work they created palm-groves of nearly 300.000 date trees irrigated by a dense network of channels under the monotonous grating sound of the pulley and cords, the 'Song of the Wādī M'Zāb', which, kept in ceaseless motion by donkeys and camels, take up in leather buckets the water of some 3000 wells over 200 feet deep. These plantations requiring an enormous investment of work and energy are not to be regarded, however, from the point of view of economic returns; in fact, their maintenance is made possible only by the gains of the Mozabite merchants established in the towns all over Algeria. It is a deep-rooted religious particularism which makes their upkeep, commercially considered, a luxury, a sacred duty of the Mozabite community.
The approximately 50.000 Mozabites live in a loose confederation of seven small urban settlements which grew up between the XIth and XVIIth centuries. Several families tracing their origin to a common ancestor form a clan *(qabīla)*, inhabit their particular quarter and have their own particular cemetery to which they devote their own proper cult. Each town constitutes a kind of theocratic republic governed by two assemblies: one, the *halqa* (circle) of twelve religious heads *(iᶜazzāben)*; and the other one, of laymen in charge of the administration and minor police affairs. For a long time civil and penal jurisdiction lay exclusively in the hands of the *iᶜazzāben* and rested on their interpretation of the Koran and *hadīth* (Tradition of the Prophet), compiled in numerous but rather confused collections until Sheikh ᶜAbd al-ᶜAzīz († 1808) of the town of Beni Isgen codified them in the 10 volumes of his *Kitāb al-Nīl*. His code, however, was still lacking in clarity until the appearance of the extensive commentary by the learned Sheikh Atfiyāsh (1820-1913) on the basis of which justice is now administred (Two studies in French of the *Kitāb al-Nīl* and of the commentary by Zeys, Paris 1886 and Algiers 1887/88). The occasionally appearing lacunae have to be filled by the *iᶜazzāben* through decisions taken by common

consent *(ittifaqāt)*. Following the incorporation into the Algerian administration of the Mozabite territory (1882) after it had already been declared (1853) a French protectorate, certain reforms were introduced into this somewhat antiquated system, but most of them remained practically unobserved, so that the French authorities thought it preferable to exempt the Mozabites from the innovations introduced (1959) into the traditional legislation regulating marriage and divorce in Algeria. Hardly more successful from the time they were opened in 1915, proved the few elementary schools with French as the language of instruction, inadapted both by their method of teaching and the choice of the teachers to the people's ways of feeling and thinking firmly anchored in traditional concepts. Thus the old-type koranic school continued, in close connection with the mosque and under the strict supervision of the *halqa*. It remained built upon the mechanical memorizing of the Koran and a rudimentary knowledge of Arabic grammar and writing, and was supplemented only for a few of the very best by a slightly higher theological training.

In recent years certain modernizing trends, inspired by Sheikh Buyūd Ibrāhīm, the head of the *halqa* of Guerrara (appr. 6000 inh.), became noticeable in the field of public education. In the early 'fifties, very cautiously at the beginning and in the face of the obstinate opposition of the older generation, he set up an organization modelled after the pattern of a political party, of small units or cells meeting regularly for discussions of religious, economic, social and educational questions of local significance. In this way he succeeded step by step in having, except in Beni Isgen (ca. 7000 inh.), a school reform programme accepted, which, notwithstanding its firm roots in Ibādite religious principles and ethics, separates school and teacher from the control of the mosque and emphasizes the awakening of the pupil's intellectual faculties as opposed to thoughtless learning by heart. Another fruit of the aims guiding Sheikh Buyūd's groups of reformers is the creation of a new type of high-school in Guerrara, which prepares for the study at the universities of al-Azhar in Cairo and al-Zaytūna in Tunis. Being the only one of its kind in an Ibādite community, it is attended also by young men of the Ibādites in the island of Jarba (Tunisia) and the Jabal Nafūsa (Tripolitania). So far these efforts at raising the educational level have remained limited to the male youth, with the exception of a three-grade girls' school established in 1954 in a private house in Ghardaia, the principal town (appr. 16.000 inh.) of the Mozabite country. In 1962 Sheikh Buyūd was designated to represent the Mozabite community in the 'Provisional Executive', the governing body in Algeria, for the period between the conclusion of the armistice and the installation of the government of the Algerian Republic.

The isolation of their homeland has never prevented the Mozabites from gaining a place in Algerian economic life. In Turkish times certain occupations such as the running of public baths, of slaughterhouses or mills were almost exclusively in their hands. Down to this day about one-sixth of the male population - the women are not allowed ever to leave the Wādī M'Zāb - seek, and achieve success on the markets of the larger Algerian towns in various commercial enterprises. The family supplies the capital and receives the profits which are realized. Hardly ever one of those Mozabite merchants feels sufficiencly attracted by the atmosphere of modern life so as not to return after some time to the old home, be it even Beni Isgen, still surrounded by its high, medieval walls, where smoking and photographing are still prohibited and strangers are not permitted to stay over night.

MOZARABS, a term derived from the Arabic *mustaʿriba* ('would-be Arabs') and, designating arabized non-Arabs or the native Christians of Latino-Iberian or Gothic origin in al-Andalus*, who after the Arab conquest had preserved their faith but in their way of life became almost completely assimilated to the conquerors. Like the non-Moslem communities in the Arab East they had to pay a special tax, lived in quarters of their own under their own laws, were subject to the jurisdiction of their own judge *(qāḍī al-naẓarā'*, judge of the Christians) and governed by their own officials *(kumis*, from Latin comes). They spoke the current Romance dialect evolved from Low Latin, but the educated among them soon began to use Arabic as their second language and frequently added an Arabic name, or at least the Arabic *ibn* (son of), to their Christian name unless they changed it into a pure Arabic name thought to have a certain assonance as e.g. Rocemundo into Rabīʿ. This process of arabization became particularly manifest in the towns where many Mozarabs worked as scribes in government offices, also at the higher hierarchical levels, especially in the financial departments, while in such centres of learning as Toledo, Cordova or Seville quite a few attained outstanding rank in the field of philosophy, science or literature. These scholarly Mozarab groups used Latin as fluently as Arabic but wrote it in Arabic characters.
Notwithstanding the social and educational differences in its midst, the Mozarab community constituted a distinct cultural unity within the Arabo-Islamic society. Later conversions and emigration make it difficult to evaluate its numerical importance or its proportion to the Moslem majority at any given time, but upon the whole it was seldom lacking in loyalty to the established régime, at least outwardly if not always in full sincerety. Occasionally there occured Mozarab revolts in the wake of general internal unrest, but religious antinomies played no, or only a secondary rôle in such movements, which were mainly of a political order. Once, in the middle of the IXth century, the Christian community of Cordova under the spell of three ecstatic ascetics, the priests Perfectus and Eulogius and the monk Isaac, was seized by a peculiar wave of religious hysteria which went so far that a number of people were driven to seek voluntary martyrdom by publicly blasheming Muhammad and Islam.
Towards the end of the IXth century an increasing current of Mozarab emigration began to set in, encouraged by the Christian kings, who wanted to re-populate the territories they had conquered and which many of the Moslem inhabitants had left. Still later, when under Almoravid* and Almohad* rule a wave of intolerance swept over al-Andalus, a great many Mozarabs who refused conversion to Islam were expelled or voluntarily emigrated into León and Castile. There the new settlers

constituted an important link between the Arabo-Islamic and Latin-Christian spheres of culture. The monasteries which they established in their new homelands became the seats of an education considerably above the general standard prevailing there at that time. Their Latin manuscripts with explanations and comments in Arabic, which have been preserved reflect the exact methods followed by these Mozarab monks. The themes and forms of Arabic poetry introduced through this and similar channels have left lasting traces in the contemporay popular poems and literary prose of northern Spain and the South of France. Mozarab architecture, rooted in Visigothic and Byzantine traditions and developed in contact with Arab Moslem art, gave rise in the West to new techniques in vaulting, arching and brick-work decoration, which for a long time remained in favour.

M.T.L.D. see MOVEMENT FOR THE TRIUMPH OF LIBERTY AND DEMOCRACY

MUDEJARS, *mudajjanūn* (from *dajana*, to take up one's abode), 'those who stayed on', a Hispano-Arabic term denoting those Moslems who remained in the land that in the course of the gradual reconquest of the Iberian peninsula became Christian territory, but retained their religion, their laws and particular practices. As time went on they became in their outward way of life more or less assimilated to their Christian surroundings and hispanized in many cases their Arabic names. Even their Arabic language was gradually overshadowed by, and at last completely abandoned for, the current Romance dialect which, however, they never ceased to write in Arabic script. This process that started with the cession of Toledo (1085) by Emir Yahyā al-Qādir of the house of the Dhū al-Nūn* to King Alfonso VI of Castile, continued its course throughout some four hundred years in territories continually widened by the conquests of Ṣaragossa (1118), Lisbon (1147), Cordova (1236), Seville (1248), Murcia (1266) and finally Granada (1492). All this time the legal status assigned to the Mudejars by a number of special charters (span. *fueros)* was that of a sort of second-rate, but benevolently treated citizens, comparable to the position of the Christians in the Arab countries. Still, every shrinkage of the area under Moslem government entailed a movement of emigration into the North African Moslem countries. After the fall of Granada, the legal, social and economic situation of the Mudejars, or Moriscos* as they were thenceforth called, rapidly deteriorated, until between 1609 and 1614 the last of them were expelled from Spanish soil.

Yet throughout the long preceding period most of them lived prosperously as industrial husbandmen, while quite a few, highly skilled craftsmen, excelled in the carving or inlaying of wood and ivory, the tooling of leather, in artistic metalwork, ceramics, enamelling and weaving, whose aesthetic and technical inventiveness was greatly appreciated. From among them also came remarkable architects and sculptors who frequently were commissioned with the construction of churches, palaces and private houses for their wealthy Christian compatriots. Thus developed in the Spanish towns a particular Mudejar style distinctly appearing in many a fine monument in Toledo, Cordova, Seville or Valencia, whose influence reached beyond the Pyrenees and left its traces in the Gothic and Renaissance architecture of southern Europe. The Mudejars also evolved and cultivated a poetry and literary prose of their own which has become known as the Aljamiado* literature.

MUHAMMAD IBN ʿABD ALLĀH, a Moroccan sultan (1757-1790) of the ʿAlawid* dynasty, who after the three decades of anarchy under Sultan Ismāʿīl's* successors reestablished the authority of government and the discipline in the army, reconstituted the dislocated financial system and gave a new incentive to the stagnating economic activities. Still in his early youth he was appointed governor of Marrakesh by his father, Sultan ʿAbd Allāh Ibn Ismāʿīl, and showed his ability in winning the confidence of the people. Preferring whenever possible negotiation to the use of force, he soon succeeded in policing the plains on the Atlantic coast with their towns as far north as Tangier, and made the port of Safi safe again for foreign trade. As sultan he continued this conciliatory policy on a country-wide scale. Adroitly playing upon the tribal rivalries, he gained the good-will of some of the influential chieftains, thus counterbalancing the unruly temper of his professional negro soldiery (*ʿAbīd al-Bukhārī**). He established a chain of fortresses on the roads connecting Meknès, Fez and Marrakesh with the sea, and modernized the antiquated fortifications of the major ports, all of which he heavily armed with artillery. Then he went about his long cherished project of a naval rearmament by purchasing a number of warships from Sweden, England and Turkey. It is uncertain to what extent this haphazardly acquired navy, consisting of allegedly 50 vessels manned with 5000 sailors and 2000 gunners, would have stood a serious test, but it strengthened without doubt his prestige in the country as well as abroad. So did the series of his commercial agreements and treaties of friendship in particular with Austria, Denmark, England, Sweden, the United States of America and Venice; the minting of a high standard coinage; and finally the military conquest of Mazagan from the Portuguese (1769).
Muhammad Ibn ʿAbd Allāh's most noteworthy achievements were those which made his name known as one of Morocco's greatest builders. There is hardly a town of any importance where he did not construct, restore or embellish mosques, theological schools, mausolea or sanctuaries of local saints. For himself he set up three new residences, one in Marrakesh, the *Dār al-Baiḍa*' ('The White House', today a hospital); one in Meknès of the same name (today an educational institution); and a third one in Rabat. The work of his life, however, was the creation of a new city - Mogador, formerly a fortified Portuguese settlement, laid out and erected by one of the most capable contemporary French architects, especially called to Morocco for this task. By the choice of the site, the design of the street pattern, the arrangement of the residential and business sections, the situation of the public buildings, and a number of details, Mogador comes surprisingly near to modern town-planning concepts, while architectural inventiveness fused occidental and Moresque forms into a decorative style of its own.

Sīdī Muhammad ʿAbd Allāh's reign meant for his country a period of long-missed order, peace and well being. He was succeeded by his son Mūlāy al-Yazīd (1790-1792), who after an extremely troublesome youth - his father had to send him four times on a pilgrimage to the Holy Cities to keep him out of Morocco - and two not less troublesome years on the throne, in which his sanguinary despotism came dangerously near to reducing his father's work to ruins, was killed in fighting a revolt conducted by one of his brothers.

MUHAMMAD al-SHAYKH al-MAHDĪ, the first ruler (1554-1557) of the Moroccan dynasty of the Saʿdians* (1554-1659), a family of *sharīfs** (descendants of the Prophet Muhammad), which in the years of the dwindling authority of the Wattāsids* held a leading position in the plain of the Sūs in south-western Morocco. There its chief, AbūʿAbd Allāh Ibn Ahmad al-Qā'im, stood in the forefront of the resistance against the Portuguese encroachment upon Moroccan soil, to which under the battle-cry of the Holy War he had called up a number of mountain clans in the Atlas and some religious brotherhoods* and influential marabouts*. After his death (1517) his sons Abū al-ʿAbbās Ahmad al-Aʿraj and Muhammad al-Shaykh al-Mahdī took his place and steadily expanded their influence. Ahmad al-Aʿraj established his seat at Marrakesh, and Muhammad al-Shaykh at Tarudant, the principal town in the Sūs, which he strongly fortified (1523), a partition of power which for a while worked more or less smoothly. An occasional sharper dissent was appeased by the pious men around them, so that the warfare against the Portuguese could successfully be continued, while the Wattāsid government had to face a common front of increasingly numerous Saʿdian followers submitting to its authority more in name than in fact. Yet when Muhammad al-Shaykh drove the Portuguese from Agadir (1541), Safi and Azemmour, and was widely hailed as the victor over the Christan invader, and found himself again in conflict with his brother, reconciliation was no longer possible. In the inevitable clash of arms Ahmad al-Aʿraj was defeated and disappeared from the political stage, but only to come forth a few years later in the ranks of his brother's enemies.

Thenceforth Muhammad al-Shaykh felt strong enough to unveil his aspiration to the throne in undisguised rebellion. Twice, halfway between Marrakesh and Fez on the slopes of the Middle Atlas, he dispersed a Wattāsid army commanded by Sultan Abū al-ʿAbbās Ahmad (1524-1545 and 1547-1550), who fell into his hands and for two years remained in Saʿdian captivity, but he could not take Fez, the Wattāsid capital. There, the groups of theological scholars firmly upheld the Wattāsid cause in public opinion and refused to let the rebels enter. Thus it became possible for the sultan's uncle Abū al-Hasan ʿAlī*, or Bū Hassūn as he was generally called, to push them back into Marrakesh. Then he enforced a settlement imposing on Muhammad al-Shaykh, in exchange for the city of Meknès, the release of the sultan (1547). The success of the loyalists was of short duration. Subtly manoeuvring the various local factions and eliminating his most tenacious opponents by assassination, the Saʿdian regained within two years sufficient strength to lay siege to Fez, which surrendered almost without resistance. Yet his triumph too came to an early end. By an attempt, which completely miscarried, to expand his territory eastwards over Tlemcen into Algeria, by then a province of the Ottoman empire, he lost two sons on the battlefield, and dangerously weakened his army. His failure paved the way for an alliance between the Turks and Bū Hassūn who had left Fez just before its fall, and with Turkish help defeated the Saʿdian troops near Taza. He found the gates of Fez open and was acclaimed sultan by the people (1554). Together with Ahmad al-Aʿraj he still succeeded in conquering Meknès, but a few months later both of them were decisively beaten. Bū Hassūn fell fighting, al-Aʿraj surrendered and Muhammad al-Shaykh al-Mahdī was the undisputed ruler of Morocco.

To secure his hard-won position against any vicissitudes of fortune was now his prime objective. He began by enlisting the well-armed Turkish soldiery which under Bū Hassūn had fought against him, making it his body-guard and the nucleus of his army. His next step was the extermination of all whom he suspected of Wattāsid sympathies. At the same time he moved the seat of government out of the midst of the fickle populace of Fez into the safer atmosphere of Marrakesh. Then, forgetting his rôle as the protagonist in the war against the infidels, he concluded a treaty with Spain for a common, large-scale offensive against the Turks in Algeria, which should rid him once and for ever from these dangerous neighbours. It did not bring the hoped-for result, but the Spanish alliance was to remain for the coming decades the cardinal point of Saʿdian foreign relations. By the same radical inversion of the religio-political course he had observed during the long years of his struggle for power, he abolished the fiscal privileges of the marabouts, brotherhoods and also of the tribal chieftains in the Atlas, many of them his one-time companions-in-arms, and imprisoned, exiled or executed whomsoever he found refractory.

Muhammad al-Shaykh holds his place in Moroccan history by his unswerving, though wholly unscrupulous tenacity in preserving the unity of the country which the weakness of his predecessors had brought to the verge of disintegration. He firmly implanted the rule of his house, but the violent end of his life prevented him from enjoying the fruits of his efforts. While engaged in subduing some rebellious mountain tribes he was murdered by a traitor introduced into his Turkish body-guard by the beylerbey of Algeria, and his head sent to Constantinople. He was succeeded by his son Abū ʿAbd Allāh al-Ghālib Billāh (1557-1574).

MUHAMMAD V IBN YŪSUF, Sultan, later assuming the title of King *(malik)*, of Morocco (1927-1961), the youngest of Sultan Mūlāy Yūsuf Ibn al-Hasan's (1913-1927) three sons, chosen to succeed to the throne by the French Protectorate* authorities because they thought that the seventeen-year old sovereign could easily be moulded into a docile 'protégé'. In the first years of his reign it seemed in fact that the inexperienced and rather timid youth whom his carefully sifted surroundings kept as much as possible out of touch with the country's life, would unreservedly follow the lines traced by French policy. He signed the so-called Berber Edict*; apparently ignored the excitement it called forth; and maintained a cautious distance from the awakening nationalist movement which in 1934 gave birth to the first political party in Morocco, the Bloc of Moroccan Action*. Its aims were moderate and merely directed towards more freedom for the play of national life within the framework of the Protectorate, but the French authorities judged its activities inopportune and the sultan ratified its dissolution. Its two successors, the 'National Party' and the 'Popular Movement', resumed the claims in more radical terms which had their resonance in street riots in Casablanca, Fez, Meknès and Marrakesh, exploited by nazi and fascist propaganda. He approved their severe repression, including the banishment of the party leaders ʿAllāl al-Fāsī and Muhammad al-Wazzānī. Still, as the events were soon to show, his sympathies were with the youthful nationalists and the cause they fought for, but he realized the futility of violent action and was resolved to discourage it. Thus at the outbreak of the war in 1939 he had the nation's loyalty to France solemnly proclaimed in all mosques, and his word was faithfully obeyed. The disturbances ceased and Morocco remained quiet even after the French capitulation.

The landing of the Allies changed this situation and new prospects came into sight. Sultan Muhammad refused to side with the Vichy government and to lend his name for a Moroccan rising against the American forces, that the Governor-General had planned. Instead, in a private conversation with President Roosevelt at Anfa near Casablanca in June 1943, he discussed the abrogation of the Protectorate and received the President's formal promise for full-hearted support in the course of the general settlement upon the end of the war. It was his first undisguised move as the interpreter of the national aspirations, and the impression on public opinion was great. In December, the nationalist groups, no longer satisfied with liberal piecemeal reforms, joined in a new party, took as its name 'Independence' *(Istiqlāl*)* and made independence the cardinal point of its programme. They found the Free French régime of General de Gaulle as inaccessible as had been its predecessors. Its answer was that Morocco remained inseparably bound to France, it silenced the claims with mass arrests and had the troops deal with the excited crowds at the cost of many killed and wounded. Relying on Roosevelt's word and anxious to appease the spreading unrest, Sultan Muhammad complied with the French request and disavowed the hot-headed fighters for independence. He was understood. By then they knew that he felt wholly with them, whatever he might be compelled to do under the pressure of the moment, for from his palace there not only reached them exhortation to patience but also moral and material encouragement in all sorts of ways.

With the premature death of Franklin D. Roosevelt, deeply mourned in Morocco, died also the hope in the promised support, the only one that could be expected, and Muhammad Ibn Yūsuf came openly into the forefront. It was the 'Sultan of the Istiqlāl' who in April 1947 at Tangier in a resounding speech emphasized the country's territorial, spiritual and emotional unity and - the prestige of the Arab League was then at its peak - its solidarity with all Arab peoples and all Moslems.

At the same time his son Hassan, chief of the 'Hassanian Scouts' (founded 1945) and his daughter Princess Lalla 'Ā'isha, unveiled, harangued the exalted Tangier youth. The word 'independence' was left unpronounced but the hint, in this context, at a possible future Franco-Moroccan 'alliance' in the sultan's simultaneous declaration to the press could not be mistaken, and in fact evoked sharp protests on the part of France. Thenceforth he was to the people, excepting some great heads of tribes and of religious brotherhoods* to whom the Protectorate meant the protection of their political and economic privileges, the incarnation of courage, tenacity and intelligence, coupled with deep attachment to Islam and the ideals of Arabism. To an influential section of French public opinion commanding a loud, popular press - in Morocco the French 'colons'; in France powerful banking, mining and commercial concerns with important investments in Morocco, and most of the right-wing political groups opposed to any change in the structure of the French colonial empire - he was the reactionary, theocratic despot who resisted all guidance to modern progress and must be made to surrender or else be removed. To the nationalist militants he was the leader who in Tangier had defined the goal: termination of the Protectorate first, and then an alliance based on mutually recognized common interests or, as it was soon expressed, 'independence within interdependence'. Their number grew, their organization consolidated and its antennae reached into the close surroundings of the sultan and Prince Hassan.

In this atmosphere the tension between the Palace and the Regency, where a policy of the strong hand was the key-note, did not take long to assume a sharpness which barred all ways to an understanding. Sterile, too, proved the sultan's direct contacts with the French Government and the President of the Republic on his visit to Paris in October 1950. In March 1951, the Resident-General, encouraging the ambitions of the powerful tribal lord in the High Atlas, Tihāmī al-Glāwī*, staged the semblance of a Berber revolt, drew a cordon of troops around the royal residence and confronted the sultan with the alternative of either abdication or the repudiation of all nationalist activities. Fearing the outbreak of the popular passion and new bloodshed he yielded. Again he was understood by the people, who resented his humiliation as an insult inflicted upon all of them, and the various political groups, bridging personal rivalries and party strife, constituted a front of common action. Twice more in the following year the sultan addressed an appeal to France for a settlement which would link both countries on an equal standing: in a memorandum to the President of the Republic and in a public speech on the anniversary of his accession to the throne, but with the same disappointing outcome. Soon afterwards Casablanca became the scene of sanguinary riots leading to others in Beni Mellal and Rabat, and soon afterwards in Oujda behind which the French police thought to have discovered the hand of his son Hassan. The long-expected moment to bring about his elimination had arrived. With the blessing of the Regency, Tihāmī al-Glāwī in alliance with 'Abd al-Haiy al-Kattānī, the head of the influential Kattānīya* brotherhood, rallied his clientèle, camped his warriors under the walls of Rabat, demanded Sultan Muhammad's destitution, and after short hesitation the French government gave its consent. On August 20, 1953, tanks and machine-guns were in position in the streets of Rabat, Muhammad V was declared deposed and with his family flown first to Corsica then to Madagascar, while his uncle Sīdī Muhammad Ibn ʿArafa was proclaimed sultan.

The belief, in France and among the French colony in Morocco, that Muhammad Ibn Yūsuf would soon be out of his people's mind once he was out of their sight, revealed itself soon as a dangerous illusion. Five years ago his Tangier speech had made him in a political battle the protagonist who knew how to inspire confidence and command obedience. Now, an emotional assimilation of pity, passion and religion made him the martyr of his fight for country and people, whose fate was felt as the fate of every Moroccan, whose liberation meant the liberation of Morocco, whom popular fervour elevated into the spheres of myth. Townspeople, peasants, tribes and the crowds in the slums were united in the same deep indignation and in the same firm will to enforce reparation. Terror bands sprang up, bombs were thrown in the streets, railways sabotaged, French goods boycotted, French shops set on fire and twice Ibn ʿArafa miraculously escaped attempts on his life. French counter-terrorists, the 'Présence Française', retaliated, more troops were sent over from France and Algeria, but shooting, assassination and guerilla continued in spite of ruthless police rule, martial law, incarcerations and death sentences. Recruiting began in the Rif for an 'Army of Liberation' which branched out into the Middle Atlas, attacked French outposts and ambushed military convoys.

Gradually the conviction ripened in Paris that there was no way out of the impasse unless the dialogue with the legitimate monarch in exile could be resumed. On September 7, 1955, high-ranking French emissaries left for Madagascar, were followed by a Moroccan delegation, and pourparlers started. Three weeks later Ibn ʿArafa was persuaded to move, pending his formal abdication, into the international zone of Tangier, whereupon the throne was declared vacant and a Council of Regency was set up in order to conduct the negotiations, so at least was the French plan, for an agreement which Muhammad Ibn Yūsuf should approve prior to his return. It took one more month to realize that this was the wrong way, and that nobody else could speak in his place. Then he was received with full honours at Nice, proceeded to St. Germain near Paris, and in a few days the solution was at hand. On the 6th of November 1955, the Declaration of La Celle-St. Cloud terminated the Protectorate and laid down for the new Franco-Moroccan relationship the basis he had repeatedly, yet in vain proposed in the past: independence within interdependence. On November 16, after two years and three months of absence and two days before the twenty-eighth anniversary of his reign, Sultan Muhammad V was greeted on Moroccan soil as the liberator by thousands of enraptured Moroccans.

In the story of the liberation the sultan's speech at Tangier in 1947 and his removal in August 1953 were unquestionably, in his own words, two essential markstones, but they cannot overshadow the part played by quite a number of the nationalist leaders and last but not least, by the broad, anonymous many. Yet it was his great historic merit, in which no one else shared, to have refined and rationalized the ecstasy springing from high-strung, most probably ephemeral emotions and turned it into enduring, unconditional loyalty. The nation had made him the symbol of the struggle, but now that it was won, a spontaneous political sense and ability in dealing with the problems, human and material, inevitably arising after the years of convulsion, made him the symbol of national unity. He let it not be questioned that in the re-born State his was the final authority; its exercise, however, was not by the easy way of coercion, but arbitration between divergent opinions and movements, and the balancing of the various interests and aspirations. He spoke cordially with the peasants and himself ploughed on the wheel of a tractor the first furrows on a newly cleared piece of land; he visited the Berber mountain hamlets, the tribes on the fringe of the desert, and the *sūqs* in the small towns. His ear was open to the claims for protection of the time-honoured customs; to the call for moderate reforms; and to the plans of advanced social and economic innovations. He solemnly addressed an assembly of the Moroccan Trade Union* (U.M.T.) on the celebration of the first of May and received in audience a deputation of the officially illegal communist party.

Deeply religious and proud of his descent from the Prophet, he never failed to exalt his position as the head of the Moroccan community of Moslems; to attend in pomp the Friday prayer with his court and the high governement officials; to emphasize his regard for the customs and institutions which tradition has made a part of the Islamic code of morals; and to nominate for his Council of the Throne only men known for their piety. Yet he turned rigorously against the practices of certain popular and religious brotherhoods; had his children educated in accordance with modern methods of thought, his daughters appear unveiled in public and take the lead in the emancipation of women. He called upon a French cultural mission to provide professors for the new faculties of Letters, Science and Law in Rabat; caused the scholars of the ancient Qarawīyīn* Academy to include up-to-date disciplines in its curriculum, and had them, for the first time in its history, invite a non-Moslem French sociologist to lecture. He changed the title of Sultan, borne during centuries by the Moroccan rulers into King *(malik)* lest it should call to mind the idea of oriental despotism; created a Consultative Assembly in which the various political, economic and social shades were reflected; and instituted a Council for the preparation of a Constitution embodying the principles of western democracies. He still remained the sole dominant figure in political life, whose words or actions were never the object of criticism. It was his conviction that there was no necessary contradiction between modernism and traditionalism as long as the aim at rejuvenation took into due account the national heritage of true cultural and ethical values. And he was believed by the people.

King Muhammad V died suddenly on February 26, 1962 and was succeeded by his son, King Hassan II.

MULATHTHAMŪN al-, the veiled ones or veil-wearers (from *lithām*, veil), a term by which the Arab authors denoted certain Berber tribes of the Sanhāja* group in the Sahara, in particular the Lamtūna* and Lamta, who used to veil their heads or faces. This custom is still followed today by the Tuaregs *(Tawāriq)* of southern Algeria. After the Almoravid* occupation of al-Andalus* under Yūsuf Ibn Tāshufīn* (1061-1107) the Sanhāja tribesmen in the conquering army retained this attire which thus became a special mark of distinction for the victors, affording them a privileged position in their contacts with the population and the authorities. It seems that it was frequently misused by others trying to secure under its cover immunity from persecution for all sorts of offences.

MŪLĀY, or *Maulāy*, My Lord, from *maulā*, transliterated also *mawlā*, meaning in the Koran 'helper, protector' as an epithet of God (e.g. Sura II, 286), commonly used in the Arab West presumably since about the middle or end of the XIVth century as a title prefixed to the name of the sultan*, his close relatives and high-ranking dignitaries. Around this time the term appears in the writings of European chroniclers and also occasionally in the Latin, Italian or Aragonian texts of the treaties concluded between Christian states and Arab rulers, but only since about the middle of the XVIth century in the documents issued by the Arab chancelleries. In Morocco, the title *mūlāy*, equivalent to *sīdī (sayyidī*, Monseigneur), denotes especially religious pre-eminence and preceeds the name of a saint, of a *sharīf** (a descendant of the Prophet) and of the sultan, or king since 1957. In popular mind it has preserved its traditional prestige nearly unaltered down to this day.

MŪLĀY ISMĀ'ĪL, ABŪ al-NASR, the second 'Alawid* sultan of Morocco (1672-1727) and one of the dynasty's outstanding figures. Successor to his brother Mūlāy al-Rashīd* (1664-1672), he was at first recognized only in the capital Meknès, where he had held the office of a governor; then in Fez and in the area of the Gharb controlled by these two cities. Everywhere else he was confronted with the resistance of his closest relatives. He had to face the open revolt of one of his nephews in alliance with his own brother, both of whom were supported by sympathizers all over the Anti Atlas, and had a solid foothold in the plain of the Sūs with the town of Tārūdānt, as well as south of the High Atlas in the valley of the Dar'a and the Tāfīlālt. It took Mūlāy Ismā'īl fifteen years of almost uninterrupted fighting to subdue the pretenders. A few years afterwards one of his sons stirred up a second rebellion in the Sūs but was beaten, captured, had one hand and one foot cut off and died of his wounds. Thereupon another son roused again the Sūs, then in the Dar'a area, but was also overcome and put to death.
The source which fed these uprisings was a deep-going insurrectional movement shaking the whole tribal population in the Middle Atlas, for the most part branches of the great Sanhāja* family. It sprang from the contest for power between Mūlāy Ismā'īl's predecessor and the Dilā'yūn* brotherhood, firmly rooted in Sanhāja tribal society, which had ended with the destruction by the victorious 'Alawids of the order's

venerated seat at Dilā'. The embittered tribes in the mountains, momentarily weakened but soon recovering their fighting spirit, descended into the tableland of the Tādlā and even menaced the capital Meknès. They were driven back, but others on the southern slopes of the High Atlas joined in the rising, moved into the Dadès valley and rallied the rebellious princes. In a pitiless warfare dragging on from the day of his accession to the throne throughout nearly twenty years, Mūlāy Ismā'īl at last mastered the insurgents in the mountains, while exploiting the rivalries of the local chieftains in the plains to impose his authority, although often more in name than in fact. The mountain districts south of Marrakesh were never brought under complete obedience.

Mūlāy Ismā'īl's success, in pacifying most of the country, was due on the whole to his unbending energy and to the military organization he had conceived and whose perfection he pursued consistently. Its nucleus was a highly-trained negro corps, the so-called *'Abīd al-Bukhārī**, recruited from among the population of black slaves brought into Morocco in the years following the conquest of the Sudan by the Sa'dian* Ahmad al-Mansūr* (1578-1603). Independently of this troop of unquestioning devotion Mūlāy Ismā'īl remodelled the traditional contingent of Arab tribes by incorporating into its ranks a number of Ma'qil* clans whose bloodties, real or alleged, with his family were to strengthen its not always unshakable loyalty. A third, war-experienced type of soldiery was formed by the enlistment of Christians converted to Islam, adventurers or liberated prisoners, who were regimented in a special body of troops used for the most risky kind of expeditions. A system of fortified places along the great highways; a network of strongholds among unruly tribes; and military camps grouped around the principal cities constituted the framework of the army. The chroniclers, while finding much praise for the efficiency of this military apparatus, have also left vivid descriptions of Mūlāy Ismā'īl's unscrupulous duress in wielding it, and of the mass executions of insurgents, of the cruel treatment of prisoners, many of whom he killed with his own hands.

With strategic considerations as much in mind as the manifestation of might and grandeur, he set about a complete transformation of Meknès, which was to be turned into a most formidable fortress and a royal seat surpassing by its dimensions and splendour every other ruler's residence of his time and of the past. For these constructions thousands of craftsmen and workers from all over Morocco were pressed into service, besides the prisoners of war and the captives brought in by pirates. Heavy ramparts over twenty miles long, reinforced by massive towers and bastions, constituted an outer circumvallation broken only by a few monumental gates, richly decorated with arabesque patterns and glazed tiles, and provided at the same time with an intricate defence system. Vast underground storage rooms, vaulted silos and water reservoirs; enormous stables for his mounted garrison and depots of arms and equipment; barracks for the numerous body-guard; a camp for military parades; two large mosques; buildings for the chancellery and lodgings for the clerks; enormous pleasure gardens with the audience halls and the palaces of the sultan and of his harem which, it is said, made him the father of some 800 children; and the residences of the high dignitaries and their own suites. All this confusing agglomeration, in the fifty years of its erection often modified and enlarged by additional auxiliary buildings, was protected by a second, inner arrangement of fortified walls and constituted the royal city proper. Some of it has been preserved and, several times remodelled, is still inhabited by members of the dynasty or has been adapted for various kinds of usages, but most of it is in ruins. Surrounded by another set of high walls stands out the sanctuary with the tomb of the great builder. Imposing, without doubt, by the mass of the material assembled, shaped and set up by one single will, this rather inorganic arrangement falls short, however, of the aesthetic requirements of architectural conception, artistic inventiveness and quality of workmanship.

Mūlāy Ismāʿīl's attitude to the European Powers was that of what may be called a splendid isolation, strongly tinged by his contempt of the Christians. Yet Morocco maintained a seemingly quite profitable although, not very extensive trade, both legitimate and by smuggling, foremost with England and Holland, and to a minor extent with Spain, Portugal and France. This trade lay mainly in the hands of European merchants in Salé and Tetuan and comprised the export of hides, sugar, honey and Sudanese gold, ivory and ostrich feathers, and the import of textiles, arms, gunpowder and all sorts of tools, with, on both sides, a certainly equal amount of freebooting. The negotiations for the redemption or the exchange of the victims of this piracy constituted the main task of the European consular agents in Morocco. Politically the contacts moved, in general, along smooth lines except for the Holy War, or rather guerilla, carried on with the sultan's tacit consent against the Christian enclaves on the coasts by the marabouts* and the population under their influence. Although conducted only on a local scale, these enterprises resulted within a decade (1681-1689) in the recovery of al-Mamūra and Larache from Spain, and of Tangier from England. Upon the whole, and notwithstanding their religious background, they were regarded both in Morocco and at the European courts as not very serious intermezzi in a mutually pursued policy of admitting the coexistence of two contradictory worlds. At any rate they did not make Mūlāy Ismāʿīl hesitate to ask in marriage, without demanding her conversion to Islam, the daughter of his famous contemporary Louis XIV of France. His ambassador, received with all marks of distinction, returned with the king's reply suggesting that the sultan should first turn Roman Catholic, whereupon the affair was dropped.

Mūlāy Ismāʿīl's achievements did not survive him. His death inaugurated a thirty-year period of struggles for the inheritance and of the most ruinous disturbances in the country's history.

MUQADDAM, plur. *muqaddamūn*, literally designating one placed before somebody or something, whence a superior or principal. In a specific sense *muqaddam* means the superior of the branch seat *(zāwiya**) of a religious brotherhood*. He is appointed by the head *(shaykh)* of the order or approved by him following his election by the other brethren. Thereupon he receives a special initiation confirmed by a certificate

(ijāza)* which authorizes him to confer the initiation himself upon new adepts.
In Morocco, *muqaddam* is the title of a lower-grade civil servant in the rural administration. In a few Berber tribes the elected head *(amghar)* of the assembly of the community also bears this title.

MURĀBITŪN, the members (sing. *murābit)* of half-religious, half-soldierly communities stationed in a fortified frontier outpost *(ribāt*)* where they devoted themselves to a kind of monastic way of life combining pious practices with military exercises. In the middle of the XIth century such a brotherhood, inspired by the word of its spiritual leader, ʿAbd Allāh Ibn Yāsīn*, started amongst the Sanhāja* tribes of the Sahara a crusading movement, which under Yūsuf Ibn Tāshufīn* carried the *murābitūn* (Almoravids*) to the conquest of an empire comprising Morocco, western Algeria and al-Andalus.

MURĀDID BEYS, a line of Tunisian *beys** (1640-1702), so called after Bey Murād, a former military slave, Muratto Corso (the Corse), converted to Islam, who distinguished himself in the army and in the service at the Dey's* court, ascended to the highest offices and received the title of pasha. In 1631 he resigned and was succeeded by his son Muhammad, generally known as Hammūda Pasha, who under the aging Dey Usta Murād († 1640), himself a Christian renegade from Genoa, practically ruled the country. He created a strong élite troop which was blindly devoted to him, ruthlessly eliminated all potential rivals and with an iron hand maintained peace and order. Under Dey Usta Murād's weak successors the function of the dey lost all but a merely honorary significance so that Bey Hammūda Pasha, when resigning in 1659 could without any more ado delegate his powers to his three sons who reigned each one over a part of the state and in turn designated members of the family as successors. In 1702 Bey Murād III and all his relatives lost their lives in a military revolt whose leader assumed the office of the bey and had the titles of dey and pasha bestowed upon himself. He was succeeded (1705) by another military commander, Husayn Ibn ʿAlī, who made the office of the bey, with all attributes of sovereignty, except a nominal recognition of Ottoman overlordship, hereditary in his family, and thus became the founder of the Husaynid* dynasty of Tunisia.

MURTAZIQA, sing. *murtaziq*, the mercenary troops in al-Andalus* at the time of the Umayyads. Besides their pay in cash *(rizq*, also denoting the honorary allowances accorded to members of the ruling family and to certain high officials in addition to their regular salary) they received an amount covering their expenses for food, in the case of cavalry also for the fodder of their horse, and were entitled to quarters in special barracks of their own. Each man was entered in a register *(dīwān)* kept up-to-date by a special government department which also handled the general administration and finances having regard to these troops, and was responsible for their military value and constant preparedness for battle. In the course of time it was found necessary to enrol a continuously growing number of North Africans, mainly Berbers, who came over by entire clans under their chieftains, attracted by the comparatively high pay, and in the years of the weakening central authority gained increasing influence upon the conduct of the affairs of the state.

MŪSEM, the colloquial form of the literary *mawsim*, in French texts spelt *moussem*, a term denoting in the Arab West the traditional birthday celebration of a local saint, which every year is held at his real, or presumed, burial place venerated as a shrine by the population of the environs. Following the special prayers, the sacrifice of one or several sheep and the offering of pious gifts to the saint's descendants and the guardians of the sanctuary, the ceremony turns into a popular feast with primitive entertainments, songs, dances and occasionally equestrian games. The *mūsem* receives, however, also an often considerable economic significance for the region by the annual fair taking place on this occasion.

MUSTANSIR al-, ABŪ ʿABD ALLĀH MUHAMMAD, the second ruler (1249-1277) of the dynasty of the Hafsids* in Tunisia, successor to his father Abū Zakariyyā' (1228-1249)*. He was the first of his line to bear the title of Caliph and *Amīr al-Mu'minīn* (Commander of the Faithful), and a few years later (1259) was officially recognized in this dignity by the Sharīf of Mecca upon the final collapse of the no more than symbolic ʿAbbāsid caliphate under the Mongol conquest of Baghdad. At the outset of his reign he had to remove two pretenders to the throne from among his family: the first, one of his cousins, supported by a clique of courtiers resenting the employment in high functions of the many new-comers from al-Andalus*, was quickly defeated and executed; the second, his own brother Abū Ishāq Ibrāhīm, in alliance with some Bedouin chiefs, was also beaten but found refuge at the court of Granada, returned after al-Mustansir's death and ascended the throne (1279-1283). More serious were the rebellions of a number of strong and turbulent Arab tribes, but after their submission al-Mustansir had his authority firmly established and could expect to look forward to a period of peaceful development. Then, however, St. Louis, King of France, at the head of the seventh crusade which had sailed to deliver Jerusalem, suddenly changed his course, steered off for Tunisia and disembarked his troops (July 18, 1270) at Carthage or rather at the uninhabited place among the ruins called al-Muʿallaqa. No plausible explanation for this diversion, which came as a complete surprise to his knights, is to be found except, perhaps, that Louis IX, a deeply religious man and a mystic, may have hoped to achieve al-Mustansir's and his people's conversion. In fact, upon the King's orders the crusaders remained entrenched in their camp and refrained from any offensive action. King Louis died of dysentery soon after the landing and the command was taken over by his brother Charles of Anjou, King of Sicily, and his son Philippe III, the new King of France. In the meantime al-Mustansir proclaimed the Holy War and assembled his army, but after two unsuccessful encounters made peace with the Christian princes (November 1270), who left Tunisian soil in return for the payment of a comparatively not too heavy contribution and some concessions regarding the stay in Tunisia of certain monastic orders and their right to preach in the churches of the Christian settlements. The Hafsid prestige both in Africa and in Europe was in no way affected by this interlude: in Morocco the Marīnid* Abū Yūsuf Yaʿqūb* and in Tlemcen the ʿAbd al-Wādid* Yaghmurāsan multiplied the manifestations of their esteem for the Tunisian monarch; Baibars, the Mamlūk sultan of Egypt (1260-1277), offered a military alliance; messengers of goodwill came from the negro kings of Central Africa. At the other end of the globe, the King of Norway made ouvertures for the negotiation of a trade and navigation agreement; the commercial conventions with Genoa, Pisa, Venice and Marseille were renewed and extended; two royal princes of Castile fought in the ranks of the Tunisian army against the crusaders. Understanding and tolerance marked the relationships with the courts of King James I of Aragon, who let his men serve in the caliph's militia; and, after conclusion of a peace treaty with the crusaders, of Charles of Anjou, the King of Sicily, to whom, upon his request, al-Mustansir sent one of his best physicians. To this favourable position in the international field corresponded inside the country security, order and general well-being. Seconded by his all-powerful chief of the chancellery and of public finances, Ibn Abī al-Husayn, who during almost his entire reign remained his counsellor and commander of the Aragonian mercenary troops, al-Mustansir successfully pursued a policy of religio-political equilibrium. It maintained the balance, on the one hand, between the strict adherents of the Almohad* doctrine, pillars of the régime, and the equally rigorous Malikite theologians who commanded a large following among the masses; and, on the other, between the Andalusian immigrants, many of them highly cultured and possessed of abilities which commended them for most, and even the key positions in the government services, and the native Berber and Arab notables, who at times very vividly manifested their resentment of this intrusion. Andalusian scholars and men of letters gave their imprint to intellectual life; Andalusian architecture and craftsmanship to the palaces and gardens of the high dignitaries. Al-Mustansir himself, although far from extravagant, enlarged and embellished his fortified residence *(qasaba*)* built by his father; and erected a beautiful palace in the midst of vast gardens at Bizerta. He set up a mosque and one of the city gates in Monastir, much visited by pilgrims to the tombs of the holy men within its precincts. For the water supply of Tunis he had an aqueduct of Roman times restored, a new one erected and a large reservoir constructed. By the time of his death the loyalty to the dynasty was firmly implanted, and remained alive, regardless of the mutual antagonism among its members which thenceforth for a hundred years to come characterized the Hafsid period of Tunisian history.

MUWAHHIDŪN al-, see ALMOHADS

MUWALLADŪN, sing. *muwallad* (from *wallada*, to bear, to beget) literally the adopted ones, a term used in al-Andalus* for all those among the native Ibero- Celtic or Visigoth population who embraced Islam after the Arab conquest. Although their conversion theoretically entitled them to civil rights equal to those of all other Moslems, they were obliged to seek the patronage of a member of the ruling Arab class, a differentiation very much like that which had become the rule in the eastern sections of the caliphate and like those rooted in the racial pride of the 'true Arabs'. Numerically the class of the *muwalladūn* constituted the most important sector of the population: peasants and fishermen; artisans; small merchants; and the mass of the urban proletariat. As time went on, quite a few made their way up, became wealthy traders and landowners, court dignitaries and high military officers or gained renown in the spheres of letters and learning, so that gradually the notion of their social inferiority disappeared. In the upper classes, most *muwalladūn* families arabized their names and tried to make people forget their non-Arab descent by inventing an appropriate genealogical tree. Nevertheless a certain ethnical solidarity, conscious or not, never entirely disappeared within the groups of common origin and especially at times of inner unrest became manifest in the formation of military or political factions.

N

NAKŪR see SĀLIHIDS

NĀSIR IBN, AHMAD IBN MUHAMMAD, called *al-Khalīfa*, a Moroccan scholar and mystic (1647-1717), a son of the founder of the still flourishing Nāsirīya* fraternity, and its real organiser. He was born in Tāmgrūt (near Zagora in the Darʿa valley, south of the High Atlas) and was one of the most distinguished disciples of his father, whom he succeeded at the head of the main seat of the Nāsirīya. He undertook four times the pilgrimage to the Holy Cities, acquiring on these occasions numerous adepts in Algeria, Tripolitania, Egypt and Arabia, so that the fraternity considerably expanded, and began to gain the spiritual, intellectual and political prestige which it was to enjoy for over two hundred years to come. As a further fruit of his voyages Ibn Nāsir left a book of travel *(rihla*)* conveying interesting information on the opinions and ways of teaching of the Egyptian and Arabian scholars with whom he had contacts during his stays in the Arab East. (Parts of it translated into French by A. Berbrugger, contained in his 'Voyages dans le sud de l'Algérie et des Etats barbaresques . . ', Paris 1846, together with parts of alʿAyyāshī's* *rihla)*.

NĀSIRĪ al-, AHMAD IBN KHĀLID, a Moroccan historian and man of letters (1835-1897), a descendant of the founder of the Nāsirīya* fraternity, of which he himself was a member. He studied in his home town Salé, then entered government service and in the course of a rather uneventful career in various provincial towns collected and elaborated the material for his comprehensive Moroccan history, under the abridged title of *Kitāb al-Istiqsā* (appr. Exhaustive Treatise). He dedicated the work to Sultan Mūlāy al-Hasan (1873-1894), but did not find the hoped-for appreciation, probably because from the official point of view the merits of the rulers, particularly of the more recent ones, were somewhat neglected in comparison with those of some contemporary figures in public life. Only a few years later was the author able to have the book published in Cairo with some additions to the first manuscript (Translations into French by E. Fumey, 'Chronique de la dynastie ʿalaouie au Maroc', Paris 1906/7; A. Graulle, 'Les Origines', 1923; A. Graulle & G. S. Colin, 'Les Idrisides & les Almoravides', 1925; Ismael Hamet, 'Les Almohades & les Mérinides, 1927 and 1934; and Muhammad al-Nāsirī, 'Les Saʿdiens', 1936; all in Archives Marocaines, Rabat).
Except for the chronicle of his own days al-Nāsirī only compiled previous historiographic or biographic texts, occasionally quoting them verbally without mentioning their authors. He was the first one to use also to a certain extent European sources of reference, a fact which in the then prevailing atmosphere of xenophobia exposed him to severe reproof.

Little valued in Morocco at the time of its appearance, the *Kitāb al-Istiqsā* became after the author's death one of the most widely-read books of its kind in the country.

NĀSIRĪYA a religious brotherhood* *(tarīqa)* founded by Muhammad Ibn Nāsir al-Darʿaī (1603-1674) at Tāmgrūt in the Wādī Darʿa near Zagora in southern Morocco, whose family subsequently claimed *sharīfian** nobility by a, hardly probable, descent from the Prophet Muhammad's uncle Abū Tālib. A disciple of one of the holy men (marabout*) who in a spiritual chain of several generations had lived at Tāmgrūt, he took over after the master's death the leadership of his small community. He insisted on the most rigid observance of the word of the Koran and of the Tradition of the Prophet *(hadīth)*; rejected the mystical chants, dances and other ecstatic practices, excepting the prolonged recitation of prayers, which were essential features of many brotherhood rituals; and followed closely the teaching of the great religious scholar and mystic al-Jazūlī*. He ist still one of the highly popular saints in the southern parts of Morocco.
The actual organization of the brotherhood and the formulation of its rules was the work of his son Ahmad Ibn Muhammad Ibn Nāsir (†1717). Having pledged, after some hesitation, his loyalty to Sultan Mūlāy Ismāʿīl (1672-1727) he was able unhindered to build up and spread his father's doctrine. His missionaries trained at Tāmgrūt, disseminated among the tribes of the Middle Atlas, in the Rif and in the plains of the Sūs, prepared the ground for the more than one hundred branch-seats *(zāwiya**) which sprang up in practically every larger Moroccan town, each one headed by one of the many sons, grandsons and great-grandsons of the founder. Tāmgrūt soon became a widely reputed centre of theological scholarship and literary activities. Special places are held in its annals by the second chief of the brotherhood, Ahmad Ibn Muhammad who wrote an interesting account of his travels *(rihla**) in the Arab East on the occasion of his four pilgrimages to the Holy Cities; and by its fourth head, Muhammad al-Makkī, the author of several studies on his ancestors, of a long versified story of Muhammad Ibn Nāsir's life, as well as of a biographical dictionary on the outstanding men of religion and letters in the Wādī Darʿa, which is the oldes history of the Nāsirīya. Its continuation into recent times is contained in the work of another member of the family, the *Kitāb al-Istiqsā*, by the historian Ahmad al-Nāsirī* (1835-1897). A further claim to scholarly merits the Nāsirīya could found on its library of allegedly some 10.000 volumes. Started by Muhammad Ibn Nāsir, who copied with his own hand manuscripts he was not able to acquire, it seems to have attained some importance already at the time of his son, who erected a special building for the collection. It has never been catalogued. In the course of time most of the manuscripts and books were dispersed and found their way into private hands. Only a modest portion is still shown with pride to visitors at Tāmgrūt.
The Nāsirīya's spiritual and scholarly prestige was reflected in the economic domain. Pious foundations in its favour; the donations of the pilgrims; and the payments by which the caravan trade between

central Morocco and the Sudan bought the safety of the roads across the mountains through the brotherhood's intervention with the tribal chieftains - all contributed to make the Nāsirīya the largest landowner in the fertile Daʿra valley. Simultaneously its political influence increased, flexibly adjusted to the varying degree of authority commanded by the central government, and to the fluctuations of power in the world of the tribes, where arguments of a pecuniary nature consolidated loyalties or appeased hostilities. The same cautious attitude was observed towards the régime of the Protectorate*, all the more so as the partition into two zones with often divergent ideologies and interests divided also the territorial spheres of Nāsirīya following. In the Spanish zone, most of the branches supported, wholeheartedly or not, the rising (1924-1926) of Abdelkrim (ʿAbd al-Karīm*), the 'Emir of the Rif'; and later sided with General Franco when he started his revolution (1936), helping recruit volunteers or informants. In the French zone, in the plains they cautiously changed from a non-committal reserve to an undemonstrative co-operation, whereas in the mountains they conformed themselves to the much entwined lines of conduct of the great chieftains. As soon as the movement for the abolition of the Protectorate gained momentum, a great many Nāsirīya adherents joined one or other of the nationalist parties, and quite a few took up arms in the patriotic struggle for liberation when the deposition of Sultan Muhammad V* (1953) brought the tension to an open outbreak. In the last few decades the loss of some branches to other brotherhoods, mainly the Darqāwa* and Tijanīya*, has numerically somewhat reduced the position of the Nāsirīya, but its standing among the broad rural population and also among some of the urban middle-class groups has remained unimpaired.

NASRIDS, or Banū Nasr, also called Banū al-Ahmar, sultans of Granada (1232-1492), the last Moslem dynasty of al-Andalus*. They were descended from the ancient Khazraj tribe of Medina, some of whose clans had come to Spain with the first Arab conquerors and settled in the area north of Jaén. Upon the collapse of the Almohad* régime in al-Andalus, Muhammad Ibn Yūsuf Ibn Nasr, nicknamed Ibn al-Ahmar (Son of the Red One), gained possession of Jaén, Cadiz, Granada, Algeciras and soon afterwards of Malaga and Almeria. He set up his residence in Granada, called *Qalʿat al-Hamrā'* (Red Castle) which under his successors became the treasure of Moorish art universally known as the Alhambra. He assumed the title of sultan with the epithet *al-Ghālib bi Allāh* (Conqueror by the Grace of God), but had to buy recognition from his powerful neighbour, the King of Castile, by the payment of a heavy tribute. To neutralize this somewhat dangerous suzerainty his son Muhammad II (1273-1302) concluded an alliance with the Moroccan Sultan Abū Yūsuf Yaʿqūb*, on the strength of which a garrison of Morrocan mercenaries remained permanently stationed in Nasrid territory in exchange for the cession of Algeciras and a few smaller but strategically important places. He thus inaugurated a diplomacy of manoeuvering among the ever changing political and military currents in Spain and Morocco, which his successors skilfully continued by sacrificing occasionally a town or portion of land, but regaining them when the constellation was favourable. The Nasrid kingdom survived for 260 years under a line of 21 rulers, while one after the other of the petty Moslem states in al-Andalus succumbed to the Christian reconquerors.

Temporarily some of the Nasrid princes even shook off both the Castilian overlordship and the Moroccan tutelage. There was the warlike Abū al-Walīd Ismāʿīl (1314-1325) who carried his arms deep into Christian territory and took back most of the areas his predecessors had lost. There was Muhammad V who after a short reign (1354-1358) was forced to abdicate by a conspiracy of his courtiers supported by Castile, and found a hospitable reception at the Marīnid* court at Fez, but during his seven-year stay there secured Castilian help and expelled the usurpers. He started the second part of his reign (1365-1390) by a sudden attack on his Spanish allies and, assisted by the Moroccan fleet, captured Algeciras which in the meantime had been conquered by the Christians. Then, exploiting the confused situation in Morocco under boy-sovereigns in the hands of tutors and generals contending with one another for every fraction of power, he came forth as arbitrator but before long was the dictator without whose order or permission nothing could be done and who deposed and installed the sultans at will.

The following hundred years of Nasrid history are an imbroglio of dynastic feuds, treason and bloodshed, and of sultans dethroned by a cousin or nephew whom after a while they again overthrew, so that five of them reigned twice and one, Muhammad VIII, three times between 1429 and 1444. This troubled period saw also the rise and fall of the great family of the Banū Sarrāj (Abencerrajes in Spanish chronicles and novels) and their wholesale murder in a hall of the Alhambra, which is still known by their name. This scene, much interwoven by legend, inspired in the XIXth century the French painter Henri Regnault, enthusiastic admirer of moresque architectural and ornamental airy exuberance, to his 'Execution without Trial' (now in the Louvre). The end of the Nasrids became inevitable when in 1469 through the union of Castile and Aragon a strong Spanish kingdom arose, an event whose historic significance for his dynasty Sultan ʿAlī Abū al-Hasan (Span. Alboacen, 1461-1482 and 1483-1485) failed to conceive. He invaded Spanish territory, was driven back (1482) and overthrown by his own son Muhammad XI Abū ʿAbd Allāh (Span. Buabdil). A year later, Muhammad renewed the incursions into Spain, was likewise repelled and taken prisoner, whereupon his father regained possession of the throne, but shortly afterwards resigned in favour of his brother Muhammad XII al-Zaghall (The Valiant). However, Abū ʿAbd Allāh, released from captivity, revolted against his uncle, occupied part of the city of Granada, so that two sultans reigned simultaneously. This was the moment for the Spanish army to strike, but it took six more years before the decisive blow fell. Muhammad al-Zaghall who in vain had appealed for help to his allies in Africa, surrendered in 1490 and withdrew to Tlemcen. Abū ʿAbd Allāh continued the resistance but on January 2, 1492 the Christian troops made their entry into the last Moslem town on Spanish soil. The last Nasrid

was given asylum in Fez, where he died in 1533. A century later his descendants still lived there, as reported by Arab historians, but in misery and on public charity.
The Nasrids, whatever their merits or demerits as rulers, made Granada a flourishing centre of craftsmanship and trade and one of the most beautiful cities of their time with, it is said, some 500.000 inhabitants. For more than 200 years their court was the splendid meeting place of men of letters and scholars. To this day, their residence, the world-famous Alhambra, speaks of the creative genius of their architects and artisans, whose work counts among the most splendid achievements of Arab medieval civilization.

NATIONAL COUNCIL OF THE ALGERIAN REVOLUTION, generally referred to under the intitials C.N.R.A. (Conseil National de la Révolution Algérienne). It was created by the Summam Valley Congress* in August 1956 with a membership originally of 34, later of 54. When the insurrection expanded, the number of members was increased to about seventy co-opted from among the Army of National Liberation* (A.L.N.) and, at least in principle, from among political groups of all parts of the country. It was supposed, for the duration of the revolution and until a regular National Congress could convene, to reflect the Algerian nation as a whole, and conceived, in a sense, as the parliament of the Front of National Liberation* (F.L.N.). As such it was the sovereign forum which deliberated on all matters of importance and whose decisions, considered as the expression of the people's will, were binding for all. It designated and discharged the members of the supreme executive organ of the F.L.N., the Committee of Coordination and Execution*, which in August 1958 became the Provisional Government of the Algerian Revolution* (G.P.R.A.). The C.N.R.A. established its seat in Tunis but also met in Cairo and Tripoli upon convocation by the Provisional Government. It could, however, assemble also upon the request of two-thirds of its members, especially in the course of the protracted negotiations with France in 1961 and 1962. The atmosphere within its midst was by no means always devoid of frictions rooted in conflicting social and political ideologies, as well as in differences of temperament, background or war-time experiences. The same divergencies did not fail to mirror themselves within the Provisional Government, dividing both policy-making bodies into what roughly may be called 'moderates' and 'radicals' of various shades. These clashes of opinions and convictions, carefully veiled while the struggle for the common goal lasted, came sharply into the open once the fighting ceased and the principles had to be determined on which the new State and its social order were to be founded.

NATIONAL UNION OF POPULAR FORCES, *al-Ittihād al-Watanī li'l-Quwwāt al-Sha'bīya*, generally referred to as U.N.F.P., the initials of its designation in French, 'Union Nationale des Forces Populaires', a political party in Morocco, called into existence in September 1959 as a result of the secession from the *Hizb al-Istiqlāl** of its left-wing members. Their disagreement with its allegedly too conservative and autocratic leanings and its tendency to emphasize the interests of the bourgeois classes at the expense of the broad urban and rural population, began to show soon after the victorious termination of the common struggle for independence. These currents, for a while only vague and inarticulate, found three dynamic organizers commanding a wide popular hearing: Mahdī Ben Barka, one of the founders of the *Istiqlāl* and since its reappearance in 1955 on the political stage its acting secretary, who from humble origin had worked his way up to the position of a college professor; Mahjūb Ibn Saddīq, a former railway worker and secretary-general of the Moroccan Federation of Labour; and Muhammad al-Basrī, a theologian, commonly known as the '*fqih*' (colloquial for *faqih)*, and in the years of the armed resistance against the French Protectorate* the chief of a clandestine fighting force. Others on the upper party level joined them. A foremost rôle owing to their following among the working classes was played by ʿAbd al-Rahīm Būabid (Ibn AbīʿUbayd), a lawyer specializing in questions of labour organization; and another lawyer, ʿAbd al-Rahmān Yūsufī, who had made a name by his success in recruiting and leading his men in the Liberation Army. All efforts to check the refractory movement by excluding, wherever possible, members of doubtful orthodoxy were in vain. It spread and increased in vehemence until finally the *Istiqlāl* Cabinet was forced to resign. Its successor was headed by ʿAbd Allāh Ibrāhīm, in more or less open sympathy with the opposition, as Prime Minister and Minister of Foreign Affairs; and 'Abd al-Rahīm Būabid as Deputy-Prime Minister and Minister of National Economy (December 1958).

One month later the dissenters took the first step towards separation by setting up their own 'autonomous regional committees of the *Istiqlāl* party', which were grouped into a 'National Confederation' by Mahdī Ben Barka, Muhammad al-Basrī and Mahjūb Ibn Saddīq. The break was consummated in September 1959 by the publication of the charter of the National Union of Popular Forces. Its press - two dailies, *al-Tahrīr* (The Liberation) and *al-Ra'y al-ʿAmm* (Public Opinion) - widely circulating especially in the urban working-class quarters, outlined its demands in terms meant to leave no doubt about its determination to pursue them without compromise: on the economic level, systematic and far-going State intervention, possibly nationalization of private enterprise, foreign or national, in the vital sectors of industrial production, marketing and banking; and on the political level, a Constituent Assembly based on general elections, with power to promulgate a Constitution providing for legislation by Parliament, universal suffrage and ministerial responsibility.

It was in particular the political side of these claims, involving radical changes in the structure of a theocratic monarchy, which placed on a totally different plane what so far had been, at least on the surface, the struggle between two rival parties. It turned one of them into an open offender against the prerogatives of the Crown, and the other into their loyal defender. It thus gave to the Istiqlālists in the King's and Crown Prince Hassan's entourage a free hand to accuse the new party and with it the Cabinet whose mouthpiece in fact it was, of sapping the nation's spiritual and secular foundations. Hardly three months after the Party had made its appearance, *al-Tahrīr* was suspended, Muhammad al-Basrī and ʿAbd al-Rahmān Yūsufī were arrested for lack of respect due to the Crown and for having attacked the institutions of the monarchy. There followed other arrests of prominent party members close to the government under the charge - subsequently abandoned - of having plotted against the life of the Crown Prince. Mahdī Ben Barka thought it safer to go abroad while there was still time. He returned in May 1962 and participated in the second party congress, but soon afterwards left Morocco again. The frictions between, on the one hand, the court and the groups enjoying the confidence of the Crown Prince, and, on the other ʿAbd Allāh Ibrāhīm's government by then almost completely identifying itself with the Party, became increasingly critical. Their disturbing effects upon public life began to assume disquieting proportions, and finally the King dismissed the Cabinet (May 1960). The National Union of Popular Forces declined the King's offer to participate in the new Cabinet, presided over by himself with the Crown Prince as Vice-President. It also refused to sit on the Constitutional Council appointed by royal decree for drafting a constitution.

After King Muhammad's* death (February 26, 1961) the Party continued in its attitude of non-cooperation. In the rural districts its influence was affected by the growth of the Popular Movement*, but with large sections of the urban population especially in Rabat, Casablanca, Safi, Marrakesh, Tetuan and Tangier its prestige remained undiminished. Its members abstained from voting in the referendum (December 1962) for the constitution promulgated by King Hassan II, but in the election (May 1963) for the Lower Chamber of the National Assembly it obtained 27 of the 140 seats. In July, two weeks before the municipal elections - of particular significance since two thirds of the Upper Chamber were to be elected from among the municipal councillors - the police claimed to have discovered a conspiracy of high treason and a plot to assassinate the King. Country-wide arrests included twentyone of the elected deputies of the Party, among them al-Basrī and Yūsufī. Thereupon the National Union of Popular Forces decided to boycott the municipal elections. In March 1964 al-Basrī was sentenced to death but, the sentence having been commuted to imprisonment for life, he was pardoned by the King in 1965 and set free together with a number of other party members. Since then cautiously established contacts between the Crown and the Party under the leadership of ʿAbd al-Rahīm Būabid tend to bring about its renewed participation in the country's political life.

NEO-DESTOUR, the only political party in Tunisia since the end of the French Protectorate*, which in the early thirties grew out of a schism in the ageing Destour*, cast it more and more in the shade and at last completely absorbed it. The split was brought about by a group of dynamic young intellectuals led by the two brothers Habīb and Muhammad Bourguiba (Abū Ruqaiba), Salāh Farhāt, Tāhir Safir and Mahmūd Matīrī, most of whom during their university years in

France had shown more or less active left-wing sympathies. Back home, they felt deeply disappointed at the atmosphere in the party, at its lack, in their eyes, of élan, and its remoteness from the real life of the people. In 1930 Habīb Bourguiba, future president of the Tunisian Republic, then 27 years old and at the beginning of a lawyer's practice, started to develop their ideas in the party paper 'La Voix Tunisienne'. Politically coinciding, upon the whole, with those underlying the official party programme - independence, a parliamentary government, full civil rights, no privileges for foreigners - they tended towards changes in the cultural, social and economic structure. They were incompatible, however, with the conservative frame of mind prevailing among the majority of the members: renovation of the educational system in accordance with modern, occidental principles; emancipation of women and their participation in public life; adoption, although selective and gradually, of the ways of thinking, the modes of life and the techniques characterizing western civilization. On this platform were to be rallied the urban and rural masses - small merchants and artisans, peasants and labourers - for collective, tenacious, yet flexible action against the colonial régime and its Tunisian beneficiaries, the big landlords, rich traders and certain notables, whether men of religion or laymen.

The untiring call to this shade of nationalism with its westernizing and democratic tinge and its unconcern with the Pan-Arab ideologies then stirring the Arab world in the East, increasingly widened the gap between the older, conservative members and the younger, progressist opposition which significantly called itself the 'Group of Tunisian Action' *(Jamā'at al-'Amal al-Tunisī)*. In 1934 they founded a paper of their own, *al-'Amal al-Tunisī*, edited by Habīb Bourgiba which formulated their programme in more incisive tones. Notwithstanding a temporary suspension its circulation widened and, coupled with a forceful propaganda by word of mouth, swelled their ranks in town and country. At a party congress in March 1934 a new Executive Committee was elected, consisting exclusively of Bourguibists with Mahmūd Matīrī as president and Habīb Bourguiba as secretary-general. The old Destour continued, but the Neo-Destour, as it became commonly known, thenceforth held the first rôle on the political stage.

In the same year Bourguiba and his closest collaborators were interned in a camp on the fringe of the desert, but the new party did not cease to expand. Immediately upon their release in the spring of 1936 they began to build it up on a broad popular base of local cells - from 65 or 70 they soon increased to some 400 - which were grouped into regional federations with a National Council of 73 elected members at the head. The National Congress, consisting of the delegates of the cells, functioned in theory as the supreme authority, but actually a ten-member Policy Committee, elected by the Congress, exercised an undisputed control. Scout troops and uniformed youth associations spread Bourguiba's word among peasants and workers, while two newspapers, the *'Amal al-Tunisī* in Arabic, and its counterpart in French, the 'Action Tunisienne', carried it into the bourgeois classes. The Congress in November 1937 was attended by seven hundred delegates representing a memberschip allegedly of nigh on 100.000. In the meantime, Bourguiba had gone to Paris and initiated negotiations intended to lead Tunisia to independence in a community of Franco-Tunisian interests, co-operation and friendship, but the negotiations were thwarted by the powerful 'lobby' of the French colons. In Tunisia the disappointment was great, and with it a radical combativeness came to the surface, grew in force and finally escaped the control of the Council until in April 1938 it broke out in heavy street riots with much bloodshed in their wake. The French authorities reacted with the utmost severity. A state of siege was proclaimed, the Party was outlawed and six of its leaders, among them Bourguiba and Salāh Ben Yūsuf, at that time his faithful lieutenant but later his deadly enemy, were arrested and held for trial at a military court. The number of the less conspicuous members who were imprisoned amounted, it was said, to more than 3000 and the Neo-Destour went underground. Upon the outbreak of the war the six were deported to an island off Marseille, and following the defeat of France transferred first to Chalons-sur-Saône, then in short succession confined to three different fortresses, later assigned a residence near Nice and in 1942 released by the Germans to Rome.

Bourguiba was honourably received by the Italian government, but attempts to win him over to the side of the Axis Powers failed. Equally unsuccessful the Germans remained when after the occupation in November 1942 of eastern Tunisia they tried to draw the Party into their camp, although upon the whole Tunisian public opinion proved rather receptive to German propaganda. Still, the Party re-consolidated its ranks and several of its members held seats in a Tunisian cabinet constituted without the agreement - of little weight anyway at that time - of the Vichy-French Resident. In April 1943 Bourguiba was permitted to return to Tunis and given an enthusiastic reception by the people, but when a month later the Allies entered the city the new Free-French governor re-established the colonial régime in its former rigour and forbade all political activities of a nationalist shade.

Bourguiba who had only been saved by American intervention from being accused of collaboration with the enemy, left the country secretly on a fishing-craft for a point on the coast of Tripolitania, whence on foot and by camel he crossed the desert, and having after much hardship reached Cairo set his mind on enlisting international support for the cause of Tunisia. He spoke in public meetings, wrote in the press and established contacts at every level, first in Egypt and then in the other countries of the Arab East, and finally went to America in quest of sympathizers in United Nation circles. Back again in Cairo he kept in close touch with the newly founded Arab League; signed on behalf of his party the Pact of the Arab West*, and for a while was the secretary of the Maghrib Bureau*. However, the manifold conflicting interests and ambitions he had to contend with, further confirmed his conviction that Tunisia could expect the fulfilment of her aspirations only from the pursuit of a realistic, specifically Tunisian policy uninfluenced by pan-Arab theories whatsoever. Much of what in times to come colour-ed Neo-Destourian political philosophy, social and economic orientation - all that for which later the term 'Bourguibism' was coined - had its roots in these years in Cairo. By the end of 1949 he was home again, everywhere acclaimed as the 'Supreme Combatant' for national liberation.

During his absence the Party, with Salāh Ben Yūsuf as secretary-general, officially dissolved but silently tolerated as time went on, recovered its strength and rekindled the national feeling. The Protectorate authorities had meant to calm the increasing restlesness by a programme of administrative reforms allowing to Tunisians a voice - not a very far-reaching one - in the conduct of local affairs, but after a short phase of easing tensions both the Neo-Destour and the clan of the French settlers again hardened their attitude. When Bourguiba returned he found the situation at a deadlock, and thus in March 1950 he reassumed his pilgrimage of propaganda, this time in France. He put forward a formula of 'seven demands' comprising self-government through parliamentary institutions and a freely consented Franco-Tunisian association based on the respect of Tunisian sovereignty and of clearly circumscribed, equitable French cultural, economic and strategic interests. He lectured in political clubs, arranged discussions in academic societies, carefully avoiding an explicit mention of independence as well as any allusion to armed action if France persisted in refusing an amicable settlement, although this alternative was always present in his mind, as shown by his correspondence and his publications. His appeals found resonance and a new Tunisian cabinet was formed in which Salāh Ben Yūsuf and Mahmūd Matīrī represented the Neo-Destour. It was entrusted with the negotiations, while Bourguiba set out for another goodwill campaign which took him to India, Indonesia, Egypt, England, Denmark and after a short stay in Paris to Washington, San Francisco, Rome, Constantinople, again to Paris and finally in January 1952 back to Tunis.

There he found a highly critical situation. The negotiations which had dragged on with many ups and downs were brusquely broken off by France, and at a clandestine party congress no voice of moderation was heard. Everywhere the party cells stirred up protest manifestations and strikes which quickly led to violence and the usual, harsh repressions with wounded and killed and mass imprisonments of party members in their wake. Salāh Ben Yūsuf, at the instance of Bourguiba, flew to Paris to submit a request for intervention to the secretariat of the United Nations. Thus, unlike four of his colleagues in the cabinet, he was able to avoid arrest, escaped into Belgium and thence to Cairo where he represented the Neo-Destour in Arab nationalist organizations during the following three years. Bourguiba, however, displaying to the full his oratory verve, stimulated the crowd to unflinching resistence, but a fortnight after his arrival was assigned with some fifty other prominent Neo-Destourians a residence under police control in the coastal town of Tabarka near the Algerian border, whence two months later they were taken to Ramada in the Algero-Tunisian desert. After a two-months stay there he was deported, this time alone, to one of the small volcanic islands of La Galite, a hundred miles off the coast between Bizerta and Tabarka. In Tunisia, disturbances grew into countrywide organized terror: bands of guerilla fighters (*fellagha**) damaged railway-lines, blew up bridges, set fire to factories and public buildings. The Neo-Destour, or rather what was left of its leadership, remained practically the sole valid mouthpiece on the political plane of public opinion, in whose mind Bourguiba, president in exile, was as present as ever.

When at last the French government saw the need for arriving at an understanding, he was transferred in May 1954 into decent quarters on the island of La Goix on the coast of Britanny, soon afterwards into the Chateau de la Ferté in the region of Orléans and then to Chantilly, near Paris, still under surveillance but thenceforth merely as a matter of form. He communicated with the Party and was in contact with the French Prime Minister; gave interviews to the Press; spoke over the radio and urgently called for an end to violence and for conciliatory attitudes. Throughout the long and intricate discussions in which Muhammad Masmūḏī and Mongi Slim (Mūnajī Salīm) were the official Neo-Destour spokesmen, he advised and guided behind the scene, insisting that the only realistic line of action was one that sought a solution by stages. The first step was a convention which in six voluminous sections and numerous provisos established internal autonomy but explicitly excepted all military matters and foreign relations. As soon as it was initialled Bourguiba left France and on June 1, 1955 held a triumphant entry into Tunis, although under the influence of Salāh Ben Yūsuf, still secretary-general of the Party and back in Tunis, some rigidly pan-Arab groups decried it as 'a step backward' leaving Tunisia's fate inextricably tied to French interests and betraying the ideal of Arab unity. Yet further steps followed in quick succession: approval of Bourguiba's policy and Salāh Ben Yūsuf's expulsion from the Party by a Neo-Destour national congress, held at Sfax in November 1955; the formation of a new cabinet in which the Neo-Destour occupied five of the six seats; a new agreement with France by which Tunisia was to have an army of her own; the solemn proclamation of independence (March 20, 1956), leaving open, however, a number of questions regarding Franco-Tunisian 'interdependence'; another agreement conceding to Tunisia a free hand in international affairs; and finally membership in the United Nations. In the elections for the Constituent Assembly (March 25, 1956) the Neo-Destour carried four-fifths of the votes and one year later more than nine-tenths in the municipal elections. In the following year the Constituent Assembly abolished the monarchy and entrusted Bourguiba, as president of the Party and Prime Minister of the first independent Tunisian government, with the functions of Head of State. On November 8, 1959 he was elected President of the Republic by universal suffrage with an overwhelming majority.

It was in this last phase, which sealed the victory of a thirty-year struggle, that Salāh Ben Yūsuf embarked on a desperate warfare against the Party and its leader, his erstwhile long-time companion in arms. Making his headquarters in Cairo under the banner of pan-Arabism he recruited - presumably with a more than merely moral encouragement from the Egyptian side - an 'Army of Liberation' which continued the familiar guerilla tactics indiscriminately against all that was French and Neo-Destourian. Terrorism reappeared; bands of killers, the 'Black Sword', infested the towns; bombs were thrown against public buildings and the Party's offices; Europeans and party members were kidnapped and murdered; and several plots to assassinate Bourguiba and to overthrow the régime were discovered just in time. Yūsufist propaganda branded the Party's social reform programme as anti-Islamic and its negative attitude towards an Arab union as anti-Arab. It found ways also into the units of the Algerian Army of Liberation* (A.L.N.) stationed on the Tunisian border, and into some political and religious circles in Morocco. Gradually, however, the fighting spirit weakened; the sources of support began to dry up; the Egyptian authorities strongly advised Salāh Ben Yūsuf to depart from Cairo; and the unrest calmed down. Once more, in March 1961, a dramatic meeting in Zürich brought the two enemies face to face but they separated unreconciled. After that, Salāh Ben Yūsuf was no longer heard of until he was found assassinated in a hotel room in Frankfort (August 14, 1961). A few months later a Moroccan political weekly opened its columns to some one-time Yūsufist partisans grouped in a 'National Democratic Front of Tunisia', who in the most vehement tones voiced their opposition to what they called the Neo-Destourian despotism, but without any practical effect. Another group of Yūsufists established its seat in Constantine and, silently tolerated by the Algerian government, carried on an equally violent anti-Bourguibist propaganda in its periodical *Al-Ahrār* but found no larger audience than did its Moroccan counterpart.

In the meantime the Neo-Destour carried out a systematic process of remodelling its structure, designed to secure a far-going concentration of policy-making and administrative authority within its own organization and through it in the machinery of government. Appointed officials replaced the elected bodies at regional level; reliable party members assumed the responsible positions in the trade unions, professional and cultural associations, youth and sport clubs; a party school for training in group leadership has solidly implanted everywhere the party doctrine and party discipline. In the National Assembly and the municipal councils the Party holds incontestable positions; it supervises the press; controls every sector of public life, and steers public opinion. This one-party rule, firmly handled by Habīb Bourguiba, rests on the all-domineering prestige which he commands not only among the enlightened bourgeoisie but also among the broad middle-class and throughout the countryside. In March 1963 the National Council decided on a second reorganization, intended to intensify still further the interpenetration of Party, society and State. By introducing into the membership a distinction between 'militants' representing a political élite, and simple 'adherents', the party base is to be greatly broadened and ramified. The Policy Committee is replaced by a Central Committee of 30 to 40 members, which has to include the Head of State. It elects a Presidential Body of five or six members, the de facto governing organ. A number of Coordination Committees link on a regional level all the cells to one another with the local branches of the various professional and cultural associations, and this whole network with the party leadership. Occasionally there appear, no doubt, internal frictions and divergencies of opinion - twice they resulted in the temporary exclusion from the Party of Muhammad Masmūdī - but it does not seem as if the Neo-Destour would need to fear any rival.

NORTH AFRICAN STAR, *al-Najm Shamāl Ifrīqīya*, generally quoted under its French name 'Etoile Nordafricaine', originally a closely knit labour association founded in 1925/26 in Paris by an Algerian member of the Central Committee of the French Communist Party, ʿAlī ʿAbd al-Qādir, for the protection of the material, social and educational interests of the North African proletariat which populated the slums in the outskirts of Paris and other industrial centers of France. In 1927 it had a new highly energetic young tribune at its head, Messali (Masālī) al-Hajj, a native of Tlemcen, fervently religious and in his younger years an adherent of the Darqāwā* brotherhood. He had served as a soldier in the First World War and after demobilization made a poor living as a labourer in various trades, married a Frenchwoman, and desirous of attaining a higher level of education, became a zealous attender of evening courses at the Sorbonne. Using a natural eloquence, in Arabic as fluently as in French, for orchestrating his propaganda in mass-meetings and through pamphlets, he built up a coherent organization which ran its own paper in French, voicing its very radical demands for social reforms coupled with those for the independence of the North African countries. Dissolved in 1929 under the accusation of subversive activities, the North African Star went underground. In 1933 Messali, assisted by Belkacem Krim (Karīm Bilqāsim), the future Vice-President of the Provisional Algerian Government* (G.P.R.A.), reconstituted it, but it was again banned and its leaders were sentenced and imprisoned for anarchistic conspiration. Released in 1935 Messali resumed his party propaganda, temporarily disguised under the name of National Union of North African Moslems, but having to fear a new arrest thought it safer to exercise the leadership for a while from Geneva through the intermediary of his lieutenants. He returned soon afterwards and implanted the North African Star - or the National Union for North African Moslems - in Algeria, where he was triumphantly received.
In the meantime he had formulated a detailed programme, published in his new journal *al-Umma* (The Nation), designed for all the countries of the Arab West. It emphasized their Islamo-Arab character and demanded their full independence, calling with equal force for universal suffrage, radical land reforms and an agrarian credit system, a modern labour and social security legislation. Within a year of campaigning, however, more and more of the leftist colours faded, and the religious and nationalistic aspects were more and more stressed. In the same measure Messali lost the support he had been given by the French communists, then in the left-wing coalition government of the Front Populaire, averse to the emancipation of any part of the French Empire. In January 1937 the Party was once more declared illegal. Two months later Messali decided to continue his struggle on a new platform, returned to Paris and set up the Algerian People's Party*.

NORTH AFRICAN UNITY AND ACTION FRONT, established at a meeting in January 1952 at Chantilly (France), called by Messali al-Hajj (Masālī al-Ḥajj), the leader of the Algerian Movement for the Triumph of Democratic Liberties* (M.T.L.D.). It was attended by the representatives of a number of nationalist parties in the Arab West, among them Sheikh Brahimi (Ṭālib al-Bashīr al-Ibrāhīmī), president of the Association of the Algerian ʿUlamā'*; Farhat Abbas, the head of the Democratic Union of the Algerian Manifesto* (U.D.M.A.); Muhammad Masmūdī of the Tunisian Neo-Destour*; and Hassan al-Wazzānī of the Moroccan Democratic Party of Independence* (P.D.I.). The 'Front', set up in Cairo with the purpose of uniting all nationalist efforts in Tunisia, Algeria and Morocco, but in fact in competition with the Maghrib Bureau*, stood under the nominal leadership of the old war-lord of the Rif, Abdelkrim (Muhammad Ibn ʿAbd al-Karīm*), after his resignation as president of the latter, yet was actually guided by Sheikh Brahimi. It formulated its aims in a common declaration of its members, but aside from the resonance its demands found in certain left-wing European circles, it obtained no practical results and soon disappeared.

O

OIL AND NATURAL GAS IN THE SAHARA, discovered around 1950 in what at that time were believed to be but moderately remunerative deposits in the vastness of the central desert, are now for Algeria and Libya a factor of vital importance, both as a much needed support of the precarious state finances and by the rôle they are bound to play in their industrial development.
In ALGERIA the first geological surveys were undertaken by the Standard Oil Company of New Jersey and the Royal Dutch Shell, but only the latter, undeterred by the climatic and geographical difficulties, continued prospecting on a major scale. When promising results began to appear, more candidates, in particular from among the 'independent' American oil firms of Texas, turned up and were granted prospecting licences. Also French enterprise, until then a rather hesitant observer, resolutely stepped in and in a short time built up a highly efficient technical and financial apparatus of its own. With a view to protect the national interests, the French government simultaneously had Parliament vote the creation in 1957 of the 'Organisation Commune des Régions Sahariennes' (O.C.R.S.) and in 1958 a 'Code Pétrolier Saharien', and set up the 'Bureau de Recherches de Pétrole' (B.R.P.), each of which became instrumental in regulating outside competition and in restricting foreign operators to a minority partnership with a French firm. By the end of 1958 there were in various types of associations 15 foreign and 22 French companies engaged in surveying, prospecting, drilling and different phases of extraction, whereas of the investments - approximately 1.3 billion Dollars at the end of 1962 - three-quarters were French capital, private or state-owned shares, and foreign participation, in terms of ascertained oil and natural gas reserves, amounted to about ten per cent.
This structure underwent certain modifications through the agreement of Evian (March 20, 1962) which established the guiding principles of the co-operation between France and the thenceforth independent Algerian Republic. The O.C.R.S. was replaced by the 'Organisme Saharien', an autonomous body within the framework of Algerian sovereignty under a Franco-Algerian board of directors. It was put in charge of the study, construction and upkeep of all public works serving the exploitation of the Saharan oil and natural gas as well as of the administrative supervision of the oil concerns in accordance with the 'Code Pétrolier', which, with slight formal adaptations, remained in force. Two departments of the Algerian government, the 'Bureau Algérien des Pétroles' and the 'Direction des Carburants', were to handle matters connected with the technical and financial aspects of Algerian public interests in the oil industry. Further were stipulated, after long and tenacious bargaining, the revenues which Algeria was to derive from oil and natural gas: 1) a royalty of 12.5 per cent of the value on the oil-

NORTH-WEST AFRICA

ATLANTIC OCEAN
MEDITERRANEAN SEA
Ben-Slimane
Ait Amar
Khénifra
Béchar
Essaouira
Kettara
Kenadsa
Djerada
Uixan
Oran
Beni-Saf
Zaccar
Béjaïa
Algiers
Skikda
Tamera
Djérissa
Annaba
Dj. Onk
Hassi R'mel
Hassi Messaoud
Bir Tlacsin
Ohanet
Edjelé
Dahra
Zelten
Berga
En Bazzane
Thara
Tibaradine

MINERALS III

Coal
Oil
Gas
Iron ore

Boundary
Gas pipeline
Oil pipeline
Oil, moved by rail

0 100 200 300 400 Miles

fields of the extracted products; 2) a tax of 50 per cent levied on the companies' profit after deduction of the royalties; 3) the dividends from a stock of shares of three of these companies, ceded by the French government from its own holdings. Within a year, however, this arrangement was found in Algeria, while more or less satisfactory from the strictly financial point of view, inadequate with regard to the possibilities of other substantial contributions of the sub-soil wealth to the country's economic development, and new negotiations became necessary. They centered around two principal Algerian claims: the obligation to be imposed upon the oil concerns to invest the major portion of their benefits in Algerian industrial projects; and majority state-participation in newly founded oil or gas transportation or processing enterprises. To emphasize its demands which met, not unexpectedly, with strong resistance, the Algerian government set up two semi-public institutions, the 'Société Nationale de Recherches et de l'Exploitation de Pétrole' and the 'Société Nationale des Hydrocarbures' for the construction of pipe-lines, refineries and gas liquefaction.

The era of the great Saharan oil development opened with the discovery between 1954 and 1956 of two vast petroliferous zones which were soon to reveal themselves as among the richest in the world. One covers the tracts of desert around the former French camel-corps outpost of Fort Polignac, of mainly archeological interest by its prehistoric rock drawings, until the derricks were springing up on the oil fields of Edjeléh Zarzaitine, Tinguentourine, ʿAin Amenas, El-Adeb Larrache, Ohanet or Tin Fouyé. The second, sixty miles to the south-east of the small town of Wargla, comprises the deposits of Hassi Massaoud, El-Gassi, El-Aghreb, Rhourde-al-Baguel and Gassi-Touil. At the same time there were found, in some cases beneath the oil-bearing strata, enormous pockets of natural gas at Hassi R'mel some 350 miles south of Algiers; shortly afterwards, in the sand-dunes around the oases of ʿAin Salah, Djaret and Hahar-El-Hammar; and, although so far only indicated by boring, near the Tunisian border on the northern outskirts of the basin of Fort-Polignac at Gassi Touil, Mezla, Hassi Touareg, Rhourde-Nousse and Alrar. Altogether the Saharan oil reserves are estimated at close on 800 million metric tons. Production, which amounted in 1960 to 8.5 million tons and in 1961 to 15.5 million, rose in 1962 to 20 million, reached 24 million in 1963 and is expected to attain by 1965, 50 million. For this rapidly growing output the pipelines conveying the crude oil from the Fort-Polignac basin to La Skhira in Tunisia on the Gulf of Gabès, and from Hassi Massaoud to Bougie became insufficient. In June 1963 the 17 concerns operating on the fringe of the Hassi Massaoud area, or rather the T.R.A.P.A.L. (Transport de Pétrole en Algérie), the oil conveying company they had just founded, submitted plans for a line to the new industrial zone of Arzew on the coast near Oran. However, the Algerian government, insisting on, but being refused, the absolute majority in the company, decided in April 1964, after prolonged negotiation with German, American, Italian and British firms, to have the construction undertaken by a British contractor with the help of a loan from the Kuwait 'Fund for Assistance to the Arab countries' and long-term credits supplied by an Arab bank and British concerns, but for the

account of its own government-controlled 'Société Nationale des Hydrocarbures' which will assume the exploitation of the line.
Algeria's great chance, however, in the process of building up an up-to-date national industry lies in the reserves of natural gas. They have not yet been fully determined, but the latest finds seem to justify their evaluation at not very far from 2000 billion cubic metres. In any case they will be sufficient for quite some time to come for the country's own needs and those of its Tunisian and Moroccan neighbours. These are expected to attain, according to a probably somewhat over-optimistic Algerian estimate, in a few years the equivalent of 80 million tons of coal and in 20 years about 100 million cubic metres of gas per year. The common utilization of the Saharan gas resources has indeed been under discussion among the three states since they achieved independence, but in the meanwhile there are still practically unlimited quantities for which Europe offers a ready market. So far there exists only one gas pipeline, which evacuates the deposits of Hassi R'mel to Arzew, Oran and Algiers, and one liquefaction plant at Arzew with a capacity of treating annually one-and-a-half billion cubic metres to be transported by specially adapted ships. Great-Britain contracted for two-thirds, and France for one-third of the output, while Spanish, Italian, German and Swiss industries also appeared as important potential consumers. Thus a number of newly created concerns started to investigate the possibilities of conveying without previous liquefaction large volumes of gas by combining overland and submarine conduits. By the end of 1963 three projects of this type of feeder-line systems were under closer study; one, through Morocco to Tangier and across the Straits to Gibraltar; the second, from Mostaganem on the Algerian coast to the Spanish port of Cartagena; and the third, from Hassi R'Mel to Cape Bon in Tunisia and thence to Marsala in Sicily. Algeria will have to be prepared, however, to meet serious competition in the supply of natural gas to Europe-very soon from Holland, and in not too distant a future from Libya.
In LIBYA promising findings of geological research, started around 1950, resulted between 1953 and 1955 in the demand for prospecting permits by thirteen oil companies, and in May 1957 for the first time in the striking of natural gas in the Fezzan by the Mobil Oil of Canada Ltd. In October the Esso Standard (Libya) Inc. struck oil in western Libya and one year later the Oasis Oil Company of Libya, a subsidiary of the Ohio Oil Company, at about 100 miles from the coast. In June 1959, the Esso reported that at the same distance from the coast a test well at Zelten in Cyrenaica had produced oil at the rate of 17.500 barrels a day from a depth of less than 6000 feet; and in July, that another well not far off was showing a productive capacity of 15.000 barrels a day from a similar depth. In December, the Oasis Oil Company struck oil near the Cyrenaican coast, and the Libyan American Company in the Syrtica Desert. By the end of 1959 altogether eighty-four prospecting concessions had been granted, and some twenty oil-fields were actually under operation by eight companies. A few months later there was awarded for the first time an offshore permit for under-water prospecting in the Gulf of the Sirte. In October 1961 the King solemnly opened the first thirty-inch pipeline connecting the Zelten

oilfields with an oil-loading station at Mars al-Burayqa on the Gulf. Another, ramified pipeline system began functioning in November 1962, and a third one in August 1963, both leading to a new loading terminal on the Gulf at Ras al-Sidr. According to the Libyan Ministry of Petroleum Affairs the quantity of the crude oil produced by 321 wells with a tested production capacity of 470.000 barrels daily amounted in 1963 to 18 million tons as compared with 9 million in 1962 and is expected to attain 35 million tons in 1964.

The revenues accruing to the Libyan Treasury under the Petroleum Law of 1955 consist, aside from the concession fees, in royalties of 12 1/2 per cent of the value of the oil at the well-head from the moment commercial production begins, and in a share in the profit on a fifty-fifty basis after deduction of the cost of exploration and development and an amortization allowance, together at a rate not exceeding 20 per cent. Under the pressure of competion for new concessions several companies spontaneously agreed to more than these legal payments. Thus in some cases the royalties were raised to 17 percent; in others a part of the permissible deductions was reliquinshed; or the government was offered a one-third partnership in the exploitation of newly discovered deposits; or the company declared its readiness to construct at its own expense a petro-chemical plant. Since under the Petroleum Law one quarter of each concession has to be returned to the government at the end of five years from the date of its grant, and another quarter within eight years, and a further third at the end of the tenth year, the government is free to grant a new concession on the surrendered area with the possibility of securing more favourable terms either from the same or from another concessionaire. By the end of 1963 these revenues fully balanced the country's trade deficit.

Principal Concerns operating in the Algerian Oil- and Natural Gas-Industry:

B.R.P. Bureau de Recherches de Pétrole, a French semi-public institution operating through subsidiary companies.

C.A.M.E.L. Compagnie Algérienne du Méthane Liquide - Shareholders: C.O.N.S.H. (50%); S.N.-R.E.P.A.L. (15%); C.F.P.A. (11%); B.R.P. (10%); Air Liquide (7%); French banks (7%).

C.E.P. Compagnie d'Exploitation Pétrolière - Shareholders: B.R.P. (51%); various French investors (49%).

C.F.P. (A). Compagnie Française des Pétroles (d'Algérie) - Shareholders: Compagnie Française des Pétroles (85%); various French investors (15%).

C.O.N.S.H. International Methan Ltd. - Shareholders: Continental Oil Corp. of America; Royal Dutch Shell; Stockyard Corp. of Chicago.

C.P.A. Compagnie des Pétroles d'Algérie - Shareholders: the Royal Dutch Shell (65%); French private investors (35%).

C.R.E.P.S. Compagnie pour la Recherche et l'Exploitation du Pétrole du Sahara - Shareholders: various French investors (65%); Royal Dutch Shell (35%).

El-Paso France Afrique - A subsidiary of the American El-Paso Natural Gas Corp.

'Independent' American Oil Concerns e.g. City Service Company, Sinclair, Philipps G.G., etc.

S.E.G.A.N.S. Société d'Etude du Transport et de la Valorisation des Gaz Naturels du Sahara - Shareholders: S.N.-REPAL (35%); C.F.P.(A.) (35%); B.R.P. (30%).

S.E.H.R. Société d'Exploitation des Hyrdocarbures d'Hassi R'Mel - Shareholders: S.N.-R.E.P.A.L. (51%); C.F.P.(A). (49%).

S.E.M. Société d'Etudes du Méthane Liquide - Shareholders: C.R.E.P.S. (25%); C.P.A. (50%); El-Paso Natural Gas Corp. (8.75%); 'independent' American oil concerns (16.25%).

S.E.M.A.R.E.L. Société d'Etudes de Marchés Européens de Gaz de Hassi R'Mel Transports par Canalisation - Shareholders: Société Commerciale du Méthane Saharien (40%); Gaz de France (40%); B.R.P. (20%).

S.E.T.R.E.L. Société d'Etudes de Transport du Gaz de Hassi R'Mel en Europe - Shareholders: S.E.G.A.N.S. (50%); Gaz de France (50%).

S.M.T. Société Méthane Transport - Shareholders: Several shipping companies (36.6%); French banks (28.8%); S.E.G.A.N.S. (19%); Gaz de France (9.6%); Méthane Liquide, a branch of Air Liquide (5.8%).

S.N.P.A. Société Nationale des Pétroles d'Aquitaine - Shareholders: B.R.P. (50.7%); C.E.P. (7.3%); French private investors (42%).

S.N.-R.E.P.A.L. Société Nationale de Recherches de Pétrole en Algérie - Shareholders: French Government (40.51%); Algerian Government (40,51%); various French private investors (18.98%).

S.O.M.O.S. Société des Monomètres de Synthèse - Shareholders: El-Paso Natural Gas Corp. (50%); Société des Pétroles d'Aquitaine and S.N.-R.E.P.A.L. (together 50%).

T.R.A.P.A.L. Société pour le Transport des Hydrocarbures Sahariens au Litoral Algérien - Shareholders: 15 concerns operating in the area of Hassi Massaoud.

T.R.A.P.S.A. a branch of C.R.E.P.S. for the evacuation of the oil from its oil fields.

Principal Oil Concerns operating in Libya:

Amerada Petroleum Co. of Libya
Ausonia Mineraria Italiana (A.M.I.)
B.P. Exploration Co. (Libya) Ltd.
Compagnia Ricerche Idrocarburi (C.O.R.I.), a subsidiary of the Italian government-owned Ente Nazionale Idrocarburi (E.N.I.)
Compagnie des Pétroles Total (Libye)
Continental Oil Co. of Libya
Elwerath
Esso Standard (Libya) Inc.
Gulf Oil Co. of Libya
Libyan-American Oil Co.
Libyan Atlantic Oil Co.
Libya Shell N.V.

Mobil Oil of Canada Ltd.
Nelson Bunker Hunt Corp.
Oasis Oil Co.
Pan American Libya Oil Co.
Philipps Petroleum Co.
Texaco Overseas - California Asiatic

ORGANISATION SECRETE, also called Organisation Spéciale or Organisation de Sécurité, usually referred to by the initials O.S., set up around 1946 by Muhammad Būdiaf and Husain Ait Ahmad. Originally it was conceived as the militant arm of Messali al-Hajj's (Masālī al-Hajj) Algerian People's Party* (P.P.A.) for the purpose of training revolutionary combat groups and the preparation of terrorist activities. Forcefully inspired by Ahmad Ben Bella (Ibn Ballā) it expanded within a year or two from the region in Oran into Kabylia, where a similar secret organization had come to life under Belkacem Krim (Karīm Bilqāsim), and soon practically all over the northern and eastern regions of Algeria. It laid out stocks of war material including machine guns, explosives, binoculars and first-aid supplies and had its supreme command and chief of sections and subsections.
It is uncertain whether, or to what extent, the O.S. had its hands in the various violent incidents in the course of the electoral campaigns of 1947 and 1948; but in the following two years it was without doubt responsible for several daring terrorist acts which finally led to its discovery in 1950 by the police, the arrest and trial in 1952 of quite a number of its members. Some of the prominent chiefs, however, escaped to Cairo, among them Ben Bella, or found hiding places in the Kabylian and Aurès mountains, whence they continued, each one in his own way, their subversive propaganda. This was a severe blow to the O.S. but by no means its end. In March 1954 a group of them - the 'Nine Historical Chiefs of the Revolution' or 'Club of the Nine' - organized the Revolutionary Committee for Unity and Action* (C.R.U.A.) and from it in turn sprang the leading political organization of the Algerian revolution, the Front of National Liberation* (F.L.N.) whose nucleus consisted of the mass of O.S. adherents. Quite a number of the protagonists found their death in combat, others ended in French prisons, but a few, such as Ahmad Ben Bella, Muhammad Khidr, Muhammad Būdiaf or Lakhdar Ben Tubbal later had their seats in the Provisional Government of the Algerian Republic* (G.P.R.A.).

O.S. see ORGANISATION SECRÈTE

OU or OULD, in Berber names the equivalent of the Arabic *ibn*, son of, possibly the berberized form of the Arabic *awlād*, children (sing. *walad*).

P

PACT OF THE ARAB WEST, concluded in January 1948 in Cairo by the delegates of seven Moroccan, Algerian and Tunisian nationalist parties with the purpose of bringing about combined action for the unconditional recognition of their countries' sovereignty and subsequent negotiations with France for economic, military and cultural co-operation. Particular stress was laid in the pact upon the pan-Arab ideology and the community of the moral and material interests of all peoples of the Arab world. Its sole practical result was the organization of the Maghrib Bureau* in Cairo.

P.D.C. see DEMOCRATIC CONSTITUTIONAL PARTY

P.D.I. see DEMOCRATIC PARTY OF INDEPENDENCE

PARTI POPULAIRE ALGERIEN see ALGERIAN PEOPLE'S PARTY

PARTI SOCIALISTE DEMOCRATE see SOCIALIST DEMOCRATIC PARTY

PARTY KINGS, *Mulūk al-Tawā'if* (Span. '*Reyes de Taifas*'), a term denoting the numerous petty rulers of the city-states and small territories into which al-Andalus* disintegrated, first at the time of the crumbling caliphate of the Spanish Umayyads, then again at the end of the Almoravid* era and finally under the last Almohads*. These miniature potentates came from the midst of the captains of the slave soldiery (*saqāliba**), Arab notables, Berber chiefs of clans or the Mozarab* gentry, who seized power and made themselves independent as soon as the central government began to weaken. Some of them were soon ousted by a more daring rival, but others founded regular, though short-lived dynasties. Their sons and grandsons, heirs to the often considerable wealth which they had ammassed, were lavish builders, munificent patrons of poets and scholars, and frequently distinguished by high cultural refinement. Their residences became intellectual and artistic centres greatly contributing to the splendid efflorescence of Arab arts, letters and philosophy, whose fruits were carried over into North Africa in the days soon to come when al-Andalus became a part of the great Almoravid and Almohad empires. Yet while these 'kingdoms' lasted, they were unceasingly involved in mutual, sterile feuds, with the result that the weaker ones were either absorbed by the stronger ones such as the ʿAbbādids* of Seville, the Dhū al-Nūn* of Toledo and the Hammūdids* of Malaga, or came under the vasallage of the kings of Castile and León until all of them were gradually swept away by the great Christian 'reconquista' of the Iberian peninsula.

THE PARTY KINGS

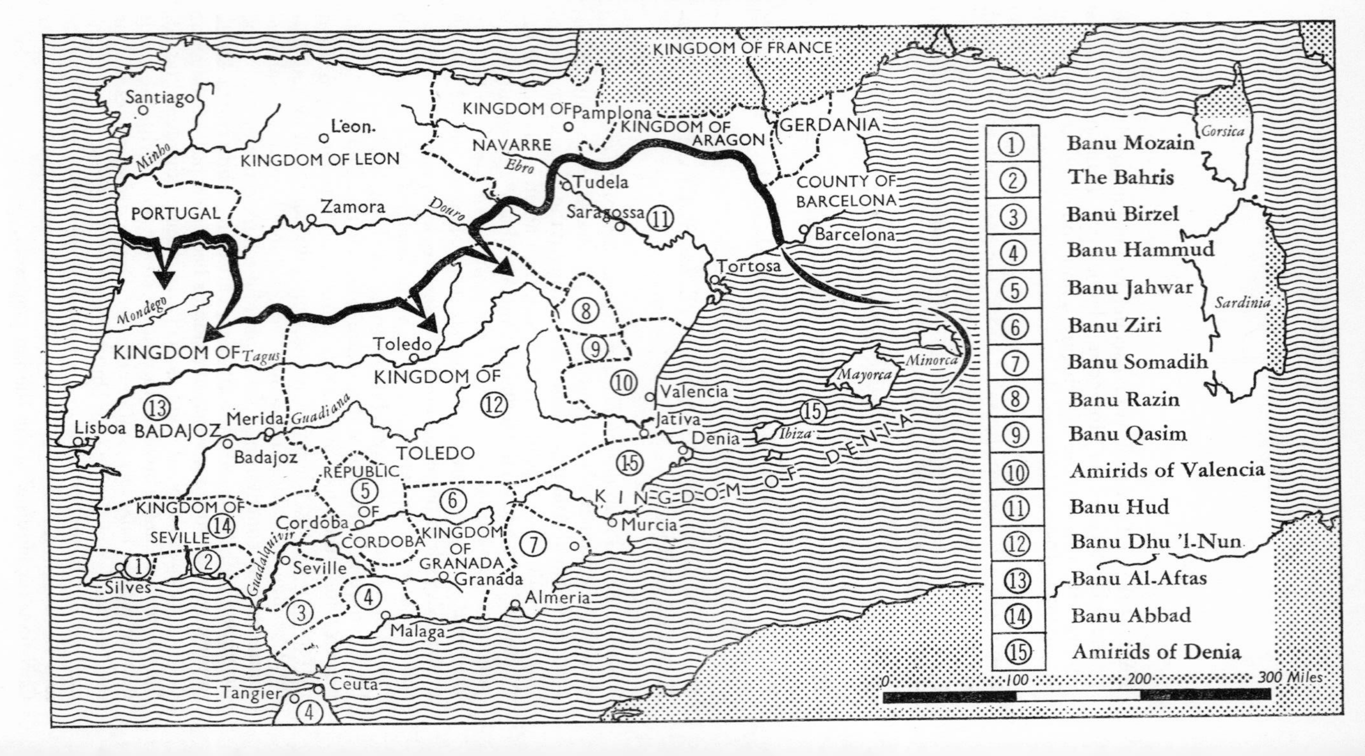

PARTY OF NATIONAL REFORMS, *Hizb al-Islah al-Watanī*, a nationalist party in Morocco, established in June 1936 in the zone of the Spanish Protectorate* by ʿAbd al-Khāliq Torrès (al-Tarrīs) in collaboration with the two brothers, Mahdī and Tayyib Benūna. It pursued upon the whole the same aims as its sister party in the French zone, the Bloc of Moroccan Action*, but, given the different situation, using somewhat different means. The rather favourable attitude towards the Moroccan nationalists of General Franco's new régime and the occasionnally quite substantial subsidies it granted them for their cultural institutions seemed to justify their hope that it would show more understanding for their aspirations than the preceding democratic government. The Party set up cells in all larger localities, founded youth groups, built schools, engaged Egyptian teachers - no adequate Moroccan teaching personnel being at that time available - and sent numerous students to Egypt. Torrès, who owned a printing plant in Tetuan, placed the publications he controlled, the daily *Al-Hayat* (The Life), the politico-philosophical review *Al-Maghrib al-Jadīd* (New Morocco, founded 1935) and the weekly magazine *Al-Rif* at the service of the Party which added (1937) another journal, *Al-Hurrīya* (Liberty, with the subtitle 'Organe du Parti Réformiste National Marocain').
From the beginning the Party moved whole-heartedly in the currents of the Spanish fascist ideology, in accord with popular opinion upon which the German propaganda of the pre-war years had not failed to exercise its effects. Impressed by the first German victories and taking too literally the assurances of German sympathies for Moroccan nationalism, Torrès suddenly changed his policy towards Spain, demanded the immediate abrogation of the Protectorate and went to Berlin to ask for support. He returned empty-handed, and the Party, fallen into disgrace with the Spanish authorities, was forced to reduce its public activities. The German defeat left it near dissolution, and Torrès had to withdraw for a while from political life. Yet his voice continued to carry weight in nationalist circles.
The hour of the Party's renaissance came when the Arab League, with which it was Spanish policy to cultivate cordial relations, invited a Moroccan delegation to the session of its Cultural Committee at Cairo in March 1946. Torrès himself did not participate but exercised decisive influence upon the preparatory work. Shortly before, he had assembled in his home in Tetuan all prominent party members and together with Benūna prepared a complete reorganization without the former fascist leanings, and established close collaboration with the political leaders in the French zone, particularly with those of the *Istiqlāl**. Soon, however, the tolerance of the Spanish authorities again gave way to all sorts of repressive measures, so that most of the leaders found it advisable to move into the safer atmosphere of the international city of Tangier. In February 1948 serious disturbances broke out in Tetuan when it became known that Torrès, returning from a vehement anti-Spanish campaign in Egypt, was refused permission to enter the Spanish zone and had to remain for some time in Tangier. The Party was dissolved and declared illegal, its papers were suppressed and many of its members arrested.
Nevertheless the Party survived and joined (April 1951) the National

Moroccan Front (a temporary association of several nationalist parties), which was to enlist international goodwill for the Moroccan cause at the assembly of the United Nations in New York. Finally the reconciliation with the Spanish authorities was brought about, the party paper *Al-Umma* (The Nation), made its appearance, and the Spanish government subsidized the 'free schools' (Etablissements de l'enseignement libre, *Mahad al-Hurr*) which Torrès had established in the international zone of Tangier. These friendly contacts, greatly furthered by the Spanish-French tensions of those years, were crowned by a visit paid by Torrès to General Franco (February 1953), and left the Party free not only to extend assistance to the *Istiqlāl* leaders banished from the territory of the French Protectorate, but also to expand its own activities into the French Zone. After the deposition of Sultan Muhammad V* (August 29, 1953), it organized active foci of resistance against the puppet sultan Muhammad Ibn ʿArafa and his sponsors. Following the return of Muhahammad V from exile (16 November 1955) and the abrogation of the Protectorate, the Party of National Reforms fused with the *Istiqlāl*.

POPULAR MOVEMENT, *al-Haraka al-Schaʿbīya*, a political party in Morocco, emerging in still inarticulate forms, without program or name, soon after the achievement of the country's independence, originally in the Rif regions among the former fighting forces of the Army of Liberation, but quickly spreading also among the people of the Atlas and the Tāfīlālt. The movement, at this stage, merely embodied the resentment felt by certain groups at the dominating position in the conduct of the affairs of the state, usurped, as as they thought, by the members of the *Istiqlāl** party, who had never participated in actual combat. Apparently actuated by one of the minor lieutenants in the Liberation Army, Haddū Rifī, the leading spirits were Doctor ʿAbd al-Karīm Khatīb, a well-known physician of Casablanca, and Mahjūb Ahardhān, one-time captain in the French army, then governor of the Province of Rabat. The movement rapidly gained a growing number of adherents and even more tacit sympathizers, especially in the army, but made also many powerful enemies. Thus, when in September 1957 it came forth with a party program, it was immediately banned, allegedly because of illegal formation, and Mahjūb Ahardhān was removed from office. Yet the tension in the mountain districts increased, and in October 1958 broke out in serious disturbances on the occasion of the funeral of a commander of the Army of Liberation, assassinated in Fez, which was attended by 5000 tribesmen and solemnly conducted by Doctor Khatīb and Mahjūb Ahardhān. A few days later both of them were arrested. This was the signal for the flaring up of a popular rising directed against the régime of the *Istiqlāl* party, which started at Ulmis, the main town of Ahardhān's native region in the northern slopes of the Middle Atlas, and penetrated southwards into the valleys of the High Atlas as far as the borders of the Sahara. Two months later (24th December 1958) a new cabinet under ʿAbd Allāh Ibrāhīm, head of the left-wing group within the *Istiqlāl*, was constituted, Doctor Khatīb and Mahjūb Ahardhān were set free and the Popular Movement was formally recognized. In the government formed by King Muhammad V* under the vice-presidency of the Crown-Prince

(May 20, 1960), Dr. Khatīb was entrusted with the Ministry of Public Works and Social Affairs, while Mahjūb Ahardhān and six other party members were assigned seats in the Constitutional Council instituted in November 1960. Ahardhān and his collegues, however, resigned when the Council elected the *Istiqlāl* leader ʿAllāl al-Fāsī as Chairman and attributed important functions to a number of other Istiqlālists (January 19, 1961). Subsequently (June 1961) Dr. Khatīb was invested by King Hassan II with the Ministry of African Affairs and Mahjūb Ahardhān first with the Ministry of Defense, and later with the Ministry of Agriculture.

The Popular Movement is primarily a peasants' party which recruits its members mainly from the midst of the small landholders in the mountain areas. It has been expanding, however, more and more into the plains among the mass of the landless labourers as well as into the fringes of the larger towns with their extremely poor, semi-rural slum-settlers who find it impossible to make a living in their villages on the scanty family property. The party wants to secure for the peasantry a measure of influence upon the social and economic policy, adequate to its position as the overwhelming majority of the population. This implies the demand for a more commensurate distribution of public expenditures for roads, schools or medical services for the village; a more effective technical and financial assistance to the village communtiy; and the rational guidance in the establishment of agricultural co-operatives and in the transformation into co-operative exploitation of the ancient and out-of date collective tribal or village properties.

In the parliamentary elections (May 1963) - the first ones held in Morocco - the Popular Movement did not nominate candidates but recommended to its members to vote for those of the new government-sponsored 'Front de la Défence des Institutions Constitutionelles'*.

P.P.A. see ALGERIAN PEOPLE'S PARTY

PROTECTORATE IN MOROCCO, comprising a French and a Spanish zone, the internationally adopted designation of the régime which France by the treaty of Fez on March 30,1912 imposed on Sultan ʿAbd al-Hāfiz (1909-1912) and terminated by negotiations with Sultan Muhammad V* (1927-1961) and the subsequent Declaration of La Celle St. Cloud on 6, November 1955. According to the first article of the treaty it was the purpose of the Protectorate to introduce the administrative, judicial, educational, economic, financial and military reforms judged necessary by France. It recognized explicitly the Sultan's sovereignty over the entire Moroccan territory, but de facto reduced it to a hardly disguised fiction. On the international plane he was bound by all engagements contracted by France in his name, while the validity of those he might enter into on his own initiative was subordinated to previous French consent. Correspondingly restricted was his power of decision in internal matters. A French Resident-General proposed the legislative measures and regulations which he had to promulgate, whereas no other royal decree or ordinance came into force without the Resident-General's approval. This control permeated the entire governmental apparatus, which apparently run by Moroccans, was in fact closely supervised by a French Secretary-General and a hierarchy of advisers and '*contrôleurs civils*' attached to the Moroccan officials, from the vizier down to the administrators of the remotest district.

ʿAbd al-Ḥāfiz does not count among the outstanding figures of his line, but it seems hardly probable that a more far-seeing and energetic sultan could have brought the intricate story of the establishment of the Protectorate to a happier end for his country. France, firmly implanted in Algeria and Tunisia, had for quite a time spared no efforts to secure the same position in Morocco and thus to round off her colonial empire in North Africa. The beginning was made with a policy of 'peaceful penetration', actively sustained by the propaganda of a semi-official Committee of Morocco in Paris and the 'lobby' of powerful banking and industrial concerns. It led to two agreements (1901, 1902) with Sultan ʿAbd al-ʿAzīz (1894-1908) which provided for military assistance in the suppression of the dangerous revolt of Bū Ḥmāra*, and substantial loans guaranteed by the revenues of custom duties and postal services which were placed under French control. By simultaneous arrangements in the international field France conceded in return for a free hand in Morocco an undisputed preponderance to Italy (1902) in Libya, and to Great Britain (1904) in Egypt, while two secret conventions (1904, 1905) with Spain outlined the territorial limits of the interests which Spain on historical grounds claimed to have in Morocco. Just when the issue seemed close at hand this diplomatic game was suddenly upset by a German move in the form of a spectacular speech made by Kaiser Wilhelm II on an impromptu visit to Tangier (March 1905) which in unmistakable terms assured the Sultan of Germany's goodwill and support against foreign covetuousness. It was sufficient to shift for the time being the 'Moroccan question' out of the reach of a French solution and onto the international level of the Algeciras Conference* (1906).

Nevertheless, the presence of French troops in Morocco continued. In the course of spreading tribal disturbances they occupied first Oujda and the north-eastern frontier area; then Casablanca; and gradually the whole Shawīya plain on the Atlantic coast. Germany sought, and found a pretext for sharp diplomatic protests and a well-orchestrated, violent press campaign in an incident created over mass desertions of Germans from the Légion Etrangère, but after an arbitration in favour of France by the International Court at The Hague, an understanding was arrived at which recognized the 'particular interests of France in the consolidation of peace and order in Morocco'. Yet still the anarchy grew there. The French forces extended their operations from Oujda westward into the Mulūya valley and upon Sultan ʿAbd al-Ḥāfiz's request for help, entered Meknès and Fez, while Spanish troops on the strength of a new agreement (1910) with the Sultan occupied the region of Larache and Qasr al-Kabīr. The moment appeared opportune for Germany to build up her own African empire by way of a colonial bargain, and as a demonstration of firmness the gunboat 'Panther' was dispatched to Agadir (July 1911). In November the bargain was made. Germany was given access to vast regions on the Congo and to the Cameroons; and France freedom of action in Morocco, on condition that commercial equality was preserved. The other signatory Powers of the Act of Algeciras consented, except the United States which insisted on special terms, and Sultan ʿAbd al-Hāfiz, left alone face to face with France, had no choice but to sign the treaty of Fez. Thus the French Protectorate was in due form established.

There remained the secret understanding with Spain of 1904 and 1905. It was embodied, without the Sultan's participation, in a new convention (November 27, 1912) which became the legal basis of the Spanish Protectorate, delimited its area - 8500 square miles as compared with the 157.000 square miles of the French zone - and determined its full administrative, economic and financial autonomy. International agreements concluded by France in the name of Morocco were not binding for the Spanish zone without the consent of Spain. The Sultan appointed as his representative *(khalīfa)* a Viceroy holding by delegation sovereign powers, but this appointment was restricted to a selection between two candidates which the Spanish government designated. The *khalīfa* with a Council of 12 Moroccan notables, the Grand-Vizier and several ministers with their seat in Tetuan, headed, under the supervision of the Spanish High Commissioner, a half-Moroccan, half-Spanish system of administration. Spanish liaison-officers *(interventores)* connected it with a purely Spanish counterpart responsible directly to the High Commissioner, which functioned as actual government. Diplomatic relations, military matters and internal security were exclusively in the hands of Spain. The contacts between the Spanish and French Protectorate authorities were upon the whole smooth, although in France there were at all times voices which took care not to let it be forgotten that Spain's position in Morocco rested on agreements with France and not with the Sultan. Spain, on the other hand, recognized the independence and unity of Morocco such as it resulted from the joint French-Moroccan declaration of La Celle St. Cloud, only after prolonged negotiations with the Sultan in a separate declaration signed in Madrid on April 7, 1956 by Sultan Muhammad V and General Franco.

The interpretation given in France and in Spain to the flexible formula of the Protectorate varied with the varying constellation and interaction in public life of the political, military, financial and ideological trends: a title to permanent annexation or mandate for a temporary co-sovereignty; a mission for a sort of paternalistic guidance to cultural and technical progress or an instrument for economic exploitation at the highest possible profits; or, as a rule, a combination of all of this. To most of the Moroccan people it was, in the words of a French observer, 'the sale to the Christians of a part of the land of Islam', and they took up arms against the foreigner not yet, as a few decades later, in the name of national liberation, but under the flag of the Holy War *(jihād)*. Well over twenty years of hard fighting were necessary to master the tenaciously resisting mountain tribes and such fierce warlords as Abdelkrim (ʿAbd al-Karīm*), the 'President' of the 'Rif Republic', or the 'Mahdi' Ahmad al-Hība who had taken the place of his father, the warrior-mystic Mā' al-ʿAinain*. At the same time an adroitly calculated dispensation of favours secured the allegiance of some of the great feudal lords such as the house of the Glāwa* or of families of old scholarly and reli-

gious prestige such as the Kattānī*, and gradually the cautious neutrality of the religious brotherhoods*.
The complex aspects of the Protectorate régime find their reflection in the widely different valuation of the social, cultural and economic results it produced. It has certainly undisputed achievements to its credit, especially in the French zone thanks to the spadework done by its first Governor-General, the broad-minded and perspicacious marshall Lyautey: construction of roads, bridges and railways; irrigation works and electric power plants; medical and hygienic services; and an administration and fiscal organization which definitively effaced the distinction between *bilād al-makhzan** and *bilād al-sība*. Although primarily designed with a view to the consolidation of the authority of the protecting Power, it all took the country a good step forward along the lines of a general development. Yet there were other features which evoked bitter criticism on the Moroccan side. There grew up, planned for a wealthy European population, new town sections with tree-bordered avenues, churches and schools, modern apartment buildings and well-equipped shops, gardens and sports grounds; but separated by a distance of sometimes two to three miles, there stood, like another world which they were not to meet, the ancient Moroccan city behind its medieval walls, overcrowded, nearly untouched by improvements and with an ever growing maze of miserable huts and petrol-can shacks in the outskirts. And there remained, left to themselves, the antiquated Moroccan schools, far too few in the towns, still less in the villages, with old-fashioned teachers and thoroughly inadequate classrooms, for which the only reform considered advisable was the teaching of French, or Spanish. The instruction in these languages was well taken care of, so that today they are among the urban population quite fluently spoken and understood. Super-imposed on this rudimentary educational structure were a few colleges and institutions of higher training based on French - or Spanish - curricula and intended for a social élite and, though much later, also for the sons of other carefully selected families, whose upbringing in an occidental cultural atmosphere was meant to produce a young intelligentsia of advocates and supporters of the foreign régime. The foundation of a private, Moroccan school on whatever level depended upon a special permission granted very reluctantly, and only if the programme of instruction followed strictly the French or Spanish pattern. A completely free field, however, was enjoyed, as a French author termed it, by 'the captains of industry whose lieutenants were generals', and, he might have added, all those who were permitted to acquire vast estates of the best land practically on their own terms. Yet no other mistake of the Protectorate Powers was as serious as their misjudgement of the forces that finally would be released by the united, nation-wide struggle for emancipation from the foreign tutelage. The cost of their mistake was heavy before they realized that the concepts and methods of an anachronistic colonialism would have to give way to a policy of economic and cultural co-operation.

PROTECTORATE IN TUNISIA, the relationship, very closely resembling colonial rule, between France and Tunisia from 1881 until

1956. The diplomatic background of its beginning was the accord reached at the Congress of Berlin (1878) among the Great Powers, which allowed France to realize her long-pursued aim of integrating her financial and economic preponderance in the Regency of Tunisia with an internationally recognized political structure. Thenceforth events moved quickly: a trivial raid of some Khumir tribesmen across the Algerian border (1880); two French army groups, one which landed at Bizerta, and the other which penetrated into the area of Le Kef; an ultimatum to Bey Muhammad as-Sadoq (al-Sādiq); and the conclusion on May 12, 1881 of the treaty of Kassar Said (also called of The Bardo). This treaty, which introduced the term 'Protectorate' into the political vocabulary, stipulated that France would assume the protection of the Bey, the dynasty and the State from all dangers which might arise, as well as the protection in foreign countries of Tunisian nationals and Tunisian interests; that consequently the French army might occupy all points considered essential for the preservation of internal order and for the security of the frontiers and coasts; and finally that the Bey would not accomplish any act of international character without a previous understanding with France. As a result, the French Governor-General representing the French governement was appointed Tunisian Minister of Foreign Affairs, and the French Commander-in-Chief invested with the functions of Minister of War. The next step was the convention signed on June 8th, 1883 at La Marsa by which the Bey bound himself to introduce such administrative, judicial and financial reforms as were considered advisable by the French government; nor to contract any loans on behalf of the Regency without its authorization.

According to the official French interpretation the Bey - His Royal Highness, Pasha, Bey, Possessor of the Kingdom (or Regency) of Tunis - remained the absolute monarch, responsible to God alone, who by accepting the ensemble of those clauses had not renounced any of his sovereign rights but only delegated them in part, temporarily and for indefinite duration, to France for the sake of expert guidance in the conduct of the affairs of the state and the supervision of the apparatus of government. However, on its way of translation into practice, this theory of guidance and supervision became the principle that the Bey had to take all legislative and executive measures which the Governor-General recommended, and that the latter's approval was prerequisite to the validity of those which he took on his own initiative. On this basis the Protectorate authorities set up a complex, double system of government: Tunisian, on the one hand, and French on the other, both closely interlocked, but the latter embodying its actual exercise and the former hardly more than reflecting a semblance of influence.

The process, at least at the beginning, went on without particular frictions. By a series of decrees the Bey broke up the traditional concentration of all administrative powers in the hands of the Grand Vizier and his immediate collaborator, the 'Vizier of the Pen'. Instead were created individual directorates and ministries, each one under a vizier who was either a high French civil servant or a Tunisian with a French adviser, and all staffed on the upper levels exclusively, and on the lower levels for the most part, with French officials. The Grand Vizier, or, as he thenceforth was referred to, the Prime Minister, was supposed to coordinate the activities of the Viziers - called Ministers - and presided over the Cabinet Council, but his actual functions were never clearly defined, so that his prestige depended primarily on his personality. On the regional and local planes the governmental structure was left unmodified. In the towns and the rural districts, the sole responsible agents of the central authority were the caids *(quwwād* sing. *qā'id**), appointed by the Bey and assisted by a number of scribes for the discharge of their administrative and judicial duties and in particular the collection of taxes and maintenance of public order. As intermediaries between them and the people stood the sheikhs, elected by the notables in every village and town quarter, subject to confirmation by the Bey. This pattern held also room for communal councils, but on a very small scale and with very restricted competencies: one in Tunis whose members were elected, and five in rural communities whose members were appointed by the Bey. Of equally not more than symbolic significance was the so-called 'Grand Council', created in 1922, repeatedly remodelled and finally consisting of a French and Tunisian section, each of 53 elected members. This was to be consulted on matters of fiscal, economic and social bearing. Yet the factor which determined, centralized, directed and superintended the operation of this governmental machinery was the French Secretary-General. Officially attached to the Prime Minister, but responsible only to the Governor-General, he was at the head of a wide-spread hierarchy of French experts, advisers and 'Contrôleurs Civils' whose voice was decisive in every department and every office from top to bottom.

Within this political and administrative framework, French economic ambitions soon found remunerative opportunities in the spheres of agriculture*, mining* and trade. Between 1892 and 1906 some 250.000 acres of crown domains and domains of the state - the two were difficult to differentiate - were allotted by way of sale or long lease on easy terms to French settlers, individuals and large concerns. Owing to the facilities offered by a government-controlled 'Fond de Colonisation' the French holdings had increased by 1914 to about one million acres. Liberally granted financial assistance by a public mortgage-loan institute, the 'Caisse Foncière', made possible large-scale investments: experimental stations, motorized equipment or local irrigation installations, introduction of modern methods of cultivation, plantation of olive and fruit trees, and of vineyards which in 1881 covered a surface of 2500 acres and in 1914 of about twenty times as much.

Along similar lines moved the exploitation of mineral resources, an exclusive field of French enterprise. From the beginning of the extraction until 1913 the annual output of the phosphate deposits rose from 70.000 metric tons (1902) to two million metric tons; of iron ores from 98.000 tons (1908) to 590.000 tons; and of zinc from 10.000 tons (1902) to 60.000 tons. The situation was inverse with regard to industry*. From the point of view of influential French industrial and banking circles it was far more profitable to keep the Tunisian market open to

French textiles, paper, glass and all sorts of small machinery and metalware than to encourage such production in Tunisia and thus promote competition. A de facto French monopoly of the import of manufactured goods and of the export of agricultural and mining products became within a short time the dominant feature of Tunisian over-sea trade. It was borne for the main part by French shipping and handled by the ports of Tunis, Sousse and Sfax, constructed between 1888 and 1899 by French engineering firms and controlled by French capital, while Bizerta was built up to a naval base of prime strategic importance. Some groups from among the intellectual youth perceived from the very beginnings the final aims of this policy intent to turn their country, if not in name yet in fact, into a French colony. Their first reaction took shape in a still loose association, the so-called Mouvement Bourgeois de Tunisie*, which in the first years of this century crystallized into the first Tunisian nationalist organization, the Young Tunisia Party*. However, in French eyes, the carefully elaborated and steadily strengthened pattern of government had lost nothing of its efficicacy and served almost unaltered as model for the organization of the Protectorate in Morocco* in 1912. France, without doubt, is fully entitled to claim as her merit - and the Tunisians do not fail to acknowledge it - much of the spadework accomplished during her presence and on her initiative in the improvement of public education, hygiene, social welfare, public security and general cultural advancement. Yet it took long years of embittered struggle, many victims and great material losses, reflected in the party history of the Destour* and Neo-Destour*, before she realized that the colonial régime was out-dated and no longer tenable. On June 3, 1955 a Franco-Tunisian convention was signed which laid down the terms of internal autonomy. After further, protracted negotiations full independence was proclaimed on March 20, 1956.

PROVISIONAL GOVERNMENT OF THE ALGERIAN REPUBLIC, usually quoted under its initials G.P.R.A. (Gouvernement Provisoire de la République Algérienne), the Algerian government-in-exile and executive organ of the Front of National Liberation* (F.L.N.), which made itself known for the first time in a proclamation of September 19, 1958 and remained in office, at least nominally, until August 1962. It was in fact the enlarged and renamed Committee of Coordination and Execution* (C.C.E.) and like it responsible to the 'parliament' of the revolution, the National Council of the Algerian Revolution* (C.N.R.A.) which designated, and could dismiss, its members by a two-third majority. At the time of its creation it was presided over by Farhat Abbas, and consisted of sixteen ministers and secretaries of state, but among them four *wilaya* (district) commanders of the Army of Liberation* who were permanently engaged in action in the field, and five of the nine 'historical chiefs' - Ben Bella, Ait Ahmad, Būdiaf, Khidr and Bitat - who were in French captivity. It was immediately recognized by Tunisia, Morocco, the United Arab Republic, Iraq, the Sudan, Communist China, Pakistan and soon afterwards by Guinea, Ghana, Liberia, Ethiopia and Mali. In December 1959 the

C.N.R.A. reduced it to ten members, but its various departments rapidly expanded and a year later occupied several well-sized buidings in the central quarters of Tunis. By then it had spread a network of official and unofficial agents abroad as well as an efficient system of espionage and counter-espionage. Through an up-to-date broadcasting station it maintained communication with the fighting forces 'in the interior' and last but not least a steady flow of propaganda. Its vice-premier and minister of foreign affairs, Belkacem Krim, the only one of the 'historical chiefs' still alive and at liberty, travelled to China, deliberated with Kruschev in Moscow, and headed the Algerian mission to the United Nations in New York.

In the course of the protracted peace negotiations with France the majority of the C.N.R.A. found Farhat Abbas too moderate, and his attitude too much tinged by 'bourgeois' concepts, so that after a twenty-day session at Tripoli he was replaced by Ben Yūsuf Ben Kedda, one of the F.L.N.'s left-wing protagonists and a convinced advocate of Fidel Castro's socio-economic order which he had observed functioning on a visit to Cuba. When at last the end of the struggle came in sight and the five imprisoned leaders were released, the G.P.R.A. held its first plenary meeting in Rabat on March 22, 1962. Thenceforth, however, all sorts of frictions in its midst, rooted in divergent political, social and economic ideologies, differences in character and education, and contradictory personal ambitions, which had been kept in check while the war was on, did not take long to come into the open. They found their echo in the C.N.R.A., in the army and among the former guerilla fighters, and soon took a highly critical turn. By the end of June the split could no longer be bridged: Muhammad Khidr resigned and Ahmad Ben Bella abruptly left Tunis, while the commander-in-chief, Colonel Būmedienne, whom Ben Kedda had deposed, was in hardly disguised insurrection. On the 3rd of July the G.P.R.A. made its solemn entry into Algiers, but the two dissident ministers were absent, and although it was given an enthusiastic reception by the city crowds it had practically lost all authority. Three weeks later Ben Bella, Khidr, Būmendjel and some of their adherents supported by Colonel Būmedienne and a number of the tribal chieftains, announced from their headquarters at Tlemcen the creation of the 'Political Bureau' as the new directing body of the F.L.N. Belkacem Krim and Muhammad Būdiaf with some Kabyle notables, however, established their seat at Tizi-Ouzou in the Kabylia and prepared an organization of armed resistance against their 'Benbellist' opponents. Last-minute attempts at bringing about a compromise and to reconstitute the cabinet failed, and on the 7th of August Ben Kedda in the name of the G.P.R.A. - or what of it was still in existence - turned over its prerogatives to the Political Bureau. On September 29th 1962, the newly elected Algerian National Assembly designated the first governement of the Algerian Republic with Ahmad Ben Bella as Premier.

P.S.D. see SOCIALIST DEMOCRATIC PARTY

Q

QĀDĪ IBN al-, AḤMAD IBN MUḤAMMAD, a Moroccan man of letters, historian, biographer and poet (1552-1615), descended from a reputed family of theological scholars whose members for generations had held high administrative and religious functions. Aḥmad Ibn al-Qāḍī studied in Marrakesh and Fez, then undertook the pilgrimage to the Holy Cities and prolonging his stay in the Arab East joined the circles of the then best-known savants in the various centres of learning. He returned to Morocco at the time of the great victory over the Portuguese in the so-called Battle of the Three Kings* (1578) and the proclamation of Sultan Abū al-ʿAbbās Aḥmad al-Manṣūr* (1578-1603) who was to be thenceforth his most liberal patron. A few years later Ibn al-Qāḍī set out again for a voyage to Egypt, but the ship was captured by Spanish or Portuguese pirates and he was made prisoner, losing all the notes he had taken along, and suffering, as he relates, great hardship, until he was ransomed by the sultan. Having been invested for a time with the office of a cadi in Salé and in Marrakesh, he subsequently took residence in Fez, where he spent the rest of his life engaged in teaching. His tomb is in Fez near the *Bāb al-Gīsa (Bāb ʿAjīsa)*.

Most of the fourteen works by Ibn al-Qāḍī's pen are known today only by their titles. One among those that have been preserved is an eulogistic biography of Sultan al-Manṣūr, inspired by the author's gratitude for his rescue from the hands of the pirates, but neither of particular literary nor historical interest. What little of original, factual information it contains, was carefully selected and used by al-Ifrānī* in his *Nuzhat al-Hadī*. Of real value, also from a modern point of view, however, are his two extensive biographical dictionaries. One is the *Durrat al-Hijāl fī Ghurrat Asmā' al-Rijāl* (appr. Biographies of the famous Men), a compilation of the celebrities in the Islamic countries, which continues down to the beginning of the XVIIth century the well known work of the Syrian biographer Ibn Khallikān (1211-1282), the *Wafayāt al-Aʿyān*, and is based on information Ibn al-Qāḍī collected during his stay in the Arab East. The second is the *Jadhwat al-Iqtibās fī man Halla min al-Aʿlām Madīnat Fās* (appr. Biographies of the Visitors of the City of Fez) which consists of a historico-topographical description of Fez; and a collection of biographical studies, arranged in alphabetical order, of the outstanding men of letters and scholars born in Fez or having lived there from the days of the Marīnids* down to his own time.

QĀDIRĪYŪN al-, a family of sharīfian notables in Fez, immigrated from Granada in the early XVth century, which in the last two to three hundred years has occupied a noteworthy place in Moroccan intellectual life. Among those who contributed to the building up of the family's prestige count in particular the historian Muḥammad al-ʿArbī (1646-1694) and his brother ʿAbd al-Salām (1638-1698), the former regarded as one of the foremost Moroccan genealogists. Besides numerous didactic poems, a genre that was then much in vogue, and some treatises on the lives and miracles of certain popular saints, he left a comprehensive study on the sharīfian families of Fez, including all their major and minor branches in the country, *al-Durr al-Sanī* (abridged title), which is still a primary source of information on Moroccan history. His achievement was equalled by his grandson Muhammad Ibn al-Tayyib (1712-1773), a saintly man devoted only to prayer and scholarly efforts, refusing all honours and only resorting to a modest office when forced to provide for the necessities of daily life. He wrote on a considerable number of theological, hagiographic and biographical subjects, but his great work is a dictionary of the famous men of the XVIIth and XVIIIth centuries in the world of Islam. It concentrates on Morocco, and as a kind of background material gives accounts, year by year, of the principal political events. It exists in two versions, which show only slight difference, the *Nashr al-Mathānī* etc. (appr. The Perfume of the Koranic Verses) and the *Iltiqāt al-Durar* etc. (appr. the Fishing of Pearls) the former partly translated into French (first by A. Graulle and Maillard, then by Michaux-Bellaire, Paris, 1913 and 1917), testifying both to its author's conscientiousness in the elaboration of his source material, and no less to his piety by the profusely interspersed moralizing exhortations, which make its reading somewhat difficult.

QĀ'ID, plur. *quwwād*, by occidental authors often spelt *caid*, originally meaning a leader in the widest sense of the word, but soon restricted to that of a military chief as already in the early times of the ʿAbbāsid caliphate for the commander of a body of a hundred soldiers (cf. the centurio in the Roman-Byzantine army). In the Arab West, *qā'id* became the title, on the one hand, of an officer of the highest grade in the military hierarchy, e.g. *qā'id al-aʿinna*, general of cavalry, or *qā'id al-bahr*, naval commander; and, on the other hand, of a high-ranking official invested simultaneously with military and civil functions, such as the governor of a province or of an important fortified place. In the larger cities the authority was occasionally divided between two *quwwād:* one, who exercised the command in the district of the fortifications proper, the *qā'id al-qasaba*;* and the second, who held the executive power in the civil sections of the town, the *qā'id al-madīna*. The residence of these officials, the *dār al-qā'id*, often also served as the main prison in their territory. Under weaker sultans a *qā'id* once in a while acquired far-reaching influence - and considerable wealth - and even succeeded in making his office quasi-hereditary during a generation or two, but by far more frequent were the cases of sudden disgrace followed by imprisonment and even execution. Towards the end of the Middle-Ages, when the enlistment for the sultan's army of Christian mercenaries, mainly Aragonians and Catalonians, had become an established practice, the *qā'id* commanding this soldiery, as a rule, was appointed by the King of Aragon or the ruler of Catalonia to whom between half and three-quarters of his pay - the amount was determined by diplomatic negotiations - had to be turned over. Christians or Christian converts to Islam *(ʿulūj* or *āʿlāj*, sing. *ʿilj)*, either adventurers seeking their fortune in the sultan's service, or former captives of pirates, frequently attained the position of a *qā'id* in the army or as commanders of the sovereign's body-guard.

In Algeria under the Turkish régime the *qā'id* was the civil, military and judiciary authority of a district, appointed by the Bey* usually from among the Turkish notables. He was especially responsible for the entry of the taxes, a task for the discharge of which he depended, however, greatly upon the chiefs of the tribes in the area. In Morocco, as time went on, the function of the *qā'id* consisted also mainly in the collection of taxes and in the recruitment among the tribal population of the sultan's mounted body-guard, but gradually lost its former significance. Towards the end of the last century the *qā'id* appears as a kind of representative of the central government attached to the chieftains of the larger tribes. In the years of the Protectorate* he was submitted to close French or Spanish control, and thus vanished whatever of his former prestige had remained. In the present system of Moroccan public administration, which was worked out by gradual reforms since the achievement of independence, the *qā'id* is a rural district official subordinate to a 'super-*qā'id*' in the hierarchy of the Ministry of Interior. A subsequently organized '*qā'id* school' aims at the theoretical and practical training of these civil servants for present-day government tasks. In Tunisia, the *qā'id* was in charge of the collection of taxes and of certain administrative and judicial functions within his particular territory until the re-organization of the public administration in 1955 assigned his duties to various specialized government departments.

QARAWĪYĪN al-, the Great Mosque of Fez, one of the largest, most famous and, judging from descriptions and photographs of the interior - non-Moslems are not admitted - most beautiful sanctuaries of Islam. Its oldest parts were built between 859 and 862 on a piece of land donated by Fātima Umm al-Banīn, the daughter of a wealthy merchant, Muhammad al-Fihrī al-Qayrawānī. He had left his home-town al-Qayrawān for Fez and settled in the quarter of the Qayrawānians, so-called after the emigrants from the Aghlabid* capital who in the days of Idrīs II* (†828) had made their home there. The original bare and primitive structure was later several times enlarged and splendidly adorned until it could hold some 20.000 worshippers under its roof supported by 270 marble and porphyry columns. It was the pride of all Moroccan dynasties to see their names inscribed on the walls of its prayer hall as the munificent contributors to its enrichment, and have their biographers praise the works of art which were their share - the fourteen gates covered with raised pattern in bronze relief; elaborate chandeliers of wrought brass; a hundred astronomical clocks; a richly sculptured marble fountain-basin; pavillions in the courtyard resembling those in the Court of the Lions in the Alhambra of Granada; a *mimbar* (preacher's pulpit) of carved and inlaid wood; and many other pieces counted among the best specimens of Arabic craftsmanship.

The Academy connected with the mosque held for many centuries an outstanding rank in the intellectual life not only of Morocco but everywhere in the Arab world and made Fez what may be called the 'university town' of the Arab West. Favoured by the patronage of the rulers and fructified by the long, intimate cultural relations between Morocco and al-Andalus*, there flourished theological and philosophical speculation and encyclopaedic scholarly activities embracing practically every branch of contemporary science. With the decline of the Golden Age of Arabic research and learning, however, the flow of independent study came to a standstill at the Qarawīyīn, just as it did on the seats of higher knowledge in Tunis, Cairo or Baghdad. The output of books was as great as before, if not greater, but with rare exceptions was confined to compilations and summaries of earlier works without adding anything new, and to a wide range of biographical writings, practically reduced to enumerations of data and events. The profane sciences were abandoned, and in the field of theology ruled a sterile formalism. Teaching came to mean the recitation by the professor (*ʿālim*, plur. *ʿulamā'*) of a few time-honoured texts which the student (*tālib*, plur. *tullāb*, coll. *tolba*) memorized until after five or six years he received - without examination - a certificate (*ījāza**) stating what lectures he had attended, what books he had read, and attesting that thenceforth he was qualified to teach in his own name. His board and lodging was provided for by pious foundations, and instruction remained free as before. The career, however, which stood open to him was in the great majority of cases that of a preacher (*khatīb*) and imam (leader in prayer) at one of the smaller mosques, or teacher at a primitive Koranic school (*maktab*) or of a minor clerk in a public office, while the *ʿulamā'* had to supplement their meager remuneration by serving as cadis, muftis and court or government officials. Yet nursed by the esprit de corps of professors and graduates the prestige of the Qarawīyīn as the focus of all wisdom and the bulwark of orthodoxy continued undiminished, and public opinion shared without questioning the conviction of the circles presiding over its destiny that any innovation whatsoever would open the doors to the materialism of the West and undermine the ethical foundation on which Islamic society rested.

From the beginning of the XIXth century onwards there arose now and then a voice suggesting a loosening of the rigid traditionalism, but only to be soon again silenced, until the introduction under Sultan Mūlāy al-Hasan (1873-1894) of the lithographic reproduction of manuscripts, and with it of the use of some kind of text-books, marked the first step towards a modernization of the method of instruction. A few more decades still went by until also its spirit began to reflect the ideas of enlightened religiousness, which emanated from the great Salafīya* reform movement and permeated the intellectual Moslem world from Syria to Morocco. These ideas had ardent advocates among the younger groups of the professorial body - in their foremost ranks ʿAllāl al-Fāsī, the future leader of the Istiqlāl* party - and were zealously propagated by a growing number of alumni and students, but the troubled period of the French Protectorate* did not provide a climate for more than superficial changes. When, however, in the new era of independence the lines were traced in accordance with up-to-date principles for the redevelopment of the entire national system of public education, the Qarawīyīn, too, celebrating its eleven hundredth anniversary, found the way paved for deep-going modifications of its pedagogical structure. Their basic feature lay in the division into two sections: one, a modern faculty of Islamic theology and jurisprudence; the other, a regular high school with an annex for girls, preparing for studies on university level. At the same time the students' activities were moved from the mosque into new premises with adequate class-rooms and dormitories in the midst of a campus with sports grounds. Only the collection of some 1600 ancient manuscripts has remained in its venerable surroundings.

QASABA, colloquially kasba, and in this spelling usually rendered in occidental texts, a type of military architecture in the Arab West, which originated in the Almohad* empire (1133-1269) and subsisted in its traditional form until well into the XIXth century. The *qasaba*, to some extent comparable to a widely spread-out citadel, was a section of the city and surrounded by its own strong fortifications which contained within their precincts the palace of the ruler or governor, and a pavilion for his audiences and ceremonious receptions; the quarters of his body-guard; the governmental offices with the residences of the dignitaries and the mass of the clerks; various dependencies including store-rooms, gardens and baths; a mosque and sometimes also a *madrasa* (a higher theological school); a library and, in the capital, the mausolea of the dynasty, as in Marrakesh the beautiful necropolis of the Saʿdian* sultans and their family. The *qasaba* constituted within the city walls proper an essential, well protected element of the government apparatus and a second defence system against the attacks of an enemy army or of rebellious tribes, but also an efficient instrument for policing an often turbulent and easily excitable urban population.
In more recent years the *qasaba* lost its military significance. Most of the ramparts decayed or were razed, the moats were filled in and the heavy gates demolished except those to which their monumental structure and elaborate arabesque reliefs or coloured glazed tiles impart artistic value. Here and there, especially in Tunisia, a *qasaba* was later restored, as the one in Tunis, once famous for the splendid palace of the Hafsid* rulers; or the one in Sousse which was turned into a museum; or the *qasaba* of Gafsa, built upon an ancient Byzantine foundation, which after its repair was again thoroughly destroyed in the Second World War. Yet, as a rule, the site itself melted into the rest of the town but is still known as the Kasba quarter, a designation which in the Algerian cities came into use for the aggregate of the old Moslem sections as opposed to the modern parts of European construction and inhabited mainly by the European population.
In the early XVIIIth century the original *qasaba*, the fortress-town, began to develop, as it were, a miniature replica in the fertile valleys and southern slopes of the High Atlas. There the chieftains of the great Berber tribes or influential lords of the region set up each one his own kasba - a huge castle, built of stamped earth, with high thick walls, with massive, crenellated towers decorated with geometrical patterns of sunbaked and whitewashed bricks. Around it settled their numerous servants, agricultural labourers and clients with their families. Similar but much smaller forts were erected by the various rulers, by the ʿAlawid* Sultan Ismāʿīl

(1672-1727) alone about seventy, which served to secure - not always successfully - inner peace and order, and in particular to protect the peasantry in the plains from the incursions of predatory mountain tribes. Yet neither the builders of the seigniorial strongholds nor the military architects of the garrison posts seem to have intended their imposing structures to last. Rains, frost and storms have fissured their walls, stripped off parts of the roof and broken out steps of the stairs, leaving most of them empty shells, no longer habitable except perhaps for some lonely watchman. They stand out in their reddish brown, inserted in the moving green of a palmgrove along the course of a river, or silhouetted against the dark, rocky waves of the mountain tablelands.
There is, finally, in the villages on the northern as well as the southern flanks of the Atlas, the least pretentious specimen of the kasba type: the house of the headman, conspicuous by its size, its turrets and its strong doors. It is the assembly place of the village elders, there the village receives its guests, and there the women and children sought refuge in case of a raid by a band of robbers or of a warlike encounter with the people of a neighbouring village - quite frequent events in a not too distant past.

QUBBA, the round or oval cupola roofing the small, cubic edifice erected over the tomb of a saint. By extension the word designates the entire structure even if the cupola is replaced, as occasionaly occurs, by a pyramid.

QUNFUDH IBN-, ABŪ al-ʿABBĀS AHMAD, a Tunisian historiographer and religious scholar, also versed in astronomy, astrology and mathematics (appr. 1340-1406). He was born in Constantine of a family in which for several generations one or the other member had held the office of *khatīb* (preacher of the Friday sermon), whence his surname Ibn al-Khatīb under which he was mainly known during his life time. He studied in Tlemcen and spent several years travelling in Morocco, everywhere in close contact with the circles of the holy men (marabout*) and religious brotherhoods*, before finally settling in Tunis. There he was invested first with the office of the *khatīb* of the Kasba *(qasaba*)* then also with those of a cadi and mufti (expert in Islamic jurisprudence). Ranking high in the favour of Sultan Abū Fāris ʿAbd al-ʿAzīz* (1394-1434) he had free access to the government archives, and on this basis compiled a history of the Hafsid* dynasty from its origin until the early years of the fifteenth century, the *Fārisīya fī Mabādi' al-Dawla al-Hafsīya* (parts translated by Charbonneau, Journal Asiatique, 1848-52), whose concise and strictly chronological form makes it a very serviceable source of information. A work on Abū Madyan*, the great patron saint of Tlemcen, and his disciples; a versified treatise on the science of medicine; and commentaries in verse on writings on religious or astrological subjects are among the numerous, although less valuable products of his pen.

QUTB, literally meaning a stake or pole or pivot, as a term of Islamic mysticism the designation of one who has reached the highest stage on the path of sanctity. According to general belief the world remains unaware of his exalted state during his earthly life, yet one or the other of those holy men may already himself have revealed it in advance like Abū Madyan* (1126-1197), who down to this day is held in high veneration in the Arab West. Immediate succession upon the death of the *qutb* prevents any vacancy in this supreme position. Dhū al-Nūn (†860), the Egyptian scholar and prominent exponent of mystical teaching, is counted among the first of this line.

QŪTĪYA IBN al-, ABŪ BAKR MUHAMMAD IBN ʿUMAR, a Hispano-Arab historian and grammarian (†977), descended allegedly from one of Caliph ʿUmar's freedmen and a Visigothic princess *(Qūtīyun*, a Goth). Born in Seville, he studied first in his home town and subsequently in Cordova, where he was invested with the office of cadi (judge), simultaneously taught grammar and devoted himself to historical and philological research. His outstanding work is the *Ta'rīkh Fath al-Andalus* (The History of the Spanish Conquest) which leads from the time of the rise of Islam down to the reign of Caliph ʿAbd al-Rahmān III* (912-961) and constitutes a valuable source of information on the history of the Arabs in Spain (Spanish translation by Julián Ribera, Madrid, 1912). Another work of his pen which has been preserved is a grammatical treatise, the *Kitāb al-Afʿāl* (Book of Verbs), the first one to deal with the rules of the conjugation of Arabic verbs.

QUZMĀN IBN, ABŪ BAKR, a Hispano-Arab minstrel (1078/80-1160). Born in Cordova, he set out, while still a youth, on a wandering life which took him all over al-Andalus*, with frequent returns to his native town. He made his living by singing the praise of wealthy patrons and, if necessary, by entertaining the large public in the manner of a street singer, never omitting to evoke the pity of his hearers by extolling his own talent - doubtless real but decidedly one-sided - and emphasizing his unmerited poverty. Borrowing from popular poetry the form of the *zajal** (a type of Andalusian folksongs consisting of rhymed stanzas) which he elevated to literary rank, he made free use of the vernacular idiom mixing Arabic, Romance and Berber elements. The sensual and erotic, even lascivious way of expressing his homage is in part to be ascribed to the general taste of his time. Ibn Quzmān finished his agitated and far from virtuous life in a mosque at Cordova where, at the age of seventy, he took over the function of *imām* (leader of the congregation in prayer). The greater part, altogether 159 pieces, of the collection of his poems, entitled *Isābat al-Aghrād fī Dhikr al- Aʿrād* (Achievements of Aims by remembering Virtues) and prefaced by the poet in literary Arabic, has been preserved, but only one manuscript is extant. It was written in Palestine - an illustration of the wide range of the interest in Ibn Quzmān's songs. Those that have come down to us were translated first into Latin as a preparatory step to a Spanish translation of about one third of them - a task somewhat complicated by the intricacies of the poet's vocabulary (A. R. Nykl, El Cancionero de Aben Guzman (Ibn Quzmān), Madrid, 1933).

R

RĀBĪAʿ IBN ZAID, or Recemundo by his Christian name, a Hispano-Arab statesman at the court of Caliph ʿAbd al-Rahmān III (912-961) and Bishop of Elvira *(Ilbira*, the Roman and Visigothic Iliberris). While still a young cleric he was employed as a scribe in the chancellery at Cordova, but his mastery of Latin and of the niceties of scholarly Arabic, as well as his high general culture, did not fail to attract the attention of the caliph. He was made bishop and entrusted by ʿAbd al-Rahmān with a mission to the German Emperor Otho I (938-983) or *Huttu* as he was called by the Arab historiographers; and shortly afterwards with a second one to the Byzantine Emperor Constantine VII (912-959). From his expedition to the East he brought back for the caliph's new residence, *Madīnat al-Zahrā'*, a richly sculptured fountain of green onyx with a gold-decorated marble basin, both, according to contemporary chroniclers, of outstanding beauty and priceless value. He stood in equally high favour with ʿAbd al-Rahmān's son and successor, Caliph al-Hakam II (961-976) who particularly admired his wide knowledge in the fields of philosophy and astronomy, and to whom he dedicated his well-known 'Calendar of Cordova'.

RAHMĀNĪYA, a religious brotherhood* founded towards the end of the XVIIIth century in the Kabylia (Algeria) by Muhammad ʿAbd al-Rahmān (†1793) of the Ait Smāʿīl, a tribe in the Jurjura mountains. He began his religious studies in Algiers and continued them at the theological academy of al-Azhar in Cairo, where he soon became deeply engaged in mystical speculation and also joined an Egyptian brotherhood. After a long stay abroad he returned to his homeland and, as he claimed, inspired by the Prophet Muhammad, formulated the rules of a brotherhood of his own, which within a short time attracted numerous adherents. Summoned before the supreme religious court at Algiers under the accusation of diffusing heretical beliefs, he was absolved thanks to the intervention of the Turkish authorities, but soon afterwards died. Legend has it that a miracle doubled his dead body, one being taken away by the Turks and buried at a place near Algiers, the other one remaining in his tomb at the fraternity's seat *(zāwiya*)*, whence his surname Abū Qabraīn (The Man with the two Tombs). After his successor's death, quarrels among the members of his family about the leadership brought about several dissensions in the brotherhood whose prestige, however, did not cease to grow and became a main factor in the long-lasting resistance of the Kabyles* against the French occupation of Algeria. It was the eighty-year old Rahmānīya head, Muhammad 'Amziān Ibn al-Haddād, and his son al-ʿAzīz, who in 1871 proclaimed the Holy War against the French intruders and thus started the most tenacious of the many tribal risings. After its suppression al-ʿAzīz, sent into exile, escaped and settled in Jidda, but the Rahmānīya branched out further under various names into Algeria, western Tunisia and the oases along the fringe of the Sahara. Although in the course of time it had lost much of its former vitality, it still counts quite a number of faithful adherents.

RASHĪD al-, IBN al-SHARĪF, the founder (1664-1672) of the reigning ʿAlawid* dynasty of Morocco. From early youth opposed in bitter enmity to his brother Mūlāy Muhammad, who after his father's abdication became the head of the ʿAlawid clan (1635), he sought safety for a while with the strong Dilā'yūn* brotherhood. Then, wandering about in the country, he rallied adherents and finally attacked his brother who was killed in the fighting. Mūlāy al-Rashīd took over his succession, strengthened the friendship his brother had set up in north-eastern Morocco with the Maʿqil* chieftains and concluded further alliances with some strong Berber tribes in the region. He established the nucleus of a government at the town of Taza, well protected behind the fortifications which the Saʿdian* Sultan Ahmad al-Mansūr* had erected. After two unfruitful assaults upon Fez, at that time a sort of independent city-republic under the leadership of an Arab chieftain, he turned into the Rif, forced some of the hostile mountain people under his obedience, and, feeling safe in his rear, again laid siege to Fez. This time the city opened its gates to him and acclaimed him as sultan (1666). Step by step he imposed his authority upon the whole northern part of the country, then moved southwards into the Middle Atlas and in a short campaign conquered and destroyed Dilā' (1668) and dispersed the fraternity's militant adherents. The following year he seized Marrakesh, more or less autonomous, like Fez, under a tribal chieftain. Leading his troops from success to success into the plains of the Shawīya (from the Atlantic coast inland between the lower course of the Bū Ragrāg and the Umm al-Rabīʿ) and southwards into the Sūs, he took the town of Tārūdānt. Thence he continued into the Tazarwalt, then went up into the Anti Atlas and occupied the territory held by the heirs of the marabout* prince al-Samlālī*, whereupon he returned to Fez (1671). A tragic fate did not allow him to ripen the fruits of his circumspectly planned strategy which he pursued with unswerving energy: the year after, in Marrakesh at the celebration of the ʿId al-Kabīr (the Great Feast, marking the end of the Pilgrimage to Mecca) his horse, suddenly shying, smashed his head when running against a tree. He was temporarily buried in Marrakesh but his brother, Mūlāy Ismāʿīl* who succeeded him and completed his work of unification, had his body put to rest at the sanctuary of a much venerated saint, Sīdī ʿAlī Ben Hārāzim (†appr. 1164) in the surroundings of Fez.

RĀZĪ al-, AHMAD IBN MUHAMMAD, the first of the great Andalusian historiographers (888-955). His father, a much travelled and highly cultured Persian merchant from the town of al-Rayy - whence the family name al-Rāzī - had open doors at the court of Cordova and occasionally was even entrusted by the emir with missions in al-Andalus* and abroad, in a field which might today be called public relations. Returning from such a voyage to the South of the country, and accompanied by his wife and three-year old son Ahmad, he suddenly died.

Ahmad Ibn Muhammad al-Rāzī studied religious science in Cordova, but soon developed a strong inclination for the investigation of the Andalusian past, and seems to have gained access to sources of information otherwise hardly available. The only data on his method of arranging the material he collected, are a few short notes left by his son ʿĪsā al-Rāzī, but the results of modern studies show unequivocally that this was the first attempt undertaken in al-Andalus to write history not in the form of an assemblage of tales more often than not of a legendary character, but to record events in their social and political context. None of al-Rāzī's works has been preserved, although the titles and subjects of a number of them are known through the frequent references by later authors. Among them are a comprehensive history of al-Andalus under the Umayyads down to his time, continued and in parts completed by his son ʿĪsā; a treatise on the Andalusian *mawālī** (the natives converted to Islam); an extensive genealogy of the great Arab families in al-Andalus; and a detailed description of Cordova which was used by later geographers, and reproduced in the form of a free Spanish version (Cronica de Moro Rasis, 1852), itself based on a Portuguese translation of the XIVth century, both of doubtful accuracy. It was only the recent discovery and exploration of an important fragment of Ibn-Hayyān's* *Muqtabis* which brought to light numerous verbatim quotations from al-Rāzī's History of al-Andalus and made it possible to appreciate the full value of his work for much of our knowledge of the earlier Hispano-Arab period.

RELIGIOUS BROTHERHOODS, *turuq*, sing *tarīqa*, an Islamic institution which originated in the Arab East, and infiltrated into North Africa around the XIIIth century where it reached its peak between the end of the XVth and the beginning of the XVIIth century. Throughout several hundred years it played a foremost rôle in the spiritual, social and political life of the countries of the Arab West, and down to the present day has retained a certain though steadily diminishing significance. The brotherhood is built upon the mystical teaching (*tarīqa*, lit. meaning a path, in this particular sense the path of spiritual perfection which leads the soul to absorption in the Divine Being, and by extension designating also the community which follows this path) of a saint (marabout*), which his adepts elaborated or adorned and clothed in a particular ritual. Seen under the angle of its spiritual affiliation with the Master, the brotherhood may indeed be regarded as going back to the saint whom it venerates as its founder and whose name it bears, although its actual constitution as an organized association may have taken place in much later days. Its doctrine and rules may move entirely within the limits of orthodox dogma and interpretations but may also have absorbed heretical, especially Khārijite and even pre-Islamic pagan elements. In any case, the absolute faith in the divinely inspired, unfailing leadership of the supreme chief; the rigid hierarchical structure; the strict obedience binding the members; and multiple ramifications, constitute the weight of the collective action

the brotherhood is able to exercise.
Its germ cell is the saint's abode or mausoleum with the quarters of his adepts, the *zāwiya**. This modest community, supported by the pious gifts of the simple folks in the surroundings, might either vegetate for a while and disappear for want of new adherents, or it might grow, gain in prestige and come to wealth through pious donations *(habūs, plur. ahbās)* by high-ranking patrons and even the sovereign. Then the *zāwiya* might branch out, set up daughter-houses, small ones among the tribes in the mountains, larger ones in the countryside and in the towns, which in turn might flourish, expand and become each one a new mother-house. Thus, as time goes on, one or the other brotherhood, by its hold upon the masses and the position of some of its members at court, in the army or government, might command a moral influence making it a factor of power - informal but none the less impossible to neglect. Yet notwithstanding their great number, the diversity of their rituals and the different levels of their social standing, the tenets of most of the important brotherhoods spring from either one of the two outstanding schools of mystical thought: the Jazūlīya, formulated by the Moroccan Muhammad Ibn ʿAbd al-Rahmān al-Jazūlī*, and the Qādirīya, founded by ʿAbd al-Qādir al-Jīlānī of Baghdad.
The spiritual and temporal head of the brotherhood is the sheikh. He is credited as a rule with sharīfian* descent (i.e. from the Prophet Muhammad) and endowed with the *baraka* (the supernatural gift by the grace of God of a bliss-dispensing force) transmitted as through the links of a mystical chain from the saintly founder, which he will confer upon the successor he designates, by divine inspiration, as a rule from among the members of his family. He leads the religious exercises; initiates the neophytes; and determines the attitude and conduct of the brotherhood in all worldly matters. His theological erudition and his wisdom in the guidance on the way to mystic experience; the number and standing of the disciples he attracts; the trust he inspires by his miraculous help in times of need; his ability as a mediator in the minor or major conflicts among families, clans or tribes - all this perpetuates the prestige of the brotherhood and, last but not least, consolidates and increases its wealth. Conversely, his falling short of his task might rapidly bring about the brotherhood's decadence.
A coadjutor *(khalīfa)* assists the sheikh and represents him on occasions when his person should not appear directly involved. An intendant *(wakīl)* administers the current affairs such as the supervision of the landed property, the collection of the yearly voluntary contributions or the distribution of alms. A number of mandatories *(muquaddamūn,* sing. *muqaddam**) direct under his control the daughter-*zāwiyas* or are in charge of missionary work. Occasionally one or the other *muqaddam*, obeying the mystical call, secedes from the main body and builds up his *zāwiya* into a new confraternity which may or may not continue to feel spiritually tied to the parent community. A system of initiation *(bayʿa)* by degrees solidly integrates the brethren *(ikhwān,* colloquially *khouan)*, who otherwise live their normal social and family life. They are bound, however, to observe the order's moral precepts, in parti-

cular as far as they enjoin unconditional assistance in the fulfilment of specific duties, whatever they may be, assigned to anyone of them by the sheikh or the *muqaddam*. At fixed intervals they assemble for the common religious exercises. In general, these are based on the recitation *(hizb)* of Koranic texts, of special prayers and of selected passages of mystical writings, and comprise certain devotional acts as an approach to the communion of the soul with God. As widely as the social and intellectual character of the individual brotherhoods differs, so, too, does their ritual vary along a much-graded scale from refined symbolism to crudely naive superstition: mechanical repetition *(dhikr)* - up to a thousand times and more - of certain invocatory phrases, liturgical chanting, monotonous music and rhythmical movements or dancing, all finally generating a state of common trance *(hāl)*. There were, on the other hand, quite a few *zāwiyas*, reputed foci of religious study, striving to harmonize mystical longing and rational thought, which drew some of the best minds within their circle of teachers and disciples, often in successful competion with the officially patronized theological schools *(madrasa)*. They also were the soil on which grew up an extensive literary activity dealing with the stories and miracles of the more widely known saints and the biographies of the sheikhs of the brotherhood, thus in many cases opening up an interesting insight into the contemporary cultural and political situation.

In the course of history, the closely coherent, two-dimensional structure - vertical, from the sheikh down over the *muqaddamūn* into the mass of the brethren; and horizontal, from the urban centres into the peasantry of the plains and the tribes in the mountains, regardless of state boundaries - made this fabric of emotional religion with its threads deeply anchored in popular piety far more than a merely social and cultural phenomenon. In the XVth and XVIth centuries, when the sultans proved unable to stem the Portuguese and Spanish penetration on the Atlantic and Mediterranean coasts, it was the voice of the sheikhs which through the network of the *zāwiyas* carried the call to the Holy War far into the interior, rallied the brethren and directed the fighting until the invaders were forced out. This warlike spirit was manifest also in internal disturbances - dynastic conflicts, revolts of pretenders to the throne or seditions of tribal leaders - and never let the brotherhoods, divided among themselves by doctrinal divergencies, stand aside as neutral spectators. It carried some ambitious and energetic sheikhs to a practically independent overlordship in large sections of the country, so that, as in the case of Muhammad al-Hajj of the Dilā'yūn* in Morocco, the conquest of the throne came to be quite a realistic aspiration. It conveyed a forceful impulse to the resistance in Algeria against the French occupation from 1830 onward throughout nearly five decades. In Morocco, during the first quarter of the present century in the struggle against the establishment of the French and Spanish Protectorates*, the brotherhoods, through all sorts of clandestine channels, smuggled arms and provided information, shelter and food to the guerilla fighters, most of whom were their adherents. In the measure, however, as the foreign rule seemed to take lasting root, this combativeness began to give way, to a kind of colourless indifference and as time went on even

to co-operation, certainly cautious and not always reliable, but upon the whole intent to keep the population docile and quiet.
This change could not fail to provoke a sharp, twofold reaction in addition to the ever-present hostility on the part of scholastic theology. It emanated, on the one hand, from the progressive religious circles such as the Salafīya* or the Association of the Algerian ʿUlamā'*, and on other, from the political organizations of the intellectual youth. Both strove to awaken the masses from their apathy and ignorance: the former, in order to lead them out of their world of superstitions to the concepts of pure faith; and the latter, to imbue them with the desire for national emancipation. Soon they found themselves united in a common front against the brotherhood institution and against the foreign power whose interests its submissive attitude served. In recent years, especially since the achievement of independence, the brotherhoods have lost their political influence and, with a few exeptions, much of their significance in the spheres of spiritual life. Their present number may be estimated at a few hundred and the number of their adherents at several hundred thousand, but a precise evaluation is hardly possible since many of them, particularly the smaller ones, have assumed the forms of philanthropic, mutual-aid or occupational associations. Some have combined in a sort of general brotherhood federation which was presided over until his death (September 1962) by Muhammad ʿAbd al-Haiy al-Kattānī*.

REVOLT IN THE SUBURB, commonly used term to designate a sedition (814 or 818) in the densely inhabited suburb *(rabad)* of Cordova on the left bank of the Guadalquivir under the reign of Emir al-Hakam I (796-822). The dissatisfaction with his despotic régime found a particularly fertile soil in this quarter of the town with its mixed population of artisans, small merchants and students of theology and canon law *(fuqahā')* at the Great Mosque nearby across the river, and a numerous, easily excitable populace of undefined occupations. Already in 805, on the occasion of a conspiracy against the emir, discovered through treachery and very severely suppressed, the atmosphere there had grown tense. Especially after the imposition of a new kind of taxation, disturbances provoking every time a series of capital punishments followed one another and marked the critical situation. One day, in March 818, in the wake of such an incident, al-Hakam on his return through the streets of the suburb from a hunting trip was insulted by the mob and had to retreat in haste behind the walls of his palace, which the turbulent crowd, overrunning his bodyguard, almost succeeded in taking by assault. In the very last minute a cavalry detachment under the command of one of his nephews saved the situation.
Three days long the suburb was left to the pilfering and murdering soldiery. Then three hundred notables were executed and nailed to crosses; some 20.000 families, according to the probably somewhat exaggerated figure transmitted by chroniclers, except the *fuqahā'*, were expelled from Cordova; and the *rabad* was levelled to the ground. Most of the *rabadī*, as they were henceforth called - while al-Hakam himself was given the nickname *al-Rabadī* by his biographers - found a new home in

Morocco, mainly in Fez, where Idrīs II* settled them in a quarter of their own (*Madīnat* or also *ʿIdwat al-Andalusiyīn*, the town or the bank of the Andalusians). Others - though they may well have belonged to a group of Cordovan emigrants who had left the city in the course of the preceding troubles - went as far as Alexandria, probably together with a fleet of corsairs from the coasts of southern Spain. They made themselves masters of the town, rallied a number of sympathizers from the surroundings, and founded an autonomous republic based upon a kind of Islamic puritanism. Forced to withdraw (827) by the ʿAbbāsid governor of Egypt, they crossed over to Crete*, then a Byzantine possession, conquered the island and remained in power for more than a century and a half.

REVOLUTIONARY COMMITTEE FOR UNITY AND ACTION, Comité Révolutionnaire pour l'Unité et l'Action (C.R.U.A.), set up in utmost secrecy in March 1954 in Algiers after several preparatory meetings in Berne, Cairo, Tripoli and various places in Algeria by a group of nine Algerian patriots all belonging to the 'Organisation Secrète' (O.S.*). The eldest of them was forty-two years of age, the youngest twenty-eight. Later, they became known as the 'Nine Historical Chiefs of the Algerian Revolution' or also as the 'Club of the Nine': Muhammad Khidr, Husain Ait Ahmad and Ahmad Ben Bella (Ibn Ballā) - refugees in Cairo and in close contact with Colonel Gamal ʿAbd al-Nāsir; Muhammad Būdiaf, Rabah Bitat and Belkacem Krim (Karīm Bilqāsim) - hiding in Algeria; ʿUmar Ben Bulaid, Murād Didūsh and Muhammad Larbi (al-ʿArabī) Muhammadī - moving more or less freely in Algeria but soon to find their death fighting or in French captivity. According to what they later termed their 'moral contract' there was never to be any sort of hierarchical distinction among them, and this colleagueship, as they agreed, should remain the fundamental principle of the supreme command throughout the revolutionary struggle. Their purpose, announced in an unsigned, mimeographed pamphlet and propagated for a few months by an equally primitive and anonymous periodical, 'The Algerian Patriot', was to reconcile the two enemy factions into which the 'Movement for the Triumph of Democratic Liberties'* (M.T.L.D.), the great nationalist party of Messali al-Hajj (Masālī al-Ḥajj), had split; to associate the Algerian patriots with the Tunisian and Moroccan nationalist movements; and then to start the common fight for 'the destruction of French colonialism'.
The unifying efforts of the 'Club' were unsuccessful, but its three members in Cairo, the nucleus of the 'External Delegation'* with Ahmad Ben Bella as the leading spirit, secured financial help from the Arab League's 'Special Fund for Aid to the Liberation Movement of the Arab West', provided arms, and orchestrated the propagandistic support of the 'Voice of the Arabs' of the Cairo Radio. Undetected by the French intelligence service, the 'interior' members consolidated the underground network of cells of the Algerian People's Party* (P.P.A.) into a well-structured terrorist apparatus, the future Army of National Liberation* (A.L.N.), which was firmly anchored in a territorial division of the whole of Algeria into six *wilayas* (districts) - the Aurès-Nemecha

Mountains, North Constantine, Kabylia, the departments of Algiers and Oran, and the Sahara - each one subdivided into zones, sectors and sub-sectors. This operational arrangement, to which later was added an autonomous sector of the City of Algiers and two zones in the Tunisian and Moroccan border areas, was kept up all through the seven years of the insurrection.
At a last meeting on the 10th of October the six chiefs inside Algeria determined one o'clock in the morning of November 1st for the first terror acts which were to mark the start of the rebellion. The same day, throughout Algeria tracts 'To the Algerian People' announced the constitution of the A.L.N. and of the Front of National Liberation* (F.L.N.) as its political section. Simultaneously was established an 'External Delegation of the 'F.L.N.'*. Two years later this still rudimentary organization was given solid forms at the Summam Valley Congress*.

RIBĀT, plur. *ribātāt* (derived from the verb *rabata,* to bind, to tie together and, figuratively, to assemble and tether the mounts and keep them ready for battle), an Arabic term used in North Africa and al-Andalus* to denote the strongholds erected at strategically important points along the frontiers and the coastline. They were garrisoned with pious volunteers *(ahl al-ribāt, murābitūn*)* and observed a half-ascetic, half-soldierly mode of community life. Permanent or temporary service in the ranks of these warrior monks, closely connected with the concept of the Holy War *(jihād)*, constituted a highly meritorious act. It was of essential significance for the preservation of a constant military preparedness and held a basic place in the organisation of the armed forces. The establishment and maintenance of such fortifications and the reinforcement of their defensive value, as well as the provision of food or other necessities of life for their garrisons was regarded equally as a work of religious merit. Some of them were built up into powerful fortresses with a regular arsenal and contained besides the rows of windowless cubicles opening towards a covered gallery forming the quarters for the soldiers, a mosque or several smaller prayer places with a minaret used also as signal tower. From the VIIIth century onwards, when the first and still primitive type of *ribāt* seems to have been built, this defensive system was constantly strengthened all along the North African and Andalusian coasts as well as in the interior. Most of them have disappeared or fallen into ruins, with few exceptions particularly in Tunisia, from which an impression of their one-time importance can be gained. Thus for instance the *ribāt* of Monastir, originally built in 796 by a governor of the ʿAbbāsid caliphs and later enlarged and remodelled; or the one at Sousse, erected in the IXth century by an Aghlabid* emir, popularly called Ksar *(al-qasr,* the fortress) which is today a museum; or the one at Sfax, also an Aghlabid construction which in the XIth and XIIth centuries the Zīrid* emirs selected as their burial place. In Morocco, the remembrance of the *Ribāt al-Fath* (of the Victory), erected perhaps on the site of an older stronghold by the Almohad* ruler Yūsuf Yaʿqūb al-Mansūr (1184-1199) survives in the name of the city of Rabat.
In al-Andalus in the course of time a shift took place in the sense of

the term *ribāt*, so that it ceased to denote the locality, for which the word *rābita* (plur. *rawābit)* came into use, and assumed the meaning of a defensively conducted Holy War. In North Africa *ribāt* retained its original significance, while *rābita*, although somewhat later, began to mean the abode of a holy man, the *murābit* (marabout*) devoting himself, perhaps with a few disciples, to an ascetic life of pious practices but no longer comprising the idea of warlike tasks.

RIHLA, literally 'journey', in a wider sense a travelling account, especially of a pilgrimage to the Holy Cities *(hajj)*, and as a literary genre very much in favour particularly in the Arab West, beginning from the later Middle-Ages until well into recent times. In its more or less standardized form the *rihla* is built up on the description of the countries and towns visited, indicating the distances, depicting the famous mosques, places of study and palaces of the rulers. Inserted are biographical notes on the local celebrities, alive or of the past; information on institutions, practices and customs that struck the authors; and narrations of events of a historic, political or simply anecdotic nature, which he witnessed or was told of. Often he uses this framework also for speaking of his own scholarly achievements and successful activities in an official function. While in their majority the *rihla* books make a somewhat monotonous reading, the ensemble of the numerous details they contain shed a vivid light on the society of their time and the intellectual, economic and political currents in its midst. Among outstanding works of this type merit mention those by Ibn Battūta*, Ibn Jubayr* and al-Ghassānī*.

RŪGĪ al-, JALĪL, frequently spelt Rogui, a tribesman of the Arab Ruwāga in the coastal plain of the Gharb in north-western Morocco, who at the time of Sultan Sīdī Muhammad ʿAbd al-Rahmān (1859-1873) incited the people of the area of al-Had Kurt (south of Wazzān) to revolt against the government, assuring them that by the grace of God, no harm whatsoever would befall them. Armed with clubs and wooden sticks they attacked the town of al-Had Kurt, killed the caid *(qā'id*)*, pillaged shops and devastated fields. They were easily beaten by the troops sent by the sultan, and Jalīl al-Rūgī tried to find refuge at the sanctuary in the holy town of Mūlāy Idrīs, but was killed. His head and hands were cut off and sent to Marrakesh were they were exposed to the public.
In Morocco, *al-rūgī* came to be used as a sort of epithet or nickname affixed to the name of a revolutionary leader such as Bū Hmāra*, ʿAbd al-Qarīm* (Abdelkrim) and others.

RUSHD IBN, ABŪ al-WALĪD MUHAMMAD IBN AHMAD, better known in occidental literature as Averroës, the form in which his name was made familiar by the scholastics in medieval Europe, an outstanding Hispano-Arab philosopher (1126-1198). He came from a distinguished Cordovan family of jurists and received an education which embraced, as was customary in the upper-class society of his days, theology and jurisprudence, medicine, mathematics, astronomy and philosophy. He served as cadi *(qādī)* in Seville and Cordova, then, after a serious illness and some years of travelling, was summoned to Marrakesh by the Almohad* ruler Abū Ya'qūb Yūsuf*, who appointed him court physician and subsequently chief-cadi in Cordova. For some time he continued in favour with Yūsuf's successor Abū Yūsuf Ya'qūb al-Mansūr*, but then fell into disgrace, apparently because of his too openly manifested unorthodox philosophical ideas, was banished from the city and had much to suffer from the satirical attacks of the theologians and all sorts of offences from the populace. After a while he was pardoned and recalled to Marrakesh, where he spent the rest of his life in retirement.

Ibn Rushd covered in his scholarly activities a wide range of subjects. He wrote on astronomy and grammar; composed a manual on the law of inheritance; in the field of music he dealt with the theory of sound; and in a commentary on Plato's *Republic* he laid down his system of politics. His contribution to medicine comprised sixteen books, among which the encyclopaedic *Kullīyāt fī al-Tibb* (The Universal of Medicine), translated fifty years after his death into Latin under the title '*Colliget*'. Repeatedly printed, it was in use until the end of the Middle Ages at the universities of Bologna, Padua, Montpellier and Paris. The great fruit of his philosophical learning appears in his commentaries on Aristotle, some of them even in a series of three - a long, an intermediate and a summary - for which, however, knowing no Greek, he had to rely on translations. A special place in this line of thought, where he speaks in his own name is occupied by the *Fasl al-Maqāli* (abridged title), a tract, small in size but indispensable for understanding the currents moving philosophical thinking, both Islamic and Christian, throughout the second half of the Middle Ages. (Translations into German by M. J. Müller in Philosophie und Theologie von Averroes, München, 1875; into Spanish by Miguel Asin Palacios, El averroismo teologico de Santo Tomas de Aquina, Saragossa, 1904; into English by G. F. Hourani, Averroes - On the harmony of Religion and Philosophy, London, 1961).

There can be no discrepancy, Ibn Rushd emphasizes, between philosophy and religion. The philosopher's search for truth, always based on Koranic Revelation, might in certain cases be governed by allegorical interpretations and not by the literal meaning, particularly where human qualities are attributed to the deity. This exegesis in the light of reason, however, remains the domain of the scholar, while the simple minded mass of the people, in need of protection from fatal errors and confusion, must be left to their naive belief in the plain and verbal sense of the sacred text worded by divine wisdom so as to lead them to piety and morality. This thesis, while a well-known element in the teaching of Islamic mysticism, flows in Ibn Rushd's argumentation from his discernment of the capacities of the human mind. Falsely, and because some translators misunderstood certain terms, it has made him appear as the author of the so-called theory of the double truth - that there is a difference between the postulates of faith, and what reason would accept as true - thus fathering on him free-thought and unbelief.

First in importance among Ibn Rushd's philosophical works ranks his *Tahāfut al-Tahāfut* (in the medieval Latin translation *Destructio Destructionis;* English translation by S. van den Bergh, The Incoherence of the

Incoherence, Oxford, 1954), a refutation of al-Ghazzālī's vehement attack on the philosophers and on rationalism in his *Tahāfut al-Falāsifa* (Incoherence of the Philosophers). Quoting al-Ghazzālī's words in detail, and formulating his criticism section by section, he penetrates into the intricacies of the controversial issues in which scholastic speculation was involved. The polemic evoked little resonance in Islamic learned society, which in general disagreed with the whole body of his doctrines and had no interest in their diffusion. It is due to this attitude that they have reached us only in very few Arabic manuscripts. Yet it was within the circle of Jewish scholars in Spain, in southern France and in Sicily where they were passionately studied, translated into Hebrew or copied from the Arabic original in Hebrew letters. The first Latin versions (around 1217) go back to Michael the Scot in Toledo, a centre of Arabic learning still long after it had come into Spanish hands (1085), and were followed by the translation of the Great Commentary on Aristotle's *De anima*, which he made in Palermo for Emperor Frederic II of Hohenstaufen. Thenceforth, this translating activity continued and opened to 'Averroism' the doors to the schools of thought of Latin Christendom. There were quite a number of points to which one of its greatest thinkers, St. Thomas Aquinas, the Doctor Angelicus (1225-1274), gave a place in his famous *Summa theologiae*, although understandably a great many others were irreconcilable with Christian ideology. Yet Ibn Rushd's authority as a commentator of Aristotle remained undisputed among the Christian universities well into the XVIth century.

RUSTUMIDS, a dynasty of *imāms* (spiritual and secular leaders) of the Ibādite sect, one of the moderate branches of the heterodox Khārijite doctrine, who reigned over the city-state of Tāhart (776-908). Its founder was ʿAbd al-Rahmān Ibn Rustum, offspring of a noble Iranian family, who under the first Ibādite *imām* in North Africa, Abū al-Khattāb al-Maʿāfirī*, was governor of al-Qayrawān but had to flee when the town was reconquered by the troops of the Baghdad caliph (761). Welcomed by the Ibādite communities in western Algeria, mainly Berbers of the Zanāta* family of tribes, he rebuilt the old settlement of Tāhart (near present-day Tiaret, appr. 140 miles south-west of Algiers), at that time in ruins, and was elected *imām* (776-784). For some 130 years Tāhart remained the religious and intellectual focus of Khārijism in the western regions of North Africa, but its voice carried weight deep in the Arab East among the sect's widely dispersed adherents.
Hemmed in by the strong Idrīsid* and Aghlabid* states, the miniature Rustumid theocracy had no military or political ambitions. Yet well aware, on the one hand of their dependency for survival on a protector and, on the other, of the interest this rôle might hold in the power constellation in the Western world of Islam, the *imāms* turned their eyes towards al-Andalus*. The second of the line, ʿAbd al-Wahhāb (784-823), seizing the occasion of the accession to the throne of the Umayyad Emir ʿAbd al-Rahmān II (822-852)*, sent three of his sons as ambassadors of friendship to Cordova, where they were given a splendid reception. Two members of the Rustumid family entered the emir's service and attained high distinction: one in the army as a commander in the

victorious battle against the invading Normans (844); the other, in the civil administration with the rank of Vizier. ʿAbd al-Rahmān's successor, Emir Muhammad (852-886) continued to cultivate the friendship with the third *imām*, Abū Saʿīd al-Aflah (823-868) and then with his son, Abū al-Yaqzān Muhammad (868-894), both of whom, relying, as it seems, fully on their ally's political wisdom and military force, let themselves be guided by his advice in all matters concerning the affairs of their state. By following this line of conduct, Tāhart, upon the whole, was able to enjoy peace and prosperity for more than a century, except for some minor disturbances caused either by frictions with neighbouring Berber clans and occasional doctrinal dissensions or dynastic rivalries under the last *imāms*.

In the cultural framework of this time, Tāhart meant more than the spiritual leadership of a sect and of theological speculation. In the atmosphere of puritanism, simplicity of the forms of material life, and tolerance, emanating from the upper strata of religious doctors around the *imām*, there grew up and spread a sincere taste for science in the wider sense, and a desire for knowledge. This was reflected in the systematic acquisition of scholarly manuscripts from the seats of learning in the Arab East, and in the afflux of students from abroad. Tāhart, however, was also a market centre with far more than a mere local significance. Situated in the midst of a fertile agricultural region at the intersection of several caravan roads and disposing of a small harbour of its own - it is not known how the *imāms* had secured it - for the shipment of wheat to Spain, it developed a flourishing trade in the hands of a curiously mixed population: Berbers from all over North Africa between Tripolitania and the Atlantic coast of Morocco; Arabs from every part of the east; Sunnites as well as adherents of various Shīʿite shades; and also some Christian groups who so far had refused conversion to Islam. The imamate collapsed under the onslaught of the Kutāma* mountain tribes led by Abū ʿAbd Allāh al-Shīʿī, the fore-runner of the Fātimid Mahdī ʿUbaydullāh (908). The last *imām* Yaʿqub Ibn al-Aflah with his son Abū Sulaymān and some followers escaped but most of the other members of his family were killed. Three years later the people of Tāhart drove out the conquerors, but after a short-lived independence the town came under the rule of a Fātimid lieutenant, the Miknāsa* chieftain Masāla Ibn Habūs. A number of the inhabitants emigrated and joined the Ibādite colony in Sadrāta near the desert town of Wargla (in an oasis some 400 miles south of Algiers), trying to bring Tāhart back to new life there, but Sadrāta, too, was conquered by the Hammādid* Emir al-Nāsir (1062-1088). Thereupon most of the people sought safety in the desolate, stony highland of the Shabka (some 100 miles west of Sadrata), where the Ibādite community has survived in the Wādī M'Zab down to this day, known as Mozabites*. Of Sadrāta only ruins have have remained, partly brought to light (1950) out of the sands, among them three large houses, apparently luxuriously decorated in their time, some pottery and fragments of sculptured ornaments. Also the site of the main mosque is recognizable and together with the tomb of Imām Yaʿqūb Ibn al-Aflah is still visited by Ibādite pilgrims.

List of Rustumid Rulers:

ʿAbd al-Rahmān Ibn Rustum	776-784
ʿAbd al-Wahhāb Ibn ʿAbd al-Rahmān	784-823
Abū Saʿīd al-Aflah Ibn ʿAbd al-Wahhāb	823-871 (868?)
Abū Bakr Ibn al-Aflah	871 (868?)
Abū al-Yaqzān Muhammad Ibn al-Aflah	871 (868?)-894
Abū Hātim Yūsuf Ibn Muhammad, first reign	894-?
Yaʿqūb Ibn al-Aflah, first reign	?
Abū Hātim Yūsuf Ibn Muhammad, second reign	?
Yaʿqūb Ibn al-Aflah, second reign	906-908

S

SABʿĪN IBN, ʿABD al-HAQQ, one of the outstanding Hispano-Arab philosophers and mystics (1217-1269), honoured by the contemporary learned circles with the epithet *Qutb al-Dīn* (the Pole of Religion). Only few events of his life are known. He was born in Murcia but left Spain for Ceuta where he founded a religious brotherhood* *(tarīqa)*. While on pilgrimage he interrupted his travel in Tunis, but his stay there was cut short by the unfriendly attitude of the theologians at the religious academy of the Zaytūna, and so he continued his way to Arabia. Received with all marks of distinction by the Sharīf of Mecca he took residence there but soon afterwards died.
His doctrine is expounded in his *Asrār al-Hikma al-Mashriqīya* (Mysteries of the Illuministic Philosophy), while another treatise develops his ideas in the field of the theory of music. Ibn Sabʿīn became in particular known to the Christian scholastics by the so-called Answers to the Sicilian Questions *(al-Ajwiba ʿan al-As'ila al-Siqillīya)* written in response to a request which Emperor Frederick II of Hohenstaufen addressed to him from his court at Palermo, and which deal extensively with such subjects as the eternity of matter, the nature of the soul, the object of theology and a number of similar philosophical and metaphysical issues.

SAʿDIANS, Banū Saʿd, a Moroccan dynasty (1554-1659) issued from a sharīfian* clan (descendants of the Prophet Muhammad) which presumably around the end of the XVth century had immigrated from the Hijāz into the Wādī Darʿa in southern Morocco. At the time of the Wattāsid* sultan Abū ʿAbd Allāh, called al-Burtūqālī (1505-1524), its head, Abū ʿAbd Allāh Ibn Ahmad al-Qā'im rallied some religious brotherhoods* and influential marabouts*, all of the spiritual family of the mystic al-Jazūlī*, under the flag of the Holy War against the Portuguese occupation of increasingly wider parts of the country. With their support and aided by his prestige as a sharīf, it did not take him long in gaining a sort of inofficial leadership among the tribes of the region. Soon finding the field too limited for his ambition, he and his two sons, Abū al-ʿAbbās Ahmad al-Aʿraj and Abū ʿAbd Allāh Muhammad al-Shaykh al-Mahdī*, with their following of saintly men and some tribal groups moved westwards, established their headquarters near Tārūdānt, the principal town in the plain of the Sūs, and with changing luck waged a kind of guerilla warfare against the Portuguese and their allies from among the local chieftains. After his death (1517) his sons continued the struggle with more success and increased the number of their warriors, pushed the Portuguese back into a narrow strip on the coast, fortified Tārūdānt and, while still recognizing the sultan's sovereignty, made themselves more or less independent masters of the region. Then by the force of arms, ruse and treason Ahmad al- Aʿraj occupied Marrakesh (1523) where he set up his court, and assigned Tārūdānt as

residence to his brother Muhammad al-Shaykh.
Skilfully exploiting the esteem enjoyed by the sharīfian nobility and at the same time emphasizing his devotion to al-Jazūlī, at that time the most widely venerated popular saint in southern Morocco, for whom and his own father he erected a beautiful mausoleum in Marrakesh, he brought most of the tribes in the High and Middle Atlas onto his side. Two attempts of the Wattāsid government to curb the menacingly growing Saʿdian power ended in a compromise (1533 and 1537) arranged by the religious doctors of Fez. It left to the two brothers practically a free hand in the entire south, but their never very solid concord, already once before superficially patched up by the saintly men around them, definitively turned into enmity. Ahmad al- Aʿraj, beaten in open battle, was forced to withdraw into the Tāfīlālt (1540) and soon afterwards joined the Wattāsid camp. In the meantime Muhammad al-Shaykh had taken up again the Holy War with much stronger forces, conquered Agadir (1541) and occupied Safi and Azemmour, both evacuated by their Portuguese garrisons.
This success marked the beginning of Muhammad al-Shaykh's thirteen-year struggle against the dissolving Wattāsid régime and its allies, the Ottoman beylerbegs of Algeria. The outcome was his recognition as sultan, his assumption of the title of Caliph and the disappearance of the last Wattāsids. Soon afterwards he was assassinated. During his short reign (1554-1557) he traced the orientation of Saʿdian policy in the next five decades: alliance with Spain as a counterpoise against Turkish pressure; curtailing the aspirations after secular power of the religious fraternities and marabouts; a strong army based on a war-trained and well-equipped corps of mercenaries; and a firm system of taxation. As long as his successors adhered to these lines, the State prospered and its international prestige stood high; with their abandonment it collapsed.
Muhammad al-Shaykh's son, Sultan and Caliph Mūlāy ʿAbd Allāh al-Ghālib (1557-1574) had to defend his title to the succession against several pretenders in his closest family, and he did it with radical efficiency: a few were thrown into prison; his brother who had sought Turkish help in Tlemcen was assassinated; so was his nephew, the governor of Meknès; two other brothers, Abū Marwān ʿAbd al-Malik and Abū al-ʿAbbās Ahmad, escaped to Constantinople and took service in the Ottoman army. Twenty years later they had their names connected, each one in a different way, with the most successful period of the Saʿdian era. Mūlāy ʿAbd Allāh strengthened the alliance with Spain by the cession of certain strategic points on the coast of the Rif, and by avoiding an intervention in favour of the Moriscos* (designation of the Moslems in Spain after the reconquest by the Christian Powers) revolting against enforced conversion. Thus he forestalled the Turkish plans of invading northern Morocco, but aroused the indignation of the marabouts and religious brotherhoods, whose hold upon the masses grew irresistably firmer. He faced open dissidence with severity and appeased the populace by manifestations of a perhaps not thoroughly sincere piety and the erection or restoration of mosques and theological schools.
He was succeeded by his son Abū ʿAbd Allāh Mūlāy Muhammad al-Mutawakkil (1574-1576) against whom however his uncle Abū Mar-

wān ʿAbd al-Malik, immediately came forth as pretender. ʿAbd al-Malik, much travelled, impregnated with Turkish culture and ranking high at the court of Constantinople, obtained from Sultan Murād in exchange for the recognition of Ottoman sovereignty, the command over a Turkish expeditionary corps which was to pave his way to the overthrow of his nephew. He defeated him at the gates of Fez and entered the city (1576), installed his brother Abū al-ʿAbbās Ahmad as governor, then occupied the capital Marrakesh while Mūlāy Muhammad sought refuge first with some of the marabouts in the Atlas and then in Spain. Coldly received he continued into Portugal, where King Sebastian concluded with him a pact for, as he was made to believe, his restoration, but in the King's mind for the Portuguese conquest of Morocco. In the meanwhile ʿAbd al-Malik, acclaimed as Sultan, hired a corps of mercenaries and rallied a number of tribal chiefs and religious brotherhoods. Then, although forced by a severe illness to turn over the command to Abū al-ʿAbbās Ahmad, he set out to confront the Portuguese who had landed in Arzila and Tangier, but did not live to see the overwhelming Moroccan victory in the so-called Battle of the Three Kings*, in which also both his adverseries, Don Sebastian and Mūlāy Muhammad met their death.

Abū al-ʿAbbās Ahmad, thenceforth Ahmad al-Mansūr* (The Victorious), hailed as sultan by his army and immediately recognized by the whole country, inaugurated an era of peace and prosperity, which lasted throughout the quarter of a century of his reign (1578-1603). Aided by the prestige which the success of his arms had won for him he managed to extricate himself from the obligation to Turkey incurred by his brother, so that the sovereignty of Morocco was no longer called into question. The considerable amount of the ransom for all the Portuguese nobles taken prisoners on the battle-field, and later on, the conquest of the Sudan (1591) with the ensuing afflux of gold, combined with a skilful economic policy put the public finances on a solid basis. All this and a strong military organization secured to Morocco the standing of a Great Power whose voice was seriously counted with in its dealing with Europe and the Ottoman Empire.

With his death his work fell to pieces and the country sank into a state of anarchy endangering its very existence. A seven-year incessant contest for the heritage opposed one against another his sons Abū Fāris, Muhammad al-Ma'mūn al-Shaykh and Abū al-Maʿālī Mūlāy Zaidān. They gained alternately, now one, then another an ephemeral recognition by the people of Fez or of Marrakesh while the loser awaited under Spanish or Turkish protection his turn for dispossessing his rivals. Out of this struggle there finally emerged one Saʿdian line at Fez, which with al-Ma'mūn al-Shaykh and his son and grand-son continued until 1626; and one at Marrakesh under Mūlāy Zaidān (1603-1628), which lived on one generation longer until the last Saʿdian, Ahmad al-ʿAbbās (1654-1659), was assassinated in a revolt, and Marrakesh occupied by an Arab tribe. Neither of the two exercised sovereign power very far beyond the city precincts and only through a well-paid body-guard of foreign mercenaries and by playing off one against the other the different antagonistic urban factions. Morocco had split into virtually independent smaller or larger territorial units of fluid boundaries, such as the city-republic of Rabat-Salé under the hegemony of the Hornachero* clan, or the marabout emirates of al-ʿAyyāshī*, al-Samlālī* or Abū Mahallī* or the Dilā'yūn* brotherhood. Mūlāy Zaidān alone among his brothers and cousins with unfaltering tenacity tried to stop the centrifugal forces but the disintegrating process was already too far advanced.

Notwithstanding the confusion of this inextricable interplay of local and regional power groups, in which every notion of an ordinate, country-wide conduct of public affairs vanished, the economic activities of the population at large seem hardly to have suffered. Judging from reports of contemporary European travellers and government agents, English, Dutch, Spanish and Portuguese merchants purchased and shipped from the ports of Safi, Agadir, Massa, Tangier and Tetuan important quantities of sugar from the large plantations in the Sūs; hides and wool; oil, salt and spices; honey, wax and camel's hair fabrics. Their partners were the great merchants of Fez and Marrakesh as well as the Hornacheros of Rabat-Salé and the marabout-princes. This trade was partly legitimate and carried on under official licences, some of it by strong, semi-public enterprises such as the Barbary Company in England (constituted 1585) which held the monopoly of the commerce with Morocco. Not the least of it was illegitimate, done by so-called 'interlopers' and smugglers, especially the sale of fire-arms to the various dissident groups, and easily changed into piracy. High-sea robbery, a regular profession of the Moriscos of Salé, but to a not much lesser extent practised also by English and Spanish marauders, had its counter-part in privateering by states at war with each other. It was thus that Mūlāy Zaidān lost his library - and his harem - which a French ship was commissioned to take to Agadir from Salé whither the sultan had fled when attacked by Abū Mahallī: the ship was captured by a Spanish privateer, and the books, taken as booty to Spain, were never returned in spite of long-drawn tripartite negotiations between Morocco, France and Spain. They are today in Madrid in the Escurial Library.

The unglorious end of the Saʿdian dynasty found Morocco fractionized into an indeterminable entanglement of half-religious, half-secular domains, tribal districts and city areas, all under equally ephemeral, illusory sovereignties. Its last members were undoubtedly insignificant, weak figures, but those who preceded them and had been able to conceive and pursue a distinct policy of their own, had steered the country clear of an imminent, two-fold danger: either of falling victim to the Spanish and Portuguese colonial expansion, or of being absorbed by the expanding Ottoman Empire. It was due to this policy that the successors of the Saʿdians, the presently reigning ʿAlawid dynasty, were able to reforge the unity of the country and preserve its independence.

The Saʿdian Rulers:

Abū ʿAbd Allāh Muhammad al-Shaykh al-Mahdī	1554-1557
Mūlāy ʿAbd Allāh al-Ghālib	1557-1574
Abū ʿAbd Allāh Mūlāy Muhammad al-Mutawakkil, surnamed al-Maslūkh	1574-1576
Abū Marwān ʿAbd al-Malik	1576-1578
Abū al-ʿAbbās Ahmad al-Mansūr, surnamed al-Dhahabī	1578-1603

Marrakesh Branch:

Abū al-Maʿālī Mūlāy Zaidān	1603-1628
Abū Marwān ʿAbd al-Malik	1628-1631
Al-Walīd Ibn Zaidān	1631-1636
Muhammad al-Shaykh Ibn Zaidān al-Asghar	1636-1654
Ahmad al-ʿAbbās Ibn Muhammad al-Shaykh	1654-1659

Fez Branch:

Mūlāy al-Ma'mūn al-Shaykh	1610-1613
ʿAbd Allāh al-Shaykh Ibn al-Ma'mūn	1613-1624
ʿAbd al-Malik Ibn al-Ma'mūn	1624-1626

SAHNŪN, the nickname (after the name of a certain lively bird, an allusion to his quick mind) under which the theological scholar ʿAbd al-Salām Ibn Saʿīd (776-854) has become known. Born in Homs (Syria) of a poor family, the son of a simple soldier, he came in his early youth to al-Qayrawān, where he had his first scholarly training. He continued his studies in Egypt with disciples of Mālik Ibn-Anas, the founder of one of the four basic schools of juridico-theological thought; then, regardless of all difficulties which poverty put in his way, travelled to Medina and joined the circle around Mālik himself who at that time was already near the end of his life. After a stay in Syria, he returned to al-Qayrawān and soon attracted an increasing number of students, Arabs and Berbers, from the North African countries as well as from al-Andalus*, thus greatly contributing to the spread of the Mālikite teaching and its implantation on both sides of the Mediterranean. His unyielding firmness in doctrinal questions repeatedly brought him into serious conflicts with powerful antagonists and even led him for a while into prison. Yet in the course of a change in the inner political constellation, he was appointed cadi in al-Qayrawān, a position only reluctantly assumed, in which his meticulous conscientiousness and humane attitude especially towards the humbler classes gained for him a profound popular esteem bordering on veneration.

Sahnūn left one fundamental work, the *Mudawwana*, an exegesis of Mālikite thought, based on the treatise of his contemporary, Asad Ibn al-Furāt*, the *Asadīya.* In the course of its elaboration he exercised utmost care in dealing with any matter which might be open to doubt, consulting with other reputed theological doctors and expounding his reasons when formulating a statement. The *Mudawanna* was often commented upon and held for several centuries an undisputed prior place at the Andalusian and North African religious academies.

SĀ'IFA, a term (comp. *saif*, summer), denoting in *al-Andalus** the incursions undertaken regularly in the summer months into the neighbouring Christian countries which were regarded as territories in a permanent state of war *(dār al-harb)* with the Moslem governments. Compared with the considerable military and financial efforts required by the preparation and organization of these expeditions, the practical results which they achieved were small in significance except for their moral effects and the devastations inflicted upon the enemy by the burning of his villages, the pilfering of his harvest or the cutting down of his fruit trees. The sole tangible gain consisted in the prisoners, male and female, who were distributed as slaves to the troops after deduction of a part for the State. Yet neither for the ruler nor for the troop commanders, selected from among the most distinguished generals and the royal princes, nor for the rank and file, was it military glory or the prospect of booty which supplied the incentive for these warlike undertakings, but primarily religious merit attached to the fulfilment of the duty of the Holy War *(jihād)* against the unbelievers for the purpose of advancing the realm of Islam.

SALAFĪYA, derived from the verb *salafa*, to precede, to be over; resp. from the noun *al-aslāf*, the predecessors, the ancestors, and denoting a spiritual movement in Islam, which aimed at the clearance of the faith from superstitions and accretions springing from political or materialistic motives. This re-established, unaltered creed was to constitute the guiding principle in religious as well as secular matters, for the individual as well as for society as a whole, in any single Moslem state as well as within the entire community of Islam. Rooted in the teaching of the Arabian reformer ʿAbd al-Wahhāb (1720-1792) and the writings of the theologian Muhammad ʿAbduh (1849-1905), the *Salafīya* began to gain ground in the Arab West around the turn of the century among the theological doctors at the academies of the Qarawīyīn* in Fez and the Zaytūna in Tunis, and also in Algeria where it later became a driving force in the movement promoted by the Association of the Algerian ʿUlamā'*. It assumed real importance in the 'twenties under the impulsion of Sheikh al-Dukkālī, who returned to Morocco, his native country, after a prolonged stay at the centres of theological learning in the Arab East. Preceded by the reputation of his piety, and aided by an extraordinary eloquence, he preached in towns and villages against the inveterate superstitious practices and in particular against the religious brotherhoods* which he branded as the guardians - and main beneficiaries - of these popular superstitions. As a result the brotherhoods lost in fact a great many adepts and supporters, although regaining most of them shortly afterwards. About the same time, the *Salafīya* doctrine with its various philosophical, moral, sociological and political aspects was given an academic formulation by the much esteemed teacher at the Qarawīyīn in Fez, Muhammad Ben Larbi Alawi (Ibn al-ʿArabī al-ʿAlawī). A group of enthusiastic students, among them several of the future protagonsists of Moroccan nationalism such as ʿAllāl al-Fāsī or Muhammad Lyazidi (al-Yazīdī) carried his word in their public lectures and pamphlets into the circles of a like-minded youth in every larger Moroccan city. In this atmosphere, what originally was the reaction of theologians against the overgrowth of heterodox deviations did not take long in assuming a growing political significance, particularly owing to the opposition against the religious orders considered - and in many cases justly so - to be the willing and seldom disinterested instruments of the régime of the Protectorate*. Thus, while the Salafīya as a religious movement began the lose momentum it became one of the driving forces of the awakening Arab nationalism.

SĀLIHIDS, an Arab dynasty of emirs in North-Africa (early VIIIth until the middle of the XIth century) ruling over the fertile area extending on both sides of the mouth of the river Nakūr on the Mediterranean coast halfway between Melilla and Tetuan. Its founder, Sālih Ibn Mansūr, of a family of South Arabian origin, was a companion-in-arms of ʿUqba Ibn Nāfiʿ, the commander of the first Arab expedition into North Africa (670-683), who with his people settled in this region of prosperous villages inhabited by the Berber Ghumāra. Subsequently the Caliph invested him with the governorship which under his descendants became hereditary. About 760 one of them, Saʿīd Ibn Idrīs, established his residence in the newly founded town of Nakūr - today the village of Adjir, the birthplace of the Berber warlord ʿAbd al-Karīm* - and developed a flourishing trade with the Andalusian ports. While the ties of the Sālihids with the caliphs gradually loosened, those with the Umayyad emirs, later caliphs of al-Andalus*, grew steadily stronger. Sālihid warriors repeatedly fought on the side of the Umayyads against their Christian neighbours, and Nakūr developed into a valuable political and military Umayyad point of support on the African coast. Strict adherents of the orthodox Sunnite creed, the Sālihids also made their little principality a focus of resistance against first the Khārijite, then the Fātimid heterodoxies.
When Nakūr was sacked and burnt down by the Normans (858) and the womenfolk of the palace taken into captivity, the emir of Cordova, Muhammad I (852-886), bought them back and returned them to the emir Sālih Ibn Saʿīd. Again, when Nakūr was captured by the Berber Miknāsa* in alliance with the Fātimids, and Saʿīd Ibn Sālih was killed in battle (917), his three surviving sons were received with full honours in al-Andalus. One of them, Sālih Ibn Saʿīd, surnamed *al-Yatīm* (The Orphan), shortly afterwards regained his heritage and solemnly placed it under Umayyad protection, but under his successor Nakūr was once more destroyed by the Miknāsa. Rapidly rebuilt, it was conquered again (935), and the ruler, Emir Abū Ayyūb Ismāʿīl, lost his life. The townspeople, however, revolted and killed the Fātimid governor, sent his head to Cordova as a token of loyalty and recalled a member of the Sālihid family to the throne. Thenceforth the fate of Nakūr did not attract any longer the interest of the chroniclers, but coins with the inscription of its name, dating from the early years of the XIth century, have been found and show that the Sālihid emirs continued to hold their place until their domain disappeared under the onslaught of the Almoravids* (1061-1147).

SAMLĀLĪ al-, ABŪ al-HASAN ʿALĪ, popularly known as Bū Hassūn (†1659) and also called the Emir of the Sūs (the large, fertile plain stretching from the Atlantic coast inland between the High and the Anti Atlas), one of the most prominent of the saintly men (marabouts*) in Morocco in the last years of the Saʿdian* dynasty. He was a member of the Samlāla clan, one of the branches of the Gazūla tribe, the same from which had come forth two centuries earlier the great mystical teacher al-Jazūlī*, and was born in the Sāhil, the coastal strip in the southern sector of the Sūs, in the town of Massa. On this spot, as legend has it, the great general of the Arab conquest of North Africa, ʿUqba Ibn Nāfiʿ († 683), drove his horse into the waves of the Ocean, calling God to witness that there was no more land for him to conquer. No information on al-Samlālī's early career has been transmitted. When his name appears in history, he had already gained unquestioned spiritual and political ascendency in the Sāhil. Partly by clever manoeuvering and partly owing to the superior number of warlike followers he eliminated the most dangerous of his rivals, the marabouts Abū Mahallī* and Abū Zakariyyā'al-Mannānī, solidly implanted his authority throughout the entire region of the Sūs and established his seat in the town of Tārūdānt. Then he carried his preaching, emphasized by the sword, deep into the interior up the Wādī Darʿa and occupied Sijilmāsa. An attempt to take hold of the oases and the palmgroves of the Tāfīlālt brought him into collision with the clan of the ʿAlawids* who were settled there since the middle of the XIIIth century and, supported by their prestige as sharīfs*, firmly refused to give ground. The conflict was temporarily appeased through intervention of the powerful Dilā'yūn* brotherhood*, but broke out again and ended with al-Samlālī's retreat from the Tāfīlālt and the Wādī Darʿa. His adversary, the ʿAlawid chieftain Mūlāy ʿAlī al-Sharīf, who soon afterwards fell into his hands, was kept for some time in honorable captivity and finally released for a substantial ransom.

Al-Samlālī stood far above the level of most of the many marabout warlords of those days. He built up the territories, assembled and controlled by his strong-willed personality, into an organized body politic extending over the greater part of the Anti Atlas and the plain of the Sūs. He maintained a lively caravan trade with the Sudan and Senegal, and equally profitable overseas relations from the port of Massa with England and Holland. The remembrance of his prosperity, perhaps somewhat embellished by legend, still lives on in the regions which constituted his principality, well protected by a military force whose arms were supplied mainly by Dutch shippers. The significance which the Dutch attached to their mercantile transactions with the marabout-emir is best illustrated by the official mission conducted by Admiral de Ruyter trying, apparently in vain, to negotiate for preferential conditions. Al-Samlālī's sons lost their heritage (1670) to the first ʿAlawid Sultan Mūlāy al-Rashīd* (1664-1672).

SANHĀJA, a wide-spread and probably the most warlike of the great historic Berber family of tribes. As early as the third century some of their branches together with other affiliated tribes such as the Hawwāra, Lamta, Lamtūna*, Massūfa and Juddāla seem to have started migrating westwards - their original homeland has so far not been precisely determined - and steadily penetrated into the Sahara. Gradually but continuously the Sanhāja advanced into Mauretania, spread further into the Sudan and the region of the Niger, partly pushing back the native peoples, partly setting up a sort of sovereignty over the various Negro princedoms, in particular over the oldest and strongest of them, the kingdom of Ghana. Converted to Islam, although of a shade still strongly tinged with beliefs and practices of their pagan past,

they carried their creed among the peoples under their rule. In the VIIIth and IXth century several quite important confederations of various Sanhāja tribes, nomads or in early stages of transition to a semi-sedentary mode of life, were predominant in the western parts of the Sahara. In Mauretania (al-Shingīt) the Massūfa and Lamtūna united with other, smaller groups all belonging to the so called *Mulaththamūn** or veil wearers, set up a tribal kingdom which from the first quarter of the ninth until the beginning of the Xth century constituted a stabilizing force within the fluctuating desert society, controlling and policing the caravan trade to the Atlantic and Mediterranean ports. It was broken up by internal rivalries, but a new confederation came into being towards the middle of the XIth century under the joint leadership of the then most powerful members of the Sanhāja family in this region, the Juddāla and Lamtūna. In their midst the triumphal religio-military advance of the Almoravids* had its origin.
During these times, in stages which are not known, numerous groups, mainly Gazūla, Lamta and Haskūra, partly remaining nomads and partly settling down, migrated into the plains of the Moroccan coasts on the Atlantic south of the Sūs. Others moved north-eastwards onto the slopes of the Middle Atlas in the area of Taza and further on into the Rif. Still others occupied the oases around Sijilmāsa, later turned eastwards and spread over a considerable section of the present-day Algerian department of Constantine, where in the early Xth century one of their branches, the Kutāma, became a pillar of the rising Fātimid power and brought about the downfall of the Aghlabid* emirate. The name of the Kutāma disappeared, but their descendants, the Kabyles*, constitute today a most active element in the political texture and intellectual life of Algeria.
From the Algerian Sanhāja sprang the dynasty of the Zīrids* (end of the Xth until the middle of the XIIth century) who played a foremost rôle in the military and political as well as the economic and cultural history of North Africa, and to a lesser extent also in al-Andalus* where from the ruins of the Umayyad caliphate they built up their throne in Granada. Of Sanhāja blood, too, was a second family of rulers in northern Algeria and Tunisia, the Hammādids*, related to the Zīrids, yet almost permanently opposed to them in tenacious rivalry. Driven by their impulse of expansion and conquest, the Sanhāja inevitably infringed upon the territories of other groups or confederations of tribes, and became involved in conflicts growing in the course of time into hereditary enmities which, such as those with the Zanāta*, left their mark on the entire period of the Middle Ages in North Africa.

SANŪSĪYA, a politico-religious brotherhood*, deeply inspired by the Wahhābi doctrine of the return to the unaltered purity and the simple pious way of life of early Islam, and, like Wahhābism, originally imbued by a highly militant spirit. The Sanūsīya, strongly represented among the Arab and Berber tribes in Cyrenaica (Libya), has communities in the Sudan, in Arabia and even in India. Its founder, Sayyid Muhammad Ibn ʿAlī al-Sanūsī, descended from a Berber family in Algeria, studied at several theological academies in North Africa, then went to Mecca, where he formulated the tenets of a school of his own and gathered his first disciples. Leaving Mecca in 1834 with a group of adepts, he wandered back to North Africa and settled on the southern slopes of the Jabal al-Akhdar in Cyrenaica, whence his missionaries carried his words all over the desert into the villages of the oases and among the nomad tribesmen. They did not take long to attract a numerous membership and set up more and more branch-seats, each of which became a centre of spiritual guidance and of further missionary work. At the same time, in accordance with the master's teaching, they were to stimulate improvements in the cultivation of the land and in the tending of livestock; to arbitrate tribal conflicts; and to maintain peace and order along the caravan routes. These tasks the network of *zāwiyas** very efficiently fulfilled, and almost completely supplanted in Cyrenaica the weak and unpopular Turkish administration. After some time, however, the increasingly hostile attitude of the Constantinople government, which perhaps not entirely without ground feared that there might be crystallizing the nucleus of a theocracy after the Wahhābi pattern in Arabia, made it appear wiser to Muhammad Ibn ʿAlī to move (1855) his headquarters to the oasis of Jaghabūb just across the Egyptian border.

His son and successor, Sayyid Muhammad al-Mahdī, systematically continued the foundation of *zāwiyas*, which soon numbered over a hundred and thus steadily expanded and consolidated the Sanūsīya's religious and political influence, but at the same time re-awakened Turkish suspicion. Again the main seat of the brotherhood had to be transferred, now into the outlying oasis of Kufra, deep in the south of the Cyrenaican desert. Muhammad al-Mahdī, venerated by the faithful as a sage and a saint, died in 1901, but was believed to be still living in concealment and to return at the chosen time. He was succeeded by his nephew, Sayyid Ahmad al-Sharīf - his own son, Sayyid Idrīs, the future King of Libya, was not yet of age - who gained the favour of the Sultan by following his call to the Holy War and leading the Sanūsī brethren against the invading Italian armies (October 1911), at first side by side with the Turkish troops, and carrying on the warfare even after Turkey had already been forced to renounce her sovereignty over the Libyan provinces (Treaty of Ouchy, October 1912). Also in the First World War he remained faithful to the Sultan and penetrating into Egypt with the help of Turkish artillery and German submarines, drove the British garrisons out of Sollum and Marsa Matruh. Repelled, however, a few months later he resigned the leadership of the order in favour of his cousin, Sayyid Idrīs, while his brother kept on harassing the French in the Fezzan. A German submarine took him safely to Constantinople, whence he went to Damascus and subsequently to Medina. There he died in 1933.

Sayyid Idrīs, having made peace with the British and the Italians, was officially recognized by both as the supreme chief of the Sanūsīya and at the end of the war also as the secular ruler - under Italian tutelage - over the Cyrenaican desert and the oases. He was accorded the title of Emir with the right to his own flag, and granted, besides a personal allowance, substantial subsidies for the chieftains of his tribes, while his uncle Safī al-Dīn al-Sanūsī was appointed president of the Cyrenaican 'parliament' which had been instituted by the Italian administration. In July 1922, an assembly of Tripolitanian notables elected Sayyid Idrīs Emir of Tripolitania, but by the end of the year owing to rapidly sharpening frictions with the new Fascist Governor he left for Cairo, accompanied by his dignitaries and soon followed by some of the influential Sanūsī shaykhs. Others found a temporary home in Syria, the Sudan and Tunisia. There he remained in exile for almost a quarter of a century but all the time in close contact with the various branches of the brotherhood, in whose eyes the nimbus of his spiritual and secular leadership continued undiminished. Yet the mass of the Sanūsī warriors, led by one of their most daring chieftains, ʿUmar al-Mukhtar, and provided with arms and ammunition by the *zāwiyas* in Egypt and the Sudan, rose against the foreign domination and kept up a pitiless guerilla for nearly a decade until the Italians put up a barbed wire barrier all along the border and cut off the supply. When at last ʿUmar Ibn Mukhtar was captured and hanged on a public square - in the memory of the Libyans he lives on as a national hero - and the Sanūsī fighters were completely worn out by the loss of lives and the destruction of their herds, the 'pacification' of Libya was secured, until Italy in June 1940 entered the Second World War.

Then a 'Libyan Arab Force', recruited by Sayyid Idrīs from among his Sanūsī communities outside the Italian sphere of power and incorporated into the British army in Egypt, took part in the successful desert campaigns against the common enemy, with the result that in 1942 the British Secretary of State for Foreign Affairs, Anthony Eden, in the House of Commons solemnly declared, that 'at the end of the war the Sanūsī in Cyrenaica should under no circumstances fall again under Italian domination'. They did not, in fact, but from November 1942 onwards for about eight years Cyrenaica remained under 'temporary' British military administration. However, by the end of 1947 Amīr Idrīs - as his people called him, or His Eminence, as he was addressed by the British Administrator - returned to Cyrenaica and instituted a National Congress under the chairmanship of one of his brothers, and in July 1949 with British approval proclaimed a Cyrenaican Constitution and appointed a Cyrenaican government. Thenceforth the fate of the Sanūsī is closely linked with the story of how the United Nations General Assembly on November 21, 1949 resolved that Libya, the former Italian colony, comprising Cyrenaica, Tripolitania and the Fezzan, was to become an independent and sovereign state, and how on Christmas eve 1951 it was declared a federal monarchy with Sayyid Muhammad Idrīs al-Sanūsī, head of the Sanūsī brotherhood, as its first hereditary ruler.

SAQĀLIBA, Hispano-Arabic term (comp. the medieval Latin 'esclavus') denoting originally the captives brought back by the Germans from their expeditions against the Slavonic tribes in south-eastern Europe and sold as slaves in al-Andalus*. They embraced Islam, and of warlike temper but simple-minded and blindly devoted to their master, they constituted an ideal soldiery from whose ranks the ruler recruited a strong and reliable body-guard. Later, a second source of supply was provided by the North African pirates raiding the Italian and

Greek coasts for more of those valuable military slaves. The *Saqāliba* were the principal instrument in the hands of the caliph for enforcing peace and order in the country and compelling the refractory nobility to obedience. Their importance as an essential factor of stability in the state inevitably also led to a change in their status. In the course of time many of their captains gained access to the civil administration, acquired property, often considerable wealth and power rooted in a strong feeling of class solidarity. Quite a few also turned towards higher education, became liberal patrons of poets, and some even aimed at literary fame for themselves. Between the Xth and XIIth century the *Saqāliba* played a rôle of considerable significance in the political and economic life of the country until they were gradually absorbed by the other elements of the population.

SHARĪF, noble, illustruous, plur. *ashrāf* or *shurafā'* (by occidental authors often renderd as 'shorfa' or in French spelling 'chorfa'), a title by which the descendants of the Prophet Muhammad by his daughter Fātima and her husband ʿAli Ibn Abī Tālib have been honoured. Soon after the Arab conquest of North Africa a number of sharīfian families settled in these remote parts of the caliphate, where they contributed greatly to the spread of Islam and stood in the forefront of the fight against the Khārijite heresy or other heterodox doctrines, and at all times were staunch supporters of orthodox sunnite teaching. Only during the Fātimid era in Tunisia (Xth century) a number of them were on the side of these shīʿite caliphs.
In Morocco, since the establishment of the sharīfian Idrīsid* dynasty (788-974), the country's first independent rulers, the prestige attached to this religious aristocracy has remained almost undiminished, notwithstanding the innumerable many who in the course of the centuries found access into its ranks often on the ground of a somewhat disputable, more often still of a patently self-fabricated genealogy. Of sharīfian descent is the reigning house of the ʿAlawids*; so were their immediate predecessors, the Saʿdians*; so are in the towns most of the old patrician families as well as many of the broad middle-class groups; and also quite a few among the rural population. With the same illustrious ancestry was credited everyone of the innumerable saints by their unquestioningly believing reverers. The sharīfian nobility has at all times been strongly represented among religious dignitaries, in scholarly circles and the high officialdom. In no other Arab country has that branch of biographical literature which deals with the history of the sharīfian families and the lives of their members enjoyed such a rich harvest. The value of these works, at least in their majority, lies only to a minor extent in the portraying abilities of their authors or the originality of the characters and their achievements, but mainly in the light occasionally shed on the social, political and general cultural environment. From this point of view they were made the subject of a modern analytical study (E. Lévi-Provençal, Les Historiens des Chorfa, Paris, 1922) based in numerous cases on still unpublished manuscripts.

SHARQĀWĪYA, a religious brotherhood*, one of the offshoots of the

Jazūlīya*, founded about 1600 by the marabout* Sīdī Mahammad Ibn Abī al-Qāsim al-Sharqī in Boujad (Abū al-Jaʿd in the Tādlā, the table-land extending north-west from the Middle Atlas along the course of the river Umm al-Rabīʿ). The high reputation of saintliness enjoyed by its heads, all members of the Sharqāwa family, which is reflected in the contemporary biographical literature, secured to the fraternity far beyond its proper area a great moral prestige and also at times a noteworthy political influence making itself felt as late as the first quarter of the present century. Certain reforms introduced towards the end of the XVIIIth century by a great-grandson of the founder, Muhammad al-Muʿtā Ibn ʿAbd al-Malik, author of a collection of prayers in 40 volumes, assimilated the Sharqāwīya closely to the Nāsirīya* brotherhood.

SHOTT, in the Arab West colloquially for *shatt* (in French texts spelt *chott)*, originally meaning a sand-bank or shoal, then in a wider sense used in the Arab East, particularly in Mesopotamia, for a broad stream (comp. *Shatt al-ʿArab* formed by the confluence of the Euphrates and Tigris). In Morocco, Algeria and Tunisia *shott* denotes the vast, shallow depressions in the border regions of the desert and in the steppe, some of them below sea-level, and during the rainy periods filled with brackish, muddy water in their deeper parts, while saline efflorescences cover the rest of the marshy surface. The special kinds of herbs and shrubby plants growing on the salty soils in and around them make these areas excellent pastures for camels.

SLAUGHTER OF THE DITCH see WAQʿAT al-HUFRA

SMALA see ZMĀLA

SOCIALIST DEMOCRATIC PARTY, usually referred to as P.S.D., the initials of its French designation 'Parti Socialiste Démocratique', a Moroccan political party which was established by Rashīd Ridā Guedīra in April 1964, when it appeared that internal dissensions were dangerously weakening the Front for the Defence of the Constitutional Institutions* (F.D.I.C.), the precarious government majority in the Lower Chamber. The new party, which enjoys the strong moral support of the groups around the Crown, is intended to attract the adherence of the peasants and workers and to draw them away from the two opposition parties, the *Istiqlāl** and the National Union of Popular Forces* (U.N.F.P.).

SULAYM, an Arabian tribe originally belonging to the Qays ʿAylān confederation, of which some groups around the time of the rise of Islam migrated into Mesopotamia, while the others remained in their pasture grounds in Central and North Arabia. In the IXth cent. the latter adhered to the socio-religious Qarmatian revolutionary movement and in the course of its suppression were deported together with the Banū Hilāl*, also fanatical Qarmatians, into the Egyptian border regions east of the Nile. Although submitting, at least in name, to the

Fātimid conquerors of Egypt, their unruliness and predatory disposition made both of them a highly undesirable element, particularly dangerous for the flourishing caravan trade, so that the fourth Fātimid caliph al-Mustansir (1036-1094), by gifts of money and robes of honour to their chieftains, induced them to leave Egypt and invade the territory of his unfaithful vassal, the Zīrid* emir al-Muʿizz, the ruler of what today is Tunisia, and following a then current practice, invested them in advance with all the country they might occupy (about 1052). They overran Lybia, but while the Banū Hilāl assailed the Zīrid realm, the Sulaym remained in Tripolitania.

There they stayed until some two hundred years later the first Hafsid* emir in Tunisia, Abū Zakariyyā' Yahyā* (1228-1249) called them into his country in order to have them dislodge a troublesome Hilālite branch, the Riyāh. They came, drove the Riyāh into eastern Algeria, and remained in the steppes of southern Tunisia, continuing their nomadic way of life. Their two main branches, more often than not opposed to each other in embittered feuds, the Kuʿūb - themselves split into two rival clans, the Awlād Abī al-Layl and the Awlād Muhalil - and the Banū Mirdās, soon gained supremacy over most of the regional Berber tribes, and gradually forced back northwards most of the sedentary population. By their number and warlike spirit they constituted a fighting force of appreciable value for the Hafsid government as long as their loyalty lasted; but, involved in all dynastic quarrels, siding now with one, now with another of the adverse parties, suddenly changing camps without apparent reason, they were responsible for much of the almost ceaseless internal unrest in Hafsid Tunisia. Still more damaging perhaps to the country's economy was their irrepressible rapacity: no village and even none of the smaller towns were safe from their raids unless they bought their safety by substantial contributions or took into their pay a rival faction to protect them from the aggressors.

It is noteworthy, however, that at times there arose in their midst an active resistance, inspired by motives of a religious nature, against such brigandage, as towards the end of the XIIIth century among the Kuʿūb clan of the Abī al-Layl. It was one of its members, the mystically inclined Qāsim Ibn Marā, who rallied a number of like-minded followers and, after his preaching had proved unsuccessful, forced, arms-in-hand, his refractory fellow-tribesmen off the great caravan roads and the larger villages, until he was assassinated by a chieftain of the enemy sister-clan, the Awlād Muhalil.

Descendants of the Sulaym, with some negroid admixture, still live today in southern Tunisia and Algeria as peaceful goat-, sheep-and camel breeders.

SULTAN, *sultān* as the title of a ruler made its appearance in the Arab West about the XIth century in al-Andalus* at the courts of the numerous city princes, the so-called Party Kings* *(mulūk al-tawā'if)*, at the time of the disintegration of the Umayyad caliphate. When most of these ephemeral miniature states came under Almoravid* and then Almohad* régime, the new sovereigns did not retain this title for themselves but left it as a mark of distinction to the other members of the family and the influential tribal chieftains. By another change in the notion of its prestige in the successor-states of the Almohad empire - Morocco, Tunisia under the Hafsids*, and the ʿAbd al-Wādid* realm of Tlemcen - the official historiographers and the court society, soon followed by public opinion, began to regard it again as the exclusive privilege of the head of the State. It took, however, some time before it was used, occasionally in the combination *al-malik al-sultān* (King-Sultan) or *al-maulā al-sultān* (Lord-Sultan), in the documents of the court chancellery, on coins and in inscriptions on public buildings; or transformed into *soldanus*, *soldanum* or *soldano* under the pen of the European redactors of the Latin or Italian texts of their governments' correspondence with the Arab sovereign. It was not until August 1957 that Muhammad V* of Morocco replaced his title of Sultan by that of King.

SUMMAM VALLEY CONGRESS, secretly held in August 1956 by partisans of the Algerian Revolution* at a remote site in the valley of the Summan River in the heart of the Kabylia mountain land. Suggested by Belkacem Krim (Karīm Bilqāsim), the commander of the rebel forces in the *wilaya* (district) Kabylia, and in particular by his brilliant and uncompromisingly radical lieutenant Ramdān Abbān - the circumstances of his death two years later have never been elucidated - it was convened by the common consent of the other commanders in the Army of National Liberation* (A.L.N.) and of the External Delegation* of the Front of National Liberation* (F.L.N.), forcefully inspired by Ahmad Ben Bella (Ibn Ballā) later President of the Algerian Republic. Yet contrary to his wish it was decided not to meet at the delegation's seat in Cairo but, notwithstanding the danger of discovery, somewhere in Algeria so as not to keep the military chiefs too long and too far away from their men. For the sake of security, place and date had to be determined, or changed, in the last minute, so that Ben Bella and his colleagues waited three weeks in Italy for the signal where and when to depart, but could not be notified in time. When Ben Bella two months later - in fact shortly before he fell into French captivity while flying from Rabat to Tunis - learned that the Conference had been held, he did not hide his discontent and contested the validity of some of its decisions taken in his absence. It may have been his five-year imprisonment and separation from the other leaders which prevented the conflict from coming to light already then in all the sharpness which it took on within the Provisional Government of the Algerian Republic* (G.P.R.A.) after his liberation.
The programme of action decided upon by the Congress was later currently referred to in Algeria as the 'platform of the Summam valley'. It provided, within the framework of the F.L.N. as the sole organization representing the Algerian people, a new structure with clearly delimited competencies, made necessary by the territorial expansion the rising had gained since it was started two years before by the 'nine historical chiefs' of the Revolutionary Committee for Unity and Action* (C.R.U.A.). Thus took its origin the National Council of the Algerian Revolution* (C.N.R.A.), assumed to express the sovereign will of the

nation, and deciding supremely in all matters of importance to the national struggle. A five-men Committee of Coordination and Execution* (C.C.E.), a sort of war-cabinet appointed by, and answerable to the National Council, was entrusted with the over-all strategy. To it, in turn, was to be responsible the External Delegation in Cairo in charge of the supply from abroad of war material and whatever other assistance. The Congress emphasized the principle of collective leadership at all levels as it had first been established by the 'Nine', and determined that primary consideration should be given to the political targets to which the military operations were to be subordinated.

At the same time an extensive document reviewed the genesis of the national movement in Algeria; gave an analysis of the trend and activities of the different political and labour organizations and of their relations to the F.L.N.; and concluded with detailed instructions as to the means to be used in the battle and the measures to be taken in order to confer upon the fighting forces the standing of a regular belligerent army in conformity with international law. Finally, the objectives of the revolt were redefined: recognition of an independent, sovereign and indivisible Algerian nation; establishment of a democratic, socialist republic guaranteeing equal rights to all its citizens without discrimination as to race or religion; and eventually the conduct of negotiations with France by the F.L.N. as the sole responsible partner representing the Algerian people. All points of the programme were unanimously accepted.

T

TĀFARĀJĪN IBN, ABŪ MUHAMMAD ʿABD ALLĀH, a chancellor *(hājib)* at the Hafsid* court in Tunis and an outstanding figure in the annals of the dynasty († 1364). His first known ancestor, Abū Hafs ʿUmar Ibn Tāfarājīn, a faithful companion-in-arms of the Mahdi Ibn Tūmart*, the founder of the Almohad* doctrine, and of his successor ʿAbd al-Mu'mīn* (1133-1163), held high government functions in Fez and Marrakesh. So did his descendants in various parts of the Almohad empire. When by the middle of the XIIIth cent. the Almohad secular power was giving way under the pressure of the Marīnids*, the Tāfarājīn family moved into Tunisia and was received with honours by the Hafsid Caliph al-Mustansir* (1249-1277), who considered himself and his country as the trustees of the Almohad spiritual heritage. Thenceforth one or the other member of the Tāfarājīn was seen in a leading position in the Hafsid army or civil administration. ʿAbd Allāh Ibn Tāfarājīn enjoyed the particular confidence of Caliph Abū Bakr* (1318-1346) who made him first his vizier, then Sheikh of the Almohads *(Shaykh al-Muwahhidīn)* and finally head of the chancellery. Simultaneously he extended the sphere of authority of this office *(hijāba)* in a measure which in fact conveyed to Ibn Tāfarājīn veritable dictatorial powers, especially since the appointment of his brother as commander of the army. After Abū Bakr's death, Ibn Tāfarājīn supported one of the caliph's sons in the struggle for the throne, but then by a sudden change of colours subtly paved the way for its almost effortless conquest by the Marīnid sultan Abū al-Hasan ʿAlī*, and riding at his right hand took part in his triumphant entry into Tunis (1347). The year after, however, found him in the camp of the rebellious faction headed by an offspring of the last Almohad sovereign Abū Dabbūs. Just in time before the revolt collapsed he took a ship for Alexandria and set out on the pilgrimage to the Holy Cities. Again, one year later, after the Marīnid had withdrawn, he suddenly re-appeared, accompanied by an influential chieftain of the Sulaym*, and with him and his men by a skilful coup de main occupied Tunis. They deposed the new Hafsid caliph, had him put to death, and his young brother, Abū Ishāq Ibrāhīm II (1350-1369) proclaimed caliph in his stead. Ibn Tāfarājīn as the caliph's tutor, was thenceforth the real master in the country, in fact the vice-roy, as he was called in his correspondence with foreign powers. Knowing how to gain and sustain the favour of the masses and to foil the machinations of rivals; when to disappear from the political stage and when to re-emerge; whom to choose as an ally and for how long - thus he held his position until his death. He died suddenly after the marriage of his daughter with the caliph and was buried in Tunis in a *madrasa* (theological school) he had founded.

TANGIER STATUTE, a diplomatic instrument drawn up in December 1923 by France and Great Britain, signed in 1924 by Spain and subsequently, with exclusion of Austria, Germany and the Soviet Union, by the other signatories of the Act of Algeciras*, except by the United States feeling bound by President Wilson's famous XIV points. The Statute practically detached the area of Tangier and its surroundings (about 170 square miles) from Moroccan territory - then under French and Spanish Protectorate* - and made it a special zone under international régime, for which it provided permanent neutrality, demilitarization and the open-door principle, i.e. economic freedom with full equality for all signatories. It recognized the Sultan's sovereignty over his Moroccan subjects, symbolized in the person of a representative *(mandūb)*, but vested the supreme supervision of the administration in a Committee of Control composed of the delegates of the signatory Powers. The highest executive was to be appointed by France; a Mixed Court of European judges administered justice; a Legislative Assembly of 9 Moroccan and 17 European members under the chairmanship of the *mandūb* was entrusted with certain minor administrative and legislative functions.

From the Moroccan point of view the Statute did not involve an essential innovation. By virtue of numerous treaties between the sultans and the maritime Christian states, Tangier, the point of the shortest crossing to Europe, had been for centuries one of the rare places where European traders and shippers were permitted to settle, establish warehouses and do business while the rest of the country was practically closed to non-Moslem foreigners. Since the end of the XVIIIth century, Tangier, not the capital Fez, was the seat of the European consulates - raised to the rank of legations in 1860 - and soon afterwards began the series of conventions which, following the pattern of the so-called 'capitulations' in the Ottoman Empire, exempted the nationals of the European Powers from the jurisdiction of Moroccan courts and conferred it upon their consuls. The diplomatic and consular corps with its numerous staff, and a wealthy foreign colony connected through manifold contacts with the native bourgeoisie created, as time went on, a specific cosmopolitan atmosphere sharply contrasting with the traditional and rigorously Islamic mode of life and set of attitudes in other Moroccan towns. Yet, Tangier was also the stage of an imbroglio of political intrigues manipulated in the capitals of the great colonial empires, and the sultans soon knew how to exploit the antagonism, open or covered, of these contradictory interests and ambitions. They were perfectly satisfied with the peculiarities of the situation in Tangier, kept carefully in the background and had their sovereignty marked merely by the presence of a Pasha whose rôle was limited to the transmission of messages between the court at Fez and the foreign diplomats. Seen in the light of world politics and the efforts to maintain a balance of power, the Statute may well be regarded as an expedient which answered its purpose.

In the second World War, when in 1940 luck seemed to have irrevocably turned against the armies of the Allies, the Spanish government thought the time favourable for the incorporation of the zone of Tangier into the territory under Spanish Protectorate. It declared the international régime incapable of discharging any longer its obligations, particularly as regarded the guarantee of neutrality; abolished its institutions and offices and took over its administration. The victory of the Allies terminated this Spanish interlude. In August 1945 at a conference held in Paris, France, Great Britain, the Soviet Union and the United States set the Statute temporarily again in operation but, pending a new formulation, with additional seats at the Control Committee for American and Soviet members - the Soviet Union refused to participate in any meeting for the duration of the Franco régime - and thereupon Spain withdrew. The provisional arrangement lasted eleven years. They made Tangier one of the post-war world's most lively financial centres thanks to the unlimited freedom in the movements of capital and transactions in whatever currency; without taxation of commercial profits and income taxes; with a thriving traffic by sea and by air; with Arabic, French, Spanish and Anglo-Saxon schools, newspapers and cultural institutions; with a population of some 200.000, a quarter of them foreigners, and with nearly a thousand banking and trading concerns. In 1956, following the recognition of Moroccan independence, an international conference with the participation of a Moroccan delegate, which met first in Fedala (on the coast 15 miles south of Casablanca) and then in Tangier, declared the Statute abolished. The international zone was made a province of the kingdom and the *mandūb* was replaced by a provincial governor. The privileges were permitted to remain in force but thenceforth as a grant by a Royal Charter of September 1957. The generally anticipated abrogation of the Charter followed in April 1959. Notwithstanding the measures intended to facilitate the transition, the effect was that most of the foreign commercial and financial establishments closed, that business stagnated and unemployment spread. A certain revival began to set in with the creation in January 1962 of a free-trade zone after the pattern of Hamburg and Beirut, coupled with a development project comprising the extension of the port and the installation of new industries. A further impulse is expected from the decision of King Hassan II to transfer for the summer months his residence and the seat of government from Rabat to Tangier.

TIJĀNĪ al-, ABŪ MUHAMMAD ʿABD ALLĀH IBN IBRĀHĪM, a Tunisian writer and chronicler (XIII/XIVth cent.). No biographical data are known except that he was closely attached to Abū Zakariyyā' Ibn al-Lihyānī, the 'Sheikh of the Almohads' *(Shaykh al-Muwahhidīn)* and future Hafsid* caliph (1311-1317), who upon his accession to the throne appointed him head of the chancellery. A few years before, he had accompanied his protector on an - unsuccessful - expedition against the island of Djerba on the Gulf of Gabès, at that time in the possession of the Aragonian family of the Lauria. He remained with him for a while in Gabès, whence they intended to undertake the pilgrimage to the Holy Cities. On the voyage through Tripolitania, interrupted by many and prolonged halts, al-Tijānī fell ill and had to be taken back to Tripoli and then by sea to Tunis. On this occasion he lost his entire and, as it seems, rather important library which he had taken along on camel-back so as to have it continually at hand. The fruit of this journey is his *Rihla** (book of travels), a minute description of the itinerary with numerous historical, geographical, economic and sociological details, keenly observed and conscientiously verified, which make the work a valuable source of information. In order to stimulate the interest of the reader, the author inserted a great many poetical quotations and even verses of his own creation. (French translation of extracts by A. Rousseau, Paris, Journal Asiatique, 1852-53). A second work by al-Tijānī, the *Tuhfat al- ʿArūs wa Nuzat al-Nufūs* (appr. The Adornment of the Bride and the Recreation of the Souls), is a compilation of poems and tales in prose by various authors, some by members of his family and by himself, others of the early centuries of Islam, mainly of erotic character.

TIJĀNĪYA, a religious brotherhood*, widely spread in Algeria and Morocco, founded in 1795 by Sīdī Abū al- ʿAbbās Ahmad Ibn Muhammad al-Tijānī (1737-1815), who was born in the village ʿAin Mādī (in the Algerian Sahara some 40 miles west of the oasis-town of Laghouat) of a family claiming descent from the Prophet and hence sharīfian* rank. He studied religious sciences at all the great centres of theological learning and mystical thought, in Fez, Tlemcen, Mecca, Medina and Cairo, and finally, returning to his home country, spent several years in the Algero-Moroccan fringe areas of the Sahara. There he formulated the rules of the brotherhood in accordance with the injunction received, as he felt, in mystical communion with the Prophet. His teaching took root among the tribes of the Sahara, passed into the Senegal and into the Sudan and began to infiltrate northwards. Then he moved to Fez. In spite of the strong undercurrents in Moroccan policy of Wahhābi puritanism with its rejection of the entire brotherhood concept, Sultan Mūlāy Sulaymān (1792-1822) received him as honoured guest. He assigned him a seigneurial residence, which was built by the sultan's father but, believed to be haunted by evil genii *(jinn)*, stood empty and was avoided by the people until al-Tijānī made it the meeting place of his adepts. Thence he carried his word, continually travelling and preaching, into ever larger sections of Morocco and Algeria. He died in Fez and lies buried there in the imposing Tijānī *zāwiya** but the main seat of the brotherhood has remained in ʿAin Mādī. In his memory, the widow of one of the later heads, a Frenchwoman, set up a sort of small-sized museum surrounded by gardens at Dār Sī Ahmad Tijānī, a nearby place, some four miles distant.
From Ahmad al-Tijānī's direct inspiration by the Prophet flows the Tijānīya's negation of all spiritual affinities with whatsoever other religious fraternity, and hence the interdiction of associating with any of them, binding its active adherents *(ashāb*, sing. *sāhib)* as well as the wider groups of sympathizers *(ahbāb*, sing. *habīb)*. This exclusiveness conjointly with a further tenet which enjoins, in conformity with the Tradition of the Prophet *(hadīth)*, strict obedience to the legal authority in the State - provided the precepts of Islam are observed - made the Tijānīya a valuable factor of government in counterbalancing the often refractory spirit of other brotherhoods and their prestige among the tribes. Its dogmatically anchored faith in the wisdom of the rightful ruler explains, at least to a considerable extent, the favour in which it was held at all times by the Moroccan sultans, several of whom are known to have

been in close touch with Tijānīya circles, and one of them, Mūlāy ʿAbd al-Hāfiz (1909-1912), to have composed an ode in praise of its founder. It determined, on the other hand, the Tijānīya's particular attitude in public life, which has often been interpreted as political indifference, especially when compared with the aggressive competition for secular power, marking the history of most of the other brotherhoods. More appropriately it might be qualified as the manifestation of a complete espousal of the policy, internal and foreign, adopted by the sovereign. Thus, along these as a rule rather intricate lines, Tijānīya chiefs throughout the last century fought and made peace with the Darqāwa* brotherhood, the Turks, Abdelkader* and the French in Algeria, without interests of their own being implied in any manner. Similarly, at the time of the Protectorate* they closely followed the cautious conduct of Sultan Muhammad V*, and although generally regarded as unpolitical, were carefully watched by both the French and Spanish authorities. Since the achievement of independence, the Tijānīya seems to have further expanded, at least in Morocco, among the rural population but also in the towns, where it counts a noteworthy proportion of adherents among the bourgeois classes and the intellectual groups in the various fields of social or economic activities.

TRADE-UNIONISM. The soil on which in the second quarter of this century an autochtonous organized labour movement in the Arab West was born and began to grow up, had until not very long before been a social and economic order of tradition-bound immobility. Under the leadership of the narrow circles of high dignitaries, tribal chieftains, wealthy merchants and men of religion it rested primarily on a peasantry to which an antiquated landholding system and equally archaic methods permitted no more than the scantiest livelihood; on sheep-and camel-breeding nomad and semi-nomad primitive tribal communities; and on modest handicraft and small trade, hereditary for generations in the same families and rigidly enclosed in ancient guilds and corporations. In this pattern, which remained practically unchanged well into the French régime a labour class was absent. Then, however, foreign capital investments brought into being industrial, mining and large-scale farming establishments; roads were constructed, port installations modernized and European residential districts built. All work requiring skill was done by Europeans, while the mass of unskilled labourers came, with their families, from the villages, the tribes and the bottom strata of the townspeople. They crowded together in agglomerations of shanties and miserable huts, which they set up around or near the centres of these new activities, and gradually assimilated to an urban mode of life of the most precarious kind.
Since the end of the Second World War these internal population shifts of a permanent nature were accompanied by a steady current of temporary migrations, fed by the same groups, to the labour markets in France and to a lesser degree, of Belgium and Germany. They have kept there an Algerian, Moroccan and Tunisian labour force, constantly renewed but never much less than half a million people. Simultaneously and in the degree to which the French administration was implanting, at first

in the principal cities and then also in the smaller towns, elementary schooling on occidental lines and with it a certain knowledge of French, there emerged an increasing number of minor clerks employed in public services and private enterprise, as well as of workers in manufacturing and commercial jobs demanding only modest qualifications. For quite a time this evolving labour proletariat was but an amorphous crowd unconscious of any solidarity of material and moral interests. Strong emotional ties kept every one bound to his often far away community of clan or tribe. To seek protection outside its spheres, to recognize ideologies alien to its traditions and to submit voluntarily to a discipline beyond its patriarchal authority were inconceivable thoughts. Here and there, however, the pressure of the progressing proletarization began to awaken a new 'class-consciousness' that made the ideas underlying trade unionism acceptable, but obstacles of a different kind arose on their way to realization.

The French administration, on the one hand, was opposed to the formation of native unions, fearing - not without ground as it was soon to appear - that they would not take long to join the ranks of the increasingly militant Arab nationalism. The local European unions, on the other, in so far as they were affiliated with the socialist sector of the French C.G.T. (Conféderation Générale des Travailleurs) clearly manifested their reluctance against an Arab adherence, either because they were afraid it would submerge them, or because of some sort of ethnic or religious prejudice. Only those which belonged to the communist C.G.T. sector (C.G.T.U., i.e. Unionists) held, primarily for propagandistic purposes, the door open for Arab members. Not before the fusion in 1934 of both sectors into the new and entirely communist-led C.G.T. was this differentiation effaced, but then the resistance came from the side of the nationalist leaders most of whom, by conviction or for reasons of their political strategy, were averse to communist infiltration. At last, and step by step, and with repeated vacillations the French authorities accorded the Arab workers the right to constitute their own unions.

The story of a purely native labour movement in the Arab West, and as a matter of fact in the Arab world, starts in TUNISIA. It began when in December 1924 the Arab dockhands in Tunis struck for wages equal to those of the dockers in Marseille and were left nearly without support by the only labour organization in the country, the 'Union des Syndicats' built upon an exclusively European membership and attached to the C.G.T. The strike was at the point of breaking down when a dynamic leader, Muhammad 'Alī, took the situation in hand. He had taken part in the Italo-Turkish campaign in Libya (1911) as Enver Pasha's driver and after a stay in Germany, where he pursued the study of economics, returned to Tunisia. He formed the strikers into a union of their own, then created others in some of the mining and industrial districts, and within a few months had them all affiliated under the roof of the General Conferation of Tunisian Workers (Conféderation Générale des Travailleurs Tunisiens, C.G.T.T.). Muhammad 'Alī's success was of short duration. Demands for higher pay of other groups by Arab workers resulted in new strikes not sanctioned by the Union des Syndicats; in clashes between European and Arab workers; in the dissolution by the authorities of the C.G.T.T.; and in his exile in November 1925. He left for Egypt, then went secretly to Morocco but was arrested in Tangier and sent back to Egypt, where he continued his studies while gaining his livelihood as a truck driver. A few years later he lost his life in an accident at the wheel of his car on the road from Jidda to Mecca. Notwithstanding the more or less open hostility from European quarters, the local unions of the former C.G.T.T. continued and encouraged the formation of others. Most of them gradually adhered to the C.G.T., since 1932 the sole authorized central organization, not without soon being marked in varying degrees by communist leanings.

After its first short-lived phase of independent existence, initiated, perhaps prematurely, by Muhammad ʿAlī, Tunisian trade-unionism had to let two decades elapse before entering the next one. The impulse was given by Farhāt Hāshid, the secretary of the local C.G.T. branch of Sfax, the important shipping center of the Gafsa phospate mines. Born of a fishermen's family on the Kerkena islands, Farhāt Hāshid made his way from a day labourer to a clerk in a government office, a position which he gave up in order to gain freedom of action in the trade union movement and in the lines of the Neo-Destour Party*. His energy and capacity for organization, coupled with a remarkable gift for winning the ear of the people, soon made him a prominent figure in public life. Visualizing what a decisive rôle in the struggle for independence might be assigned to the labour proletariat, provided it could be consolidated on a national platform and become conscious of its moral and tactical weight, he set all his efforts on this task. Trusting in his lead the Sfax dockers' union was the first to secede from the French-managed C.G.T., and in quick succession others throughout the country followed. Farhāt Hāshid grouped them in one single 'Union of the Autonomous Unions' which shortly afterwards he built up (June 1945) into the Union Générale des Travailleurs Tunisiens (U.G.T.T.), structured by occupational categories as a federation of ten member unions, regionally subdivided into twelve sectors, and directed by a Committee of Administration, elected by, and responsible to a National Council. After a sequence of tenaciously sustained strikes which seriously endangered important French interests, official recognition was obtained. In the increasingly embittered struggle against the French rule it stood hand in hand with the Neo-Destour, forcefully inspired by Farhāt Hāshid, thenceforth its secretary-general until his assassination by French counter-revolutionary terrorists (1952).

His successor was the young and impetuous Ahmad Ben Salāh, a brilliant speaker and fervently believing in the nation-wide social, economic and cultural rejuvination he had planned in his study years in France. Then, however, he lost no time in propagating his programme, to be carried out by a socialist party he intended to create. Its boldness not only aroused resistance of the bourgeois groups in the Neo-Destour but also scared quite a few of his colleagues in the union, who argued, perhaps rightly, that it might discourage foreign capital investment. By the end of 1956 his opponents had brought into life a rival union, the U.T.T. (Union des Travailleurs Tunisiens) and Ahmad Ben Salāh was forced to resign and subsequently appointed Secretary of State of the

Plan and of Finances. His place was taken by one of the Neo-Destour's executive officers, whereupon the U.T.T. ceased to exist. The U.G.T.T. has ever since remained integrated in the system of the oneparty state. A pro-communist labour union, the U.S.T.T. (Union Syndicale des Travailleurs Tunisiens) which came into existence in 1946 - in fact the Tunisian branch of the C.G.T. assuming a label of national tinge in order to compete with, and eventually absorb the U.G.T.T. - disappeared in 1956 soon after the proclamation of independence.

In MOROCCO the seed of trade unionism was sown in 1934 when the country's first nationalist party, the Bloc of Moroccan Action* *(al-Kutla al-ʿAmal al Maghribī)* submitted to the French Protectorate* authorities its 'Programme of Reforms' in which the freedom to constitute trade unions was included. This remained without response but two years afterwards the C.G.T. set up a Moroccan sector - later the Union Générale des Syndicats Confedérés du Maroc (U.G.S.C.M.) of communist sympathies - which, although on paper open to Europeans only, soon had about a thousand Moroccan members in the phosphate mining* district of Khouribga. In 1938, as the aftermath of a strike and serious troubles in the mines, the admittance of Moroccans to workers' unions was forbidden, a measure which, however, seems to have not been earnestly enforced, for from 1943 onwards more and more Moroccans appear in the various U.G.S.C.M. branches, some of them even on responsible posts. Apprehensive of the consequences of such exposure to communist indoctrination, the Istiqlāl* party at first tried to stem the current. After some time, however, by a complete reversal advocated in particular by ʿAbd al-Rahīm Būabid, well-versed in the field of labour unions, it strongly encouraged these enrolments. In fact, it found a ready response to its call to a common struggle for the national aims and recruited its very shock troops from the midst of organized labour. In this atmosphere the demand for national trade unions, a decade and a half after its first rather academic formulation, gradually ripened into realization.

It was a five-years' process, initiated and tenaciously pursued by a railway worker, Mahjūb Ibn Saddīq, and a coal miner, Tayyib Ibn Būazza, both of whom held influential positions in the U.G.S.C.M., had abandoned their communist affiliations and joined the Istiqlāl. In 1952, just as they were about to set up an autonomous union of exclusively Moroccan membership and to prepare the secession from the U.G.S.C.M., they were sentenced to a two-year imprisonment for allegedly having incited the violent riots which broke out in Casablanca upon the news of Farhāt Hāshid's assassination and were followed by the proscription of the U.G.S.C.M. Immediatly after their release in 1954, while popular excitement at the sultan's deposition (August 1953) had reached its height and the Istiqlāl was crippled by the imprisonment or exile of its leaders, they formed a 'Committee for the Study of Free Trade Unions in Morocco'. Thereupon at a secret meeting held in Casablanca by 45 workers' delegates in March 1955, an all-Moroccan labour organization, the Moroccan Workers' Union (Union Marocaine du Travail, U.M.T.) was constituted and its governing body elected with Mahjūb Ibn Saddīq as secretary-general and Tayyib

Ibn Būazza as his deputy. The U.M.T.'s first proclamation was a claim for the sultan's immediate reinstatement and for Moroccan independence. Without waiting for the official authorization which was accorded a few months later, local committees in every town, and cells in every larger industrial establishment started to enroll. Notwithstanding the sharp antagonism which they encountered on the part of the U.G.S.C.M., the membership amounted at the time of the sultan's return (November 1955) to some 40.000. By the middle of 1956 it was estimated at some 300.000 industrial wage-earners and some 200.000 agricultural labourers - practically the whole Moroccan labour force - in a structure of some 600 occupational unions, a number of local and regional sectors, and linked together by a system of federations. Under the firm, sometimes critizised as authoritarian, direction of a strongly centralized administration with Mahjūb Ibn Saddīq and Tayyib Ibn Būazza at the head, the U.M.T., during the following three years closely and very actively supported the Istiqlāl's policy in issues of national importance. However its leftist orientation frequently brought it into conflict with the party's more moderate elements, and directed its approach to socio-economic problems towards solutions which in the eyes of many were inspired by too radical concepts.
The U.M.T. edifice was too intimately connected with the Istiqlāl's party machinery not to be affected by its frictions, and when these towards the end of 1958 assumed critical proportions, it too began to show fissures which soon irreparably widened. Mahjūb Ibn Saddīq was one of the principal artisans of the split in the party and of the programme of far-going social and economic reforms which the new National Union of Popular Forces* made its platform. His dynamism and prestige drew along most of the urban labour proletariat into the rows of the opposition, yet he was unable to prevent the more and more outspoken resentment at his rigid ways of holding the reins from crystalizing into open defection. The strong docker's union of Casablanca was the first to withdraw and a number of minor ones followed its example. After a short autonomous existence their integration was undertaken by a Liaison and Coordination Committee under the patronage of the Istiqlāl, and in March 1960 the Union Générale des Travailleurs Marocains (U.G.T.M.) was constituted. Three months later it was accorded legal status, notwithstanding Ibn Saddīq's violent protests and the obstacles raised by ʿAbd al-Rahīm Būabid, at that time minister of national economy. Although numerically of much lesser importance than its rival, the U.G.T.M. has broken the monolitic structure of Moroccan trade unionism.
In ALGERIA the national labour movement is a child of the revolution. Before its outbreak in 1954 the Arab workers were either not organized or belonged to the Algerian sectors of French unions: the socialist-minded Force Ouvrière (F.O.); the Catholic Confédération Française des Travailleurs Chrétiens (C.F.T.C.); the communist Union Générale des Syndicats Algériens (U.G.S.A.); or a few French not-federated unions. Most of the Algerians in France were enrolled in the C.G.T. The thought of starting an independent Arab - or practically Moslem - labour federation, implanted in Algeria and abroad under the flag of

the national cause, was first raised early in 1953 by the Movement for the Triumph of Democratic Liberties* (M.T.L.D.), the party of Messali al-Hajj, at that time still at the height of its influence but no longer under his undisputed control. It did, in fact, disintegrate a year or so later and the plans could not materialize, but Messali's new Algerian National Movement* (M.N.A.) took them up again. In February 1956 Muhammad Ramdani, a faithful Messalist and member of the Algiers city council, set up the first purely Arab unions among the street-car men and power-plant workers, then others in the building trades, among the dockers and the hospital staff. He federated them in the Union Syndicale des Travailleurs Algériens (U.S.T.A.), while Messali al-Hajj recruited a numerous membership in France. In Algeria, however, it had soon to give way to a rival federation, the Union Générale des Travailleurs Algériens (U.G.T.A.) which was created one month afterwards by ʿAbd al-Qādir Amranī, another Algiers city councillor, but sympathizer with Messali's antagonists in the Front of National Liberation* (F.L.N.). In the climate of the growing nationalist exaltation and aided by F.L.N. pressure, the U.G.T.A. drew into its orbit most of the Arab workers and small employees. Whole-heartedly espousing the cause of the rebellion, it appointed as secretary-general one of the F.L.N. protagonists, Ayssat Idir who was shortly afterwards arrested, but while in prison was elected into the supreme revolutionary executive, the Committee of Coordination and Execution (C.C.E.)*. Its outspoken insurrectional attitude in the general strikes and boycotts at the end of 1956, which introduced the ten or twelve months of terrorism and anti-terrorism of the 'Battle of Algiers' set an early end to its existence. Before the year was over, the U.G.T.A. was banned and all its leaders who could not escape in time were in internment camps. Yet with the help of the Moroccan U.M.T. and the Tunisian U.G.T.T. the fragments were joined together in Tunis, whence from a make - shift office throughout the revolution clandestine but increasingly tighter connections with the mass of Algerian labour were kept functioning. Upon the conclusion of the armistice the U.G.T.A. moved back into Algiers, stronger than ever before. Since then it has forcefully expanded and carefully avoided siding with any of the factions into which the contest for power had torn asunder the ranks of the F.L.N. while the Algerian Republic was in the making.

Since the days of their appearance the two world-spanning organizations in the field of international trade unionism, the pro-communist World Federation of Trade Unions (W.F.T.U., founded 1945), and its opponent, the International Confederation of Free Trade Unions (I.C.F. T.U., founded 1949), strongly backed by the American Federation of Labour (A.F.L.) have both striven hard to attract the Arab unions - of a membership estimated at about one million - and to draw them into their ideological spheres. In the Arab West, the I.C.F.T.U. has doubtlessly won the race notwithstanding the spade-work undertaken in prewar years with some success by the C.G.T. for the spread of communist influence. In Tunisia, Farhāt Hāshid neutralized such trends in the local unions which he federated, and then led the U.G.T.T. to the affiliation with the I.C.F.T.U., thereby winning for Tunisian trade

unionism valuable American assistance. In Morocco also two months after its foundation the U.M.T. was a member of the I.C.F.T.U. but, unlike its Tunisian counterpart, without neglecting to cultivate relations with Moscow and Peking. It was host in 1959 at its headquarters in Casablanca to the communist-sponsored conference of the 'International Council for Solidarity with the Workers and the People of Algeria' created by the W.F.T.U. in 1957 at its Fourth Congress in Leipzig. In Algeria, the U.G.T.A. joined the I.C.F.T.U. in the first year of its existence, secured, however, a few months later also a seat in the Executive Committee of the W.F.T.U. Unable to have its candidates for instruction in trade union functions accepted by the western non-communist unions except in Western Germany - in 1959 its delegates to the sixth congress of the I.C.F.T.U. in Bruxelles were even refused the Belgian visa - it sent its trainees, estimated at well over a thousand, into the countries behind the Iron Curtain, yet not into the Soviet Union. There they stayed on, expecting the day of independence, in the meantime earning their livelihood in different kinds of jobs. It remains to be seen, whether and to what extent, their exposure to communist indoctrination will after their return influence the political attitude of the Algerian proletariat.
The third of the great ideological currents in world politics, 'positive neutrality', has also, primarily under the Pan-Arab label, attained an increasing significance as a factor in trade unionism in the Arab West. Its principal exponent is the Confederation of Arab Trade Unions with headquarters in Cairo, actively patronized by Gamal ʿAbd al-Nāsir. Founded by the Congress of Arab Workers at Damascus in 1956 with the aim of affiliating all organized Arab labour between the Persian Gulf and the Atlantic, it was warmly welcomed in Algeria as ally in leading labour circles. In 1958 an agreement was concluded with Mahjūb Ibn Saddīq for cooperation with the U.M.T. in all matters of significance to the working classes. To the same range of thought belongs the declaration issued about two years later conjointly by the representatives of the trade unions in most of the countries of the Arab East and those of Tunisia, Algeria and Morocco, emphasizing the solidarity of all Arab workers in the pursuit of their common interests. In a still broader avenue move the attempts at building up an independent Trade Union Confederation of the African Peoples, in which the U.M.T. again plays a leading rôle. The Tunisian U.G.T.T. rather seems to favour the plan of an African Regional Section developed by the International Confederation of Free Trade Unions in order to meet the desire for emancipation permeating the labour masses in the developing countries, and at the same time to maintain their links with the world of the West.

TUFAYL IBN, ABŪ BAKR MUHAMMAD IBN ʿABD al-MALIK, called Abubacer - the latinized form of Abū Bakr - by the scholastics, one of the eminent Hispano-Arab philosophers with strong mystical leanings († 1185) and equally conversant with medicine, mathematics and astronomy besides being gifted with remarkable literary talent. Only scarce information on his life has been transmitted, except that he was born in Cadiz, served as secretary to the governor of Granada, then was summoned to the Almohad* court at Marrakesh and appointed personal physician to Abū Yaʿqūb Yūsuf* (1163-1184). Ranking high in the ruler's favour he held this position until, advanced in age, he resigned, recommending as his successor the young Ibn Rushd* whom he strongly encouraged to study, and comment upon, Aristotelian philosophy, advice for which he well merited, as the future was to show, a grateful remembrance in the history of Arabic scholarship. Ibn Tufayl died in Marrakesh and was buried with the highest honours.

Most of Ibn Tufayl's minor writings are lost, but the work of his life, which has been preserved, the philosophic romance *Hayy Ibn Yaqzān* (The Living One, Son of the Vigilant) has secured for him a lasting place of fame. The author imagines a new-born child - Hayy Ibn Yaqzān - all alone on an uninhabited island. The naked and helpless creature is nursed by a gazelle, meant as the symbol of sympathy and love uniting all beings, and in a rhythm of seven times seven years repeats the evolution of mankind, progressing from the stages of a hunter, a tamer of wild animals, an artisan and finally by the observation of the physical phenomena of nature, to the maturity of the perfect philosopher. Like Ibn Bājja's* 'solitary', the hero of Ibn Tufayl's story follows the path of contemplative speculation in the search for truth; learns how to distinguish matter from the 'spiritual forms'; becomes conscious of the real essence of man and of the source of his sufferings and felicity, until at last he is able to apprehend the eternal verities, and, guided by the 'One Agent Intellect' - the Supreme Spiritual Being - perceives the vision in the highest spheres of the Divine Splendour.

At this point there arrives a stranger from a neighbouring island: Absāl, who with his companion Salāmān had been living there among a people blindly obeying the rules of a Law without understanding their meaning, bound up in the trivialities of a commonplace existence, and barred by mental inertia from the attainment of the higher levels of happiness. Salāmān, the man of practical opportunism, adapts himself to the situation and is made the ruler of the island, whereas Absāl, the mystic, seeking perfection in the retirement of spiritual contemplation, leaves for the twin-island where he expects to find the solitude he desires. Soon, however, he and Hayy Ibn Yaqzān discover their union in the aspiration after the same sublime and eternal goal. Animated by the noble impulse to lift Salāmān's people to their own spiritual height, they set out for his island. They are received with great honours and begin their philosophical preaching which only results in creating confusion and discord, the rapid cooling off of friendship and its transformation into undisguised hostility. Now they realize that it was a mistake to interfere with the conventional beliefs of the masses, and that perfection cannot be achieved by the ordinary ways of human teaching. They return to their island, understanding that beatitude is accessible only to the few who renounce the profane ambitions of the world, and in the meditations of the solitary philosopher's striving for illumination by the 'Agent Intellect'.

Ibn Tufayl borrowed the names of his characters from a short tale by the Persian philosopher Ibn Sīna (Avicenna, † 1037), called the 'Mystical Allegory of Hayy Ibn Yaqzān' which is known, however, by some quotations and a summary, contained in the writings of a Persian author of the XIIIth century. His literary merit was the original manner of expounding his philosophy. The work enjoyed great popularity and was many times translated, first into Hebrew and then into Latin (Philosophus Autodidactus, abridged title, Oxford 1671). From the Latin text as well as from the Arabic original several translations were made into modern European languages: Dutch (1672); English (1708); French (L. Gauthier, Hayy ben Yaqdhān, roman philosophique d'Ibn Thofail, Alger 1900, 2nd ed. Paris 1936); Russian (1920); Spanish (G. Palencia, El filosofo autodidacto, Madrid 1934). It has been suggested that the figure of Hayy Ibn Yaqzān might have inspired Daniel Defoe for his Robinson Crusoe.

TULAYTULĪ al-ABŪ al-QĀSIM SĀʿID IBN AHMAD, frequently called 'Qādī Sāʿid' or the 'Cadi of Toledo', Hispano-Arab scholar of encyclopaedic erudition (1029-1070). He was born in Alméria, began his studies in Cordova and continued them in Toledo, where he soon became known for his erudition, particularly in the fields of law, mathematics, astronomy and history, and was appointed cadi of the city under the reign of the Dhū al-Nūn*. The only extant work from his pen is the *Tabaqāt al-Ummam* (Classification of Nations), a voluminous history of the development of science in eight different countries. It was obiously meant for the larger, uncritical public seeking rather entertainment than historical truth, but regarded mistakenly by later authors as a source of authentic information.

TŪMART IBN, a religious reformer (†ca 1130) and the founder of the politico-spiritual Almohad* *(al-Muwahhidūn)* movement which was at the root of one of the most powerful empires of the Arab West. He was born in a village of the Hargha tribe, a member of the Berber confederation of the Masmūda*, on the northern slopes of the Anti Atlas. Later, in the course of his mission he added to his name the name of the Prophet, Muhammad, while his biographers, spreading over every phase of his life a veil of pious legends, attributed to his father an Arab descent and the name of the Prophet's father, ʿAbd Allāh. In spite of his bodily weakness given already in young years to a severely self-denying, almost ascetic way of life, and passionately applying his remarkable intelligence to religious study, he left, presumably in his early thirties, for the centres of learning in the Arab East. During a stay of some ten years he familiarized himself thoroughly with the currents in theology, philosophy and jurisprudence, which moved the contemporary world of Islam, in particular the teaching of the great al-Ghazzālī, acquiring at the same time a perfect knowledge of the subtleties of the Arabic language. Yet all information which has been transmitted as to his stay there, or as to when and how he conceived and formulated his own doctrine, must be considered more or less conjectural.

This doctrine may be summed up as the rigorous affirmation of the Islamic dogma of the Unity of God *(tawhīd*, from *wāhid*, one, whence the name *al-Muwahhidūn*, Unitarians, converted into the Spanish form Almohades, generally accepted in occidental literature). From it follows that attributes inherent in, and inseparable from the essence of the Deity - The Merciful *(al-Rahmān)* or the The Generous *(al-Karīm)* or The Just *(al-ʿAdl)* etc. - must not be imagined in terms of human nature. Such anthropomorphism, Ibn Tūmart taught, was equivalent to atheism, and to take up the sword against those who were guilty of it, was the duty of every Moslem, a duty more sacred than the Holy War *(jihād)* against the unbelievers. A set of the strictest puritan rules for the conduct of private and public life; and the return to the study, almost completely fallen into disuse in the jurisprudence of the Arab West, of the Koran and the Tradition of the Prophet *(hadīth)* as the sole source of all law among Men, completed the *muwahhid* doctrine. At a later stage Ibn Tūmart incorporated into his teaching the belief in the coming of the *Mahdī*, deeply rooted in the minds of the Berbers, and declared to be the Infallible *Imām*, the God-guided leader and saviour - the *Mahdī*. On his way home from the East Ibn Tūmart, still all alone, stayed some time in Egypt and, probably between 1110 and 1115, went by sea from Alexandria to Tunisia. Then he wandered westwards from town to town and in the manner of an itinerant missionary preached to the simple people in the streets, to the learned in the mosques, modulating his eloquence in accordance. Slowly advancing he came to Tunis, to Constantine and to Bougie, in some places reverently listened to and accepted by the scholarly circles as one of their own, in others derided or driven away as a disturber of peace and order. A few disciples, however, had begun to follow him on his peregrinations and remained his devoted companions throughout the rest of his life, among them al-Baidhāq* who was to become his most enthusiastic biographer, and ʿAbd al-Mu'min*, the future ruler of the Almohad empire. Together the small group continued, leaving everywhere nuclei of adherents: from Bougie to Tlemcen, from there to Taza and further on to Fez and finally to Marrakesh, the Almoravid* capital. They lived in the most frugal manner, inexorable critics of a society which, as they saw it, was indulging in sinful luxury, loose morals and disregarding the most elementary precepts of religion. Proselytizing for their tenets with an ardour that could not fail to turn them, at least in the eyes of the authorities, from exalted religious reformers into political agitators, they were expelled first from Fez, then from Marrakesh, then withdrew to Aghmāt and from there, narrowly escaping arrest, into Ibn Tūmart's homeland, seeking refuge with the Masmūda of the Atlas. They were friendly received and found their first influential supporter, the chieftain of the strong Hintāta tribe, Faskāt ū-M'zāl, later called after one of the Prophet's companions, Abū Hafs ʿUmar*, the ancestor of the Hafsid* dynasty in Tunisia (1236-1575). In these mountains of difficult access and among tribal groups hardly more than nominally incorporated into the structure of the Almoravid state, Ibn Tūmart began to preach not only his doctrine, but open revolt against the godless régime, first at his native village amongst the Hargha clans and then all over the High and Anti Atlas.

Firmly upheld by the veneration and blind obedience of the neophytes, whose number quickly increased, he fitted the principle of the *Mahdī* leadership into the federative order of Berber tribal society with its hierarchy of consultative assemblies of notables. Thus he set up a new half-spiritual, half-political and military organization embracing within a short time most of the Masmūda family of tribes, which was sufficiently strong to suppress without pity all internal opposition and prepare the Holy War against the Almoravid rulers. The mountain passes and Tinmāl (or Tīnmallal), the center of the Almohad community, were fortified, and several attempts to subdue the rebels failed. Their first offensive action against Marrakesh was repelled with heavy losses after a forty-days' siege of the city, but ʿAbd al-Mu'min led the troops back into their mountains and the Almohad élan remained unshaken. Soon afterwards the *Mahdī* died and was buried in Tinmāl. His death was kept secret, allegedly during three years, until ʿAbd al-Mu'min, his designated successor, had established his authority. Ibn Tūmart laid down the Almohad doctrine and rite in a book, probably originally written in Berber language, (Arabic version *Al-Tawhīd*, Algiers 1903) and in a number of letters which are still extant and bear witness to his fanatic reformatory zeal.

TUNISIA, *Al-Jumhurīya al-Tūnisīya* (The Republic of Tunisia), comparable in shape to a distorted quandrangle, has a surface of 48.000 sq. miles - one-eighteenth of neighbouring Algeria and less than one-third of Morocco - and some four million inhabitants. On two sides the quadrangle is made up by an 800-mile long coast which at Cape Bon is only 80 miles distant from Sicily. The two land frontiers, neither determined by geographical factors nor resulting from historic development, are merely the heritage of an arbitrary administrative division between the former Turkish provinces *(ojaks* or regencies) of Tripoli, Tunis and Algiers. They reach deep into the Sahara through wide, open spaces, facing Tripolitania in the East and South-East, and Algeria in the West.

From oldest times the advantageous configuration of the coasts, much indented in parts by the promontories which the mountains of the interior project into the sea, and soft, sandy beaches elsewhere, invited the establishment by sea-faring traders of permanent settlements. Favoured by easy inland communications, they grew into prosperous towns where the Berber tribes of the countryside marketed their olives, dates, fruit and cattle. Most of them survived more or less unaffected behind their fortifications the turbulent centuries of the Middle Ages and remained under Berber or Arabic dynasties, as in the Punic, Roman and Byzantine eras, the meeting place of urban and rural interests, customs and ways of thought, except that Islam became the common spiritual background and Arabic the vehicle of the interchanges. However, the steadily flowing currents in the fields of technical skills, artistic concepts and theological speculation from the great medieval cities of the Arab East and later, in the wake of the Christian reconquest of Moslem Spain, the long continuing stream of Andalusian immigration kept the balance tilted in favour of the bourgeois element notwithstanding the steady afflux of village people. Neither did the three centuries of Turkish rule

TUNISIA

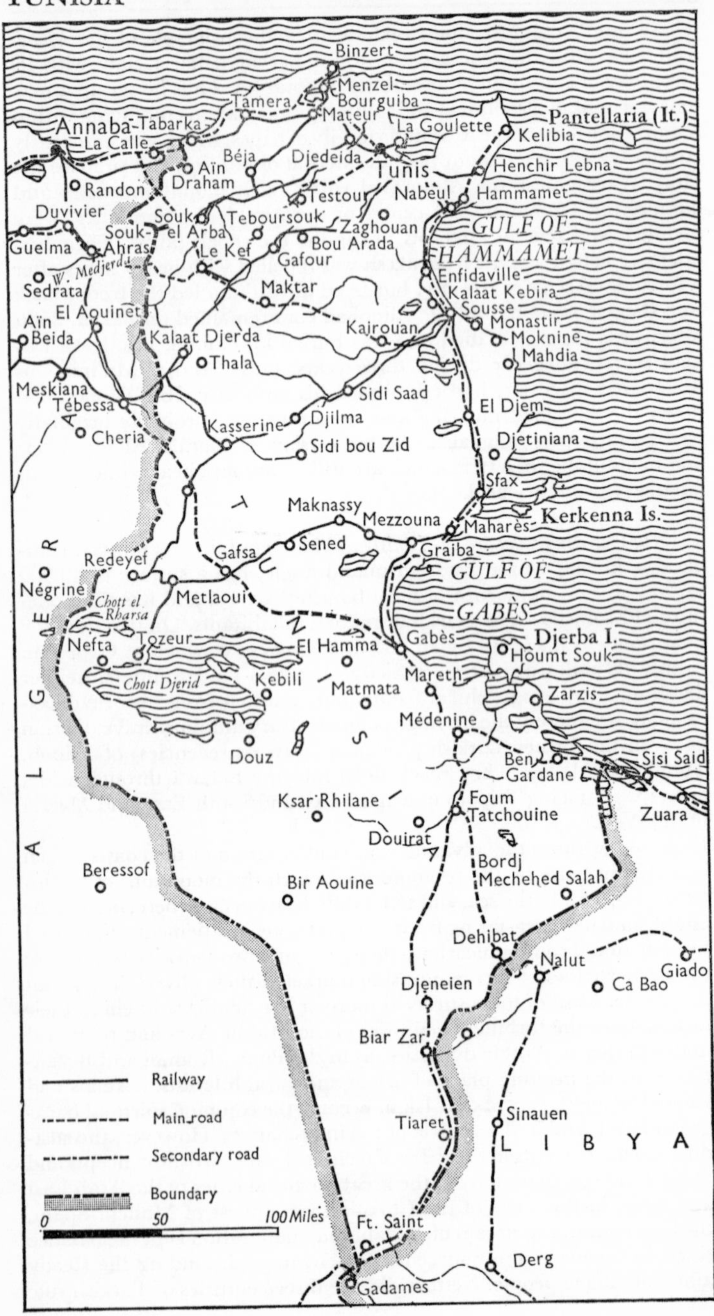
Binzert
Menzel
Bourguiba
Tamera
Mateur
Annaba
Tabarka
La Calle
La Goulette
Pantellaria (It.)
Kelibia
Béja
Aïn
Draham
Djedeida
Tunis
Henchir Lebna
Randon
Testour
Nabeul
Hammamet
Duvivier
Souk
el Arba
Teboursouk
Zaghouan
GULF OF
HAMMAMET
Guelma
Souk-
Ahras
Le Kef
Bou Arada
Gafour
W. Medjerda
Sedrata
Maktar
Enfidaville
Kalaat Kebira
Sousse
Monastir
Moknine
Mahdia
El Aouinet
Aïn
Beida
Kalaat Djerda
Kairouan
Thala
Meskiana
Tébessa
Sidi Saad
El Djem
Cheria
Kasserine
Djilma
Sidi bou Zid
Djetiniana
Sfax
Maknassy
Mezzouna
Maharès
Kerkenna Is.
Redeyef
Gafsa
Sened
Graiba
GULF OF
GABÈS
Négrine
Metlaoui
Chott el
Rharsa
Nefta
Tozeur
El Hamma
Gabès
Djerba I.
Houmt Souk
Chott Djerid
Kebili
Matmata
Mareth
Zarzis
Médenine
Douz
Ben
Gardane
Sisi Said
Ksar Rhilane
Foum
Tatchouine
Zuara
Douirat
Bordj
Mechehed Salah
Beressof
Bir Aouine
Dehibat
Nalut
Giado
Djeneien
Ca Bao
Biar Zar
Sinauen
Tiaret
L I B Y A
A L G E R I A
T U N I S I A
Railway
Main road
Secondary road
Boundary
0
50
100 Miles
Ft. Saint
Derg
Gadames

nor the seventy-five years of the French Protectorate* change to any noteworthy extent the traditional picture of this provincial town-life. Under the French régime, it is true, modern sectors were built for the new European population at some distance from the 'old town' and rebuilt after the destruction they had suffered in the Second World War, but there were practically no contacts between the two communities.

On their short northern portion the shores harbour today only one unimportant fishing hamlet, Tabarka, once a Phoenician trading post, in Roman times a thriving port and under the Turks a strong fortress and the seat of a remunerative Genoese coral-diving enterprise. At Cape Blanc, the site of a powerful military radar station, the coastline turns sharply southwards and through a narrow canal gives access to a wide deep-water lagoon. There lies the city of Bizerta (appr. 45.000 inh.), once a Phoenician town; some two thousand years later the pleasure residence of the Hafsid* sultan al-Mustansir*; and a few hundred years later a Turkish stronghold. The French converted the area on the sea, including the canal and the lagoon, the so-called Lake of Bizerta, into an air and naval base, considered of prime strategic importance as long as Tunisia was still a French Protectorate, but by the end of 1962 its gradual evacuation and retrocession was agreed upon between the French and Tunisian governments. In the framework of the present Tunisian Ten-Year Development Plan the military installations, in particular the great arsenal on the Lake at Menzel Bourguiba (formerly Ferryville) are to be turned into industrial plants and a series of workshops.

Between Cape Portofarina and Cape Bon the Gulf of Tunis reaches deep into the land. There, on another large lagoon, the Lake of Tunis *(Al-Bahaira,* The Little Sea), connected since time immemorial by a waterway across the sandbank of La Goulette *(Fam al-Wādī,* The River's Mouth) another Phoenician settlement was to become the city of Tunis. While its stronger neighbour and rival Carthage has long ago fallen into ruins, Tunis (appr. 500.000 inh.) has been since the beginning of the Hafsid reign the country's political, administrative and economic capital whose venerable academy of the Zaytūna mosque has held for centuries a foremost rank in the world of Islamic scholarship. By the end of the last century, a channel, 22 feet deep and six miles long, was pierced across the shallow lake, basins for the port were dug and the excavated materials were used for the construction of two dams flanking the channel, over one of which now runs a street-car line. Around the Gulf and all over the peninsula of Cape Bon French and Italian settlers planted in the early years of the Protectorate vineyards which cover about 90.000 acres and yield on the average some twenty million gallons of wine, consumed exclusively by the European population and exported mainly to France.

At the northernmost point of the vertical side of the quadrangle begins the soft curve of the Gulf of Hammamat and then swings into the semicircle of the Gulf of Gabès, the Minor Syrtis of antiquity, which rests, as it were, its one end on the Kerkenna Islands and the other on the island of Jerba. A modern road leads from Tunis to the Libyan frontier, in parts doubled by a small-gauge railway, borders the sea and connects the numerous towns and the clusters of villages around them: Sousse (40.000 inh.) whence Hannibal in the Second Punic War set out for the defence of Carthage against the assault of the Romans, and centuries later the Aghlabid* army for the conquest of Sicily, today the seat of a prosperous oil-pressing industry and the principal port for the shipping of esparto grass; Monastir (15.000 inh.), named after the fortified Byzantine monastery converted into its Moslem counterpart, a *ribāt**, with the nearby summer residence at Skanès of President Bourguiba; al-Mahdīya (12.000 inh.) on a long stretch of rocky peninsula, built up from the stones of Phoenician and Roman ruins by the first Fātimid caliph, the Mahdi ʿUbaydullāh, today a center of fish-canning industries; Sfax (60.000inh.) of the same respectable age, which as early as the tenth century traded in Tunisian oil with the cities of Italy, and today counts dispersed in the surrounding district, some 400 oilpresses besides being the port whence the largest tonnage is shipped from Tunisia, mainly phosphates, oil, and cereals; finally Gabès (25.000 inh.), embedded in palm groves of some 200.000 trees. Some 35 miles west of Sousse, in the midst of a wide barren plain, lies the holy city of Qairouan (al-Qayrawān) on the site where ʿUqba Ibn Nāfiʿ on his advance into North Africa had set up his headquarters and built the first mosque in Berber territory. The Mosque of Sīdī ʿUqba, several times rebuilt and lavishly embellished in the course of centuries, is still one of the most highly venerated sanctuaries in the Arab West. Qairouan, residence of the caliph's governors, the spiritual and intellectual metropolis of the Arab West in the days of the Aghlabid* and Zīrid* emirs, was thoroughly destroyed in the XIth century by the invading Banū Hilāl* and today only feebly reflects its one-time glory, but has acquired a reputation by the particular type of carpets woven by its women on about a thousand hand-looms. The immediate hinterland of this coast is a ribbon of plains and softly undulating hill-lands, the Sahil. It is the country, as generally recognized, of the world's best olive groves: altogether 21 million of Tunisia's total of 26 million trees of which six million stand in the area of Sfax; two million around Sousse, Monastir and Mahdīya; and four to five million in the plains of Tunis and Bizerta. Taking into account the alternation of poor and rich years the Tunisian olive groves yield an average harvest of more than 4000 metric tons of olives treated by some 2000 presses and assign to Tunisia the second place among the olive-oil exporting countries. Yet, olives, although the principal arboricultural product are by far not the only one of importance for Tunisia's economy: there are various fruits grown all over the eastern regions, altogether over three million trees.

Landwards the hilly waves of the Sahil rise slowly to about 2000 feet, come closer together, link into short chains and form a highland which further to the West separates into the two Algerian mountain ranges, the Atlas of the Tell and the Atlas of the Sahara. It spreads from south-west to north-east and, looked at on a relief map, invites the comparsion, often used in geographical descriptions, with a dorsal spine ('La Dorsale') supporting the country's physical structure. Occasionally it culminates in higher summits such as the Jabal Zaghūan (4300 ft), whose many sources supply Tunis with much of its drinking water; the Jabal Gorra (3000 ft); or the highest mountain in Tunisia, the Jabal Shambī (5000 ft) near the Algerian border. Broad, well-watered valleys with good soils cross its northern sector and there quite a number of villages and small agricultural market towns such as Toboursūk (6000 inh.), Le Kef (14.000 inh.) or Zaghuān (7000 inh.) grew up in the early Middle Ages, built from the stones of the nearby ancient ruins some of which by their imposing dimensions bear witness to a one-time considerable wealth.

Further on, the highland changes into another mountainous region, the Tell, traversed by the fertile plains of the river system of the Mejerda with its many affluents. These plains, bordered by dense forests, are Tunisia's granary chosen by the French 'colons' for laying out the largest and richest of their cereal-growing estates. The Mejerda, Tunisia's longest water course (some 170 miles), has its head-waters in Algeria and flows into the Gulf of Tunis in a wide, swampy estuary. Screening it off to the North arise the Khumirīya and Mogod Mountains with their half a million acres of forests, one third of them cork oaks which yield a yearly average of 35.000 to 40.000 quintals of cork. The name of Khumirīya became current only about three hundred years ago when the four Khumir tribes, probably descendants of the Sanhāja* Berbers, but completely arabized, shook off the overlordship of the Shābbīya brotherhood (established at La Chebba, al-Shābba, halfway between al-Mahdīya and Sfax), left their homeland in the coastal plains, and wandered about for a time until they settled in these mountains and now make their living as horse-breeders and wood-cutters.

South of the 'dorsal' highland begin the steppes with the salt marshes of the *shotts** and oases of the Jarīd. The vast, monotonous tracts of the steppes, divided into wide-stretched hollows by long, rocky crests, are the pasture grounds of the sheep-and camel-breeding nomads and the land of the esparto grass (stipa tenacissima), a much used raw material in the European manufacture of paper, of which yearly from 80.000 to 100.000 tons are exported. The cutting of the grass, its transport by camel, its handling and loading at the port provide a livelihood for some 300.000 people. Near the Algerian border, wedged in between the Shott al-Gharsa and the Shott al-Jarīd, extends the Bilād al-Jarīd (shortly called al-Jarīd), the country of the datepalms. Of Tunisia's three-and-a-half million date trees which yield approximately 35.000 to 40.000 metric tons of dates, about two-thirds grow there in the four great oases of Tozeur, Nefta, al-Wadiān and al-Hamma, watered by nearly a thousand natural springs and artesian wells and protected by a system of embankments against the sands of the shifting dunes of the desert.

On a density map of the population the darkest shades appear in the regions turning towards the sea: in the North, around Bizerta and Tunis; in parts of the peninsula of Cape Bon and in the valley of the Mejerda river; and in the East, all along the coastal ribbon of the Sahil and reaching into the islands of the Kerkenna group and of Jerba. The lighter shades, occasionally sprinkled with darker spots, become apparent in the fertile highland of the Tell but gradually fade towards the steppes and turn into white in the vast blank of the desert. This population, such as the Arab armies encountered it on the conquering advance around the end of the seventh century, was of unmixed Berber stock except in the towns, where in the course of time various other ethnical groups had left their traces. In the new province of the Arab empire, Islam took root comparatively soon, beginning in the towns and gradually radiating among tribes, although often in the heterodox Khārijite version. Sunnism, the official creed of the caliphate, finally prevailed over the heresy which has lived on only among the few Ibādite sectarians on the islands of Jerba. It was also the urban society which, taking its lead from al-Qayrawān, first adopted Arabic, the language of religion, of the law and public administration, of business and learning. Far more slowly and over detours which could not yet be elucidated but are mirrored in considerable idiomatic variations, the process of arabization found its way into the villages. Apparently it was carried among the nomads only by the waves of the invasion of the Banū Hilāl* and Sulaym* in the eleventh century. Today, Berber is spoken by hardly more than 40.000 to 50.000 people in the southern regions of the country. More intricate is the story of how out of tribal particularism and the struggle of local power groups, of dynastic contests for supremacy, of Turkish military rule and of the pressure of European colonial expansion the Tunisians evolved the consciousness of a national and political individuality:

647 First Arab raids into the South of Tunisia, then a Byzantine province.

670 ʿUqba Ibn Nāfiʿ lays out a fortified camp, the future city of al-Qayrawān, and builds there the first mosque in North Africa. Under Kusaila and later under the leadership of the Kāhina the Berbers bring the Arab advance to a halt but in 702 Hassān Ibn Nuʿmān at the head of a re-enforced army occupies Carthage, quenches Berber resistance and puts an end to Byzantine authority.

702-801 Tunisia, incorporated in the caliphate, is administered by governors residing in al-Qayrawān. Islam in the form of orthodox Sunnism takes root in the urban centres, whereas the heterodox Khārijite doctrine spreads in the countryside, especially in the South. Foundation in Tunis of the Zaytūna Mosque (734) and aggrandizement of the Great Mosque of Sīdī ʿUqba in al-Qayrawān, both of which are to develop into reputed centres of Islamic scholarship. The second half of the century witnesses a series of Khārijite tribal revolts in the course of which the rebels occupy al-Qayrawān several times.

801-909 Dynasty of the Aghlabid Emirs
Although recognizing ʿAbbāsid suzerainty, the Aghlabid emirs rule practically in full independence over an area which at times extends westwards into Central Algeria and eastwards as far as Tripoli and deep into southern Tunisia. An expedition under the flag of the Holy War results in the conquest of Sicily. Foundation of a new residence at ʿAbbāssīya and later of a second one at al-Raqqāda. Period of great prosperity.

909-973 Fātimid Rule

In the name of the first Fātimid caliph, the Mahdī ʿUbaydallāh, the Berber Kutāma tribesmen conquer al-Qayrawān (909) and the last Aghlabid is forced to flee from Tunisia. Foundation of the Fātimid residence at al-Mahdīya. The religious doctors remain hostile to Fātimid heterodoxy, while heavy taxes create increasing dissatisfaction among the population at large. In 943 Abū Yazīd, 'the man of the donkey', at the head of Khārijite tribes in eastern Algeria, overruns the country, occupies al-Qayrawān, Tunis and Sousse, but at last is defeated and the force of Khārijism is definitively broken. Under the Fātimid caliph Ismāʿīl al-Mansūr Tunisia enjoys again years of fruitful economic, intellectual and artistic activities. In 973 his son al-Muʿizz transfers the seat of the central Fātimid government to Egypt.

973-1167 Dynasty of the Zīrid Emirs

Abū al-Futūh Buluggīn of the Sanhāja Banū Zīrī, whose family had loyally fought for the Fātimid cause against the attempts of the Spanish Umayyads to gain hegemony in North Africa, is appointed vice-roy of a territory comprising Tunisia and the later Algerian department of Constantine. Under his immediate successors Zīrid power and with it general prosperity reach their height: over-sea trade continues lively, religious studies as well as the arts flourish. Around 1045 Emir al-Muʿizz breaks with the Fātimids, rejects heterodoxy and recognizes the spiritual supremacy of the ʿAbbāsid caliphs; thenceforth Sunnism remains the predominant creed in Tunisia. Prosperity rapidly declines under the impact of the invading Banū Hilāl and Sulaym Bedouins. Al-Qayrawān is destroyed and the government organization is dislocated. The authority of the Zīrid emirs is reduced to their residence al-Mahdīya and the narrow coastal strip, whereas the rest of the country is split into numerous city-states under continuously changing local chieftains. Finally the Normans of Sicily invade al-Mahdīya (1148) and other towns on the coast, but have to give way to the conquering Almohads (1160).

1160-1236 Almohad Rule

For the following years Tunisia is a province of the vast Almohad empire but still exposed to tribal raids and devastations. By 1184 it falls under the sway of the Banū Ghāniya, a Berber family established in Majorca, and fierce enemies of the Almohads, who notwithstanding temporary setbacks firmly hold southern Tunisia, some of the smaller coastal towns as well as Tunis. Order is restored at last in 1236 by the Almohad governor ʿAbd al-Wāhid Ibn Abī Hafs.

1236-1574 Hafsid Dynasty

ʿAbd al-Wāhid's son, Abū Zakariyyā', severs his allegiance to the Almohads. His descendants rule over a territory extending over Tunisia, the eastern parts of Algeria and Tripolitania. Almost incessant family feuds favour the establishment by dissident Hafsid princes of emirates at Bougie and Constantine; rise of autonomous city-states under local notables; occupation, twice in succession (1347-49 and 1357) of Tunis by the Marīnid sultans of Morocco; and growth of the influence of nearly independent Arab chieftains.

Periodically, energetic Hafsid sultans such as Abū Bakr (1318-1346), Abū al-ʿAbbās Ahmad (1370-1394) and Abū Fāris (1394-1434) and his immediate successors command sufficient authority to keep the realm united. Abū Fāris brings the ʿAbd al-Wādids of Tlemcen under Hafsid vasallage. Trade with the principal markets of the Arab East and Central Africa and especially with the Italian city-republics, with Sicily and Aragon flourishes, but so does Christian and Moslem piracy in the western Mediterranean. The skill and mercantile talent of the Moslem immigrants from al-Andalus (Moriscos) further the growth of a well-to-do bourgeois middle-class, and European commercial establishments in Tunisian ports increase in number and importance. Rapid decline of the authority of the Hafsid sovereigns at the end of the XVIth century. Tunisia becomes a stake in the Spanish-Turkish contest for possession of the North African coasts, out of which the Turks come forth as victors. With Sultan Mūlāy Muhammad the Hafsid dynasty ends.

1574-1590 The Régime of the Pashas

Tunisia, thenceforth an Ottoman 'Regency', is governed by a Pasha appointed for a three-year term of office, and assisted by a council *(dīwān)* of the officers commanding the garrisons in the larger towns.

1590-1640 The Régime of the Deys

In the course of a military revolt the members of the *dīwān* are assassinated and a new *dīwān* is instituted which elects from its midst, theoretically subject to confirmation by the Porte, the Head of the State with the title Dey. The function of the Pasha is reduced to the symbolic rôle of the Sultan's representative. A main source of the Dey's revenue flows from freebooting and the slave trade, controlled principally by Christian renegades, many of whom accede to key positions in the army and public administration but maintain also lively commercial relations with the French and Italian ports. The Englishman Ward - Yūsuf Rais after his conversion - builds up a Tunisian naval force. Morisco immigration reaches a new peak with the expulsion from Spain of the last Moslems and Jews, and gives a fresh incentive to economic activities. Upon the death of the Dey Usta Murād, the Bey (high military and civil officer) Hamūda Pasha seizes full powers.

1640-1702 The Murādid Beys

Under the reign of the Murādid line, called after Hamūda Pasha's father, Murād Pasha the title Dey, as some decades earlier that of Pasha, is divested of all but a merely honorary meaning. For three generations the supreme authority remains in the hands of his descendants until Mūrad III falls victim to a military conspiracy and with his entire family is put to death.

1705-1957 The Husaynid Beys

After a three-year struggle for power Husayn Ibn ʿAlī is recognized by the Porte as head of the Regency. Thenceforth the succession remains hereditary in the Husaynid family. Continuous internal disturbances and conflicts with the Deys of Algiers throughout the XVIIIth century. Development among the renegade groups of an influential military and civil servant caste branching out into the wealthy merchant and landowning classes, and thriving on legitimate trade and on piracy. The peasantry and urban masses live in poverty and ignorance. Introduction of reforms in the XIXth century by liberal-minded rulers such as Ahmad Bey (1839-1855) and his successors Muhammad Bey (1855-1859) and Bey Muhammad as-Sadoq (1859-1883) who promulgate the 'Fundamental Pact' (1857) and a Constitution *(dustūr)* in 1861. Yet the economic situation deteriorates, prosperity declines through misrule and dissipation, and indebtedness to foreign, mainly French, banks lead to the control of the State finances by an 'International Finance Commission'. In vain the progressive Grand Vizier Khair al-Dīn attempts to forestall French influence by reaffirming Ottoman suzerainty. Bey Muhammad as-Sadoq signs the Treaty of Kassar Said (1881) and the Convention of La Marsa (1883), which establish the French Protectorate in Tunisia.

Towards the close of 1881 reluctance to submit to the foreign rule - which although initially tended to appear as what today might be called technical assistance to an underdeveloped country - became noticeable among the young middle-class intelligentsia. It took shape in the Mouvement Bourgeois de Tunisie* but was not yet able to find the way to coherent and uniform expression. As, however, the Tunisian élite, both of Islamic-religious and of western-academic schooling, felt more and more ousted from ever wider fields of public life, the discontent assumed more definite forms, especially when it became increasingly manifest that the expected promotion of the country's cultural and economic advancement had to rank behind the interests of the French 'colons' and of metropolitan finance and big industry. Yet not before the turn of the century were the demands for emancipation from the French tutelage dressed in a precise political program and made the platform of the Young Tunisia Party*, the pacemaker of militant Tunisian nationalism. The Protectorate authorities thoroughly misjudged the potential force of the movement. Pretexting some labour troubles and street riots in Tunis they deported the leaders and arrested some members and sympathizers. The organization, however, continued clandestinely throughout the First World War, although still confined to a comparatively small number from among the educated circles. After their spokesmen had tried in vain at the Paris Peace Conference to assert for Tunisia the right to self-determination they called on the Bey to initiate negotiations for the gradual abrogation of the Protectorate and to re-enact the Constitution of 1861. The reaction of the French authorities was thoroughly negative, as could not otherwise be expected, but in the country the disappointment evoked loud resonance. A new party programme was drawn up in 1922 and out of the soil prepared by the 'Young Tunisians' there grew up the Destour* (Liberal Constitutional Party). It branched out rapidly and widely, but within a few years under the influence of a right-wing majority of upper-and middle-class merchants and landowners and men of religion remained uncompromising where questions of a religious bearing were involved, and assumed an increasingly cautious attitude in the thenceforth interconnected issues of independence and liberal reforms. Against them stood a youthful, progressively minded minority of rather laicizing tendencies with Habīb Bourguiba, twenty-five years later President of the Republic, in the forefront. It saw as the target of the national struggle the simultaneous achievement of the freedom from foreign encroachment and of the liberation of the mass of the people from ignorance, backwardness and the domination by age-old vested interests. In March 1934, the two camps separated and the Neo-Destour* made its appearance on the political stage. Ḥabīb Bourguiba was its secretary-general, and soon afterwards its president. Within a year or two it built up a country-wide, solidly structured organization and took ever firmer root first in the towns, but soon also among the peasantry and the workers in the mining districts.

The growth of the Neo-Destour; its emergence as the protagonist in the battle against the French régime; its rôle in the subsequent negotiations with the French government; and finally its ascent to the position of the sole policy-making factor in the state - these may well be the headings of some of the principal chapters in the story of the birth and the infant years of the Republic of Tunisia. The first part of the story is the account of reforms, promised to appease the popular unrest and watered down, indefinitely postponed or revoked under the pressure of the influential cliques of the 'colons'; of strikes and uproar countered by mass trials and martial law; of the confusion and destruction in the war years which made in turn Vichy France, the Germans, the Allies and the Free French masters of the country; the deposition of Bey Muhammad al-Munsif because of his sympathies for the Neo-Destour; the imprisonment or internment in concentration camps of the party leaders; Bourguiba's long years in exile - throughout 1934, from 1938 to 1943, and from 1952 to 1955 - and his 'public relations' tour over half the world; the alliance between the Neo-Destour and the Tunisian Trade Unions; the spread of terrorism and counter-terrorism; and finally the laborious negotiations which at last resulted on June 3, 1955 in the grant of internal autonomy and on March 20, 1956 in the proclamation of independence. The interpretation of what was called the Franco-Tunisian 'interdependence' was left to the future: the question of the French base at Bizerta and of the French garrisons still maintained in some Tunisian towns; the much entangled relations between the French and Tunisian treasuries; or the financial and technical assistance which France was to extend the young State in the making.

The second part of the story deals with the work confronting the Tunisian leaders, upon whom it fell to build up the new social, economic and cultural structure for the country and to secure for it a commensurate place in the international political pattern. The French tutelage had undoubtedly helped in many respects towards the adoption of modern concepts and attitudes, but there was much in the heritage that made this work far from easy: the depressing poverty of the rural masses; in agri-, culture*, antiquated methods of production and hence low yields except on the large estates which were in foreign hands; an inadequately developed industry* except in the branch of mining* also under foreign control, and a school system that left more than half of the boys and nearly all the girls without elementary education. There was among the educated classes an élite of high standard, but rather small in view of the tasks ahead. Besides, it was divided as to principles, methods and rhythm, required to guide the process of evolving a new order. It reflected opinions which ranged from cautious conservatism of strong religious shades to uncompromising radicalism in the eyes of its opponents very near to atheism. Divergences came to the surface also on the plane of external politics with regard to the position Tunisia was to assume in the 'Arab family'. They separated the partisans, on the one hand, of a Greater Maghrib - the close alliance of Tunisia, Algeria and Morocco - and, on the other, of some form of a much farther extended pan-Arab union under Egyptian hegemony. The way out was obviously difficult. It had to take many detours and was often one of trial and error.

The start was made with the elections for a Constituent Assembly on the platform of National Unity. The Neo-Destour won all the seats, and Habīb Bourguiba constituted the first government of independent Tunisia, all of whose members were Neo-Destourians, some of them prominent in Tunisian trade unionism*. A 'national reform programme' was elaborated and was initiated by the abrogation of polygamy and the granting to women of the right to vote - they used it two months later in the municipal elections in which the party obtained an overwhelming majority. One year later the Constituent Assembly abolished the monarchy (May 25, 1957); declared Tunisia a Republic; confiscated the property of the Bey and of his numerous family; and, pending the promulgation of the Constitution, elected Bourguiba Head of State while leaving him in charge of presiding over the Cabinet of Ministers - or rather Secretaries of State - responsible to him alone. His formal election (November 1959) as President of the Republic was one of the first acts of the new Legislative Assembly elected by universal suffrage with the women voters appearing unveiled at the polls. To broaden and intensify the contacts between the government - or the Party - and the various strata of the population, a country-wide network of cultural and occupational satellite organizations was created or, as far as some of it dated from French times, 'tunisified' and integrated within the party system: the Tunisian Union of Artisans and Merchants (Union Tunisienne de l'Artisanat et du Commerce, U.T.A.C.); the National Union of Tunisian Agriculturists (Union Nationale des Agriculteurs Tunisiens, U.N.A.T.); the Tunisian Women's Association; the General Union of Tunisian Students (Union Générale des Etudiants Tunisiens); and the Association of Tunisian Boy Scouts which soon had over 20.000 members.

There was, however, one oppositional movement that could not be prevented from assuming extremely violent forms. It was inspired by Bourguiba's former comrade-in-arms of the Neo-Destour but later his deadly enemy, Salāh Ibn Yūsuf with the group of malcontents around him. Its seat was at first in Cairo, subsequently in Rabat and Constantine, and temporarily chilled Tunisia's relations with Egypt and Morocco.

Far more serious were the frictions heightening at times into sharp conflicts in the Franco-Tunisian 'inter-relationship'. Partly they arose out of the fighting in Algeria. They ranged from minor but repeated frontier violations by French troops in the pursuit of Algerian revolutionaries to the capture of Ben Bella and his travel companions flying from Rabat to a meeting with Bourguiba in Tunis, and culminated in the bombing by the French air force of the border town of Sakiet Sīdī Yūsuf (February 1958), which killed a number of women and children and destroyed over a hundred houses and shops. Tunisia, on the other hand, supplied the Algerian revolutionaries with arms, ammunition and war material and gave hospitality to an army of some 100.000 men. Other tensions developed early in 1958 when Tunisia requested the withdrawal of the French garrisons still in the country and the evacuation of Bizerta. The garrisons were withdrawn, but Bizerta was not evacuated. Tunisia reopened the Bizerta question in 1959, and after dilatory pourparlers brought it up again in January 1960 with the same negative result. The situation worsened and in August 1961 popular exitement came to a climax. Uniformed youth troops tried to storm the French barbed-wire barriers, and the result was some 600 Tunisians and some 30 French dead. It needed the intervention of the United Nations' Security Council and one year of strenuous negotiations until France agreed to the transfer of the port and the arsenal 'within a reasonable time'. They were turned over on October 15, 1963.

The suspension from the end of 1957 until March 1963 of French financial assistance could to some extent be balanced from American, German, Italian, Russian and other sources, but inevitably retarded the implementation of the comprehensive programme of reforms. Still, new elementary schools were established, mainly in the countryside, at the annual rate of 600 classrooms for some 25.000 pupils, and gradually French was replaced by Arabic as the language of instruction. There is so far no university in Tunisia, apart from the Academy of the Zaytūna Mosque with two sections, one of the strictly religious disciplines, the other of Arabic literature. There are, however, an 'Institut des Hautes Etudes' for Law, Letters and Social Sciences; a 'Centre d'Etudes des Sciences Humaines', established in 1956, and a 'School of Administration', which are planned to develop into a university in the near future.

New industrial enterprises were created on the basis of a partnership between the State and large foreign concerns. Deep - going changes in the out-of-date system of agricultural land tenure, schemes for soil improvements, the rationalization of the methods of production and the provision of decent housing for the peasantry were initiated. A Ten-Year Development Plan (1962-1971) was elaborated and its first phase, a three-year 'pre-plan' set in operation. Its extension into a second, five-year phase was prepared when friendly relations with France were resumed early in 1963.

It would be premature to attempt a forecast as to when and to what extent all the new industries will prove commercially profitable, or how soon the agricultural reforms will actually increase and improve the harvest. More important is what may be called their social productivity - the fact that they supply new means of earning to quite a number of workers and at the same time open their eyes to modern techniques. It would be equally out of place to find all too many faults with certain flaws and inefficiencies in the public administration, and the authoritarian character of the one-party régime, at least as long as the blemishes of the past have not been made up for.

TUNISIAN PARTY see YOUNG TUNISIA PARTY

TURMEDA ANSELMO, a Catalan monk (born ca 1353) from Majorca and in his time a well-known man of letters who after some studies in Greek and Hebrew at the university of Lérida left for Tunis. There, without compulsion and obviously moved by sincere conviction, in a solemn assembly of the court before Sultan Abū al-ʿAbbās* (1370-1394) he abjured his faith and embraced Islam. Appointed to a government position he soon acquired full mastery of Arabic and served as interpreter *(tarjumān)* in the negotiations with European ambassadors. Notwithstanding several attempts undertaken by high ecclesiastic authorities and even by the King of Aragon to win him back, ʿAbd Allāh al-Tarjumān, the former Fra Anselmo Turmeda, refused to tear himself away from his new self-chosen home-country, but, held in high favour also by Sultan Abū Fāris* (1394-1434) continued his ascending career in the sovereign's close surroundings. At the same time he seems to have gone rather deeply into the intricacies of the argumentation used in the polemics between Christian and Muslim apologetics, as appears from his *Tuhfat al-Arīb* (abridged title, appr. The Adornment of the Clever Man, French translation in Revue Tunisienne, 1906), a short, but, compared with the great majority of similar treatises, logically constructed refutation of the Christian creed and justification of the Islamic dogmas. Other works of his pen in Catalan verse of a more popular, half-religious, half-philosophical character have been preserved partly in the original, partly in a contemporary French translation. Al-Tarjumān died at an unknown date, probably over 70 years old, and is buried in Tunis.

U

U.D.M.A. see DEMOCRATIC UNION OF THE ALGERIAN MANIFESTO

U.G.T.A., abbreviation for Union Générale des Travailleurs Algériens, see TRADE UNIONISM

U.G.T.T., abbreviation for Union Générale des Travailleurs Tunisiens, see TRADE UNIONISM

U.M.T., abbreviation for Union Marocaine du Travail, see TRADE UNIONISM

ʿUMĀRA IBN ABĪ, AHMAD IBN MARZŪQ, called the impostor, a Tunisian ruler (1283-1284) whose reign for the first time broke the almost uninterrupted line of the Hafsid* dynasty (1228-1574). A poor tailor in Bougie, he gained a following at first in Morocco among the Arab tribe of the Maʿqil* by claiming to be the *Mahdī*, the God-guided Saviour; and then in the region of Tripoli where he managed to pass for al-Fadl, a son of the Hafsid caliph al-Wāthiq (1277-1279), whom his uncle, Caliph Abū Ishāq Ibrāhīm (1279-1283) had deposed and put to death. Ibn Abī ʿUmāra, supported by several tribal groups, especially the Kuʿūb, a Sulaym* branch, found recognition in Gabès, then made himself master of al-Qayrawān and Sfax, and finally, as al-Fadl, was proclaimed caliph. Abū Ishāq Ibrāhīm, deserted by most of his troops, had to abdicate. The usurper held his entry into the capital Tunis, defeated an army commanded by the dethroned ruler's son, who along with three of his brothers was killed, while their father was taken prisoner and executed. Only the fifth son, Abū Zakariyyā', escaped to Tlemcen and was cordially received at the court of his brother-in-law, Abū Saʿīd ʿUthmān, who, however, recognized Ibn Abī ʿUmāra as the legitimate ruler. Abū Zakariyyā', in an effort to recover his heritage, rallied some Bedouin tribes and, meeting with little resistance, seized the towns and region of Bougie and Constantine. It was this move which shortly was to lead to the first partition of the Hafsid realm. In the meantime Ibn Abī ʿUmāra's lucky star rapidly paled. His first-hour allies, the Kuʿūb, turned their favour to Abū Ishāq's youngest brother, Abū Hafs ʿUmar*, and gained a number of tribes for his cause. The pseudo-Fadl, unable to quench the insurrection which spread with increasing momentum, hid a few days in Tunis but was soon discovered, confessed his fraud and was beheaded. Abū Hafs ʿUmar was solemnly recognized as the rightful sovereign (1284-1295).

U.N.F.P. see NATIONAL UNION OF POPULAR FORCES

UNION DÉMOCRATIQUE DU MANIFESTE ALGÉRIEN see DEMOCRATIC UNION OF THE ALGERIAN MANIFESTO

UNION NATIONALE DES FORCES POPULAIRES see NATIONAL UNION OF POPULAR FORCES

U.P.A. see ALGERIAN POPULAR UNION

UNION POPULAIRE ALGÉRIENNE see ALGERIAN POPULAR UNION

URJŪZA, a genre of didactic treatises, composed in verse for the purpose of aiding the student's memory and named after its use of the so-called *rajaz*, a simple and easily adaptable meter. The *urjūza*, which until not very long ago held an old-established place in the text-books for lower-grade study especially of grammar and jurisprudence, appeared also quite frequently in unsophisticated books on history, intended for a public that neither noticed nor most probably would have minded the author's fanciful play with events and popular figures of the past. This latter type of poetry, if its quality still permits calling it so, inverted the ancient practice of assigning numerical values with different powers to the letters of the alphabet, and expressed the dates by an assemblage of letters which then were fitted more or less successfully into rhythm and rhyme. Nevertheless there were at all times, even up to the end of the last century, men of truly scholarly standing who did not disdain the form of *urjūza* for one or the other of their writings, mainly of a biographical character. As an illustration may serve the versified biography of Ahmad Ibn Muhammad Tijānī, the founder of the Tijānīya* fraternity, written by a Moroccan cadi in 1844 and the subject of a long, scholarly commentary published in Cairo in 1887 by a highly reputed theologian of Rabat.

WAQʿAT al-HUFRA, rendered in occidental texts by the 'Slaughter of the Ditch' and denoting the suppression, or perhaps prevention, of the outbreak (797) of a revolt in Toledo against Emir al-Hakam I (796-822). In the excited days of al-Hakam's struggle with his uncles ʿAbd Allāh and Sulaymān, the sons of the first Umayyad emir ʿAbd al-Rahmān I*, over the succession to the throne, the public opinion in Toledo, a town always unruly and difficult to handle, did not hide its hostility to the new monarch. It is not certain whether or not the general unrest had already crystallized into a concrete plan for rebellious action, but the commander of the town, ʿĀmrūs Ibn Yūsuf, one of the emir's most faithful generals, decided to eradicate once for all every seditious inclination. He invited the outstanding citizens - 700 according to some sources, 5000 according to others - to a feast in his new castle, and as soon as a guest passed through the heavy gateway his head was cut off and he was thrown into a nearby ditch especially dug for the purpose. For a short time the people of Toledo remained quiet, but the hatred fermented under the surface and broke out in new revolts every two or three years.

WATTĀSIDS, Banū Wattās, a Berber dynasty in Morocco (1472-1554), issued from a branch of the Zanāta* family of tribes and thus related to the Marīnids*, their predecessors on the throne (1244-1465). Having slowly migrated from their pasture grounds on the northern fringes of the Sahara through southern Tripolitania and Algeria, they settled in the XIIIth century in eastern Morocco and in the hilly regions of the Rif. After a period of wavering loyalty under the first Marīnids they became faithful supporters of the dynasty which for several generations selected from among them most of its high-ranking dignitaries. In the years of its decadence and the general anarchy which followed the assassination of its last forceful sovereign, Abū ʿInān Fāris (1351-1358)*, the heads of the great Wattāsid family, in name regents or tutors of a child-potentate or the governors of a town, were actually the masters of the country, more often than not at war with one another and with the refractory Arab chiefs of the plains.

In the first quarter of the XVth century, one of the family, Abū Zakariyyā' Yahyā Ibn Zaiyān, the governor of Salé, had the one-year old Marīnid ʿAbd al-Haqq* proclaimed sovereign and assumed the functions of regent which he continued to hold also after his ward had come of age until he met his death fighting against some revolting Berbers. His place was taken first by one of his cousins, who was killed while trying to suppress another tribal sedition, and then by his son Yahyā. In the same year, ʿAbd al-Haqq had Yahyā and the other members of the Wattāsid clan assassinated (1458), with the exception of two brothers whom he could not lay hands on. One of them, Muham-

mad al-Shaykh, was to ascend the throne of Morocco as the first Wattāsid sultan (1472-1505).
In the area of Arzila (on the Atlantic coast, some 40 miles south of Tangier), among a population devoted to his cause, Muhammad al-Shaykh assembled troops and began to wage war against ʿAbd al-Haqq who, however, was assassinated (1465) in Fez by a seditious mob which proclaimed *Imām* (secular and spiritual leader) the head of the sharīfian Idrīsid* family. Muhammad al-Shaykh turned his arms against this new rival but was beaten at the gates of Meknès. Thereupon he concluded an armistice with the Portuguese who in the meantime had advanced along the Atlantic coast and had occupied Arzila and Tangier. Then he continued the struggle against the *Imām* and drove him behind the walls of Fez. After a two-year siege the city surrendered and the Idrīsid imamate collapsed (1472).
Muhammad al-Shaykh, officially the sole ruler, exercised actual power only within rather narrow limits. His attempts to dislodge the Portuguese from Ceuta, lost at the time of the last Marīnids, and from Arzila, failed. Neither could he prevent them from setting up a sort of commercial protectorate over the Atlantic ports of Safi (1481) and Azemmour (1486); nor from building the sea fortress of al-Brija al-Jadīda (1502), which was to develop into the town of Mazagan; and the one, south of Cape Guir (1505) that was to grow into the town of Agadir (Sainte Croix du Cap de Gué or Cap Ghir in contemporary sources). He was unable to forestall the loss to Spain of Melilla (1497) which ever since has remained Spanish territory, and of Mers al-Kabīr on the Algerian coast (1505). Nor could he impose his authority in the Rif region upon the Jabal Alam, south-east of Tetuan. There the principality of Shashāwan (span. Xauen), founded by another Idrīsid *sharīf*, enjoyed a practically complete independence and under the flag of the Holy War sustained by Moslem refugees (Moriscos*) from Granada, opposed for some sixty years to the Christian invaders a most tenacious resistance. A similar self-government was established in Tetuan, also by Moriscos who rebuilt the town from the ruins which were left after its destruction by the Castilian navy (1399). Unsubmissive, too, remained the emirate of the Marīnid side-line at Dabdū in the mountains south of Taūrīrt. Only by giving in marriage two of his sons to two Marīnid daughters could Muhammad al-Shaykh achieve there the semblance of sovereignty. He was equally unsuccessful in the southern sections where Nāsir Ibn Shantūf, a chieftain of the great Hintāta tribe, a Masmūda* branch, moved down from the High Atlas into the plains of Marrakesh and took hold of the city and the surrounding region, refusing to recognize a more than nominal Wattāsid overlordship.
The structure of the State loosened further at a rapidly accelerating rate during the reign of Muhammad al-Shaykh's son, Abū ʿAbd Allāh Muhammad (1505-1524) surnamed al-Burtūqālī, the Portuguese, because of his long stay in Portugal. The Portuguese not only fortified the places where they had gained a footing but also brought into their obedience the major tribes of the hinterland. Penetrating from Agadir eastwards they made most of the chieftains in the plain of the Sūs

their allies, and even pushed forth dangerously near Marrakesh (1515) and south of the High Atlas into the areas of the Wādī Darʿa. They established friendly relations with a number of clans, but it was there, near present-day Zagora, that the resistance against the invaders took its origin. There, too, at the same time began a struggle which ultimately carried a new dynasty, the Saʿdians*, to power. It was started by one Abū ʿAbd Allāh Ibn Ahmad al-Qā'im, the chief of the sharīfian family of the Banū Saʿd*, who with his two sons, Ahmad al-Aʿrāj and Muhammad al-Shaykh al-Mahdī, moved from the Darʿa valley into the Sūs, rallied some tribes by the call to the Holy War and attacked the Portuguese at Azemmour and at Safi. After his death (1517) his sons set up their residence in Tārūdānt (some 50 miles east of Agadir) and ten years later took possession of Marrakesh (1523). Shortly before Muhammad al-Burtūqālī's death (1524) they were masters of nearly all southern Morocco.

Under al-Burtūqālī's weak and unsteady son, Abū al-ʿAbbās Ahmad (1524-1549 with a short interruption), the Saʿdians openly severed all ties of allegiance. He followed his grandfather's example, made peace with the Portuguese and attacked his revolting vassals who, however, inflicted a series of defeats upon his dwindling forces and finally made him prisoner. They also successfully continued the war against the infidels, conquered Agadir, occupied Azemmour and Safi, which the Portuguese evacuated without giving battle. While Abū al-ʿAbbās Ahmad was in the enemy's hands, his uncle Abū al-Hassan ʿAlī, commonly called Bū Hassūn, the very soul of the resistance, had as a matter of form placed another of his nephews on the throne, continued the war, and succeeded, through the intermediary of some influential religious orders, in having Abū al-ʿAbbās Ahmad set free in return for the surrender of Meknès. He could not prevent the fall of Fez (1550), notwithstanding the strife opposing the two Saʿdian brothers, one of whom even fought on Wattāsid sides. Most of the Wattāsids were either deported into the oases on the fringe of the desert and subsequently killed or fled to Spain and Portugal, where some of them embraced Christianity and withdrew into monastic life. Bū Hassūn, too, escaped and after a long peregrination in the quest of allies which took him first to Spain; then into Germany to Emperor Charles V in whose army he served for a while; and again into Spain, then to Lisbon and finally, intercepted by pirates on the way back to Africa, into captivity to Algiers. There he persuaded the Turkish beylerbey to organize an expedition against the Saʿdian usurpers of the Marīnid throne, reconquered Fez with Turkish help and maintained himself in power for a few months, but at last succumbed to the Saʿdians who by then were already masters of nearly the entire Wattāsid possessions.

As little as their immediate predecessors, the last Marīnids, did the Wattāsids command a sufficient measure of either prestige or organisational capacity to integrate in a system of government the various power groups often contending with one another for supremacy within fluid regional limits: bellicose mountain tribes and their ephemeral alliances; ambitious notables or theological doctors manipulating a fickle urban populace; great chieftains in the plains, supporting now one, now another pretender to the throne; and everywhere in the country the still growing number of holy men (marabouts*) and religious brotherhoods*, whose word was law within the ever widening circles of their devotees. Still, the unstability of its structure and its aversion to any authority beyond jealously circumscribed territorial or tribal confines in no way affected the vitality of this society nor its - although often dormant - community consciousness. These became forcefully manifest in the years of the Portuguese invasion. When the call to the Holy War resounded, everywhere, spontaneously, guerilla fighters banded together and, unorganized, without plan, in ever shifting groupings, but unceasingly and tenaciously harassed the invaders, checked their advance and ultimately achieved their withdrawal. Here and there, especially in the areas of the Atlantic ports held by the Portuguese, advantage was found in maintaining commercial relations serving the trade between the interior of Africa and Europe. On the constantly changing political stage alliances, mostly of a very short duration, were sought by some of the petty city potentates or by members of the dynasty in the course of its struggle for survival. They did not, however, alter the general picture to any noteworthy extent.

Y

YAHYĀ IBN IBRĀHĪM, al-JADDĀLĪ, a Berber chieftain (†1056) of the Juddāla tribe and head of a Sanhāja* confederation of tribes, constituted in the first half of the XIth century by the Juddāla, Lamtūna* and Massūfa. Returning from the pilgrimage to the Holy Cities and desirous of leading his tribes, still only rather superficially observing the precepts of Islam, onto a way of life more in accord with the teaching of the Prophet, he took the theologian ʿAbd Allāh Ibn Yāsīn* to his people. The tribesmen listened to the preaching but without actually changing their deep-rooted, semi-pagan customs and practices, and soon after Yahyā Ibn Ibrāhīm's death, drove the reformer from their midst. Their new chief, however, elected from the tribe of the Lamtūna, Yahyā Ibn ʿUmar al-Lamtūnī, his brother Abū Bakr Ibn ʿUmar and a few other adherents followed ʿAbd Allāh Ibn Yāsīn into a *ribāt** (fortified monastery) founded, according to some authors by him, according to others by Yahyā Ibn Ibrāhīm. This was the origin of the great Almoravid* movement.

YAHYĀ IBN YAHYĀ al-LAITHĪ, a Hispano-Arab theologian and jurist (†849), born from a family of Berber origin which had settled in Spain soon after the Arab conquest. He went, like many young students of religious science, to Medina and became a zealous adherent of Mālik Ibn Anas (713-795), the great scholar of Islamic canon law, who, it is related, honoured him by the sobriquet 'the wise man of al-Andalus'. After his return he made his home in Cordova where his erudition, piety and minute observance of the Islamic code of ethics, coupled with a remarkable firmness of mind soon established not only his unquestioned authority within the juridico-theological circles, but also his popularity with the masses and his standing at court. His influence was instrumental in making the rigorous Mālikite school of thought the ruling doctrine of law in al-Andalus*, and it was he who practically controlled all appointments to the office of cadi. Relentlessly he stigmatised what he considered to be a sinful display by the upper classes of luxury, laxity of morals and disregard for the teaching of the Prophet, and their patronage of poets, astrologers, musicians and singers. Suspected of implication in the subersive movement against Emir al-Hakam I (796-822) which culminated in the so-called Revolt of the Suburb* (818) in Cordova, he had temporarily to leave the capital, but later was permitted to return with undiminished prestige. Yahyā Ibn Yahyā, although of a scholarly calibre by far surpassing the average, may be regarded as the prototype of the *faqīh* class which throughout the Umayyad régime gave its imprint to public life in al-Andalus.

YAZĪD ABŪ, MAKHLAD IBN KAYDAD, a Berber sectarian leader (ca 880-947) of the Banū Īfran*, a branch of the great Zanāta* group.

He was born in the Sudan of a negro mother but spent his youth in the small town of Tozeur (in the depression of the Shatt Jarīd in central Tunisia) and there joined the Ibādite Nukkār sect of the Kharijite heterodoxy. Desirous of acquainting himself more thoroughly with the doctrine, he moved to Tāhart, the seat of the Rustumid* *Imāms* and a center of Khārijite learning, where he made a modest livelihood by teaching and interpreting the Koran. Upon the conquest of Tāhart by the Fātimid apostle Abū ʿAbd Allāh al-Shīʿī he returned to Tozeur, at that time already in Fātimid hands, and started a religio-political propaganda against the - from the Khārijite point of view - heretical Fātimid régime and its heavy and - as he claimed - illegal system of taxation. Thrown into prison but set free by his adherents, he went with them nortwards among the Zanāta tribes of the Algerian mountain region of the Aurès and Hodna. Though crippled and of frail constitution, he travelled indefatigably on his donkey all over the country - hence called 'The man of the donkey' *(sāhib al-himār)* - and by his extreme austerity, fanaticism and eloquence not only acquired a rapidly spreading spiritual prestige as the 'Sheikh of the Believers', but at the same time recruited an army of Zanāta warriors, strong enough for regular military action against the Fātimid government.
Pilfering, devastating and murdering, Abū Yazīd's tribes broke forth (943) from their mountains, rushed down over the plains of eastern Algeria and Tunisia, forced al-Qayrawān to surrender and even had the highly reputed Sunnite scholars of the Great Mosque, much against their own judgement, it is true, sanction his cause. He installed his governors in the conquered towns, laid siege to the Fātimid residence al-Mahdīya (on the coast, south east of al-Qayrawān) and established friendly relations with the Umayyad court at Cordova, as rigorously orthodox as the religious doctors of al-Qayrawān but welcoming him, regardless of his heresy, as an ally against the rival Fātimid caliphate. Intoxicated, however, by his success, Abū Yazīd gave up his ascetic way of life, became overbearing and dictatorial, until he was left by many of his follwers. After eight months of heavy fighting, the siege of al-Mahdīya had to be raised, the conquered towns were evacuated and Abū Yazīd, desperately resisting, withdrew with the last faithful remainder of his community into a fortress in the Hodna mountains. Defending every foot of ground with utmost tenacity against his overwhelmingly superior assailants he finally was seriously wounded, taken prisoner and ignominiously killed, while his two sons escaped to al-Andalus*. Abū-Yazīd's short-lived power completely collapsed, but while it lasted it shook the Fātimid realm to its very foundations.

YOUNG TUNISIA PARTY, later called simply Tunisian Party, the first nationalist organization in Tunisia. It was formed around 1908 by ʿAlī Bāsh Hamba and Bashīr Sfar (Safar), the leading spirits of the liberally-minded 'Alumni of the Sādiqī College' (Les Anciens du Collège Sādiki) and of the conservative 'Khaldūnīya', the two groups into which the Mouvement Bourgeois Tunisien* had split and which they reunited under the roof of the new party. They were joined by Bashīr Sfar's former student and close friend, Sheikh ʿAbd al-ʿAzīz al-Thaʿālībī, much travelled in Turkey, Egypt and Arabia, and one of the protagonists of the Salafīya* Islamic renaissance movement eloquently propagated in the columns of his paper *Sabīl al-Rashad* (Road to Truth). Prior to the Party's actual establishment Bashīr Sfar had outlined its aims in an address delivered on the occasion of a public ceremony in 1906, which may be briefly summarized as the demand for equality of rights without distinction between native Tunisians and French citizens living in Tunisia, and the transfer into Tunisian hands of the administrative and economic control of Tunisian affairs. The 'Young Tunisia' party, modelled in many respects after the pattern of the Young Turks, recruited its membership almost exclusively in the ranks of the liberal intelligentsia - lawyers, higher-grade officials, journalists, all with rare exceptions issued from French universities. Its organ, the weekly 'Le Tunisien', was in fact published in French and only after some time Sheikh al-Thaʿālībī prepared an Arabic edition. By its outspoken modernistic tendencies the Party evoked the sharp antagonism of the traditionalist religious circles and their following - the 'Old Turbans' as they were derisively called - and failed to find a more than very limited audience in the broader public which still had little understanding for the meaning of Tunisian nationalism.

This atmosphere rapidly changed under the impact of the excitement stirred up in all strata of the population by the Italian invasion of Tripolitania (1911), the territory of a Moslem sister nation. Within the Party strong pan-Islamic currents came to the surface; the people at large awakened to the nationalist ideologies; and the resentment against the French colonial régime spread and began to take root. In the heightening tension some otherwise not particularly serious incidents assumed critical proportions. The inclusion in the general land registry of a Moslem cemetery provoked violent street riots, military intervention with a great number of killed and wounded, and the proclamation of a state of war. A boycott by the Moslems of the street-cars in Tunis was followed by the strike of the Moslem workers and employees of the - Italian-owned - street-car company, both animated by a Committee of Action of the Party, and continued in spite of their interdiction by the Protectorate* authorities. The French riposte was the deportation of ʿAlī Bāsh Hamba, Sheikh al-Thaʿālībī and their nearest collaborators (1912). The Party, deprived of its leadership, remained for some time inactive but then started an underground propaganda, tenaciously pursued notwithstanding some more arrests, among others of Sheikh Ahmad Tawfīq al-Madanī, who subsequently was to play a foremost rôle in the Algerian Revolution* as the secretary-general of the Association of the Algerian ʿUlamā',*. ʿAlī Bāsh Hamba settled in Constantinople, was appointed political adviser to the Grand Vizier, and during the years of the first World War directed the press campaigne against the Allies, in particular France, and for the Tunisian emancipation, until his death in 1918 on the day of the entry of the allied troops into Constantinople. Sheikh al-Thaʿālībī, who shortly before the outbreak of the war was permitted to return to Tunis, cautiously took up his relations with the clandestine party organizations and upon the ending of hostilities appeared again openly on the political stage, taking a principal part in the revival of the nationalist movement which in 1920 crystallized in the *Hizb al-Hurr al-Dustūrī*, commonly called Destour*, the Liberal Constitutional Party.

YŪSUF IBN TĀSHUFĪN, the first Almoravid* ruler (1061-1106), a cousin of the two Lamtūna* chieftains Yahyā Ibn ʿUmar and Abū Bakr Ibn ʿUmar, who together with the theologian ʿAbd Allāh Ibn Yāsīn* created the religious movement which carried the Almoravids (*Murābitūn**) to power. Entrusted with the military command in the conquered regions in southern Morocco by Abū Bakr who had to appease some of his always restless tribal groups in the desert, he directed his efforts towards the consolidation of the new possessions. He laid down the basis of public administration, organized the tribesmen and built up coherent army formations. To mark the beginning of the new order, he transferred the seat of his government from the former residence at the town of Aghmāt in the Middle Atlas to a fortified camp in the plain (1062) which in a short time was to develop into the city of Marrakesh. Having thus started the transformation into a state of what until then was hardly more than a loose agglomeration of territories overrun by nomad tribes, he persuaded Abū Bakr upon his return to go back to his desert people and reassume the raids against the Negro kingdoms. Then he set systematically upon the expansion of his domain over northern Morocco.
Between 1063 and 1082 one after the other of the principalities held by Miknāsa* or Maghrāwa* emirs or by some of the other smaller Zanāta* groups, fell into the hands of Yūsuf Ibn Tāshufīn and his Almoravid generals: Fez - occupied, lost again and at last definitively taken (1069) - then, by gradual advance eastwards and northwards, the Mulūya region on the eastern slopes of the Rif; the region of Taza; Tangier and Melilla. Then followed the occupation of the Rif; of the Sālihid* domain, the city and port of Nakūr which was completely destroyed; of Oujda and Agadir (1082) which together with Tagrart, the fortified camp he set up on the outskirts of the old town, was to develop into the city of Tlemcen. Then, pushing eastwards, he took Oran and Tenès and went as far as Algiers. Having reached the territories of related, sedentary Sanhāja* family members, the Zīrids* and Hammādids*, he stopped, installed his governors in the various sections of his new realm, and returned to Marrakesh.
It was about this time that the rulers of Seville, Badajoz and Granada - the Abbādid* Muʿtamid, the Aftasid* al-Mutawakkil and the Zīrid ʿAbd Allāh - sent repeated and increasingly urgent appeals to Yūsuf Ibn Tāshufīn for help against the dangerously proceeding offensive of Alfonso VI, King of Castile and León. After careful preparation, and having entrusted the African empire to his son as regent, he led his troops into the Holy War for the defence of Islam. At al-Zallāqa*, the modern Sagrajas near Badajoz, the joint Almoravid and Andalusian army inflicted a heavy defeat on Alfonso (1086). Informed of his son's sudden death, Yūsuf returned to Morocco, leaving in al-Andalus* 3000 of his warriors who were, however, unable to prevent the recovery of the Castilians and to protect the Arab city-states from the daring

raids of the 'Cid', Rodrigo el Campeador, the Spanish knight of epic fame. Once more Almoravid help was requested and once more Yūsuf crossed the Straits (1088). This time, his expedition was a failure, mainly due to the discord among the Andalusian princes. Deeply irritated by the lack of pious zeal, he caused the religious doctors of al-Andalus to issue a series of *fatwā's* (formal answer to a question of Islamic law) which were confirmed by reputed scholars in the Arab East, condemning the Andalusian princes for their disregard of the word of the Koran and declaring that they had forfeited their right to reign over a Moslem country. A third time he went over to Spain (1090), deposed the Zīrid ʿAbd Allāh of Granada and the Hammūdid* Tamīm of Malaga, then, leaving the command of the army to one of his generals, he went back to Morocco. In the course of the following year Seville was conquered, its ruler al-Muʿtamid taken prisoner and most of al-Andalus passed into Almoravid hands; only the Cid, master of Valencia, remained undefeated. For the fourth time Yūsuf went to Spain (1097) in order to lead the operations personally. It took five more years to overcome the resistance of Valencia, sustained after the Cid's death by his widow Jemena, and to achieve the conquest of the rest of al-Andalus with the exception of Saragossa, where the Banū Hūd still retained a nominal sovereignty.

Thus Yūsuf Ibn Tāshufīn's statesmanship and forceful personality, rooted in profound religious conviction, carried him, the simple and practically uneducated warrior of the Sahara, in the last years of his life to a triumph the like of which it was not given to many to enjoy. He forged Morocco out of a multitude of loose tribal emirates, opposed to one another in herditary feuds. He achieved the unification of Arab Spain, divided into the innumerable city-states of the 'Party Kings'* and embodied it into his empire. Although one of the most powerful Moslem monarchs of his time, he never ceased to recognize the spiritual overlordship of the Baghdad caliph.

Z

ZAHĪR, plur. *zahā'ir* or *zahrawāt*, in French texts usually spelt *dahir*, the designation in the Arab West of a document issued by the sultan. In Tunisia under the Hafsids* the term was used to denote letters patent for nomination to a high office or other government function. In Morocco *zahīr* means a royal decree invested with the force of law.

ZAHRĀWĪ al-, ABŪ al-QĀSIM KHALAF IBN ʿABBĀS, called Albucasis or Abulcasis in the Latin West, generally considered the greatest Arab surgeon of the Middle Ages († ca 1013). He was born in al-Zahrā', a suburb of Cordova, and was appointed court physician to the Umayyad caliph Hakam II (961-976). Al-Zahrāwī made his reputation by the *Tasrīf li man ʿAjaz ʿan al-Ta'ālīf* (freely translated 'A simplified medical Handbook'), especially by the part which deals with surgery, a field in general rather neglected by Arab physicians. In this work he describes some operations he had performed, which until then were unknown, and supplies interesting illustrations of the instruments which he used. Partly translated into Latin (published in Venice 1497, Basel 1541, Oxford 1778) it served for many years as standard textbook at the medical schools of Europe.

ZAJAL, a type of love-songs and ballads, which originated in al-Andalus* towards the end of the IXth century. It quickly came into favour with the broad masses in country and town as well as with the higher classes, and at court was cultivated by a great many professional poets or minstrels, among whom Ibn-Quzmān* († 1160) gained particular fame. From its homeland it spread into North Africa and the Arab East and flourished well until the end of the Middle Ages. Down to this day the *zajal* still finds an audience in the popular quarters of the Moroccan towns. The appeal of this new folk-poetry was probably a reaction against the predominance of the classical ode *(qasīda)*, more and more felt as antiquated and no longer suitable to express the feeling and thinking of a time and society which had nothing in common with the heroic age. Structurally the *zajal* consists of an introductory couplet and a free number of stanzas, each one usually of four lines. The first three rhyme among themselves and the last one with the couplet so that one master-rhyme runs through the whole poem as illustrated by the scheme: a-a-b-b-b-a; c-c-c-a; d-d-d-a; etc. The *zajal* uses only the dialect; a composition of the same structure but in literary Arabic was called *muwashsha*, but here, too, a couplet in colloquial language often forms the end. *Zajal* and *muwashsha*, unlike the *qasīda*, were not recited but sung, probably to the accompaniment of lute-players and flautists, by singers or songstresses, with the audience taking up in chorus the fourth line of each stanza.

The *zajal* and the *muwashsha* sing in lyric tunes the courtly, platonic or spiritual love, the lover's tender submission to the whims of his beloved one and their tender sensibility to the beauties of nature, whereby often certain stereotyped characters - the moralist, the envier or the slanderer - introduce a dramatic element by disturbing the idyll. Both may also dwell on sensual love and its aberrations in terms of a crude and lascivious realism, so that modern translators preferred to refrain from rendering the full contents of such pieces. By the XIIIth or early XIVth century the *zajal* had found its way into Christian Spain - in Castilian language but in its original metrical and strophical structure - where it enjoyed the same popularity as in al-Andalus. Whether or to what extent there existed a relationship between the *zajal* and the poetical creation of the first troubadours and trouvères of southern France has been in recent years a subject of much controversial discussion which still remains without generally accepted result.

ZAIYĀNĪ al-,ABŪ al-QĀSIM IBN AḤMAD, a Moroccan statesman and historian (1734-1833?), born in Fez of a family descended from the Zaiyān (or Izayan), a group of Berber tribes in the Middle Atlas in the area of Khenifra. Having terminated his theological studies, he accompanied his parents on the pilgrimage to the Holy Cities. They arrived after a shipwreck on the Red Sea, in which they lost all their belongings except the 300 gold pieces carried by the mother in her sash. On the return journey they remained some time in Cairo, where al-Zaiyānī became interested in alchemy. Then they crossed from Alexandria to Livorno, continued by land to Barcelona, thence to Gibraltar and finally arrived in Fez almost completely destitute. Al-Zaiyānī entered government service and gained the favour of Sultan Muhammad Ibn ʿAbd Allāh (1757-1790). Having shown remarkable ability in negotiating with refractory tribal chieftains, he was entrusted with increasingly important tasks and finally with a diplomatic mission to the court of Constantinople, where he secured valuable friendships for his country and for himself. Upon his return he was appointed governor first of Taza then of Sijilmāsa, but after Muhammad Ibn ʿAbd Allāh's death fell into disgrace and was put into prison by the new sultan, Mūlāy Yazīd (1790-1792), yet a few weeks later released and again commissioned to persuade some recalcitrant tribes to submit to the central authority. Less successful this time, he was bastinadoed and re-imprisoned. Mūlāy Yazīd's successor, Mūlāy Sulaymān (1792-1822), well aware of al-Zaiyānī's experience in tribal affairs and anxious to gain support in the struggle for the throne against his brothers, set him free, and sent him out to enlist the help of the great chieftains. Attacked, however, in the mountains by clans of the opposite camp and forced to flee, al-Zaiyānī did not return to his sovereign but went to Tlemcen. He rented a house near the mausoleum of the famous mystic Abū Madyan*, where he spent about a year-and-a-half working on his books. Then he travelled by sea via Algiers and Tunis to Constantinople, was splendidly received and after a while undertook another pilgrimage, but the ship which was to carry him back from Alexandria to Algiers was driven by a storm to Rhodos and thence sailed to a Syrian port. Having lost in the course of this perilous voyage the merchandise he had bought in the East with the hope of profitable commercial transactions, he finally came home to Morocco, again left almost without means, but once more found a most honourable reception and was appointed vizier. He died at the age of 99 years and lies buried in Fez.

Three among al-Zaiyānī's fifteen works present a particular interest. One, *al-Turjumān al-Muʿarib an duwal al-Mashriq wa'l Maghrib* (The eloquent Interpreter of the States of the Orient and the Occident, French translation of extracts by O. Houdas, 'Le Maroc de 1631-1812', Paris, 1886) deals in succinct form with the entire history of the world of Islam and in detail with the Ottoman Empire and the dynasties of the Arab West and al-Andalus*, thus constituting to some extent a continuation of al-Īfranī's* *Nuzhat al-Hādī*. While in this book al-Zaiyānī simply recorded historical facts and data in the manner of the chronologists, foregoing all elaboration of style, he reveals a remarkable literary refinement and a sharp critical sense in his second historic work, the *Bustān al-Ẓarīf fī Dawlat Awlād Mawlāy ʿAlī al-Sharīf* (appr. Concise History of the Descendents of ʿAlī, the Noble) which is mainly a history of the reigning ʿAlawid* dynasty. The third of his books deserving special mention is the *Turjumānat al-Kubrā* (appr. The Great Interpretation) which combines the characteristics of a book of travel *(rihla*)* with a wealth of historic, literary and biographical material. It is based partly on his own observation, partly gathered together by painstaking research and substantiated by the conscientious indication of his sources of reference. A 'map of the seas' drawn by himself was added to the original manuscript (French translation of the part containing a description of Morocco by Coufourier, 'Une description géographique du Maroc d'Az-Zyāny', Paris 1906).

ZAKARIYYĀ' YAHYĀ, ABŪ-, the founder (1228-1249) of the Hafsid* dynasty in Tunisia. In his young years he served in several Andalusian towns as troop commander in the Almohad* army and later in Gabès under the orders of his brother Abū Muhammad, Almohad governor of Tunis. Subsequently he was appointed to the governorship in the place of his brother who had refused to recognize the new sovereign al-Ma'mūn (1227-1232). He renounced his allegiance upon al-Ma'mūn's repudiation of the Almohad doctrine, assumed the title of emir and a few years later declared his full sovereignty taking care to legitimize this step by claiming to preserve the continuity of the Almohad religio-political principle. Then he occupied all the territory of Constantine, Bougie and Algiers; imposed an alliance bordering on vasselage upon the emir of Tlemcen, Yaghmurāsan of the ʿAbd al-Wādids*; and subdued the recalcitrant Berber and Arab tribes of Tunisia and central Algeria. With his authority in this vast domain firmly founded upon a well-organized army and administration conceived in the Almohad spirit and Almohad traditions, his prestige made itself felt in the rapidly disintegrating Almohad empire as well as in al-Andalus*. His influence was decisive in the nomination of the governors of such important places in Morocco as Sijilmāsa, Tangier, Qasr al-Kabīr or Ceuta, who directly or indirectly remained under his obedience. The city-prince of Valencia,

a weak successor of Ibn-Mardanīsh* in war with the King of Aragon, sought his help - in a lengthy and elaborate poetical missive - against stronger rivals and submitted to Tunisian sovereignty; so did the princes of Seville, Xeres, Tarifa and Almeria. Also the Nasrid* sultans of Granada and Malaga, at that time still at the height of their power, paid homage in return for assistance against their Christian neighbours. Even the strong Marīnid* chieftain Abū Yahyā Ibn ʿAbd al-Haqq, then just beginning the struggle for the Almohad throne, found it to his advantage to submit to Hafsid suzerainty.
Equally fortunate was Abū Zakariyyā's policy of consolidating and expanding the peaceful relations with the great oversea trading centres in Italy, France and Sicily. Commercial treatises, minutely negotiated, were concluded - their Latin versions have been preserved - with Venice, Pisa, Genoa and Marseille (between 1231 and 1236) and somewhat later also with Aragon. They specify mutual protection of the maritime traffic from piracy; determine the conditions of establishing in Tunisian ports Christian commercial settlements, including hostels, churches, public baths and cemeteries; regulate the privileges and jurisdiction of consular representatives; and the kind and quantities of the merchandise to be imported or exported as well as the taxes imposed upon these transactions. The profits derived from the flourishing trade resulting from these conventions were reflected by the revenues of the Tunisian treasury and hence by architectural improvements and embellishments of the capital: remodelling the fortified government quarters and the emirs' residence *(Qasaba**, Kasba); construction of the mosque called *al-Muwahiddīn* (of the Almohads) also called *Jāmiʿ al-Qasaba* (Mosque of the Kasba), the name which it still carries today; extension of the covered *sūq* (the market) of which only the *Sūq al-ʿAttarīn* (of the spice and perfume merchants) has been preserved unchanged; foundation of the first *madrasa* (theological academy) in the Arab West, intended to re-consolidate and firmly implant among the educated classes the Almohad doctrine; or establishment in his palace of a library containing allegedly some 30.000 manuscripts.
Abū Zakariyyā' suddenly died at the age of fifty and was succeeded by his son Abū ʿAbdallāh Muhammad al-Mustansir (1249-1277), who had been designated heir apparent *(walī al-ʿahd)* shortly before his father's death.

ZAKARIYYĀ', ABŪ, al-WARJLĀNĪ, the principal historiographer (second half of the XIth until beginning of XIIth cent.) of the Ibādite imamate of Tāhart, built up by the Rustumid* dynasty (776-908), himself a member of the North African Ibādite branch of the heterodox Khārijite sect. Very little is known about his life beside the fact that he came from the town of Wargla, near Sadrāta (in an oasis about 380 miles south-west of Algiers), a centre of the Ibādite sectarians. He seems to have died and been buried in Sadrāta. His work, *al- Sīra wa Akhbār al-A'imma* (appr. Biographies and Traditions of the Imams) contains valuable information on the development of the Ibādite African community, of the rise and fall of the Rustumids, and on the lives and achievements of Ibādite theologians. It was referred to byArab historiographers as late as the XVIth century and has been partly translated into French (E. Masqueray, Chronique d'Abou Zakaria, Algiers, 1878).

ZANĀTA, a much ramified Berber family of tribes who at a period and in stages that have remained unknown, but certainly before the conquest of North Africa by the generals of the first Umayyad caliphs, had migrated from southern Tunisia and Tripolitania westwards through the steppes and the fringe of the Sahara, and then further on along the Algerian highlands. Some remained in the regions of Tiaret and Tlemcen, others moved onwards into Morocco, some of them taking to a sedentary or semi-sedentary mode of life, others continuing as nomads. All their numerous, never very solidly coherent groups, in particular the strong and warlike Maghrāwa*, Miknāsa* and later the Banū Īfran*, at times allied, at times enemies, played a history-making rôle in these parts of the Arab West. In the second half of the VIIth century Maghrāwa warriors were among the troops of the Umayyad general ʿUqbah Ibn Nāfiʿ. A few years later another Zanāta tribe, the Jawāra, led by a mystically inspired woman, the legendary Kāhina*, violently opposed the advancing Arab armies in the area between the Aurès and the sea. In the first years of the VIIIth century tribesmen of the Miknāsa fought under Tāriq Ibn Ziyād, himself a Berber in Arab service, in the expedition across the Straits, which marked the beginning of the Arab era in Spain.
Following their comparatively quick though hardly very deep-going conversion to Islam the majority of the Zanāta, like most of the Berber population, adhered to the combative Khārijite heterodoxy, less on doctrinal grounds than because it rallied under the banner of religion the forces of resistance against the incorporation into the - orthodox - Arab empire. In the course of the VIIIth century the Miknāsa held a foremost rank in a revolt of a Khārijite tribal coalition which defeated the Umayyad army in the so-called Battle of the Nobles*; the Banū Īfran constituted the community of the Khārijite 'Caliph' Abū Qurra*; various Zanāta sections built up the Rustumid Khārijite theocracy in Tāhart; and if the Maghrāwa supported Idrīs I*, the founder of the first organized commonwealth in Morocco, although his preaching came close to sunnite orthodoxy, their primary motive was his opposition to the ʿAbbāsid caliphate. As time went on, however, Khārijism lost its emotional hold on the masses. Its last, somewhat anachronistic call to arms resounded at the end of the tenth century among the Banū Īfran through the mouth of the 'Prophet' Abū Yazīd*, yet no longer against the expansionist policy, for quite some time abandoned, of Baghdad, but against the new Fātimid empire in the making.
Thenceforth the key-note in the history of the Zanāta came not from the sphere of religion but sprang from an irreconcilable - and inscrutable - hatred which from generation to generation opposed them to the kindred Sanhāja*. It ranged them in the hundred-year contest for power between the Fātimids and the Umayyads of al-Andalus* on the side of the latter, and made the Sanhāja protagonists of the Fātimid cause. Thus, at least, appears the picture seen in a broad perspective. Its details are blurred by the rivalries often setting one against the other

not only Maghrāwa, Miknāsa and Banū Īfran as more or less compact units, but also within each of them ambitious and influential chieftains and their clans with the ensuing changes and re-changes of camps. It all resulted in displacements of large Zanāta sections into central and western Morocco and into al-Andalus, and in the birth and decay of ephemeral Zanāta emirates of either Umayyad or Fātimid obedience. By the middle of the eleventh century the decline of Andalusian influence on the one hand, and on the other, the shift of Fātimid interests away from the Arab West to the East, and in its wake the invasion of Arab Bedouins, the Banū Hilāl* and Sulaym*, ended this chapter of Zanāta history. Before the next one could begin, a century and a half had to pass which witnessed the rise and fall of the powerful Almoravid* (1061-1147) and Almohad* (1133-1269) empires.
When in the irreversibly progressing disintegration of all central authority under the last Almohad sovereigns the Zanāta emerged again as a factor capable of intervening in the events of their time, it was in new, or at least until then unnoticed, tribal configurations. Two clans of the Banū Wasān tribe, the ʿAbd al-Wād* (1236-1550), in the areas of present-day western Algeria with Tlemcen as capital, and the Marīnids* (1244-1465) in Morocco, closely related but, true to Zanāta nature, embittered enemies, shaped their throne and consolidated it by force of arms, the use of the growing currents of popular mysticism and saint-veneration, and the enlistment of one or the other of the Arab chieftains. For a time it seemed as if an energetic and far-seeing Marīnid sultan such as Abū al-Hasan ʿAlī* or his son Abū ʿInān Fāris* would overwhelm his ʿAbd al-Wādid neighbours and even the Hafsid* realm of Tunisia and unite the entire Arab West in one Zanāta empire. Yet the development of territory-bound different traditions and inconsistent material and intellectual interests was already too far advanced for such attempts to materialize. One more Zanāta offspring, the Wattāsids*, also issued from the Banū Wasān, gave a line of sultans (1472-1554) to Morocco. They were eclipsed by the Saʿdians*, an Arab dynasty of sharīfian* descent, while the ʿAbd al-Wād found an inglorious end in the struggle for hegemony between Spain and the Ottoman empire. At that time the vitality of the Zanāta was spent. They seem to have melted into the mass of Arab Bedouin tribes for thenceforth their name is no longer mentioned by the historiographers unless to record their fame in the past.

ZARKASHĪ al-,ABŪ ʿABD ALLĀH MUHAMMAD, a Tunisian historiographer of the XVth century, presumably the author of the *Ta'rīkh al-Dawlatain al-Muwahhidīya wa al-Hafsīya* (French translation by E. Fagnan, Histoire des Almohades et des Hafsides attribué a Zerkechi, Constantine, 1895) which concentrates on the events in Tunisia under the Hafsid* sultans especially during the reign of Sultan Abū ʿAmr ʿUthmān (1435-1488) but ends with the year 1477. Since it is practically the only source of detailed information on the history of Tunisia and Tlemcen in the fifteenth century, it is of considerable value for the knowledge of this period in an important part of the Arab West. No biographical data of the author have come down to us.

ZĀWIYA, literally an angle as a geometrical term (from the verb *zawā*, to draw together) as well as the corner of a building, then designating also the cell of a Christian monk and still later, in a purely Islamic sense, a small room for the performance of the ritual prayers in distinction from the regular mosque. Towards the end of the XIIth century the word began to be used in the Arab West, at first interchangeably with *rābita*, for the abode, as a rule situated on the outskirts of a town, of a saintly man *(murābit**, marabout*) and a selected number of his disciples. Connected with it was a primitive prayer-hall serving also for the gatherings of the people coming to listen to his word. His livelihood and the upkeep of the place was provided for by pious gifts and, depending upon the weight attached to his voice in public opinion, by donation of a piece of State land *(iqtāʿ**) by the sovereign. A disciple or faithful servant took care of the everyday needs. Usually it was there, too, that the saint was buried. His tomb, a simple whitewashed cubicle with a cupola *(qubba**) over the sarcophagus became a shrine which did not cease to attract devotees from the closer or wider surroundings. Its precincts remained an inviolable refuge open to everybody persecuted for whatever reason by a private enemy or the public authority.

Frequently the *zāwiya* grew into a considerable agglomeration of various buildings: a mosque; hostels for pilgrims; living quarters for the adepts who long after the master's death continued in the sacred environment to strive for spiritual perfection; and lodgings for numerous novices whom they introduced into his teaching. As time went on, one or the other *zāwiya* developed into an institution of higer religious education, partly supplementary to, partly in competition with the courses delivered by the official doctors of religion *(fuqahā*, sing. *faqīh)* at the Great Mosque of the city. Inversely, in the XIVth and XVth centuries, when a sovereign established a *madrasa* (theological academy) he often set up simultaneously, and in close association with it, a *zāwiya*, and thus took a step further towards the interpenetration of the scientific-dogmatic and the emotional - mystic conceptions of piety, characteristic during centuries of the spiritual life in the Arab West.

According to the esteem in which a *zāwiya* was held on the ground of the virtue, wisdom and nearness to God to which it was believed to lead, its sphere of moral, educational and social influence might widen from a local to an ever larger, regional significance. With the diffusion, from about the XVth century onward, of the religious brotherhood* movement, the head of a particularly distinguished *zāwiya*, if possessed of organizing ability and credited with descent from its saint - more often than not rather a spiritual affinity than one by virtual descent, but for the mass of the people a meaningless differentiation - might work up the ritual practices of his community into a system of formal rules, establish a hierarchical order of initiates for collective action, and thus make his *zāwiya* the motherhouse of a new brotherhood. This took its name from the *zāwiya's* saint in whom legend and, based thereon, hagiographical authors, more susceptible to pious fiction than actual facts, did not take long to see its true, divinely inspired founder.

It is in this sense as the seat of a brotherhood that *zāwiya* as a religious term has retained its meaning.

ZAYDŪN IBN, ABŪ al-WALĪD AHMAD, a Hispano-Arab poet (1003-1071) born in Cordova, an offspring of the Banū Makhzūm, a clan of the Quraysh, the Prophet's tribe. While still a youth, his poetical gifts supported by an excellent education gained for him great popularity, and his noble descent a position of first rank in the circle around the council of patricians, which under Jahwarid* leadership conducted the government of Cordova after the destitution of the last Umayyad caliph (1031). Soon, however, his courtship of Wallāda, an Umayyad princess, equally renowned for her beauty and poetical talent, brought him into conflict with a dangerous rival, Ibn ʿAbdūs, vizier of Abū al-Hazm Ibn Jahwar, against whom, regardless of the consequences, he made freely use of all the satirical power of his pen in verse and prose. Accused by Ibn ʿAbdūs of treasonable pro-Umayyad activities, he was thrown into prison. There he wrote some of his most touching poems to his beloved - in vain, for her favour went to her other worshipper. After a dramatic escape from prison and several years of an eventful wandering life, yet unable to forget his disappointment in love, he returned to Cordova after Abū al-Hazm's son Abū al-Walīd had succeeded to the government. He was received with honours and entrusted with various diplomatic missions to the other city-potentates in al-Andalus*, but again fell into disgrace and resumed his career as singing knight errant.
His fame spread, and finally he was invited by the ruler of Seville, the ʿAbbādid* prince al-Muʿtadid (1042-1069), known as patron of arts and letters as much as by his sagacity as statesman, whom it did not escape what advantage he could derive from Ibn Zaydūn's inside knowledge of the situation at the various Andalusian courts. Thus the poet was made minister of state, and continued in this position also under Muʿtadid's son and successor, al Muʿtamid (1069-1091), who bestowed upon him the honorary title of *Dhū al-Wizāratayn* (Possessor of the two Vizirates, i.e. that of the State and that of the pen). When Muʿtamid conquered Cordova - greatly helped, it is said, by Ibn Zaydūn's Cordovan friends - and transferred his residence there, the poet at last saw the fulfilment of his ardent desire of returning to his native town and was given an enthusiastic welcome. It was not in his stars to enjoy his home-coming very long. This time it was not a love affair but the statesman Ibn ʿAmmār*, envious of his prestige, who made the prince decide to send him back to Seville under an honorary pretext. There he died soon afterwards, deeply mourned by the whole population.
Ibn Zaydūn's poetry is distinguished by the lyric strain and the love for the beauties of nature which imbue it. Some of his letters, (translated into Latin, Leipzig 1755, Kopenhagen 1889), which count among the specimens of the best Arabic epistolary style and open valuable insight into the complex political situation of his world.

ZĪRIDS, a dynasty of emirs (end of the Xth until the middle of the

XIIth century) in the northern section of present-day Algeria, Tunisia and Libya, issued from the tribe of the Talkāta, a sedentary branch of the Berber Sanhāja*. In the contest for hegemony in North Africa between the Umayyad caliphs of al-Andalus* and the Fātimids they were faithful Fātimid partisans, while their own hereditary enemies, the Berber Maghrāwa* of the Zanāta* group, fought on the side of the Umayyads. Probably with the help of architects lent by the Fātimid caliph al-Qā'im (934-946), who may have wished to increase the power and prestige of his allies, the Sanhāja chieftain Zīrī Ibn Manād al-Talkātī built in the Titterī mountains some 80 miles south-east of Algiers, the stronghold of Ashīr (935) that was to develop into a well-sized, heavily fortified town. Thanks to Zīrī and his warriors, Caliph al-Qā'im and his successor Caliph al-Mansūr (946-953) subdued the revolt of the Khārijite 'prophet' Abū Yazīd Makhlad Ibn Kaydad* and his allied Zanāta tribes, which shook the Fātimid throne to its very foundation. Zīrī Ibn Manād, appointed governor of a region covering approximately present-day Algeria north of the desert, fell fighting against a former Fātimid vassal, the Maghrāwa chieftain Muhammad Ibn al-Khair, who had changed over to the Umayyad camp (971). His head was sent as a trophy to Caliph al-Hakam's court at Cordova.

In the same year, Zīrī Ibn Manād's son Abū al-Futūh Buluggīn (or Bulukkīn), who assumed the Arabic name Yūsuf, twice defeated the Zanāta, occupied most of the towns which they controlled along the Algerian coast and inland as far west as Tlemcen, and transplanted many of their inhabitants to his capital Ashīr. In reward for his services Caliph al-Muʿizz (953-975) made him viceroy of a territory comprising present-day Libya, Tunisia and the Algerian department of Constantine, as well as of all further regions which he might wrest from the Zanāta. Buluggīn tranferred the seat of the government to al-Qayrawān, but left his family and most of his retinue in Ashīr. Then he set out on a conquering expedition into the heart of the Zanāta lands which took him as far as Ceuta. Refraining from an attack on this well-defended Umayyad possession, he turned southwards, gained hold of Fez (979) and Sijilmāsa and invaded the country of the Barghawāta on the Atlantic coast of Morocco, but died on his way home (984). His son al-Mansūr (984-995) soon after his father's death entrusted his uncle Hammād with the governorship of Ashīr and the western sections of the realm (987/88) and established his residence first at al-Raqqāda, the one-time Aghlabid* pleasure seat, and subsequently at Sabra al-Mansūrīya, a foundation of the Fātimids at the gates of al-Qayrawān.
A split in the family followed the accession to the throne of al-Mansūr's son Bādīs (995-1016), whose title was contested by his grand-father, Buluggīn's brother, Zāwī Ibn Zīrī. The pretender, forced to abandon his claim and to leave the country, was received with honours at the Umayyad court in Cordova and became the founder of a Zīrid line reigning in Granada. A second family conflict of equally far-reaching consequences broke out between Bādīs and Hammād who demanded full

independence. It was settled only by Bādīs' son al-Muʿizz (1016-1062), who consented to a partition of the Zīrid territory (1017) and recognized the house of the Hammādids* as rulers of equal rank. Al-Mansūr's move to al-Mansūrīya marked the social, economic and cultural transformation which within three generations had changed a community based on traditional tribal order into an organized state of which its chroniclers have left a vivid, although in some instances perhaps somewhat too exuberant picture. Its peasants cultivated wheat, olives, sugar-cane and cotton; its artisans produced all sorts of fabrics, carpets, woodwork and ceramics, its merchants traded with the African countries, Spain, Sicily, Egypt, Syria and Iraq. Its treasury could rely on a well functioning fiscal system which supplied to the prince the means for a brilliant court life; for the embellishment of the Great Mosque of al-Qayrawān - some of the fine bronze chandeliers and the *maqsūra* (space set apart for the sovereign) of exquisitely carved wood are still there; and for the construction of costly palaces of which, except a few columns subsequently built into the Qayrawān mosque, nothing has remained. It may have been this prosperity and the confidence in his power, perhaps also the influence of the rigidly sunnite circles of al-Qayrawān, which led al-Muʿizz to renounce obedience to his schismatic Fātimid sovereigns by assuming full secular authortiy and recognizing the spiritual supremacy of the orthodox ʿAbbāsid caliphate of Baghdad (about 1045).

The Fātimid riposte was to release upon the Zīrid territories the strong and highly warlike Arab tribes of the Banū Hilāl* and Sulaym*, kept with difficulty under control in their pasture ground in Upper Egypt. It was an operation meant, perhaps, not so much to redress the situation as to inflict a punishment on the rebellious vassal, but which resulted in lasting changes in the ethnical and political structure of this part of North Africa. In wave after wave the invaders - the warriors followed by their families and herds - swept over the Cyrenaica and Tripolitania into southern Tunisia, drawing others behind them, pilfering, burning and destroying everything on their way. Al-Muʿizz, after vain attempts at damming the devastating flood by negotiation, was beaten and withdrew to the greater safety of al-Mahdīya, strongly fortified on a narrow peninsula, leaving his sumptuous residence and the city of al-Qayrawān defenceless to be plundered (1057). In Gabès, Sfax, Gafsa and other, smaller towns ephemeral leaders, buying the benevolence of the Bedouin chieftains, arose to power but lost it soon again to a more successful rival. Only in Tunis the former governor of the town, Ibn Khurāssān, built up a small independent principality which maintained good-neighbourly relations with the Arabs around it, and under his successors subsisted until Tunisia was incorporated in the Almohad* empire (1159).

The Zīrid rule, thenceforth a shadow of its former splendour, maintained itself one more century over a strip of the coast with some small ports whose people made a scanty living from the traffic with the coastal towns of al-Andalus and Sicily, or more often than not from piracy. When the Normans had become masters of Sicily (1091) and began to look for footholds on the African coast, they met with only weak resistance. King Roger II imposed his sovereignty on al-Hasan Ibn ʿAlī (1121-1167) and subsequently occupied al-Mahdīya (1148) but was forced out by the Almohad ruler ʿAbd al-Mu'min* (1159). Al-Hasan, re-installed by the victors as their vassal, was deposed again (1167), lived in hiding until his death. He was the last of the Zīrid line.

1. Zīrī Ibn Manād al-Talkātī †971
2. Abū al-Futūh Buluggīn 971-984
3. al-Mansūr 984-995
4. Bādīs 995-1016
5. al-Muʿizz 1016-1062
6. Tamīm 1062-1108
7. Yahyā 1108-1116
8. ʿAlī 1116-1121
9. al-Hasan 1121-1167

ZIRYĀB, the sobriquet (meaning a kind of black-feathered bird, probably an allusion to his dark complexion) under which the musician and singer Abū al-Hasan ʿAlī Nāfiʿ (789-857) holds a pre-eminent place in the history of Hispano-Arabic music and in the annals of Cordovan fashion and elegance. He was a freedman of unknown origin at the court of Baghdad, where his beautiful voice and talent for lute-playing aroused the interest of the great musician Ibrāhīm al-Mawsilī. Received into the circle of al-Mawsilī's pupils, he drew upon himself his master's jealousy by his extraordinary success and finally was obliged to leave Baghdad. During a short stay at al-Qayrawān he was invited to Cordova by the Umayyad Emir ʿAbd al-Rahmān II* (822-52) who bestowed upon him a princely salary and admitted him into his immediate entourage. An accomplished artist and theorist, gifted with an astounding musical memory and equally remarkable pedagogic faculties, Ziryāb attracted numerous disciples from all parts of the country. Through the medium of his school which lent nationwide resonance to his inventiveness, the five-string lute in the place of the one with three cords, became the dominant instrument, and Andalusian music was given those particular shades that were to mark it off lastingly from all other Arabic musical expression. In Morocco it still enjoys the favour of a broad public. Bel-esprit, appreciated as a poet, conversant with the most various topics in the fields of literature, history, astronomy and geography Zyriāb held a unique position within the social élite of the most splendid city of al-Andalus*, eager to follow his lead as to the colour and style of his dress, the cut of his hair and beard, the way of setting the table and the gastronomical refinements he had learned in Baghdad or devised himself.

ZMĀLA, plur. *zumūl* in French texts spelt *smala,* designating in the Arab West the encampment of a tribe or of an important tribal leader with his family, retinue, bodyguard and servants. A well-known camp of this type, by its size rather an ambulant residential tent-town, was the *zmāla* of Emir ʿAbd al-Qādir Ibn Muhyī al-Dīn* (Abdelkader), the tenacious opponent of the French in the long-drawn warfare for

the conquest of Algeria. Having lost to the French troops all the towns he had garrisoned, he moved his *zmāla* which contained, it is said, some 50.000 people, from place to place on the Algerian Highlands and for a long time evaded his pursuers. The final conquest of his *zmāla* (May 16, 1843) resulted in the capture of 4000 prisoners, among them the families of his most faithful adherents and his treasury while he himself, defended by his guard, escaped into Morocco.
Under the Turkish régime in Algeria such military camps which were garrisoned with tribes exempted from the payment of taxes, had the task of securing peace and order in the area assigned to them.

ZUHR IBN, an Andalusian family of six generations of scholars (XIth to XIIIth cent.), originally immigrated from Arabia. Their name appears for the first time as that of a well-known jurist noted for his piety († 1030). He was the father of a wealthy and much honoured physician who practised in several Andalusian towns and for some time also in al-Qayrawān and Cairo. His son Abū al-ʿAlā', mentioned by the Latin chroniclers of the Middle Ages variously as al-Aboali, Abueli and Ebilula or Abuleizor and Abulelizor, attained real fame as physician and stood in great honour at the ʿAbbādid* court in Seville. After the conquest of Seville by the Almoravids* (1091) he entered the service of the victor, Yūsuf Ibn Tāshufīn*, who appointed him vizier († 1130 in Seville or Cordova).
The most illustrous member of the family was Abū al-ʿAlā's son, Abū Marwān ʿAbd al-Malik Ibn Zuhr (1091-1161), called Avenzoar. Born in Seville, well versed in theology, canon law and literature, he soon acquired great reputation for his erudition as a physician. Like his father he served in high functions under the Almoravids and after their downfall continued under their successors, the Almohads*, and was made vizier by ʿAbd al-Muʿmin* (1133-1163), who distinguished him by his personal friendship. He was the first to recommend tracheotomy and artificial nutrition. The best known of his medical works is *al-Taysīr fi'l Mudāwāt wa'l Tadbīr* (The Facilitation of Therapeutics and Diet). It was first translated into Hebrew, and this version was somewhat later used in Venice for a Latin translation which was repeatedly reprinted and widely used in the Occident as late as the XVIIth century.
Avenzoar's son, Abū Bakr Muhammad (1110-1198), also highly reputed for his medical knowledge, especially as a practitioner, was also esteemed as a poet. He was the personal physician of the Almohad ruler Abū Yūsuf Yaʿqūb al-Mansūr* (1184-1199) but died, poisoned by a jealous court dignitary of Marrakesh. Abū Yūsuf Yaʿqūb preached the sermon at the funeral. The last outstanding scion of the Ibn Zuhr family was Abū Bakr's son Abū Muhammad ʿAbd Allāh (1181-1205), like all his ancestors an excellent physician and enjoying a distinguished standing at the Almohad court at Marrakesh. He, too, met his death through poison when travelling from Marrakesh to Rabat. All members of the family were buried in Seville.

APPENDICES

LIST OF MAPS

POLITICAL PARTIES AND GROUPINGS IN THE ARAB WEST

Political party-life has its origin in the efforts at achieving national independence. Some of the smaller parties and loose groupings subsequently disappeared or merged with stronger ones. There crystallized a one-party system in Tunisia (Neo-Destour) and in Algeria (Front of National Liberation), and a multi-party system in Morocco. In Libya, where none of the political movements ever reached the stage of a solid organization, political party-life was suppressed soon after the attainment of independence. Since then it has not reappeared.

Designation in English	Designation in Arabic	Designation in French
	ALGERIA	
North African Star	*al-Najm Shamāl Ifrīqīya*	Etoile Nordafricaine
Association of the Algerian ʿUlamā'		Association des Oulémas Algériens
Algerian People's Party	*Hizb al-Shaʿb al-Jazā'ir*	Parti Populaire Algérien
Algerian Popular Union		Union Populaire Algérienne
Friends of the Manifesto and of Liberty	*Asdiqā' al-Bayān*	Amis du Manifeste et de la Liberté
Democratic Union of the Algerian Manifesto	*al-Ittihād al-Dimuqrātī li'l Bayān al-Jazā'ir*	Union Démocratique du Manifeste Algérien
Movement for the Triumph of Liberty and Democracy		Mouvement pour le Triomphe de la Liberté et la Démocratie
Common Front for the Defence of, and Respect for Liberty		Front commun pour la Défense et le Respect de la Liberté
Front of National Liberation	*Jabha al-Harīr al-Watanīya*	Front de Libération Nationale
Algerian National Movement		Mouvement National Algérien
	MOROCCO	
Bloc of Moroccan Action	*Kutla al-ʿAmal al-Maghribī*	Comité d'Action Marocaine

Party of National Reforms	*Hizb al-Islah al-Watanī*	Parti des Réformes Nationales
Istiqlāl Party	*Hizb al-Istiqlāl*	Parti de l'Istiqlāl
Democratic Party of Independence subsequently changed into	*Hizb al-Shūrā wa'l Istiqlāl*	Parti Démocratique de l'Indépendance
Democratic Constitutional Party	*Hizb al-Dustūr al-Dimuqrātī*	Parti Démocratique Constitutionel
Movement of Moroccan Unity	*Haraka al-Wahda al-Maghribīya*	Mouvement d'Unité Marocaine
Popular Movement	*al-Haraka al-Shaʿbīya*	Mouvement Populaire
National Union of Popular Forces	*al-Ittihād al-Watanī l'il Quwwāt al-Shaʿbīya*	Union Nationale des Forces Populaires
Front for the Defence of the Constitutional Institutions		Front de Défense des Institutions Constitutionelles
Socialist Democratic Party		Parti Socialiste Démocratique

TUNISIA

		Mouvement Bourgeois de Tunisie
Young Tunisia Party		Parti Jeune Tunisien
Destour Party	*Hizb al-Hurr al-Dustūrī*	Destour
Neo-Destour		Néo-Destour

LIBYA

National Front	*al-Jabha al-Watanīya*
Youth League	*Rabita al-Shabāb*
National Congress	*al-Mu'tamar al-Watanī*
National Party	*al-Hizb al-Watanī*
United National Front	*al-Jabha al-Watanīya al-Mutahida*
Free National Bloc	*al-Kutla al-Watanīya al-Hurra*
Egyptian Tripolitanian Union Party	
Tripolitanian National Congress	

PLACE NAMES
in
Algeria (A) Libya (L) Morocco (M) Spain (S) Tunisia (T)

In Occidental Languages	In Arabic
Alcazarquivir (M)	al-Qasr al-Kabīr
Algeria	Barr al-Jazā'ir
Algiers	al-Jazā'ir
Arzila (M)	Asīlā
Aurès mountains (A)	Awrās
Azemmour (M)	Azammūr
Badajoz (S)	Batalyaws
Benghazi (L)	Banghāzi
Biskra (A)	Biskara
Bizerta (T)	Bansart
Blida (A)	Bulayda
Bône (A)	Būna, or Bilād al-ʿUnnāb
Bougie (A)	Bijāya
Carthage (T)	Qartājanna
Casablanca (M)	Dār al-Baīdā'
Chaouia (M)	Shāwīya
Chechaouene (M)	Shabshāwān
Chélif river (A)	Shalaf
Chella (M)	Shālla
Ceuta (M)	Sabta
Collo (T)	al-Qull
Constantine (A)	Qusantīna
Cordova (S)	Qurtuba
Cyrenaica (L)	Barqa
Djerba island (T)	Jarba
Djérid oases (T)	Jarīd
Fez (M)	Fās
Gabès (T)	Qābis
Gafsa (T)	Qafsa
Guadalquivir river (S)	al-Wādī al-Kabīr
Guadiana river (S)	al-Wādī Ānā
Granada (S)	Gharnāta
Kerkenna islands (T)	Qarqina

Lake of Tunis (T)	al-Buhaira
Larache (M)	al-Arā'ish
Lisbon	al-Ushbūna
Louis Gentil (M)	Yūsūfīya
Mahdia (T)	al-Mahdīya
Marrakesh (M)	Marrākush
Mazagan (M)	al-Jadīd
Meknès (M)	Miknāsa
Melilla (M)	Malīlīt
Mogador (M)	al-Sūirāt
Monastir (T)	Munastīr
Murcia (S)	Mursīya
Oujda (M)	Wajda
Oum Er Rebia river (M)	Umm al-Rabīʿ
Rabat (M)	Rabāt
Rio de Oro (M)	Saqīyat al-Hamrā'
Safi (M)	Asfī
Sahel	al-Sāhil
Salé (M)	Slā
Santarem (S)	Shantarūm
Santaver (S)	Shantabarīya
Sétif (A)	Satīf
Seville (S)	Ishbīliya
Sfax (T)	Safāqus
Silves (S)	Shilb
Sicily	Siqilliya
Sijilmassa ruins (M)	Sijilmāsa
Sousse (T)	Sūsa
Tangier (M)	Tanja
Taza (M)	Tāzā
Tetuan (M)	Titawān
Tiaret (A)	Tāhart
Tlemcen (A)	Tilimsān
Tobruk (L)	Tubrūq
Tozeur (T)	Tauzar or Tūzar
Tripoli (L)	Tarābulus
Tunis	Tūnis
Wargla (A)	Warjalān

READING SUGGESTIONS

The following short list is meant only as an indication where to obtain more ample information on the subjects dealt with in the entries of this book. Since practically all the works mentioned hereunder provide also an extensive bibliographical material in their own particular fields, its repetition here was thought to be unnecessary.

Alleg Henri, *La Question*, Paris 1958.

Ashford D. E., *Political Change in Morocco*, Princeton 1961.

Barbour Neville, *A Survey of North West Africa (The Maghrib)*, London 1959.

Barrat Robert, *Justice pour le Maroc*, Paris 1953.

Bedjaoui Mohammed, *La Révolution algérienne et le Droit*, Bruxelles 1963.

Behr Edward, *The Algerian Problem*, London 1961.

Benabdellah Abdelaziz, *Les Grands Courants de la Civilisation du Maghreb*, Rabat 1958.

Berque Jaques, *Structures sociales du Haut Atlas*, Paris 1955.

—, *Al-Yousi, Problèmes de la Culture Marocaine au XVII ème Siècle*, La Haye 1958.

—, *Les Arabes*, Paris 1959.

—, *Le Maghrib entre Deux Guerres*, Paris 1962.

Boudiaf Mohamed, *Où va l'Algérie?*, Paris 1964.

Bourdieu Pierre, *Sociologie de l'Algérie*, Paris 1958.

Bourguiba Habib, *La Tunisie et la France*, Paris 1954.

Brockelmann C., *Geschichte der islamischen Völker und Staaten*, Berlin 1943.

Bromberger Serge, *Les Rebelles Algériens*, Paris 1958.

Bromberger Serge & Merry a.o., *Barricades et Colonels*, Paris 1960.

Brunschvig Robert, *La Berbérie Orientale sous les Hafsides*, Paris 1940/47.

Clark M. K., *Algeria in Turmoil*, New York 1959.

Corbin Henri, *Histoire de la philosophie islamique*, Paris, 1964.

Despois Jean, *La Tunisie Orientale et Basse Steppe*, Paris 1955.

Drague Georges, *Esquisse d'histoire réligieuse du Maroc*, Paris 1951.

Encyclopaedia of Islam, Leiden.

al-Fāsī ʿAllāl *The Independence Movements in Arab North Africa*, Washington 1954.

Favrod Charles Henri, *La Révolution Algérienne*, Paris 1959.

Feraoun Mouloud, *Le Fils du Pauvre*, Paris 1954.

Fernau Friedrich Wilhelm, *Arabischer Westen*, Stuttgart 1959.

Fisher Godfrey, *Barbary Legend*, Oxford 1957.

Franchon Y., *Le Maroc, d'Algéciras a la souveraineté économique*, Paris 1957.

Garas Félix, *Bourguiba et la naissance d'une nation*, Paris 1956.

Guernier Eugène, *La Berbérie*, Paris 1950.

Guillot J., *Le Développement économique de l'Algérie, in Cahiers de l'Institut de Science Economique Appliquée*, No 108, Paris 1960.

Hole E. C., *Andalus: Spain under the Muslims*, London 1958.

L'Inititiation à l'Algérie, several authors, Paris 1957.
L'Initiation à la Tunisie, several authors, Paris 1950.
International Bank for Reconstruction and Development, *The Economic Development of Libya*, Baltimore 1960.
Julien Ch. André, *L'Afrique du Nord en Marche*, Paris 1953.
Khadduri Majid, *Modern Libya*, Baltimore 1963.
Lacouture Jean et Simone, *Le Maroc à l'Epreuve*, Paris 1958.
Landau Rom, *Moroccan Drama*, San Francisco 1956.
—, *Muhammad V, King of Morocco*, Rabat 1957.
Lévi-Provençal E., *L'Islam d'Occident*, Paris 1948.
—, *La Civilisation Arabe en Espagne*, Paris 1948.
—, *Histoire de l'Espagne Musulmane*, Paris 1950/53.
—, *Seville musulmane au début du XIIIème siècle: Le Traité d'Ibn Abdun*, Paris 1948.
Le Tourneau Roger, *Evolution politique de l'Afrique du Nord Musulmane*, Paris 1962.
Mahdi Muhsin, *Ibn Khaldun's Philosophy of History*, London 1957.
Mandouze André, *La Révolution Algérienne par les Textes*, Paris 1961.
Marçais Georges, *Manuel d'Art Musulman*, Paris 1926.
—, *Tlemcen, Paris* 1950.
Monès H., *La chute du califat umayyad de Cordoue*, Cairo 1948.
Montagne Robert, *La Naissance du Prolétariat Marocain*, Paris 1951.
—, *Révolution au Maroc*, Paris 1953.
Nouschi André, *La Naissance du Nationalisme Algérien (1914-1954)*, Paris 1963.
Rézette Robert, *Les Partis Politiques Marocains*, Paris 1955.
Roolvink R., *Historical Atlas of the Muslim Poeples*, Amsterdam 1957.
Roy Jules, *La Guerre d'Algérie*, Paris 1960.
Spuler Bertold, *Geschichte der islamischen Länder*. I. Abschnitt, *Die Chalifenzeit*, Leiden 1952. III. Abschnitt, *Neuzeit*, Leiden-Köln 1959. (*Handbuch der Orientalistik*. 6. Band)
Terrasse H., *L'Art hispano-mauresque des origines au XIIIe siècle*, Paris 1937.
—, *Histoire du Maroc des origines à l'établissement du Protectorat Français*, Casablanca 1950.
—, *Islam d'Espagne, une rencontre de l'Orient et de l'Occident*, Paris 1958.
Tillion Germaine, *L'Algérie en 1957*, Paris 1957.
Yacef Saadi, *Souvenirs de la Bataille d'Alger*, Paris 1964.

PERIODICALS

L'Afrique et l'Asie, Paris
Civilisations, Bruxelles
Maghreb, Paris
Orient, Paris
Politique Etrangère, Paris
Synthèses, Bruxelles
Tiers Monde, Paris

Middle Eastern Affairs, New York
Foreign Affairs, New York
International Affairs, London
World Today, London
The Moslem World, Hartford
Middle East Journal, Washington

Neues Afrika, München
Orient, Hamburg
Welt des Islams, Leiden

Afrika, Rotterdam

Oriente Moderno, Roma

Among the dailies consistently publishing news on North African current events and problems: The Times, London; The New York Times, New York; Le Monde, Paris; Neue Frankfurter Zeitung, Frankfurt; Neue Züricher Zeitung, Zürich.